PENGUIN BOOKS

THE PENGUIN GUIDE TO AMERICAN
MEDICAL AND DENTAL SCHOOLS

Harold R. Doughty is currently a management and educational consultant. He was formerly executive vice president and chief operating officer at American Commonwealth University; vice president for admissions, financial aid, and enrollment services at United States International University; director of admissions and summer sessions at New York University; and director of admissions and freshmen development at Adelphi University. His *Guide to American Graduate Schools* and *The Penguin Guide to American Law Schools* are also available from Penguin.

THE PENGUIN
GUIDE TO
AMERICAN
MEDICAL
AND DENTAL
SCHOOLS

Harold R. Doughty

PENGUIN BOOKS

PENGUIN BOOKS
Published by the Penguin Group
Penguin Putnam Inc., 375 Hudson Street,
New York, New York 10014, U.S.A.
Penguin Books Ltd, 27 Wrights Lane,
London W8 5TZ, England
Penguin Books Australia Ltd, Ringwood,
Victoria, Australia
Penguin Books Canada Ltd, 10 Alcorn Avenue,
Toronto, Ontario, Canada M4V 3B2
Penguin Books (N.Z.) Ltd, 182–190 Wairau Road,
Auckland 10, New Zealand

Penguin Books Ltd, Registered Offices:
Harmondsworth, Middlesex, England

First published in Penguin Books 1999

1   3   5   7   9   10   8   6   4   2

LIBRARY OF CONGRESS CATALOGING IN PUBLICATION DATA
Doughty, Harold R.
The Penguin guide to American medical and dental schools /
Harold R. Doughty.
p.   cm.
ISBN 0 14 02.7515 0
1. Medical colleges—United States—Directories.   I. Title.
R735.A4D68   1999
610'.71'173—DC21   98–45438

Printed in the United States of America
Set in Times Roman

CONTENTS

PREFACE

This guide is designed to provide prospective medical, dental, and osteopathic students with the basic information they need to select the appropriate health professional school. It describes all nationally accredited/approved medical, dental, and osteopathic professional schools in the United States, each of which has been contacted at least once. Additional material was obtained from the Internet and other supplemental resources.

Each entry contains information concerning the professional school's parent institution and the professional schools' admission and degree requirements, standards, enrollment and faculty size (when available), tuition charges, financial-aid opportunities and deadlines, library and housing facilities, and, wherever possible, material related to joint-, combined-, and dual-degree programs and to the NIH/institutional M.S.T.P./D.S.T.P. While this book has been prepared especially for the first-year medical/dental student, there is also information about high-school-student preparation and admission requirements for B.A./B.S.-M.D./D.D.S. combined-degree programs and postbaccalaureate premedical programs for those wishing to enhance their academic preparation through intensified basic medical science training. High school counselors, premed advisers, college faculty, administrative officers, and potential medical/dental students will also find this information useful.

It should be noted that *The Penguin Guide to American Medical and Dental Schools* is intended only as a first source of information. The student is encouraged to seek advice from premed advisers, undergraduate science faculty members, and especially any medical/dental professional he or she knows and to consult catalogs, bulletins, professional guides, and Web sites for the most up-to-date information on the institutions that interest him or her. Careful analysis of the data summarized should enable the applicant to become more aware of the opportunities available and then narrow the selection to the specific state or geographic area and then to the institutions, public or private, he or she is most likely to find most suitable and which present the greatest chance of gaining an acceptance. But the most important ingredient in the whole selection process is still the applicant's brutally frank self-appraisal of his or her academic ability and objectives as well as his or her motives for undertaking professional study and whether they are sufficient to sustain the medical/dental student for the next four to seven years.

The author wishes to express his indebtedness to the professional-school deans, admission officers, and their assistants who provided the information presented. Further revisions of this guide are planned, and corrections and suggestions are welcomed.

H. R. D.

INTRODUCTION

THE PROFESSIONAL SCHOOL

All study beyond the undergraduate level is essentially "professional" in nature. The graduate school of arts and science was created primarily to train college teachers and scholars, even though most of those who hold master's and doctoral degrees do not enter higher education. But graduate training in fields other than the humanities and sciences is designed for specific occupations.

Although there are no agreed demarcations, it can be fairly stated that some sixteen disciplines are the predominant arenas of postbaccalaureate professional study: architecture, business, dentistry, education, engineering, forestry, law, library science, medicine, nursing, optometry, pharmacy, public health, social work, theology, and veterinary medicine. Cases can be made for including under this label such fields as journalism and physical therapy.

Even this list could be winnowed further. The origins of formal education for just three professions predate those of all others by many decades. Training for them—law, medicine, theology—has developed independently of most forms of graduate study. Indeed, the law schools still speak of work for the first law degree as "undergraduate," as if candidates could enter directly from high school. Many other programs are still struggling for full recognition of their professional status and often remain as mere departments of a larger division.

Make no mistake. The designation of an academic subdivision as a department or institute, and not that of a school or college is a distinction important beyond simple academic snobbery. Professional "schools" within broader institutions have more stature than departments. They have independent administrations and faculties, sometimes even their own boards of trustees. Often they are able to detach their fund-raising activities from their parent institutions and thus have greater latitude in distribution of monies separated from contributors. There is greater unity of purpose. Faculties of medical/dental schools are typically better paid than those in most other academic fields.

And in the current atmosphere of student specialization and vocationalism, professional schools have the upper hand in determining the direction of their institutions, while many other university units struggle with enrollment and fiscal problems. The following pages outline professional schools and their programs and briefly describe factors to be considered in the selection process.

SELECTING A MEDICAL OR DENTAL SCHOOL

Professional schools often have been accused of unduly restricting enrollment at times of expanding need. Now, having moved to meet urgently expressed national needs, institutions find themselves the targets of the reverse criticism: Some say they have gone too far and now must start reducing the number of students they enroll. There looms the previously unbelievable prospect of a surplus of doctors and dentists in some areas of the country, while in other regions, particularly rural areas, there are still shortages. According to one estimate, if in the United States the rate of enrollment and graduation continues at its current level, by 2000 there will be half again as many doctors as in 1980 and a slight decrease in dentists. In a nation headed toward zero population growth, this prediction has been used as justification by federal agencies to attempt to limit aid for professional education to loan programs.

The result of these trends will be to make professional

study even more difficult to undertake than it already is. Medical schools, for example, are talking tentatively about charging tuition that actually covers instructional expenses, meaning annual tuition could soon reach as high as $35,000–$40,000 at some private institutions! This cost does not even include living expenses; financial aid is far from munificent, and federal cutbacks can be anticipated.

Admission standards, too, may escalate still further, putting even the least glossy medical/dental schools out of reach of all but the most capable applicants. But in the meantime, some students of above-average, if unspectacular, aptitude and credentials have reason to be hopeful about gaining entrance to some publicly supported school as long as they are not unrealistically fussy about location and "image."

COST, SIZE, LOCATION. The costs for professional medical and dental study vary widely, depending principally on the field and the type of institutional or public support. Annual tuition ranges from about $5,000 to $20,000 at publicly supported schools and from $22,000 to $33,000 at private schools, all escalating at an average rate of nearly 5 percent a year. In general, tuition has been increasing by 6–7 percent each year. (Always check with the institution in question regarding current tuition charges.)

Student bodies of professional schools are customarily in the 300–800 range, but a few exceed 1,000 in enrollment. Dental and osteopathic schools' enrollments tend to be on the lower side of this range, while medical schools tend to be on the higher side. Women make up about 35–45 percent of the total medical/dental school, with the percentage being a little higher in medical schools and a little lower in both dental and osteopathic schools. Underrepresented minorities make up about 3–5 percent of medical/dental school enrollment; other minorities, 8–10 percent. In many cases, even private schools, give some preference to state residents, thereby severely restricting the options available to many well-qualified candidates. The ratios of resident/nonresident range from 100% resident enrollment at several state institutions to a high at one private institution of 15% resident to 85% non-resident.

The great majority of professional schools are affiliated with universities. Increasingly, formerly independent medical and dental schools are being absorbed into larger institutions or are joining with other institutions to form new entities. (In one recent case the school just closed its doors.)

Only the most populous states have schools offering all three types of professional medical study. There are medical/dental schools in forty-five states, the District of Columbia, and Puerto Rico. Even with this broad geographic base, medical/dental students can probably expect to enroll at an institution farther away from home than their undergraduate colleges were.

ADMISSION

The professional schools of medicine, dentistry, and osteopathic medicine set rigorous entrance requirements and thus avoid the separate step of "admission to candidacy," not to mention the high attrition rate, of many graduate schools. It is not possible, therefore, to suggest that any college graduate can gain admission to some medical/dental professional school as is the case with some graduate schools. Nevertheless, admission is not always as difficult as is commonly supposed if students have the appropriate academic preparation and GPA and are willing to consider professional schools without regard to location or presumed reputation. (Since most professional schools must meet fairly high minimum criteria to retain accreditation by the appropriate professional associations, it is probably safe to say that few truly "marginal" schools exist.) Several factors influence the decisions of admission committees, and these should be understood by the potential applicant.

PREPARATION. Some schools are willing to consider applicants who do not hold bachelor's degrees certifying completion of a four-year undergraduate program. Schools of dentistry, for example, sometimes admit students with as little as two years of undergraduate study, though nearly all medical schools require the bachelor's degree. Even in the case of the B.A./B.S.-M.D. joint-degree programs, you rarely see undergraduate students entering medical school without completing a four-year baccalaureate program. Undergraduate preparation generally follows the curricula laid down by the preprofessional committee, and these programs tend to emphasize the natural and/or physical sciences. This does not mean that the diversity of academic background provided by study in the humanities and social sciences is to be minimized. In fact, the completion of course work in English, the humanities, the behavioral sciences, and the social sciences is required for medical-school admission nearly as often as biology, chemistry, and physics. However, in medical school you will discover that the vast majority of students have majored in one of the sciences or engineering. Some dental and osteopathic schools suggest in their catalogs that general liberal arts studies are more important for their students than a specialized science major, but this is by no means a significant number of schools.

CREDENTIALS. In addition to official transcripts of

undergraduate, and any graduate study completed, applicants are nearly always expected to provide one to three letters of recommendation and MCAT or DAT scores. In many cases, the letters of recommendation may be replaced totally or in part by the recommendations of the undergraduate preprofessional faculty committee.

Nearly all schools of dentistry, medicine, and osteopathic medicine demand the results of an appropriate entrance examination prepared and/or administered by their professional associations. In some joint-degree programs the results of an appropriate standardized entrance exam prepared and/or administered by a professional association or testing agency may also be required. The addresses of these associations/agencies follow:

Dental Aptitude Test (DAT)—applications available from either the chosen dental school or from the Department of Testing Services, American Dental Association, 211 East Chicago Avenue, Suite 1840, Chicago, IL. 60611-2678; phone: (312)440-2689.

Graduate Management Admissions Test (GMAT)—applications available from Graduate Management Admissions Test, P.O. Box 6101, Princeton, NJ 08541-6101; phone: (601)771-7330.

Graduate Record Examination (GRE)—application available from Graduate Record Examinations, Education Testing Service, P.O. Box 6000, Princeton, NJ 08541-6000; phone: (609)771-7670, or in the California Bay Area, phone: (510)654-1200.

Law School Admission Test (LSAT)—applications available from Law School Council, Box 2000, Newtown, PA 18940; phone: (215)968-1001.

Medical College Admission Test (MCAT)—applications available from MCAT Program Office, P.O. Box 4065, Iowa City, IA 52243; phone: (319)337-1276.

Test of English as a Foreign Language, Test of Spoken English, Test of Written English (TOEFL, TSE, TWE)—applications available from TOEFL, P.O. Box 6151, Princeton, NJ 08541-6151; phone: (609)771-7100.

DEADLINES. Medical and dental schools customarily accept applications for admission starting in June of the year preceding the proposed term of entrance. Most medical schools set closing dates for the receipt of completed applications in December, although for some schools this date may be flexible. Dental and osteopathic schools may accept applications as late as May or until the class is filled. After receipt of the preliminary report from the application service, a supplemental, secondary, or formal application may be sent to those who pass the initial screening. In the case of many dental schools the applicant will be contacted by phone and advised to submit supplemental materials. All professional schools restrict entrance for beginning students to the fall term, or occasionally to the summer (for those accepted into combined-, joint-, or dual-degree programs).

COMMON APPLICATION PROCESSING SERVICES. In an effort to ease the burden on students intent on applying for admission to multiple schools and to cut their own clerical cost, most medical and dental schools have subscribed to the services of centralized processing agencies. These services accept academic credentials and other data from applicants, summarizing them in uniform formats and passing them on to the designated schools. The clearinghouses do not offer advisement and do not make admission decisions; that still remains the province of the schools themselves. The student, after ascertaining whether the schools in which he or she is interested and wishes to employ the relevant service, should write to the service listed below:

American Association of Colleges of Osteopathic Medicine Application Service (AACOMAS): AACOMAS, 6110 Executive Boulevard, Suite 405, Rockville, MD 20852; phone: (301)468-0990, or obtain an ACCOMAS Application Request Card from a participating osteopathic school or from a premedical adviser in an undergraduate college.

American Medical College Application Service (AMCAS): AMCAS, Section for Student Services, AAMC, 2450 N St. N.W., Suite 2011, Washington, D.C. 20037-1131; phone: (202)828-0600, or obtain an AMCAS Application Request Card from a participating medical school or from a premedical adviser in an undergraduate college.

American Association of Dental Schools Application Service (AADSAS): AADSAS, 1625 Massachusetts Avenue, N.W., #101, Washington, D.C. 20036; phone: (202)667-9433, or request an AADSAS Application Request Card from a participating dental school or from a predental adviser in an undergraduate college.

There is a fee associated with these application processing services, usually escalating with the number of schools to which the materials are to be sent. Most schools, after receiving the preliminary report, require supplementary materials. Most expect payment of an official application fee as well.

STANDARDS. It is probably safe to say that between 15 and 25 percent of the applicants to the health-profession schools are accepted for admission; for medical schools the percentage is a little lower, and for dental and osteopathic schools it is a little higher. Allowing for duplication of applications, available statistics suggest that an even larger percentage of students may eventually gain entrance to some medical/dental schools.

Most health-profession schools seek students with a minimum undergraduate grade-point average of "B." The phrase generally used in their printed material is "for serious consideration a GPA of . . . is required." Depending on the degree of competition created by the number of applicants in any given year, this may be interpreted to mean an average as low as a "C plus," or 2.50 (A = 4) GPA, or as high as an "A minus," or 3.5 GPA. In any event, it is generally agreed that the grade-point average is the single most reliable predictor of success in postbaccalaureate professional studies. While the scores on the various entrance exams are undeniably important in the deliberations of the admissions committees, students should not expect strong

scores to outweigh mediocre grades in undergraduate course work, even if the degree is from a prestigious institution.

INTERVIEWS. All medical/dental schools, after they have conducted a preliminary screening of all Application Processing Service Reports and supplemental materials received, will invite a certain percentage of candidates for an on-campus qualifying interview. These interviewees are generally considered the semifinalist applicants, but this is not universal.

FINANCIAL ASSISTANCE

Professional medical and dental study is expensive, and although various forms of aid are available, most students must plan to meet costs through loans or their own resources. Most financial assistance is based on demonstrated and documented need. Some schools have research assistantships, fellowships, and stipends for M.D.-Ph.D. and M.S.T.P. students. Many medical and dental schools also provide a limited number of scholarships, grants, and tuition waivers from institutional funds; the size of these awards are generally tied to the student's academic achievement. However, the basic component in all financial-aid packages will be loans. In addition to the loan resources of the schools themselves, low-cost loans are widely available through government agencies, some banks, private lending groups, professional associations, and private or community groups.

The Federal Health Professions Educational Assistance Act has established scholarship and loan programs for majority as well as minority students. Students apply for government-sponsored loan programs through the individual medical and dental schools to which they seek admission or through the parent institution's financial aid office, in general must submit an FAFSA. Information about alternative loan programs can be obtained from banks and private agencies as well as from the medical and dental schools themselves. Many schools assist the spouses of students in obtaining local or institutional employment. Although part-time employment is normally out of the question for most first- and second-year students, given the workload, this possibility should be explored in the form of summer fellowships and externships.

THE STRUCTURE OF PROFESSIONAL STUDY OF MEDICINE AND DENTISTRY

Programs leading to the first degree in medicine and dentistry require four years of full-time study. Since practice in the medical and dental professions demands both clinical skills and a thorough understanding of the physical and natural sciences, students in these fields can expect balanced study in both these aspects of training. The first two years traditionally are spent in work in the basic and preclinical sciences, while the last two are devoted largely to clinical work. There are some newly designed curricula which incorporate or integrate basic medical sciences with the clinical experience. Although in some of these innovative and integrated curricula there is a still a heavy reliance on the basic medical sciences, the difference is that they are being taught throughout the entire four-year program. While there are no foreign-language requirements required for the degree, a few medical programs have thesis requirements. In general, during the first two years of medical/dental study, the summers are free.

Most medical and dental schools offer advanced study beyond the first degree in both clinical and research specializations. Such programs are generally administered by the graduate schools of the institutions with which the professional schools are affiliated, and students usually must meet admission and degree requirements established by both the graduate and the professional divisions. Sometimes graduate work is given through the professional school itself, especially if the school is located at a medical center separate from the main campus of the parent institution.

Programs leading to professional degrees are demanding, and standards of performance are rigorous, but the rewards are substantial. If the applicant is realistic in selecting a school consistent with his or her interests and aptitudes, the experience will test his or her mind and spirit and lead to lifelong fulfillment.

UNDERSTANDING THE ENTRIES

The information on the following pages describes the structure and content of the institutional entries that make up the main portion of this volume. For the entries to be of maximum value, it is important that the reader properly interpret the data provided. The entries contain the kinds of basic information a potential applicant is likely to seek in choosing a medical/dental school.

Careful examination of the school descriptions should aid the student in reaching realistic preliminary decisions. Since admission standards and requirements, course offerings, and financial-aid opportunities are subject to frequent revision, it is not to be assumed that the entries can replace individual school bulletins/catalogs.

Several points must be kept in mind. First, the listed institutions were contacted or researched to obtain figures on enrollment, faculty size and percentages of applications accepted, and the number of NIH awards/ grants and financial-aid awards. When possible, information for the 1998–99 academic year were used.

Second, all institutions in this guide are accredited by the appropriate U.S. professional/accrediting associations.

Third, every effort has been made to render these data understandable without reference to elaborate indexes of codes and abbreviations. However, some symbols other than abbreviations for degrees and commonly required entrance examinations have been used. One symbol regularly used throughout this book is the "virgule," or slant line, as in "teaching/research"; as employed here, the virgule means only "and/or."

The following pages describe in some detail the kinds of information to be found under each entry, in the same order. Not all items listed below are included in every entry, either because they are not relevant or because specific data were not available.

GENERAL CHARACTERISTICS OF THE PARENT INSTITUTION

Name of parent institution. In the case of about 90 percent of all accredited medical/dental schools, the school is a part of a larger institution, either a college or a university. This introductory institutional information (founding date, location, environment, enrollment, library size, etc.) has been included to establish a general atmosphere in which the medical/dental school functions. The colleges and universities are arranged in alphabetical order according to the most important word in the institutional title. (The reader should use the contents to assist in locating a particular college/school of interest.)

Mailing address of the main campus. The name of the city and state in which the main campus is located; the Internet web sites were included when available.

Founding date. Usually this represents the year the institution was chartered but sometimes the year classes were started or the year of the opening of another institution from which the present one developed. Occasionally, historical data or other points of interest were included.

Location in direction and miles from nearest major city. Direction from the nearest major city is given in appropriate capital letters (NW, SE). The mileage given is the approximate road distance. Sometimes the city named is relatively small but sufficiently well known and is given only to establish the general location of the main campus.

Type of control. If the institution is supported primarily by public funds, it is called public. Occasionally, private institutions receive substantial amounts of financial support from the state or city government but decision-making powers are retained by the board of trustees. In other cases, individual divisions of universities are totally or mostly supported by public funds. In these instances, control is often shared. When appropriate, the type of control is noted.

Many private institutions are sponsored by religious denominations, and such an affiliation is mentioned. Although few such colleges and universities restrict enrollment to members of the sponsoring churches, students may be expected to adhere to certain basic social or curricular requirements.

Semester, quarter, trimester. The semester system (the system used by almost all medical/dental schools) provides study during two terms of a nine- to ten-month academic year and, usually, during one or more summer sessions. The quarter system divides the calendar year into four equal terms, the trimester into three. Under all systems, students typically attend classes for about nine to ten months. For no apparent historical reason, Western colleges and universities most often operate on the quarter system; those in the East, on the semester. The trimester is still relatively uncommon but has found favor in some sections.

Library. This figure is the total number of bound volumes in the institution's collections; when available, figures for microforms and current periodicals/subscriptions are also included. When there are special collections or several libraries at different centers, the figure represents the combined number of volumes. Information concerning the number of personal-computer work stations is also included.

Special programs. There are two programs noted in this section. The first relates to a baccalaureate-medical/dental program linking the medical/dental school to one of the parent university's undergraduate institutions; the annual undergraduate tuition costs are also included. The other program is the postgraduate program for adults and underrepresented minorities, aimed at upgrading the scientific skills of applicants. In most cases, the phone number of the program director or coordinator is included.

Special facilities. Included in this category are special centers/institutes at the parent institutions of interest to a potential medical/dental student.

The University's NIH rankings. This information is provided to enable an applicant to get a sense of the breadth of research possibilities available university-wide. The author reviews only the top 150 domestic higher-educational institutions for the 1997 calendar year to obtain this ranking information.

Other graduate schools/colleges. To provide a sense of the educational environment in which the medical/dental school functions, this information is included, as are the total university/college enrollment figures.

GENERAL CHARACTERISTICS OF THE MEDICAL/ HEALTH SCIENCE CENTER/HOSPITAL COMPLEX

Name and mailing address of the major medical center/health science center/hospital complex. The name, mailing address, and the telephone number and web site were included here, when available, to assist the applicant in locating the major health/medical facility connected with the medical/dental school.

Founding date. This usually represents the year the institution opened, merged, or moved to the current site.

Council of Teaching Hospitals. The information provided shows the hospital's participation in this significant teaching-hospital organization.

Schools located at medical/health-science center. All the parent institution's schools/colleges located at the facilities are noted here.

Nationally recognized programs and nationally recognized medical centers/hospital complexes. Over the past several years, there has been an ongoing effort to rate/rank medical centers/hospital complexes overall, as well as certain medical specialties associated with the medical center/hospital complex. The eighteen medical specialties cited were obtained from a list of the top 45 U.S. hospitals housing these specialties. The medical centers/hospital complexes are from two separately prepared lists, one with the top 20 noted, the other with the top 25 ranked. It should be understood that no single evaluation is ever perfect, nevertheless these results have been included in this entry to provide guidance for medical school candidates who are looking for access to specific research facilities or a particular medical specialty as part of his/her medical/residency training experience. This item is an element in the Medical/Dental School Selection Checklist.

GENERAL CHARACTERISTICS OF THE MEDICAL AND DENTAL SCHOOLS

Name of the medical/dental school. The schools are arranged in alphabetical order according to the main institutional affiliation. An index with cross-references to help the reader locate a school by either its major institutional name or its specific school name is found at the end of this book. For example, for Albert Einstein College of Medicine, see Yeshiva University, New York, NY. Several other institutional indexes can be found in the back of the book to provide for further assistance in locating a specific medical/dental school.

Mailing address of the school. The name, P.O. box, street, city, and state in which the school/college is located; the zip code, telephone, Internet web sites, and E-mail address are included when available.

Founding date. This is usually the year the school was chartered/founded/established, the year classes were started, or the year of the opening of another institution from which the present one developed. Occasionally, historical data or other points of interest were included.

Location. Most medical/dental schools affiliated with a university or college are located on or near the main campus. For schools not on the main campus, the location is given in miles from the nearest major city or from the campus. Directions from the nearest major city are given in appropriate capital letters (NW, SE).

Semester, quarter, trimester, phase, or year system. The semester system (the one used by almost all medical/dental schools) provides study during two terms of a nine-to-ten-month academic year and, usually, during one or more summer sessions. (The quarter system divides the calendar year into four equal terms, the trimester into three; the phase and the four-year systems are made up of a series of steps to be successfully completed before advancing to the next phase or year.) Under all systems, students typically attend classes for about nine to ten months during the first two years and sometimes year-round for the final two years.

Library. This figure is the total number of bound volumes/microforms in the medical/dental school's collections; when available, figures for current periodicals/subscriptions and the number of computer work stations are included.

Affiliated hospitals. In general, the basic sciences are taught within the medical/dental school or university hospital complex. The clinical experiences are provided not only through the university's hospitals but through the school's affiliated hospital system. As many affiliated hospitals are listed here as possible, along with informa-

tion about national recognition or nationally recognized specialities.

Special facilities/programs. Included under this category are special centers, institutes, summer-abroad programs, faculty/student exchange, internships/externships, prematriculation summer session, and programs for underrepresented minorities. This list is not intended to be exhaustive, but only to note distinctive offerings and suggest the scope of possibilities. Since this information is not always available, its absence does not necessarily mean that special facilities/programs do not exist at a given institution.

Annual tuition charges. Many public institutions use the term "fees" rather than "tuition," often with additional "tuition" for out-of-state students. This semantic distinction is often employed to maintain the illusion of low-tuition/low-cost institutions. The cost of tuition and/or fees at public institutions is always greater for nonresidents than for residents, while there is no such distinction at private colleges and universities. A separate category of "fees" was added here when it became quite clear that in some circumstances tuition appeared relatively low but there were substantial additional expenses, especially for dental students. Throughout this book, "annual" refers to the academic, not the calendar, year. It also should be remembered that tuition charges are constantly on the rise, increasing at an annual rate of 5–6 percent at most institutions. This fact should be anticipated when possible. The charges indicated are customarily for the 1998–99 year.

On- and off-campus housing availability. Many institutions are unable to provide data for on-campus housing availability for medical/dental students per se. If the medical/dental school is located on or near the campus, it may be assumed that the students are eligible for some on-campus housing. The figure given for married-student housing should be interpreted as family units (apartments), while the figure for single students refers to individual spaces only. "On-campus housing" means institutionally owned or controlled housing and does not include private accommodations. Medical/dental students who choose to live in institutional housing must remember that they are usually expected to observe the restrictions in force for all residents and that there may be housing-application deadlines. A few institutions indicated that only off-campus housing was available.

Annual on- and off-campus housing expenses. This figure is for the academic year and relates only to the expenses taken from the financial-aid budget for both university-owned or -operated housing and private accommodations. The cost described is generally for the mid-range, and cost variations depend on the nature of accommodations. Unless otherwise specified, figures are for rent or room charges only, not board.

Housing deadlines and contacts. This notes the deadlines if applicable and the office(s) to contact for both on- and off-campus housing information. If only one office is mentioned, it generally provides information for both institutional and private accommodations. If no housing information is supplied, then generally the admissions office is the appropriate office to contact for either on- or off-campus housing information.

Enrollment. Figures are for medical/dental students only. These figures are usually broken down into first-year and total enrollments and the percentages of men and women for the combined total. Beginning with "first-year statistics," the enrollment information refers to just first-year-enrolled students.

Faculty. This is the total number of faculty teaching courses on a full- and/or part-time/volunteer basis. This is often the least reliable data of all, for obvious reasons. In general, full-time represents permanent faculty; part-time represents part-time or adjunct appointments and volunteers.

Types of degrees conferred. Abbreviations were used for all medical/dental, scientist training programs and joint-/dual-degree programs. Please consult the Key to Abbreviations index for specific definitions.

Recruitment practices. This section indicates the specific individual at either the medical/dental school or the health center charged with diversity responsibility and includes phone numbers.

ADMISSION REQUIREMENTS

Credentials required in support of application. This paragraph lists all documents, entrance examinations, and other requirements needed for an admission decision. In general, any supplemental applications, recommendations, and financial-aid requests should be sent directly to the medical/dental school. Test scores and official transcripts (one official transcript for each college or university attended) must be sent to the application processing service, where they are processed and then forwarded to the medical/dental schools. At last count there were only sixteen medical schools that did not use an application processing service, and four of them use the University of Texas Medical Dental Application Center. Ninety-eight percent of medical and about 60 percent of the dental schools expect applicants to hold a bachelor's degree from an accredited institution when enrolling. A number of schools admit students with fewer than four years of undergraduate study, although typically these schools had combined-degree programs with their own undergraduate schools/colleges. Even with these combined programs, the medical school seldom permits a student to enter the medical program with less than the equivalent of four years of undergraduate study. Official transcripts of previous undergraduate and graduate study (when applicable) may also be required as part of the supplemental materials requested by the schools to be sent to the medical/dental school's admissions office.

The MCAT/DAT is required for all medical/dental schools. Each school treats multiple-choice test results differently; some average the scores, others take the highest, still others take the results of the last test taken.

Always contact the school you are considering before retaking any test to ensure that the results will be used to your advantage.

Most schools request one letter of recommendation from the premed committee or three letters of recommendation from science faculty members and one from a practicing professional. Ordinarily, the applicant is asked to have the recommendations sent directly to the school. In some cases, the application must include the names of the persons willing to send recommendations; the school then takes the responsibility of obtaining the recommendation.

Additional requirements for admission. Personal statements, essays, and résumés may also be given consideration. In general, supplementary materials are requested only after a preliminary review/evaluation and the school wishes to add another dimension to the applicants' profiles before sending out the invitations for on-campus interviews.

International applicants. International students are more likely to apply to, and enroll in, dental/osteopathic programs than they are to enter a M.D. program. Nevertheless, information with reference to TOEFL/TSE/TWE and services that will translate and evaluate foreign credentials has been included. Many institutions have their own international application and an international students office. The international applicant should consult with this office early in the process for it will have the most comprehensive and current information pertaining to the international student admissions process, application deadlines, and application fees. In most cases the international applicant must demonstrate English proficiency and the ability to pay all school expenses (room, board, tuition, etc.) while staying in the United States, before his/her application can be considered complete, then reviewed for admission and, if accepted, have the necessary entry documents (visas) issued.

Early Decision Program (EDP). Many medical schools, but only a few dental schools, have an EDP. Specific information has been supplied regarding time lines and procedures. In some instances, the only way a nonresident can apply to a state-supported medical school is through the EDP.

Dual-/joint-/combined-degree programs; M.S.T.P. In many cases, a joint-degree applicant must apply to, and be accepted by, both schools or both degree programs. In some cases the MCAT/DAT can be substituted for the master's/Ph.D. entrance exam, while a few joint-degree programs require the MCAT/DAT and either the GRE or GMAT. At some institutions the decision to apply for a second degree can be put off until the end of the first year. Several schools have joint-degree students start the graduate program in the summer prior to enrollment in the medical/dental school. About 80 percent of the medical schools have M.D.-Ph.D. programs, but there are only a few joint programs at either the dental or osteopathic schools. For M.S.T.P./D.S.T.P./institutional M.S.T.P. candidates, each school has a unique admissions procedure; phone numbers for the Program Director/Coordinator are included. (See index of current NIH-supported programs.)

Bachelor- M.D./D.D.S./D.M.D. applicants. There are at least thirty-three institutions that have a joint program with undergraduate institutions. (Please refer to the index for a current list.) This section contains the required high school preparation, required or suggested entrance exams, special conditions, and deadlines.

Transfer applicants/advanced standing students. A few medical schools accept transfer applicants from other LCME-accredited institutions, but only on a space-available basis and under certain extenuating circumstances. Dental schools consider advanced-standing students more frequently, and some dental schools have specific two- or three-year programs for graduates of foreign dental schools.

Office and dates of application. This refers to the office of the school from which application forms and current information on policies and procedures can be obtained. Closing dates for filing applications should be carefully observed. All supporting materials should also be received by their deadlines as well. In some cases, no firm deadlines are set, but priority/preferred dates are suggested. The applicant is advised to apply well in advance of these dates.

Application fee. This information was not always available. Its absence should not be interpreted to mean that no application fee is required.

Telephone and fax numbers and E-mail addresses. The numbers listed in both the admission requirements and the financial-aid sections are general contact numbers for both the medical/dental school and, in many cases, the university's financial aid office and a contact at the university for information regarding federally sponsored programs.

ADMISSION STANDARDS AND INSTITUTIONAL RECOGNITION

Prospective medical/dental students should consider a variety of factors in making their choice among schools. This section attempts to present factors that may assist the reader in determining the appropriate institutional fit. Among these factors are the number of resident/nonresident applications received, interviewed, and accepted; the median MCAT/DAT; the median UGPA; attrition rates; and two, three or four ranking/rating sources. The ranking sources may include one or all of the following: the *Barron's Guide,* which includes the 20 most prestigious U.S. Medical Schools; the *Gorman Report* with its rating score (Scale: very strong 4.51–2.99; strong 4.01–4.49; good 3.61–3.99; acceptable plus 3.01–3.49; adequate 2.51–2.99; marginal 2.01–2.49); *U.S. News & World Report*'s ranking of the top 25 medical schools and the top 25 medical schools for primary care; the ranking of medical/dental schools by the number of National Institutes of Health awards, including the total in-

stitutional dollars received. This data should help to give the applicant a more comprehensive perspective.

Medical/dental schools can be assessed as to quality in a variety of ways. The accrediting bodies fiercely resist any rating of their accredited schools beyond a simple statement of accreditation. Qualities that make one kind of school desirable to one student may not be as important to another. The quality of credentials of the groups of applicants to different institutions varies widely, and the degree of difficulty of admission must be interpreted accordingly. In other words, the most highly regarded institutions naturally attract applications from superior students in greater numbers than do the less favored schools. Therefore, the standards at a top medical/dental school cannot be assumed to be the same as those at less prestigious institutions.

Caution must be taken in equating the difficulty of admission with the quality of program. While there is clearly some relationship between the strength of the student body and the effectiveness of the program, this is less true on the professional-school level than on the undergraduate level. Limited facilities or state laws may restrict enrollment and therefore produce an image of quality due to the low number of applicants interviewed and then accepted. On the other hand, some schools may be able to accept larger proportions of their applicants without a reduction in the quality of the student body. Contrary to the assumption of many applicants, the grade-point average and MCAT/DAT median scores are not absolute "floors" or cutoff scorers. As with the descriptions of admissions policies, the inclusion of information about ranking and ratings is offered merely as a guide to help the applicant begin to focus his/her search for the right school. These data are only a part of the puzzle. What school is best for me? is a complex question. A selection checklist at the end of this introductory section helps the reader pull together the remaining factors needed to start the selection process.

FINANCIAL AID

The basic philosophy behind financial aid/student assistance as it is practiced at most professional schools is quite simple. The assumption is that three not so equal partners support the educational endeavor of the medical/dental student. The first one, and by far the largest partner, is the federal government, then the student and his/her parents, followed by the medical/dental school. It should become quite clear to the reader that the foundation undergirding most financial-aid policy is that the student is expected to finance his/her medical/dental education with only a minimum reliance on institutional scholarships/grants, tuition waivers, etc. Only the most highly endowed schools are able to extend sizable amounts of merit-based funding to members of the incoming class, and even then it is almost always part of an aid package that contains as much as 60–80 percent short- and long-term loans.

Types of aid administered by the school/college. Scholarships, fellowships, grants-in-aid, assistantships, stipends, and tuition waivers are the most common forms of assistance available. (Very few schools have all the above-mentioned forms of gift aid.) As listed here, merit-based grants are offered by institutional funds, gifts, contributions, or aid programs administered by the medical/dental school of the university. Most have to be renewed each year.

Nevertheless, some conclusions can be drawn about actual aid available. Scholarships rarely have service requirements, and the term "fellowship" is often used in lieu of "scholarship." Thus, an entry reading "Scholarships, fellowships, grants, tuition waivers; teaching/research assistantships" means that no service is required in exchange for the first four forms of aid, while those who hold assistantships are expected to assume some additional responsibilities. Duties may involve direct assistance in research to a particular faculty member or general responsibilities within a faculty area, such as grading papers or assisting in demonstrations. Fellowships and assistantships typically carry a tuition-remission privilege, some may also include an annual stipend. Since fellowships are generally regarded as the more prestigious of the two types of award, the stipend is often larger than for assistantships, and the tasks assigned may be more challenging in nature. Both types of awards are subject to broad variations between faculty, specialties, and schools. Many schools assist students in obtaining summer internships and externships. Since scholarships/fellowships generally include renewals for returning students as well, it should not be assumed that all those listed are solely for entering students.

To whom to apply and closing date. It is often necessary to apply to different persons, offices, or committees for the several kinds of aid available. If no deadline date is set, it is wise to apply as soon as possible after January 1, but certainly no later than February 15. Early applications receive maximum consideration. Scholarships and fellowships are often awarded through a central committee of the school; assistantships may also be granted by the graduate department offering study in the proposed joint-degree field. As a result, it may be necessary to contact as many as two or three persons or offices to obtain information about various forms of aid at the medical/dental school and in the university/college. In general, an applicant applies to the school via some form of financial-aid application for scholarships, fellowships, grants, and tuition waivers and to either the medical/dental school or the university/college for federally sponsored programs/loans. In some instances (depending on history and tradition), the medical/dental school may administer all aspects of the financial-aid process. In all cases, the second, if not the first, step in the aid process is to submit the FAFSA to a federal processor. This free federal document is used by all schools/colleges/universities to determine an accepted student's need to attend a particular school. In this entry the phrase "use" or "submit FAFSA" means that the applicant should submit the FAFSA in time for the processing center to return the necessary information to the school/

college/university (processing generally takes six weeks) prior to the financial-aid deadline.

Some schools/colleges do have merit and non-need-based scholarship programs. Generally, all accepted students are automatically considered for these programs during some phase of the acceptance process. For a few schools a special institutional scholarship/fellowship application is required. In all cases, the final authority is the medical/dental school's admissions/financial-aid office, and they must be contacted to receive the most current information.

Percentage of students receiving aid other than loans. The percentages given here relate to the total number of enrolled students receiving some form of financial assistance.

When information was available, a figure for total indebtedness for four years of medical/dental school is given. As a general rule of thumb, your debt picture after four years of school is found by taking the total financial-aid budget used by the school for one year and multiplying it by a factor of three or three and one-half. This will be your approximate debt picture upon graduation. There may be loan-forgiveness programs available for graduates willing to start their practice in rural or underrepresented areas, in public health, or in the military. Each program is unique, so contact the financial-aid office for the most current information, program regulations, and employment conditions.

DEGREE REQUIREMENTS

For M.D./D.D.S./D.M.D. degrees. The programs normally are completed in four years, though in rare instances this time frame can be accelerated by attending summer sessions. There are also some decelerated programs that are extended to five years. For most joint-degree programs the time needed to accomplish both

degrees is usually reduced by between one-half and two full years, and the number of credits required for both degrees may also be reduced. On the other hand, concurrent-degree programs may reduce the time required to complete both degrees but not the number of credits.

KEY TO ABBREVIATIONS

EXAMINATIONS AND OTHER ABBREVIATIONS

AACOMAS	American Association of Colleges of Osteopathic Medicine Application Service
AADA	American Association of Dental Schools
AADSAS	American Association of Dental Schools Application Service
AAMC	Association of American Medical Schools
ACT	American College Testing Program
AEGD	Advanced Education in General Dentistry
ALP	MEDLOANS Alternative Loan Program
AMA	American Medical Association
AMCAS	American Medical College Application Service
AOA	American Osteopathic Association
AP	Advanced Placement
CDA	Commission on Dental Accreditation
CEEB	College Entrance Examination Board
CLEP	College-Level Examination Program
CSS	College Scholarship Service
DAT	Dental Admission Test
D.S.A.	Dental Scientist Award Program
D.S.T.P.	Dental Scientist Training Program
ECFMG	Educational Council for Foreign Medical Graduates
ED	U.S. Department of Education
EDP	Early Decision Program
ETS	Educational Testing Service
FADHPS	Financial Assistance for Disadvantaged Health Professions Students
FAF	Financial Aid Form
FAFSA	Free Application for Federal Student Aid
FAT	Financial Aid Transcript
FDSLP	Federal Direct Student Loan Program
FFS	Family Financial Statement
FSLS	Federal Supplemental Loans for Students
FSSL	Federal Stafford Student Loan
FUSSL	Federal Unsubsidized Stafford Student Loans
FWSP	Federal Work-Study Program
GAPSFAS	Graduate and Professional School Financial Aid Service
GMAT	Graduate Management Admissions Test

GPA	Grade Point Average
GRE	Graduate Record Examination
GSL	Guaranteed Student Loans
HEAL	Health Education Assistance Loan
HPSL	Health Professions Student Loans
LCME	Liaison Committee on Medical Education
LDS	Loans for Disadvantaged Students
LSAT	Law School Admissions Test
MCAT	Medical College Admissions Test
Med-MAR	Medical Minority Applicant Registry
MELAB	Michigan English Language Assessment Battery
M.S.P.	Medical Scientist Program
M.S.T.P.	Medical Scientist Training Program
NBME	National Board of Medical Examiners
NHSC	National Health Service Corps Scholarship Program
NIH	National Institutes of Health
NIRMP	National Intern and Resident Matching Program
PAEG	Prueba de Admisiones para Estudios Graduados
PAT	Perceptual Ability Test
PCL	Primary Care Loans (formerly HPSL)
SAAC	Student Aid Application for California
SAT	Scholastic Assessment Test
SDS	Scholarships for Disadvantaged Students
SREB	Southern Regional Education Board
TOEFL	Test of English as a Foreign Language
TSE	Test of Spoken English
TWE	Test of Written English
UGPA	Undergraduate Grade Point Average
USMLE	U.S. Medical Licensing Examination
VA	Veterans Administration
WAMI	Wyoming, Alaska, Montana, Idaho
WICHE	Western Interstate Commission for Higher Education
WWAMI	Washington, Wyoming, Alaska, Montana, Idaho

DEGREES

AEGD	Advanced Education in General Dentistry	M.A.	Master of Arts
B.A.	Bachelor of Arts	M.B.A.	Master of Business Administration
B.S.	Bachelor of Science	M.D.	Doctor of Medicine
D.D.S.	Doctor of Dental Surgery	M.P.H.	Master of Public Health
D.M.D.	Doctor of Dental Medicine	M.S.	Master of Science
D.O.	Doctor of Osteopathic Medicine	M.S.D.	Master of Science in Dentistry
D.P.H.	Doctor of Public Health	M.T.M.H.	Master of Tropical Medicine and Hygiene
GPR	General Practice Residency	Ph.D.	Doctor of Philosophy
J.D.	Doctor of Jurisprudence		

KEY ORGANIZATIONS
AND WEB SITES

AACOM & AACOMAS
American Association of Colleges of Osteopathic Medicine and American Association of Colleges of Osteopathic Medicine Application Service
5550 Friendship Boulevard, Suite 310
Chevy Chase, Maryland 20815
Telephone: (301)968-4190
http://www.aacom.org

AADSAS Application
1625 Massachusetts Avenue, N.W., Suite 600
Washington, D.C. 20036-2212
Telephone: (202)667-9433; fax: (202)667-0642
E-mail: aadsas.appl@aads.jhu.edu

American Association of Dental Schools
1625 Massachusetts Avenue, N.W.
Washington, D.C. 20036-2212
Telephone: (202)667-9433; fax: (202)667-0642
http://www.aads.jhu.edu

American Dental Association
211 East Chicago Avenue, Suite 840
Chicago, Illinois 60611
Phone: (312)440-2795; fax: (312)440-2800
http://www.ada.org/index.html

DAT
Department of Testing Service
American Dental Association
211 East Chicago Avenue
Chicago, Illinois 60611-2678
Telephone: (800)621-8099
Test application information: (312)440-4650

Membership and Publication Orders
Association of American Medical Colleges
Washington, D.C. 20037-1129
Telephone: (202)828-0416; fax: (202)828-1123
http://www.aamc.org

Minority Student Information Clearinghouse
Division of Community and Minority Programs
Association of American Medical Colleges
2450 N Street, N.W.
Washington, D.C. 20037-1126

AMCAS
Section for Students Services
Association of American Medical Colleges
2501 M Street, N.W., Lobby 26
Washington, D.C. 20037-1300
Telephone: (202)828-0600
http://www.aamc.org
E-mail: AMCAS@aamc.org

Staff, Women in Medicine Program
Division of Institutional Planning and Development
Association of American Medical Colleges
2450 N Street, N.W.
Washington, D.C. 20037-1126
http://www.aamc.org

Department of Women in Medicine
American Medical Association
515 North State Street
Chicago, Illinois 60610
Telephone: (312)464-4392
http://www.ama.org

Department of Examination Services
Federation of State Medical Boards
400 Fuller Wiser Road, Suite 300
Euless, Texas 76039-6855
Telephone: (817)571-2949
http://www.fsmb.org

Health Resource Center
One Dupont Circle, N.W., Suite 800
Washington, D.C. 20036-1193
Telephone: (202)939-9320

MCAT
P.O. Box 4056
Iowa City, Iowa 52243
Telephone: (319)337-1357

Program Administrator
Medical Scientist Training Program
National Institutes of Health
45 Center Drive, MSC 6200
Bethesda, Maryland 20892-6200
Telephone: (301)594-3830

Test of English as a Foreign Language (TOEFL)
P.O. Box 6154
Princeton, New Jersey 08541-6151
Telephone: (609)771-7100
http://www.toefl.org

Federal Student Aid Information Center
U.S. Department of Education

P.O. Box 84
Washington, D.C. 20044
Telephone: (800)4-Fed-Aid
http://www.ed.gov/offices/OPE/Students

USMLE Secretariat
3750 Market Street
Philadelphia, Pennsylvania 19104-3190
Telephone: (215)590-0960

National Health Service Corps Scholarship Program
U.S. Public Health Recruitment
8201 Greensboro Drive, Suite 600
McLean, Virginia 22102

University of Texas System
Medical and Dental Application Center
702 Colorado, Suite 6400
Austin, Texas 78701
Telephone: (512)499-4785; fax: (512)499-4786

World Education Service (Midwest office)
P.O. Box 11623
Chicago, Illinois 65061-0623
Telephone: (312)222-0882; fax: (312)222-1217

World Education Service (New York City office)
P.O. Box 745 Old Chelsea Station
New York, New York 10113-0745
Telephone: (212)966-6311; fax: (212)966-6395

Selected Lending Organizations

AAMC MEDLOANS Program
Division of Student Affairs and Education Services
Association of American Medical Colleges
2450 N Street, N.W.
Washington, D.C. 20037

The Access Group
1411 Foulk Road
P.O. Box 7430
Wilmington, Delaware 19803-0430
Telephone: (800)282-1550; fax: (302)477-4080

CitiAssist
P.O. Box 22945
Rochester, New York 14692
Telephone: (800)745-5473
http://www.citibank.com/student

CollegeReserve Loan
USA Group
Telephone: (800)538-8492
http://www.usagroup.com

Medical/Dental School

	1st Choice	2nd Choice	3rd Choice	4th Choice
Name of Medical/Dental School				
Geographic location				
Public/private				
Size of parent institution				
Year school founded				
Size of college/university				
Library size				
Special facilities				
Special programs				
NIH ranking				
Total NIH funds received				
Hospital/medical/center recognized in Top 20,				
Hospital/medical/center recognized in Top 25				
# of specialities recognized				
Total school/college enrollment				
Tuition				
Total additional fees				
On-campus housing available				
Approximate living expenses				
# of full-time faculty				
Degrees offered				
Application deadlines				
# of resident applications received				
# of residents interviewed				
# of residents accepted				
# of residents enrolled				
# of applications received by nonresidents				
# of nonresidents interviewed				
# of nonresidents accepted				
# of nonresidents enrolled				
Median MCAT/DAT scores				
My scores				
Median GPA				
My GPA				
Science GPA				
My science GPA				
My chances of being accepted resident				
My chances of being accepted nonresident				
Is school in Top 25?				
Is school in Top 25 in primary care?				
Gorman rating				
NIH ranking				
Total NIH funding level				
% of total enrollment receiving financial aid				
Average size of scholarship/grants				
Average debt after graduation				

Selection Checklist

5th Choice	6th Choice	7th Choice	8th Choice	9th Choice	10th Choice

Application Calendar

(This form should be used after completing the "Selection Checklist.")

	1st Choice	2nd Choice	3rd Choice	4th Choice
Academic prep required:				
Biology, # of credits				
General chemistry, # of credits				
Organic chemistry, # of credits				
Physics, # of credits				
Mathematics, # of credits				
English, # of credits				
Foreign Language, # of credits				
Electives, # of credits				
Number of years/credits required for consideration				
Testing date required				
Test registration date required				
Test fee required				
DAT/MCAT Web site				
Processing service used				
Processing service fee				
AACOM/AADSAS/AMCAS Web site				
Date appl. requested from nonparticipating school				
Official transcript requested				
EDP				
Supplemental materials deadline				
Institutional application fee				
Personal statement required				
Personal statement completed				
Premed/dent adviser recommendation required				
2,3,4 letters of recommendation required				
On-campus invitational interview time frame				
Notification date				
Response date				
Deposit due				
Date credit report requested				
Financial-aid deadlines				
FAFSA deadline (min. six weeks prior to FA deadline)				

and Checklist

5th Choice	6th Choice	7th Choice	8th Choice	9th Choice	10th Choice

THE PENGUIN
GUIDE TO
AMERICAN
MEDICAL
AND DENTAL
SCHOOLS

UNIVERSITY OF ALABAMA AT BIRMINGHAM

Birmingham, Alabama 35294
Internet site: http://www.uab.edu

Founded 1970. Public control. Quarter system. Library: 1,567,700 volumes; 1,181,772 microforms; 5,100 periodicals/subscriptions; 210 work stations. Special facilities: Alabama Congenital Heart Disease Diagnosis and Treatment Center, Center for Health Promotion, Deep South Occupational Health & Safety Education Resource Center, Injury Control Research Center, Lister Hill Center for Health Policy, Sparkman Center for International Public Health Policy, Vision Science Research Center. University's ranking by NIH awards in domestic institutions of higher education was 19th, with 442 grants; total dollars awarded $121,996,615.

The university's graduate school includes: Graduate School of Management, School of Arts and Humanities, School of Education, School of Engineering, School of Health Related Professions, School of Nursing, School of Public Health, School of Social and Behavioral Sciences, School of Dentistry, School of Medicine, School of Optometry.

Total university enrollment at main campus: 15,275.

Medical Center

701 20th Street South
Birmingham, Alabama 35294
Telephone: (800)822-8816
E-mail: hf@hsf.uab.edu

Founded 1945. Located in Birmingham. Public control. Member of Council of Teaching Hospitals. Schools located at Medical Center: School of Dentistry, School of Medicine, School of Nursing, School of Optometry, School of Public Health, School of Health Related Professions. Special facilities: Arthritis Center, Cardiovascular Research and Training Center, Comprehensive Cancer Center, Comprehensive Stroke Center, Cystic Fibrosis Research Center, Diabetes Research and Training Center, Institute of Dental Research. Nationally recognized programs in AIDS, Cardiology, Gastroenterology, Geriatrics, Neurology, Otolaryngology, Urology.

School of Medicine

100 Volker Hall
Birmingham, Alabama 35294-0019
Telephone: (205)931-2330; fax: (205)934-8724
Internet site: http://www.uab.edu/uasom
E-mail: ghand@uasom/.los/uab/edu

Established 1859. Upper-division branch campuses created in 1969 at Huntsville and Tuscaloosa. Semester system. Library: 240,000 volumes/microforms; 3,000 current periodical/subscriptions. Affiliated hospitals: University Hospital, Children's Hospital, Cooper Green Hospital, Eye Foundation Hospital, Capstone Medical Center, DCH Regional Medical Center, Veteran's Hospital, AMI West Alabama Hospital, Bryce State Hospital/Partlow State School and Hospital. Special programs: summer programs for underrepresented minorities; prematriculation summer sessions.

Annual tuition (M.D.): residents $6,108, nonresidents $18,324. Limited housing available at medical center; preference given to married students. Annual on-campus housing cost: $8,052 (room and board). Contact Admissions Office for both on- and off-campus housing information. Medical students tend to live off-campus. Off-campus housing and personal expenses: approximately $9,000–$10,000. Additional costs: approximately $4,000.

Enrollment: 1st-year class 165 (EDP 15, M.D.-Ph.D. 9); total full-time 702 (men, 65%, women, 35%); no part-time students. First-year statistics: 17% out of state; 60 colleges represented; 32% women; 10% underrepresented minorities; 8% other minorities; undergraduate majors represented: 46% biology, 33% from engineering, math, other sciences.

Degrees conferred: M.D., M.D.-Ph.D. (Anatomy, Biochemistry, Biophysics, Cell Biology, Genetics, Immunology, Microbiology, Molecular Biology, Neurosciences, Pathology, Pharmacology, Physiology); has M.S.T.P.

RECRUITMENT PRACTICES AND POLICIES. School has diversity program and actively recruits women/minority applicants. Participates in Med-MAR. Diversity contact: Coordinator, Minority Enhancement Program; phone: (205)934-2330.

ADMISSION REQUIREMENT FOR UAB EARLY-MEDICAL-SCHOOL-ACCEPTANCE APPLICANTS. Open to residents only. Submit application, SAT/ACT, official high school transcripts, and 2 letters of recommendation to Office of Enrollment Management by February 1. Early applications encouraged. Phone: (205)934-8152

ADMISSION REQUIREMENTS FOR FIRST-YEAR APPLICANTS. Preference given to state residents. *Undergraduate preparation.* Suggested premed courses: 2 courses in biology, 2 courses in inorganic chemistry, 2 courses in organic chemistry, 2 courses in physics, 2 courses in college math, 2 courses in English. Bachelor's degree from an accredited institution required. In most cases applicants must have bachelor's degree awarded prior to enrollment. *Has EDP for state residents only;* applicants must apply through AMCAS (official transcripts should be sent by mid-May) between June 1 and August 1. Early applications are encouraged. Submit secondary/supplemental application, a personal statement, and 2 recommendations to Admissions Office within 2 weeks of receipt of application. Notification normally begins October 15. *Regular application process.* Apply through AMCAS (file after June 1, before December 1); submit MCAT (will accept MCAT test results from 1995, MCAT essay required; if more than 1 MCAT taken, highest is used), official transcripts for each school attended (should show at least 90 semester credits/135 quarter credits, submit transcripts by mid-May to AMCAS), service processing fee. Submit secondary application within 2 weeks of receipt, a personal comment/statement (1 page only), and 2 recommendations to Admissions Office. Dual-degree applicants must apply to, and be accepted by, both schools. Interviews are by invitation only and generally for final selection. First-year students admitted in fall only. Rolling admission process: Notification usually starts in October (letters of acceptance are sent out on the 15th of each month) and is finished when class is filled. Applicant's response to offer and 1st deposit due within 2 weeks of receipt of acceptance letter. School does maintain an alternate/waiting list. Application fee, $65. Phone: (205)934-2330. MSTP information number: (205)934-4092.

ADMISSION REQUIREMENTS FOR TRANSFER APPLICANTS (state residents only). Accepts transfers from other accredited American/foreign medical schools. Admission limited to space available.

ADMISSION STANDARDS AND RECOGNITION. *For M.D.:* number of applicants: residents 536; nonresidents 1,507; number of interviews: residents 379, nonresidents 176; number enrolled: residents 138, nonresidents 27; median MCAT 9.8 (verbal reasoning 9.8; biological sciences 8.9; physical sciences 9.7); median GPA 3.55 (A = 4). Attrition rate: generally less than 3%. Barron's ranking of the 20 most prestigious U.S. medical schools: not listed; Gorman rating 3.67 (scale: good 3.61–3.99); *U.S. News & World Report* ranking: not ranked in the Top 25 of all medical schools; not ranked in the Top 25 of all primary-care programs; medical-school ranking by NIH awards was 15th; total dollars awarded $101,837,056.

FINANCIAL AID. Scholarships, medical scholarship (state residents only), minority scholarships, grants-in-aid, institutional loans, HEAL, alternative loan programs, NIH stipends, federal Perkins loans, Stafford subsidized and unsubsidized loans, and service commitment scholarship programs offered through Financial Aid/Medical Students Services Office. Assistantships may be available for dual-degree candidates. For medical scholarships the selection criteria place heavy reliance on MCAT and undergraduate GPA; phone: (205)934-4384. All accepted students are sent financial-aid information and forms. Early applications are encouraged. For financial-aid information contact Financial Aid/Medical Students Services; phone: (205)934-8707. Use FAFSA for all federal programs (Title IV school code # 001052); also submit Financial Aid Transcript and Federal Income Tax forms. Approximately 22% of 1st-year class received scholarships/grants-in-aid. Approximately 76% of current students receive some form of financial assistance. Average debt after graduation $53,000.

DEGREE REQUIREMENTS. *For M.D.:* satisfactory completion of 4-year program. Accelerated M.D. available. All students must pass USMLE Step 1 prior to entering 3rd year; all students must pass USMLE Step 2 prior to the awarding of M.D.; clinical clerkship. *For M.D.-Ph.D.:* generally a 7-year program; candidacy, dissertation, oral defense, final exam.

School of Dentistry
Box 16 SDB
UAB Station
1919 Seventh Avenue, South
Birmingham, Alabama 35294-0007
Telephone: (205)934-3387; fax: (205)975-5364
Internet site: http://www.uab.edu/sdentistry.htm

Established 1945. Located on main campus at medical center. Basic sciences are presented in first 2 years. Library: 210,000 volumes/microforms; 2,900 current periodicals/subscriptions. Special facilities: Research Center in Oral Biology, Oral Cancer Research Center, Institute of Dental Research. Postgraduate specialties: Endodontics, General Dentistry, Dental Public Health, Oral and Maxillofacial Surgery, Orthodontics, Orthopedics, Pediatric Dentistry, Periodontics, Prosthodontics.

Annual tuition: residents $5,163; nonresidents $15,489; fees $2,329; equipment and supplies $5,200. Limited housing available at medical center. Annual on-campus housing cost: $8,052 (room and board). Contact Admissions Office for both on- and off-campus housing information. Dental students tend to live off-campus. Off-campus housing, food, transportation, and personal expenses: approximately $1,073 per month.

Enrollment: 1st-year class 55 (men 40%, women 15%; total full-time 244). First-year statistics: 4 from out of state; 3 states represented; average age 24; 3 underrepresented minorities; 3 other minorities.

Degrees conferred: D.M.D., B.S.-D.M.D., D.M.D.-M.S. (Oral Biology); D.M.D.-Ph.D. (Anatomy, Biochemistry, Biophysics, Microbiology, Pharmacology, Physiology).

RECRUITMENT PRACTICES AND POLICIES. School has diversity program and actively recruits women/minority applicants. Diversity contact: Admissions Office; phone: (205)934-3387.

ADMISSION REQUIREMENTS FOR FIRST-YEAR APPLICANTS. Preference given to state residents and applicants from neighboring states; U.S. citizens and permanent residents only. *Undergraduate preparation.* Suggested predent courses: 4 courses in biology with labs, 2 courses in inorganic chemistry with labs, 2 courses in organic chemistry with labs, 2 courses in physics with labs, 2 courses in college math, 2 courses in English, at least 10 courses in nonsciences. The junior-college transfer-credit limit is 70 credits. Will consider applicants with only 3 years of undergraduate preparation; prefer applicants who will have bachelor's degree prior to enrollment, all enrolled students have bachelor's degree awarded prior to enrollment. For serious consideration an applicant should have a 2.5 GPA or better. *Application process.* Apply through AADSAS (file after June 1, before January 15); submit official transcripts for each school attended (should show at least 90 semester credits/135 quarter credits), service processing fee; at the same time as you send in AADSAS materials, submit official DAT scores directly to Admissions Office. TOEFL required of an applicant whose native language is other than English. Submit the following materials only after being contacted by an admissions officer: an application fee of $25, a secondary/supplemental application, official transcripts, predental committee evaluation or 2 recommendations from professors in your major field of study, photograph, and Verification of Residency form to Admissions Office within 2 weeks of receipt of supplemental materials. Interviews are by invitation only and generally for final selection. Dual-degree applicants must apply to, and be accepted by, both schools. First-year students admitted in fall only. Rolling admission process. Notification starts in December and is finished when class is filled. Applicant's response to offer and $200 deposit due within 30 days if accepted prior to February 1; response and deposit due within 2 weeks if received after February 1. School does maintain an alternate list. Admissions office phone: (205)934-3387; fax: (205)975-5364.

ADMISSION REQUIREMENTS FOR ADVANCED-STANDING APPLICANTS. Accepts transfers from other accredited U.S. dental schools into the 3rd year of study. Admission limited to space available. There is no Advanced-Standing Program for graduates of foreign schools of dentistry. Contact the Admissions Office for current information.

ADMISSION STANDARDS. *For D.M.D.:* number of applicants 646; number enrolled 55; median DAT: ACAD 17.94, PAT 16.14; median GPA 3.45 (A = 4); median sciences GPA 3.4 (A = 4). Gorman rating 4.25 (scale: strong 4.01–4.49); ranked in the Top 35 of all U.S. dental schools.

FINANCIAL AID. Scholarships, merit scholarships, minority scholarships, grants-in-aid, institutional loans, state loan programs, DEAL, HEAL, HPSL, alternative loan programs, federal Perkins loans, Stafford subsidized and unsubsidized loans, and armed forces service commitment Scholarship programs are available. Assistantships/fellowships may be available for combined degree candidates. Institutional financial aid applications and information are given out at the on-campus (by invitation) interview. For merit scholarships, the selection criteria place heavy reliance on DAT and undergraduate GPA. Contact the Financial Aid Office for current information; phone: (205)934-3387. For need-based programs use FAFSA (Title IV school code # 001052); also submit Financial Aid Transcript, Federal Income Tax forms, and Use of Federal Funds Certification. Approximately 87% of current students receive some form of financial assistance. Average award $19,558.

DEGREE REQUIREMENTS. *For D.M.D.:* satisfactory completion of 4-year program. *For D.D.S.-M.P.H.:* generally a 5-year program. *For D.M.D.-M.S.:* generally a 4½–5½-year program; thesis/nonthesis option; research project. *For D.M.D.-Ph.D.:* generally a 6–7-year program; candidacy, dissertation, oral defense, final exam.

ALLEGHENY UNIVERSITY OF THE HEALTH SCIENCES

Philadelphia, Pennsylvania 19102-1192
Internet site: http://www.auhs.edu

Formed by combining the Medical College of Pennsylvania and Hahneman Medical School and Hospital in 1993. Name changed to Allegheny University of the Health Sciences in 1996. Located Philadelphia, Pittsburgh, and Erie. Private control. Semester system. Library: 210,000 volumes; 2,500 current periodicals/subscriptions; 200 work stations.

The university's other graduate colleges/schools: School of Health Professions, School of Nursing, School of Public Health.

Total university enrollment: 3,040.

Allegheny Health, Education and Research Foundation (AHERF)

Broad and Vine Streets, MS #300
Philadelphia, Pennsylvania 19102

Founded 1996. Private control. Member of Council of Teaching Hospitals. The health system includes the Graduate Health System (Philadelphia and New Jersey), the Forbes Health System (Pittsburgh), Allegheny Valley Hospital (Natrona Heights), Cannonsburg General Hospital (Cannonsburg). Nationally recognized programs: Cancer, Gastroenterology, Geriatrics, Neurology, Orthopedics, Otolaryngology.

MCP-Hahneman School of Medicine

2900 Queen Lane Avenue
Philadelphia, Pennsylvania 19129
Telephone: (215)991-8202; fax: (215)843-1766
Internet site: http://www.aushs.edu
E-mail: admis@ef.allegheny.edu

Medical College of Medicine founded 1850; Hahneman founded 1848. Combined, they form the largest medical school in U.S. Semester system. Full-time, day study only. Special programs: B.A.-M.D. program (Lehigh University); B.S.- M.D. program (Villanova University); has postbaccalaureate/M.D. program for adults in conjunction with Bryn Mawr College, Bennington College, Columbia University, Duquesne University, Goucher College, University of Pennsylvania, West Chester University. Special programs: summer programs for underrepresented minorities; prematriculation summer sessions.

Annual tuition (M.D.): $24,500. Limited on-campus rooms and apartments available for both single and married students. Annual on-campus housing cost: $5,000 (room only), $7,200 (room and board). Contact Graduate Office for both on- and off-campus housing information. Phone: (215)762-8495. Medical students tend to live off-campus. Off-campus housing and personal expenses: approximately $10,000–$12,000.

Enrollment: 1st-year class 250 (EDP 15); total full-time 1,124 (men 55%, women 45%); no part-time students. First-year statistics: 43% out of state; 37% women; 16% underrepresented minority; undergraduate majors represented: biology, chemistry, and sciences form the vast majority of majors.

Faculty: full- and part-time 3,600.

Degrees conferred: M.D., M.D.-B.A., M.D.-B.S., M.D.-M.P.H., M.D.-M.S. (Clinical Microbiology, Laboratory Animal Science [M.L.A.S.], Microbiology and Immunology, Molecular and Cell Biology, Pharmacology, Radiation Sciences); M.D.-Ph.D. (Biomedical Engineering, Cardiovascular Biology, Microbiology and Immunology, Molecular Pathobiology, Neurosciences, Pharmacology, Physiology, Radiation Sciences).

RECRUITMENT PRACTICES AND POLICIES. School has diversity program and actively recruits women/minority applicants. Participates in Med-MAR. Diversity contact: Director of Minority Affairs; phone: (515)991-8215. Early Assurance Program available in conjunction with Chatham College, Colby-Sawyer College, Duquesne University, Gannon University, Indiana University of Pennsylvania, Allegheny University, Monmouth University, Muhlenberg College, Rosemont College, Ursinus College, West Chester University, Widener University, Wilkes University.

ADMISSION REQUIREMENT FOR BACHELOR-M.D. APPLICANTS. Open to Lehigh and Villanova University students only. Submit application, SAT (at least 1,350 combined score), official high school transcript (rank in class, top 10%), 3 letters of recommendation. Apply to Bachelor's/M.D. Program Coordinator, Lehigh University (610)785-3100), Villanova University (610)519-4833, by February 1.

ADMISSION REQUIREMENTS FOR FIRST-YEAR APPLICANTS. *Undergraduate preparation.* Suggested premed courses: 2 courses in biology, 2 courses in inorganic chemistry, 2 courses in organic chemistry, 2 courses in physics, 2 courses in English, 2 courses in college math, 2 courses in humanities, 2 courses in social sciences. Bachelor's degree from an accredited institution required; 98% of applicants had bachelor's degree awarded prior to enrollment. *Has EDP;* applicants must apply through AMCAS (official transcripts sent by mid-May) between June 1 and August 1. Early applications are encouraged. Submit secondary/supplemental application, a personal statement, 2 recommendations to Office of Admission and Recruitment within 3 weeks of receipt of application. Notification normally begins October 1. *Regular application process.* Apply through AMCAS (file after June 1, before December 1); submit MCAT (will accept MCAT test results from 1995; MCAT essay required; if more than 1 MCAT taken, highest is used), official transcripts for each school attended (should show at least 90 semester credits/135 quarter credits; submit transcripts by mid-May to AMCAS), service processing fee. Submit supplemental application, a personal comment/statement, and 2 recommendations to Office of Admission and Recruitment within 2–3 weeks of receipt of supplemental materials. Dual-degree applicants must apply to, and be accepted by, both schools; see graduate-school requirements below. Interviews are by invitation only and generally for final selection. First-year students admitted in fall only. Rolling admission process. Notification starts October 15 and is finished when class is filled. Applicant's response to offer and 1st deposit due within 3 weeks of receipt of acceptance letter. Application fee $55; phone: (215)991-8100; E-mail: admmed@auhs.edu.

ADMISSION REQUIREMENTS FOR TRANSFER (Fifth Pathway) APPLICANTS. Accepts transfers from other accredited American/foreign medical schools. Admission limited to space available. Submit application, application fee, official transcripts from current medical school, and personal statement regarding reason for transfer. Third-year transfers must have taken and passed Step 1 of USMLE.

ADMISSION REQUIREMENTS FOR GRADUATE/DUAL-DEGREE APPLICANTS. Official transcripts, 3 letters of recommendation, GRE General Test (some programs accept MAT in lieu of GRE), interview (some programs) required in support of graduate-school application. TOEFL required for foreign applicants whose native language is not English. Graduates of unaccredited institutions not considered. Application deadlines are degree-specific; contact the M.D.-M.S., M.D.-Ph.D. Program Coordinator for the latest information; phone (215)991-8570.

ADMISSION STANDARDS AND RECOGNITION. *For M.D.:* number of resident applicants, 1,497, nonresidents 11,041; number of state residents interviewed 443; nonresidents 613; number of residents enrolled 152, nonresidents 94; median MCAT N/A; median GPA 3.51(A = 4). Attrition rate: generally less than 3%. Gorman rating 3.39 (scale: acceptable plus 3.01–3.59); medical-school ranking by NIH awards was 58th; total dollars awarded $29,778.248.

FINANCIAL AID. Merit scholarships (half tuition), minority scholarships (full and half tuition), HEAL, alternative loan programs, federal Perkins loans, Stafford subsidized and unsubsidized loans, service commitment scholarship programs, and federal W/S are available. Assistantships may be available for dual-degree candidates. For merit and minority scholarships, selection criteria place heavy reliance on MCAT and undergraduate GPA; all accepted students are considered for these scholarships. For all financial-aid information contact the Office of Student Financial Aid; phone: (215)991-8210; E-mail: iannuzzij@wpo.mcphu.edu. Use FAFSA for all federal programs (Title IV school code # 003271); also submit Financial Aid Transcript and Federal Income Tax forms. Approximately 85% of 1st-year class receives some form of financial assistance.

DEGREE REQUIREMENTS. *For B.A./B.S.-M.D.:* a 6–7-year program. *For M.D.:* satisfactory completion of 4-year program. Accelerated M.D. available. All students must pass USMLE Step 1 prior to entering 3rd year; all students must pass USMLE Step 2 prior to awarding of M.D. *For M.S.-M.D.:* generally a 4½–5½-year program; thesis/nonthesis option; research project. *For M.D.-M.P.H.:* a 5-year program. *For M.D.-Ph.D.:* generally a 7-year program; candidacy, dissertation, oral defense.

UNIVERSITY OF ARIZONA

Tucson, Arizona 95721
Internet site: http://www.Arizona.edu

Founded 1885. Located 100 miles SW of Phoenix, near the international border. Coed. Public control. Semester system. Library: 3,907,000 volumes; 4,624,000 microforms; 26,000 periodicals/subscriptions.

The university's graduate colleges/schools: The Graduate college includes everything but School of Medicine. College of Agriculture, College of Architecture, College of Business and Public Administration, College of Education, College of Engineering and Mines, College of Fine Arts, College of Humanities, College of Nursing, College of Pharmacy, College of Science, College of Social and Behavioral Sciences, School of Health Related Professions, College of Medicine. The university's ranking by NIH awards in domestic higher education was 43rd, with 242 grants; total dollars awarded $60,060,182.

Total university enrollment at main campus: 34,777.

University of Arizona Health Sciences Center

1501 North Campbell Avenue
Tucson, Arizona 85724
Telephone: (520)694-8888
Internet site: http://www.ahsc.arizona.edu

Completed 1971. Public Control. Member of Council of Teaching Hospitals. Schools located at medical center: College of Medicine, School of Health Professions, School of Nursing, School of Pharmacy. Special facilities: Arizona Arthritis Center, Arizona Cancer Center, Arizona Center on Aging, Arizona Emergency Medicine Research Center, Arizona Poison and Drug Information Center, Arizona Prevention Center, Center for Pharmaceutical Economics, Center for Toxicology, Respiratory Sciences Center, Steele Memorial Children's Research Center, University Heart Center.

College of Medicine
P.O. Box 245075
Tucson, Arizona 85724-5075
Telephone: (520)626-6214; fax: (520)626-4884
Internet site: http://www.ahsc.arizona.edu/pre-med

Established 1967. Located in downtown Tucson. Semester system. Library: 165,000 volumes/microforms; 3,500 current periodicals/subscriptions. Special programs: summer programs for underrepresented minorities; prematriculation summer sessions.

Annual tuition (M.D.): Arizona residents and residents of Alaska, Montana, Wyoming, $7,360. Limited on-campus housing available. Annual on- and off-campus housing cost: $6,000–$7,400 (room only). Contact Admissions Office for both on- and off-campus housing information. Medical students tend to live off-campus. Additional cost: approximately $2,500.

Enrollment: 1st-year class 100. First-year statistics: 0% out of state; 49% women; average age 24; 10% underrepresented minorities.

Faculty: full-time 500, part-time/volunteers 800.

Degrees conferred: M.D., M.D.-M.P.H., M.D.-Ph.D. (Anatomy, Biochemistry, Cell Biology, Genetics, Immunology, Microbiology, Molecular Biology, Neurosciences, Pharmacology, Physiology).

RECRUITMENT PRACTICES AND POLICIES. School has diversity program and actively recruits women/minority applicants. Diversity contact: Program Coordinator, Office of Minority Affairs; phone: (606)262-7146.

ADMISSION REQUIREMENTS FOR FIRST-YEAR APPLICANTS. Preference given to state residents of Arizona, Alaska, Montana, and Wyoming; U.S. citizens and permanent residents only. *Undergraduate preparation.* Suggested premed courses: 2 laboratory courses in biology/zoology, 2 laboratory courses in general chemistry, 2 laboratory courses in organic chemistry, 2 laboratory courses in physics, 2 courses in English; will not accept either CLEP or AP credits. Bachelor's degree from an accredited institution required; all applicants have bachelor's degree awarded prior to enrollment. *Does not have EDP. Application process.* Apply through AMCAS (file after June 15, before November 1); submit MCAT (will accept MCAT test results from 1995), official transcripts for each school attended (should show at least 90 semester credits/135 quarter credits, submit transcripts by mid-May to AMCAS), service processing fee. Submit supplemental application, a personal statement, and 2 recommendations to Admissions Office within 2–3 weeks of the receipt of supplemental materials; no application

fee required. Interviews are by invitation only and generally for final selection. Dual-degree applicants must apply to, and be accepted by, both schools; contact the Admissions Office for current information and specific requirements for admission. First-year students admitted in fall only. Rolling admission process: Notification starts on January 30 and is finished when class is filled. Applicant's response to offer is due within 2 weeks of receipt of acceptance letter; phone: (520)626-6214; fax: (520)626-4884.

ADMISSION REQUIREMENTS FOR TRANSFER APPLICANTS. Accepts transfers from other accredited U.S. medical and osteopathic schools. Admission limited to space available and restricted to state residents and certified and funded WICHE applicants. Contact the admissions office for current information and specific requirements for admission.

ADMISSION STANDARDS AND RECOGNITION. *For M.D.:* number of state-resident applicants 588, nonresidents 463; number of state residents interviewed 528, nonresidents 3; number of state residents accepted 118, nonresidents 0; number of residents enrolled 100, nonresidents 0; median MCAT 9.3 (verbal reasoning 9.4; biological sciences 9.3; physical sciences 8.6); median GPA 3.55 (A = 4). Gorman rating 3.42 (scale: acceptable plus 3.01–3.59); medical ranking by NIH awards was 54th; total dollars awarded $31,633,067.

FINANCIAL AID. State scholarships, minority scholarships, institutional and state loans, HEAL, alternative loan programs; federal Perkins loans, Stafford subsidized and unsubsidized loans, and armed forces service commitment scholarship programs are available. Assistantships/fellowships may be available for dual-degree candidates. All accepted students are considered for merit scholarships. Selection criteria place heavy reliance on MCAT and undergraduate GPA. For financial-aid applications and information, contact the Financial Aid Office; phone: (520)626-7145. For need-based programs, use FAFSA (Title IV school code # 001083); also submit Financial Aid Transcript and Federal Income Tax forms. Approximately 85% of current students receive some form of financial assistance.

DEGREE REQUIREMENTS. *For M.D.:* satisfactory completion of 4-year program. All students must pass USMLE Step 1 prior to entering 3rd year; all students must pass USMLE Step 2 prior to awarding of M.D.; clinical clerkship. *For M.D.-M.P.H.:* generally a 5–6-year program. *For M.D.-Ph.D.:* generally a 7-year program; candidacy, dissertation, oral defense.

UNIVERSITY OF ARKANSAS

Little Rock, Arkansas 72204-1099
Internet site: http://www.ualr.edu

Located in the city of Little Rock. Coed. Public control. Semester system. Library: 394,780 volumes; 691,612 microforms; 2,626 periodicals/subscriptions; 100 work stations.

The university's graduate school includes: College of Arts Humanities and Social Sciences, College of Business Administration, College of Education, College of Professional Studies, College of Sciences and Engineering Technology.

Total university enrollment at main campus: 11,000.

University of Arkansas for Medical Sciences

Little Rock, Arkansas 72205-7199

Occupied present facilities in 1957; renamed in 1975. Public control. Member of Council of Teaching Hospitals. Schools located at medical center: College of Health Related Professions, College of Nursing, College of Pharmacy, Graduate Institute of Technology, School of Medicine. Special facilities: Arkansas Cancer Research and Treatment Center, Jones Eye Institute, T. H. Barton Institute for Medical Research. Nationally recognized programs in Otolaryngology.

School of Medicine

4301 West Markham Street
Little Rock, Arkansas 72205-7199
Telephone: (501)686-5354; fax: (501)686-5873
Internet site: http://www.uams.edu
E-mail: TSouth@comdeanl.uams.edu

Established 1879. Special programs: summer programs for minorities; prematriculation summer sessions.

Annual tuition (M.D.): residents $8,098, nonresidents $16,196. On-campus rooms and apartments available for single students only. All 1st- and 2nd-year students are required to live on campus. Annual on-campus housing cost: single students $2,435 (room only). Contact Graduate Housing Office for both on- and off-campus housing information; phone: (501)686-5850.

Enrollment: first-year class 150; total full-time 554 (men 62%, women 38%). First-year statistics: 0% out of state; 52% women; 11% underrepresented minorities; 80% in science majors.

Degrees conferred: M.D., M.D.-M.S., M.D.-Ph.D. (Anatomy, Biochemistry, Neurosciences, Pharmacology, Physiology).

RECRUITMENT PRACTICES AND POLICIES. School has diversity program and actively recruits women/minority applicants. Diversity contact: Associate Dean for Minority Affairs; phone: (501)686-5123.

ADMISSION REQUIREMENTS FOR FIRST-YEAR APPLICANTS. Applicants restricted to state residents only and to nonresidents with strong ties to state who are U.S. citizens and permanent residents. *Undergraduate preparation.* Suggested premed courses: 2 courses in biology with labs, 2 courses in general chemistry with labs, 2 courses in organic chemistry with labs, 2 courses in physics with labs, 2 courses in college math, 3 courses in English. Bachelor's degree from an accredited institution required; 98% of applicants have bachelor's degree awarded prior to enrollment. *Does not have EDP. Application process.* Apply through AMCAS (file after June 1, before November 1); submit MCAT (will accept MCAT test results from 1995), official transcripts for each school attended (should show at least 90 semester credits/ 135 quarter credits, submit transcripts by mid-May to AMCAS), service processing fee. Submit an application fee of $10, supplemental application, a personal comment/statement, preprofessional committee evaluation, and 2 recommendations from science faculty to Admissions Office within 2–3 weeks of receipt of supplemental materials. Interviews are by invitation only and generally for final selection. Dual-degree applicants must apply to, and be accepted by, both schools; contact the Admissions Office for current information and specific requirements for admissions. First-year students admitted in fall only. Rolling admission process: Notification starts on December 15 and is finished when class is filled. Applicant's response to offer and $100 deposit due within 3 weeks of receipt of acceptance letter.

ADMISSION REQUIREMENTS FOR TRANSFER APPLICANTS. Accepts transfers from other accredited U.S. medical schools who are state residents or nonresidents who have strong ties to the state. Admission limited to space available. Contact the Admissions Office for current information and specific requirements.

ADMISSION STANDARDS AND RECOGNITION *For M.D.:* number of full-time state-resident applicants 431; nonresidents 459; number of state residents interviewed 431; nonresidents 28; number of state residents enrolled 139; nonresidents 0; median MCAT 9.7 (verbal reasoning 9.4; biological sciences 9.4; physical sciences 8.9); median GPA 3.64 (A = 4). Gorman rating 3.45 (scale: acceptable plus 3.01–3.59).

FINANCIAL AID. Scholarships, merit scholarships, minority scholarships, HEAL, alternative loan programs, federal Perkins loans, Stafford subsidized and unsubsidized loans, and armed forces scholarship programs are available. Assistantships/fellowships may be available for dual-degree candidates. All accepted students are considered for scholarships; the selection criteria place heavy reliance on MCAT and undergraduate GPA. Contact the Financial Aid Office for current information; phone: (501)686-5813. For most financial assistance and all federal programs, submit FAFSA to a federal processor (Title IV school code # E00600); also submit Financial Aid Transcript and Federal Income Tax forms. Approximately 80% of 1st-year class receive some form of financial assistance. Average debt after graduation $53,000.

DEGREE REQUIREMENTS. *For M.D.:* satisfactory completion of 4-year program. All students must pass USMLE Step 1 prior to entering 3rd year; all students must pass USMLE Step 2 prior to awarding of M.D. *For M.D.-M.S.:* generally a 5–6-year program. *For M.D.-Ph.D.:* generally a 7-year program.

BAYLOR COLLEGE OF MEDICINE
Houston, Texas 77030

Founded 1903. Private control. Quarter system. Library, 260,000 volumes; 4,500 current periodicals/subscriptions. Special facilities: DeBakey Heart Center, Huffington Center on Aging, Center for Medical Ethics and Health Policy.

Texas Medical Center
Holcombe Boulevard
Houston, Texas 77030

Private control. Member of Council of Teaching Hospitals. Schools located at medical center: Baylor College of Medicine, Graduate School of Biomedical Sciences, College of Pharmacy, Dental School, Nursing School, School of Public Health. Special facilities: over 50 specialties centers. Nationally recognized programs in AIDS, Cancer, Cardiology, Endocrinology, Gastroenterology, Gynecology, Neurology, Ophthalmology, Orthopedics, Otolaryngology, Pulmonary Diseases, Rehabilitation, Urology.

Baylor College of Medicine
One Baylor Plaza
Houston, Texas 77030
Telephone: (713)798-4842; fax: (713)798-5563
Internet site: http://www.bcm.tmc.edu
E-mail: melodym@bcm.tms.edu

Established in Dallas in 1900. Relocated to Houston in 1943. Separated from Baylor University in 1969. Quarter system. Affiliated hospitals: Harris County Hospital District, Methodist Hospital, St Luke's Episcopal Hospital, Texas Children's Hospital, Veterans Affairs Medical Center. Special Programs: summer programs for underrepresented minorities; prematriculation summer sessions.

Annual tuition: residents $6,550, nonresidents $19,500. Near-campus housing available; 1 residency hall. Contact Admissions Office for both on- and off-campus housing information. Medical students tend to live off-campus. Off-campus housing and personal expenses: approximately $12,000–$15,000.

Enrollment: 1st-year class 168 (EDP 5; M.D.-Ph.D., approximately 10–12 yearly); total full-time 677 (men, 60%, women, 40%). First-year statistics: 76% out of state; 24 states represented; 40% women; 23% minorities; 36 undergraduate majors represented; 70% were science majors.

Faculty: full-time 1,470; part-time/volunteers 1,836

Degrees conferred: M.D., B.S.-M.D. (with Rice University); M.D.-M.P.H., M.D.-Ph.D. (Audiology and Bioacoustics, Biochemistry, Biomedical Engineering [with Rice University], Cardiovascular Sciences, Cell Biology, Cell and Molecular Biology, Developmental Biology, Microbiology and Immunology, Molecular and Human Genetics, Molecular Physiology and Biophysics, Molecular Virology, Neurosciences, Pharmacology); has M.S.T.P.

RECRUITMENT PRACTICES AND POLICIES. School has diversity program and actively recruits women/minority applicants. Diversity contact: Senior Associate Dean; phone: (713)746-6457.

ADMISSION REQUIREMENT FOR BACHELOR-M.D. APPLICANTS. Open to both state residents and nonresidents. Submit application, SAT I or ACT, plus 3 SAT II subject tests, official high school transcripts with rank in class (for serious consideration rank should be in top 5% of class), and 3 letters of recommendation. Apply to Rice University's Admissions Office, 6100 Main

Street, Houston, Texas 77035, after November 1, before December 1. Notification date is April 15. Application fee $25.

ADMISSION REQUIREMENTS FOR FIRST-YEAR APPLICANTS. *Undergraduate preparation.* Suggested premed courses: 2 courses in biology with labs, 2 courses in general chemistry with labs, 2 courses in organic chemistry with labs, 2 courses in English. Bachelor's degree from an accredited institution required; all applicants have bachelor's degree awarded prior to enrollment. Does not use AMCAS. *Has EDP;* applicants must apply between June 1 and August 1. Early applications are encouraged. Submit application, official transcripts, MCAT, a personal statement, and 2 recommendations (1 from preprofessional committee) to Admissions Office. Application fee $35. Notification completed by October 1. *Regular application process.* Apply directly to the college with either paper or electronic application; submit MCAT (will accept MCAT test results from 1995), official transcripts for each school attended (should show at least 90 semester credits/135 quarter credits), a personal statement, preprofessional committee evaluation, 2 recommendations from science faculty, and application fee of $35 to Admissions Office after June 1, before November 1. Interviews are by invitation only and generally for final selection. A second interview is required for M.S.T.P. Dual-degree applicants must apply to, and be accepted by, both schools; contact the Admissions Office for current information and specific requirements for admission. First-year students admitted in fall only. Rolling admission process. Notification starts in October and is finished when class is filled. Applicant's response to offer and $100 deposit due within 2 weeks of receipt of acceptance letter. School does maintain an alternate list. Phone: (713)798-4842; fax: (713)798-5563. M.S.T.P. contact: (713)798-5264.

ADMISSION REQUIREMENTS FOR TRANSFER APPLICANTS. Accepts transfers from other accredited U.S. medical schools only into the 1st clinical year of study. Admission limited to space available. Contact the Admissions Office for current information and specific requirements.

ADMISSION STANDARDS AND RECOGNITION. *For B.S.-M.D.:* number of state residents interviewed 18, nonresidents 21; number of residents enrolled 10, nonresidents 4. *For M.D.:* number of state-resident applicants 1,622, nonresidents 2,049; number of state residents interviewed 428, nonresidents 178; number of residents enrolled 127, nonresidents 41; median MCAT 11.0 (verbal reasoning 11.0; biological sciences 11.0; physical sciences 11.0); median GPA 3.7 (A = 4). *Barron's Guide* placed Baylor among the Top 25 most prestigious U.S. medical schools; Gorman rating 4.33 (scale: strong 4.01–4.49); *U.S. News & World Report* ranking: ranked in the Top 25 of all U.S. medical schools; not ranked in the Top 25 in primary-care programs; medical ranking by NIH awards was 23rd, with 372 awards/grants; total dollars awarded $94,479,287.

FINANCIAL AID. Scholarships, merit scholarships, minority scholarships, grants-in-aid, institutional and state loans, HEAL, alternative loan programs, NIH stipends, federal Perkins loans, Stafford subsidized and unsubsidized loans, federal W/S, and service commitment scholarship programs are available. Assistantships/fellowships may be available for dual-degree candidates. For merit scholarships, the selection criteria place heavy reliance on MCAT and undergraduate GPA. Contact the Financial Aid Office for current information; phone: (713)798-4603. For most financial assistance and all federal programs, submit FAFSA to a federal processor (Title IV school code # 015170); also submit Financial Aid Transcript and Federal Income Tax forms. Approximately 77% of current students receive some form of financial assistance. Average debt after graduation $68,000.

DEGREE REQUIREMENTS. *For B.S.-M.D.:* an 8-year program. *For M.D.:* satisfactory completion of 4-year program. All students must pass USMLE Step 1 prior to entering 3rd year; all students must pass USMLE Step 2 prior to awarding of M.D. *For M.D.-M.P.H.:* generally a 5–6-year program. *For M.D.-Ph.D., M.S.T.P.:* generally a 7-year program.

BOSTON UNIVERSITY
Boston, Massachusetts 02215
Internet site: http://www.bu.edu

Founded 1839. Located in city of Boston. Private control. Semester system. Library: 1,949,000 volumes; 3,444,000 microforms; 28,800 periodicals/ subscriptions. Special programs: B.A./B.S.-M.D. program (annual undergraduate tuition $20,570).

The university's other graduate colleges/schools: College of Communication, College of Engineering, Graduate School of Arts and Sciences, Henry M. Goldman School of Graduate Dentistry, Metropolitan College, Sargent College of Allied Health Professions, School for the

Arts, School of Education, School of Management, School of Medicine, School of Social Work, School of Theology. The university's ranking by NIH awards in domestic higher education was 33rd, with 263 grants; total dollars awarded $73,596,334.

Total university enrollment at main campus: 30,400.

Boston University Medical Center
88 East Newton Street
Boston, Massachusetts 02118

Located in the south end of Boston. Private Control. Member of Council of Teaching Hospitals. School of Medicine, Schools located at medical center: the Dental School, School of Public Health. Special facilities: Center for Advancement in Health and Medicine, University Hospital. Nationally recognized programs in AIDS, Endocrinology, Geriatrics, Neurology, Ophthalmology.

School of Medicine
80 East Concord Street
Boston, Massachusetts 02118
Telephone: (617)638-4630
Internet site: http://med-amsa.bu.edu
E-mail: presch@bu.edu

Established 1848. Located in Boston between Boston City Hospital and Boston University Medical Center Hospital. Library: 110,200 volumes/microforms; 1,100 current periodicals/subscriptions. Special programs: summer programs for underrepresented minorities, prematriculation summer sessions.

Annual tuition: $31,500. No on-campus housing available. Contact Admissions Office for off-campus housing information. Off-campus housing and personal expenses: approximately $10,790.

Enrollment: 1st-year class 135 (EDP 3); total full-time 640 (men 61%, women 39%). First-year statistics: 39% women; average age 22; 11% minorities; 67% science majors.

Degrees conferred: M.D., B.S.-M.D., M.D.-M.A., M.D.-M.B.A., M.D.-M.P.A., M.D.-M.P.H., M.D.-M.S., M.D.-Ph.D. (Anatomy, Biochemistry, Biomedical Engineering, Biophysics, Cell Biology, Genetics, Immunology, Microbiology, Molecular Biology, Neurosciences, Pathology, Pharmacology, Physiology).

RECRUITMENT PRACTICES AND POLICIES. School has diversity program and actively recruits women/minority applicants. Diversity contact: Associate Dean for Student and Minority Affairs; phone: (617)638-4163.

ADMISSION REQUIREMENT FOR BACHELOR-M.D. APPLICANTS. Open to both state residents and nonresidents. Submit application, SAT I or ACT, SAT II in English composition with writing sample, math I or II, and chemistry; official high school transcripts with rank in class; letters of recommendation. Interviews are required but are by invitation only. Apply to Admissions Office after September 1, before December 1. Application fee $50. Phone: (617)353-9695. Notification normally between March 15 and April 15. Applicant's response to offer and $400 deposit due by May 1.

ADMISSION REQUIREMENTS FOR FIRST-YEAR APPLICANTS. Preference given to U.S. citizens and permanent residents only. *Undergraduate preparation.* Suggested premed courses: 2 courses in biology with labs, 2 courses in inorganic chemistry with labs, 2 courses in organic chemistry with labs, 2 courses in physics with labs, 2 courses in the humanities, 2 courses in English; 1 course in calculus strongly recommended. Bachelor's degree from an accredited institution required; 75% of applicants have bachelor's degree awarded prior to enrollment. *Has EDP* for state residents only; applicants must apply through AMCAS (official transcripts sent by mid-May) between June 1 and August 1. Early applications are encouraged. Submit secondary/supplemental application, a personal statement, and 2 recommendations to Admissions Office within 2 weeks of receipt of application. Notification normally begins October 1. *Regular application process.* Apply through AMCAS (file after June 1, before November 1); submit MCAT (will accept MCAT test results from 1995), official transcripts for each school attended (should show at least 90 semester credits/135 quarter credits; submit transcripts by mid-May to AMCAS), service processing fee. Submit an application fee of $95, supplemental application, a personal comment/statement, preprofessional committee evaluation, and 2 recommendations from science faculty to Admissions Office within 2–3 weeks of the receipt of supplemental materials. Interviews are by invitation only and generally for final selection. Dual-degree applicants must apply to, and be accepted by, both schools; contact the Admissions Office for current information and specific requirements for admission. Phone: (617)638-4633. First-year students admitted in fall only. Rolling admission process. Notification starts in February and is finished when class is filled. Applicant's response to offer and first deposit of $500 due June 15. School does maintain an alternate/waiting list.

ADMISSION REQUIREMENTS FOR TRANSFER APPLICANTS. Accepts transfers from other accredited

U.S. medical schools. Admission limited to space available through attrition. Contact Admissions Office for current information and specific requirements for admission.

ADMISSION STANDARDS AND RECOGNITION. *For B.A./B.S.-M.D.:* number of state-resident applicants 81, nonresidents 932; number of state residents interviewed 6, nonresidents 102; number of residents enrolled 4, nonresidents 14; median GPA 4.0 (A = 4). *For M.D.:* number of state-resident applicants 919, nonresidents 10,667; number of state residents interviewed 288, nonresidents 965; number of residents enrolled 51, nonresidents 87; median MCAT 9.4 (verbal reasoning 9.3; biological sciences 9.8; physical sciences 9.6); median GPA 3.5 (A = 4). Gorman rating 4.44 (scale: strong 4.01–4.49); *U.S. News & World Report* ranking: not ranked in Top 25 of all U.S. medical schools; medical ranking by NIH awards was 32nd, with 177 awards/grants; total dollars awarded $57,444,649.

FINANCIAL AID. Limited scholarships available, institutional loans, HEAL, alternative loan programs, federal Perkins loans, Stafford subsidized and unsubsidized loans, and service commitment scholarship programs are available. Assistantships/fellowships may be available for dual-degree candidates. All accepted students considered for scholarships; the selection criteria place heavy reliance on MCAT and undergraduate GPA. Contact the Financial Aid Office for current information and deadlines; phone: (617)638-5130. For most financial assistance and all federal programs, submit FAFSA to a federal processor (Title IV school code # 002130); also submit Financial Aid Transcript and Federal Income Tax forms. Approximately 90% of current students receive some form of financial assistance. Average debt after graduation $131,000.

DEGREE REQUIREMENTS. *For BA/B.S.-M.D.:* a 7-year program. *For M.D.:* 4-year program. All students must pass USMLE Step 1 prior to entering 3rd year; all students must pass USMLE Step 2 prior to awarding of M.D. *For M.D.-Masters:* generally a 5–6½-year program. *For M.D.-Ph.D.:* generally a 7-year program.

Goldman School of Dental Medicine
100 East Newton Street, Room 305
Boston, Massachusetts 02118
Telephone: (617)638-4780
Internet site: http://www.dental.bu.edu/DENTAL

Founded in 1963; D.M.D. program established in 1974. Located at Boston University Medical Center. Special programs: APEX Program places dental interns into affiliated dental practices. Postgraduate specialties: Endodontics, General Dentistry, Oral and Maxillofacial Surgery, Orthodontics, Pediatric Dentistry, Periodontics, Prosthodontics.

Annual tuition: $30,888; fees $2,100; equipment and supplies $5,064. On-campus rooms and apartments available for both single and married students. Contact Office of Housing for both on- and off-campus housing information; phone: (617)353-3511. Dental students tend to live off-campus. Off-campus housing, food, transportation, and personal expenses: approximately $15,569.

Enrollment: 1st-year class 91; total full-time 607. First-year enrolled student information: 78 from out of state; 16 states represented; 4 foreign countries; 34 women; average age 25; 6 underrepresented minorities; 35 other minorities.

Faculty: full-time 73, part-time/volunteers 217.

Degrees conferred: D.D.S., baccalaureate-D.D.S. (College of Arts and Sciences, Boston University).

RECRUITMENT PRACTICES AND POLICIES. School has diversity program and actively recruits women/minority applicants. Diversity contact: Office of Minority Affairs; phone: (617)638-4787.

ADMISSION REQUIREMENT FOR BACHELOR-D.D.S. APPLICANTS. For specific information and applications contact: Program Director, College of Arts and Sciences, Room 109, Boston University.

ADMISSION REQUIREMENTS FOR FIRST-YEAR APPLICANTS. Preference given to state residents; U.S. citizens and permanent residents only. *Undergraduate preparation.* Suggested predent courses: 3 courses in biology with labs, 2 courses in inorganic chemistry with labs. 2 courses in organic chemistry with labs, 2 courses in physics with labs, 2 courses in college math, 4 courses in English. The junior-college transfer-credit limit is 60 credits. Will consider applicants with only 3 years of undergraduate preparation; prefer applicants who will have a bachelor's degree prior to enrollment; 98% of applicants have bachelor's degree awarded prior to enrollment. *Application process.* Apply through AADSAS (file after June 1, before March 1), submit official transcripts for each school attended (should show at least 90 semester credits/135 quarter credits), service processing fee; at the same time as you send in AADSAS materials, submit official DAT scores directly to the Office of Predoctoral Admission. TOEFL may be required of an applicant whose native language is other than English. Submit the following materials only after being contacted by an Admissions Officer: an application fee of $50, a supplemental application, official transcripts, DAT scores, predental committee evaluation or 2 recommendations from professors in your major field of study, and photograph to Office of Predoctoral Admissions within 2 weeks of receipt of supplemental materials but no later than March 1. Interviews are by invitation only and generally for final selection. First-year students admitted in fall only. Rolling admission process. Notification starts on December 1 and is finished when class is filled. Applicant's response to offer and $2,000 deposit due within 15 days if accepted prior to January 31; response and deposit due within 2 weeks if received after February 1. School does maintain an alternate list; phone: (617)638-4787; fax: (617)638-4798.

ADMISSION REQUIREMENTS FOR ADVANCED-STANDING APPLICANTS. Accepts transfers from other accredited U.S. dental schools into the 3rd year of study only. Admission limited to space available. There are no advanced-standing credits for graduates of foreign schools of dentistry. Contact the Office of Predoctoral Admissions for current information and specific requirements.

ADMISSION STANDARDS AND RECOGNITION. *For D.D.S.:* number of applicants 2,646; number enrolled 91; median DAT: ACAD 17; PAT 17; median GPA 3.16 (A = 4), median sciences GPA 3.10 (A = 4); Gorman rating 4.31 (scale: strong 4.01–4.49); this placed the school in the Top 30 of all U.S. dental schools; the dental school's ranking by NIH awards was 20th among dental schools, with 12 awards/grants received; total value of all awards/grants $1,799,424.

FINANCIAL AID. Limited scholarships, institutional loans, state loan programs, DEAL, HEAL, alternative loan programs, federal Perkins loans, and Stafford subsidized and unsubsidized loans are available. Most financial assistance is based on demonstrated need and is in the form of loans. Submit institutional financial-aid applications after being accepted. Contact the Financial Aid Office for current information; phone: (617)638-5130. For most financial assistance and all need-based programs, submit FAFSA to a federal processor (Title IV school code # 002130); also submit Financial Aid Transcript, Federal Income Tax forms, and Use of Federal Funds Certification. Approximately 54% of current students receive some form of financial assistance. Average award $3,023.

DEGREE REQUIREMENTS. *For baccalaureate-D.D.S.:* a 7-year program. *For D.D.S.:* satisfactory completion of 4-year program.

BROWN UNIVERSITY
Providence, Rhode Island 02912
Internet site: http://www.brown.edu

Founded 1764. Private control. Semester system. Special facilities: Biomedical Center, Center for Dynamic Systems, Center for Environmental Studies, Center for Latin American Studies, East Asian Language and Area Center, Geology-Chemistry Research Center, Haffenreffer Museum of Anthropology, Hunter Psychological Laboratory, Institute for Brain and Neural Systems, Institute for International Health, Institute of Life Science, Population Studies and Training Center. Library: 2,225,000. Special programs: B.A.-M.D. (PLME) program (annual undergraduate tuition $21,592); postbaccalaureate premedical program for adults is restricted to Brown alumnae, Rhode Island residents only; contact Program Director; phone: (401)863-3452. The university's ranking by NIH awards in domestic higher education was 82nd, with 107 awards/grants received; total value of awards/grants received $22,057,571.

The university's graduate school includes the Center for Environmental Studies, Center for Old World Archaeology and Art, Center for Portuguese and Brazilian Studies, Division of Applied Mathematic, Division of Engineering.

School of Medicine
97 Waterman Street, Box G-A212
Providence, Rhode Island 02912-9706
Telephone: (401)863-2149; fax (401)863-2660
Internet site: http://www.brown.edu
E-mail: MedSchool_admissions@brown.edu

Medical program established in 1880; the M.D. accredited in 1975. Special facilities: Biomedical Center, Cancer Research Center, Center for Alcohol and Addiction Studies, Center for Biomedical Computing, Center for Biomedical Ethics, Center for Clinical Oncology, Center for Gerontology and Health Care Research, Center for Statistical Science, Center for Surgical Research, International Health Institute. Special programs: Brown/Dartmouth Medical Program, Program in Liberal Medical Education, summer programs for underrepresented minorities. Affiliated hospitals: Emma Pendleton Bradley Hospital, Butler Hospital, Memorial Hospital of Rhode Island, Miriam Hospital, Rhode Island Hospital, Roger Williams Medical Center, VA Medical Center, Women and Infants Hospital of Rhode Island.

Annual tuition: $24,984. On-campus rooms and apartments available for single students only. Annual on-campus housing cost: single students $4,800 ($9,000 including board). Contact Housing Office for both on- and off-campus housing information; phone: (401)863-

2251. Medical students tend to live off-campus. Off-campus housing and personal expenses: approximately $15,000.

Enrollment: 1st-year class 78 (PLME), 10–15 M.D.-Ph.D.; total full-time 317 (men 47%, women 53%). First-year statistics: 92% out of state; 54% women; 12% minority.

Faculty: full-time/part-time/volunteers 1,425.

Degrees conferred: B.A.-M.D. (PLME), M.D., M.D.-M.S., M.D.-Ph.D. (Artificial Organs, Biochemistry, Biomaterials, Cell Biology, Cellular Technology, Ecology and Evolutionary Biology, Epidemiology and Gerontology, Molecular Biology, Neurology, Pathobiology).

RECRUITMENT PRACTICES AND POLICIES. School has diversity program and actively recruits women/minority applicants. Diversity contact: Associate Dean, Office of Minority Affairs; phone: (401)863-3335.

ADMISSION REQUIREMENT FOR BACHELOR-M.D. (PLME) APPLICANTS. Open to residents and nonresidents. Minimum high school units recommended: 4 years of English, 3 years of mathematics, 3 years of foreign language, 2 years of lab sciences beyond freshman year, 1 year of the arts, 1 year of academic electives. Submit application, SAT I, and SAT II (3 achievement) or ACT, official high school transcripts, letters of recommendation. Apply to Admissions Office after November 1, before January 1. Rolling admissions process. Notification normally begins December 15, latest date April 3. Applicant's response to offer is due May 1. Application fee $55. Phone: (401)863-2149. During first 4 years of B.A.-M.D. (PLME) financial aid is awarded through the university's Financial Aid Office.

ADMISSION REQUIREMENTS FOR M.D.-Ph.D. APPLICANTS. Applicants restricted to premed students at Brown University, Bryn Mawr College, or Columbia University; Early Identification Programs at Providence College, Tougaloo College, Rhode Island College, and University of Rhode Island. *Undergraduate preparation.* Suggested premed courses: 1 course in biochemistry, 2 courses in biology with labs, 2 courses in general chemistry with labs, 1 course in organic chemistry with labs, 2 courses in physics with labs, 1 course in calculus and 1 course in probability and statistics, 2 courses in social and behavioral sciences. Bachelor's degree from an accredited institution required; all applicants have bachelor's degree awarded prior to enrollment. *Application process.* Apply after August 15, before March 1; submit MCAT, official transcripts for each school attended (should show at least 90 semester credits/135 quarter credits), a personal statement, preprofessional committee evaluation and 2 recom-

mendations from science faculty, and an application fee of $60 to Admissions Office. Interviews are by invitation only and generally for final selection. First-year students admitted in fall only. Rolling admission process. Notification starts on January 1 and is finished by April 15. Applicant's response to offer due within 3 weeks of receipt of acceptance letter. Phone: (404)863.2149; E-mail: MedSchool_Admission@brown.edu.

ADMISSION REQUIREMENTS FOR APPLICANTS REQUESTING ADVANCED STANDING. Accepts transfers from other accredited U.S. and Canadian medical schools and Rhode Island residents attending foreign medical schools into the 3rd year only. Admission limited to space available. Contact the Admissions Office for current information and specific requirements.

ADMISSION STANDARDS AND RECOGNITION. *For B.A.-M.D. (PLME):* number of state-resident applicants 53; nonresidents 2,188; number of residents enrolled 5; nonresidents 73. *For M.D.-Ph.D.:* number of state-resident applicants 65; nonresidents 2,264; number of state residents interviewed 3; nonresidents 90; number of residents enrolled 7, nonresidents 61; median GPA 3.45 (A = 4). Gorman rating 4.14 (scale: strong 4.01–4.49); medical ranking by NIH awards was 71st, with 82 awards/grants; total dollars awarded $17,682,297.

FINANCIAL AID. During the first 4 years of B.A.-M.D. program financial assistance is administered through the university's financial aid office; the final 4 years of financial aid is administered through the School of Medicine's Office of Admissions and Financial Aid. Scholarships, merit scholarships, minority scholarships, grants-in-aid, institutional loans, HEAL, alternative loan programs, NIH stipends, federal Perkins loans, Stafford subsidized and unsubsidized loans, and service commitment scholarship programs are available. Assistantships/fellowships may be available for M.D.-Ph.D. degree candidates. For all M.D.-Ph.D. programs contact the Office of Admissions and Financial Aid for current information; phone: (401)863-1142. For most financial assistance and all federal programs, submit FAFSA to a federal processor (Title IV school code # E00059); also submit Financial Aid Transcript and Federal Income Tax forms. Approximately 70% of current students receive some form of financial assistance. Average debt after graduation $75,000.

DEGREE REQUIREMENTS. *For BA-M.D. (PLME):* an 8-year program. *For M.D.:* satisfactory completion 4-year program. All students must pass USMLE Step 2 prior to awarding of M.D. *For M.D.-M.S.:* generally a

4½–5½-year program. *For M.D.-Ph.D.:* generally a 7–8-year program.

STATE UNIVERSITY AT BUFFALO
State University of New York
Buffalo, New York, 14260-1608
Internet site: http://www.buffalo.edu

Founded 1846. Public control. Semester system. Library: 2,991,000 volumes; 4,740,453 microforms; 21,000 periodicals/subscriptions; 300 PC work stations. Special facilities: Center for Assistive Technology, Center for Applied Molecular Biology and Immunology, Center for Behavioral and Social Aspects of Health, Center for Hearing and Deafness, Center for Research and Education in Special Environments, Center for Studying the Aging, Center for Structural Biology, Periodontal Disease Research Center, Research Center for Oral Biology, Research Institute on Addiction, Roswell Park Cancer Institute, Toxicology Research Center. The university's ranking in domestic higher education by NIH awards/grants was 80th, with 119 awards/grants received; total dollars awarded $22,392,455.

The university's graduate schools include: Faculty of Arts and Letters, Faculty of Natural Sciences and Mathematics, Faculty of Social Sciences, Graduate Programs in Biomedical Sciences at Roswell Park, Graduate School of Education, School of Architecture and Planning, School of Dental Medicine, School of Engineering and Applied Sciences, School of Health Related Professions, School of Information and Library Studies, School of Law, School of Management, School of Medicine, School of Nursing, School of Pharmacy, School of Social Work.

Total university enrollment at main campus: 26,500.

School of Medicine and Biological Sciences
40 Biomedical Education Building
Buffalo, New York 14214-3013
Telephone: (716)829-3466; fax: (716)829-2798
Internet site: http://www.smbs.buffalo.edu
E-mail: jrosso@ubmedc.buffalo.edu

Established 1846. Located on the Main Street campus at the northeast corner of the city. Semester system. Library: 270,000 volumes/microforms; 2,700 current periodicals/subscriptions. Affiliated hospitals: Buffalo General Hospital, the Children's Hospital of Buffalo, Erie County Medical Center, Mercy Hospital, Millard Fillmore Health System (a member of the Council of Teaching Hospitals), Sisters of Charity Hospital, Buffalo VA Medical Center. Special programs: Early Assurance Program for underrepresented minorities; prematriculation summer sessions.

Annual tuition: residents $11,505, nonresidents $22,605; fees $665. On-campus rooms available for single students. Annual on-campus housing cost: single students $9,865. Contact university's Housing Bureau for both on- and off-campus housing information; phone: (716)645-2171. Medical students tend to live off-campus. Off-campus housing and personal expenses: approximately $14,500.

Enrollment: 1st-year class 139 (EDP 10); total full-time 586 (men 55%, women 45%). First-year statistics: 1% out of state; 46.8% women; average age 25; 6% minorities; 62% science majors.

Faculty: full-time 750.

Degrees conferred: M.D., M.D.-M.B.A., M.D.-M.P.H. (SUNY at Albany), M.D.-M.S., M.D.-Ph.D. (Anatomy, Biochemistry, Biophysics, Cell Biology, Immunology, Microbiology, Molecular Biology, Pathology, Pharmacology, Physiology); has M.S.T.P.

RECRUITMENT PRACTICES AND POLICIES. School has diversity program and actively recruits women/minority applicants. Diversity contact: Assistant Dean, Minority Affairs; phone: (716)729-2812.

ADMISSION REQUIREMENTS FOR FIRST-YEAR APPLICANTS. Preference given to western New York State residents, state residents; U.S. citizens, and permanent residents only. *Undergraduate preparation.* Suggested premed courses: 2 courses in biology with labs, at least 1 course in inorganic chemistry with labs, 2 courses in organic chemistry with labs, 2 courses in physics with labs, 2 courses in English. Bachelor's degree from an accredited institution required; 98% of applicants have bachelor's degree awarded prior to enrollment. *Has EDP;* applicants must apply through AMCAS (official transcripts sent by mid-May) between June 1 and August 1. Early applications are encouraged. Submit secondary/supplemental application, a personal statement, and 2 recommendations to Admissions Office within 2 weeks of receipt of application. Interviews are by invitation only and generally for final selection. Notification normally begins October 1. *Regular application process.* Apply through AMCAS (file after June 1, before October 15), submit MCAT (will accept MCAT test results from last 4 years); official transcripts for each school attended (should show at least 90 semester credits/135 quarter credits, submit transcripts by mid-May to AMCAS), service processing fee. Submit an application fee of $65, a supplemental application, a personal statement, preprofessional committee evaluation, and 2 recommendations from science faculty to Admissions Office within 2–3 weeks of the receipt of supplemental materials. Interviews are by invitation only and generally for final selection. M.S.T.P. applicants must submit a supplemental application; contact either the Admissions Office (phone: (716)829-3467) or the M.S.T.P. Office (phone: (716)829-3236) for current information and specific requirements for admission. First-year students admitted in fall only. Rolling admission process. Notification starts October 15 and is finished when class is filled. Applicant's response to offer and $100 deposit due within 2 weeks of receipt of acceptance letter. School does maintain an alternate list.

ADMISSION REQUIREMENTS FOR TRANSFER APPLICANTS. Rarely considers transfer applicants except under conditions of extreme hardship. Contact the Admissions Office for current information and any modification in policy.

ADMISSION STANDARDS AND RECOGNITION. *For M.D.:* number of state-resident applicants 2,689, nonresidents 702; number of state residents interviewed 471, nonresidents 13; number of residents enrolled 134, nonresidents 1; median MCAT 10.4 (verbal reasoning 9.3; biological sciences 10.2; physical sciences 10.0); median GPA 3.65 (A = 4). Gorman rating 4.36 (scale: strong 4.01–4.49); school's medical ranking by NIH awards/grants was 84th, with 62 awards/grants received; total dollars awarded $11,650,372.

FINANCIAL AID. Scholarships, merit scholarships, minority scholarships, grants-in-aid, institutional loans, tuition assistance programs, HEAL, alternative loan programs, NIH stipends, federal Perkins loans, Stafford subsidized and unsubsidized loans, and service commitment scholarship programs are available. M.S.T.P. students receive both a tuition waiver and a stipend. Most financial aid is based on demonstrated need. Financial-aid applications and information are sent to all accepted students. For scholarship assistance, the selection criteria place heavy reliance on MCAT and undergraduate GPA. Contact the Financial Aid Office for current information; phone: (716)829-3724. For most financial assistance and all federal programs, submit FAFSA, before May 15 for priority consideration, to a federal processor (Title IV school code # 002837); also submit Financial Aid Transcript and Federal Income Tax forms. Approximately 85% of current students receive some form of financial assistance. Average debt after graduation $55,000.

DEGREE REQUIREMENTS. *For M.D.:* satisfactory completion of 4-year program. All students are encouraged to take the USMLE Step 1 and Step 2, but it is op-

tional. *For M.D.-M.B.A.:* generally a 5-year program. *For M.D.-M.P.H.:* generally a 4½–5-year program. *For M.D.-Ph.D., M.S.T.P.:* generally a 7–8-year program.

School of Dental Medicine
327 Squire Hall
Buffalo, New York 14214-3008
Telephone: (716)829-2839; fax: (716)883-3517
Internet site: http://www.sdm.buffalo.edu
E-mail: robert_joynt@sdm.buffalo.edu

Established 1892. Joined SUNY system in 1962. Located on main campus. Semester system. First 2 years dedicated to basic sciences. Affiliated hospitals: Buffalo General Hospital, Children's Hospital of Buffalo, Buffalo VA Medical Center, Erie County Medical Center, Millard Fillmore Hospital, Roswell Park Center Institute. Special facilities: Periodontal Research Center, Solevary Research Center, Laser Research Center. Postgraduate specialties: Endodontics, General Dentistry (AEGD), Dental Public Health, Oncology, Oral and Maxillofacial Pathology, Oral and Maxillofacial Surgery, Orthodontics, Pediatric Dentistry, Periodontics, Prosthodontics, Restorative Dentistry.

Annual tuition: residents $10,840, nonresidents $21,949; fees $2,500; equipment and supplies $1,790. On-campus rooms available for single students. Annual on-campus housing cost: single students $9,865. Contact university's Housing Bureau for both on- and off-campus housing information; phone: (716)645-2171. Dental students tend to live off-campus. Off-campus housing, food, transportation, and personal expenses: approximately $9,200.

Enrollment: 1st-year class 86. First-year enrolled-student information: 11 from out of state; 11 states represented; 26 women; average age 24; no underrepresented minorities; 16 other minorities.

Faculty: full-time 74, part-time 104.

Degrees conferred: D.D.S., B.S.-D.D.S. (Canisius College, LeMoyne College, St. Lawrence University, Utica College of Syracuse University, SUNY College at Genesseo), D.D.S.-M.S. (Biomaterials, Oral Sciences, Orthodontics), D.D.S.-Ph.D. (Oral Biology); has D.S.T.P.

RECRUITMENT PRACTICES AND POLICIES. School has diversity program and actively recruits women/minority applicants. Diversity contact: Admissions Office.

ADMISSION REQUIREMENT FOR B.S.-D.D.S. APPLICANTS. Contact each undergraduate institution listed above for applications, current information, and requirements for admission.

ADMISSION REQUIREMENTS FOR FIRST-YEAR APPLICANTS. Preference given to state residents; U.S. citizens and permanent residents only. *Undergraduate preparation.* Suggested predental courses: 2 courses in biology with labs, 2 courses in inorganic chemistry with labs, 2 courses in organic chemistry with labs, 2 courses in physics with labs, 2 courses in English; courses in statistics, computer science, psychology, and humanities are strongly encouraged. The junior-college transfer-credit limit is 60 credits. Will consider applicants with only 3 years of undergraduate preparation; preference given to applicants who will have bachelor's degree prior to enrollment; all enrollees had bachelor's degree awarded prior to enrollment. *Application process.* Apply through AADSAS (file after June 1, before February 15); submit official transcripts for each school attended (should show at least 90 semester credits/135 quarter credits); service processing fee; at the same time as you send in AADSAS materials, submit an application fee of $50, official college and high school transcripts, official DAT scores, and predental committee evaluation or 3 recommendations from professors to Admissions Office. TOEFL may be required of an applicant whose native language is other than English. Interviews are by invitation only and generally for final selection. Dual-degree applicants must apply to, and be accepted by, both schools. First-year students admitted in fall only. Rolling admission process: Notification starts in December and is finished when class is filled. Applicant's response to offer and $150 deposit due within 30 days if accepted prior to December 31; response and deposit due within 14 days if received after January 1. Phone: (716)829-2839 or (716)829-2862.

ADMISSION REQUIREMENTS FOR ADVANCED-STANDING APPLICANTS. Accepts transfers from other accredited U.S. and Canadian dental schools into the 2nd year only. Preference given to state residents. Admission limited to space available. There is an international dental program of advanced standing for graduates of foreign schools of dentistry. Contact the Admissions Office for current information and specific requirements.

ADMISSION STANDARDS AND RECOGNITION. *For D.D.S.:* number of applicants 963; number of residents enrolled 71, nonresidents 11; median DAT: ACAD 18.9, PAT 17.8; median GPA 3.23 (A = 4), median sciences GPA 3.20 (A = 4). Gorman rating 4.58 (scale: very strong 4.51–4.99); this placed the school in the Top 15 of all U.S. dental schools; the dental school's ranking by NIH awards was 7th among dental schools, with 23 awards/grants received; total value of all awards/grants $4,625,531.

FINANCIAL AID. Scholarships, New York State Regents scholarships for Professional Education (minority program), grants-in-aid, Dental Scientist Awards, institutional loans, state loan programs, DEAL, HEAL, alternative loan programs, federal Perkins loans, Stafford subsidized and unsubsidized loans, and military service commitment scholarship programs are available. Assistantships/fellowships may be available for combined-degree candidates. Institutional financial-aid applications and information are generally available at the on-campus interview (by invitation). For scholarship assistance, the selection criteria place heavy reliance on DAT and undergraduate GPA. Contact the Financial Aid Office for current information; phone: (716)829-2839. For most financial assistance and all need-based programs submit FAFSA to a federal processor (Title IV school code # 002837); also submit Financial Aid Transcript, Federal Income Tax forms, and Use of Federal Funds Certification. All current students receive some form of financial assistance. Average award resident $19,592, nonresident $29,135.

DEGREE REQUIREMENTS. *For B.S.-D.D.S.:* a 7- or 8-year program. *For D.D.S.:* satisfactory completion of 4-year program. *For D.D.S.-M.S.:* generally a 4½–5½-year program. *For D.D.S.-Ph.D.:* generally a 7-year program.

UNIVERSITY OF CALIFORNIA AT DAVIS
Davis, California 95616-5201
Internet site: http://www.ucdavis.edu

Founded 1868. Located 12 miles W of Sacramento. Public control. Quarter system. Library: 2,700,000 volumes; 3,450,000 microforms; 47,100 periodicals/subscriptions.

The university's other graduate colleges/schools: College of Engineering, Graduate School of Management, School of Medicine, School of Veterinary Medicine. The university's ranking by NIH awards in domestic higher education is 45, with 253 awards/grants; total dollars received $58,826,426.

Total university enrollment at main campus: 23,100.

University of California at Davis Medical Center
2315 Stockton Boulevard
Sacramento, California 95817

Located Sacramento, California. Public Control. Member of Council of Teaching Hospitals. Nationally recognized programs in AIDS, Cancer, Orthopedics, and Pulmonary Disease.

School of Medicine
Davis, California 95616
Telephone: (916)752-2717
Internet site: http://www-med.ucdavis.edu

Established 1968. Located on main campus. Quarter system. Library: 142,000 volumes/microforms; 3,700 current periodicals/subscriptions. Affiliated hospitals: Kaiser Foundation Hospital, David Grant Hospital, Sutter Hospital, Highland General Hospital. Special programs: prematriculation summer sessions.

Annual tuition/fees: resident student fees $8,922, nonresident tuition and student fees $17,326. On-campus rooms and apartments available for both single and married students. Annual on-campus housing cost: single students $6,690 (room and board), married students $5,800 (room only). Contact Student Housing Office for both on- and off-campus housing information; phone: (916)752-2033. Medical students tend to live off-campus. Off-campus housing and personal expenses: approximately $11,782.

Enrollment: 1st-year class 93; total full-time 424 (men 59.4%, women 40.6%). First-year statistics: none from out of state; 51.1% women; average age 26; 8% minorities; 65% science majors.

Faculty: full-time approximately 500, part-time/volunteers 1,500.

Degrees conferred: M.D., M.D.-M.A., M.D.-M.B.A., M.D.-M.P.H. (UC Berkeley), M.D.-M.S., M.D.-Ph.D. (Biochemistry, Biomedical Engineering, Cell Biology, Genetics, Immunology, Microbiology, Molecular Biology, Neurosciences, Pathology, Pharmacology, Physiology).

RECRUITMENT PRACTICES AND POLICIES. School has diversity program and actively recruits women/minority applicants. Diversity contact: Assistant Dean, Minority Affairs, phone: (916)752-8119.

ADMISSION REQUIREMENTS FOR FIRST-YEAR APPLICANTS. Applicants restricted to state residents and WICHE Professional Student Exchange Program candidates; U.S. citizens and permanent residents only. *Undergraduate preparation.* Suggested premed courses: 2 courses in biology with labs, 2 courses in inorganic chemistry with labs, 2 courses in organic chemistry with labs, 2 courses in physics with labs, 1 course in college math, 2 courses in English. Bachelor's degree from an accredited institution required; all applicants have bachelor's degrees awarded prior to enrollment. Does not have

EDP. *Application process.* Apply through AMCAS (file after June 1, before November 1), submit MCAT (will accept MCAT test results no more than 2 years old), official transcripts for each school attended (should show at least 90 semester credits/135 quarter credits, submit transcripts by mid-May to AMCAS), service processing fee. Submit an application fee of $25, supplemental application, a personal statement, preprofessional committee evaluation, and 2 recommendations from science faculty to Admissions Office within 2–3 weeks of the receipt of supplemental materials. Interviews are by invitation only and generally for final selection. Dual-degree applicants must apply to, and be accepted by both schools; contact the Admissions Office for current information and specific requirements for admission. First-year students admitted in fall only. Rolling admission process: Notification starts on October 15 and is finished when class is filled. Applicant's response to offer due within 2 weeks of receipt of acceptance letter. Phone: (916)752-2717.

ADMISSION REQUIREMENTS FOR TRANSFER APPLICANTS. Accepts transfers from other accredited U.S. medical schools who are California residents. Admission limited to space available. Contact the Admissions Office for current information and specific requirements.

ADMISSION STANDARDS AND RECOGNITION. *For M.D.:* number of state-resident applicants 4,389, nonresidents 775; number interviewed 684; number of residents enrolled 93, nonresidents 0; median MCAT 11.9 (verbal reasoning 11.9; biological sciences 11.9; physical sciences 11.9); median GPA 3.40 (A = 4). Gorman rating 4.45 (scale: strong 4.01–4.49); *U.S. News & World Report* ranking: ranked in the Top 15 in primary-care programs; medical ranking by NIH awards was 61st, with 139 awards/grants; total dollars awarded $28,718,519.

FINANCIAL AID. Regents scholarships, fellowships, opportunity grants, UC grants, institutional loans, HEAL, alternative loan programs, federal Perkins loans, Stafford subsidized and unsubsidized loans, and service commitment scholarship programs are available. Assistantships/fellowships may be available for dual-degree candidates. All accepted students are considered for merit scholarships; the selection criteria place heavy reliance on MCAT and undergraduate GPA. Contact the Financial Aid Office for current information; phone: (916)752-6618. For most financial assistance and all federal programs, submit FAFSA to a federal processor (Title IV school code # 001313); also submit Financial Aid Transcript and Federal Income Tax forms. Approximately

83% of current students receive some form of financial assistance. Average scholarship/grant $5,723. Average debt after graduation $49,900.

DEGREE REQUIREMENTS. *For M.D.:* satisfactory completion of 4-year program. All students must pass USMLE Step 1 prior to entering 3rd year; all students must pass USMLE Step 2 prior to awarding of M.D. *For M.D.-master's.:* generally a 4½–6-year program. *For M.D.-Ph.D.:* generally a 7-year program.

UNIVERSITY OF CALIFORNIA AT IRVINE

Irvine California 92717
Internet site: http://www.uci.edu

Founded 1965. Located 40 miles S of Los Angeles. Public control. Quarter system. Special facilities: Cancer Research Center, Developmental Biology Center, Institute for Brain Aging and Dementia, Institute for Mathematical Behavioral Science, Institute of Transportation Studies. Library: 1,500,000 volumes; 2,143,825 microforms; 17,500 periodicals/subscriptions; 178 PC computer work stations. Special programs: Postbaccalaureate premedical program for adults and underrepresented minorities; for information contact Program Coordinator; phone: (714)856-4603. The university's ranking by NIH awards in domestic higher education was 57th, with 202 grants; total dollars awarded $43,851,048.

The university's Office of Research and Graduate Studies includes: Graduate School of Management, School of Biological Sciences, School of Engineering, School of Humanities, School of Physical Sciences, School of Social Ecology, School of Social Sciences, School of the Arts.

Total university enrollment at main campus: 17,221.

University of California at Irvine Medical Center

101 The City Drive
Orange, California 92668

Public control. Member of Council of Teaching Hospitals.

College of Medicine

P.O. Box 4089, Medical Education Building
Irvine, California 92697-4089
Telephone: (714)824-5388, (800)824-5388; fax: (714)824-2485
Internet site: http://www.com.uci.edu
E-mail: RESchiei@uci.edu

Established 1896 as a private institution; joined UC system in 1965. Located main campus. Quarter system. Affiliated hospitals: Children's Hospital of Orange County, Long Beach VA Hospital, Memorial Hospital of Long Beach.

Annual tuition and student fees: resident student fees $9,291.50, nonresident tuition and student fees $16,995.50. On-campus rooms and apartments available for both single and married students. Annual on-campus housing cost: single students $6,500 (room only). For on-campus housing information contact Housing Office; phone: (714)824-6811; for off-campus housing information, phone: (714)824-7247. Medical students tend to live off-campus. Off-campus housing and personal expenses: approximately $10,686.

Enrollment: 1st-year class 92; total full-time 396 (men 56%, women 44%). First-year statistics: none from out of state; 51% women; average age 24; 21% minorities; 78% science majors.

Faculty: full-time, 800; part-time/volunteers, 1900.

Degrees conferred: M.D., M.D.-M.B.A., M.D.-Ph.D. (Anatomy, Biochemistry, Biophysics, Microbiology, Molecular Biology, Pharmacology, Physiology); has M.S.T.P.

RECRUITMENT PRACTICES AND POLICIES. School has diversity program and actively recruits women/minority applicants. Diversity contact: Assistant Dean for Outreach, Student Affairs; phone: (714)856-4771.

ADMISSION REQUIREMENTS FOR FIRST-YEAR APPLICANTS. Preference given to state residents and applicants from Alaska, Idaho, Montana, Wyoming; U.S. citizens and permanent residents only. *Undergraduate preparation.* Suggested premed courses: 3 courses in biology with labs, 2 courses in general chemistry with labs, 2 courses in organic chemistry with labs, 2 courses in physics with labs, 1 course in calculus, 1 course in biochemistry. Bachelor's degree from an accredited institution required; all applicants have bachelor's degrees awarded prior to enrollment. Does not have EDP. *Application process.* Apply through AMCAS (file after June 1, before November 1); submit MCAT (will accept MCAT test results that are no older than 3 years), official transcripts for each school attended (should show at least 90 semester credits/135 quarter credits, submit transcripts by mid-May to AMCAS), service processing fee. Submit an application fee of $40, supplemental application, a personal statement, preprofessional committee evaluation, and 2 recommendations from science faculty to Admissions Office within 2–3 weeks of the receipt of supplemental materials. Interviews are by invitation only and generally for final selection. Dual-degree applicants must apply to, and be accepted by, both schools; contact the Admissions Office for current information and specific requirements for admission. Supplemental application required for M.S.T.P. M.S.T.P. phone: (714)824-5264; E-mail: mstp@uci.edu. First-year students admitted in fall only. Rolling admission process. Notification starts on November 15 and is finished when class is filled. Applicant's response to offer due within 2 weeks of receipt of acceptance letter. Admissions Office phone: (714)825-4605.

ADMISSION REQUIREMENTS FOR TRANSFER APPLICANTS. College of Medicine does not generally accept transfer applicants. Contact the Admissions Office for current information.

ADMISSION STANDARDS AND RECOGNITION. *For M.D.:* number of state-resident applicants 4,360, nonresidents 436; number of state residents interviewed 458, nonresidents 0; number of residents enrolled 92, nonresidents 0; median MCAT 10.5 (verbal reasoning 9.2; biological sciences 10.7; physical sciences 10.4); median GPA 3.63 (A = 4). Gorman rating 4.34 (scale: strong 4.01–4.49); medical school ranking by NIH awards was 67th, with 98 awards/grants; total dollars awarded $22,848,211.

FINANCIAL AID. Regents scholarships, merit scholarship, minority scholarships, grants, institutional loans, HEAL, alternative loan programs, federal Perkins loans, Stafford subsidized and unsubsidized loans, and service commitment scholarship programs are available. Assistantships/fellowships may be available for dual-degree candidates. Financial-aid applications and information are given out at the on-campus interview (by invitation). For merit scholarships, the selection criteria place heavy reliance on MCAT and undergraduate GPA. Contact the Financial Aid Office for current information; phone: (714)824-4601. For most financial assistance and all federal programs, submit FAFSA to a federal processor (Title IV school code # 001314); also submit Financial Aid Transcript and Federal Income Tax forms. Approximately 87% of current students receive some form of financial assistance. Average debt after graduation $49,000.

DEGREE REQUIREMENTS. *For M.D.:* satisfactory completion of 4-year program. All students must pass USMLE Step 1 prior to starting clinical clerkship; all students must pass USMLE Step 2 prior to awarding of M.D. *For M.D.-Ph.D.:* generally a 7-year program.

UNIVERSITY OF CALIFORNIA AT LOS ANGELES

Los Angeles, California 90024-1301
Internet site: http://www.ucla.edu

Founded 1919. Located in the Westwood section of Los Angeles. Public control. Quarter system. Library: 6,200,000 volumes; 6,300,000 microforms; 94,000 periodicals/subscriptions. The university's ranking by NIH awards in domestic higher education was 10th, with 616 grants; total dollars awarded $158,361.652.

The university's graduate division includes: College of Letters and Sciences, Graduate School of Education and Information Science, John E. Anderson School of Management, School of Engineering and Applied Science, School of Nursing, School of Public Health, School of Public Policy and Social Research, School of the Arts and Architecture, School of Theater, Film and TV, School of Dentistry, School of Medicine.

Total university enrollment at main campus: 32,625.

UCLA Medical Center

10833 Le Conte Avenue
Los Angeles, California 90095-1730
Internet site: http://www.medctr.ucla.edu

Public Control. Member of Council of Teaching Hospitals. Special facilities: Brain Research Institute, Neuropsychiatric Institute, LA County Cardiovascular Research Laboratory, Reed Neurological Research Center. Nationally recognized programs in AIDS, Cancer, Cardiology, Endocrinology, Gastroenterology, Geriatrics, Gynecology, Neurology, Ophthalmology, Orthopedics, Otolaryngology, Pediatrics, Psychiatry, Pulmonary Disease, Rehabilitation, Rheumatology, Urology. *U.S. News & World Report* placed UCLA Medical Center among the Top 20 in the U.S.

School of Medicine

Los Angeles, California 90095-1720
Telephone: (310)825-6081
Internet site: http://www.medsch.ucla.edu

Established 1951. Quarter system. Library: 471,000 volumes/microforms; 6,000 current periodicals/subscriptions. Affiliated hospitals: LA County Harbor Hospital, VA Hospital of West Los Angeles, Olive View Medical Center, Santa Monica Hospital, Cedars-Sinai Medical Center. Special programs: prematriculation summer sessions.

Annual tuition and student fees: resident student fees $9,258, nonresident tuition and fees $17,652. On-campus rooms and apartments available for both single and married students. Annual on-campus housing cost: $8,000 (room and board). Books, supplies, equipment, and personal expenses: approximately $8,000–$9,000.

Enrollment: 1st-year class 145, Drew/UCLA Program 24; total full-time 701 (men 57%, women 43%). First-year statistics: 36.9% women; average age 24; 28% minorities; 56% science majors.

Degrees conferred: M.D., B.S.-M.D. (UC Riverside), M.D.-M.P.H., M.D.-Ph.D. (Anatomy, Biochemistry, Biomedical Engineering, Biomathematics, Biophysics, Cell Biology, Experimental Pathology, Genetics, Immunology, Medical Physics, Microbiology, Molecular Biology, Neurosciences, Pathology, Pharmacology, Physiology); has M.S.T.P.

RECRUITMENT PRACTICES AND POLICIES. School has diversity program and actively recruits women/minority applicants. Diversity contact: Office of Student Support; phone: (310)825-3575.

ADMISSION REQUIREMENT FOR BACHELOR-M.D. APPLICANTS. Preference given to state residents. Submit application, SAT I and 3 SAT IIs, official high school transcripts, letters of recommendations. Apply to Student Affairs Office, UC Riverside, CA 92521-0121 after November 1, before November 30. Notification date is March 1. Applicant's response to offer and deposit due date is May 1. Application fee $40. Phone: (909)787-4333.

ADMISSION REQUIREMENTS FOR FIRST-YEAR APPLICANTS. Preference given to state residents; U.S. citizens, and permanent residents only. *Undergraduate preparation.* Suggested premed courses: 2 courses in biology with labs, 2 courses in chemistry with labs, 2 courses in physics with labs, 1 course in college math, 2 courses in English; courses in Spanish, computer skills, and humanities recommended. Bachelor's degree from an accredited institution required; all applicants have bachelor's degree awarded prior to enrollment. Does not have EDP. *Application process.* Apply through AMCAS (file after June 1, before December 1); submit MCAT (must have been taken within the last 3 years), official transcripts for each school attended (should show at least 90 semester credits/135 quarter credits, submit transcripts by mid-May to AMCAS), service processing fee. Submit an application fee of $40, supplemental application, a personal statement, preprofessional committee evaluation, and 2 recommendations from science faculty to Admissions Office within 2–3 weeks of the receipt of supplemental materials. Interviews are by invitation only and generally for final selection. Dual-degree applicants must apply to, and be accepted by, both schools; contact the

Admissions Office for current information and specific requirements for admission. First-year students admitted in fall only. Rolling admission process. Notification starts on January 15 and is finished when class is filled. Applicant's response to offer and $100 deposit due within 2 weeks of receipt of acceptance letter. School does maintain an alternate list. Admissions Office phone: (310)825-6081.

ADMISSION REQUIREMENTS FOR TRANSFER APPLICANTS. Accepts transfers from other accredited U.S. medical schools into the 3rd year and only if space is available. Contact the Admissions Office for current information and specific requirements for admission.

ADMISSION STANDARDS AND RECOGNITION. *For B.S.-M.D.:* number of state-resident applicants 52, nonresidents 0; number of state residents interviewed 52, nonresidents 0; number of residents enrolled 24, nonresidents 0. *For M.D.:* number of state-resident applicants 1,636, nonresident 4,128; number of state residents interviewed 773, nonresidents 127; number of residents enrolled 128, nonresidents 17; median GPA 3.66 (A = 4). *Barron's Guide* placed School of Medicine among the Top 25 most prestigious U.S. medical schools; Gorman rating 4.85 (scale: very strong 4.51–4.99); *U.S. News & World Report* ranking: School of Medicine ranked in the Top 25 of all U.S. medical schools, ranked in the Top 25 in primary-care programs; medical ranking by NIH awards was 16th, with 373 awards/grants; total dollars awarded $96,757,742.

FINANCIAL AID. Regents scholarships, grants, institutional loans, HEAL, alternative loan programs, NIH stipends; federal Perkins loans, Stafford subsidized and unsubsidized loans, and service commitment scholarship programs are available. Assistantships/fellowships may be available for dual-degree candidates and for the M.S.T.P. All financial aid is based on documented need. Contact the Financial Aid Office for current information and source book *Pennies From Heaven;* phone: (310)825-4181, E-mail: fao@deans.medsch.ucla.edu. For most financial assistance and all federal programs, submit FAFSA to a federal processor (Title IV school code # E00374); also submit Financial Aid Transcript, Federal Income Tax forms, and CSS Profile form. Approximately 85% of current students receive some form of financial assistance. Average debt after graduation $51,600.

DEGREE REQUIREMENTS. *For B.S.-M.D.:* a 7-year program. *For M.D.:* satisfactory completion of 4-year program. All students must pass USMLE Step 1 prior to entering 3rd year; all students must pass USMLE Step 2 prior to awarding of M.D. *For M.D.-M.P.H.:* generally a 5-year program. *For M.D.-Ph.D., M.S.T.P.:* generally a 7-year program.

School of Dentistry

Room A3-042 HS
108333 Le Conte Avenue
Los Angeles, California 90095-1762
Telephone: (310)794-7971; fax: (310)825-9808

Established 1960. Located in the Center for Health Sciences on main campus. Curriculum is vertical tier and competency based. Library: share biomedical library. Affiliated dental facilities: Harbor/UCLA Medical Center, Roybal Pediatric Dental Clinic, Wilson-Jennings-Bloomfield UCLA Venice Dental Center, Mobile Clinic program. Postgraduate specialties: Endodontics, Maxillofacial Prosthodontics, Oral and Maxillofacial Surgery, Orthodontics, Pediatric Dentistry, Periodontics, Prosthodontics.

Annual tuition and fees: resident $10,517, nonresident $18,911; equipment and supplies $9,255. On-campus apartments available for single students. Contact On-campus Housing Assignments Office for on-campus housing information; phone: (310)825-4271; Community Housing Office for off-campus housing information; phone; (310)825-4491. Dental students tend to live off-campus. Off-campus housing, food, transportation, and personal expenses: approximately $11,778.

Enrollment: 1st-year class 95 (men 52, women 43). First-year statistics: 8 underrepresented minorities; 57 other minorities.

Faculty: full-time/part-time/volunteers 400.

Degrees conferred: D.D.S., D.D.S.-M.P.H., D.D.S.-M.S. (Oral Biology), D.D.S.-Ph.D. (Oral Biology).

RECRUITMENT PRACTICES AND POLICIES. School has diversity program and actively recruits women/minority applicants. Diversity contact: Office of Enrichment and Retention; phone: (310)206-1718.

ADMISSION REQUIREMENTS FOR FIRST-YEAR APPLICANTS. Preference given to state residents and WICHE-approved residents; U.S. citizens and permanent residents only. *Undergraduate preparation.* Suggested predent courses: 2 courses in biology with labs, 2 courses in inorganic chemistry with labs, 2 courses in organic chemistry with labs, 2 courses in physics with labs, 1 course in biochemistry, 2 courses in English, 1 course in psychology. The junior-college transfer-credit limit is 70 credits. Will consider applicants with only 3 years of un-

dergraduate preparation; prefer applicants who will have a bachelor's degree prior to enrollment; all enrollees had bachelor's degree awarded prior to enrollment. *Application process.* Apply through AADSAS (file after June 1, before January 1); submit official transcripts for each school attended (should show at least 90 semester credits/135 quarter credits), service processing fee; at the same time as you send in AADSAS materials, submit official DAT scores (must be taken 1 year prior to year of anticipated enrollment) directly to the Admissions Office. Submit the following materials only after being contacted by an Admissions Officer: an application fee of $75, a secondary/supplemental application, official transcripts, and predental committee evaluation or 3 recommendations from professors in your major field of study to Admissions Office within 2 weeks of receipt of supplemental materials. Interviews are by invitation only and generally for final selection. First-year students admitted in fall only. Rolling admission process. Notification starts in December and is finished when class is filled. Applicant's response to offer and $200 deposit due within 30 days if accepted prior to January 31; response and deposit due within 2 weeks if received after February 1. School does maintain an alternate list. Admissions Office phone: (310)794-7971.

ADMISSION REQUIREMENTS FOR ADVANCED-STANDING APPLICANTS. Does not accept transfer applicants. There is no advanced-standing program for graduates of foreign schools of dentistry. Contact the Admissions Office for current information.

ADMISSION STANDARDS AND RECOGNITION. *For D.D.S.:* number of applicants 1,471; number enrolled 95; median DAT: ACAD 21, PAT 19; median GPA 3.4 (A = 4), median sciences GPA 3.3(A = 4). Gorman rating 4.85 (scale: very strong 4.51–4.99); this placed the school in the Top 10 of all U.S. dental schools; the dental school's ranking by NIH awards was 15th among dental schools, with 15 awards/grants received; total value of all awards/grants $2,795,677.

FINANCIAL AID. Regents scholarships, dean's dental scholarship fund, minority scholarships, grants, institutional loans, Cal State graduate fellowships, state loan programs, DEAL, HEAL, alternative loan programs, federal Perkins loans, Stafford subsidized and unsubsidized loans, and military service commitment scholarship programs are available. Assistantships/fellowships may be available for combined-degree candidates. For merit scholarships, the selection criteria place heavy reliance on DAT and undergraduate GPA. Contact the Financial

Aid Office for current information; phone: (310)825-6994. For most financial assistance and all need-based programs, submit FAFSA to a federal processor no later than March 2 (Title IV school code # E00375); also submit Financial Aid Transcript, Federal Income Tax forms, CSS Profile form, and Use of Federal Funds Certification. Approximately 92% of current students receive some form of financial assistance. Average award $21,290–$23,250.

DEGREE REQUIREMENTS. *For D.D.S.:* satisfactory completion of 4-year (45-month) program. *For D.D.S.-M.P.H.:* generally a 5-year program. *For D.D.S.-M.S.:* generally a 4½–5½-year program. *For D.D.S.-Ph.D.:* generally a 6–7-year program.

UNIVERSITY OF CALIFORNIA AT SAN DIEGO

La Jolla, California 92093
Internet Site: http://www.ucsd.edu

Founded in 1964. Public control. Quarter system. Special facilities: California Space Institute, Cancer Center, Center for Astrophysics and Space Sciences, Center for Energy and Combustion Research, Center for Human Information Processing, Center for Iberian and Latin American Studies, Center for Magnetic Recording Research, Center for Research in Computing and the Arts, Center for Molecular Genetics, Center for Research in Language, Center for United States–Mexican Studies, Cray C90, Intel Paragon Supercomputer, Thinking Machine CM-Z, DEC Alpha Fany, Institute for Biomedical Engineering, Institute for Global Conflict and Cooperation, Institute for Geophysics and Planetary Physics, Institute for Neural Computation, Institute for Nonlinear Science, Institute for Pure and Applied Physical Sciences, Institute for Research on Aging, Intercampus Institute for Research and Particle Accelerators, Laboratory for Comparative Human Cognition, Laboratory for Mathematics and Statistics, Scripps Institution of Oceanography, San Diego Supercomputer Center. Library 2,300,000 volumes, 2,416,000 microforms, 200 PC work stations in all libraries. Special programs: postbaccalaureate premedical program for adults and underrepresented minorities; contact Assistant Director, Health Careers Opportunity Program; phone: (619)534-4170. The university's ranking by NIH awards in domestic higher education was 15th, with 507 grants; total dollars awarded $139,664,360.

The university's Office of Graduate Studies also includes the Graduate School of International Relations and Pacific Studies and Scripps Institution of Oceanography.

Total university enrollment at main campus: 18,119.

UC at San Diego Medical Center
200 West Arbor Drive
San Diego, California 92103

Located in San Diego. Public Control. Member of Council of Teaching Hospitals. Nationally recognized programs in AIDS, Cardiology, Orthopedics, Pulmonary Disease, Urology.

School of Medicine
Office of Admissions, 0621 Medical Teaching Facility
9500 Gilman Drive
La Jolla, California 92093-0621
Telephone: (619)534-3880; fax: (619)534-5282
Internet site: http://medschool.ucsd.edu
E-mail: mlofftus@ucsd.edu

Established 1968. Located on main campus. Quarter system. Affiliated hospitals: UCSD Medical Center, VA Hospital, Naval Regional Medical Center, Mercy Hospital, Sharp Hospital, Kaiser Permamente Foundation Hospitals and Clinics, Green Hospital of Scripps Clinic.

Annual tuition and fees: resident student fees $9,287.50, nonresident tuition and fees $17,681.50. Limited on-campus housing available. Contact Housing Office for both on- and off-campus housing information; phone: (619)534-2952. Medical students tend to live off-campus. Off-campus housing and personal expenses: approximately $12,036.

Enrollment: 1st-year class 122; total full-time 493 (men 57%, women 43%). First-year statistics: 1% out of state; 40% women; average age 25; 11% minority; 52% biology and chemistry majors.

Degrees conferred: M.D., M.D.-M.P.H. (San Diego State University), M.D.-Ph.D. (Biochemistry, Biomedical Engineering, Biophysics, Cell Biology, Genetics, Immunology, Microbiology, Molecular Biology, Neurosciences, Pathology, Pharmacology, Physiology), has M.S.T.P.

RECRUITMENT PRACTICES AND POLICIES. School has diversity program and actively recruits women/minority applicants. Diversity contact: Assistant Dean for Development; phone: (619)534-4184.

ADMISSION REQUIREMENTS FOR FIRST-YEAR APPLICANTS. Preference given to state residents; U.S. citizens, and permanent residents only. School participates in WICHE Professional Student Exchange Program. *Undergraduate preparation.* Suggested premed courses: 2 courses in biology with labs, 2 courses in inorganic chemistry with labs, 2 courses in organic chemistry with labs, 2 courses in physics with labs, 2 courses in college-level math (calculus, statistics, computer science), 2 courses in English. Bachelor's degree from an accredited institution required; all applicants have bachelor's degree awarded prior to enrollment. Does not have EDP. *Application process.* Apply through AMCAS (file after June 1, before November 1); submit MCAT (must have been taken within last 3 years), official transcripts for each school attended (should show at least 90 semester credits/135 quarter credits, submit transcripts by mid-May to AMCAS), service processing fee. Submit an application fee of $40, supplemental application, a personal statement, preprofessional committee evaluation, and 2 recommendations from science faculty to Admissions Office within 2–3 weeks of the receipt of supplemental materials. Interviews are by invitation only and generally for final selection. Dual-degree applicants must apply to, and be accepted by, both schools; contact the Admissions Office for current information and specific requirements for admission. M.S.T.P. contact: Office of Student Affairs; phone: (800)925-8704, (619)534-0689. First-year students admitted in fall only. Rolling admission process. Notification starts on October 15 and is finished when class is filled. Applicant's response to offer and $100 deposit due within 2 weeks of receipt of acceptance letter. School maintains an alternate/waiting list. Phone: (619)534-3880; fax: (619)534-5282.

ADMISSION REQUIREMENTS FOR TRANSFER APPLICANTS. Accepts transfers from other accredited U.S. medical schools. Admission limited to space available. Contact the Admissions Office for current information and specific requirements for admission.

ADMISSION STANDARDS AND RECOGNITION. *For M.D.:* number of state-resident applicants 1,233, nonresidents 4,115; number of state residents interviewed 563, nonresidents 286; number of residents enrolled 121, nonresidents 1; median MCAT 11.0 (verbal reasoning 10.4; biological sciences 11.0; physical sciences 11.4); median GPA 3.66 (A = 4). *Barron's Guide* placed School of Medicine among the Top 25 most prestigious U.S. medical schools; Gorman rating 4.49 (scale: strong 4.01–4.49); *U.S. News & World Report* ranking: ranked in the Top 25 of all U.S. medical schools; was ranked in the Top 25 in primary-care programs; medical ranking by NIH awards was 12th, with 366 awards/grants; total dollars awarded $108,965,495.

FINANCIAL AID. Regents scholarships, academic merit scholarships, minority scholarships, grants-in-aid, institutional loans, HEAL, alternative loan programs, NIH stipends, federal Perkins loans, Stafford subsidized and unsubsidized loans, and service commitment scholarship programs are available. Assistantships/fellowships may be available for dual-degree candidates. Financial-aid applications are sent to all accepted applicants. For merit scholarships, the selection criteria place heavy reliance on MCAT and undergraduate GPA. Apply to the Financial Aid Office within 2 weeks of the receipt of the financial-aid application. For financial-aid information contact the Student Financial Services Office; phone: (619)534-4664. For most financial assistance and all federal programs, submit FAFSA to a federal processor (Title IV school code # 001317); also submit Financial Aid Transcript and Federal Income Tax forms. Approximately 77% of current students receive some form of financial assistance. Average debt after graduation $48,114.

DEGREE REQUIREMENTS. *For M.D.:* satisfactory completion of 4-year program; completion of independent study project. *For M.D.-M.P.H.:* generally a 4½–5½-year program. *For M.D.-Ph.D., M.S.T.P.:* generally a 6–7-year program.

UNIVERSITY OF CALIFORNIA AT SAN FRANCISCO
San Francisco, California 94143
Internet site: http://www.ucsf.edu

Founded 1864. Public control. Graduate-only institution. Special facilities: Cardiovascular Research Institute, Cancer Research Institute, Francis I. Proctor Foundation for Research in Ophthalmology, Hormone Research Laboratory, Institute for Health and Aging, Institute for Health Policy Studies, Laboratory of Radiobiology, Langley Porter Psychiatric Institute, Metabolic Research Unit, Reproductive Endocrinology Center, George Hooper Foundation for Medical Research. Library: 691,400 volumes; 160,732 microforms; 5,400 periodicals/subscriptions; 275 PC work stations. University's ranking by NIH awards in domestic higher education was 4th, with 752 grants. Total dollars awarded $215,160,185.

The university's other graduate schools include: Graduate Division, School of Dentistry, School of Nursing, School of Pharmacy.

Total university enrollment at main campus: 3,695.

UCSF/Stanford Health Sciences Center
Five Thomas Mellon Drive
San Francisco, California 94034

Member of Council of Teaching Hospitals. Nationally recognized programs in AIDS, Cancer, Cardiology, Endocrinology, Gastroenterology, Geriatrics, Gynecology,

Neurology, Ophthalmology, Orthopedics, Otolaryngology, Pediatrics, Psychiatry, Pulmonary Disease, Urology. *U.S. News & World Report* placed the Medical Center among the Top 20 in the U.S.

School of Medicine

P.O. Box 0408
San Francisco, California 94143
Telephone: (415)476-4044
Internet site: http://www.som.ucsf.edu

Established in 1864 as Toland Medical College; affiliated with the University of California in 1873. Quarter system. Affiliated hospitals: UC Hospital, San Francisco General Hospital, VA Hospital, Mount Zion Hospital, Children's Medical Center.

Annual tuition and student fees: residents $9,940, nonresidents $18,924. On-campus rooms and apartments available for both single and married students. Contact Student Housing Office for both on- and off-campus housing information; phone: (415)476-2231. Medical students tend to live off-campus. Off-campus housing and personal expenses: approximately $14,395.

Enrollment: 1st-year class 141, UC at Berkeley program 12; total full-time 666 (men 46.4%, women 53.6%). First-year statistics: 56.3% women; average age 24; 21% underrepresented minorities; 54% other minorities; 64% science majors.

Degrees conferred: M.D., M.D.-M.P.H., M.D.-M.S., (joint medical program with U.C. Berkeley), M.D.-Ph.D. (Anatomy, Biochemistry, Biophysics, Cell Biology, Genetics, Immunology, Microbiology, Molecular Biology, Neurosciences, Pathology, Pharmacology, Physiology); has M.S.T.P.

RECRUITMENT PRACTICES AND POLICIES. School has diversity program and actively recruits women/minority applicants. Diversity contact: Associate Dean, Administration; phone: (415)476-4044.

ADMISSION REQUIREMENTS FOR FIRST-YEAR APPLICANTS. Preference given to state residents, U.S. citizens, and permanent residents only. *Undergraduate preparation.* Suggested premed courses: 2–3 courses in biology with labs, 2–3 courses in general chemistry with labs, 2–3 courses in organic chemistry with labs, 2–3 courses in physics, bachelor's degree from an accredited institution required; all applicants have bachelor's degree awarded prior to enrollment. Does not have EDP. *Application process.* Apply through AMCAS (file after June 1, before November 1); submit MCAT (must have been taken within last 2 years), official transcripts for each school attended (should show at least 90 semester credits/

135 quarter credits, submit transcripts by mid-May to AMCAS), service processing fee. Applications for M.S.T.P. and UC San Francisco/UC Berkeley Joint Program are included in secondary application materials. Submit an application fee of $40, supplemental application, a personal comment/statement, preprofessional committee evaluation, and 2 recommendations from science faculty to Admissions Office within 2–3 weeks of the receipt of supplemental materials, but no later than December 1. Interviews are by invitation only and generally for final selection. Joint-degree applicants must apply to, and be accepted by, both schools; for current information and specific requirements for admission, contact the Graduate Office, Health and Medical Science Program, 570 University Hall, # 1190, Berkeley, California, 94720; phone: (510)642-5671. First-year students admitted in fall only. Rolling admission process. Notification starts on December 15 and is finished when class is filled. Applicant's response to offer and $100 deposit due within 2 weeks of receipt of acceptance letter. School does maintain an alternate/waiting list. Phone: (415)476-4044.

ADMISSION REQUIREMENTS FOR TRANSFER APPLICANTS. School of Medicine does not consider transfer applicants.

ADMISSION STANDARDS AND RECOGNITION. *For M.D.:* number of state-resident applicants 3,121, non-residents 2,626; number of interviews 524; number of residents enrolled 109, nonresidents 32; median MCAT 11.4 (verbal reasoning 11.0; biological sciences 12.0; physical sciences 11.0); median GPA 3.74 (A = 4). *Barron's Guide* placed the School of Medicine among the Top 25 most prestigious U.S. medical schools; Gorman rating 4.92 (scale: very strong 4.51–4.99); *U.S. News & World Report* ranking: ranked in the Top 25 of all U.S. medical schools, ranked in the Top 25 in primary-care programs; medical ranking by NIH awards was 4th, with 622 awards/grants; total dollars awarded $180,293,976.

FINANCIAL AID. Regents scholarships, merit scholarships, minority scholarships, grants-in-aid, institutional loans, HEAL, alternative loan programs, NIH stipends, federal Perkins loans, Stafford subsidized and unsubsidized loans, and service commitment scholarship programs are available. Assistantships/fellowships may be available for dual-degree candidates. All accepted applicants are considered for scholarships; the selection criteria place heavy reliance on MCAT and undergraduate GPA. Contact the Financial Aid Office for current application information; phone: (415)476-4181. For most financial assistance and all federal programs, submit FAFSA to a federal processor (Title IV school code

001319); also submit Financial Aid Transcript and Federal Income Tax forms. Approximately 75% of current students receive some form of financial assistance. Average debt after graduation $49,600.

DEGREE REQUIREMENTS. *For M.D.:* satisfactory completion of 4-year program. All students must pass USMLE Step 1 prior to entering 3rd year; all students must take USMLE Step 2 and record a score prior to awarding of M.D. *For M.D.-master's:* generally they are 4½–5½-year programs. *For M.D.-Ph.D., M.S.T.P.:* generally a 7-year program.

School of Dentistry
513 Parnassus, Room S-630
San Francisco, California 94143-0430
Telephone: (415)476-2738
Internet site: http://itsa.ucsf.edu
E-mail: dental@itsa,ucsf.edu

Established 1881. Share the health sciences library. Special programs: summer programs for underrepresented minorities; prematriculation summer sessions. Postgraduate specialties: Dental Public Health, Geriatric Dentistry, Oral and Maxillofacial Surgery, Orthodontics, Pediatric Dentistry, Periodontology, Prosthodontics.

Annual tuition and fees: resident student fees $8,799, nonresident tuition and fees $17,783; equipment and supplies $7,200. On-campus rooms and apartments available for both single and married students. Contact Housing Office for both on- and off-campus housing information; phone: (415)476-2231. Dental students tend to live off-campus. Off-campus housing, food, transportation, and personal expenses: approximately $11,800.

Enrollment: 1st-year class 80. First-year enrolled student information: 8 from out of state; 49 men, 31 women; average age 25; 7 underrepresented minorities; 45 other minorities.

Degrees conferred: D.D.S., B.S.-D.D.S., D.D.S.-M.S. (Oral Biology), D.D.S.-Ph.D. (Bioengineering, Epidemiology, Oral Biology), D.S.T.P. (1 of 3 in U.S.); has D.S.A. program.

RECRUITMENT PRACTICES AND POLICIES. School has diversity program and actively recruits women/minority applicants. Has a Health Careers Opportunity Program (HCOP). Diversity contact: Admissions Office; phone: (415)476-2737.

ADMISSION REQUIREMENTS FOR FIRST-YEAR APPLICANTS. Preference given to state residents; U.S. citizens and permanent residents only. *Undergraduate preparation.* Suggested predental courses: 2 courses in biology with labs, 2 courses in inorganic chemistry with labs, 2 courses in organic chemistry with labs, 2 courses in physics with labs, 1 course in college math, 2 courses in English. The junior-college transfer-credit limit is 60 credits. Will consider applicants with only 3 years of undergraduate preparation; prefer applicants who will have a bachelor's degree prior to enrollment; all enrollees had bachelor's degree awarded prior to enrollment. *Application process.* Apply through AADSAS (file after June 1, before January 1), submit official transcripts for each school attended (should show at least 90 semester credits/135 quarter credits), service processing fee; submit the following materials only after being contacted by an admissions officer: an application fee of $40, a UCSF supplemental application, official transcripts, official DAT scores (taken no later than 1 year prior to date of anticipated enrollment), and predent committee evaluation or 2 recommendations from science professors to Admissions Office within 2 weeks of receipt of supplemental materials, but no later than November 1. Interviews are by invitation only and generally for final selection. Dual-degree applicants must apply to, and be accepted by, both schools. Contact the Admissions Office for current information and specific requirements for admission. First-year students admitted in fall only. Rolling admission process. Notification starts on January 1 and is finished when class is filled; no later than April 15. Applicant's response to offer and $200 deposit due within 30 days if accepted prior to April 1; response and deposit due within 2 weeks if received after April 1. Phone: (415)476-2737. For current information with reference to Dental Scientist Training Program (DSTP) and Institutional Dental Scientist Award Program (DSA), contact Program Director, Office of Graduate Affairs, 513 Parnassus Avenue, S619-D, San Francisco, California 94143-0430.

ADMISSION REQUIREMENTS FOR ADVANCED-STANDING APPLICANTS. Does not accept transfer applications.

ADMISSION STANDARDS AND RECOGNITION. *For D.D.S.:* number of applicants 1,624; number enrolled 80; median DAT: ACAD 20.8, PAT 19; median GPA 3.52 (A = 4), median sciences GPA 3.50 (A = 4). Gorman rating 4.92 (scale: very strong 4.51–4.99); this placed the school in the Top 5 of all U.S. dental schools; the dental school's ranking by NIH awards was 2nd among dental schools, with 50 awards/grants received; total value of all awards/grants was $12,311,280.

FINANCIAL AID. Regents scholarships, university scholarships, minority scholarships, Cal State graduate fellowships, grants-in-aid, institutional loans, state loan programs, DEAL, HEAL, alternative loan programs, federal Perkins loans, Stafford subsidized and unsubsidized loans, and armed forces service commitment scholarship programs are available. Assistantships/fellowships may be available for combined-degree candidates. For regents and university scholarships, the selection criteria place heavy reliance on DAT and undergraduate GPA. Contact the Financial Aid Office for current information; phone: (415)476-4781. For most financial assistance and all need-based programs, submit FAFSA to a federal processor (Title IV school code # 001319); also submit Financial Aid Transcript, Federal Income Tax forms, and Use of Federal Funds Certification. Approximately 93% of current students receive some form of financial assistance. Average award resident $21,388, nonresident $31,783.

DEGREE REQUIREMENTS. *For D.D.S.:* satisfactory completion of 4-year program. *For D.D.S.-M.P.H.:* generally a 5-year program. *For D.D.S.-M.S.:* generally a 4½–5½-year program. *For D.D.S.-Ph.D.:* generally a 7–8-year program.

CASE WESTERN RESERVE UNIVERSITY
Cleveland, Ohio 44106
Internet site: http://www.cwru.edu

Formed as a result of a merger between Case Institute of Technology and Western Reserve University in 1967. Located 5 miles E of Cleveland. Private control. Semester system. Library: 1,900,000 volumes; 2,181,000 microforms; 14,100 periodicals/subscriptions; 45 PC computer work stations. Special programs: B.A./B.S.-M.D. program (annual undergraduate tuition $17,100). The university's ranking by NIH awards in domestic higher education was 16th, with 479 grants; total dollars awarded $135,848,540.

The university's other graduate schools: Frances Payne Bolton School of Nursing, Mandel School of Applied Sciences, School of Dentistry, School of Graduate Studies, School of Law, Weatherhead School of Management.

Total university enrollment at main campus: 9,750.

University Hospitals of Cleveland
University Circle
Cleveland, Ohio 44106

Adjoining the Case Western Reserve University Campus. Private control. Member of the Council of Teaching Hospitals. Nationally recognized programs in Cardiology, Cancer, Endocrinology, Gastroenterology, Geriatrics, Gynecology, Neurology, Ophthalmology, Otolaryngology, Pediatrics, Rheumatology.

School of Medicine
10900 Euclid Avenue
Cleveland, Ohio 44106-4920
Telephone: (216)368-3450; fax: (216)368-4621
Internet site: http://www.cwru.edu

Established 1943. Located on the university's main campus, 5 miles E of downtown Cleveland. Library: 150,000 volumes/microforms; 3,000 current periodicals/subscriptions. Affiliated hospitals: University Hospitals of Cleveland, Metro Health Medical Center, St. Luke's Hospital, Veterans Affairs, Cleveland Medical Center, Mt. Sinai Medical Center, Henry Ford Health System (Detroit, Michigan). Special programs: summer programs for underrepresented minorities; prematriculation summer sessions.

Annual tuition: $24,500. Graduate housing about 10 minutes from campus. Graduate housing cost: $400 per month for room, $200 per month board. Contact Admissions Office for graduate housing information; phone: (216)368-3780. Medical students tend to live off-campus. Off-campus housing and personal expenses: approximately $13,259.

Enrollment: 1st-year class 138 (EDP 35); total full-time 574 (men 58.4%, women 41.6%). First-year statistics: 40% out of state; over 20 states represented; 41.3% women; average age 24; 18% minorities; 60% science majors.

Degrees conferred: M.D., B.S.-M.D., M.D.-Ph.D. (Biochemistry, Biomedical Engineering, Biophysics, Cell Biology, Genetics, Immunology, Microbiology, Molecular Biology, Neurosciences, Pathology, Pharmacology, Physiology); has M.S.T.P.

RECRUITMENT PRACTICES AND POLICIES. School has diversity program and actively recruits women/minority applicants. Diversity contact: Associate Dean; phone: (216)368-7212.

ADMISSION REQUIREMENT FOR BACHELOR-M.D. APPLICANTS. Preference given to state residents. Minimum high school preparation: 1 year of biology, 1 year of chemistry, 1 year of physics, 4 years of mathematics. Submit application, SAT I, 3 SAT IIs, ACT assessment, official high school transcripts with rank in class, and letters of recommendation to the Office of Undergraduate Admission by January 1. Notification date is April 15. Applicant's response to offer and $200 deposit due within 3 weeks of receipt of acceptance letter. Application fee: none. Phone: (216)368-4450. For financial aid information contact the university's Office of Financial Aid; phone: (216)368-4530.

ADMISSION REQUIREMENTS FOR FIRST-YEAR APPLICANTS. Applicants must be U.S. citizens and permanent residents only. *Undergraduate preparation.* Suggested premed courses: 2 courses in biology with labs, 2 courses in inorganic chemistry with labs, 2 courses in organic chemistry with labs, 2 courses in physics with labs, 2 courses in English. Bachelor's degree from an accredited institution required; 97% of applicants have bachelor's degree awarded prior to enrollment. *Has EDP;* applicants must apply through AMCAS (official transcripts sent by mid-May) between June 1 and August 1. Early applications are encouraged. Submit supplemental application, a personal statement, and 2 recommendations to Office of Admissions within 2 weeks of receipt of application. Notification normally begins October 1. *Regular application process.* Apply through AMCAS (file after June 1, before October 15); submit MCAT (must have been taken within the last 3 years), official transcripts for each school attended (should show at least 90 semester credits/135 quarter credits, submit transcripts by mid-May to AMCAS), service processing fee. Submit an application fee of $60, supplemental application, a personal comment/statement, preprofessional committee evaluation, and 2 recommendations from science faculty to Admissions Office within 2–3 weeks of the receipt of supplemental materials. Interviews are by invitation only and generally for final selection. Dual-degree applicants must apply to, and be accepted by, both schools; contact the Admissions Office for current information and specific requirements for admission. First-year students admitted in fall only. Rolling admission process. Notification starts on October 15 and is finished when class is filled. Applicant's response to offer due within 4 weeks of receipt of acceptance letter. School does maintain an alternate list. Phone: (216)368-3450.

ADMISSION REQUIREMENTS FOR TRANSFER APPLICANTS. Transfer students are not normally considered. Contact the Admissions Office for current information.

ADMISSION STANDARDS AND RECOGNITION. *For B.A./B.S.-M.D.:* number of state-resident applicants 750; number of residents interviewed 60; number residents enrolled 25; median SATs 1,480, ACT 33; median GPA 4.35 (A = 4). *For M.D.:* number of state-resident applicants 6,708, nonresidents 1,211; number of state residents interviewed 408, nonresidents 543; number of residents enrolled 84, nonresidents 54; median MCAT 10.0 (verbal reasoning 10.0; biological sciences 10.0; physical sciences 10.0); median GPA 3.50 (A = 4). Gorman rating 3.90 (scale: good 3.61–3.99); the school's medical ranking by NIH awards was 10th, with 413 awards/grants; total dollars awarded $122,225,805.

FINANCIAL AID. Scholarships, merit scholarships, minority scholarships, grants, institutional loans, HEAL, alternative loan programs, NIH stipends, federal Perkins loans, Stafford subsidized and unsubsidized loans, and armed forces service commitment scholarship programs are available. Assistantships/fellowships may be available for dual-degree candidates. Financial-aid applications and information are mailed to all serious candidates in January. Most financial aid is based on demonstrated need. For scholarships, the selection criteria place heavy reliance on MCAT and undergraduate GPA. Contact the Financial Aid Office for current information; phone: (216)368-3666. For most financial assistance and all federal programs, submit FAFSA to a federal processor (Title IV school code # E0079); also submit Financial Aid Transcript and Federal Income Tax forms. A typical financial-aid package consists of 30–40% grant plus 60–70% loan. Approximately 87% of current students receive some form of financial assistance. Average debt after graduation $79,800.

DEGREE REQUIREMENTS. *For B.S.-M.D.:* an 8-year program. *For M.D.:* satisfactory completion of 4-year program. All students must pass USMLE Step 1 prior to entering 3rd year; all students must pass USMLE Step 2 prior to awarding of M.D. *For M.D.-M.S.:* generally a 4½–5½-year program. *For M.D.-Ph.D.:* generally a 7-year program.

School of Dentistry
10900 Euclid Avenue
Cleveland, Ohio 44106-4905
Telephone: (216)368-3200; fax (216)368-3204
Internet site: http://www.crwu.edu

Established 1892. Located at the Health Science Center since 1969. Special programs: dental externships, summer programs for underrepresented minorities; prematriculation summer sessions. Affiliated hospitals: University Hospital, Metro Health System, Veterans Administration Hospital, Free Medical Clinic of Greater Cleveland. Postgraduate specialties: Endodontics, General Dentistry, Oral and Maxillofacial Surgery, Oral Medicine, Orthodontics, Pediatric Dentistry, Periodontics.

Annual tuition: $24,800; fees $890; equipment and supplies $4,700. On-campus single rooms and single-occupancy apartments available. Contact Housing Office for both on- and off-campus housing information; phone: (216)368-3780. Dental students tend to live off-campus. Off-campus housing, food, transportation, and personal expenses: approximately $9,400.

Enrollment: 1st-year class 62. First-year enrolled student information: 48 from out of state; 18 states represented; 19 women; average age 24; 17 minorities.

Faculty: full-time 33, part-time/volunteers 200.

Degrees conferred: D.D.S., D.D.S.-M.B.A., D.D.S.-M.S., D.D.S.-Ph.D. (Anatomy, Biochemistry, Microbiology, Pathology, Pharmacology, Physiology); has M.S.D.

RECRUITMENT PRACTICES AND POLICIES. School has diversity program and actively recruits women/minority applicants. Diversity contact: Minority Coordinator; phone: (216)368-3201.

ADMISSION REQUIREMENTS FOR FIRST-YEAR APPLICANTS. Preference given to state residents; U.S. citizens, and permanent residents only. *Undergraduate preparation.* Suggested predental courses: 2 courses in biology with labs, 2 courses in inorganic chemistry with labs, 2 courses in organic chemistry with labs, 2 courses in physics with labs, 2 courses in English. The junior-college transfer-credit limit is 60 credits. Will consider applicants with only 3 years of undergraduate preparation; prefer applicants who will have a bachelor's degree prior to enrollment; 80% of enrollees had bachelor's degree awarded prior to enrollment. *Application process.* Apply through AADSAS (file after June 1, before March 1); submit official transcripts for each school attended (should show at least 90 semester credits/135 quarter credits), service processing fee; at the same time as you send in AADSAS materials, submit official DAT scores, application fee of $35, official transcripts, and predental committee evaluation or 2 recommendations from science professors directly to the Admissions Office. Interviews are by invitation only and generally for final selection. Combined-degree applicants must apply to, and be accepted by, both schools. Contact the Admissions Office for current information and specific requirements for admission. First-year students admitted in fall only. Rolling admission process. Notification starts on December 1 and is finished when class is filled. Applicant's response to offer and $1,000 deposit due within 30–45 days if accepted prior to January 31; response and deposit due within 2 weeks if received after February 1. School does maintain an alternate list. Phone: (216)368-2460; fax: (216)368-3204. For graduate-degree information, contact the Office of Graduate Studies, phone: (216)368-3731.

ADMISSION REQUIREMENTS FOR ADVANCED-STANDING APPLICANTS. Accepts transfers from other accredited U.S. and foreign dental schools. Admission limited to space available. There is an advanced-standing program for graduates of foreign schools of dentistry. Contact the Admissions Office in writing for current information and specific requirements for admission.

ADMISSION STANDARDS AND RECOGNITION. *For D.D.S.:* number of applicants 2,201; number enrolled 62; median DAT: ACAD 18.21, PAT 17.35; median GPA 3.14 (A = 4), median sciences GPA 3.0 (A = 4). Gorman rating 4.45 (scale: strong 4.01–4.49); this placed the school in the Top 20 of all U.S. dental schools.

FINANCIAL AID. Scholarships, merit scholarships, minority scholarships, grants-in-aid, institutional loans, state loan programs, DEAL, HEAL, alternative loan programs, federal Perkins loans, Stafford subsidized and unsubsidized loans, and armed forces service commitment scholarship programs are available. Assistantships/fellowships may be available for combined-degree candidates. A tuition stabilization plan is available. Institutional financial-aid applications and information are given out at the on-campus interview (by invitation). For merit scholarships, the selection criteria place heavy reliance on DAT and undergraduate GPA. Contact the Financial Aid Office for current information; phone: (216)368-3256. For most financial assistance and all need-based programs, submit FAFSA to a federal processor (Title IV school code # E0078); also submit Financial Aid Transcript, Federal Income Tax forms, and Use of Federal Funds Certification. Approximately 77% of current students receive some form of financial assistance. Average award $34,000.

DEGREE REQUIREMENTS. *For D.D.S.:* satisfactory completion of 4-year program. *For D.D.S.-M.B.A.:* generally a 5-year program. *For D.D.S.-M.S.:* generally a 4½–5½-year program. *For D.D.S.-Ph.D.:* generally a 6–7-year program. *For M.S.D.:* 54-credit program; thesis, oral defense.

UNIVERSIDAD CENTRAL DEL CARIBE

School of Medicine
Call Box 60-327
Bayamón, Puerto Rico 00960-6032
Telephone: (809)740-1611, X210; fax: (809)269-7550
Internet site: http://www.uccaribe.edu

Founded 1976. Located at the health center in downtown Bayamón. Private control. Semester system. Library: 26,385 volumes; 467 periodicals/subscriptions; 20

PC work stations. Principle teaching hospital is Dr. Ramón Ruíz Arnau University Hospital.

Annual tuition: residents $17,800, nonresidents $24,000. No on-campus housing available. Contact Admissions Office for off-campus housing information. Off-campus housing and personal expenses: approximately $6,000–$8,000.

Enrollment: 1st-year class 60; total full-time 246 (men 53%, women 47%). First-year statistics: 20% outside Puerto Rico, 52.5% women; average age 25.

Degree conferred: M.D.

RECRUITMENT PRACTICES AND POLICIES. School has diversity program and actively recruits women applicants. Diversity contact: Dean of Admissions and Student Affairs; phone: (809)740-1611.

ADMISSION REQUIREMENTS FOR FIRST-YEAR APPLICANTS. Preference given to residents of Puerto Rico. *Undergraduate preparation.* Suggested premed courses: 2 courses in biology with labs, 2 courses in inorganic chemistry with labs, 2 courses in organic chemistry with labs, 2 courses in physics with labs, 2 courses in college math, 3 courses in English, 6 courses in Spanish, 12 courses in behavioral/social sciences/humanities. Bachelor's degree from an accredited institution required; 97% of applicants have bachelor's degree awarded prior to enrollment. Does not have EDP. *Application process.* Apply through AMCAS (file after June 1, before December 15); submit MCAT (will accept test results that are no more than 3 years old), official transcripts for each school attended (should show at least 90 semester credits/135 quarter credits, submit transcripts by mid-May to AMCAS), service processing fee. Submit an application fee of $50, a supplemental application, a personal statement, preprofessional committee evaluation, and 2 recommendations from science faculty to Admissions Office within 2–3 weeks of the receipt of supplemental materials. Interviews are by invitation only and generally for final selection. First-year students admitted in fall only. Rolling admission process. Notification starts on January 15 and is finished when class is filled. Applicant's response to offer and $100 deposit due within 10 days of receipt of acceptance letter. Admissions Office phone: (809)740-1611, x210.

ADMISSION REQUIREMENTS FOR TRANSFER APPLICANTS. Accepts transfers from other accredited U.S. medical schools. Admission limited to space available. Contact the Admissions Office for current information and specific requirements for admission.

ADMISSION STANDARDS AND RECOGNITION. *For M.D.:* number of P.R. resident applicants 431, nonresidents 656; number of residents interviewed 136, nonresidents 20; number of residents enrolled 47, nonresidents 12; median MCAT N/A; median GPA 3.12 (A = 4). Gorman rating 3.03 (scale: acceptable plus 3.01–3.59); medical school ranking by NIH awards was 120th, with 2 awards/grants; total dollars awarded $2,928,608.

FINANCIAL AID. Commonwealth scholarships, federal scholarships, HEAL, alternative loan programs, federal Perkins loans, Stafford subsidized and unsubsidized loans, and armed forces service commitment scholarship programs are available. Financial-aid applications and information are given out at the on-campus interview (by invitation only). For scholarships, the selection criteria place heavy reliance on MCAT and undergraduate GPA. Contact the Financial Aid Office for current information; phone: (809)740-1611. For most financial assistance and all federal programs, submit FAFSA to a federal processor (Title IV school code # 014999); also submit Financial Aid Transcript and Federal Income Tax forms. Approximately 75% of current students receive some form of financial assistance. Average debt after graduation $50,000.

DEGREE REQUIREMENTS. *For M.D.:* satisfactory completion of 4-year program.

UNIVERSITY OF CHICAGO
Chicago, Illinois 60637-1513
Internet site: http://www.uchicago.edu

Founded 1890. Private control. Quarter system. Library: 5,850,000 volumes; 2,178,000 microforms; 45,500 periodicals/subscriptions; 158 work stations. The university's ranking in domestic higher education by NIH awards was 24th, with 324 grants received; total dollars awarded $92,852,332.

The university's other graduate divisions/schools: Divinity School, Division of Social Sciences, Division of the Humanities, Division of the Biological Sciences, Division of Physical Sciences, Graduate School of Business, Law School, School of Social Services Administration, Irving B. Harris Graduate School of Public Policy Studies.

Total university enrollment at main campus: 12,200.

University of Chicago Medical Center
5841 South Maryland
Chicago, Illinois 60637

Private Control. Member of Council of Teaching Hospitals. Facilities include Bernard Mitchell Hospital, Chicago Lying In Hospital, Wyler's Children Hospital, Center for

Advanced Medicine. Special facilities: National Cancer Research Center, National Diabetes Research Training Center, National Clinical Nutrition Research Unit, Special Center for Research in Arteriosclerosis, Joseph P. Kennedy, Jr. Mental Retardation Research Center, Clinical Pharmacology Center. Nationally recognized programs in AIDS, Cancer, Cardiology, Endocrinology, Gastroenterology, Geriatrics, Gynecology, Neurology, Orthopedics, Otolaryngology, Pulmonary Disease, Rheumatology, Urology. US News Hospital/Medical Center national rankings for all hospitals placed University of Chicago Medical Center in the Top 20 of all U.S. Hospital/Medical Centers.

Pritzker School of Medicine

924 East 57th Street, BLSC 104
Chicago, Illinois 60637-5416
Telephone: (773)702-1937; (773)702-2598
Internet site: http://pritzker.bsd.uchicago.edu
E-mail: fernada@prufrock.bsd.uchicago.edu

Established 1927 and is part of the university's Division of Biological Sciences. Located on main campus. Library: 996,000 volumes/microforms; 7,000 current periodicals/subscriptions. Special facilities: Biological Sciences Research Center, Jules Knapp Institute for Molecular Medicine, McLean Center for Clinical Medical Ethics, Berman and Hannah Friend Center for Family Health Care. Affiliated hospitals: University of Chicago Hospitals, Louis A. Weiss Memorial Hospital, MacNeal Hospital.

Annual tuition: $21,660. On-campus rooms and apartments available for both single and married students; approximately 1,100 apartments. Contact Admissions Office for both on- and off-campus housing information. Medical students tend to live off-campus. Off-campus housing and personal expenses: approximately $12,056.

Enrollment: 1st-year class 104 (EDP 5, M.S.T.P. approximately 10); total full-time 420 (men 44.5%, women 45.5%). First-year statistics: 60% out of state; 48% women; average age 25; 15% minorities; 62% science majors.

Faculty: full-time 650.

Degrees conferred: M.D., M.D.-M.A., M.D.-M.B.A., M.D.-J.D., M.D.-Ph.D. (Anatomy, Biochemistry, Cell Biology, Genetics, Immunology, Molecular Biology, Neurosciences, Pathology, Pharmacology, Physiology); has M.S.T.P.

RECRUITMENT PRACTICES AND POLICIES. School has diversity program and actively recruits women/minority applicants. Diversity contact: Director of Student Programs, phone: (312)702-1939.

ADMISSION REQUIREMENTS FOR FIRST-YEAR APPLICANTS. Preference given to U.S. citizens and permanent residents only. *Undergraduate preparation.* Suggested premed courses: 2 courses in biology with labs, 2 courses in inorganic chemistry with labs, 2 courses in organic chemistry with labs, 2 courses in physics with labs; 1 course in biochemistry is strongly recommended. Bachelor's degree from an accredited institution required; all applicants have bachelor's degrees awarded prior to enrollment. *Has EDP;* applicants must apply through AMCAS (official transcripts sent by mid-May) between June 1 and August 1. Early applications are encouraged. Submit secondary/supplemental application, a personal statement, and 2 recommendations to Admissions Office within 2 weeks of receipt of application. Notification normally begins October 1. *Regular application process.* Applications are initiated through AMCAS (file after June 1, before December 1); submit MCAT (scores must be no older than 3 years), official transcripts for each school attended (should show at least 90 semester credits/135 quarter credits, submit transcripts by mid-May to AMCAS), service processing fee. A supplemental application is sent to every applicant who submits an application through AMCAS. Submit the supplemental application and an application fee of $55, a personal statement, preprofessional committee evaluation, and 2 recommendations from science faculty to Admissions Office within 2–3 weeks of the receipt of supplemental materials, but not later than January 7. Interviews are by invitation only and generally for final selection. Dual-degree applicants must apply to, and be accepted by, both schools; contact the Admissions Office for current information and specific requirements for admission. First-year students admitted in fall only. Rolling admission process. Notification starts on October 15 and is finished when class is filled. Applicant's response to offer and $100 deposit due within 30 days of receipt of acceptance letter. School does maintain an alternate list. Phone: (773)702-1937; fax: (773)702-2598.

ADMISSION REQUIREMENTS FOR TRANSFER APPLICANTS. Accepts transfers from other LCME-accredited U.S. medical schools into the 2nd and 3rd years but only with compelling reasons. Admission limited to space available. Contact the Admissions Office for current information and specific requirements.

ADMISSION STANDARDS AND RECOGNITION. *For M.D.:* number of state-resident applicants 1,258, nonresidents 7,451; number of state residents interviewed 158, nonresidents 401; number of residents enrolled 47, nonresidents 57; median MCAT 10.7 (verbal reasoning

10.0; biological sciences 10.5; physical sciences 10.3); median GPA 3.59 (A = 4). *Barron's Guide* placed Pritzker School of Medicine among the Top 25 most prestigious U.S. medical schools; Gorman rating 4.88 (scale: very strong 4.51–4.99); *U.S. News & World Report* ranking: ranked in the Top 25 of all U.S. medical schools; ranked in the Top 25 in primary-care programs; medical school rankings by NIH awards was 19th, with 298 awards/grants received; total dollars awarded $87,933,721.

FINANCIAL AID. Scholarships, merit scholarships, minority scholarships, grants-in-aid, institutional loans, HEAL, alternative loan programs, NIH stipends, federal Perkins loans, Stafford subsidized and unsubsidized loans, and service commitment scholarship programs are available. Assistantships/fellowships may be available for dual-degree candidates. All accepted applicants are sent financial aid information after January 1. All interviewed applicants receive additional information. Contact the Financial Aid Office for current information; phone: (773)702-1938. For most financial assistance and all federal programs, submit FAFSA to a federal processor (Title IV school code # G10141); also submit Financial Aid Transcript and Federal Income Tax forms. Approximately 82% of current students receive some form of financial assistance. Average debt after graduation $64,100.

DEGREE REQUIREMENTS. *For M.D.:* satisfactory completion of 4-year program. Passage of USMLE is not required for graduation. *For M.D.-M.S.:* generally a 4½–5½-year program. *For M.D.-Ph.D., M.S.T.P.:* generally a 7–8-year program.

UNIVERSITY OF CINCINNATI
Cincinnati, Ohio 45221
Internet site: http://www.cu.edu

Founded 1819. Coed. Private control. Quarter system. Library: 1,980,000 volumes; 2,919,000 microforms; 21,500 periodicals/subscriptions; 436 work stations. The university's ranking in domestic higher education by NIH awards was 58th, with 182 grants; total dollars awarded $43,510,859.

The university's Division of Research and Advanced Studies includes: College-Conservatory of Music, College of Business Administration, College of Design, Architecture, Art and Planning, College of Education, College of Engineering, College of Nursing and Health, College of Pharmacy, McMicken College of Arts and Sciences, School of Social Work, College of Law.

Total university enrollment at main campus: 35,500.

University of Cincinnati Medical Center
234 Goodman Street
Cincinnati, Ohio 45267
Internet site: http://medcenter.uc.edu

Public Control. Member of Council of Teaching Hospitals. Schools located at medical center: College of Medicine, College of Nursing and Health, College of Pharmacy. Nationally recognized programs in AIDS, Cancer, Cardiology, Endocrinology, Gastroenterology, Geriatrics, Gynecology, Neurology, Otolaryngology, Pulmonary Disease.

College of Medicine
P.O. Box 670552
231 Bethesda Avenue
Cincinnati, Ohio 45267-0552
Telephone: (513)558-7314; fax: (513)558-1165
Internet site: http://www.med.uc.edu

Established 1819. Library: 125,000 volumes/microforms; 2,800 current periodicals/subscriptions. Affiliated hospitals: University Hospital, VA Medical Center, Children's Hospital, Medical Center and Christ Hospital, Good Samaritan Hospital. Special facilities: Area Health Education Center (for underserved and urban communities); Center for Cardiovascular Materials, Center for Environmental Genetics, Institute of Molecular Pharmacology and Biophysics. Special programs: summer programs for underrepresented minorities; prematriculation summer sessions.

Annual tuition: residents $10,971, nonresidents $19,632. Limited on-campus housing available. Contact Admissions Office for both on- and off-campus housing information. Medical students tend to live off-campus. Off-campus housing and personal expenses: approximately $13,788.

Enrollment: 1st-year class 160; total full-time 637 (men 63.7%, women 36.3%). First-year statistics: 17% out of state; 40.7% women; average age 24; 23% underrepresented minorities; 12% other minorities; 78% science majors.

Clinical faculty: full-time 650.

Degrees conferred: M.D., M.D.-M.S. (Blood Transfusion Medicine, Environmental Health, Genetic Counseling, Radiological Sciences), M.D.-Ph.D. (Cell Biology, Developmental Biology, Environmental Health, Molecular, Cellular and Biochemical Pharmacology, Molecular and Cellular Physiology, Molecular Genetics, Biochemistry and Microbiology, Neurosciences, Pathobiology and Molecular Medicine); has P.S.T.P.

RECRUITMENT PRACTICES AND POLICIES. School has diversity program and actively recruits women/minority applicants. Diversity contact: Assistant Dean for Admissions and Student Affairs, phone: (613)558-7314.

ADMISSION REQUIREMENTS FOR FIRST-YEAR APPLICANTS.

Preference given to first-time applicants, state residents; U.S. citizens, Canadian residents, and permanent residents only. *Undergraduate preparation.* Suggested premed courses: 2 courses in biology with labs, 2 courses in general chemistry with labs, 2 courses in organic chemistry with labs, 2 courses in physics with labs, 1 course in college math, 2 courses in English. Bachelor's degree from an accredited institution required; all applicants have bachelor's degree awarded prior to enrollment. *Has EDP;* applicants must apply through AMCAS (official transcripts sent by mid-May) between June 1 and August 1. Early applications are encouraged. Submit secondary/supplemental application, a personal statement, 2 recommendations to Admissions Office within 2 weeks of receipt of application. Notification normally begins October 1. *Regular application process.* Apply through AMCAS (file after June 1, before November 15); submit MCAT (scores must be from the last 2 years) and official transcripts for each school attended (should show at least 90 semester credits/135 quarter credits, submit transcripts by mid-May to AMCAS), service processing fee. A supplemental application is sent to selected applicants. Submit an application fee of $25, the supplemental application, a personal statement, preprofessional committee evaluation, and 2 recommendations from science faculty to Admissions Office within 2–3 weeks of the receipt of supplemental materials. Interviews are by invitation only and generally for final selection. Dual-degree applicants must apply to, and be accepted by, the College of Medicine and the Medical Science Scholars program; contact the Admissions Office for current information and specific requirements for admission. First-year students admitted in fall only. Rolling admission process. Notification starts on October 15 and continues on the 15th of each month until the class is filled. Applicant's response to offer due within 2 weeks of receipt of acceptance letter. School does maintain an alternate list. Phone: (513)558-7314; fax: (513)558-2380. Contact Physician Scientist Training Program (P.S.T.P) through their web site: http://www.med.uc.edu/pstp/index.htm.

ADMISSION REQUIREMENTS FOR TRANSFER APPLICANTS.

Accepts transfers from other accredited U.S. and Canadian medical schools. Admission limited to space available. Contact the Admissions Office for current information and specific requirements for admission.

ADMISSION STANDARDS AND RECOGNITION.

For M.D.: number of state-resident applicants 1,507, nonresidents 3,280; number of state residents interviewed 480, nonresidents 162; number of residents enrolled 126, nonresidents 25; median MCAT 9.7 (verbal reasoning 9.4; biological sciences 9.9; physical sciences 9.7); median GPA 3.45 (A = 4). Gorman rating 3.70 (scale: good 3.61–3.99); College of Medicine's ranking by NIH awards was 43rd, with 175 awards/grants; total dollars awarded $42,524,633.

FINANCIAL AID.

Scholarships, merit scholarship, minority scholarships, grants-in-aid, institutional loans, HEAL, alternative loan programs, federal Perkins loans, Stafford subsidized and unsubsidized loans, and service commitment scholarship programs are available. Assistantships/fellowships may be available for dual-degree and P.S.T.P. candidates. Financial-aid packets mailed to all accepted applicants after January 1. Apply by May 1 to the college's Financial Aid Office; for current information contact the Financial Aid Office; phone: (513)558-6797. For most financial assistance and all federal programs submit FAFSA to a federal processor (Title IV school code # E00385); also submit the NEED ACCESS diskette, a Financial Aid Transcript, and Federal Income Tax forms. Approximately 80% of current students receive some form of financial assistance. Average debt after graduation $63,600.

DEGREE REQUIREMENTS.

For M.D.: satisfactory completion of 4-year program. All students must pass USMLE Step 1 prior to entering 3rd year; all students must pass USMLE Step 2 prior to awarding of M.D. *For M.D.-M.S.:* generally a 4½–5½-year program. *For M.D.-Ph.D., P.S.T.P.:* generally a 7-year program.

UNIVERSITY OF COLORADO HEALTH SCIENCE CENTER

4200 East 9th Avenue
Denver, Colorado 80262
Telephone: (303)372-0000
Internet site: http://www.uchsc.edu

Founded 1885, relocated to Denver in 1911. Public control. Semester system. Library: 2,500,000 volumes; 250,000 microforms; 1,650 periodicals/subscriptions; 20 work stations. The health science center's ranking in domestic higher education by NIH awards was 81st, with 124 grants; total dollars awarded $22,228,077. Member of Council of Teaching Hospitals. Schools located at health science center: School of Dentistry, School of Medicine,

School of Nursing, School of Pharmacy. Total enrollment at health science center: 2,156. Special facilities: John F. Kennedy Center for Developmental Disabilities, Saban Building for Cellular Research, Webb-Waring Institute for Biomedical Research. Nationally recognized programs in Geriatrics, Pulmonary Disease, Rehabilitation.

School of Medicine
4200 East 9th Avenue, C-297
Denver, Colorado 80262
Telephone: (303)315-7361, 315-7679, 315-4355; fax: (303)315-8494
Internet site: http://www.uchsc.edu
E-mail: joey.seamans@uchsc.edu

Established 1883. Quarter system. Library: 161,000 volumes/microforms; 2,100 current periodicals/subscriptions. Affiliated hospitals: University Hospital, Colorado General Hospital, VA Hospital, Denver General Hospital.

Annual tuition: residents $12,544, nonresidents $53,358; fees $1,805. No on-campus housing available. Contact Student Assistance Office for off-campus housing information; phone: (303)315-7620. Medical students must live off-campus. Off-campus housing and personal expenses: approximately $11,000.

Enrollment: 1st-year class 130; total full-time 519 (men 57%, women 43%). First-year statistics: 19% out of state; 47.3% women; average age 26; 20% minorities; 78% science majors.

Faculty: full-time 1,000, part-time/volunteers 2,500.

Degrees conferred: M.D., M.D.-M.B.A., M.D.-Ph.D. (Biochemistry, Biophysics, Cell Biology, Immunology, Microbiology, Molecular Biology, Neurosciences, Pharmacology, Physiology); has M.S.T.P.

RECRUITMENT PRACTICES AND POLICIES. School has diversity program and actively recruits women/minority applicants. Diversity contact: Assistant Chancellor, Diversity; phone: (303)315-8558.

ADMISSION REQUIREMENTS FOR FIRST-YEAR APPLICANTS. Preference given to state residents and WICHE Program applicants; U.S. citizens and permanent residents only. *Undergraduate preparation.* Suggested premed courses: 2 courses in biology with labs, 2 courses in general chemistry with labs, 2 courses in organic chemistry with labs, 2 courses in physics with labs, 2 courses in college math, 1 course in English. Bachelor's degree from an accredited institution required; all applicants have bachelor's degree awarded prior to enrollment. Does not have EDP. *Application process.* Apply through AMCAS (file after June 1, before December 1); submit MCAT (will accept MCAT test results from 1995), offi-

cial transcripts for each school attended (should show at least 90 semester credits/135 quarter credits, submit transcripts by mid-May to AMCAS), service processing fee. Submit an application fee of $70, a supplemental application, a personal statement, preprofessional committee evaluation, and 2 recommendations from science faculty to Admissions Office within 2–3 weeks of the receipt of supplemental materials. Interviews are by invitation only and generally for final selection. Dual-degree applicants must apply to, and be accepted by, both schools; contact the Admissions Office for current information and specific requirements for admission. M.S.T.P. phone contact: (303)315-8986. First-year students admitted in fall only. Rolling admission process. Notification starts on October 15 and is finished when class is filled. Applicant's response to offer and $200 deposit due within 2 weeks of receipt of acceptance letter. School does maintain an alternate list. Admissions Office phone: (303)315-7361.

ADMISSION REQUIREMENTS FOR TRANSFER APPLICANTS. Accepts transfers from other accredited U.S. medical schools who are Colorado residents. Admission limited to space available. Contact the Admissions Office for current information and specific requirements for admission.

ADMISSION STANDARDS AND RECOGNITION. *For M.D.:* number of state-resident applicants 757, nonresidents 1,943; number of state residents interviewed 480, nonresidents 243; number of residents enrolled 105, nonresidents 24; median MCAT 10.0 (verbal reasoning 9.9; biological sciences 9.9; physical sciences 9.9); median GPA 3.6 (A = 4). Gorman rating 3.85 (scale: good 3.61–3.99); the college's ranking by NIH awards was 20th, with 305 awards/grants received; total dollars awarded $86,549,524.

FINANCIAL AID. Scholarships, minority scholarships, Colorado graduate grants, institutional loans, HEAL, HPSL, primary-care loans, alternative loan programs, NIH stipends, federal Perkins loans, Stafford subsidized and unsubsidized loans, and service commitment scholarship programs are available. Assistantships/fellowships may be available for dual-degree candidates. Financial-aid applications and information are given out at the on-campus interview (by invitation). For merit scholarships, the selection criteria place heavy reliance on MCAT and undergraduate GPA. Contact the health sciences center's Financial Aid Office for current information; phone: (303)315-8364. For most financial assistance and all federal programs, apply after January 1, before March 15, and submit FAFSA to a federal processor (Title IV school code # 004508); also submit Financial Aid Transcript and Federal Income Tax forms. Approximately 80% of current students receive some form of financial assistance. Average debt after graduation $73,398.

DEGREE REQUIREMENTS. *For M.D.:* satisfactory completion of 4-year program. *For M.D.-M.B.A.:* generally a 5-year program. *For M.D.-Ph.D., M.S.T.P.:* generally a 7-year program.

School of Dentistry
Box C-284
4200 East 9th Avenue
Denver, Colorado 80262
Telephone: (303)315-8893; fax: (303)315-8892
Internet site: http://www.uchsc.edu/sd/sd/program.html

Established 1967. Located at the health science center. Postgraduate specialties: General Dentistry (AEGD).

Annual tuition: residents $6,980, nonresidents $23,700; fees $1,800, equipment and supplies $7,400. No on-campus housing available. Contact Student Assistance Office for off-campus housing information; phone: (303)315-7620. Dental students must live off-campus. Off-campus housing, food, transportation, and personal expenses: approximately $11,000.

Enrollment: 1st-year class 36. First-year enrolled student information: 11 from out of state; 6 states represented; 9 women; average age 27; 3 from underrepresented minority; 2 from other minorities.

Faculty: full-time/part-time 50, volunteers 300.

Degree conferred: D.D.S.

RECRUITMENT PRACTICES AND POLICIES. School has diversity program (HCOP) and actively recruits women/minority applicants. Diversity contact: Office of Multicultural Enrichment; phone: (303)315-8550.

ADMISSION REQUIREMENTS FOR FIRST-YEAR APPLICANTS. Preference given to state residents, U.S. citizens, and permanent residents only. *Undergraduate preparation.* Suggested predental courses: 2 courses in biology with labs, 2 courses in general chemistry with labs, 2 courses in organic chemistry with labs, 2 courses in physics with labs, 2 courses in literature/humanities, 1 course in English. The junior-college transfer-credit limit is 60 credits. Will consider applicants with only 3 years of undergraduate preparation; prefer applicants who will have a bachelor's degree prior to enrollment; all enrollees had bachelor's degree awarded prior to enrollment. *Application process.* Apply through AADSAS (file after June 1, before January 1, early applications are highly recom-

mended), submit official transcripts for each school attended (should show at least 90 semester credits/135 quarter credit), service processing fee; at the same time as you send in AADSAS materials, submit Official DAT scores (must be taken no later than October of the year preceding the year of anticipated enrollment) directly to the Admissions Office. Submit the following materials only after being contacted by an admissions officer: an application fee of $50, a secondary/supplemental application, official transcripts, predental committee evaluation or 2 recommendations from professors in your major field of study, recent photograph, Regents questionnaire, and Verification of Colorado Residency form or WICHE Certification letter to Office of Admission and Student Affairs within 2 weeks of receipt of supplemental materials. Interviews are by invitation only and generally for final selection. First-year students admitted in fall only. Rolling admission process. Notification starts on December 1 and is finished when class is filled. Applicant's response to offer and $200 deposit due within 14 days of receipt of the letter of acceptance. School does maintain an alternate list. Phone: (303)315-7259.

ADMISSION REQUIREMENTS FOR ADVANCED-STANDING APPLICANTS. Accepts transfers from other accredited U.S. dental schools, but on a space-available basis. Contact the Admissions Office for current information and specific requirements for admission.

ADMISSION STANDARDS AND RECOGNITION. *For D.D.S.:* number of applicants 914; number enrolled 36; median DAT: ACAD 18.5, PAT 18.0; median GPA 3.50 (A = 4); median sciences GPA 3.50 (A = 4). Gorman rating 4.10 (scale: strong 4.01–4.49); this placed the school in the Bottom 10 of all U.S. dental schools; the dental school's ranking by NIH awards was 31st among dental schools, with 6 awards/grants received; total value of all awards/grants was $644,183.

FINANCIAL AID. University grants, institutional loans, state loan programs, DEAL, HEAL, alternative loan programs; federal Perkins loans, Stafford subsidized and unsubsidized loans, and armed forces service commitment scholarship programs are available. Apply for financial aid as soon as acceptance letter is received. Contact the health center's Financial Aid Office for current information; phone: (303)315-8550. For most financial assistance and all need-based programs, submit FAFSA to a federal processor (Title IV school code # 004508); also submit Financial Aid Transcript, Federal Income Tax forms, and Use of Federal Funds Certification. Approximately 92% of current students receive some form of financial assistance. Average award resident $21,484, nonresident $34,510.

DEGREE REQUIREMENTS. *For D.D.S.:* satisfactory completion of 4-year program.

COLUMBIA UNIVERSITY
New York, New York 10027
Internet site: http://www.columbia.edu

Founded 1754. Located in Morningside Heights area of Manhattan. Private control. Semester system. Library: 6,260,000 volumes; 4,460,000 microforms; 63,400 periodicals/subscriptions.

The university's other graduate colleges/schools: Graduate School of Architecture, Planning and Preservation, Graduate School of Arts and Sciences, Graduate School of Business, Graduate School of Journalism, School of Dental and Oral Surgery, School of Engineering and Applied Science, School of International and Public Policy, School of Law, School of Nursing, School of Public Health, School of Social Work, School of the Arts, Teachers College. Special programs: postbaccalaureate premedical program for adults and underrepresented minorities in the School of General Studies; phone: (212)854-6340. The university's ranking in domestic higher education by NIH awards was 11th, with 521 grants received; total dollars awarded $153,982,856.

Total university enrollment at main campus: 19,900.

Columbia-Presbyterian Medical Center
161 Ft. Washington Avenue
New York, New York 10032

Opened in 1928. Private control. Member of Council of Teaching Hospitals. School of Dental and Oral Surgery is also located at medical center. Special facilities: Center for Geriatrics and Gerontology, Center for Molecular Recognition, Center for Neurobiology, Center for Psychoanalytic Training and Research, Center for NMR Spectroscopy, Center for the Study of Society and Medicine, Columbia-Presbyterian Cancer Center, Howard Hughes Medical Institute programs in Molecular Neurobiology, Structural Biology, International Institute for the Study of Human Reproduction, Institute for Comparative Medicine, Institute of Cancer Research, Institute of Human Nutrition, Irving Center for Clinical Research, Richard and Linda Rosenthal Center for Alternative/ Complementary Medicine. Nationally recognized programs in AIDS, Cancer, Cardiology, Endocrinology, Geriatrics, Gynecology, Neurology, Orthopedics, Oto-

laryngology, Pediatrics, Psychiatry, Pulmonary Disease, Rheumatology, Urology.

College of Physicians and Surgeons
Admissions Office, Room 1-416
630 West 168th Street
New York, New York 10032
Telephone: (212)305-3595
Internet site: http://www.cpmccnet.columbia.edu/dept/ps/ admissions
E-mail: pt8@columbia.edu.

Established 1767. The college was the first school to award an earned doctor of medicine in the American colonies. Library: 450,000 volumes/microforms; 4,000 current periodicals/subscriptions. Clinical teaching is at Medical Center, Roosevelt-St. Luke's Hospital Center, Harlem Hospital Center, Bassett Hospital (Cooperstown, N.Y.), Morristown Memorial Hospital (N.J.), Overlook Hospital (N.J.). Special programs: 4th-year students can serve for 3 months in hospitals in South America, Africa, or Asia.

Annual tuition: $26,674. On-campus rooms and apartments available for both single and married students in Bard Hall and Bard Haven Towers. Contact Admissions Office for both on- and off-campus housing information. Off-campus housing and personal expenses: approximately $13,104.

Enrollment: 1st-year class 149 (M.D.-Ph.D., up to 8 may be accepted); total full-time 611 (men 59%, women 41%). First-year statistics: 44% women; average age 25; 10% minorities; 69% science majors.

Degrees conferred: M.D., M.D.-M.P.H. (School of Public Health), M.D.-Ph.D. (Anatomy, Biochemistry, Biophysics, Cell Biology, Genetics, Immunology, Microbiology, Molecular Biology, Neurosciences, Pathology, Pharmacology, Physiology); has M.S.T.P.

RECRUITMENT PRACTICES AND POLICIES. School has diversity program and actively recruits women/minority applicants. Diversity contact: Associate Dean for Minority Affairs; phone: (212)305-4157, X4158.

ADMISSION REQUIREMENTS FOR FIRST-YEAR APPLICANTS. Preference to U.S. citizens and permanent residents. *Undergraduate preparation.* Suggested premed courses: 2 courses in biology with labs, 2 courses in general chemistry with labs, 2 courses in organic chemistry with labs, 2 courses in physics with labs, 2 courses in English. Bachelor's degree from an accredited institution required; all applicants have bachelor's degrees awarded prior to enrollment. Does not have EDP.

Application process. Apply directly to the college's Admissions Office after June 15, before October 15; submit MCAT (scores must have been obtained within the last 2 years); official transcripts for each school attended (should show at least 90 semester credits/135 quarter credits), an application fee of $75, a personal statement in the applicant's own handwriting, preprofessional committee evaluation, and 2 recommendations from science faculty to Admissions Office within 2–3 weeks of the receipt of supplemental materials. M.D.-Ph.D. applicants must apply to, and be accepted by, both College of Physicians and Surgeons and the Graduate School of Arts and Sciences; M.D.-M.P.H. applicants must be accepted by the college before applying to the School of Public Health; contact the Admissions Office for current information and specific requirements for admission. Interviews are by invitation only and generally for final selection. First-year students admitted in fall only. There are two rounds of notification letters. The 1st round is on February 1; the 2nd round starts in the 2nd or 3rd week of March. Applicant's response to offer due within 3 weeks of receipt of acceptance letter. School does maintain an alternate list. Phone: (212)305-3595.

ADMISSION REQUIREMENTS FOR TRANSFER APPLICANTS. Accepts transfers from other accredited U.S. and Canadian medical schools, generally no more than 1–3 students, depending on the space available. Contact the Admissions Office for current information and specific requirements for admission.

ADMISSION STANDARDS AND RECOGNITION. *For M.D.:* number of state-resident applicants 980, nonresidents 3,159; number of state residents interviewed 232, nonresidents 1,121; number of residents enrolled 42, nonresidents 108; median MCAT 11.44 (verbal reasoning 11.0; biological sciences 11.0; physical sciences 11.0); median GPA 3.65 (A = 4). *Barron's Guide* placed the college among the Top 25 most prestigious U.S. medical schools; Gorman rating 4.86 (scale: very strong 4.51–4.99); *U.S. News & World Report* ranking: the college ranked in the Top 25 of all U.S. medical schools; the college's ranking by NIH awards was 11th, with 405 awards/grants received; total dollars awarded $121,038,096.

FINANCIAL AID. Scholarships, merit scholarship, minority scholarships, grants-in-aid, institutional loans, HEAL, alternative loan programs, NIH stipends, federal Perkins loans, Stafford subsidized and unsubsidized loans, and service commitment scholarship programs are available. Assistantships/fellowships may be available for combined degree candidates. All financial aid is based on documented need. Contact the Officer of Student Financial Planning for current information; phone: (212)305-4100. For most financial assistance and all federal programs, submit FAFSA to a federal processor (Title IV school code # E00117); also submit Financial Aid Transcript and Federal Income Tax forms. Approximately 68% of current students receive some form of financial assistance. Average debt after graduation $69,250.

DEGREE REQUIREMENTS. *For M.D.:* satisfactory completion of 4-year program. *For M.D.-M.P.H.:* generally a 4½–5½-year program. *For M.D.-Ph.D., M.S.T.P.:* generally a 7-year program.

School of Dental and Oral Surgery
630 West 168th Street
New York, New York 10032
Telephone: (212)305-3478; fax (212)305-1034
Internet site: http://cpmcnet.columbia.edu/dental

Established 1852; became part of Columbia University in 1916; part of Columbia-Presbyterian Medical Center. Dental students take most of their basic science courses with the medical students. Postgraduate specialties: Endodontics, General Dentistry, Oral and Maxillofacial Surgery, Orthodontics, Pediatric Dentistry, Periodontics, Prosthodontics.

Annual tuition: $26,324; fees $1,350; equipment and supplies $3,800. Limited on-campus housing available for both single and married students. Contact Admissions Office for both on- and off-campus housing information. Dental students tend to live off-campus. Off-campus housing, food, transportation, and personal expenses: approximately $11,000.

Enrollment: 1st-year class 72. First-year enrolled student information: 44 from out of state; 12 states represented; 35 women; average age 25; 4 underrepresented minority; 48 other minorities.

Degrees conferred: D.D.S., D.D.S.-M.B.A., D.D.S.-M.P.H., D.D.S.-M.S. (Health Care Management); M.S.

RECRUITMENT PRACTICES AND POLICIES. School has diversity program and actively recruits women/minority applicants. Diversity contact: Minority Affairs Office; phone: (212)305-3573.

ADMISSION REQUIREMENTS FOR FIRST-YEAR APPLICANTS. Preference given to state residents, U.S. citizens, and permanent residents only. *Undergraduate preparation.* Suggested predental courses: 2 courses in biology with labs, 2 courses in inorganic chemistry with labs, 2 courses in organic chemistry with labs, 2 courses in physics with labs, 2 courses in English. There is no limitation on the number of junior-college transfer credits taken by the applicant. Will consider applicants with only

3 years of undergraduate preparation; prefer applicants who will have a bachelor's degree prior to enrollment; all enrollees had bachelor's degree awarded prior to enrollment. *Application process.* Apply through AADSAS (file after June 1, before December 1); submit official transcripts for each school attended (should show at least 90 semester credits/135 quarter credits), service processing fee; at the same time as you send in AADSAS materials, submit official DAT scores (DAT must be taken no later than March of year of anticipated enrollment), an application fee of $50, official transcripts, and predental committee evaluation or 3 recommendations from science professors to the Office of Admissions and Student Affairs. Interviews are by invitation only and generally for final selection. Dual-degree applicants must apply to, and be accepted by, both schools. First-year students admitted in fall only. Rolling admission process. Notification starts on December 15 and is finished when class is filled. Applicant's response to offer and $1,000 deposit due within 30 days if accepted prior to February 15; response and deposit due within 15 days if received after February 15. School does maintain an alternate list. Phone: (212)305-3478.

ADMISSION REQUIREMENTS FOR ADVANCED-STANDING APPLICANTS. Accepts transfers from other accredited U.S. dental schools. Admission limited to space available. Contact the Office of Admissions and Students Affairs for current information and specific requirements. There is an advanced-standing program for graduates of foreign schools of dentistry. The following are generally requested of all applicants from foreign dental schools: a completed application, a personal statement, official results of the National Board Examination part 1, TOEFL (score of 600 required) if English was not the language of instruction, 3 letters of recommendation, $100 application fee. Contact the Director of Advanced Standing Program for current information and specific requirements for admission; phone: (212)305-3573.

ADMISSION STANDARDS AND RECOGNITION. *For D.D.S.:* number of applicants 1,809; number enrolled 72; median DAT: ACAD 20.1, PAT 17.4; median GPA 3.18 (A = 4), median sciences GPA 3.09 (A = 4). Gorman rating 4.90 (scale: very strong 4.51–4.99); this placed the school in the Top 5 of all U.S. dental schools; the dental school's ranking by NIH awards was 33rd among dental schools, with 2 awards/grants received; total value of all awards/grants $615,557.

FINANCIAL AID. Scholarships, merit scholarships, minority scholarships, grants-in-aid, institutional loans, state loan programs, DEAL, HEAL, alternative loan programs, federal Perkins loans, Stafford subsidized and unsubsidized loans, and armed forces service commitment scholarship programs are available. Assistantships/fellowships may be available for combined degree candidates. For merit scholarships, the selection criteria place heavy reliance on DAT and undergraduate GPA. Most financial assistance is based on documented need. Contact the Financial Aid Office for current information; phone: (212)305-4100. For most financial assistance and all need-based programs submit FAFSA to a federal processor (Title IV school code # E00119); also submit Financial Aid Transcript, Federal Income Tax forms, and Use of Federal Funds Certification. Approximately 93% of current students receive some form of financial assistance. Average award $32,000.

DEGREE REQUIREMENTS. *For D.D.S.:* satisfactory completion of 4-year (45-month) program. *For D.D.S.-M.B.A.,-M.P.H.,-M.S.:* programs generally take between 4½–6 years to complete.

UNIVERSITY OF CONNECTICUT HEALTH CENTER
Farmington Avenue
Farmington, Connecticut 06030
Internet site: http://www.uchc.edu

Located 7 miles W of Hartford. Public control. Semester system. The health center's ranking in domestic higher education by NIH awards was 69th, with 145 grants received; total dollars awarded $32,690,258. Member of the Council of Teaching Hospitals. Schools located at Medical Center, School of Dental Medicine, School of Medicine.

School of Medicine
263 Farmington Avenue, Room AG-062
Farmington, Connecticut 06030-1905
Telephone: (860)679-2152; fax: (860)679-1282
Internet site: http://www.uchc.edu

Established 1968. Located at the health center. Library: 160,000 volumes/microforms; 1,200 current periodicals/subscriptions. Affiliated hospitals: University Hospital, Hartford Hospital, St. Francis Hospital, New Britain General Hospital, Connecticut Children's Hospital, Hospital for Special Care, VA Connecticut Hospital. Special programs: summer programs for underrepresented minorities; prematriculation summer sessions.

Annual tuition: residents $8,400, nonresidents $19,100; fees $3,450. Contact Office of Student Affairs for both on- and off-campus housing information. Medical students tend to live off-campus. Off-campus housing and personal expenses: approximately $15,000.

Enrollment: 1st-year class 82 (EDP 6); total full-time 338 (men 49.4%, women 50.6%). First-year statistics: 12% out of state; 46.9% women; average age 23; 11% minorities; 80% science majors.

Degrees conferred: M.D., M.D.-M.P.H., M.D.-Ph.D. (Biochemistry, Cell Biology, Immunology, Molecular Biology, Neurosciences, Pharmacology).

RECRUITMENT PRACTICES AND POLICIES. School has diversity program and actively recruits women/minority applicants. Diversity contact: Associate Dean, Minority Affairs; phone: (860)679-3483.

ADMISSION REQUIREMENTS FOR FIRST-YEAR APPLICANTS. Preference given to state residents; U.S. citizens, and permanent residents only. *Undergraduate preparation.* Suggested premed courses: 2 courses in biology with labs, 2 courses in general chemistry with labs, 2 courses in organic chemistry with labs, 2 courses in physics with labs. Bachelor's degree from an accredited institution required; all applicants have bachelor's degree awarded prior to enrollment. *Has EDP* for state residents only; applicants must apply through AMCAS (official transcripts sent by mid-May) between June 1 and August 1. Early applications are encouraged. Submit secondary/supplemental application, a personal statement, and 2 recommendations to Admissions Office within 2 weeks of receipt of application. Notification normally begins October 1. *Regular application process.* Apply through AMCAS (file after June 1, before December 1), submit MCAT (will accept MCAT test up to 3 years old), official transcripts for each school attended (should show at least 90 semester credits/135 quarter credits; submit transcripts by mid-May to AMCAS), service processing fee. Submit an application fee of $60, a supplemental application, a personal statement, preprofessional committee evaluation, and 2 recommendations from science faculty to Admissions Office within 2–3 weeks of receipt of supplemental materials, but no later than December 31. Interviews are by invitation only and generally for final selection. Dual-degree applicants should contact the Admissions Office for current information and specific requirements for admission. First-year students admitted in fall only. Rolling admission process. Notification starts on October 15 and is finished when class is filled. Applicant's response to offer and $100 deposit due within 2 weeks of receipt of acceptance letter. School does maintain an alternate list. Phone: (680)679-3874.

ADMISSION REQUIREMENTS FOR TRANSFER APPLICANTS. Accepts transfers from other accredited U.S. medical schools, preference given to state residents. Admission limited to space available. Contact the Admissions Office for current information and specific requirements for admission.

ADMISSION STANDARDS AND RECOGNITION. *For M.D.:* number of state-resident applicants 473, nonresidents 2,502; number of state residents interviewed 244, nonresidents 180; number of residents enrolled 73, nonresidents 8; median MCAT 10.0 (verbal reasoning 10.0; biological sciences 10.0; physical sciences 10.0); median GPA 3.55 (A = 4). Gorman rating 3.88 (scale: good 3.61–3.99); medical school's ranking by NIH awards was 65th, with 95 awards/grants received; total dollars awarded $24,974,946.

FINANCIAL AID. Scholarships, minority scholarships, grants-in-aid, short-term emergency institutional loans, HEAL, alternative loan programs, federal Perkins loans, Stafford subsidized and unsubsidized loans, and service commitment scholarship programs are available. Assistantships/fellowships may be available for dual-degree candidates. All financial aid is based on demonstrated need. Contact the Financial Aid Office for current information; phone: (860)679-3873. For most financial assistance and all federal programs, submit FAFSA to a federal processor (Title IV school code # G09867); also submit Financial Aid Transcript and Federal Income Tax forms. Approximately 80% of current students receive some form of financial assistance.

DEGREE REQUIREMENTS. *For M.D.:* satisfactory completion of 4-year program. All students must take the NBME before the awarding of M.D. *For M.D.-M.P.H.:* generally a 4½–5½-year program. *For M.D.-Ph.D.:* generally a 7-year program.

School of Dental Medicine
263 Farmington Avenue
Farmington, Connecticut 06030
Telephone: (860)679-3748; fax: (860)679-1899
Internet site: http://www.uchc.edu

First class entered September 1968. Located at Health Center. Special programs: externships. Affiliated facilities: University Hospital, satellite clinic in Burgdorf Health Center (Hartford).

Annual tuition: residents $7,900, New England regional residents $11,850, nonresidents $20,250; fees $3,725; equipment and supplies $2,770. Contact Office of Student Affairs for both on- and off-campus housing information. Dental students tend to live off-campus. Off-campus housing, food, transportation, and personal expenses: approximately $15,000.

Enrollment: 1st-year class 44. First-year enrolled student information: 30 from out of state; 6 states represented; 20 women; average age 24; 5 underrepresented minorities; 4 other minorities.

Degrees conferred: D.M.D., B.S.-D.D.S. (Spellman College; Morehouse College), D.M.D.-M.P.H., D.M.D.-M.D., D.M.D.-Ph.D.

RECRUITMENT PRACTICES AND POLICIES. School has diversity program and actively recruits women/minority applicants. Diversity contact: Officer of Minority Student Affairs; phone: (860)679-2175.

ADMISSION REQUIREMENT FOR BACHELOR-D.D.S. APPLICANTS. For information and application procedures contact the Program Directors or the undergraduate Admissions Office at Spellman College or Morehouse College.

ADMISSION REQUIREMENTS FOR FIRST-YEAR APPLICANTS. Preference given to state residents and New England regional residents; U.S. citizens and permanent residents only. *Undergraduate preparation.* Suggested predent courses: 2 courses in biology with labs, 2 courses in inorganic chemistry with labs, 2 courses in organic chemistry with labs, 2 courses in physics with labs; courses in English, biochemistry, cell biology, and genetics recommended. There is no junior-college transfer-credit limit. Will consider applicants with only 3 years of undergraduate preparation; prefer applicants who will have a bachelor's degree prior to enrollment; 98% of applicants have bachelor's degree awarded prior to enrollment. *Application process.* Apply through AADSAS (file after June 1, before January 15); submit official transcripts for each school attended (should show at least 90 semester credits/135 quarter credits); service processing fee; at the same time as you send in AADSAS materials, submit official DAT scores (taken not later than October of the year prior to the anticipated date of enrollment), an application fee of $60, official transcripts, and predental committee evaluation or 3 recommendations from science professors to Office of Academic and Student Affairs. Interviews are by invitation only and generally for final selection. Dual-degree applicants must apply to, and be accepted by, both schools/programs; contact the Office of Academic and Student Affairs for current information and specific requirements. First-year students admitted in fall only. Rolling admission process. Notification starts on December 1 and is finished when class is filled. Applicant's response to offer and $400 deposit due within 30 days if accepted prior to December 31; response and deposit due within 2 weeks if received after February 1. School does maintain an alternate list. Phone: (860)679-2175.

ADMISSION REQUIREMENTS FOR ADVANCED-STANDING APPLICANTS. Accepts transfers from other accredited U.S. and Canadian dental schools. Admission limited to space available. There is an advanced-standing program for graduates of foreign schools of dentistry. Contact the Admissions Office for current information and specific requirements for admission.

ADMISSION STANDARDS AND RECOGNITION. *For D.D.S.:* number of applicants 1,163; number interviewed 200; number enrolled 44; median DAT: ACAD 19.3, PAT 17; median GPA 3.36 (A = 4), median sciences GPA 3.30 (A = 4). Gorman rating 4.33 (scale: strong 4.01–4.49); this placed the school in the Top 40 of all U.S. dental schools.

FINANCIAL AID. Scholarships, minority scholarships, institutional loans, state loan programs, DEAL, HEAL, alternative loan programs, federal Perkins loans, and Stafford subsidized and unsubsidized loans are available. Assistantships/fellowships may be available for combined-degree candidates. All financial aid is based on documented need. Contact the Financial Aid Office for current information; phone: (860)379-3873. For most financial assistance and all need-based programs, submit FAFSA to a federal processor (Title IV school code # G11215); also submit Financial Aid Transcript, Federal Income Tax forms, and Use of Federal Funds Certification. Approximately 91% of current students receive some form of financial assistance. Average award resident $19,090, New England regional resident $21,838, nonresident $26,876.

DEGREE REQUIREMENTS. *For BA/BS-D.M.D.:* an 8-year program. *For D.M.D.:* satisfactory completion of 4-year program. *For D.M.D.-M.P.H.:* generally a 5–6-year program. *For D.M.D.-Ph.D.:* generally a 6–7-year program.

CORNELL UNIVERSITY
Ithaca, New York 14853-0001
Internet site: http://www.cornell.edu

Founded 1865. Located in small city in upstate New York. Private control; some divisions are statutory colleges of the State University of New York. Semester system. Library: 5,825,000 volumes; 6,770,000 microforms; 61,700 periodicals/subscriptions; 500 work stations.

The university's graduate school includes: Graduate Fields in the Law School, Graduate Fields of Agriculture and Life Sciences, Graduate Fields of Architecture Art and Planning, Graduate Fields of Arts and Sciences,

Graduate Fields of Engineering, Graduate Fields of Human Ecology, Graduate Fields of Industrial and Labor Relations, Graduate School of Medical Sciences, Professional Field of the Johnson Graduate School of Management, Professional School of Veterinary Medicine. The university's ranking in domestic higher education by NIH awards was 20th, with 393 grants; total dollars awarded $96,642,969.

Total university enrollment at main campus: 18,900.

New York Hospital-Cornell Medical Center
505 East 68th Street
New York, New York 10021-4896

Private Control. Member of Council of Teaching Hospitals. Schools located at Medical Center Medical College, Graduate School of Medical Sciences. Nationally recognized programs in AIDS, Cancer, Cardiology, Gastroenterology, Geriatrics, Gynecology, Neurology, Urology. *U.S. News & World Report*'s hospital/medical center national rankings for all U.S. hospitals placed New York Hospital-Cornell Medical Center in the Top 20.

Cornell University Medical College
445 East 69th Street
New York, New York 10021
Telephone: (212)746-1067
Internet site: http://www.med.cornell.edu
E-mail: cumc-admission@mail.med.cornell.edu

Established 1898. Located on the Upper East side of NYC. Library: 1,322,000 volumes/microforms; 1,830 current periodicals/subscriptions. Affiliated hospitals: Memorial Sloan-Kettering Cancer Center, Hospital for Special Surgery, New York Hospital Medical Center of Queens, New York Methodist Hospital, New York Community Hospital of Brooklyn, St. Barnabas Hospital, Burke Rehabilitation Center in White Plains, United Hospital Medical Center in Port Chester, Cayuga Medical Center in Ithaca. Special programs: summer programs for underrepresented minorities.

Annual tuition: $24,000; fees $555. Medical-college residences are available for both single and married students. All housing is subsidized by the college. Housing and personal expenses per year: approximately $9,700.

Enrollment: 1st-year class 101 (EDP 5); total full-time 412 (men 46%, women 54%). First-year statistics: 52% out of state; 22 states represented; 53.6% women; average age 24; 33% minorities; 75% science majors.

Faculty: full-time/part-time 1,500.

Degrees conferred: M.D., M.D.-Ph.D. (Biochemistry and Structural Biology, Cell Biology and Genetics, Clinical Epidemiology and Health Services Research, Immunology, Molecular Biology, Neurosciences, Pharmacology, Physiology and Biophysics), has M.S.T.P. (in conjunction with Rockefeller University and Memorial Sloan-Kettering Cancer Center).

RECRUITMENT PRACTICES AND POLICIES. School has diversity program and actively recruits women/minority applicants. Diversity contact: Associate Dean for Student Affairs and Equal Opportunity Programs; phone: (212)746-1058.

ADMISSION REQUIREMENTS FOR FIRST-YEAR APPLICANTS. Preference given to U.S. citizens and permanent residents only. *Undergraduate preparation.* Suggested premed courses: 2 courses in biology with labs, 2 courses in inorganic chemistry with labs, 2 courses in organic chemistry with labs, 2 courses in physics with labs, 2 courses in English. Bachelor's degree from an accredited institution required; all applicants have bachelor's degree awarded prior to enrollment. *Has EDP* for state residents only; applicants must apply through AMCAS (official transcripts sent by mid-May) between June 1 and August 1. Early applications are encouraged. Submit secondary/supplemental application, a personal statement, and 2 recommendations to Admissions Office within 2 weeks of receipt of application. Notification normally begins October 1. *Regular application process.* Apply through AMCAS (file after June 1, before October 15); submit MCAT (will accept MCAT test results from the last 2 years only), official transcripts for each school attended (should show at least 90 semester credits/135 quarter credits, submit transcripts by mid-May to AMCAS), service processing fee. Submit an application fee of $75, a supplemental application, a personal statement, preprofessional committee evaluation, and 2 recommendations from science faculty to Admissions Office within 2–3 weeks of the receipt of supplemental materials. Interviews are by invitation only and generally for final selection. Dual-degree applicants must apply to, and be accepted by, both schools; contact the Admissions Office for current information and specific requirements for admission. First-year students admitted in fall only. Rolling admission process. Notification starts on October 15 and is finished by mid-March. Applicant's response to offer and $100 deposit due within 2 weeks of receipt of acceptance letter. Admissions Office phone: (212)746-1067. M.S.T.P. contact: Tri-Institutional M.D.-Ph.D. Program, 1300 York Avenue, New York, New York; phone: (212)746-6023.

ADMISSION REQUIREMENTS FOR TRANSFER APPLICANTS. Accepts transfers from other accredited U.S. medical schools. Admission limited to space available. Contact the Admissions Office for current information and specific requirements for admission.

ADMISSION STANDARDS AND RECOGNITION. *For M.D.:* number of state-resident applicants 1,737, nonresidents 5,866; number of state residents interviewed 425, nonresidents 914; number of residents enrolled 54, nonresidents 58; median MCAT 10.6 (verbal reasoning 10.6; biological sciences 10.6; physical sciences 10.6); median GPA 3.58 (A = 4). *Barron's Guide* placed the medical college among the Top 25 most prestigious U.S. medical schools; Gorman rating 4.84 (scale: very strong 4.51–4.99); *U.S. News & World Report* ranking: the medical college was ranked in the Top 25 of all U.S. medical schools; not ranked in Top 25 in primary-care programs; the medical college's medical ranking by NIH awards was 31st, with 224 awards/grants received; total dollars awarded $64,765,733.

FINANCIAL AID. Scholarships, minority scholarships, grants-in-aid, institutional loans, HEAL, alternative loan programs, NIH stipends, federal Perkins loans, Stafford subsidized and unsubsidized loans, and service commitment scholarship programs are available. The M.D.-Ph.D. program is a fully funded program. All financial aid is based on demonstrated need. Contact the Financial Aid Office for current information; phone: (212)746-1065. For most financial assistance and all federal programs, submit FAFSA to a federal processor (Title IV school code # E00139); also submit Financial Aid Transcript and Federal Income Tax forms. Approximately 80% of current students receive some form of financial assistance. Average debt after graduation $59,200.

DEGREE REQUIREMENTS. *For M.D.:* satisfactory completion of 4-year program. Taking the USMLE optional. *For M.D.-Ph.D., M.S.T.P.:* generally a 7-year program.

CREIGHTON UNIVERSITY
Omaha, Nebraska 68178-0001
Internet site: http://www.creighton.edu

Founded 1878. Located in downtown Omaha. Private control. Roman Catholic (Jesuit) affiliation. Semester system. Library: 444,000 volumes; 123,100 microforms. Special programs: Postbaccalaureate premedical program for underrepresented minorities; contact Program Director; phone: (402)280-3185.

The university's graduate school includes: College of Arts and Sciences, Eugene C. Eppley College of Business Administration, School of Dentistry, School of Law, School of Pharmacy, and Allied Health Programs.

Total university enrollment at main campus: 6,200.

School of Medicine
2500 California Plaza
Omaha, Nebraska 68178
Telephone: (402)280-2798; fax: (402)280-1241
Internet site: http://www.creighton.edu
E-mail: medschadm@creighton.edu.

Established 1892. Located on main campus. Library: 200,000 volumes/microforms; 1,500 current periodicals/subscriptions. Affiliated hospitals: Clarkson Medical Center, Omaha Veterans Medical Center, Children's Memorial Hospital, St. Joseph's Hospital (member of Council of Teaching Hospitals), Bergan and Mercy Hospital. Special programs: summer programs for underrepresented minorities; prematriculation summer sessions.

Annual tuition: $24,254; fees $464. On-campus rooms and apartments available for married students. Contact Department of Residence Life for both on- and off-campus housing information; phone: (402)280-3016. Medical students generally live off-campus. Off-campus housing and personal expenses: approximately $12,476.

Enrollment: 1st-year class 111 (EDP 20); total full-time 463 (men 67%, women 33%). First-year statistics: 80% out of state; 32% women; average age 24; 9% minorities; 78% science majors.

Degrees conferred: M.D., M.D.-Ph.D. (Anatomy, Biochemistry, Microbiology, Pharmacology, Physiology).

RECRUITMENT PRACTICES AND POLICIES. School has diversity program and actively recruits women/minority applicants. Diversity contact: Director Minority Affairs for Health Sciences; phone: (402)280-2981.

ADMISSION REQUIREMENTS FOR FIRST-YEAR APPLICANTS. Preference given to Creighton University undergraduates and residents of states without medical schools; U.S. citizens and permanent residents only. *Undergraduate preparation.* Suggested premed courses: 2 courses in biology with labs, 2 courses in inorganic chemistry with labs, 2 courses in organic chemistry with labs, 2 courses in physics with labs, 1 course in college math, 2 courses in English. Will consider CLEP and AP credit. Bachelor's degree from an accredited institution required; all applicants have bachelor's degree awarded prior to enrollment. *Has EDP for state residents only;* applicants must apply through AMCAS (official transcripts sent by mid-May) between June 1 and August 1. Early applications are encouraged. Submit secondary/supplemental application, a personal statement, and 2 recommendations to Admissions Office within 2 weeks of receipt of application. Notification normally begins October 1. *Regular application process.* Apply through AMCAS (file after June 1, before December 1); submit

MCAT (will accept MCAT test results from 1995), official transcripts for each school attended (should show at least 90 semester credits/135 quarter credits, submit transcripts by mid-May to AMCAS), service processing fee. Submit an application fee of $65, supplemental materials, a personal statement, preprofessional committee evaluation, and 2 recommendations from science faculty to Admissions Office within 2–3 weeks of the receipt of supplemental materials. Interviews are by invitation only and generally for final selection. Dual-degree applicants must apply to, and be accepted by, both schools; contact the Admissions Office for current information and specific requirements for admission. First-year students admitted in fall only. Rolling admission process. Notification starts on October 15 and is finished when class is filled. Applicant's response to offer and $100 deposit due within 2 weeks of receipt of acceptance letter. Phone: (402)280-2798.

ADMISSION REQUIREMENTS FOR TRANSFER APPLICANTS. Accepts transfers with a compelling reason for transferring from other accredited U.S. medical schools with a Creighton University affiliation. Admission limited to space available. Contact the Admissions Office for current information and specific requirements for admission.

ADMISSION STANDARDS AND RECOGNITION. *For M.D.:* number of state-resident applicants 285, nonresidents 7,450; number of state residents interviewed 61, nonresidents 304; number of residents enrolled 23, nonresidents 88; median MCAT 9.2 (verbal reasoning 9.3; biological sciences 9.1; physical sciences 9.1); median GPA 3.6, science GPA 3.5 (A = 4). Gorman rating 3.86 (scale: good 3.61–3.99); School of Medicine ranking by NIH awards was 108th, with 19 awards/grants received; total dollars awarded $2,980,201.

FINANCIAL AID. Scholarships, grants-in-aid, institutional loans, HEAL, state loan programs, alternative loan programs, federal Perkins loans, Stafford subsidized and unsubsidized loans, and armed forces commitment scholarship programs are available. Assistantships/fellowships may be available for dual-degree candidates. All financial assistance is based on demonstrated need. For scholarships, the selection criteria place heavy reliance on MCAT and undergraduate GPA. Contact the Financial Aid Office for current information; phone: (402)280-2666. For most financial assistance and all federal programs, submit FAFSA to a federal processor (Title IV school code # 002542); also submit Financial Aid Transcript and Federal Income Tax forms. Approximately

95% of current students receive some form of financial assistance. Average debt after graduation $96,700.

DEGREE REQUIREMENTS. *For M.D.:* satisfactory completion of 4-year program. All students must pass USMLE Step 1 prior to entering 3rd year; all students must take USMLE Step 2 and receive a score prior to awarding of M.D. *For M.D.-Ph.D.:* generally a 7-year program.

School of Dentistry
2500 California Plaza
Omaha, Nebraska 68178
Telephone: (800)544-5072; fax: (402)280-5094
Internet site: http://www.creighton.edu
E-mail: dtravis@creighton.edu

Established 1905. Located on main campus. Basic science courses are jointly taught by both dental- and medical-school faculty. Special facilities: Bio-Information Center. Affiliated facilities: St. Joseph's Hospital, Omaha Professional Center, Boys Town National Research Center.

Annual tuition: $20,410; fees $1,640; equipment and supplies $4,175. On-campus rooms and apartments available for both single and married students. Contact Department of Residence Life for both on- and off-campus housing information; phone: (402)280-3016. Dental students tend to live off-campus. Off-campus housing, food, transportation, and personal expenses: approximately $12,000.

Enrollment: 1st-year class, 84. First-year enrolled student information: 73 from out of state; 18 states represented; 27 women; average age 24; 6 underrepresented minorities; 4 other minorities.

Degree conferred: D.D.S.

RECRUITMENT PRACTICES AND POLICIES. School has diversity program and actively recruits women/minority applicants. Diversity contact: Director Minority Affairs for Health Sciences; phone: (402)280-2981.

ADMISSION REQUIREMENTS FOR FIRST-YEAR APPLICANTS. Creighton has dental education compact with Idaho, North Dakota, New Mexico, Utah, and Wyoming. *Undergraduate preparation.* Suggested predent courses: 2 courses in biology with labs, 2 courses in inorganic chemistry with labs, 2 courses in organic chemistry with labs, 2 courses in physics with labs, 2 courses in English, 6 courses in nonsciences. There is no limitation on the number of junior-college credits considered. Will consider applicants with only 3 years of undergraduate preparation; prefer applicants who will have a bachelor's degree prior to enrollment; 98% of applicants have bachelor's degrees awarded prior to enrollment. *Application process.* Apply through AADSAS (file after July 1, before April 1, AADSAS deadline February 1), submit official transcripts for each school attended (should show at least 90 semester credits/135 quarter credits), service processing fee; at the same time as you send in AADSAS materials, submit official DAT scores, an application fee of $35, a supplemental application, official transcripts, predental committee evaluation or 2 recommendations from professors in your major field of study, and photograph directly to the Admissions Office not later than April 1. Interviews are by invitation only and generally for final selection. First-year students admitted in fall only. Rolling admission process. Notification starts on December 1 and is finished when class is filled. Applicant's response to offer and $200 deposit due within 30 days if accepted prior to January 31; response and deposit due within 2 weeks if received after February 1. School does maintain an alternate list. Phone: (800)544-5072, (402)280-2881; E-mail: dtravis@creighton.edu.

ADMISSION REQUIREMENTS FOR ADVANCED-STANDING APPLICANTS. Accepts transfers from other accredited U.S. and Canadian dental schools. Admission limited to space available. There is an advanced-standing program for graduates of foreign schools of dentistry. Contact the Admissions Office for current information and specific requirements for admission.

ADMISSION STANDARDS AND RECOGNITION. *For D.D.S.:* number of applicants 1,979; number enrolled 84; median DAT: ACAD 17.4, PAT 17.9; median GPA 3.26 (A = 4), median sciences GPA 3.07 (A = 4). Gorman rating 4.53 (scale: acceptable plus 3.01–3.59); this placed the school in the Top 20 of all U.S. dental schools.

FINANCIAL AID. Scholarships, minority scholarships, government grants, institutional loans, state loan programs, DEAL, HEAL, alternative loan programs, federal Perkins loans, Stafford subsidized and unsubsidized loans, and health service commitment scholarship programs are available. All financial aid is based on demonstrated need. For scholarships, the selection criteria place heavy reliance on DAT and undergraduate GPA. Contact the Financial Aid Office for current information; phone: (402)280-2731. For most financial assistance and all need-based programs, submit FAFSA to a federal processor (Title IV school code # 002542); also submit Financial Aid Transcript, Federal Income Tax forms, and Use of Federal Funds Certification. Approximately 90% of current students receive some form of financial assistance. Average award $33,000.

DEGREE REQUIREMENTS. *For D.D.S.:* satisfactory completion of 4-year program.

DARTMOUTH COLLEGE
Hanover, New Hampshire 03755
Internet site: http://www.dartmouth.edu

Founded 1769. Located 135 miles NW of Boston. Private control. Semester system. Special facilities: Fairchild Science Center, McGraw Hill Observatory (Tucson, Arizona), Nelson A. Rockefeller Center for the Social Sciences, C. Everett Koop Institute. Library: over 2,057,000 volumes; 2,378,000 microforms; 20,764 periodicals/subscriptions; 150 PC work stations.

The college's graduate units: School of Arts and Sciences, Amos Tuck School of Business Administration, Thayer School of Engineering.

Total college enrollment: 5,249.

Dartmouth-Hitchcock Medical Center
One Medical Center Drive
Lebanon, New Hampshire 03756-0001

Private control. Mary Hitchcock Memorial Hospital is a member of the Council of Teaching Hospitals. The center includes the Mary Hitchcock Memorial Hospital, Norris Cotton Cancer Center, Lahey-Hitchcock Clinic, and the White River Junction VA Hospital. Nationally recognized programs in Cancer, Cardiology, Rheumatology.

Dartmouth Medical School
7020 Rensen, Room 306
Hanover, New Hampshire 03755-3833
Telephone: (603)650-1505; fax (603)650-1614
Internet site: http://www.dartmouth.edu/dms
E-mail: dms.admissions@dartmouth.edu

Established 1797; the 4th-oldest medical school in U.S. Located on college's campus. Library: 235,000 volumes/microforms; 3,000 current periodicals/subscriptions. Affiliated hospitals/clinics: Brattleboro Retreat (VT), Family Medical Institute (Augusta, ME), Hartford Hospital (CT), the Tuba City Indian Health Service Hospital (AZ).

Annual tuition: $23,260; fees $3,900. On-campus apartments available for both single and married students. Contact Office of Rental Housing for both on- and off-campus housing information; phone: (603)646-2170.

Medical students generally live off-campus. Off-campus housing and personal expenses: approximately $12,920.

Enrollment: 1st-year class 64 (M.D.-Ph.D. 3, up to 20 students may be in Brown-Dartmouth program); total full-time 317 (men 59%, women 41%). First-year statistics: 93% out of state; 25 states represented; 50 different undergraduate institutions represented; 53% women; average age 24; 15% minorities; 60% science majors.

Faculty: full-time/ part-time/volunteers 1,000.

Degrees conferred: M.D., M.D.-M.B.A., M.D.-Ph.D. (Biochemistry, Biomedical Engineering, Cell Biology, Genetics, Immunology, Microbiology, Molecular Biology, Pharmacology, Physiology).

RECRUITMENT PRACTICES AND POLICIES. School has diversity program and actively recruits women/minority applicants. Diversity contact: Assistant Dean, Minority Affairs; phone: (603)650-1156.

ADMISSION REQUIREMENTS FOR FIRST-YEAR APPLICANTS. Preference given to New Hampshire and Maine residents; U.S. citizens, and permanent residents only. *Undergraduate preparation.* Suggested premed courses: 2 courses in biology with labs, 2 courses in inorganic chemistry with labs, 2 courses in organic chemistry with labs, 2 courses in physics with labs, 1 course in calculus; proficiency in English required. Bachelor's degree from an accredited institution required; all applicants have bachelor's degree awarded prior to enrollment. Does not have EDP. *Application process.* Apply through AMCAS (file after June 1, before November 1); submit MCAT (will accept MCAT test results from the last 3 years), official transcripts for each school attended (should show at least 90 semester credits/135 quarter credits; submit transcripts by mid-May to AMCAS), service processing fee. Submit an application fee of $60, a supplemental application, a personal statement, preprofessional committee evaluation, and 2 recommendations from science faculty to Admissions Office within 2–3 weeks of the receipt of supplemental materials, but not later than December 31. Interviews are by invitation only and generally for final selection. All interviewed applicants may apply for Brown-Dartmouth program. Dual-degree applicants must apply to, and be accepted by, both schools; information regarding dual-degree programs is included with the secondary application materials. Contact the Admissions Office for current information and specific requirements for admission. First-year students admitted in fall only. Rolling admission process. Notification starts on December 15 and is finished when class is filled. Applicant's response to offer due within 2 weeks of receipt of acceptance letter. School does maintain an alternate list. Phone: (603)650-1505; E-mail:dms. admissions@dartmouth.edu.

ADMISSION REQUIREMENTS FOR TRANSFER APPLICANTS. Accepts transfers from other accredited U.S. medical schools with a compelling need to be in Hanover. Admission limited to space available. Contact the Admissions Office in February for current information and specific requirements for admission.

ADMISSION STANDARDS AND RECOGNITION. *For M.D.:* number of state-resident applicants 66, nonresidents 7,832; number of state residents interviewed 29, nonresidents 498; number of residents enrolled 6, nonresidents 77; median MCAT 10.0 (verbal reasoning 10.0; biological sciences 10.0; physical sciences 10.0); median GPA 3.50 (A = 4). Gorman rating 4.22 (scale: strong 4.01–4.49); *U.S. News & World Report* ranked Dartmouth Medical School in the Top 25 in primary-care programs; medical school's ranking by NIH awards was 56th, with 127 awards/grants received; total dollars awarded $30,979,821.

FINANCIAL AID. Scholarships, merit scholarships, minority scholarships, grants-in-aid, institutional loans, HEAL, alternative loan programs, federal Perkins loans, Stafford subsidized and unsubsidized loans, and service commitment scholarship programs are available. All students are offered financial aid with demonstrated need. Funding may be available for dual-degree candidates. Financial-aid applications and information are given out at the on-campus interview (by invitation). All financial aid is comprised of two elements; "base loan" and scholarship; 40% of students receive scholarships. Contact the Financial Aid Office for current information; phone: (603)650-1919. For most financial assistance and all federal programs, submit FAFSA to a federal processor (Title IV school code # 002573); also submit Financial Aid Transcript and Federal Income Tax forms. Approximately 80% of current students receive some form of financial assistance. Average debt after graduation $65,000.

DEGREE REQUIREMENTS. *For M.D.:* 4-year program. Taking USMLE Step 1 and 2 is optional. *For M.D.-master's:* generally 4½–5½-year programs. *For M.D.-Ph.D.:* generally a 7-year program.

UNIVERSITY OF DETROIT MERCY
Detroit, Michigan 48219-0900

Founded 1877. In 1990 the University of Detroit and Mercy College consolidated to form a new university. Private control; Roman catholic affiliation. Semester system. Special facilities: Center for the Study of Development and Aging, Manufacturing Institute, Institute for Business and Community Services, Kellstadt Consumer Research Center, Polymer Institute, Center for Excellence in Environmental Engineering and Science. Library: 645,000 volumes; 777,000 microforms; 5,500 current periodicals/subscriptions.

The university's other graduate colleges/schools include: College of Business Administration, College of Education and Human Services, College of Engineering and Science, College of Health Professions, College of Liberal Arts, School of Law.

School of Dentistry
P.O. Box 19900
8200 West Outer Drive
Detroit, Michigan 48219-0900
Telephone: (313)494-6500; fax: (313)494-6659

Established 1932. Located in NW Detroit. Curriculum: basic and preclinical sciences are concentrated in first 2 years. Affiliated hospitals/clinics: University of Detroit Receiving Hospital, University Health Center complex. Postgraduate specialties: Endodontics, General Dentistry, Orthodontics.

Annual tuition: $22,500; fees $121; equipment and supplies $4,700. Limited on-campus housing available. Contact Director of Residential Life for both on- and off-campus housing information; phone: (313)993-1230. Dental students tend to live off-campus. Off-campus housing, food, transportation, and personal expenses: approximately $11,345.

Enrollment: 1st-year class, 74. First-year enrolled student information: 20 from out of state; 5 states represented; 26 women; average age 24; 7 underrepresented minorities; 6 other minorities.

Degree conferred: D.D.S.

RECRUITMENT PRACTICES AND POLICIES. School has diversity program and actively recruits women/minority applicants. Diversity contact: Officer of Minority Affairs; phone: (313)494-6650.

ADMISSION REQUIREMENTS FOR FIRST-YEAR APPLICANTS. Preference given to state residents; U.S. citizens and permanent residents only. *Undergraduate preparation.* Suggested predental courses: 2 courses in biology with labs, 2 courses in inorganic chemistry with labs, 2 courses in organic chemistry with labs, 2 courses in physics with labs, 2 courses in English; courses in anatomy, histology or embryology, and biochemistry are

recommended. The junior-college transfer-credit limit is 60 credits. Will consider applicants with only 3 years of undergraduate preparation; prefer applicants who will have a bachelor's degree prior to enrollment; 98% of enrollees had bachelor's degree awarded prior to enrollment. *Application process.* Apply through AADSAS (file after June 1, before December 1), submit official transcripts for each school attended (should show at least 90 semester credits/135 quarter credits), service processing fee; at the same time as you send in AADSAS materials, submit official DAT scores (taken in October of the year prior to the anticipated year of enrollment), an application fee of $35, official transcripts, predental committee evaluation or 2 recommendations from science professors, 1 recommendation from a practicing dentist, and a photograph directly to the Admissions Office. Interviews are by invitation only and generally for final selection. First-year students admitted in fall only. Rolling admission process. Notification starts in December and is finished when class is filled. Applicant's response to offer due within 30 days if accepted prior to January 31; response due within 2 weeks if received after February 1. School does maintain an alternate list. Phone: (313)494-6650.

ADMISSION REQUIREMENTS FOR ADVANCED-STANDING APPLICANTS. Accepts transfers from other accredited U.S. and Canadian dental schools. Admission limited to space available. Contact the Admissions Office for current information and specific requirements for admission.

ADMISSION STANDARDS AND RECOGNITION. *For D.D.S.:* number of applicants 1,384; number enrolled 74; median DAT: ACAD 18.0, PAT 17.0; median GPA 3.31 (A = 4), median sciences GPA 3.23 (A = 4). Gorman rating 4.23 (scale: strong 4.01–4.49); this placed the school in the Top 40 of all U.S. dental schools.

FINANCIAL AID. Scholarships, merit scholarships, minority scholarships, Michigan tuition grants, institutional loans, state loan programs, DEAL, HEAL, alternative loan programs, federal Perkins loans, Stafford subsidized and unsubsidized loans, and service commitment scholarship programs are available. Assistantships/fellowships may be available for combined-degree candidates. For merit scholarships, the selection criteria place heavy reliance on DAT and undergraduate GPA. Contact the Financial Aid Office for current information; phone: (313)446-1950 or (313)993-3350. For most financial assistance and all need-based programs, submit FAFSA to a federal processor (Title IV school code # E00635); also submit Financial Aid Transcript, Federal Income Tax forms, and Use of Federal Funds Certification. Approximately 72% of current students receive some form of financial assistance. Average award resident $27,792; nonresident $29,148.

DEGREE REQUIREMENTS. *For D.D.S.:* satisfactory completion of 4-year program.

DUKE UNIVERSITY
Durham, North Carolina 27708-0586
Internet site: http://www.duke.edu

Founded 1838. Located in a rural area 25 miles NW of Raleigh. Private control. Semester system. Library: 4,300,000 volumes; 3,000,000 microforms; 31,800 periodicals/subscriptions; 300 work stations. The university's ranking in domestic higher education by NIH awards/grants was 12th, with 552 awards/grants received; total dollars awarded $152,342,468.

The university's graduate school includes: Institute of Statistics and Decision Sciences, School of Engineering, Terry Sanford Institute of Public Policy, Divinity School, Fuqua School of Business, Nicholas School of the Environment, School of Law, School of Nursing.

Total university enrollment at main campus: 12,200.

Medical Center
Durham, North Carolina
Internet site: http://www.mc.duke.edu

Hospital opened in 1930. Located on campus. Private control. Member of Council of Teaching Hospitals. Schools located at medical center are the School of Medicine and School of Nursing. Nationally recognized programs in AIDS, Cancer, Cardiology, Endocrinology, Gastroenterology, Geriatrics, Gynecology, Neurology, Ophthalmology, Orthopedics, Otolaryngology, Pediatrics, Psychiatry, Pulmonary Disease, Rheumatology, Urology. *U.S. News & World Report*'s hospital/medical center national rankings for all hospitals placed the medical center in the Top 20 of all U.S. Hospitals.

School of Medicine
P.O. Box 3710
Durham, North Carolina 27710
Telephone: (919)684-2985; fax: (919)684-8893
Internet site: http://www.mc.duke.edu/depts/som
E-mail: medadm@mc.duke.edu

Established 1932. Located on medical center campus. Library: 239,000 volumes/microforms; 5,000 current periodicals/subscriptions. Affiliated hospitals: Duke Hospital, Durham VA Hospital, Leno Baker Children's Hospital, Durham County General Hospital.

Annual tuition: $24,650; fees $1,399. On-campus rooms and apartments available for both single and married students. Contact Office of Housing Administration for both on- and off-campus housing information; phone: (919)684-4304. Annual housing and personal expenses: approximately $14,940.

Enrollment: 1st-year class 99; total full-time 395 (men 58%, women 42%). First-year statistics: 68% out of state; 38% women; average age 24; 14% minorities; 74% science majors.

Degrees conferred: M.D., M.D.-M.A. (Medical History, Public Policy), M.D.-M.B.A., M.D.-M.P.H., M.D.-J.D., M.D.-Ph.D. (Anatomy, Biochemistry, Biomedical Engineering, Cell Biology, Genetics, Immunology, Medical History, Microbiology, Molecular Biology, Neurosciences, Pathology, Pharmacology, Physiology); has M.S.T.P.

RECRUITMENT PRACTICES AND POLICIES. School has diversity program and actively recruits women/minority applicants. Diversity contact: Professor of Pediatrics; phone: (919)681-2916.

ADMISSION REQUIREMENTS FOR FIRST-YEAR APPLICANTS. Special consideration given to state residents; U.S. citizens, and permanent residents only. *Undergraduate preparation.* Suggested premed courses: 2 courses in biology with labs, 2 courses in inorganic chemistry with labs, 2 courses in organic chemistry with labs, 2 courses in physics with labs, 2 courses in calculus, 2 courses in English. Bachelor's degree from an accredited institution required; all applicants have bachelor's degree awarded prior to enrollment. Does not have EDP. *Application process.* Apply through AMCAS (file after June 1, before October 15); submit MCAT (will accept MCAT test results if less than 3 years old), official transcripts for each school attended (should show at least 90 semester credits/135 quarter credits, submit transcripts by mid-May to AMCAS), service processing fee. Submit an application fee of $65, a supplemental application, a personal statement, preprofessional committee evaluation, and 2 recommendations from science faculty to Admissions Office within 2–3 weeks of the receipt of supplemental materials, but no later than December 1. Interviews are by invitation only and generally for final selection. Dual-degree applicants must apply to, and be accepted by, both schools; contact the Admissions Office for current information and specific requirements for admission. First-year students admitted in fall only. Notification is on March 1. Applicant's response to offer and $100 deposit due within 3 weeks of receipt of acceptance letter. School does maintain an alternate list. Phone: (919)684-2985; E-mail: medadm@mc.duke.edu.

ADMISSION REQUIREMENTS FOR TRANSFER APPLICANTS. Will not consider transfer applicants except for unusual circumstances. Contact the Admissions Office for current information and specific requirements.

ADMISSION STANDARDS AND RECOGNITION. *For M.D.:* number of state-resident applicants 297, nonresidents 6,884; number interviewed 670; number of residents enrolled 32, nonresidents 68; median MCAT 11.3 (verbal reasoning 11.0; biological sciences 11.0; physical sciences 12.0); median GPA 3.60 (A = 4). *Barron's Guide* placed School of Medicine among the Top 25 most prestigious U.S. medical schools; Gorman rating 4.78 (scale: very strong 4.51–4.99); *U.S. News & World Report* ranked the School of Medicine in the Top 25 of all U.S. medical schools; not ranked in the Top 25 in primary-care programs; the school's medical ranking by NIH awards was 8th, with 481 awards/grants received; total dollars awarded $135,826,546.

FINANCIAL AID. Scholarships, minority scholarships (preference given to state residents), grants-in-aid, institutional loans, HEAL, alternative loan programs, NIH stipends, federal Perkins loans, Stafford subsidized and unsubsidized loans, and armed forces and health service commitment scholarship programs are available. Assistantships/fellowships may be available for dual-degree candidates. M.S.T.P. candidates receive full tuition, fees, and a stipend. For merit scholarships, the selection criteria place heavy reliance on MCAT and undergraduate GPA. Contact the Financial Aid Office for current information; phone: (919)684-2985. For most financial assistance and all federal programs, submit FAFSA (as soon as possible after January 1) to a federal processor (Title IV school code # E00161); also submit Financial Aid Transcript, Federal Income Tax forms, and NEEDS ACCESS diskette. Approximately 80% of current students receive some form of financial assistance. Average debt after graduation $55,000.

DEGREE REQUIREMENTS. *For M.D.:* satisfactory completion of 4-year program. *For M.D.-M.A.:* generally a 4½–5½-year program. *For M.D.-M.P.H., M.B.A.:* generally 5–6-year programs. *For M.D.-J.D.:* generally a 6½–7-year program. *For M.D.-Ph.D., M.S.T.P.:* generally a 6–7-year program.

EAST CAROLINA UNIVERSITY
Greenville, North Carolina 27834-4353
Internet site: http://www.ecu.edu

Founded 1907. Located 85 miles E of Raleigh. Public control. Semester system. Special facilities: Center on Aging, Center for Coastal and Marine Resources, Mental Health Training Institute, East Carolina Development Institute. Library: 1,112,000 volumes; 1,588,000 microforms; 7,000 periodicals/subscriptions; 184 work stations.

The university's graduate school includes: College of Arts and Sciences, School of Allied Health Sciences, School of Art, School of Business, School of Education, School of Health and Human Performance, School of Human Environmental Sciences, School of Industry and Technology, School of Music, School of Nursing, School of Social Work.

Total university enrollment at main campus: 16,805.

East Carolina University Health Science Center
Greenville, North Carolina 27834

Located on a hundred-acre campus contiguous with Pitt County Memorial Hospital. Public control. Special facilities: Leo W. Jenkins Cancer Center, Mental Health Center, Alcoholic Rehabilitation Center, Rehabilitation Center, Area Health Education Center.

School of Medicine
Greenville, North Carolina 27858-4354
Telephone: (919)816-2202
Internet site: http://www.med.ecu.edu

Established 1972. Located at the health science center. Library: 138,000 volumes/microforms; 1,800 current periodicals/subscriptions.

Annual tuition: residents $2,030, nonresidents $21,386; fees $878. No on-campus housing available. Contact university's Housing Office for off-campus housing information; phone: (919)328-6450. Off-campus housing and personal expenses: approximately $12,400.

Enrollment: 1st-year class 72 (EDP 9); total full-time 302 (men 50%, women 50%). First-year statistics: 1% out of state; 50% women; average age 26; 77% science majors.

Degrees conferred: M.D., M.D.-Ph.D. (Anatomy, Biochemistry, Cell Biology, Immunology, Microbiology, Pathology, Pharmacology, Physiology).

RECRUITMENT PRACTICES AND POLICIES. School has diversity program and actively recruits women applicants. Diversity contact: Assistant Dean for Student Affairs; phone: (919)816-2870.

ADMISSION REQUIREMENTS FOR FIRST-YEAR APPLICANTS. Preference given to state residents and the state's underrepresented minorities; U.S. citizens and permanent residents only. *Undergraduate preparation.* Suggested premed courses: 2 courses in biology with labs, 2 courses in inorganic chemistry with labs, 2 courses in organic chemistry with labs, 2 courses in physics with labs, 2 courses in English. Bachelor's degree from an accredited institution required; all applicants have bachelor's degree awarded prior to enrollment. *Has EDP for state residents only;* applicants must apply through AMCAS (official transcripts sent by mid-May) between June 1 and August 1. Early applications are encouraged. Submit supplemental application, a personal statement, and 2 recommendations to Admissions Office within two weeks of receipt of application. Notification normally begins October 1. *Regular application process.* Apply through AMCAS (file after June 1, before November 1); submit MCAT (will not accept MCAT more than 2 years old), official transcripts for each school attended (should show at least 90 semester credits/135 quarter credits, submit transcripts by mid-May to AMCAS), service processing fee. Submit an application fee of $35, a supplemental application, a handwritten narrative, preprofessional committee evaluation, and 2 recommendations from science faculty to Admissions Office within 2–3 weeks of the receipt of supplemental materials. Two personal interviews are by invitation only and generally for final selection. Dual-degree applicants should contact the Admissions Office for current information and specific requirements for admission. First-year students admitted in fall only. Rolling admission process. Notification starts on October 15 and is finished when class is filled. Applicant's response to offer and $100 deposit due within 3 weeks of receipt of acceptance letter. Phone: (919)816-2202.

ADMISSION REQUIREMENTS FOR TRANSFER APPLICANTS. Accepts transfers from other accredited U.S. medical schools. Admission limited to space available; however, vacant positions seldom exist. Contact the Admissions Office for current information and specific requirements for admission.

ADMISSION STANDARDS AND RECOGNITION. *For M.D.:* number of state-resident applicants 1,035, nonresidents 846; number of state residents interviewed 622, nonresidents 1; number of residents enrolled 72, nonresidents 0; median MCAT 8.5 (verbal reasoning 8.6; biological sciences 8.4; physical sciences 8.1); median GPA 3.5 (A = 4). Gorman rating 3.14 (scale: acceptable plus 3.01–3.59); School of Medicine's ranking by NIH awards was 112th, with 20 awards/grants received; total dollars awarded $2,661,973.

FINANCIAL AID. Scholarships, merit scholarship, grants-in-aid, institutional loans, HEAL, alternative loan programs, federal Perkins loans, Stafford subsidized and unsubsidized loans, and armed forces service commitment scholarship programs are available. Assistantships/fellowships may be available for dual-degree candidates. Financial aid is based on demonstrated need. For merit scholarships, the selection criteria place heavy reliance on MCAT and undergraduate GPA. Contact the Office of Student Affairs/Financial Assistance for current information; phone: (919)816-2278. For most financial assistance and all federal programs, submit FAFSA to a federal processor (Title IV school code # 002923); also submit Financial Aid Transcript and Federal Income Tax forms. Approximately 65% of current students receive some form of financial assistance. Average debt after graduation $43,700.

DEGREE REQUIREMENTS. *For M.D.:* satisfactory completion of 4-year program. All students must pass USMLE Step 1 prior to entering 4th year; all students must take USMLE Step 2. *For M.D.-Ph.D.:* generally a 7–8-year program.

EAST TENNESSEE STATE UNIVERSITY
Johnson City, Tennessee 37614-0734
Internet site: http://www.east-tenn-st.edu

Founded 1911. Located 100 miles NE of Knoxville in the tricity area of Johnson City, Bristol, and Kingsport. Public control. Semester system. Library: 550,000 volumes; 1,506,000 microforms; 4,200 periodicals/subscriptions; 110 PC work stations. Special facilities: Center for Appalachian Studies, Bay Mountain Field Station, Eastman Center for Nutrition, Early Childhood Center, Institute for Public Service Evaluation and Research.

The university's School of Graduate Studies includes: College of Applied Science and Technology, College of Arts and Sciences, College of Business, College of Education, College of Nursing, College of Public and Allied Health.

Total university enrollment at main campus: 10,706.

James H. Quillen College of Medicine
P.O. Box 70580
Johnson City, Tennessee 37614-0580
Telephone: (423)439-6221; fax: (423)439-6616
Internet site: http://www.east-tenn-st.edu
E-mail: medcom@etsu-tn.edu

Established 1978. Located on main campus. Library: 90,000 volumes/microforms; 1,000 current periodicals/subscriptions. Affiliated hospitals: U.S. Veteran Affairs Medical Center, Bristol Regional Medical Center, Halston Valley Medical Center, Johnson City Medical Center, Woodbridge Psychiatric Hospital.

Annual tuition: residents $8,750, nonresidents $16,424; fees $408. On-campus rooms and apartments available for both single and married students. Contact Director of Housing for both on- and off-campus housing information; phone: (423)439-4446. Medical students tend to live off-campus. Off-campus housing and personal expenses: approximately $12,516.

Enrollment: 1st-year class 60 (EDP 8); total full-time 245 (men 56%, women 44%). First-year statistics: 7% out of state; 40% women; average age 25; 22% minorities.

Faculty: full-time 162, part-time/volunteers 542.

Degrees conferred: M.D., B.S.-M.D., M.D.-Ph.D. (Anatomy, Biochemistry, Cell Biology, Microbiology, Molecular Biology, Pharmacology, Physiology).

RECRUITMENT PRACTICES AND POLICIES. School has diversity program and actively recruits women/minority applicants. Diversity contact: Associate Dean; phone: (423)439-6269.

ADMISSION REQUIREMENT FOR BACHELOR-M.D. APPLICANTS. Applicants for combined-degree program apply during their freshmen year at East Tennessee State University. Contact the Undergraduate Admissions Office for current information and specific requirements for admission; phone: (423)439-5602; fax: (423)439-6905.

ADMISSION REQUIREMENTS FOR FIRST-YEAR APPLICANTS. Preference given to state residents; U.S. citizens, and permanent residents only. Nonresidents who are not residents of the Appalachian region are strongly discouraged. *Undergraduate preparation.* Suggested premed courses: 2 courses in biology with labs, 2 courses in general or inorganic chemistry with labs, 2 courses in organic chemistry with labs, 2 courses in physics with labs, 1 course in college math, 2 courses in English. Bachelor's degree from an accredited institution required; all applicants have bachelor's degree awarded prior to enrollment. *Has EDP;* applicants must apply through AMCAS (official transcripts sent by mid-May) between June 1 and August 1. Early applications are encouraged. Submit secondary/supplemental application, a personal statement, and 2 recommendations to Admissions Office within 2 weeks of receipt of application. Notification normally begins October 1. *Regular application process.* Apply through AMCAS (file after June 1,

before December 1); submit MCAT (test results may not be more than 2 years old), official transcripts for each school attended (should show at least 90 semester credits/135 quarter credits, submit transcripts by mid-May to AMCAS), service processing fee. Submit an application fee of $25, a supplemental application, a personal statement, preprofessional committee evaluation, and 2 recommendations from science faculty to Office of Student Affairs within 2–3 weeks of the receipt of supplemental materials. Interviews are by invitation only and generally for final selection. Dual-degree applicants must apply to, and be accepted by, both schools; contact the Office of Student Affairs for current information and specific requirements for admission. First-year students admitted in fall only. Rolling admission process. Notification starts on October 15 and is finished when class is filled. Applicant's response to offer and $100 deposit due within 2 weeks of receipt of acceptance letter. Admissions office phone: (423)439-6221; fax: (423)439-6616; E-mail: medcom@etsu-tn.edu.

ADMISSION REQUIREMENTS FOR TRANSFER APPLICANTS. Accepts transfers from other accredited U.S. medical schools, but transfer space is extremely rare. Contact the Office of Student Affairs for current information and specific requirements.

ADMISSION STANDARDS AND RECOGNITION. *For M.D.:* number of state-resident applicants 626, nonresidents 1,200; number of state residents interviewed 197, nonresidents 38; number of residents enrolled 56, nonresidents 4; median MCAT (verbal reasoning 9.7; biological sciences 8.9; physical sciences 8.9); median GPA 3.3 (A = 4). Gorman rating 3.14 (scale: acceptable plus 3.01–3.59); College of Medicine's ranking by NIH awards was 112th, with 20 awards/grants received; total dollars awarded $2,661,973.

FINANCIAL AID. Scholarships, merit scholarships, minority scholarships (state residents only), grants-in-aid, institutional loans, HEAL, alternative loan programs, federal Perkins loans, Stafford subsidized and unsubsidized loans, and service commitment scholarship programs are available. Assistantships/fellowships may be available for dual-degree candidates. Financial-aid applications and information are given out at the on-campus interview (by invitation). Most financial aid is in some form of long-term loan. Contact the college's Financial Aid Office for current information; phone: (423)439-6218. For most financial assistance and all federal programs, submit FAFSA to a federal processor (Title IV school code # E00171); also submit Financial Aid Transcript and Federal Income Tax forms. Approximately 65% of current students receive some form of financial assistance.

DEGREE REQUIREMENTS. *For BA/BS-M.D.:* an 8-year program. *For M.D.:* satisfactory completion of 4-year program. *For M.D.-Ph.D.:* generally a 7-year program.

EASTERN VIRGINIA MEDICAL SCHOOL OF THE MEDICAL COLLEGE OF HAMPTON ROADS

721 Fairfax Avenue
Norfolk, Virginia 23507-2000
Telephone: (757)446-5815; fax: (757)446-5896
Internet site: http://www.ivms.edu
E-mail: sic@worf.evms.edu

Established 1973. Located in the Hampton Roads area of Virginia and North Carolina. Private control. Library: 86,000 volumes/microforms; 1,800 current periodicals/subscriptions. Affiliated hospitals: Jones Institute for Women's Health, Diabetes Center, Center for Pediatric Research. Special programs: summer programs for underrepresented minorities in conjunction with Norfolk State University.

Annual tuition: residents $13,500, nonresidents $24,000; fees $1,208. Limited college-owned housing available. Contact Admissions Office for both on- and off-campus housing information; phone: (757)446-5961. Off-campus housing and personal expenses: approximately $10,600.

Enrollment: 1st-year class 100 (EDP 8); total full-time 416 (men 56%, women 44%). First-year statistics: 15% out of state; 31% women; average age 25; 15% other minorities.

Faculty: full-time 299, part-time/volunteers 943.

Degrees conferred: M.D., B.S.-M.D. (with the College of William and Mary, Old Dominion University, Hampton University, Norfolk State University), M.S. (Biomedical Sciences with Old Dominion University), Psy.D. (with the College of William and Mary).

RECRUITMENT PRACTICES AND POLICIES. School has diversity program and actively recruits women/minority applicants. Diversity contact: Assistant Dean for Students Affairs and Director of Minority Affairs; phone: (757)446-5869.

ADMISSION REQUIREMENT FOR B.S.-M.D. APPLICANTS. Open to both state residents and nonresidents. Contact Admissions Offices of the listed undergraduate institutions above for current admissions and financial-aid information and specific requirements for admission.

ADMISSION REQUIREMENTS FOR FIRST-YEAR APPLICANTS. Preference given to state residents; U.S. citizens, and permanent residents only. *Undergraduate preparation.* Suggested premed courses: 2 courses in biology with labs, 2 courses in general chemistry with labs, 2 courses in organic chemistry with labs, 2 courses in physics with labs, 2 courses in English. Bachelor's degree from an accredited institution required; 99% of applicants have bachelor's degree awarded prior to enrollment. *Has EDP;* applicants must apply through AMCAS (official transcripts sent by mid-May) between June 1 and August 1. Early applications are encouraged. Submit secondary/supplemental application, a personal statement, and 2 recommendations to Admissions Office within 2 weeks of receipt of application. Notification normally begins October 1. *Regular application process.* Apply through AMCAS (file after June 1, before November 15); submit MCAT (MCATs must be taken within the last 2 years), official transcripts for each school attended (should show at least 90 semester credits/135 quarter credits, submit transcripts by mid-May to AMCAS), service processing fee. Submit an application fee of $80, a supplemental application, a personal statement, preprofessional committee evaluation, and 2 recommendations from science faculty to Admissions Office within 2–3 weeks of the receipt of supplemental materials. Interviews are by invitation only and generally for final selection. First-year students admitted in fall only. Rolling admission process. Notification starts on October 15 and is finished when class is filled. Applicant's response to offer and $200 deposit due within 2 weeks of receipt of acceptance letter. Phone: (757)446-5812; fax: (757)446-5896; E-mail: sic@worf.evms.edu.

ADMISSION REQUIREMENTS FOR TRANSFER APPLICANTS. Accepts transfers from other accredited U.S. medical schools. Admission limited to space available. Contact the Admissions Office for current information and specific requirements.

ADMISSION STANDARDS AND RECOGNITION. *For B.S.-M.D.:* number of state-resident applicants 145; number of state residents interviewed 35, nonresidents 19; number of residents enrolled 10, nonresidents 3. *For M.D.:* number of state-resident applicants 1,030, nonresidents 6,248; number of state residents interviewed 300, nonresidents 260; number of residents enrolled 86, nonresidents 20; median MCAT 9.8 (verbal reasoning 10.0; biological sciences 10.0; physical sciences 10.0); median GPA 3.41 (A = 4). Gorman rating 3.12 (scale: acceptable plus 3.01–3.59); the medical school's ranking by NIH awards was 105th, with 25 awards/grants received; total dollars awarded $3,064,555.

FINANCIAL AID. Scholarships, merit scholarships, minority scholarships, grants-in-aid, low-interest institutional loans, HEAL, alternative loan programs, federal Perkins loans, Stafford subsidized and unsubsidized loans, and primary-care service commitment scholarship programs are available. Most financial aid is based on demonstrated need. Financial aid applications and information are given out at the on-campus interview (by invitation). For merit scholarships, the selection criteria place heavy reliance on MCAT and undergraduate GPA. Contact the Financial Aid Office for current information; phone: (757)446-5813. For most financial assistance and all federal programs submit FAFSA to a federal processor (Title IV school code # G10338); also submit Financial Aid Transcript and Federal Income Tax forms. Approximately 90% of current students receive some form of financial assistance.

DEGREE REQUIREMENTS. *For B.S.-M.D.:* an 8-year program. *For M.D.:* satisfactory completion of 4-year program. All students must pass USMLE Step 1 prior to entering 3rd year; all students must pass USMLE Step 2 prior to awarding of M.D.

EMORY UNIVERSITY
Atlanta, Georgia 30322
Internet site: http://www.emory.edu

Founded 1836. Located in a suburban area 6 miles NE of downtown Atlanta. Private control. Methodist affiliation. Special facilities: Carter Center, Center for Public Health Practice, Emerson Center for Scientific Computation, Emory Fertility Center, Institute for Women's Studies, Institute for African Studies, Integrated Scanning, Electron Microscopy and Microanalytical Facility, National Institute of Church Finance and Administration, Nutrition and Health Sciences Center, Vascular Surgery Center. Semester system. Library: 2,200,000 volumes; 3,076,000 microforms; 24,588 periodicals/subscriptions. The university's ranking in domestic higher education by NIH awards was 25th, with 405 awards/grants received; total dollars awarded $90,953,311.

The university's other graduate colleges/schools: Candler School of Theology, Graduate School of Arts and Sciences, Nell Hodgson Woodruff School of Nursing, Roberto C. Goizueta Business School, Rollins School of Public Health, School of Law.

Total university enrollment at main campus: 11,300.

Woodruff Health Science Center
Located on main campus. Emory University Hospital is a member of the Council of Teaching Hospitals. Nationally recognized programs in Cardiology, Neurology, Ophthalmology, Orthopedics, Urology.

School of Medicine
Medical School Administration, Room 303
Atlanta, Georgia 30322-4510
Telephone: (404)727-5660; fax: (404)727-0045
Internet site: http://www.emory.edu/WHSC
E-mail: medschadmiss@medadm.emory.edu

Established 1864 as Atlanta Medical College; changed name in 1919. Located in the Druid Hills section of Atlanta. Library: 200,000 volumes/microforms; 3,000 current periodicals/subscriptions. Affiliated hospitals: University Hospital, Grady Memorial Hospital, VA Hospital, Crawford Long Hospital.

Annual tuition: $22,810; fees $440. On-campus rooms and apartments available for both single and married students. On-campus housing is not guaranteed. Contact Department of Residential Services for both on- and off-campus housing information; phone: (404)727-8830. Medical students tend to live off-campus. Off-campus housing and personal expenses: approximately $12,840.

Enrollment: 1st-year class 112; total full-time 441 (men 62%, women 38%). First-year statistics: 49% out of state; 50% women; average age 25; 15.2% underrepresented minorities; 22% other minorities; 60% science majors.

Faculty: full/part-time/volunteers 2,500.

Degrees conferred: M.D., M.D.-M.P.H., M.D.-Ph.D. (Biochemistry, Biomedical Engineering, Biophysics, Cell Biology, Genetics, Immunology, Microbiology, Molecular Biology, Neurosciences, Pharmacology, Physiology); has M.S.T.P.

RECRUITMENT PRACTICES AND POLICIES. School has diversity program and actively recruits women/minority applicants. Diversity contact: Associate Dean/Director of Minority Affairs; phone: (404)727-0016.

ADMISSION REQUIREMENTS FOR FIRST-YEAR APPLICANTS. Preference given to state residents; the school reserves up to 5 places each year for applicants from Emory College and Oxford College of Emory University; U.S. citizens and permanent residents only. *Undergraduate preparation.* Suggested premed courses: 2 courses in biology with labs, 2 courses in inorganic chemistry with labs, 2 courses in organic chemistry with labs, 2 courses in physics with labs, 2 courses in English. Bachelor's degree from an accredited institution required; all applicants have bachelor's degree awarded prior to enrollment. Does not have EDP. *Application process.* Apply through AMCAS (file after June 1, before October 15); submit MCAT (MCAT test results must be from the last 4 years), official transcripts for each school attended (should show at least 90 semester credits/135 quarter credits; submit transcripts by mid-May to AMCAS), service processing fee. Submit an application fee of $50, a supplemental application, a personal comment/statement, preprofessional committee evaluation, and 2 recommendations from science faculty to Admissions Office within 2–3 weeks of the receipt of supplemental materials, but no later than December 1. Interviews are by invitation only and generally for final selection. Dual-degree applicants must apply to, and be accepted by, both schools; contact the Admissions Office for current information and specific requirements for admission. First-year students admitted in fall only. Rolling admission process. Notification starts on October 15 and is generally finished by mid-March. Applicant's response to offer and $150 deposit due within 2 weeks of receipt of acceptance letter. School does maintain an alternate/waiting list. Phone: (404)727-5660; fax: (404)727-0045; E-mail: medschadmiss@medadm.emory.edu.

ADMISSION REQUIREMENTS FOR TRANSFER APPLICANTS. Accepts transfers with a compelling reason from other accredited U.S. and Canadian medical schools. Some preference given to state residents. Admission limited to space available. Contact the Admissions Office for current information and specific requirements.

ADMISSION STANDARDS AND RECOGNITION. *For M.D.:* number of state-resident applicants 731, nonresidents 7,546; number of state residents interviewed 208, nonresidents 583; number of residents enrolled 56, nonresidents 56; median MCAT 10.2 (verbal reasoning 10.0; biological sciences 10.4; physical sciences 10.4); median GPA 3.69 (A = 4). Gorman rating 4.31 (scale: strong 4.01–4.49); *U.S. News & World Report* ranked the School of Medicine in the Top 25 of all U.S. medical schools; not ranked in the Top 25 in primary-care programs; Medical school's ranking by NIH awards was 30th, with 315 awards/grants received; total dollars awarded $65,123,163.

FINANCIAL AID. Scholarships, merit scholarships, 6 Robert Woodruff fellowships, minority scholarships, grants-in-aid, institutional loans, HEAL, alternative loan programs, NIH stipends, federal Perkins loans, Stafford subsidized and unsubsidized loans, and service commitment scholarship programs are available. Assistantships/fellowships may be available for dual-degree candidates. Financial-aid applications and information are given out at the on-campus interview (by invitation). For merit scholarships, the selection criteria place heavy reliance on MCAT and undergraduate GPA. Apply for financial aid after January 1, before March 1; however, contact the Financial Aid Office for the most current information; phone: (800)727-5682. For most financial assistance and all federal programs, submit FAFSA to a federal processor (Title IV school code # 001564); also submit Financial Aid Transcript and Federal Income Tax forms. Approximately 75% of current students receive some form of financial assistance. Average debt after graduation $66,852.

DEGREE REQUIREMENTS. *For M.D.:* satisfactory completion of 4-year program. All students must pass USMLE Step 1 prior to entering 3rd year; all students must take USMLE Step 2 and record a score prior to awarding of M.D. *For M.D.-M.P.H.:* generally a 5-year program. *For M.D.-Ph.D., M.S.T.P.:* generally a 6–7-year program.

FINCH UNIVERSITY OF HEALTH SCIENCES/CHICAGO MEDICAL SCHOOL
3333 Green Bay Road
North Chicago, Illinois 60064-3037
Internet site: http://www.finchcms.edu

Founded 1912. University was established in 1968, with Chicago Medical School as the core component of 3 allied units. Private control. Quarter system. Library: 87,185 volumes; 5,790 microforms; 1,050 periodicals/subscriptions; 25 PC work stations. Special facilities: Electron-microscope Facility, Protein Sequence Laboratory, Special Pathogen-Free Swine Facility, Computer Center.

The university's other graduate units: School of Graduate and Postdoctoral Studies, School of Related Health Science.

Total university enrollment at main campus: 1,440.

Chicago Medical College
3333 Green Bay Road
North Chicago, Illinois 60064-3037
Telephone: (847)578-3206, X3207.
Internet site: http://www.finchcms.edu
E-mail: jonesk@mis.finchcms.edu

Established 1912. Term system. Affiliated hospitals: Cook County Hospital, Edward Hines VA Medical Center, Mt. Sinai Hospital, North Chicago Veterans Affairs Medical Center, Illinois Masonic Medical Center, Swedish Covenant Hospital, Lutheran General Hospital, Resurrection Hospital, Henry Ford Health System (Detroit).

Annual tuition: $31,280; fees $100. No on-campus housing available. Contact Admissions Office for off-campus housing information. Off-campus housing and personal expenses: approximately $16,966.

Enrollment: 1st-year class 176 (EDP 3); total full-time 747 (men 62%, women 42%). First-year statistics: 60% out of state; 17 states represented; 40% women; average age 25; 12% minorities; 50% science majors.

Degrees conferred: M.D., B.S.-M.D. (with Illinois Institute of Technology; Chemistry, Electrical Engineering, Mechanical Engineering, Computer Science), M.D.-M.S., M.D.-Ph.D. (Anatomy, Biochemistry, Biophysics, Cell Biology, Immunology, Microbiology, Molecular Biology, Neurosciences, Pathology, Pharmacology, Physiology).

RECRUITMENT PRACTICES AND POLICIES. School has diversity program and actively recruits women/minority applicants. Diversity contact: Associate Dean, Ancillary Programs; phone: (847)578-3314.

ADMISSION REQUIREMENT FOR BACHELOR-M.D. APPLICANTS. Program is open to all U.S. citizens and permanent residents. Submit application, an application fee of $30, SAT I or ACT, official high school transcript with rank in class, and 3 letters of recommendation to the Admissions Office, Illinois Institute of Technology. Apply to Admissions Office by January 1. Interview by invitation required. Notification normally April 1. Applicant's response to offer and $100 deposit due May 1. Undergraduate phone: (312)567-3025; outside Chicago: (800)448-2329. For financial-aid information contact either Illinois Institute of Technology or Chicago Medical College. Web sites: http://www.iit.edu; www.finchcms.edu

ADMISSION REQUIREMENTS FOR FIRST-YEAR APPLICANTS. Preference given to state residents; U.S. citizens and permanent residents only. *Undergraduate preparation.* Suggested premed courses: 2 courses in biology with labs, 2 courses in inorganic chemistry with labs, 2 courses in organic chemistry with labs, 2 courses in physics with labs. Bachelor's degree from an accredited institution required; 99% of applicants have bachelor's degrees awarded prior to enrollment. *Has EDP* for state residents only; applicants must apply through AMCAS (official transcripts sent by mid-May) between June 1 and August 1. Early applications are encouraged. Submit secondary/supplemental application, a personal statement, and 2 recommendations to Admissions Office within 2 weeks of receipt of application. Notification normally begins October 1. *Regular application process.* Apply through AMCAS (file after June 1, before December 15); submit MCAT (will accept MCAT taken in the last 3 years), official transcripts for each school attended

(should show at least 90 semester credits/135 quarter credits, submit transcripts by mid-May to AMCAS), service processing fee. Submit an application fee of $65, a supplemental application, a personal statement, preprofessional committee evaluation, and 2 recommendations from science faculty to Admissions Office within 2–3 weeks of the receipt of supplemental materials. Interviews are by invitation only and generally for final selection. Combined-degree applicants must apply to, and be accepted by, both schools; contact the Admissions Office for current information and specific requirements for admission. First-year students admitted in fall only. Rolling admission process. Notification starts on November 15 and is finished when class is filled. Applicant's response to offer and $100 deposit due within 2 weeks of receipt of acceptance letter. School does maintain an alternate list. Phone: (847)578-3206; fax: (847)578-3284; E-mail: jonesk@mis.finchcms.edu.

ADMISSION REQUIREMENTS FOR TRANSFER APPLICANTS. Accepts transfers from other accredited U.S. and Canadian medical schools. Admission limited to space available. Contact Admissions Office for current information and specific requirements.

ADMISSION STANDARDS AND RECOGNITION. *For B.S.-M.D.:* number of state-resident applicants 53, nonresidents 49; number of state residents interviewed 8, nonresidents 32; number of residents enrolled 2, nonresidents 6; median SAT 1,275, ACT 27; median GPA 3.5 (A = 4). *For M.D.:* number of state-resident applicants 1,450, nonresidents 11,310; number of state residents interviewed 177, nonresidents 603; number of residents enrolled 71, nonresidents 105; median MCAT 9.0 (verbal reasoning 9.0; biological sciences 9.0; physical sciences 9.0); median GPA 3.3 (A = 4). Gorman rating 3.31 (scale: acceptable plus 3.01–3.59); the medical college's ranking by NIH awards was 101st, with 30 awards/grants received; total dollars awarded $4,789,955.

FINANCIAL AID. Grants, institutional loans, HEAL, alternative loan programs, federal Perkins loans, Stafford subsidized and unsubsidized loans, and service commitment scholarship programs are available. Assistantships/fellowships may be available for dual-degree candidates. Financial-aid applications and information are given out at the on-campus interview (by invitation). Contact the Financial Aid Office for current information; phone: (847)578-3217. For most financial assistance and all federal programs, submit FAFSA to a federal processor (Title IV school code # 001659); also submit Financial Aid Transcript and Federal Income Tax forms. Approximately 75% of current students receive some form of financial assistance. Average debt after graduation $145,000.

DEGREE REQUIREMENTS. *For B.S.-M.D.:* an 8-year program. *For M.D.:* satisfactory completion of 4-year program. All students must pass USMLE Step 1 prior to entering 3rd year; all students must pass USMLE Step 2 prior to awarding of M.D. *For M.D.-M.S.:* generally a 4½–5½-year program. *For M.D.-Ph.D.:* generally a 7-year program.

UNIVERSITY OF FLORIDA
Gainesville, Florida 32611-8140
Internet site: http://www.ufl.edu

Founded 1853. Located 75 miles SW of Jacksonville. Public control. Semester system. Library: 3,000,000 volumes; 4,200,000 microforms. The university's ranking in domestic higher education by NIH awards was 52nd, with 229 awards/grants received; total dollars awarded $49,116,997.

The university's graduate school includes: College of Agriculture, College of Architecture, College of Business Administration, College of Engineering, College of Fine Arts, College of Health and Human Performance, College of Health Related Professions, College of Journalism and Communication, College of Liberal Arts and Sciences, College of Nursing, School of Forest Resources and Conservation; College of Dentistry, College of Law, College of Pharmacy.

Total university enrollment at main campus: 38,700.

J. Hillis Miller Health Center
Opened 1956. Shands Hospital is located at health center and is a member of the Council of Teaching Hospitals. Schools located at health center: College of Dentistry, College of Health Professions, College of Nursing, College of Pharmacy, College of Veterinary Medicine. Special facilities: Center for Biotechnology Research, Center for Mammalian Genetics, Center for Structural Biology, Cancer Center, University of Florida Brain Institute, Health Policy Institute, Institute for Wound Research. Shands Hospital has nationally recognized programs in Cancer, Gastroenterology, Neurology, Otolaryngology.

College of Medicine
P.O. Box 100216
Gainesville, Florida 32610-0216
Telephone: (352)392-4569; fax: (352)846-0622
Internet site: http://www.med.ufl.edu
E-mail: robyn@dean.med.ufl.edu

Established 1956. Located on SE corner of main campus. Library: 215,000 volumes/microforms; 1,800 current periodicals/subscriptions. Affiliated hospitals: Shands Hospital at University of Florida, Gainesville Veterans Affairs Medical Center, University Medical Center (Jacksonville). Special programs: program in Medical Sciences with Florida State University, University of West Florida, and Florida Agricultural and Mechanical University; Junior Honors Medical Program (primarily for juniors at University of Florida); prematriculation summer sessions.

Annual tuition: residents $7,641, nonresidents $20,888; fees $1,723. On-campus rooms and apartments available for both single and married students. Annual on-campus housing cost: $11,911 (room and board). Contact Director of Housing Office for both on- and off-campus housing information; phone: (352)392-2161.

Enrollment: 1st-year class total 115, 73 (regular), 12 (junior honors), 30 (Program in Medical Sciences); total full-time 467 (men 54%, women 46%). First-year statistics: 4% out of state; 45% women; average age 23; 7 minorities; 55% science majors.

Faculty: full-time/part-time/volunteers 1,050.

Degrees conferred: M.D., B.S.-M.D., M.D.-Ph.D. (Anatomy, Biochemistry, Biomedical Engineering, Cell Biology, Genetics, Immunology, Microbiology, Molecular Biology, Neurosciences, Pathology, Pharmacology, Physiology); has M.S.T.P.

RECRUITMENT PRACTICES AND POLICIES. School has diversity program and actively recruits women/minority applicants. Diversity contact: Assistant Dean for Minority Relations; phone: (352)974-3393.

ADMISSION REQUIREMENT FOR PROGRAM-IN-MEDICAL-SCIENCES APPLICANTS. Restricted to Florida residents with a clear interest in primary-care specialties from underrepresented minorities and from rural areas in Florida. For complete information contact Program in Medical Sciences, Florida State University, Tallahassee, Florida 32306-4051; phone: (904)644-1855.

ADMISSION REQUIREMENTS FOR FIRST-YEAR APPLICANTS. Preference given to state residents; U.S. citizens and permanent residents only. *Undergraduate preparation.* Suggested premed courses: 2 courses in biology with labs, 1 course in inorganic chemistry with labs, 2 courses in organic chemistry with labs, 2 courses in physics with labs, 1 course in biochemistry. Bachelor's degree from an accredited institution required; all applicants have bachelor's degrees awarded prior to enrollment. Does not have EDP. *Application process.* Apply through AMCAS (file after June 1, before December 1);

submit MCAT (must be taken within the last 3 years), official transcripts for each school attended (should show at least 90 semester credits/135 quarter credits, submit transcripts by mid-May to AMCAS), service processing fee. Submit an application fee of $20, a supplemental application, a personal comment/statement, preprofessional committee evaluation, and 2 recommendations from science faculty to Admissions Office within 2–3 weeks of the receipt of supplemental materials, but not later than January 15. Interviews are by invitation only and generally for final selection. Dual-degree and M.S.T.P. applicants must apply to, and be accepted by, both schools; contact the Admissions Office for current information and specific requirements for admission. First-year students admitted in fall only. Rolling admission process. Notification starts on October 15 and is finished when class is filled. Applicant's response to offer due within 2 weeks of receipt of acceptance letter. Phone: (352)392-4569.

ADMISSION REQUIREMENTS FOR TRANSFER APPLICANTS. Transfer students rarely considered. Contact the Admissions Office for current information and specific requirements for admission.

ADMISSION STANDARDS AND RECOGNITION. *For M.D.:* number of state-resident applicants 1,454, nonresidents 877; number of state residents interviewed 306, nonresidents 22; number of residents enrolled 82, nonresidents 3; median MCAT 9.2 (verbal reasoning 9.1; biological sciences 9.4; physical sciences 9.0); median GPA 3.91 (A = 4). Gorman rating 3.80 (scale: good 3.61–3.99); medical college's ranking by NIH awards was 53rd, with 146 awards/grants received; total dollars awarded $31,763,449.

FINANCIAL AID. Limited scholarships, minority scholarships, grants-in-aid, institutional loans, HEAL, alternative loan programs, NIH stipends; federal Perkins loans, Stafford subsidized and unsubsidized loans, and service commitment scholarship programs are available. Assistantships/fellowships and tuition waivers may be available for combined-degree candidates. For scholarships, the selection criteria place heavy reliance on MCAT and undergraduate GPA. Contact the Office for Student Financial Affairs for current information; phone: (352)392-7800. For most financial assistance and all federal programs, submit FAFSA to a federal processor (Title IV school code # 001535); also submit Financial Aid Transcript and Federal Income Tax forms. Approximately 80% of current students receive some form of financial assistance. Average debt after graduation $61,200.

DEGREE REQUIREMENTS. *For Junior Honor Medical Program-M.D.:* a 7-year program. *For M.D.:* satisfactory completion of 4-year program. All students must pass USMLE Step 1 prior to entering 3rd year; all students must pass USMLE Step 2 prior to awarding of M.D. *For M.D.-Ph.D.:* generally a 7-year program.

College of Dentistry
Box 100445, J.H.M.H.C.
Gainesville, Florida 32610-0445
Telephone: (352)392-4866; fax: (352)846-0311
Internet site: http://www.dental.ufl.edu
E-mail: bennett@dental.ufl.edu

Admitted 1st class in 1972. Located on health center campus. Affiliated hospitals: Shands Hospital, Veterans Administration Medical Center (Jacksonville). Postgraduate specialties: Dental Biomaterials, Dental Public Health, Endodontics, General Dentistry, Geriatric Dentistry, Oral Biology, Oral Pathology, Oral and Maxillofacial Surgery, Orthodontics, Pediatric Dentistry, Periodontics, Prosthodontics.

Annual tuition: residents $9,100, nonresidents $22,040; fees $15; equipment and supplies $5,837. On-campus rooms and apartments available for both single and married students. Contact Director of Housing Office for both on- and off-campus housing information; phone: (352)392-2161. On- or off-campus housing, food, transportation, and personal expenses: approximately $8,332.

Enrollment: 1st-year class 78. First-year enrolled student information: 5 from out of state; 4 states represented; 27 women; average age 24; 15 underrepresented minorities; 7 other minorities.

Degrees conferred: D.M.D., B.S.-D.M.D. (with University of Florida, University of South Florida, and Florida International University).

RECRUITMENT PRACTICES AND POLICIES. School has diversity program and actively recruits women/minority applicants. Diversity contact: Office of Minority Affairs; phone: (352)392-2671.

ADMISSION REQUIREMENT FOR BACHELOR-D.M.D. APPLICANTS. For information and applications contact: Undergraduate Program Director, University of Florida, University of South Florida, and Florida International University.

ADMISSION REQUIREMENTS FOR FIRST-YEAR APPLICANTS. Preference given to state residents; U.S. citizens and permanent residents only. *Undergraduate preparation.* Suggested predental courses: 2 courses in biology with labs, 2 courses in inorganic chemistry with labs, 2 courses in organic chemistry with labs, 2 courses in physics with labs; courses in biochemistry, microbiology, and immunology are strongly recommended. The junior-college transfer-credit limit is 2 years of credit. Will consider applicants with only 3 years of undergraduate preparation; prefer applicants who will have a bachelor's degree prior to enrollment; all applicants have bachelor's degree awarded prior to enrollment. *Application process.* Apply through AADSAS (file after June 1, before October 15), submit official transcripts for each school attended (should show at least 90 semester credits/135 quarter credits), service processing fee; at the same time as you send in AADSAS materials, submit official DAT scores (must be taken in the fall of the year prior to the year of anticipated enrollment) directly to the Admissions Office. Submit the following materials only after being contacted by an Admissions Officer: an application fee of $20, a formal University of Florida application, official transcripts, DAT scores, predental committee evaluation or 2 recommendations from professors in your major field of study, photograph, and Verification of Residency form to Admissions Office within 2 weeks of receipt of supplemental materials. Interviews are by invitation only and generally for final selection. First-year students admitted in fall only. Rolling admission process. Notification starts in December and is finished when class is filled. Applicant's response to offer and $100 deposit due within 30 days if accepted prior to February 28; response and deposit due within 2 weeks if received after March 1. School does maintain an alternate list. Phone: (352)392-4866; E-mail: bennett@dental.ufl.edu.

ADMISSION REQUIREMENTS FOR ADVANCED-STANDING APPLICANTS. Accepts transfers from other accredited U.S. dental schools. Admission limited to space available in January of the 1st year. There is an advanced-standing program for graduates of foreign schools of dentistry; generally applicants are considered for admission in January only. Contact the Admissions Office for current information and specific requirements.

ADMISSION STANDARDS AND RECOGNITION. *For D.M.D.:* number of applicants 768; number enrolled 78; median DAT: ACAD 18.47, PAT 17.57; median GPA 3.32 (A = 4), median sciences GPA 3.25 (A = 4). Gorman rating 4.08 (scale: strong 4.01–4.49); this placed the school in the Bottom 10 of all U.S. dental schools.

FINANCIAL AID. Limited scholarships, grants, institutional loans, state loan programs, DEAL, HEAL, alternative loan programs; federal Perkins loans, Stafford subsidized and unsubsidized loans, and service commitment scholarship programs are available. Institutional financial aid applications and information are sent out with the acceptance letter. Contact the Financial Aid Office for current information; phone: (352)846-1384; E-mail: mike_powell@sfa.ufl.edu. For most financial assistance and all need-based programs, submit FAFSA to a federal processor (Title IV school code # 001535); also submit Financial Aid Transcript, Federal Income Tax forms, and Use of Federal Funds Certification. Approximately 95% of current students receive some form of financial assistance. Average award resident $20,570, nonresident $19,500.

DEGREE REQUIREMENTS. *For B.S.-D.M.D.:* an 8-year program. *For D.M.D.:* satisfactory completion of 4-year program.

GEORGE WASHINGTON UNIVERSITY
Washington, D.C. 20052
Internet site: http://www.gwu.edu

Founded 1821. Located in downtown Washington. Private control. Semester system. Library: 1,760,000 volumes; 2,016,600 microforms; 14,000 periodicals/subscriptions; 160 work stations. The university's ranking in domestic higher education by NIH awards was 86th, with 46 awards/grants received; total dollars awarded $20,331,162. Special programs: B.A./B.S.-M.D. program (annual undergraduate tuition $29,125).

The university's other graduate colleges/schools: Columbia College of Arts and Sciences, Elliot School of International Affairs, Graduate School of Education and Human Development, National Law Center, School of Business and Public Policy, School of Engineering and Applied Sciences.

Total university enrollment at main campus: 19,670.

Medical Center
901 23rd Street, N.W.
Washington, D.C. 20337
Internet site: http://www.gwu.mc.edu

Private control. Member of Council of Teaching Hospitals. Nationally recognized programs in Neurology, Otolaryngology, Rheumatology.

School of Medicine and Health Sciences
2300 I Street N.W., Room 615
Washington, D.C. 20037
Telephone: (202)994-3506
Internet site: http://www.gwu.edu
E-mail: medadmit@gwis2.circ.gwu.edu

Established 1825 and is 11th oldest medical school in U.S. Located at Washington Circle in the Foggy Bottom area of Washington. Library: 100,000 volumes/microforms; 1,500 current periodicals/subscriptions. Affiliated hospitals: University Hospital, Children's Hospital, National Medical Center, Fairfax Hospital, Holy Cross Hospital, National Naval Medical Center, St. Elizabeth's Hospital, VA Hospital, Washington Hospital Center.

Annual tuition: $31,500; fees $950. Limited on-campus housing available. Contact Office of Campus Life for both on- and off-campus housing information. Housing information is sent with the acceptance letter. Medical students tend to live off-campus. Average monthly rent $600. Off-campus housing and personal expenses: approximately $15,000.

Enrollment: 1st-year class 150 (EDP 2); total full-time 630 (men 49%, women 51%). First-year statistics: 99% outside of D.C.; 52.9% women; average age 23; 16% minorities; 66% science majors.

Faculty: full-time/part-time/volunteers 3,000.

Degrees conferred: M.D., B.A.-M.D. (Columbian School of Arts and Sciences), M.D.-M.P.H., M.D.-Ph.D. (Anatomy, Biochemistry, Biomedical Engineering, Cell Biology, Genetics, Immunology, Microbiology, Molecular Biology, Neurosciences, Pathology, Pharmacology, Physiology).

RECRUITMENT PRACTICES AND POLICIES. School has diversity program and actively recruits women/minority applicants. Diversity contact: Medical Director; phone: (202)944-0525.

ADMISSION REQUIREMENT FOR B.A.-M.D. APPLICANTS. Open to residents and nonresidents. Submit application, SAT I, SAT II (subject test in writing, mathematics, and a science) or ACT, official high school transcripts with rank in class, and 3 letters of recommendations. Apply to George Washington University's Admissions Office after September 1, before December 1. Application fee $50. Admissions Office phone: (800)447-3765. Supplemental application deadline is January 15. Notification normally begins in mid-March. Applicant's response and $650 deposit is due by May 1.

ADMISSION REQUIREMENTS FOR FIRST-YEAR APPLICANTS. Additional consideration given to applicants from the District of Columbia and its metropolitan area as well as the university's undergraduates; U.S. citizens and permanent residents only. *Undergraduate preparation.* Suggested premed courses: 2 courses in biology with labs, 2 courses in inorganic chemistry with labs, 2 courses in organic chemistry with labs, 2 courses in physics with labs, 2 courses in English. Bachelor's degree from an accredited institution required; all applicants have bachelor's degree awarded prior to enrollment. *Has EDP;* applicants must apply through AMCAS (official transcripts sent by mid-May) between June 1 and August 1. Early applications are encouraged. Submit secondary/supplemental application, a personal statement, and 2 recommendations to Admissions Office within 2 weeks of receipt of application. Notification normally begins October 1. *Regular application process.* Apply through AMCAS (file after June 1, before December 1); submit MCAT (will accept MCAT test results from 1995), official transcripts for each school attended (should show at least 90 semester credits/135 quarter credits, submit transcripts by mid-May to AMCAS), service processing fee. Supplemental application and additional information sent 1 week after receipt of AMCAS preliminary materials. Submit an application fee of $75, the supplemental application, a personal statement, pre-professional committee evaluation, and 2 recommendations from science faculty to Admissions Office within 2–3 weeks of the receipt of supplemental materials. Interviews are by invitation only and generally for final selection. Joint-degree applicants must apply to, and be accepted by, both schools; contact the Admissions Office for current information and specific requirements for admission. First-year students admitted in fall only. Rolling admission process. Notification starts on October 15 and is finished when class is filled. Applicant's response to offer and $100 deposit due within 2 weeks of receipt of acceptance letter. School does maintain an alternate list. Phone: (202)994-3506.

ADMISSION REQUIREMENTS FOR TRANSFER APPLICANTS. Accepts transfers from other accredited U.S. medical schools. Admission limited to space available. Contact the Admissions Office for current information and specific requirements.

ADMISSION STANDARDS AND RECOGNITION. *For B.A.-M.D.:* number of applicants 612; number interviewed 55; number enrolled 9; median SAT 1,450, ACT 32; median GPA 3.75 (A = 4). *For M.D.:* number of D.C. resident applicants 58, nonresidents 11,370; number of residents interviewed 17, nonresidents 986; number of residents enrolled 1, nonresidents 152; median MCAT 10.0 (verbal reasoning 10.0; biological sciences 10.0; physical sciences 10.0); median GPA 3.50 (A = 4). Gorman rating 4.35 (scale: strong 4.01–4.49); School of Medicine's ranking by NIH awards was 91st, with 34 awards/grants received; total dollars awarded $8,396,911.

FINANCIAL AID. Scholarships, minority scholarships, grants-in-aid, institutional loans, HEAL, alternative loan programs, NIH stipends, federal Perkins loans, Stafford subsidized and unsubsidized loans, and service commitment scholarship programs are available. Most financial assistance is based on documented need. Assistantships/fellowships may be available for joint-degree candidates. Financial aid applications and information are given out at both the on-campus and regional interviews (by invitation). For scholarships, the selection criteria place heavy reliance on MCAT and undergraduate GPA. Contact the Financial Aid Office for current information; phone: (202)994-2960. For most financial assistance and all federal programs, submit FAFSA to a federal processor (Title IV school code # E00197); also submit Financial Aid Transcript and Federal Income Tax forms. Approximately 80% of current students receive some form of financial assistance. Average debt after graduation $103,500.

DEGREE REQUIREMENTS. *For B.A.-M.D.:* a 7-year program. *For M.D.:* satisfactory completion of 4-year program. All students must pass USMLE Step 1 prior to entering 3rd year; all students must take USMLE Step 2 prior to awarding of M.D. *For M.D.-M.P.H.:* generally a 5–6-year program. *For M.D.-Ph.D.:* generally a 7-year program.

GEORGETOWN UNIVERSITY
Washington, D.C. 20057
Internet site: http://www.georgetown.edu

Founded 1789. Private control. Roman Catholic Jesuit affiliation. Semester system. Library: 2,070,000 volumes; 2,747,000 microforms; 26,470 periodicals/subscriptions. Postbaccalaureate premedical program for adults and underrepresented minorities (priority given to D.C. residents); phone: (202)687-1406. The university's ranking in domestic higher education by NIH awards was 62nd, with 185 awards/grants received; total dollars awarded $42,268,353.

The university's graduate school includes: Center for German and European Studies, Center for Latin American Studies, Edmund A. Walsh School of Foreign Service, School of Business, School of Nursing, Georgetown Public Policy Institute, Law Center.

Total university enrollment at main campus: 12,618.

Georgetown University Medical Center
4000 Reservoir Road, N.W.
Washington, D.C. 20007

Private control. Member of Council of Teaching Hospitals. School located at medical center: School of Medicine. Nationally recognized programs in Cancer, Gastroenterology, Gynecology, Neurology, Pulmonary Disease.

School of Medicine
3900 Reservoir Road, N.W.
Washington, D.C.
Telephone: (202)387-1154
Internet site: http://www.dml.georgetown.edu/schmed

Established 1851. Located on main campus. Library: 160,000 volumes/microforms; 1,830 current periodicals/subscriptions. Affiliated hospitals: Georgetown University Hospital, Lombardi Cancer Research Center, Concentrated Care Center, Georgetown Medical Centers (Rockville and Ballston), Arlington Hospital, General Hospital, Fairfax Hospital, National Naval Medical Center, Walter Reed Army Medical Center, Washington Veterans Affairs Medical Center. Special programs: prematriculation summer sessions.

Annual tuition: $26,046. On-campus rooms and apartments available for both single and married students. Contact Director of Housing Office for both on- and off-campus housing information; phone: (202)687-4560. Medical students tend to live off-campus. Off-campus housing and personal expenses: approximately $16,100.

Enrollment: 1st-year class 165; total full-time 727 (men 56%, women 44%). First-year statistics: 94% out of D.C.; 43% women; average age 24; 9.6% minorities; 75% science majors.

Faculty: full-time 572, part-time/volunteers 136

Degrees conferred: M.D., M.D.-M.B.A., M.D.-Ph.D. (Biochemistry, Biophysics, Cell Biology, Immunology, Microbiology, Molecular Biology, Neurosciences, Pathology, Pharmacology, Physiology, Tumor Biology).

RECRUITMENT PRACTICES AND POLICIES. School has diversity program and actively recruits women/minority applicants. Diversity contact: Director, Office of Minority Affairs; phone: (202)687-1602.

ADMISSION REQUIREMENTS FOR FIRST-YEAR APPLICANTS. Preference given to D.C. residents; U.S. citizens and permanent residents only. *Undergraduate preparation.* Suggested premed courses: 2 courses in biology with labs, 2 courses in inorganic chemistry with labs, 2 courses in organic chemistry with labs, 2 courses in physics with labs, 1 course in college math, 2 courses in English. Bachelor's degree from an accredited institution required; all applicants have bachelor's degree awarded prior to enrollment. Does not have EDP. *Application process.* Apply through AMCAS (file after June 1, before November 1); submit MCAT (will accept MCAT test results from 1995), official transcripts for each school attended (should show at least 90 semester credits/135 quarter credits, submit transcripts by mid-May to AMCAS), service processing fee. Submit an application fee of $60, a secondary application, a personal statement, preprofessional committee evaluation, and 2 recommendations from science faculty to Admissions Office within 2–3 weeks of the receipt of supplemental materials. Interviews are by invitation only and generally for final selection. M.D.-Ph.D. and M.D.-M.B.A. applicants must apply to, and be accepted by, both schools; contact the Admissions Office for current information and specific requirements for admission. First-year students admitted in fall only. Rolling admission process. Notification starts on October 15 and is finished when class is filled. Applicant's response to offer and $100 deposit due within 3 weeks of receipt of acceptance letter; an additional $900 prepayment due June 1. School does maintain an alternate list. Phone: (202)687-1154.

ADMISSION REQUIREMENTS FOR TRANSFER APPLICANTS. Accepts transfers from other LCME-accredited U.S. medical schools only. Admission limited to space available. Contact the Admissions Office for current information and specific requirements.

ADMISSION STANDARDS AND RECOGNITION. *For M.D.:* number of D.C. resident applicants 49, nonresidents 10,965; total number interviewed 1,523; number of residents enrolled 10, nonresidents 157; median MCAT 10.0 (verbal reasoning 10.0; biological sciences 10.0; physical sciences 10.0); median GPA 3.58 (A = 4). Gorman rating 4.38 (scale: strong 4.01–4.49); School of Medicine's ranking by NIH awards was 46th, with 168 awards/grants received; total dollars awarded $38,900,761.

FINANCIAL AID. Scholarships, merit scholarships, minority scholarships, grants-in-aid, institutional loans, HEAL, alternative loan programs, NIH stipends, federal Perkins loans, Stafford subsidized and unsubsidized loans, and service commitment scholarship programs are available. Assistantships/fellowships may be available for combined-degree candidates. Financial-aid applications and information are given out at the on-campus interview (by invitation). For scholarships, the selection criteria place heavy reliance on MCAT and undergraduate GPA. Contact the Office of Student Financial Planning for current information; phone: (202)687-1693. For most financial assistance and all federal programs, submit FAFSA to a federal processor (Title IV school code # E00518); also submit Financial Aid Transcript and Federal Income Tax forms. Approximately 85% of current students re-ceive some form of financial assistance. Average debt after graduation $113,000.

DEGREE REQUIREMENTS. *For M.D.:* satisfactory completion of 4-year program. All students must pass USMLE Step 1 prior to entering 3rd year. *For M.D.-M.B.A.:* generally a 5-year program. *For M.D.-Ph.D.:* generally a 7-year program.

HARVARD UNIVERSITY
Cambridge, Massachusetts 02138
Internet site: http://www.harvard.edu

Founded 1636. Located in Cambridge. Private control. Semester system. Library: 13,143,000 volumes; 6,755,000 microforms; 6,775 periodicals/subscriptions. Special programs: Postbaccalaureate premedical program for adults and underrepresented minorities exist in the Harvard Extension School. For information contact the Director of Health Careers Program; phone: (617)495-2926. The university's ranking in domestic higher education by NIH awards was 8th, with 583 awards/grants received; total dollars awarded $180,022,635.

The university's other graduate schools: Divinity School, Graduate School of Arts and Sciences, Graduate School of Business Administration, Graduate School of Design, Graduate School of Education, J. F. K. School of Government, Law School, School of Dentistry, School of Public Health.

Total university enrollment at main campus: 18,310.

Medical School
25 Shattuck
Boston, Massachusetts 02155-6092
Telephone: (617)432-1550; fax: (617)432-3307
Internet site: http://www.med.harvard.edu
E-mail: HMSADM@warren.med.harvard.edu

Established 1782. Located in Boston. Library: 608,900 volumes/microforms; 203,000 monographs, 3,971 current periodicals/subscriptions. Affiliated hospitals: Beth Israel Deaconess Medical Center, Brigham and Women's Hospital, Cambridge Hospital, Children's Hospital, D.V.A. Medical Center (Brockton/West Roxbury), Massachusetts Eye and Ear Infirmary, Massachusetts General Hospital, McLean Hospital, Mount Auburn Hospital, Spaulding Rehabilitation Hospital. Special associations: Center for Blood Research, Dana-Farber Cancer Institute, Harvard Pilgrim Health Care, Joslin Diabetes Center, Judge Baker Children's Center, Massachusetts Mental Health Center, Schepens Eye Research Institute. Both

Brigham and Women's Hospital and Massachusetts General Hospital are considered to be among the Top 20 hospitals in the U.S. Special programs: M.D.-Ph.D. with Massachusetts Institute of Technology Division of Health Sciences and Technology (HST), first 2 years are taught jointly by both faculties; prematriculation summer sessions.

Annual tuition: $24,150, fees $1,559. On-campus facilities available for single students. Apartments for married students can be found near the campus. Contact Admissions Office for both on- and off-campus housing information. The average cost of living in Boston is approximately $15,700.

Enrollment: 1st-year class 164; total full-time 741 (men 51%, women 49%). First-year statistics: 85% out of state; 27 states represented; 54 different undergraduate institutions represented: 54% women; average age 24; 21% minorities; 61% science majors.

Faculty: full-time/part-time/volunteers over 4,600.

Degrees conferred: M.D., M.D.-M.P.P. (with Kennedy School of Government), M.D.-M.P.H. (with School of Public Health), M.D.-Ph.D. (Biochemistry, Biomedical Engineering, Biophysics, Cell Biology, Genetics, Immunology, Microbiology, Molecular Biology, Neurosciences, Pathology, Pharmacology), M.S.T.P. (in cooperation with MIT; several programs with the Division of Medical Sciences at Harvard Medical School and 1 program with Harvard Graduate School of Arts and Sciences; all programs are sponsored by NIH).

RECRUITMENT PRACTICES AND POLICIES. School has diversity program and actively recruits women/minority applicants. Diversity contact: Associate Dean for Student Affairs; phone: (617)232-8390.

ADMISSION REQUIREMENTS FOR FIRST-YEAR APPLICANTS. *Undergraduate preparation.* Suggested premed courses: 2 courses in biology with labs, 2 courses in inorganic chemistry with labs, 2 courses in organic chemistry with labs, 2 courses in physics with labs, 2 courses in calculus, 2 courses in English. Bachelor's degree from an accredited institution required. For HST program: same as above except calculus through differential equations and calculus-based physics; biochemistry encouraged. All applicants will have bachelor's degree awarded prior to enrollment. *Application process.* Apply through AMCAS (file after June 1, before October 15); submit MCAT (will accept MCAT test results taken within the last 4 years), official transcripts for each school attended (should show at least 90 semester credits/135 quarter credits, submit transcripts by mid-May to AMCAS), service processing fee. Submit an application fee of $75, a supplemental application, a personal com-

ment/statement, preprofessional committee evaluation, and 2 recommendations from science faculty to Admissions Office within 2–3 weeks of the receipt of supplemental materials, but no later than November 15. Interviews are by invitation only and generally for final selection. M.D.-M.P.H.-M.P.P. degree applicants may apply simultaneously to both schools or they may start study at one school before applying to the other; contact the Admissions Office for current information and specific requirements for admission. First-year students admitted in fall only. Rolling admission process. Notification starts in October and is finished February 28. Applicant's response to offer due within 3 weeks of receipt of acceptance letter. Phone: (617)432-1550; E-mail: HMSADM@warren.med.harvard.edu. Formal M.S.T.P. applications are submitted during the 2nd year of medical school. Contact the M.D.-Ph.D. Program Officer for the latest information; phone: (617)432-0991, Web site: http://www.hms.harvard.edu/md_ph.d.

ADMISSION REQUIREMENTS FOR TRANSFER APPLICANTS. Transfers from other accredited U.S. medical schools are rarely considered. Contact the Admissions Office after January 1 for current information and specific requirements for admission.

ADMISSION STANDARDS AND RECOGNITION. *For M.D.:* number of state-resident applicants 747, nonresidents 3,209; number of state residents interviewed 232, nonresidents 793; number of residents enrolled 66, nonresidents 98; median MCAT 11.3 (verbal reasoning 10.7; biological sciences 11.5; physical sciences 11.7); median GPA 3.7 (A = 4). *Barron's Guide* placed the medical school among the Top 25 most prestigious U.S. medical schools; Gorman rating 4.93 (scale: very strong 4.51–4.99); *U.S. News & World Report* ranked medical school in the Top 25 of all U.S. medical schools; not ranked in the Top 25 in primary-care programs; medical school is ranked by NIH awards was 18th, with 320 awards/grants received; total dollars awarded $89,201,697.

FINANCIAL AID. All financial aid is based on documented need. Grants, institutional loans, HEAL, alternative loan programs, NIH stipends, federal Perkins loans, Stafford subsidized and unsubsidized loans, and service commitment scholarship programs are available. Assistantships/fellowships may be available for joint-degree candidates. Contact the Financial Aid Office for current information; phone: (617)432-1575; fax: (617)432-4308; E-mail: hmsfao@warren.med.harvard.edu. For most financial assistance and all federal programs, submit FAFSA to a federal processor (Title IV school code # E00472); also submit Financial Aid Transcript, Federal

Income Tax forms, and CSS Profile. Approximately 70% of current students receive some form of financial assistance. Average debt after graduation $73,300.

DEGREE REQUIREMENTS. *For M.D.:* satisfactory completion of 4-year program. All students must pass USMLE Step 1 prior to entering 3rd year; all students must pass USMLE Step 2 prior to awarding of M.D. *For M.D.-M.P.H.-M.P.P.:* generally a 5–6-year program. *For M.D.-Ph.D.:* generally an 8-year program.

School of Dental Medicine
188 Longwood Avenue
Boston, Massachusetts 02115
Telephone: (617)432-1443
Internet site: http://www.hsdm.harvard.edu
E-mail: hsdmapps@warren.med.harvard.edu

Established 1867. The first university-affiliated dental school in U.S. Located in Boston. Curriculum: Dental students participate in the New Pathways curriculum of the medical school for the first 2 years. Affiliated hospitals: Children's Hospital and Medical Center, Beth Israel Hospital, Brigham and Women's Hospital, Massachusetts General Hospital, DVA Medical Center, Forsyth Dental Center. Both Brigham and Women's Hospital and Massachusetts General are considered to be among the Top 20 hospitals in the U.S. Postgraduate specialties: Advanced General Dentistry (AGED), Oral and Maxillofacial Surgery, Oral Biology, Pediatric Dentistry.

Annual tuition: $25,250; other expenses $2,653. On-campus facilities available for single students only. Apartments for married students can be found near the campus. Contact Admissions Office for both on- and off-campus housing information. Average cost of living in Boston is approximately $15,700.

Enrollment: 1st-year class 30. First-year enrolled student information: 30 from out of state; 10 states represented; 18 women; average age 23; 0 underrepresented minorities; 19 other minorities.

Degrees conferred: D.M.D., D.M.D.-M.P.H. (School of Public Health); D.M.D.-M.M.Sc., D.M.D.-M.P.P. (Kennedy School of Government); D.M.D.-Ph.D. (Massachusetts Institute of Technology); D.M.D.-M.D. (Oral and Maxillofacial Surgery at Massachusetts General Hospital).

RECRUITMENT PRACTICES AND POLICIES. School has diversity program and actively recruits women/minority applicants. Diversity contact: Associate Dean, Minority Affairs; phone: (617)432-4246.

ADMISSION REQUIREMENTS FOR FIRST-YEAR APPLICANTS. Preference given to state residents; U.S. citizens and permanent residents only. *Undergraduate preparation.* Suggested predental courses: 2 courses in biology with labs, 2 courses in inorganic chemistry with labs, 2 courses in organic chemistry with labs, 2 courses in physics with labs, 1 course in calculus, 2 courses in English (preferably composition). The junior-college transfer credit limit is 60 credits and all credits earned must be before an applicant enters the 3rd year of a baccalaureate program. Will consider applicants with only 3 years of undergraduate preparation; prefer applicants who will have a bachelor's degree prior to enrollment; all enrollees had bachelor's degree awarded prior to enrollment. *Application process.* Apply through AADSAS (file after June 1, before January 1), submit official transcripts for each school attended (should show at least 90 semester credits/135 quarter credit), service processing fee; at the same time as you send in AADSAS materials, submit an application fee of $50, a supplemental application, official transcripts, DAT scores (prefer April test of applicant's junior year), predental committee evaluation or 3 recommendations from college professors, high school transcript, and photograph directly to the Admissions Office. Interviews are by invitation only and generally for final selection. Joint-degree applicants must apply to, and be accepted by, both schools; contact the Admissions Office for current information and specific requirements for admission. First-year students admitted in fall only. Rolling admission process. Notification starts in December and is finished when class is filled. Applicant's response to offer due within 30 days if accepted prior to January 31; response due within 2 weeks if received after February 1. School does maintain an alternate list. Phone: (617)432-1443; E-mail: hsdmapps@warren.med.harvard.edu.

ADMISSION REQUIREMENTS FOR ADVANCED-STANDING APPLICANTS. There is no formal advanced-standing program. Contact the Admissions Office for current information.

ADMISSION STANDARDS AND RECOGNITION. *For D.M.D.:* number of applicants 795; number enrolled 30; median DAT: ACAD 21.9, PAT 18.2; median GPA 3.55 (A = 4), median sciences GPA 3.56 (A = 4). Gorman rating 4.93 (scale: very strong 4.51–4.99); ranked number 1 of all U.S. dental schools; the dental school's ranking by NIH awards was 14th among dental schools, with 14 awards/grants received; total value of all awards/grants $2,860,100.

FINANCIAL AID. Scholarships, minority scholarships, institutional loans, state loan programs, DEAL, HEAL, alternative loan programs, federal Perkins loans, Stafford subsidized and unsubsidized loans, and military service commitment scholarship programs are available. All financial aid is based on demonstrated need. Assistantships/fellowships may be available for combined-degree candidates. Contact the Office of Financial Aid for current information; phone: (617)432-1527. For most financial assistance and all need-based programs, submit FAFSA to a federal processor (Title IV school code # E00508); also submit Financial Aid Transcript, Federal Income Tax forms, CSS Profile, and Use of Federal Funds Certification. Approximately 66% of current students receive some form of financial assistance. Average award $29,189.

DEGREE REQUIREMENTS. *For D.M.D.:* satisfactory completion of 4-year program. *For D.M.D.-M.P.H., M.P.P., M.M.Sc.:* generally a 5–6-year program. *For D.M.D.-M.D., Ph.D.:* generally a 7–8-year program.

UNIVERSITY OF HAWAII AT MANOA
Honolulu, Hawaii
Internet site: http://www.hawaii.edu

Founded 1907. Located in Manoa Valley, a residential area of Honolulu. Public control. Semester system. Library: 2,860,000 volumes; 5,565,000 microforms; 22,840 periodicals/subscriptions; 105 PC work stations. The university's ranking in domestic higher education by NIH awards was 96th, with 38 awards/grants received; total dollars awarded $16,342,100.

The university's graduate division includes: College of Arts and Sciences, College of Business Administration, College of Education, College of Engineering, College of Health Sciences and Social Welfare, College of Tropical Agriculture and Human Resources, School of Architecture, School of Hawaiian, Asian and Pacific Studies, School of Library and Information Studies, School of Ocean and Earth Science and Technology, School of Travel Industry Management, William S. Richardson School of Law.

Total university enrollment at main campus: 18,270.

John A. Burns School of Medicine
1960 East-West Road, Biomed T-101
Honolulu, Hawaii 96822
Telephone: (808)956-8300; fax: (808)956-9547
Internet site: http://www.hawaii.edu
E-mail: niskikim@jabsom.biomed.hawaii.edu

Established 1965; expanded to 4-year program in 1973. Located on Manoa campus. Library: 73,000 volumes/microforms; 1,400 current periodicals/subscriptions. Affiliated hospitals/clinics: Kapi'olani Medical Center for Women and Children, Kapi'olani Medical Center at Pali Moni, St. Francis Medical Center, St. Francis Medical Center-West, Queen's Medical Center, Tripler Army Medical Center, Straub Clinic and Hospital, Kuakini Medical Center, Shriners Hospital, Kaiser Medical Center, Wahiawa General Hospital, Wai'anae Coast Comprehensive Health Center, Kalihi-Palama Health Center, Rehabilitation Hospital of the Pacific. Special programs: Postbaccalaureate program (Imi Ho Ola) for potential medical-school applicants (participation guarantees admission after 12-month program); phone: (808)956-3466.

Annual tuition: residents $10,584, nonresidents $24,288; fees $107.40. No on-campus housing available. Medical students live off-campus. Contact Admissions Office for off-campus housing information. Off-campus housing and personal expenses: approximately $8,700.

Enrollment: 1st-year class 58 (EDP 1); total full-time 234 (men 53%, women 47%). First-year statistics: 5% out of state; 42.7% women; average age 25; 86% minorities; 86% science majors.

Degrees conferred: M.D., M.D.-Ph.D. (Anatomy, Biochemistry, Biophysics, Genetics, Immunology, Microbiology, Molecular Biology, Neurosciences, Pharmacology, Physiology).

RECRUITMENT PRACTICES AND POLICIES. School has diversity program and actively recruits women/minority applicants. Diversity contact: Chair, Family Practice and Community Health; phone: (808)625-2499.

ADMISSION REQUIREMENTS FOR FIRST-YEAR APPLICANTS. Preference given to state and Pacific Islands residents; for serious consideration nonresidents should have ties to Hawaii. *Undergraduate preparation.* Suggested premed courses: 2 courses in biology with labs, 2 courses in general chemistry with labs, 2 courses in organic chemistry with labs, 2 courses in physics with labs, 1 course in molecular and cell biology with lab, 1 course in biochemistry, competency in English. Bachelor's degree from an accredited institution required; 96% of applicants have bachelor's degree awarded prior to enrollment. *Has EDP for state residents only;* applicants must apply through AMCAS (official transcripts sent by mid-May) between June 1 and August 1. Early applications are encouraged. Submit secondary/supplemental application, a personal statement that indicates what the applicant can contribute to the health professions in the Pacific, and 3 recommendations to Admissions Office within 2 weeks of receipt of supplemental application. Notification normally begins October 1. *Regular application process.* Apply through AMCAS (file after June 1, before December 1); submit MCAT (will accept MCAT taken within the last 3 years), official transcripts for each school attended (should show at least 90 semester credits/135 quarter credits, submit transcripts by mid-May to AMCAS), service processing fee. Submit an application fee of $50, a supplemental application, a personal statement that indicates what the applicant can contribute to the health professions in the Pacific, preprofessional committee evaluation, and 2 recommendations from science faculty to Admissions Office within 2–3 weeks of the receipt of supplemental materials. Interviews are by invitation only and generally for final selection. Dual-degree applicants must apply to, and be accepted by, both schools; contact the Admissions Office for current information and specific requirements for admission. First-year students admitted in fall only. Rolling admission process. Notification starts on October 15 and is finished in early April. Applicant's response to offer due within 2 weeks of receipt of acceptance letter. School does maintain an alternate list. Phone: (808)956-8300; fax: (808)956-9547.

ADMISSION REQUIREMENTS FOR TRANSFER APPLICANTS. Accepts transfers from other accredited U.S. and Canadian medical schools with a competency-based learning curriculum. Admission limited to space available. Contact the Admissions Office for current information and specific requirements.

ADMISSION STANDARDS AND RECOGNITION. *For M.D.:* number of state-resident applicants 263, nonresidents 1,066; number of state residents interviewed 184, nonresidents 62; number of residents enrolled 52, nonresidents 4; median MCAT (verbal reasoning 8.87; biological sciences 9.88; physical sciences 9.12); median GPA 3.43 (A = 4). Gorman rating 3.25 (scale: acceptable plus 3.01–3.59); the school's ranking by NIH awards was 111th, with 9 awards/grants received; total dollars awarded $2,725,181.

FINANCIAL AID. Scholarships, merit scholarships, minority scholarships, grants-in-aid, institutional loans, HEAL, alternative loan programs, NIH stipends, federal Perkins loans, Stafford subsidized and unsubsidized loans, and service commitment scholarship programs are available. Assistantships/fellowships may be available for dual-degree candidates. All financial aid is based on documented need. Only U.S. citizens and permanent residents are eligible for financial assistance. For merit scholarships, the selection criteria place heavy reliance on MCAT and undergraduate GPA. Contact the Office of Financial Aid Services for current information; phone: (808)956-7251. For most financial assistance and all federal programs, submit FAFSA to a federal processor (Ti-

tle IV school code # 001610); also submit Financial Aid Transcript and Federal Income Tax forms. Approximately 70% of current students receive some form of financial assistance. Average debt after graduation $27,200.

DEGREE REQUIREMENTS. *For M.D.:* satisfactory completion of 4-year program. All students must pass USMLE Step 1 prior to entering 3rd year; all students must pass USMLE Step 2 prior to awarding of M.D. *For M.D.-Ph.D.:* generally a 7-year program.

UNIVERSITY OF HEALTH SCIENCES
Kansas City, Missouri 64106-1493

College of Osteopathic Medicine
1750 Independence Boulevard
Kansas City, Missouri 64124-1493
Telephone: (916)283-2000, (800)234-4UHS
Internet site: http://www.ush.edu

Founded 1916; relocated to current location in 1921; in 1980 the name was changed. One of the oldest osteopathic colleges. Private control. Library: 77,000 volumes/microforms; 227 current periodicals/subscriptions; 15 computer work stations. College is affiliated with 26 hospitals and 18 clinics in Missouri, Michigan, Colorado, California, Florida, Ohio, Kansas, Arizona, and Texas. Special facilities: Education pavilion completed in 1996.

Annual tuition: $23,360. No on-campus housing available. Contact Admissions Office for off-campus housing information. Off-campus housing and personal expenses: approximately $12,300.

Enrollment: 1st-year class 220; total full-time 790 (men 74%, women 26%). First-year statistics: 84% out of state; 27% women; average age 28; 10% minorities; 61% science majors.

Faculty: full-time 35, part-time/volunteers 100.

Degree conferred: D.O.

RECRUITMENT PRACTICES AND POLICIES. School has diversity program and actively recruits women/minority applicants. Diversity Contact: Admissions Office.

ADMISSION REQUIREMENTS FOR FIRST-YEAR APPLICANTS. Preference given to state residents; U.S. citizens and permanent residents only. *Undergraduate preparation.* Suggested premed courses: 3 courses in biology, 2 courses in inorganic chemistry, 2 courses in organic chemistry, 2 courses in physics, 2 courses in English. Preference given to applicants who will have a baccalaureate from an accredited institution prior to enrollment; all enrollees had bachelor's degree awarded prior to enrollment. *Application process.* Apply through AACOMAS (file after June 1, before February 1); submit MCAT (will accept MCAT from last 3 years), official transcripts for each school attended (should show at least 90 semester credits/135 quarter credits), service processing fee. After a review of the AACOMAS application and supporting documents, a decision is made concerning which candidates should receive supplemental materials. Supplemental materials, an application fee of $35, a personal statement, 3 recommendations (1 from a D.O.), and a signed and dated Participation in Osteopathic Principles and Practices Laboratory form should be returned to Admissions Office as soon as possible. Interviews are by invitation only and generally for final selection. First-year students admitted in fall only. Rolling admission process. Notification starts in October and is finished when class is filled. Applicant's response to offer and $100 deposit due within 2 weeks of receipt of acceptance letter. School does maintain a waiting list. Phone: (816)234-4847; E-mail: admissions@stuser.uhs.edu.

ADMISSION REQUIREMENTS FOR TRANSFER APPLICANTS. Accepts transfers from other accredited U.S. osteopathic medical schools. Admission limited to space available. Contact the Admissions Offices for current information and specific requirements for admission.

ADMISSION STANDARDS. *For D.O.:* number of applicants 4,500; number enrolled 220; median MCAT 8.5; median GPA 3.37 (A = 4).

FINANCIAL AID. Scholarships, merit scholarship, minority scholarships, grants-in-aid, institutional loans, NOF, HEAL, alternative loan programs, federal Perkins loans, Stafford subsidized and unsubsidized loans, service obligation scholarship programs, and military and National Health Service programs are available. Most financial aid is based on demonstrated need. Financial aid applications and information are given out at the on-campus interview (by invitation). Contact the Financial Aid Office for current information; phone: (816)283-2000. For most financial assistance and all federal programs, submit the FAFSA to a federal processor (Title IV school code # G24524); also submit Financial Aid Transcript and Federal Income Tax forms. Approximately 98% of current students receive some form of financial assistance. Average debt after graduation $110,177.

DEGREE REQUIREMENTS. *For D.O.:* satisfactory completion of 4-year program. All students must pass the National Board of Osteopathic Medical Examination Level I and II prior to the awarding of D.O.

HOWARD UNIVERSITY
Washington, D.C. 20059-0002
Internet site: http://www.howard.edu

Founded 1867. Located in an urban area of NW Washington. Private control. Semester system. Library: 1,720,000 volumes; 1,453,000 microforms; 2,800 periodicals/subscriptions. Special facilities. Special programs: B.S.-M.D. program (annual undergraduate tuition $7,005). The university's ranking in domestic higher education by NIH awards was 102nd, with 30 awards/grants received; total dollars awarded $13,037,076.

The university's graduate colleges/schools include: College of Dentistry, College of Fine Arts, College of Medicine, College of Nursing, College of Pharmacy, Graduate School of Arts and Sciences, School of Architecture, School of Business, School of Divinity, School of Education, School of Engineering, School of Social Work.

Total university enrollment at main campus: 10,248.

Howard University Center of Health Sciences
2041 Georgia Avenue, N.W.
Washington, D.C. 20060

University hospital is a member of Council of Teaching Hospitals.

College of Medicine
520 W Street, N.W.
Washington, D.C. 20059
Telephone: (202)806-6270; fax: (202)806-7934
Internet site: http://www.med.howard.edu

Opened 1868; the oldest black medical school in the U.S. and the 36th-oldest medical school. Library: 265,000 volumes/microforms; 1,750 current periodicals/subscriptions. Affiliated hospitals: District of Columbia General Hospital, St. Elizabeth's Hospital, Walter Reed Army Medical Center, U.S. Naval Medical Center, Washington Veterans Administration Medical Center, Providence Hospital, National Rehabilitation Hospital, Washington Hospital Center, Prince George's Hospital Center. Special programs: Early Entry Medical Education Program (entrance after 3 years of undergraduate education).

Annual tuition: $15,500; fees $903. No on-campus housing available. A university-owned apartment complex is nearby. Contact Admissions Office for off-campus housing information. Off-campus housing and personal expenses: approximately $13,700.

Enrollment: 1st-year class 100; total full-time 454 (men 51%, women 49%). First-year statistics: 96% from

D.C.; 46.8% women; average age 26; 77% underrepresented minorities; 16% other minorities; 73% science majors.

Degrees conferred: M.D., B.S.-M.D., M.D.-Ph.D. (Anatomy, Biochemistry, Human Genetics, Microbiology, Pharmacology, Physiology).

RECRUITMENT PRACTICES AND POLICIES. School has a diversity program and actively recruits women/underrepresented minority applicants. Diversity contact: Assistant Dean for Students Affairs; phone: (202)806-7679.

ADMISSION REQUIREMENT FOR BACHELOR-M.D. APPLICANTS. High school prerequisites: 1 year of biology, 1 year of chemistry, 1 year of physics, 2 years of math, 4 years of English, 2 years of foreign language. Submit application, SAT or ACT, official high school transcripts with rank in class, and 3 letters of recommendation to the Admissions Office by December 1. Interview by invitation only. Rolling admission process. Notification normally begins February 1. Application fee $25. For current information and specific requirements for admission, contact the Center for Preprofessional Education; phone: (202)806-7231.

ADMISSION REQUIREMENTS FOR FIRST-YEAR APPLICANTS. Preference given to U.S. citizens and permanent residents only. *Undergraduate preparation.* Suggested premed courses: 2 courses in biology with labs, 2 courses in general chemistry with labs, 2 courses in organic chemistry with labs, 2 courses in physics with labs, 2 courses in college math, 2 courses in English. Bachelor's degree from an accredited institution required; 95% of applicants have bachelor's degree awarded prior to enrollment. Does not have EDP. *Application process.* Apply through AMCAS (file after June 1, before December 15); submit MCAT (will accept MCAT test results from the last 3 years), official transcripts for each school attended (should show at least 90 semester credits/135 quarter credits, submit transcripts by mid-May to AMCAS), service processing fee. Submit an application fee of $45, a supplemental application, a personal comment/statement, preprofessional committee evaluation, and 2 recommendations from science faculty to Admissions Office within 2–3 weeks of the receipt of supplemental materials. Interviews are by invitation only and generally for final selection. Dual-degree applicants must apply to, and be accepted by, both schools; contact the Admissions Office for current information and specific requirements for admission. First-year students admitted in fall only. Rolling admission process. Notification starts on October 15 and is finished when class is filled. Applicant's response to offer and $100 deposit due within 30 days of receipt of acceptance letter. School does maintain an alternate waiting list. Phone: (202)806-6270; fax: (202)806-7934.

ADMISSION REQUIREMENTS FOR TRANSFER APPLICANTS. Rarely accepts transfer applicants. Contact the Admissions Office for current information and specific requirements.

ADMISSION STANDARDS AND RECOGNITION. *For B.S.-M.D.:* number of applicants 25; number interviewed 15; number enrolled 10; median SAT 1,300, ACT 25–29; median GPA 3.7 (A = 4). *For M.D.:* number of D. C. resident applicants 46, nonresidents 5,943; number of residents interviewed 7, nonresidents 532; number of residents enrolled 3, nonresidents 108; median MCAT 8.0 (verbal reasoning 7.6; biological sciences 8.2; physical sciences 8.0); median GPA 3.10 (A = 4). Gorman rating 3.30 (scale: acceptable plus 3.01–3.59); the medical school's ranking by NIH awards was 89th, with 20 awards/grants received; total dollars awarded $8,823,957.

FINANCIAL AID. Scholarships, minority scholarships, grants-in-aid, institutional loans, HEAL, alternative loan programs, federal Perkins loans, Stafford subsidized and unsubsidized loans, and service commitment scholarship programs are available. Assistantships/fellowships may be available for joint-degree candidates. Most financial aid is based on demonstrated need. For scholarships, the selection criteria place heavy reliance on MCAT and undergraduate GPA. Contact the Financial Aid Office for current information; phone: (202)806-6388. For most financial assistance and all federal programs, submit FAFSA to a federal processor (Title IV school code # 001448); also submit Financial Aid Transcript and Federal Income Tax forms. Approximately 85% of current students receive some form of financial assistance. Average debt after graduation $63,208.

DEGREE REQUIREMENTS. *For B.S.-M.D.:* a 6–7-year program. *For M.D.:* satisfactory completion of 4-year program. All students must pass USMLE Step 1 prior to entering 3rd year; all students must pass USMLE Step 2 prior to awarding of M.D. *For M.D.-Ph.D.:* generally a 7-year program.

College of Dentistry
600 W Street, N.W., Room 2A-1
Washington, D.C. 20059
Telephone: (202)806-0400; (202)806-0354
Internet site: http://www.howard.edu

Established 1881 as a department in the College of Medicine. Located at the Center for Health Sciences. Special programs: pre-entrance enrichment summer sessions. Postgraduate specialties: General Dentistry, Oral and Maxillofacial Surgery, Orthodontics, Pediatric Dentistry.

Annual tuition: $12,500; fees $6,932. No on-campus housing available. A university-owned apartment complex is nearby. Contact Admissions Office for off-campus housing information. Off-campus housing, food, transportation, and personal expenses: approximately $11,616.

Enrollment: 1st-year class 84; total full-time 346. First-year enrolled student information: 31 from D.C.; 22 states represented; 50 women; average age 25; 52 underrepresented minorities; 16 other minorities.

Faculty: full-time/part-time/volunteers 160.

Degrees conferred: D.D.S., B.S.-D.D.S.

RECRUITMENT PRACTICES AND POLICIES. School has diversity program and actively recruits women/underrepresented minority applicants. Diversity contact: Associate Dean for Student Affairs; phone: (202)806-0336.

ADMISSION REQUIREMENTS FOR B.S.-D.D.S. APPLICANTS. For information and applications contact the Office of Undergraduate Admissions, Howard University.

ADMISSION REQUIREMENTS FOR FIRST-YEAR APPLICANTS. U.S. citizenship is not considered a requirement for admission. *Undergraduate preparation.* Suggested predental courses: 2 courses in biology with labs, 2 courses in inorganic chemistry with labs, 2 courses in organic chemistry with labs, 2 courses in physics with labs, 1 course in college math, 2 courses in English, 7–8 courses in nonsciences. Will consider applicants with only 3 years of undergraduate preparation; prefer applicants who will have a bachelor's degree prior to enrollment; 80% of enrollees had bachelor's degree awarded prior to enrollment. *Application process.* Apply through AADSAS (file after July 1, before March 1), submit official transcripts for each school attended (should show at least 90 semester credits/135 quarter credits), service processing fee. TOEFL may be required of an applicant whose native language is other than English. Submit the following materials only after being contacted by an admissions officer: an application fee of $45 (money order only), a secondary/supplemental application, official transcripts, official DAT scores, and predental committee evaluation or 2 recommendations from science professors to Admissions Office within 2 weeks of receipt of supplemental materials. Interviews are by invitation only and generally for final selection. First-year students admitted in fall only. Rolling admission process. Notification starts on December 1 and is finished when class is filled. Applicant's response to offer and $250 deposit due within 30 days if accepted prior to January 31; response and deposit due within 15 days if received after February 1. School does maintain an alternate/waiting list. Phone: (202)806-0500.

ADMISSION REQUIREMENTS FOR ADVANCED-STANDING APPLICANTS. Will consider transfer applicants from other accredited U.S. dental schools for entrance into the 2nd year only. Admission limited to space available. Contact the Admissions Office for current information and specific requirements.

ADMISSION STANDARDS AND RECOGNITION. *For D.D.S.:* number of applicants 1,407; number enrolled 84; median DAT: ACAD 15, PAT 14; median GPA 2.88 (A = 4); median sciences GPA 2.76 (A = 4). Gorman rating 4.04 (scale: strong 4.01–4.49); this placed the school in the Bottom 10 of all U.S. dental schools.

FINANCIAL AID. Limited scholarships, minority scholarships, grants-in-aid, institutional loans, state loan programs, DEAL, HEAL, alternative loan programs, federal Perkins loans, Stafford subsidized and unsubsidized loans, and military service commitment scholarship programs are available. Institutional financial aid applications and information are given to all accepted students with the letter of acceptance. For scholarships, the selection criteria place heavy reliance on DAT and undergraduate GPA. Contact the Financial Aid Office for current information; phone: (202)806-0374. For most financial assistance and all need-based programs, submit FAFSA to a federal processor (Title IV school code # 001448); also submit Financial Aid Transcript, Federal Income Tax forms, and Use of Federal Funds Certification. Approximately 77% of current students receive some form of financial assistance. Average award $18,500.

DEGREE REQUIREMENTS. *For B.S.-D.D.S.:* a 6-year program. *For D.D.S.:* satisfactory completion of 4-year program.

UNIVERSITY OF ILLINOIS AT CHICAGO

Chicago, Illinois 60680
Internet site: http://www.uic.edu

Created in 1992 by combining the resources and facilities of two University of Illinois campuses in Chicago; the 20-year-old University of Illinois Chicago Circle campus and the Medical Center campus in existence for over 100 years. Public control. Semester system. Special facilities: Anatomy Museum, Biologic Research laboratory, Institute for Humanities, Pathology Museum, Research and Education Hospitals, Neuropyschiatric Institute, Center for Molecular Biology and Oral Diseases, Engineering Research Facility, Environmental Stress Facility, Hispanic Center for Excellence, International Center for Software Engineering, Center for Pharmaceutical Biotechnology, Center for Urban Transportation, Center for Women's Studies, Survey Research laboratory. Library: 1,600,000 volumes; 225,000 microforms. The university's ranking in domestic higher education by NIH awards was 56th, with 227 awards/grants received; total dollars awarded $45,241,326.

The university's graduate college includes: College of Architecture and Art, College of Associated Health Professions, College of Business Administration, College of Education, College of Engineering, College of Liberal Arts and Sciences, College of Nursing, College of Urban Planning and Public Affairs, Jane Addams College of Social Work, College of Dentistry, College of Medicine, College of Pharmacy, School of Public Health.

Total university enrollment at main campus: 24,584.

Health Sciences Center

1740 West Taylor Street
Chicago, Illinois 60612

Public control. Library: 525,000 volumes; 67,000 current periodicals/subscriptions. University of Illinois Hospitals and Clinics is a member of the Council of Teaching Hospitals. Nationally recognized programs in AIDS, Cancer, Geriatrics, Gynecology, Endocrinology, Neurology, Otolaryngology, Rheumatology.

College of Medicine

808 South Wood Street, Room 165
CME Medical Center 783
Chicago, 60612-7302
Telephone: (312)996-5635; fax: (312)996-6693
Internet site: http://www.uic.edu/depts/mcam

Established 1881 as College of Physicians and Surgeons of Chicago. Name changed in 1900 to College of Medicine. College has campuses in Chicago, Urbana-Champaign, Peoria, Rockford; Chicago is the largest site. Affiliated hospitals: in Peoria—Methodist Medical Center, St. Francis Medical Center; in Rockford—Rockford Memorial Hospital, St. Anthony's Medical Center, Swedish-American Hospital; Urbana is affiliated with all hospitals in east/central region; in Chicago—University of Illinois Hospital, West Side Veterans Administration Hospital, Cook County Hospital, Mercy Hospital Medical Center, Christ Hospital, Ravenswood Hospital Medical Center, St. Francis and Michael Rees Hospital. Special programs: Medical Scholars Program (Urbana-Champaign); prematriculation summer sessions.

Annual tuition: residents $12,990, nonresidents $35,170; fees $1,318. On-campus rooms and apartments available for both single and married students at Chicago and Urbana. Contact the Office of Student Affairs or Campus Housing Office at each campus for both on- and off-campus housing information. Off-campus housing and personal expenses: approximately $10,958.

Enrollment: 1st-year class 300 (approximately 75–80 students enter UIC, Chicago (EDP 15); total full-time 1,252 (men 65%, women 35%). First-year statistics: 2% out of state; 41% women; average age 24; 27% minorities; 56% science majors.

Faculty: full-time/part-time/volunteers; about 4,000 at all 4 campuses.

Degrees conferred: M.D., M.D.-M.P.H., M.D.-M.S. (offered in Chicago and Urbana; independent study programs in Peoria and Rockford), M.D.-Ph.D. (offered in Chicago and Urbana; independent-study programs in Peoria and Rockford; Anatomy, Biochemistry, Biomedical Engineering, Biophysics, Cell Biology, Genetics, Immunology, Microbiology, Molecular Biology, Pathology, Pharmacology, Physiology).

RECRUITMENT PRACTICES AND POLICIES. School has diversity program and actively recruits women/minority applicants. Diversity contact: Associate Dean and Director of Urban Health Programs; phone: (312)996-4493.

ADMISSION REQUIREMENTS FOR FIRST-YEAR APPLICANTS. Preference given to state residents; U.S. citizens and permanent residents only. *Undergraduate preparation.* Suggested premed courses: 2 courses in biology with labs, 2 courses in inorganic chemistry with labs, 2 courses in organic chemistry with labs, 2 courses in physics with labs, 1 course in social sciences. Bachelor's degree from an accredited institution required; all applicants have bachelor's degree awarded prior to enrollment. *Has EDP* for state residents only; applicants must apply through AMCAS (official transcripts sent by mid-May) between June 1 and August 1. Early applications are encouraged. Submit secondary/supplemental application, a personal statement, and 3 recommendations to Admissions Office within 2 weeks of receipt of supplemental application. Interviews are by invitation only and generally for final selection. Notification normally begins October 1. *Regular application process.* Apply through AMCAS (file after June 1, before December 1); submit MCAT (will accept MCAT test results from 1995), official transcripts for each school attended (should show at least 90 semester credits/135 quarter credits, submit transcripts by mid-May to AMCAS), service processing fee. Submit an application fee of $30, a supplemental application, a personal comment/statement, preprofessional committee evaluation, and 2 recommendations from science faculty to Admissions Office within 2–3 weeks of receipt of supplemental materials, but not later than February 15. Interviews are by invitation only and generally for final selection. Dual-degree applicants must apply to, and be accepted by, both schools; contact the Admissions Office for current information and specific requirements for admission. M.D.-Ph.D. Web site: http://www.uic.edu./~jharmon/MDPHD_HOME.html. First-year students admitted in fall only. Rolling admission process. Notification starts on October 15 and is finished when class is filled. Applicant's response to offer and $100 deposit due within 2 weeks of receipt of acceptance letter. School does maintain an alternate/waiting list. Admissions Office phone: (312)996-5635; fax: (312)996-6693; E-mail: Med-admit@mailbox.comd.uic.edu. For Medical Scholars Program information contact Director, Medical Scholars Program, 190 Medical Sciences Building (MC-714), 506 South Matthews, Urbana, Illinois 61801, phone: (217)333-8146; fax: (217)244-7078. E-mail: mspo@ux1.cso.uiuc.edu; Web site: http://soma.npa.uiuc.edu/msp

ADMISSION REQUIREMENTS FOR TRANSFER APPLICANTS. Accepts transfers from other accredited U.S. medical schools. Admission limited to space available. Contact the Admissions Office after January 1 for current information and specific requirements.

ADMISSION STANDARDS AND RECOGNITION. *For M.D.:* number of state-resident applicants 2,125, nonresidents 3,481; number of state residents interviewed 218, nonresidents 71; number of residents enrolled 266, nonresidents 13; median MCAT 9.3 (verbal reasoning 9.3; biological sciences 9.3; physical sciences 9.2); median GPA 3.41 (A = 4). Gorman rating 4.41 (scale: strong 4.01–4.49); the college's ranking by NIH awards was 57th, with 156 awards/grants received; total dollars awarded $29,901,753.

FINANCIAL AID. Scholarships, merit scholarships, minority scholarships, grants-in-aid, NIH stipends, institutional loans, HEAL, alternative loan programs, federal Perkins loans, Stafford subsidized and unsubsidized loans, and service commitment scholarship programs are available. Assistantships/fellowships may be available for joint-degree candidates. Most financial aid is based on demonstrated need. For scholarships, the selection criteria place heavy reliance on MCAT and undergraduate GPA. Contact the Office of Student Financial Aid for current information and application procedures; phone: (312)413-0127; fax: (312)996-2467. For most financial assistance and all federal programs, submit FAFSA to a federal processor (University of Illinois at Chicago's Title IV school code is # 001776); also submit Financial Aid Transcript and Federal Income Tax forms. Approximately 80% of current students receive some form of financial assistance. Average debt after graduation $65,000.

DEGREE REQUIREMENTS. *For M.D.:* satisfactory completion of 4-year program. All students must pass USMLE Step 1 prior to entering 3rd year; all students must pass USMLE Step 2 prior to awarding of M.D. *For M.D.-M.P.H.:* generally a 5–6-year program. *For M.D.-M.S.:* generally a 4½–5½-year program. *For M.D.-Ph.D.:* generally a 7-year program.

College of Dentistry
P.O. Box 5220
Chicago, Illinois 60680-5220
Telephone: (312)996-2621

Established in 1898 as the Columbian Dental College. Joined the university in 1913. Located at health science center. Special programs: Urban Health Program; prematriculation summer sessions. Postgraduate specialties: Endodontics, General Dentistry, Oral Pathology, Oral Surgery, Orthodontics, Pediatric Dentistry, Periodontics.

Annual tuition: residents $7,866, nonresidents $22,624; fees $1,616; equipment and supplies $7,000. On-campus rooms and apartments available for both single and married students. Contact Director of Housing Office for both on- and off-campus housing information; phone: (312)355-6320. Dental students tend to live off-campus. Off-campus housing, food, transportation, and personal expenses: approximately $12,000.

Enrollment: 1st-year class 64. First-year enrolled student information: none from out of state; 32 women; average age 24; 6 underrepresented minorities; 23 other minorities.

Degrees conferred: D.D.S., D.D.S.-M.S., D.D.S.-Ph.D.

RECRUITMENT PRACTICES AND POLICIES. School has diversity program and actively recruits women/minority applicants. Diversity contact: Director of Urban Health Program; phone: (312)996-3547.

ADMISSION REQUIREMENTS FOR FIRST-YEAR APPLICANTS. Preference given to state residents; U.S. citizens and permanent residents only. *Undergraduate preparation.* Suggested predental courses: 2 courses in biology with labs, 2 courses in inorganic chemistry with labs, 2 courses in organic chemistry with labs, 2 courses in physics with labs, 2 courses in English, 9 courses in nonsciences. There is no limit to the number of junior-college credits taken. Will consider applicants with only 3 years of undergraduate preparation; prefer applicants who will have a bachelor's degree prior to enrollment; 98% of enrollees had bachelor's degree awarded prior to enrollment. *Application process.* Apply through AADSAS (file after July 1, before March 1), submit official transcripts for each school attended (should show at least 90 semester credits/135 quarter credits), service processing fee; at the same time as you send in AADSAS materials, submit application fee of $40 directly to the Admissions Office. Submit the following materials only after being contacted by an Admissions Officer: a secondary/supplemental application, official transcripts, official DAT scores (test results should be from the last 3 years), and predental committee evaluation or 3 recommendations from professors (recommendations should be sent directly to Dr. Donald Rice, College of Dentistry, M/C 6211, University of Illinois at Chicago, 801 S. Paulina Street, Chicago, Illinois 60612-7211) to Admissions Office within 2 weeks of receipt of supplemental materials. Interviews are by invitation only and generally for final selection. Dual-degree applicants must apply to, and be accepted by, both the College of Dentistry and the graduate college; contact the Admissions Office for current information and specific requirements for admission. First-year students admitted in fall only. Rolling admission process. Notification starts on December 1 and is finished when class is filled, generally not later than June 1. Applicant's response to offer and $100 deposit due within 30 days if accepted prior to February 28; response and deposit due within 2 weeks if acceptance received after March 1. School does maintain an alternate/waiting list. Phone: (312)996-1020.

ADMISSION REQUIREMENTS FOR ADVANCED-STANDING APPLICANTS. Accepts transfers from other accredited U.S. and Canadian dental schools who are state residents. Admission limited to space available. Contact the Admissions Office for current information and specific requirements for admission.

ADMISSION STANDARDS AND RECOGNITION. *For D.D.S.:* number of applicants 1,366; number enrolled 64; median DAT: ACAD 17, PAT 17; median GPA 3.27 (A = 4); median sciences GPA 3.31 (A = 4). Gorman rating 4.72 (scale: very strong 4.51–4.99); this placed the college in the Top 15 of all U.S. dental schools; the dental college's ranking by NIH awards was 27th among dental schools, with 7 awards/grants received; total value of all awards/grants $881,986.

FINANCIAL AID. Scholarships, Research Scholarship Program, grants-in-aid, institutional loans, state loan programs, DEAL, HEAL, alternative loan programs, federal Perkins loans, Stafford subsidized and unsubsidized loans, and military service commitment scholarship programs are available. Assistantships/fellowships may be available for combined degree candidates. For Research Scholarship Program (includes both tuition waivers and a stipend), the selection criteria place heavy reliance on DAT and undergraduate GPA. Contact the university's Office of Financial Aid for current information; phone: (312)996-5563. For most financial assistance and all need-based programs, submit FAFSA to a federal processor (Title IV school code # 001776); also submit Financial Aid Transcript, Federal Income Tax forms, and Use of Federal Funds Certification. Approximately 80% of current students receive some form of financial assistance. Average award for residents $19,000.

DEGREE REQUIREMENTS. *For D.D.S.:* satisfactory completion of 4-year program. *For D.D.S.-M.S.:* generally a 4½–5½-year program. *For D.D.S.-Ph.D.:* generally a 6–7-year program.

INDIANA UNIVERSITY–PURDUE UNIVERSITY INDIANAPOLIS
Indianapolis, Indiana 46202-2896
Internet site: http://www.iupui.edu

Located in an urban area of Indianapolis. Public control. Semester system. Library: 700,000 volumes; 970,000 microforms; 7,000 periodicals/subscriptions. The university's ranking in domestic higher education by NIH awards was 32nd, with 303 awards/grants received; total dollars awarded $73,972,092.

The university's other graduate schools: Herron School of Art, School of Business, School of Dentistry, School of Education, School of Engineering and Technology, School of Law, School of Medicine, School of Nursing, School of Public and Environmental Affairs, School of Science, School of Social Work.

Total university enrollment at main campus: 26,900.

Indiana University Medical Center
Located about 1 mile from the center of the city. Public control. University Hospital is a member of the Council of Teaching Hospitals. Schools located at medical center are: School of Allied Health Sciences, School of Dentistry, School of Medicine, School of Nursing. Hospitals/institutes located at medical center are: Robert W. Long Hospital, University Hospital, James Whitcomb Riley Hospital for Children, Psychiatric Research Institute.

Nationally recognized programs in Cancer, Cardiology, Gastroenterology, Gynecology, Neurology, Otolaryngology, Rheumatology, Urology.

School of Medicine
Fesler Hall 213
1120 South Drive
Indianapolis, Indiana 46202-5113
Telephone: (317)274-3772; fax: (317)278-0211
Internet site: http://www.iupui.edu/it/medschl/home.html
E-mail: inmedadm@uipui.edu

Established 1903. The School of Medicine's main campus is located at the medical center, and it is responsible for the Statewide Medical Educational System. The Statewide Medical Educational System has medical programs, for the first 2 years of basic medical instruction, at Bloomington, Evansville, Fort Wayne, Gary, Lafayette, Muncie, South Bend, and Terre Haute. Affiliated hospitals: Robert W. Long Hospital, University Hospital, James Whitcomb Riley Hospital for Children, William H. Coleman Hospital for Women, VA Medical Center, Laurie D. Carter Memorial Hospital. Library: 202,198 volumes/microforms; 1,849 current periodicals/subscriptions. Special programs: graduate programs for disadvantaged and underrepresented minorities; prematriculation summer sessions.

Annual tuition: residents $12,957, nonresidents $28,332; fees $198. Very limited on-campus housing available. Contact IUPIU Department of Campus Housing Office for both on- and off-campus housing information; phone: (317)274-7200. Medical students tend to live off-campus. Off-campus housing and personal expenses: approximately $10,476.

Enrollment: 1st-year class 280 (EDP 25, B.A.-M.D., approximately 10 each year); total full-time 1,110 (men 61.5%, women 42.5%). First-year statistics: 6% out of state; 41% women; average age 24; 17% minorities; 75% science majors.

Degrees conferred: M.D., B.A.-M.D. (Rural Health Program with Indiana State University), M.D.-Ph.D. (Anatomy, Biochemistry, Biophysics, Genetics, Immunology, Microbiology, Molecular Biology, Neurosciences, Pathology, Pharmacology, Physiology), M.D.-Ph.D. Purdue University (Engineering, Medicinal Chemistry, Molecular Biology, Neuroscience at Lafayette Center for Medical Education); has M.S.P. (Most students on Bloomington campus are involved in the M.S.P.)

RECRUITMENT PRACTICES AND POLICIES. School has diversity program and actively recruits women/minority applicants. Diversity contact: Assistant Dean, phone: (317)283-4065.

ADMISSION REQUIREMENT FOR B.A.-M.D. (RURAL HEALTH PROGRAM) APPLICANTS. This is a special program for up to 10 residents from rural areas. Contact the Director, Rural Health Program, Terre Haute Center for Medical Education, Indiana State University, for current admissions and financial aid information and specific requirements for admission.

ADMISSION REQUIREMENTS FOR FIRST-YEAR APPLICANTS. Preference given to state residents; U.S. citizens and permanent residents only. *Undergraduate preparation.* Suggested premed courses: 2 courses in biology with labs, 2 courses in general chemistry with labs, 2 courses in organic chemistry with labs, 2 courses in physics with labs. Bachelor's degree from an accredited institution required; all applicants have bachelor's degree awarded prior to enrollment. *Has EDP* for state residents only; applicants must apply through AMCAS (official transcripts sent by mid-May) between June 1 and August 1. Early applications are encouraged. Submit secondary/supplemental application, a personal statement, and 2 recommendations to Admissions Office within 2 weeks of receipt of application. Notification normally begins October 1. *Regular application process.* Apply through AMCAS (file after June 1, before December 15); submit MCAT (will accept MCAT from the last 3 years), official transcripts for each school attended (should show at least 90 semester credits/135 quarter credits, submit transcripts by mid-May to AMCAS), service processing fee. A supplementary packet is sent to all students who have passed the initial review. Submit an application fee of $35, the supplemental materials, a personal comment/statement, preprofessional committee evaluation, and 2 recommendations from science faculty to Admissions Office within 2–3 weeks of the receipt of supplemental materials. Interviews are by invitation only and generally for final selection. Combined degree applicants must apply to, and be accepted by, both schools; contact the Admissions Office for current information and specific requirements for admission. First-year students admitted in fall only. Rolling admission process. Notification starts on October 15 and continues on the 15th of each month until the class is filled. Applicant's response to offer and $100 deposit due within 3 weeks of receipt of acceptance letter. Phone: (317)274-3772; fax: (317)278-0211; E-mail: inmedadm@uipui.edu. *For M.S.P.* information contact: Program Director; phone: (317)274-3441; E-mail: wbasson@uipiu.edu.

ADMISSION REQUIREMENTS FOR TRANSFER APPLICANTS. Accepts transfers from other accredited U.S. and foreign medical schools who are state residents. Admission limited to space available. Contact the Admissions Office for current information and specific requirements for admission.

ADMISSION STANDARDS AND RECOGNITION. *For M.D.:* number of state-resident applicants 752, nonresidents 1,852; number of state residents interviewed 706, nonresidents 204; number of residents enrolled 269, nonresidents 11; median MCAT 9.7 (verbal reasoning 9.7; biological sciences 9.8; physical sciences 9.6); median GPA 3.69 (A = 4). Gorman rating 4.43 (scale: strong 4.01–4.49); *U.S. News & World Report* ranked the medical school in the Top 25 of all U.S. medical schools in primary-care programs; the medical school's ranking by NIH awards was 34th, with 195 awards/grants received; total dollars awarded $55,832,734.

FINANCIAL AID. Scholarships, merit scholarships, minority scholarships, grants-in-aid, institutional loans, HEAL, alternative Loan Programs, federal Perkins loans, Stafford subsidized and unsubsidized loans, and service commitment scholarships for primary-care medical programs are available for state residents only. Assistantships/fellowships are available for M.S.P. candidates. Financial aid applications and information are sent to all accepted students. Contact the Student Financial Services Office for current information; phone: (317)274-8568; E-mail: jespode@uipui.edu. For most financial assistance and all federal programs, submit FAFSA to a federal processor (Title IV school code # 001813); also submit Financial Aid Transcript and Federal Income Tax forms. Approximately 75% of current students receive some form of financial assistance. Average debt after graduation $57,200.

DEGREE REQUIREMENTS. *For M.D.:* satisfactory completion of 4-year program and a biomedical research paper. All students must pass USMLE Step 1 prior to entering 3rd year; all students must pass USMLE Step 2 prior to awarding of M.D. *For M.D.-M.S.:* generally a 4½–5½-year program. *For M.D.-Ph.D.:* generally a 7–8-year program.

School of Dentistry
1121 W. Michigan Street, Room 105
Indianapolis, Indiana 46202-5186
Telephone: (317)274-8173; fax: (317)274-2419
Internet site: http://www.iusd.iupui.edu
E-mail: ckacius@uisd.iupui.edu

Established 1879 as a private school; joined the university in 1925. Located at the Medical Center. Library: 48,000 volumes/microforms; 640 current periodicals/subscriptions. Affiliated hospitals: James Whitcomb Riley Hospital for Children, Regenstrief Health Center, University Hospital. Postgraduate specialties: Dental Materials, Dental Sciences, Endodontics, General Dentistry, Operative Dentistry, Oral and Maxillofacial Surgery, Orthodontics, Pediatric Dentistry, Periodontics, Preventive Dentistry, Prosthodontics.

Annual tuition: residents $10,650, nonresidents $22,810; fees $106; equipment and supplies $5,600. On-campus rooms and apartments available for both single and married students. Contact Associate Director of University Housing for both on- and off-campus housing information; phone: (317)274-5159. Dental students tend to live off-campus. Off-campus housing, food, transportation, and personal expenses: approximately $14,280.

Enrollment: 1st-year class 100. First-year enrolled student information: 40 from out of state; 19 states and 2 foreign countries represented; 34 women; average age 24; 3 underrepresented minorities; 17 other minorities.

Faculty: full-time/part-time/volunteers 250.

Degrees conferred: D.D.S., D.D.S.-M.S.D., D.D.S.-Ph.D.

RECRUITMENT PRACTICES AND POLICIES. School has diversity program and actively recruits women/minority applicants. Diversity contact: Associate Dean for Minority Affairs; phone: (317)274-5625.

ADMISSION REQUIREMENTS FOR FIRST-YEAR APPLICANTS. Preference given to state residents; U.S. citizens and permanent residents only. *Undergraduate preparation.* Suggested predental courses: 2 courses in biology with labs, 2 courses in inorganic chemistry with labs, 1 course in organic chemistry with lab, 2 courses in physics with labs, 1 course in anatomy, physiology, biochemistry, 2 courses in English. The junior-college transfer credit limit is 60 credits. Will consider applicants with only 3 years of undergraduate preparation; prefer applicants who will have a bachelor's degree prior to enrollment; all enrollees had bachelor's degree awarded prior to enrollment. *Application process.* Apply through AADSAS (file after June 1, before December 1), official transcripts for each school attended (prefer a total of 90 semester credits/135 quarter credits), submit service processing fee; at the same time as you send in AADSAS materials, submit official DAT scores (must take the October test in the year prior to anticipated date of enrollment) directly to the Admissions Office. TOEFL may be required of an applicant whose native language is other than English. Submit the following materials only after being contacted by an Admissions Officer: an application fee of $35 (nonresidents $55), a supplemental application, official transcripts, predental committee evaluation or 3 academic recommendations, and current photograph to the Admissions Office within 2 weeks of receipt of supplemental materials. Interviews are by invitation only and generally for final selection. First-year students admitted in fall only. Rolling admission process. Notification starts on December 1 and is finished when class is filled. Applicant's response to offer and $500 deposit due within 45 days if accepted December 1. School does maintain an alternate list. Phone: (317)274-8173; E-mail: CKACIUS@IUSD.IUPIU.EDU.

ADMISSION REQUIREMENTS FOR ADVANCED-STANDING APPLICANTS. Accepts transfers from other accredited U.S. and Canadian dental schools. Admission limited to space available. Contact the Admissions Office for current information and specific requirements for admission.

ADMISSION STANDARDS AND RECOGNITION. *For D.D.S.:* number of applicants 1,123; number enrolled 100; median DAT: ACAD 17.3, PAT 16.6; median GPA 3.19 (A = 4), median sciences GPA 3.11 (A = 4). Gorman rating 4.43 (scale: strong 4.01–4.49); this placed the school in the Top 20 of all U.S. dental schools; the dental school's ranking by NIH awards was 32nd, among dental schools, with 6 awards/grants received; total value of all awards/grants $618,557.

FINANCIAL AID. Scholarships, minority scholarships, grants-in-aid, institutional loans, state loan programs, DEAL, HEAL, alternative loan programs, federal Perkins loans, Stafford subsidized and unsubsidized loans, and military service commitment scholarship programs are available. Contact the university's Office of Student Financial Aid for current information; phone: (317)278-GRAD. For most financial assistance and all need-based programs, submit FAFSA to a federal processor (Title IV school code # 001813); also submit Financial Aid Transcript, Federal Income Tax forms, and Use of Federal Funds Certification. Approximately 86% of current students receive some form of financial assistance. Average award for residents $22,835, nonresidents $32,456.

DEGREE REQUIREMENTS. *For D.D.S.:* satisfactory completion of 4-year program. *For D.D.S.-M.S.D.:* generally a 4½–5½-year program. *For D.D.S.-Ph.D.:* generally a 6–7-year program.

UNIVERSITY OF IOWA
Iowa City, Iowa 52242
Internet site: http://www.uiowa.edu

Founded 1847. Located 125 miles E of Des Moines. Public control. Semester system. Library: 3,651,000 volumes; 5,613,200 microforms; 37,200 periodicals/subscriptions. The university's ranking in domestic higher education by NIH awards was 27th, with 329 awards/grants received; total dollars awarded $83,660,721.

The university's graduate college includes: College of Business Administration, College of Education, College of Engineering, College of Law, College of Liberal Arts, College of Nursing; College of Dentistry, College of Medicine.

Total university enrollment at main campus: 27,500.

Health Science Campus
200 Hawkins Drive
Iowa City, Iowa 52242

Public control. University of Iowa Hospital and Clinics is a member of Council of Teaching Hospitals. Schools located at health science campus: College of Dentistry, College of Medicine, College of Nursing, College of Pharmacy. Special facilities: Medical Research Center, Center for Health Service Research, Mental Health Clinical Research Center, Cardiovascular Research Center, Diabetes and Endocrinology Research Center, Cancer Center, Alzheimer's Disease Research Center, Center for Digestive Diseases. Nationally recognized programs in AIDS, Cancer, Cardiology, Endocrinology, Gastroenterology, Geriatrics, Gynecology, Neurology, Ophthalmology, Orthopedics, Otolaryngology, Pulmonary Disease, Rheumatology, Urology. *U.S. News & World Report*'s hospital/medical center national rankings for all hospitals placed University of Iowa Hospitals and Clinics in the Top 20 of all U.S. Hospitals.

College of Medicine
100 Medicine Administration Building
Iowa City, Iowa 52242-1101
Telephone: (319)335-8052; fax: (319)335-8049
Internet site: http://www.medadmin.uiowa.edu

Established 1850. Located at health science campus. Library: 260,521 volumes/microforms; 2,583 current periodicals/subscriptions. Affiliated hospitals: University Hospital and Clinics, VA Hospital. Special facilities: Center for Macular Degeneration, Center for Health Effects of Environmental Contamination, Center for the Study of the Brain and Language, Cooperative Human Linkage Center, Iowa Cystic Fibrosis Center, Iowa Geriatric Education Center, Iowa Specialized Center for Pulmonary Research, Schizophrenia Research Center, Specialized Center for Occupational and Immunological Lung Disease. Special programs: prematriculation summer sessions.

Annual tuition: residents $8,722, nonresidents $23,360; fees $930. On-campus rooms and apartments available for both single and married students. Annual housing cost: range from $275 to $700 per month. Married students contact Family Housing Office for housing information; phone: (319)335-9199. For off-campus housing information contact the Housing Clearinghouse; phone: (319)335-3055. Off-campus housing and personal expenses: approximately $10,273.

Enrollment: 1st-year class 175 (M.S.T.P. approximately 8–10 each year); total full-time 697 (men 56%, women 44%). First-year statistics: 20% out of state; 41% women; average age 23; 10% underrepresented minorities; 8.6% other minorities; 73% science majors.

Faculty: full-time/part-time/volunteers 737.

Degrees conferred: M.D., M.D.-M.S. (Anatomy, Biochemistry, Microbiology, Pathology, Pharmacology, Preventive Medicine and Environmental Health, Radiation Biology), M.D.-Ph.D. (Anatomy, Biochemistry, Genetics, Hospital and Health Administration, Microbiology, Molecular Biology, Neurosciences, Pharmacology, Physiology and Biophysics, Preventive Medicine and Environmental Health, Radiation Biology); has M.S.T.P.

RECRUITMENT PRACTICES AND POLICIES. School has diversity program and actively recruits women/minority applicants. Diversity contact: Program Associate for Equal Opportunity Programs; phone: (319)335-8056.

ADMISSION REQUIREMENTS FOR FIRST-YEAR APPLICANTS. Preference given to state residents; U.S. citizens and permanent residents only. *Undergraduate preparation.* Suggested premed courses: 2 courses in biology with labs, 2 courses in general chemistry with labs, 2 courses in organic chemistry with labs, 2 courses in physics with labs. Bachelor's degree from an accredited institution required; all applicants have bachelor's degree awarded prior to enrollment. *Has EDP* for state residents only, applicants must apply through AMCAS (official transcripts sent by mid-May) between June 1 and August 1. Early applications are encouraged. Submit supplemental application, a personal statement, and 2 recommendations to Admissions Office within two weeks of receipt of application. Notification normally begins October 1. *Regular application process.* Apply through AMCAS (file after June 1, before November 1); submit MCAT (will accept MCAT test results from last 5 years), official transcripts for each school attended (should show at least 90 semester credits/135 quarter credits, submit transcripts by mid-May to AMCAS), service processing fee. Submit an application fee of $20, a supplemental application, a personal comment/statement, preprofessional committee evaluation, and 2 recommendations from science faculty to Admissions Office within 2–3 weeks of the receipt of supplemental materials. Interviews are by invitation only

and generally for final selection. Most dual-degree applicants must apply to, and be accepted by, both schools; contact the Admissions Office for current information and specific requirements for admission. A separate M.S.T.P. application is required. First-year students admitted in fall only. Rolling admission process. Notification starts on October 15 and is finished when class is filled. Applicant's response to offer and $50 deposit due by March 1, if accepted after February 15 response and $50 deposit is due within 2 weeks. Phone: (319)355-8052; E-mail: medicaladmissions@uiowa.edu. M.S.T.P. contact: Director, M.S.T.P., phone: (800)551-6787; E-mail: mstp@uiowa.edu.

ADMISSION REQUIREMENTS FOR TRANSFER APPLICANTS. Transfers applicants are generally not considered. However, contact the Admissions Office for current information and/or change in policy.

ADMISSION STANDARDS AND RECOGNITION. *For M.D.:* number of state-resident applicants 407, nonresidents 2,320; number of residents enrolled 140, nonresidents 35; median MCAT 9.9 (verbal reasoning 9.7; biological sciences 10.1; physical sciences 9.6); median GPA 3.6 (A = 4). Gorman rating 4.40 (scale: strong 4.01–4.49); *U.S. News & World Report* ranked the college in the Top 25 of all U.S. medical schools in primary-care programs; medical ranking by NIH awards was 27th, with 259 awards/grants received; total dollars awarded $68,047,998.

FINANCIAL AID. Scholarships, merit scholarships, minority scholarships, grants-in-aid, institutional loans, HEAL, alternative loan programs, NIH stipends, federal Perkins loans, Stafford subsidized and unsubsidized loans, and service commitment scholarship programs are available. Assistantships/fellowships may be available for dual-degree candidates. Financial aid is based solely on documented need. Contact the Office of Student Financial Aid for current information; phone: (319)335-8059. For all financial assistance and federal programs, submit FAFSA, as soon as possible after January 1, to a federal processor (Title IV school code # 001892); also submit Financial Aid Transcript and Federal Income Tax forms. Approximately 95% of current students receive some form of financial assistance. Average debt after graduation $58,582.

DEGREE REQUIREMENTS. *For M.D.:* satisfactory completion of 4-year program. *For M.D.-M.S.:* generally a 4½–5½-year program. *For M.D.-Ph.D., M.S.T.P.:* generally a 7-year program.

College of Dentistry
311 Dental Science Building North
Iowa City, Iowa 52242-1010
Telephone: (319)335-9650; fax: (319)335-7155
Internet site: http://www.uiowa.edu
E-mail: elain-brown@uiowa.edu

Established 1882. Located at health science campus. Library: 18,000 volumes/microforms; 283 current periodicals/subscriptions. Special facilities: Dows Institute of Dental Research, Center for Clinical Studies, Center for Oral and Maxillofacial Implants, Oral Health Research Clinical Core Center, Research Center on Oral Health in Aging, Specialized Caries Research Center. Special programs: summer programs for underrepresented minorities. Postgraduate specialties: Dental Public Health, Endodontics, General Dentistry, Operative Dentistry, Oral and Maxillofacial Pathology, Oral and Maxillofacial Surgery, Oral Science, Orthodontics, Pediatric Dentistry, Periodontics, Prosthodontics, Radiology and Medicine.

Annual tuition: residents $6,852, nonresidents $19,178; fees $3,299; equipment and supplies $4,093. Limited on-campus housing available. Monthly housing cost ranges from $275 to $700 per month. Married students contact Family Housing Office for housing information; phone: (319)335-9199. For off-campus housing information contact the Housing Clearinghouse; phone: (319)335-3055. Off-campus housing, food, transportation, and personal expenses: approximately $10,273.

Enrollment: 1st-year class 73; total full-time 288. First-year enrolled student information: 18 from out of state; 12 states represented; 27 women; average age 24; 8 underrepresented minorities; 7 other minorities.

Faculty: full-time 94.

Degrees conferred: D.D.S., M.S., Ph.D., has D.S.T.P. (NIH-funded program).

RECRUITMENT PRACTICES AND POLICIES. School has diversity program and actively recruits women/minority applicants. Diversity contact: Assistant Dean for Student Affairs; phone: (319)335-7164.

ADMISSION REQUIREMENTS FOR FIRST-YEAR APPLICANTS. Preference given to state residents; U.S. citizens and permanent residents only. *Undergraduate preparation.* Suggested predental courses: 2 courses in biology with labs, 2 courses in inorganic chemistry with labs, 2 courses in organic chemistry with labs, 2 courses in physics with labs, at least 10 nonscience courses. The junior-college transfer credit limit is 62 credits. Will consider applicants with only 3 years of undergraduate preparation; prefer applicants who will have a bachelor's degree prior to enrollment; 77% of enrollees had bachelor's degree awarded prior to enrollment. *Application process.* Apply through AADSAS (file after June 1, before November 1), submit official transcripts for each school attended (should show at least 94 semester credits/145 quarter credits), service processing fee; at the same time as you send in AADSAS materials, submit official DAT scores (taken not later than November 1 of the year prior to the anticipated year of enrollment), a Statement of Financial Eligibility, and 3 letters of recommendation directly to the Admissions Office. TOEFL and TSE may be required of an applicant whose native language is other than English. Submit the following materials only after being contacted by an Admissions Officer: an application fee of $20, a final application, and official transcripts to Admissions Office within 2 weeks of receipt of request. Interviews are by invitation only and generally for final selection. First-year students admitted in fall only. Rolling admission process. Notification starts on December 1 and is finished when class is filled. Applicant's response to offer and $500 deposit due within 30 days if accepted prior to January 31; response and deposit due within 2 weeks if received after February 1. Phone: (319)335-7157; fax: (319)335-7155; E-mail: admissions@uiowa.edu.

ADMISSION REQUIREMENTS FOR ADVANCED-STANDING APPLICANTS. College does not have a formal advance-standing program. However, contact the Admissions Office for current information and any changes in policy.

ADMISSION STANDARDS AND RECOGNITION. *For D.D.S.:* number of applicants 1,037; number enrolled 73; median DAT: ACAD 18.0, PAT 17.0; median GPA 3.38 (A = 4), median sciences GPA 3.28 (A = 4). Gorman rating 4.38 (scale: strong 4.01–4.49); this placed the school in the Top 25 of all U.S. dental schools; the dental school's ranking by NIH awards was 13th among dental schools, with 12 awards/grants received; total value of all awards/grants $3,234,257.

FINANCIAL AID. Scholarships, dental research/teaching awards, minority scholarships, grants-in-aid, institutional loans, state loan programs, DEAL, HEAL, alternative loan programs, federal Perkins loans, Stafford subsidized and unsubsidized loans, and military service commitment scholarship programs are available. Institutional financial aid applications and information are sent to the applicant with the letter of acceptance. For scholarships an early completed application is strongly encouraged; the selection criteria place heavy reliance on DAT and undergraduate GPA. Contact the Office of Student Financial Aid for current information; phone: (319)335-1450. For most financial assistance and all need-based programs, submit FAFSA to a federal processor (Title IV school code # 001892); also submit Financial Aid Transcript, Federal Income Tax forms, and Use of Federal Funds Certification. Approximately 96% of current students receive some form of financial assistance. Average award resident $18,500, nonresident $27,850.

DEGREE REQUIREMENTS. *For D.D.S.:* satisfactory completion of 4-year program.

JOHNS HOPKINS UNIVERSITY

Baltimore, Maryland 21218-2699
Internet site: http://www.jhu/edu

Founded 1876. Private control. Semester system. Special facilities: Center for Astrophysical Sciences, Applied Physics Laboratory, Bologna Center (Italy), Carnegie Institute, Center for Communication Programs, Center for Social Organization of Schools, Center for Non-Destructive Evaluation, Institute for International Programs, Geology Field Station, Homewood Computing Center, McCollum-Pratt Institute, Nanjing Center (PRC), Oceanographic Research Vessels, Research and Training Center in Hearing and Balance, Women's and Children's Health Policy Center, Villa Spelman (Italy). Library: 2,337,000 volumes; 3,495,000 microforms; 13,950 periodicals/subscriptions; 248 PC work stations. The university's ranking in domestic higher education by NIH awards was 1st, with 941 awards/grants received; total dollars awarded $292,159,594.

The university's other graduate colleges/schools include: G. W. C. Whiting School of Engineering, Paul H. Nitze School of Advanced International Studies, Peabody Conservatory of Music, School of Arts and Science, School of Continuing Studies (Division of Business and Management, Division of Education, Division of Liberal Arts), School of Hygiene and Public Health, School of Medicine, School of Nursing.

Total university enrollment at main campus: 13,800.

Johns Hopkins Hospital

600 North Wolfe Street
Baltimore, Maryland 21287

Private control. Hospital is a member of Council of Teaching Hospitals. Nationally recognized programs in AIDS, Cancer, Cardiology, Endocrinology, Gastroenterology, Geriatrics, Gynecology, Neurology, Ophthalmology, Orthopedics, Otolaryngology, Pediatrics, Psychiatry, Pulmonary Disease, Rehabilitation, Rheumatology, Urology. *U.S. News & World Report*'s hospital/medical center national rankings for all hospitals placed Johns Hopkins Hospital in the Top 20 of all U.S. hospitals.

School of Medicine

720 Rutland Avenue
Baltimore, Maryland 21205-2196
Telephone: (410)955-3182
Internet site: http://infonet.welch.jhu.edu

Established 1893. Located in eastern Baltimore. Library: 354,000 volumes/microforms; 3,600 current periodicals/subscriptions. Affiliated hospitals: Johns Hopkins Hospital, Johns Hopkins Bayview Medical Center, Good Samaritan Hospital, Sinai Hospital of Baltimore, Francis Scott Key Medical Center, Kennedy Kieger Institute. Special Programs: Flexible Medical Admissions Program (Flexmed) provides qualified college juniors with early acceptance and college seniors with up to 3 years deferral.

Annual tuition: $25,890; fees $1,910. On-campus rooms available for single students only. Contact Housing Office for both on- and off-campus housing information; phone: (410)516-7960. Medical students tend to live off-campus. Off-campus housing and personal expenses: approximately $14,400.

Enrollment: 1st-year class 120 (EDP 5); total full-time 477 (men 53%, women 47%). First-year statistics: 85% out of state; 46 states and foreign countries represented; 43.7% women; average age 24; 13% minorities; 63% science majors.

Degrees conferred: M.D., M.D.-M.P.H., M.D.-M.S.E. (Biomedical Engineering), M.D.-Ph.D. (Anatomy, Biochemistry, Biological Chemistry, Biomedical Engineering, Biophysics, Cell Biology, Cellular and Molecular Medicine, Epidemiology, Human Genetics, Immunology, Microbiology, Molecular Biology, Neurosciences, Pathology, Pharmacology, Physiology); has M.S.T.P.

RECRUITMENT PRACTICES AND POLICIES. School has diversity program and actively recruits women/minority applicants. Diversity contact: Assistant Dean for Student Affairs; phone: (410)955-3419.

ADMISSION REQUIREMENTS FOR FIRST-YEAR APPLICANTS. Some preference given to state residents; U.S. citizens and permanent residents only. *Undergraduate preparation.* Suggested premed courses: 2 courses in biology with labs, 2 courses in inorganic chemistry with labs, 2 courses in organic chemistry with labs, 2 courses in physics with labs, 1 course in calculus, 6 courses in humanities and social and behavioral sciences. Bachelor's degree from an accredited institution required; all applicants have bachelor's degree awarded prior to enrollment. *Has EDP;* students apply directly to the Committee on Admission between June 1 and August 1. Early applications are encouraged. Notification normally begins October 1. *Regular application process.* Apply directly to School of Medicine (file after July 1, before November 1); applicants can submit an SAT, ACT, GRE, or the MCAT, whichever one represents his/her best standardized testing skills (the MCAT is not required, however, 98% submit it anyway), official transcripts for each school attended (should show at least 90 semester credits/135 quarter credits, submit transcripts by mid-May to AMCAS), application fee of $60, supplemental application, a preprofessional committee evaluation, a personal statement, and 3 recommendations from science faculty to Committee on Admissions. Interviews are by invitation only and generally for final selection. M.D.-Ph.D. degree applicants must submit an application supplement. Contact the Admissions Office for current information and specific requirements for admission. First-year students admitted in fall only. Rolling admission process. Notification starts on November 1 and is finished by March 31. Applicant's response to offer due within 3 weeks after receipt of acceptance letter. School does maintain an alternate list. Phone: (410)955-3184; E-mail: jhusom @som.adm.jhu.edu.

ADMISSION REQUIREMENTS FOR TRANSFER APPLICANTS. Accepts transfers from other accredited U.S. medical schools. Admission limited to space available. Contact the Admissions Office after January 1 for current information and specific requirements for admission.

ADMISSION STANDARDS AND RECOGNITION. *For M.D.:* number of state-resident applicants 324, nonresidents 3,515; number of state residents interviewed 71, nonresidents 594; number of residents enrolled 18, nonresidents 101; MCAT is not required; median GPA 3.8 (A = 4). *Barron's Guide* placed School of Medicine among the Top 25 most prestigious U.S. medical schools; Gorman rating 4.92 (scale: very strong 4.51–4.99); *U.S. News & World Report* ranked the School of Medicine in the Top 25 of all U.S. medical schools; not ranked in the Top 25 for primary-care programs; medical ranking by NIH awards was 1st, with 687 awards/grants received; total dollars awarded $210,303,176.

FINANCIAL AID. Scholarships, minority scholarships, grants-in-aid, institutional loans, HEAL, alternative loan programs, NIH stipends, federal Perkins loans, Stafford subsidized and unsubsidized loans, and service commitment scholarship programs are available. Assistantships/fellowships may be available for combined degree candidates. All financial aid is based on demonstrated need. Contact the Financial Aid Office for current information; phone: (410)955-1324. For most financial assistance and all federal programs, submit FAFSA to a federal processor (Title IV school code # E00235); also submit Financial Aid Transcript and Federal Income Tax forms. As there is no financial assistance for non-U.S. citizens, they are required to establish an escrow account to cover tuition, fees, and living expenses for the entire period of enrollment. Approximately 82% of current students receive some form of financial assistance. Average debt after graduation $60,400.

DEGREE REQUIREMENTS. *For M.D.:* satisfactory completion of 4-year program. *For M.D.-M.S.E.:* generally a 4½–5½-year program; 24 credits; thesis or internship. *For M.D.-Ph.D., M.S.T.P.:* generally a 7–8-year program.

UNIVERSITY OF KANSAS
Lawrence, Kansas 66045
Internet site: http://www.ukans.edu

Founded 1886. Located 40 miles W of Kansas City; 25 miles E of Topeka (the state capital). Public control. Semester system. Library: 3,379,000 volumes; 2,900,000 microforms; 32,500 periodicals/subscriptions; 250 PC work stations. The university's ranking in domestic higher education by NIH awards was 71st, with 133 awards/grants received; total dollars awarded $27,496,345.

The university's graduate school includes: College of Liberal Arts and Sciences, School of Architecture and Urban Design, School of Business, School of Education, School of Engineering, School of fine Arts, School of Journalism and Mass Communication, School of Pharmacy, School of Law, School of Medicine, School of Social Work. The School of Graduate Studies at the medical center includes: the School of Allied Health, School of Nursing.

Total university enrollment at main campus: 27,600.

University of Kansas Medical Center
3901 Rainbow Boulevard
Kansas City, Kansas 66160
Telephone: (913)588-5000
Internet site: http://www.kumc.edu

Public control. The University of Kansas Hospital is a member of Council of Teaching Hospitals. Schools located at medical center are: Graduate Studies, School of Allied Health Professions, School of Nursing, School of Medicine. Special facilities: Cancer Center, Center for Aging, Radiation Therapy Center, Center on Environmental and Occupational Health.

School of Medicine
3901 Rainbow Boulevard
Kansas City, Kansas 66160-7301
Telephone: (913)588-5245; fax: (913)588-5259
Internet site: http://www.kumc.edu/som
E-mail: hswick@kumc.edu

Established 1899 with a 2-year program; expanded to 4 years in 1906. Located at the medical center and also in Wichita. Library: 170,000 volumes/microforms; 1,500 current periodicals/subscriptions.

Annual tuition: residents $9,494, nonresidents $22,544; fees $310. No on-campus housing available. Contact Students Service Office for off-campus housing information; phone: (913)588-6580. Off-campus housing and personal expenses: approximately $12,278.

Enrollment: 1st-year class 176 (EDP 30); total full-time 699 (men 61.4%, women 38.6%). First-year statistics: 10% out of state; 39% women; average age 24; 10% minorities; 69% science majors.

Faculty: full-time 450, part-time/volunteers 1,100.

Degrees conferred: M.D., B.S.-M.D., M.D.-Ph.D. (Biochemistry, Cell Biology, Genetics, Immunology, Microbiology, Molecular Biology, Neurosciences, Pathology, Pharmacology, Physiology).

RECRUITMENT PRACTICES AND POLICIES. School has diversity program and actively recruits women/minority applicants. Diversity contact: Associate Dean for Minority Affairs; phone: (913)588-7285.

ADMISSION REQUIREMENTS FOR FIRST-YEAR APPLICANTS. Preference given to state residents and nonresidents with significant ties to Kansas; U.S. citizens and permanent residents only. *Undergraduate preparation.* Suggested premed courses: 2 courses in biology with labs, 2 courses in inorganic chemistry with labs, 2 courses in organic chemistry with labs, 2 courses in physics with labs, 1 course in calculus, statistics, or computer science, 1–2 courses in English. Bachelor's degree from an accredited institution required; all applicants have bachelor's degree awarded prior to enrollment. *Has EDP;* applicants must apply through AMCAS (official transcripts sent by mid-May) between June 1 and August 1. Early applications are encouraged. Submit secondary/supplemental application, a personal statement, and 2 recommendations to Admissions Office within 2 weeks of receipt of application. Interviews are by invitation only and generally for final selection. Notification normally begins October 1. *Regular application process.* Apply through AMCAS (file after June 1, before October 1; prefer that applicants apply by September 1); submit MCAT (will accept MCAT test results from 1995), official transcripts for each school attended (should show at least 90 semester credits/135 quarter credits, submit transcripts by mid-May to AMCAS), service processing fee. Submit an application fee of $40, a supplemental application, a personal statement, preprofessional committee evaluation, and 2 recommendations from science faculty to Admissions Office within 2–3 weeks of the receipt of supplemental materials. Interviews are by invitation only and generally for final selection. Combined degree applicants must apply to, and be accepted by, both the School of Medicine and the School of Graduate Studies; contact the Admissions Office for current information and specific requirements for admission. First-year students admitted in fall only. Rolling admission process. Notification starts on February 1 and is finished when class is filled. Applicant's response to offer and $50 deposit due within 2 weeks of receipt of acceptance letter. Phone: (913)588-8583.

ADMISSION REQUIREMENTS FOR TRANSFER APPLICANTS. Rarely accepts transfers applicants and then only into the 3rd year. Contact the Admissions Office for current information and specific requirements for admission.

ADMISSION STANDARDS AND RECOGNITION. *For M.D.:* number of state-resident applicants 450, nonresidents 1,486; number of state residents interviewed 319, nonresidents 56; number of residents accepted 189, nonresidents 34; number of residents enrolled 157, nonresidents 19; median MCAT 9.6 (verbal reasoning 9.6; biological sciences 9.7; physical sciences 9.4); median GPA 3.6 (A = 4). Gorman rating 3.87 (scale: good 3.61–3.99); the School of Medicine's ranking by NIH awards was 78th, with 72 awards/grants received; total dollars awarded $14,853,965.

FINANCIAL AID. Scholarships, minority scholarships, grants-in-aid, institutional loans, Kansas Medical Student Loan Program, HEAL, alternative loan programs, NIH stipends, federal Perkins loans, Stafford subsidized and unsubsidized loans, and service commitment scholarship or loan forgiveness for primary-care programs are available. Assistantships/fellowships may be available for combined degree candidates. The majority of financial aid is based on demonstrated need. Contact the Office of Student Financial Aid for current information; phone: (913)588-5170. For most financial assistance and all federal programs, submit FAFSA to a federal processor (Title IV school code # 004605); also submit Financial Aid Transcript and Federal Income Tax forms. Approximately 90% of current students receive some form of financial assistance. Average debt after graduation $61,630.

DEGREE REQUIREMENTS. *For M.D.:* satisfactory completion of 4-year program. All students must pass USMLE Step 1 prior to entering 3rd year; all students must pass USMLE Step 2 prior to awarding of M.D. *For M.D.-Ph.D.:* generally a 7-year program.

UNIVERSITY OF KENTUCKY

Lexington, Kentucky 40506-0032
Internet site: http://www.uky.edu

Founded 1865. Located in the bluegrass horse-farm region of central Kentucky. Public control. Semester system. Library: 2,556,800 volumes; 5,240,000 microforms, 26,000 periodicals/subscriptions; 1,000 PC work stations. The university's ranking in domestic higher education by NIH awards was 65th, with 202 awards/grants received; total dollars awarded $36,647,898.

The university's graduate school includes: College of Communication and Information Studies, College of Human Environmental Sciences, College of Nursing, College of Social Work; graduate programs from the Colleges of Agriculture, Allied Health, Arts and Sciences, Business and Economics, Education, Engineering, Fine Arts; College of Dentistry, College of Law, College of Medicine, College of Pharmacy.

Total university enrollment at main campus: 24,400.

University of Kentucky Chandler Medical Center

800 Rose Street
Lexington, Kentucky 40536

Founded 1956. Public control. University of Kentucky Hospital is a member of Council of Teaching Hospitals. Colleges located at Medical Center are: College of Allied Health, College of Dentistry, College of Medicine, College of Nursing, College of Pharmacy. Special facilities: Ambulatory Care Center, Center for Pharmaceutical Science and Technology, Center for Membrane Sciences, Critical Care Center, Gamma Knife Center, Graduate Center for Biomedical Engineering, Sanders-Brown Center of Aging, Lucille Parker Machey Cancer Center, Mills-Davis Magnetic Resonance Imaging and Spectroscopy Center, Neurosciences Institute, Bone Marrow Transplant Program, Center on Drug and Alcohol Abuse.

College of Medicine

800 Rose Street
Lexington, Kentucky 40536-0084
Telephone: (606)323-6161; fax: (606)323-2076
Internet site: http://www.comed.uky.edu/medicine

Established 1956. Located at the medical center. Semester system. Library: 172,000 volumes/microforms; 2,000 current periodicals/subscriptions. Affiliated hospitals: University of Kentucky Hospital, Veterans Affairs Medical Center, Kentucky Clinic.

Annual tuition: residents $8,793, nonresidents $20,923; fees $393. On-campus rooms and apartments available for both single and married students. Contact Admissions Office for both on- and off-campus housing information; phone: (606)257-3721. Annual housing and personal expenses: approximately $19,300.

Enrollment: 1st-year class 95 (EDP 30); total full-time 378 (men 64%, women 36%). First-year statistics: 10% out of state; 41% women; average age 25; 16% minorities; 61% science majors.

Faculty: full-time 525.

Degrees conferred: M.D., M.D.-M.S., M.D.-Ph.D. (Anatomy, Biochemistry, Biomedical Engineering, Biophysics, Cell Biology, Genetics, Immunology, Microbiology, Molecular Biology, Neurosciences, Pharmacology, Physiology).

RECRUITMENT PRACTICES AND POLICIES. School has diversity program and actively recruits women/minority applicants. Diversity contact: Assistant Dean for Admissions; phone: (606)323-6161.

ADMISSION REQUIREMENTS FOR FIRST-YEAR APPLICANTS. Preference given to state residents; U.S. citizens and permanent residents only. *Undergraduate preparation.* Suggested premed courses: 2 courses in biology with labs, 2 courses in general chemistry with labs, 2 courses in organic chemistry with labs, 2 courses in physics with labs, 2 courses in English, 1 course in college math. Bachelor's degree from an accredited institution required; all applicants have bachelor's degree awarded prior to enrollment. *Has EDP* for state residents only; applicants must apply through AMCAS (official transcripts sent by mid-May) between June 1 and August 1. Early applications are encouraged. Submit secondary/supplemental application, a personal statement, and 2 recommendations to Admissions Office within 2 weeks of receipt of application. Notification normally begins October 1. *Regular application process.* Apply through AMCAS (file after June 1, before December 1); submit MCAT (will accept MCAT test results from 1995), official transcripts for each school attended (should show at least 90 semester credits/135 quarter credits, submit transcripts by mid-May to AMCAS), service processing fee. Supplemental applications are sent to all Kentucky residents and to nonresidents with 3.75 GPA (A = 4) and MCAT scores of 10 or higher. Submit an application fee of $30, a supplemental application, a personal comment/statement, preprofessional committee evaluation, and 2 recommendations from science faculty to Admissions Office within 2–3 weeks of the receipt of supplemental materials. Interviews are by invitation only and generally for final selection. Dual-degree applicants should contact the Admissions Office for current information and specific requirements for admission. First-year students admitted in fall only. Rolling admission process. Notification starts after interview is completed and is finished when class is filled. Applicant's response to offer and $100 deposit due within 2 weeks of receipt of acceptance letter. Phone: (606)323-6161.

ADMISSION REQUIREMENTS FOR TRANSFER APPLICANTS. Accepts transfers from other LCME-accredited U.S. medical schools. Admission limited to space available. Contact the Admissions Office for current information and specific requirements.

ADMISSION STANDARDS AND RECOGNITION. *For M.D.:* number of state-resident applicants 513, nonresidents 1,353; number of state residents interviewed 303, nonresidents 61; number of residents enrolled 86, nonresidents 6; median MCAT 9.1 (verbal reasoning 9.0; biological sciences 9.3; physical sciences 9.2); median GPA 3.55 (A = 4). Gorman rating 3.65 (scale: good 3.61–3.99); the College of Medicine's ranking by NIH awards was 60th, with 155 awards/grants received; total dollars awarded $29,160,873.

FINANCIAL AID. Scholarships, minority scholarships, grants-in-aid, institutional loans, HEAL, alternative loan programs, federal Perkins loans, Stafford subsidized and unsubsidized loans, and service commitment scholarship (Rural Kentucky Scholarship Fund) programs are available. Assistantships/fellowships may be available for dual-degree candidates. Contact the Financial Aid Office for current information; phone: (606)323-6271. For most financial assistance and all federal programs, submit FAFSA to a federal processor (Title IV school code # E00588); also submit Financial Aid Transcript and Federal Income Tax forms. Approximately 85% of current students receive some form of financial assistance. Average debt after graduation $57,265.

DEGREE REQUIREMENTS. *For M.D.:* satisfactory completion of 4-year program. All students must pass USMLE Step 1 prior to entering 3rd year; all students must pass USMLE Step 2 prior to awarding of M.D. *For M.D.-M.S.:* generally a 4½–5½-year program. *For M.D.-Ph.D.:* generally a 7-year program.

College of Dentistry
Chandler Medical Center, Room D-155
800 Rose Street
Lexington, Kentucky 40536-0084
Telephone: (606)323-6386
Internet site: http://www.mc.uky.edu/dentistry
E-mail: tdennis@pop.uky.edu

Admitted 1st class in 1962. Postgraduate specialties: General Dentistry, Oral and Maxillofacial Surgery, Orofacial Pain, Pediatric Dentistry, Periodontics.

Annual tuition: residents $7,035, nonresidents $17,865; fees $1,176; equipment and supplies $4,890. On-campus rooms and apartments available for both single and married students. Contact Admissions Office for both on- and off-campus housing information. Annual housing, food, transportation, and personal expenses: approximately $10,600.

Enrollment: 1st-year class 52; total full-time 199. First-year enrolled student information: 16 from out of state; 12 states represented; 25 women; average age 24; 4 underrepresented minorities; 5 other minorities.

Faculty: full-time 56.

Degrees conferred: D.M.D., D.M.D.-M.D. (Oral Physician Program started in 1997).

RECRUITMENT PRACTICES AND POLICIES. School has diversity program and actively recruits women/minority applicants. Diversity contact: Office of Academic and Student Affairs; phone: (606)323-6386.

ADMISSION REQUIREMENTS FOR FIRST-YEAR APPLICANTS. Preference given to state residents; U.S. citizens and permanent residents only. *Undergraduate preparation.* Suggested predental courses: 2 courses in biology with labs, 2 courses in general chemistry with labs, 2 courses in organic chemistry with labs, 2 courses in physics with labs, 1 course in college math, 2 courses in English. No limit on the number of junior-college credits that can be taken. Will consider applicants with only 3 years of undergraduate preparation; prefer applicants who will have a bachelor's degree prior to enrollment; all enrollees had bachelor's degree awarded prior to enrollment. *Application process.* Apply through AADSAS (file after June 1, before December 1), submit official transcripts for each school attended (should show at least 90 semester credits/135 quarter credits), service processing fee; at the same time as you send in AADSAS materials, submit official DAT scores directly to the Admissions Office. Submit the following materials only after being contacted by an Admissions Officer: an application fee of $25, a supplemental data form, official transcripts, predental committee evaluation, and 2 recommendations from science professors, photograph, to Office of Academic and Student Affairs within 2 weeks of receipt of supplemental materials. Preference is given to applicants whose AADSAS applications and supplemental materials are received before January 1. Interviews are by invitation only and generally for final selection. Combined degree applicants will have to apply to both the College of Dentistry and the College of Medicine. Contact the Office of Academic and Student Affairs for current information and specific requirements for admission. First-year students admitted in fall only. Rolling admission process. Notification starts in December and is finished when class is filled. Applicant's response to offer and $200 deposit due within 30 days if accepted prior to January 31; response and deposit due with 2 weeks if received after February 1. School does maintain an alternate list. Phone: (606)323-6071; fax: (606)323-1042; E-Mail: tdennis @pop.uky.edu.

ADMISSION REQUIREMENTS FOR ADVANCED-STANDING APPLICANTS. College does not have an established advanced-standing program. Contact the Academic and Student Affairs Office for current information and specific requirements for admission.

ADMISSION STANDARDS AND RECOGNITION. *For D.D.S.:* number of applicants 1,102; number enrolled 52; median DAT: ACAD 17.0, PAT 16.2; median GPA 3.21 (A = 4), median sciences GPA 3.03 (A = 4). Gorman rating 4.07 (scale: strong 4.01–4.49); this placed the school in the Bottom 10 of all U.S. dental schools; the dental school's ranking by NIH awards was 38th among dental schools, with 1 award/grant received; total value of all awards/grants $103,083.

FINANCIAL AID. Scholarships, merit scholarships, minority scholarships, grants-in-aid, research fellowships, institutional loans, state loan programs, DEAL, HEAL, alternative loan programs, federal Perkins loans, Stafford subsidized and unsubsidized loans, and military service commitment scholarship programs are available. Most financial aid is based on demonstrated need. For scholarships, the selection criteria place heavy reliance on DAT and undergraduate GPA. Contact the Financial Aid Coordinator for current information; phone: (606)323-6071. For most financial assistance and all need-based programs, submit FAFSA to a federal processor (Title IV school code # E00587); also submit Financial Aid Transcript, Federal Income Tax forms, and Use of Federal Funds Certification. Approximately 80% of current students receive some form of financial assistance. Average award for residents $11,600, nonresidents $20,100.

DEGREE REQUIREMENTS. *For D.M.D.:* satisfactory completion of 4-year program; an 8-week summer externship in private practice. *For D.M.D.-M.D.:* a 6–7-year program.

KIRSKVILLE COLLEGE OF OSTEOPATHIC MEDICINE
800 West Jefferson Avenue
Kirksville, Missouri 63501-1497
Telephone: (816)626-2121; fax: (816)626-2483
Internet site: http://www.kcom.edu

Established 1892 by Andrew Taylor Still, the founder of osteopathic medicine, as the first school of osteopathic medicine in the U.S. College is located next to the Kirksville Osteopathic Medical Center and Diagnostic and Treatment Center. Private control. Library: 75,000 volumes/microforms; 1,000 current periodicals/subscriptions; 36 computer work stations. Special facilities: Rea Cancer Treatment Center. Special programs: Southwest Center for Osteopathic Medical Education and Health Sciences of Kirksville College of Osteopathic Medicine is located on the campus of Grand Canyon University in Phoenix, Arizona.

Annual tuition: $23,000; fees $1,000. Limited on-campus rooms and apartments available for both single and married students. Annual on-campus housing cost: single students $3,500 (room only), married students $4,000. Contact Office of Student Affairs for both on- and off-campus housing information. Medical students tend to live off-campus. Off-campus housing and personal expenses: approximately $15,000.

Enrollment: 1st-year class 145; total full-time 569 (men 70%, women 30%). First-year statistics: 85% out of state; 35% women; average age 26; 4% minorities; 79% science majors.

Faculty: full-time 82, part-time/volunteers 45.

Degree conferred: D.O.

RECRUITMENT PRACTICES AND POLICIES. School has diversity program and actively recruits women/minority applicants. Contact Admissions Office for current information.

ADMISSION REQUIREMENTS FOR FIRST-YEAR APPLICANTS. Preference given to U.S. citizens and permanent residents only. *Undergraduate preparation.* Suggested premed courses: 2 courses in biology, 2 courses in general chemistry, 2 courses in organic chemistry, 2 courses in physics, 1 course in college math, 2 courses in English. Bachelor's degree from an accredited institution required; all enrollees had bachelor's degree awarded prior to enrollment. *Application process.* Apply through AACOMAS (file after June 1, before February 1, early applications are encouraged); submit MCAT (will accept MCAT test results from 1995), official transcripts for each school attended (should show at least 90 semester credits/135 quarter credits), service processing fee. After a review of the AACOMAS application and supporting documents, a decision is made concerning which candidates should receive supplemental materials. The supplemental application, an application fee of $50, a personal statement, and 3 recommendations (1 from the premed committee, 1 from a science professor, and 1 from a D.O.) should be returned to Admissions Office as soon as possible. In addition, international applicants must submit foreign transcripts to the World Education Service for translation and evaluation. TOEFL may be required of those applicants whose native language is other than English. Interviews are by invitation only and generally for final selection. First-year students admitted in fall only. Rolling admission process. Notification starts in October and is finished when class is filled. Applicant's response and acceptance fee due within 2 weeks of receipt of acceptance letter. School does maintain an alternate list. Phone: (816)626-2237; fax: (816)626-2815; E-mail: admissions@fileserver7. KCOM.edu.

ADMISSION REQUIREMENTS FOR TRANSFER APPLICANTS. Accepts transfers from other accredited U.S., U.K., Canadian, and Australian osteopathic medical schools. Admission limited to space available. Contact Office of Admissions after January 1 for current information and specific requirements for admission.

ADMISSIONS STANDARDS AND RECOGNITION. *For D.O.:* number of applicants 4,577; number enrolled 145; median MCAT 9.1, total of all sections combined 28; median GPA 3.4, median science GPA 3.35 (A = 4); the school's ranking by NIH awards/grants was 4th among osteopathic schools, with 2 awards/grants received; total value of all awards/grants $296,622.

FINANCIAL AID. Scholarships, merit scholarships, predoctoral fellowships, institutional loans, NOF, HEAL, alternative loan programs, federal Perkins loans, Stafford subsidized and unsubsidized loans, service obligation scholarship programs, and military and National Health Service programs are available. Financial aid applications and information are generally available at the on-campus interview (by invitation). For merit scholarships, the selection criteria place heavy reliance on MCAT and undergraduate GPA. Contact the Financial Aid Office for current information as soon as possible after January 1; applications are not generally accepted after May 1; phone: (816)626-2529. For most financial assistance and all federal programs, submit FAFSA to a federal processor (Title IV school code # G02477); also submit Financial Aid Transcript and Federal Income Tax forms. Average debt after graduation $131,100.

DEGREE REQUIREMENTS. *For D.O.:* satisfactory completion of 4-year program. All students must take the National Board of Osteopathic Medical Examination Level I and II prior to the awarding of D.O.

THE LAKE ERIE COLLEGE OF OSTEOPATHIC MEDICINE

1858 West Grandview Boulevard
Erie, Pennsylvania 16509
Telephone: (814)866-6641; fax: (814)866-8123
Internet site: http://www.lecom.edu

Established 1992. Three-phase curriculum. Library: 5,400 volumes/microforms; 94 current periodicals/subscriptions.

Annual tuition: in state $20,500, out of state $21,500. No on-campus housing available. Contact Admissions Office for both on- and off-campus housing information. Off-campus housing and personal expenses: approximately $13,000–$16,000.

Enrollment: 1st-year class 132; total full-time 409 (men 64%, women 36%). First-year statistics: 38% out of state; 36% women; average age 26; 13% minorities; 73% science majors.

Faculty: full-time 32, part-time/volunteers 106.

Degree conferred: D.O.

RECRUITMENT PRACTICES AND POLICIES. School has diversity program and actively recruits women/minority applicants. Contact the Admissions Office for current information.

ADMISSION REQUIREMENTS FOR FIRST-YEAR APPLICANTS. Preference given to state residents; U.S. citizens and permanent residents only. *Undergraduate preparation.* Suggested premed courses: 2 courses in biology, 2 courses in inorganic chemistry, 2 courses in organic chemistry, 2 courses in physics, 2 courses in English, 2 courses in behavioral sciences. Bachelor's degree from an accredited institution required; all enrollees had bachelor's degree awarded prior to enrollment. For serious consideration, an applicant should have at least a 2.75 GPA (A = 4) in all premed courses. *Application process.* Apply through AACOMAS (file after June 1, before December 1); submit MCAT (will accept test results from last 3 years), official transcripts for each school attended (should show at least 90 semester credits/135 quarter credits), service processing fee. After a review of the AACOMAS application and supporting documents, a decision is made concerning which candidates should receive supplemental materials. The LECOM supplemental application, an application fee of $50, a personal statement, and a premed committee letter or 2 recommendations from science faculty, 1 recommendation from a D.O. and 1 general recommendation should be returned to Admissions Office as soon as possible, but not later than March 15. Interviews are by invitation only and generally for final selection. First-year students admitted in fall only. Rolling admission process. Notification starts in December and is finished when class is filled. Applicant's response to offer and $500 deposit due within 2 weeks of receipt of acceptance letter. School does maintain an alternate list. Phone: (814)866-6641.

ADMISSION REQUIREMENTS FOR TRANSFER APPLICANTS. Accepts transfers from other accredited U.S. osteopathic medical schools. Admission limited to space available. Contact the Admissions Office for current information and specific requirements for admission.

ADMISSION STANDARDS AND RECOGNITION. *For D.O.:* number of applicants 4,100, number enrolled 132; median MCAT 7.9; median GPA 3.3.

FINANCIAL AID. Scholarships, merit scholarships, minority scholarships, grants-in-aid, institutional loans, NOF, HEAL, alternative loan programs, federal Perkins loans, Stafford subsidized and unsubsidized loans, service obligation scholarship programs, and military and National Health Service programs are available. Financial aid applications and information are generally available at the on-campus interview (by invitation). For merit scholarships, the selection criteria place heavy reliance on MCAT and undergraduate GPA. Contact the Financial Aid Office for current information; phone: (814)866-6441. For most financial assistance and all federal programs, submit FAFSA to a federal processor (Title IV school code # G30908); also submit Financial Aid Transcript and Federal Income Tax forms.

DEGREE REQUIREMENTS. *For D.O.:* satisfactory completion of 4-year program. All students must pass the

National Board of Osteopathic Medical Examination Level I and II prior to the awarding of D.O.

LOMA LINDA UNIVERSITY
Loma Linda, California 92350
Internet site: http://www.llu.edu

Founded 1905. Located San Bernardino, Redlands area, about 5 miles from each city. Private control. The university is operated by the Seventh-Day Adventist Church, with approximately 40% of its student body belonging to other religious faiths. Quarter system. Library: 299,876 volumes; 74,224 microforms; 2,500 periodicals/subscriptions; 75 PC work stations.

The university's other graduate colleges/schools include: Graduate School, School of Allied Health Professions, School of Dentistry, School of Medicine, School of Public Health.

Total university enrollment at main campus: 3,391.

Loma Linda University Medical Center
11234 Anderson Street
P.O. Box 2000
Loma Linda, California 92354
Telephone: (909)824-0800

Opened 1967. Private control. The medical center is a member of Council of Teaching Hospitals. Facilities located at Medical Center are Loma Linda University Children's Hospital, Loma Linda University Community Medical Center, Loma Linda University Behavioral Medical Center; it is a Level 1 trauma center. Nationally recognized programs in Cancer and Gynecology.

School of Medicine
Loma Linda, California 92350
Telephone: (909)824-4467; fax: (909)824-4146.
Internet site: http://www.llu.edu

Established 1909. Quarter system. Library: 287,000 volumes/microforms; 2,753 current periodicals/subscriptions. Affiliated hospitals: Jerry L. Pettis Memorial Veterans Hospital, Riverside General Hospital, White Memorial Medical (Los Angeles), San Bernardino County General Hospital, Kaiser Foundation Hospital, Glendale Adventist Medical Center.

Annual tuition: $23,944; fees $805. On-campus rooms and apartments available for both single and married students. Contact Admissions Office for both on- and off-campus housing information; phone: (909)824-4510. Medical students tend to live off-campus. Off-campus housing and personal expenses: approximately $6,530 (dormitory), $9,200 (community housing).

Enrollment: 1st-year class 150 (EDP 10); total full-time 652 (men 63%, women 37%). First-year statistics: 45% out of state; 35% women; average age 25; 7% minorities.

Degrees conferred: M.D., M.D.-M.S., M.D.-Ph.D. (Anatomy, Biochemistry, Genetics, Immunology, Microbiology, Molecular Biology, Neurosciences, Pharmacology, Physiology), has M.S.T.P. (non-NIH funded).

RECRUITMENT PRACTICES AND POLICIES. School has diversity program and actively recruits women/minority applicants. Diversity contact: Assistant Dean for Clinical Education; phone: (909)824-4271.

ADMISSION REQUIREMENTS FOR FIRST-YEAR APPLICANTS. Preference given to Seventh-Day Adventist church members; U.S. citizens and permanent residents only. *Undergraduate preparation.* Suggested premed courses: 2 courses in biology with labs, 2 courses in inorganic chemistry with labs, 2 courses in organic chemistry with labs, 2 courses in physics with labs, 2 courses in English; will not consider CLEP credit. Bachelor's degree from an accredited institution required; 99% of applicants have bachelor's degrees awarded prior to enrollment. *Has EDP* for state residents only; applicants must apply through AMCAS (official transcripts sent by mid-May) between June 1 and August 1. Early applications are encouraged. Submit secondary/supplemental application, a personal statement, and 2 recommendations to Admissions Office within 2 weeks of receipt of application. Interviews are by invitation only and generally for final selection. Notification normally begins October 1. *Regular application process.* Apply through AMCAS (file after June 1, before November 1); submit MCAT (will accept MCAT test results from 1995), official transcripts for each school attended (should show at least 90 semester credits/135 quarter credits, submit transcripts by mid-May to AMCAS), service processing fee. Submit an application fee of $55, a supplemental application, a personal statement, preprofessional committee evaluation, and 2 recommendations from science faculty to Admissions Office within 2–3 weeks of the receipt of supplemental materials. Interviews are by invitation only and generally for final selection. M.S.T.P. and combined degree applicants must apply to, and be accepted by, both schools; contact the Admissions Office for current information and specific requirements for admission. Application fees for combined degree applicants will be waived if applications are received by November 1. First-year students admitted in fall only. Rolling admission process. Notification starts on December 1 and is finished when class is filled. Applicant's response to offer and $100 deposit due within 30 days of receipt of acceptance letter.

School does maintain an alternate list. Phone: (909)824-4467.

ADMISSION REQUIREMENTS FOR TRANSFER APPLICANTS. Accepts transfers from other accredited U.S. medical schools under exceptional circumstances. Contact the Admissions Office after January 1 for current information and specific requirements.

ADMISSION STANDARDS AND RECOGNITION. *For M.D.:* number of state-resident applicants 2,344, nonresidents 2,316; number of state residents interviewed 262, nonresidents 211; number of residents enrolled 86, nonresidents 73; median MCAT 9.6 (verbal reasoning 9.5; biological sciences 9.8; physical sciences 9.6); median GPA 3.63 (A = 4). Gorman rating 4.29 (scale: strong 4.01–4.49); the school's ranking by NIH awards/grants was 109th, with 14 awards/grants received; total dollars awarded $2,875,967.

FINANCIAL AID. Scholarships, minority scholarships, grants-in-aid, institutional loans, HEAL, alternative loan programs, federal Perkins loans, Stafford subsidized and unsubsidized loans, and service commitment scholarship programs are available. Scholarships/tuition waivers may be available for dual-degree candidates. All financial aid is based on demonstrated need and the Uniform Needs Analysis. For priority financial aid consideration, apply by April 15. Financial aid applications and information are given out at the on-campus interview (by invitation) and to accepted students. For scholarships, the selection criteria place heavy reliance on MCAT and undergraduate GPA. Contact the Student Finance Office for current information; phone: (909)824-4509. For most financial assistance and all federal programs, submit FAFSA to a federal processor (Title IV school code # 001218); also submit Financial Aid Transcript and Federal Income Tax forms.

DEGREE REQUIREMENTS. *For M.D.:* satisfactory completion of 4-year program. All students must pass USMLE Step 1 prior to entering 3rd year; all students must pass USMLE Step 2 prior to awarding of M.D. *For M.D.-M.S.:* generally a 5–6-year program. *For M.D.-Ph.D.:* generally a 6–7-year program.

School of Dentistry
Loma Linda, California 92350
Telephone: (909)824-4621; fax: (909)824-4211
Internet site: http://www.llu.edu
E-mail: dentao@comail.llu.edu

Established 1953. Located at medical center. Special programs: summer programs for underrepresented minorities; international dental program for dentists trained in other countries. Postgraduate specialties: Dental Anesthesiology, Endodontics, General Dentistry, Oral Implantology, Oral and Maxillofacial Surgery, Orthodontics, Pediatric Dentistry, Periodontics, Prosthodontics.

Annual tuition and fees: $23,511, equipment and supplies $7,000. On-campus rooms and apartments available for both single and married students. Annual on-campus housing cost: $6,000–$8,100; off-campus $8,000–$10,680. Contact Dean of Students Office for both on- and off-campus housing information; phone: (909)824-4510. Dental students tend to live off-campus.

Enrollment: 1st-year class 85. First-year enrolled student information: 17 from out of state; 9 states and 1 foreign country represented; 24 women; average age 25; 9 underrepresented minorities; 43 other minorities.

Degrees conferred: D.D.S., D.D.S.-M.S., D.D.S.-Ph.D. (Anatomy, Biochemistry, Microbiology, Pharmacology, Physiology).

RECRUITMENT PRACTICES AND POLICIES. School has diversity program and actively recruits women/minority applicants. Diversity contact: Office of Diversity; phone: (909)824-4787.

ADMISSION REQUIREMENTS FOR FIRST-YEAR APPLICANTS. Preference given to state and WICHE residents as well as graduates of Seventh-Day Adventist universities/colleges; U.S. citizens and permanent residents only. *Undergraduate preparation.* Suggested predental courses: 2 courses in biology with labs, 2 courses in general chemistry with labs, 2 courses in organic chemistry with labs, 2 courses in physics with labs, 2 courses in English. Will consider applicants with only 3 years of undergraduate preparation; priority given to applicants who will have a bachelor's degree prior to enrollment; all applicants have bachelor's degree awarded prior to enrollment. For serious consideration an applicant should have at least a 2.7 GPA (A = 4). *Application process.* Apply through AADSAS (file after June 1, before December 15), submit official transcripts for each school attended (should show at least 90 semester credits/135 quarter credits); service processing fee; at the same time as you send in AADSAS materials, submit official DAT scores directly to the Admissions Office. TOEFL may be required of an applicant whose native language is other than English. Submit the following materials only after being contacted by an Admissions Officer: an application fee of $50, a supplemental application,

official transcripts, and predental committee evaluation or 3 recommendations from professors in your major field of study to Admissions Office within 2 weeks of receipt of supplemental materials. Interviews are by invitation only and generally for final selection. Combined degree applicants must apply to, and be accepted by, the Biomedical Advisory Committee. Contact the Admissions Office for current information and specific requirements for admission. First-year students admitted in fall only. Rolling admission process. Notification starts in December and is finished when class is filled. Applicant's response to offer and $1,000 deposit due within 2 weeks of the receipt of letter of acceptance. Phone: (909)824-4221, (800)422-4558; fax: (909)824-4211.

ADMISSION REQUIREMENTS FOR ADVANCED-STANDING APPLICANTS. Accepts transfers from other accredited U.S. dental schools. Admission limited to space available. There is advanced-standing program for graduates of foreign schools of dentistry. Contact the Admissions Office for current information and specific requirements for admission.

ADMISSION STANDARDS AND RECOGNITION. *For D.D.S.:* number of applicants 1,524; number enrolled 85; median DAT: ACAD 17.2, PAT 17.8; median GPA 3.19 (A = 4), median sciences GPA 3.05 (A = 4). Gorman rating 4.29 (scale: strong 4.01–4.49); this placed the school in the Top 35 of all U.S. dental schools.

FINANCIAL AID. Scholarships, merit scholarships, minority scholarships, grants-in-aid, institutional loans, state loan programs, DEAL, HEAL, alternative loan programs, federal Perkins loans, Stafford subsidized and unsubsidized loans, and military service commitment scholarship programs are available. Assistantships/fellowships may be available for combined degree candidates. All financial aid is based on documented need. For merit scholarships, the selection criteria place heavy reliance on DAT and undergraduate GPA. Contact the Financial Aid Office for current information; phone: (909)824-4509. For most financial assistance and all need-based programs, submit FAFSA to a federal processor (Title IV school code # 001218); also submit Financial Aid Transcript, Federal Income Tax forms, and Use of Federal Funds Certification. Approximately 81% of current students receive some form of financial assistance. Average award $28,957.

DEGREE REQUIREMENTS. *For D.D.S.:* satisfactory completion of 4-year program; must successfully complete parts I and II of national boards. *For D.D.S.-M.S.:*

generally a 5–5½-year program. *For D.D.S.-Ph.D.:* generally a 6–7-year program.

LOUISIANA STATE UNIVERSITY MEDICAL CENTER

New Orleans, Louisiana 70112-2223
Internet site: http://www.lsumc.edu

Founded 1967. Public control. Semester system. Library: 320,000 volumes; 8,599 microforms; 3,528 periodicals/subscriptions; 24 PC work stations. Special facilities: Pennington Biomedical Research Center, LSU Eye Center. The medical center's ranking in domestic higher education by NIH awards/grants was 99th, with 81 awards/grants received; total dollars awarded $14,179,539. The Medical center and LSU Hospital (Shreveport) are both members of Council of Teaching Hospitals. Other schools located at medical center are: School of Allied Health Professions, School of Dentistry, School of Graduate Studies, School of Medicine, School of Nursing.

Total enrollment at university's medical centers: 2,965.

School of Medicine in New Orleans

1901 Perdido Street, Box P3-4
New Orleans, Louisiana 70112-1393
Telephone: (504)568-6262; fax: (504)586-7712
Internet site: http://www.lsumc.edu

Established 1966. Library: 258,000 volumes/microforms; 3,400 current periodicals/subscriptions. Affiliated hospitals: Medical Center of Louisiana at New Orleans (Charity Hospital) University Hospital, Mercy Baptist Hospital (Baton Rouge). Special programs: Summer programs for underrepresented minorities; prematriculation summer sessions.

Annual tuition: residents $6,776, nonresidents $14,676; fees $150. On-campus rooms and apartments available for both single and married students. Annual on-campus living expenses: approximately $9,000. Contact Housing Office for both on- and off-campus housing information; phone: (504)568-6260.

Enrollment: 1st-year class 165 (EDP 8); total full-time 720 (men 57.1%, women 42.9%). First-year statistics: none from out of state; 38% women; average age 24; 31% minorities; 78% science majors.

Faculty: full-time 550, part-time/volunteers 1,500.

Degrees conferred: M.D., M.D.-M.P.H., M.D.-Ph.D. (Anatomy, Biochemistry, Cell Biology, Genetics, Immunology, Microbiology, Molecular Biology, Neurosciences, Pathology, Pharmacology, Physiology).

RECRUITMENT PRACTICES AND POLICIES. School has diversity program and actively recruits women/minority applicants. Diversity contact: Assistant Dean, Minority Affairs; phone: (504)568-8501.

ADMISSION REQUIREMENTS FOR FIRST-YEAR APPLICANTS. Accepts only state residents who are U.S. citizens or permanent residents. *Undergraduate preparation.* Suggested premed courses: 2 courses in biology with labs, 2 courses in inorganic chemistry with labs, 2 courses in organic chemistry with labs, 2 courses in physics with labs, proficiency in spoken and written English required. Bachelor's degree from an accredited institution required; 95% of applicants have bachelor's degree awarded prior to enrollment. *Has EDP* for state residents only; applicants must apply through AMCAS (official transcripts sent by mid-May) between June 1 and August 1. Early applications are encouraged. Submit secondary/supplemental application, a personal statement, and 2 recommendations to Admissions Office within 2 weeks of receipt of application. Interviews are by invitation only and generally for final selection. Notification normally begins October 1. *Regular application process.* Apply through AMCAS (file after June 1, before November 1); submit MCAT (will accept MCAT test results from the last 3 years), official transcripts for each school attended (should show at least 90 semester credits/135 quarter credits, submit transcripts by mid-May to AMCAS), service processing fee. Submit an application fee of $50, a supplemental application, a personal statement, preprofessional committee evaluation, and 2 recommendations from science faculty to Admissions Office within 2–3 weeks of the receipt of supplemental materials. Interviews are by invitation only and generally for final selection. Dual-degree applicants must apply to, and be accepted by, both schools; contact the Admissions Office for current information and specific requirements for admission. First-year students admitted in fall only. Rolling admission process. Notification starts on October 15 and is finished when class is filled. Applicant's response to offer and $100 deposit due within 2 weeks of receipt of acceptance letter. School does maintain an alternate list. Phone: (504)568-6262; fax: (504)568-7701; E-mail: web@lsumc.edu.

ADMISSION REQUIREMENTS FOR TRANSFER APPLICANTS. Accepts both resident and nonresident transfers from other accredited U.S. medical schools. Admission limited to space available. Contact the Admissions Office for current information and specific requirements.

ADMISSION STANDARDS AND RECOGNITION. *For M.D.:* number of state-resident applicants 889, nonresidents 389; number of state residents interviewed 164, nonresidents 1; number of residents enrolled 164, nonresidents 1; special program with University of New Orleans; median MCAT 9.3 (verbal reasoning 9.3; biological sciences 9.7; physical sciences 9.0); median GPA 3.4 (A = 4). Gorman rating 3.68 (scale: good 3.61–3.99); the medical school's ranking by NIH awards was 68th, with 133 awards/grants received; total dollars awarded $21,665,379.

FINANCIAL AID. Scholarships, merit scholarships, minority scholarships, grants-in-aid, state and institutional loans, HEAL, alternative loan programs, NIH stipends, federal Perkins loans, Stafford subsidized and unsubsidized loans, and service commitment scholarship programs are available. Stipends/tuition waivers may be available for combined degree candidates. Financial aid applications and information are given out at the oncampus interview (by invitation). For merit scholarships, the selection criteria place heavy reliance on MCAT and undergraduate GPA. Contact the Student Financial Aid Office for current information; phone: (504)568-4820. For most financial assistance and all federal programs, submit FAFSA to a federal processor (Title IV school code # 002014); also submit Financial Aid Transcript and Federal Income Tax forms.

DEGREE REQUIREMENTS. *For M.D.:* satisfactory completion of 4-year program. All students must pass USMLE Step 1 prior to entering 3rd year; all students must pass USMLE Step 2 prior to awarding of M.D. *For M.D.-M.P.H.:* generally a 5–6-year program. *For M.D.-Ph.D.:* generally a 7–8-year program.

School of Dentistry
1100 Florida Avenue
New Orleans, Louisiana 90119-2799
Telephone: (504)619-8579; fax: (504)619-8740
Internet site: http://www.lsusd.lsumc.edu

Established 1968. Located at the medical center. Special facilities: Center for Clinical Dental Research. Special programs: Summer externship program sessions.

Annual tuition: residents $5,736; fees $1,590; equipment and supplies $3,204. On-campus rooms and apartments available for both single and married students. Annual housing, food, transportation, and personal expenses: approximately $9,810. Contact Admissions Office for both on- and off-campus housing information.

Enrollment: 1st-year class 55. First-year enrolled student information: 1 from out of state; 22 women; average age 24; 2 underrepresented minorities; 5 other minorities.

Degree conferred: D.D.S.

RECRUITMENT PRACTICES AND POLICIES. School has diversity program and actively recruits women/minority applicants. Diversity contact: Admissions Office.

ADMISSION REQUIREMENTS FOR FIRST-YEAR APPLICANTS. Admission consideration limited to Louisiana and Arkansas residents; U.S. citizens and permanent residents only. *Undergraduate preparation.* Suggested predental courses: 2 courses in biology with labs, 2 courses in inorganic chemistry with labs, 2 courses in organic chemistry with labs, 2 courses in physics with labs, 1 course in college math, 2 courses in English. The junior-college transfer credit limit is 60 credits. Will consider applicants with only 3 years of undergraduate preparation; prefer applicants who will have a bachelor's degree prior to enrollment; all enrollees had bachelor's degree awarded prior to enrollment. *Application process.* Apply directly to School of Dentistry after September 1, before February 28. Submit a School of Dentistry application, official transcripts for each school attended (should show at least 90 semester credits/135 quarter credits), official DAT scores, predental committee evaluation or 2 recommendations from professors in your major field of study, and photograph to Admissions Office. Interviews are by invitation only and generally for final selection. First-year students admitted in fall only. Rolling admission process. Notification starts on December 1 and is finished when class is filled, but generally not later than June 15. Applicant's response to offer and $200 deposit due 15 days after the receipt of acceptance. Phone: (504)619-8579.

ADMISSION REQUIREMENTS FOR ADVANCED-STANDING APPLICANTS. Accepts transfers from other accredited U.S. dental schools who are residents of Louisiana and Arkansas. Admission limited to space available. Contact the Admissions Office for current information and specific requirements.

ADMISSION STANDARDS AND RECOGNITION. *For D.D.S.:* number of applicants 161; number enrolled 55; median DAT: ACAD 16.8, PAT 15.6; median GPA 3.36 (A = 4), median sciences GPA 3.32 (A = 4). Gorman rating 4.21 (scale: strong 4.01–4.49); this placed the school in the Top 35 of all U.S. dental schools; the dental school's ranking by NIH awards/grants was 36th among dental schools, with 2 awards/grants received; total value of all awards/grants $261,267.

FINANCIAL AID. Scholarships, merit scholarships, minority scholarships, grants-in-aid, institutional loans, state loan programs, DEAL, HEAL, alternative loan programs, federal Perkins loans, Stafford subsidized and unsubsidized loans, and military service commitment scholarship programs are available. Institutional financial aid applications and current information are available at the on-campus interview (by invitation). For merit scholarships, the selection criteria place heavy reliance on DAT and undergraduate GPA. Contact the medical center's Office of Financial Aid for current information; phone: (504)619-8556. For most financial assistance and all need-based programs, submit FAFSA to a federal processor (Title IV school code # 002014); also submit Financial Aid Transcript, Federal Income Tax forms, and Use of Federal Funds Certification. Approximately 79% of current students receive some form of financial assistance. Average award for residents $18,524, nonresidents $14,000.

DEGREE REQUIREMENTS. *For D.D.S.:* satisfactory completion of 4-year program.

Louisiana State University Hospital
1541 Kings Highway
P.O. Box 33932
Shreveport, Louisiana 71130

Public control. Hospital is a member of Council of Teaching Hospitals. The schools located at LSU Hospital are the School of Graduate Studies and the School of Medicine.

School of Medicine
P.O. Box 33932
1501 Kings Highway
Shreveport, Louisiana 91130-39932
Telephone: (318)675-5190; fax: (318)675-5244
Internet site: http://lib-sh.lsumc.edu
E-mail: shvadm@lsumc.edu

Established 1969. Library: 98,000 volumes/microforms; 1,300 current periodicals/subscriptions. Affiliated hospitals: LSU Hospital, Shreveport VA Hospital, E. A. Conway Hospital (Monroe, Louisiana).

Annual tuition: residents none, nonresidents $7,900; fees $8,125. No on-campus rooms and apartments available for both single and married students. Contact Admissions Office for off-campus housing information. Off-campus housing and personal expenses: approximately $13,940.

Enrollment: 1st-year class 100 (EDP 5); total full-time 400 (men 65.5%, women 34.5%). First-year statistics: none from out of state; 24 institutions represented; 41.6% women; average age 25; 16% minorities; 64% science majors.

Degrees conferred: M.D., M.D.-Ph.D. (Anatomy, Biochemistry, Microbiology, Pharmacology, Physiology).

RECRUITMENT PRACTICES AND POLICIES. School has diversity program and actively recruits women/minority applicants. Diversity contact: Director, Multi-Cultural Affairs; phone: (318)675-5050.

ADMISSION REQUIREMENTS FOR FIRST-YEAR APPLICANTS. Accepts state residents only who are U.S. citizens or permanent residents. *Undergraduate preparation.* Suggested premed courses: 2 courses in biology with labs, 2 courses in inorganic chemistry with labs, 2 courses in organic chemistry with labs, 2 courses in physics with labs, 2 courses in English. Bachelor's degree from an accredited institution required; 95% of applicants have bachelor's degree awarded prior to enrollment. *Has EDP;* applicants must apply through AMCAS (official transcripts sent by mid-May) between June 1 and August 1. Early applications are encouraged. Submit secondary/supplemental application, a personal statement, and 2 recommendations to Admissions Office within 2 weeks of receipt of application. Notification normally begins October 1. *Regulation application process.* Apply through AMCAS (file after June 1, before November 15); submit MCAT (will accept MCAT test results from 1995), official transcripts for each school attended (should show at least 90 semester credits/135 quarter credits; submit transcripts by mid-May to AMCAS), service processing fee. Submit an application fee of $50, a supplemental application, a personal statement, preprofessional committee evaluation, and 2 recommendations from science faculty to Admissions Office within 2–3 weeks of the receipt of supplemental materials. Interviews are by invitation only and generally for final selection. Combined degree applicants must apply to, and be accepted by, both schools; contact the Admissions Office for current information and specific requirements for admission. First-year students admitted in fall only. Rolling admission process. Notification starts on October 15 and is finished when class is filled. Applicant's response to offer and $100 deposit due within 2 weeks of receipt of acceptance letter. Admissions Office phone: (318)675-5190; E-mail: shvadm@lsumc.edu.

ADMISSION REQUIREMENTS FOR TRANSFER APPLICANTS. Accepts transfers from other accredited U.S. medical schools who are state residents. Admission limited to space available. Contact the Admissions Office for current information and specific requirements for admission.

ADMISSION STANDARDS AND RECOGNITION. *For M.D.:* number of state-resident applicants 773, nonresidents 253; number of state residents interviewed 200, nonresidents none; number of residents enrolled 100;

median MCAT 9.1 (verbal reasoning 9.0; biological sciences 9.2; physical sciences 9.0); median GPA 3.5 (A = 4). Gorman rating 3.63 (scale: good 3.61–3.99); School's ranking by NIH awards/grants was 123rd, with 54 awards/grants received; total dollars awarded $7,747,107.

FINANCIAL AID. Scholarships, merit scholarships, minority scholarships, grants-in-aid, institutional loans, HEAL, alternative loan programs, NIH stipends, federal Perkins loans, Stafford subsidized and unsubsidized loans, and service commitment scholarship programs are available. Assistantships/fellowships may be available for dual-degree candidates. All financial aid is based on demonstrated need. Financial aid applications and information available at the on-campus interview (by invitation). For merit scholarships, the selection criteria place heavy reliance on MCAT and undergraduate GPA. Financial aid application should be submitted no later than March 15. Contact the Financial Aid Office for current information; phone: (318)675-5561. For most financial assistance and all federal programs, submit FAFSA to a federal processor (Title IV school code # 002013); also submit Financial Aid Transcript and Federal Income Tax forms. Approximately 81% of current students receive some form of financial assistance. Average debt after graduation $50,717.

DEGREE REQUIREMENTS. *For M.D.:* satisfactory completion of 4-year program. All students must pass USMLE Step 1 prior to entering 3rd year; all students must pass USMLE Step 2 prior to awarding of M.D. *For M.D.-Ph.D.:* generally a 7-year program.

UNIVERSITY OF LOUISVILLE
Louisville, Kentucky 40292-0001
Internet site: http://www.louisville.edu

Founded 1798. Located 5 miles S of downtown Louisville. Public control. Semester system. Library: 1,315,000 volumes/microforms; 12,812 periodicals/subscriptions. The university's ranking in domestic higher education by NIH awards/grants was 122nd, with 46 awards/grants received; total dollars awarded $7,772,541.

The university's graduate school includes: College of Arts and Sciences, College of Business and Public Administration, College of Health and Social Services, School of Education, School of Law, School of Music, School of Nursing, Speed Scientific School, School of Dentistry, School of Medicine.

Total university enrollment at main campus: 21,200.

Health Sciences Center
530 S. Jackson Street
Louisville, Kentucky 40202

Public control. Hospital is a member of Council of Teaching Hospitals.

School of Medicine
323 East Chestnut Street
Louisville, Kentucky 40202-3866
Telephone: (502)852-5193; (800)334-8635, X5193
Internet site: http://www.louisville.edu
E-mail: mesklaoi@ulkyum.louisville.edu

Established 1833 as Louisville Medical Institute, affiliated with university in 1846. Located at Health Science Center. Affiliated hospitals: Kosair-Children's Hospital, VA Medical Center, Audubon Hospital, Jewish Hospital, James Graham Brown Cancer Center, Allient Norton Hospital, St. Anthony Hospital. Special programs: summer programs for underrepresented minorities; prematriculation summer sessions.

Annual tuition: residents $8,630, nonresidents $20,760. Rooms and apartments available for both single and married students at the medical-dental dormitory. Contact Admissions Office for both on- and off-campus housing information. Annual housing and personal expenses: approximately $13,300.

Enrollment: 1st-year class 137 (EDP 12); total full-time 564 (men 53%, women 47%). First-year statistics: 10% out of state; 46% women; average age 25; 10% minorities.

Degree conferred: M.D.

RECRUITMENT PRACTICES AND POLICIES. School has diversity program and actively recruits women/minority applicants. Diversity contact: Director of Special Programs; phone: (502)852-7182.

ADMISSION REQUIREMENTS FOR FIRST-YEAR APPLICANTS. Preference given to state residents; U.S. citizens and permanent residents only. *Undergraduate preparation.* Suggested premed courses: 2 courses in biology with labs, 2 courses in inorganic chemistry with labs, 2 courses in organic chemistry with labs, 2 courses in physics with labs, 1 course in college math or calculus, 2 courses in English. Bachelor's degree from an accredited institution required; all applicants have bachelor's degree awarded prior to enrollment. *Has EDP for state residents only;* applicants must apply through AMCAS (official transcripts sent by mid-May) between June 1 and August 1. Early applications are encouraged. Submit secondary/ supplemental application, a personal statement, and 2 recommendations to Admissions Office within 2 weeks of receipt of application. Interviews are by invitation only and generally for final selection. Notification normally begins October 1. *Regulation application process.* Apply through AMCAS (file after June 1, before November 1); submit MCAT (will accept MCAT test results from 1995), official transcripts for each school attended (should show at least 90 semester credits/135 quarter credits, submit transcripts by mid-May to AMCAS), service processing fee. Submit an application fee of $15, a supplemental application, a personal statement, preprofessional committee evaluation, and 2 recommendations from science faculty to Admissions Office within 2–3 weeks of the receipt of supplemental materials. Interviews are by invitation only and generally for final selection. First-year students admitted in fall only. Rolling admission process. Notification starts on October 15 and is finished by April 30. Applicant's response to offer and $100 deposit due within 2 weeks of receipt of acceptance letter. Phone: (502)852-5193; E-mail: mesklaoi@ulkyum.louisville.edu.

ADMISSION REQUIREMENTS FOR TRANSFER APPLICANTS. Accepts transfers from other accredited U.S. medical schools who are state residents with documented circumstances necessitating a return to Kentucky. Admission limited to space available. Contact the Admissions Office for current information and specific requirements.

ADMISSION STANDARDS AND RECOGNITION. *For M.D.:* number of state-resident applicants 513, nonresidents 1,394; number of state residents interviewed 300, nonresidents 35; number of residents enrolled 124, nonresidents 13; median MCAT 8.8 (verbal reasoning 8.9; biological sciences 8.7; physical sciences 8.7); median GPA 3.6 (A = 4). Gorman rating 4.26 (scale: strong 4.01–4.49); school's ranking by NIH awards/grants was 95th, with 43 awards/grants received; total dollars received $7,266,916.

FINANCIAL AID. Scholarships, merit scholarships, minority scholarships, grants-in-aid, institutional loans, HEAL, alternative loan programs, federal Perkins loans, Stafford subsidized and unsubsidized loans, and service commitment scholarship programs are available. Financial-aid applications and information available at on-campus interview (by invitation). For merit scholarships, the selection criteria place heavy reliance on MCAT and undergraduate GPA. Contact the Financial Aid Office for current information; phone: (502)852-5187. For most financial assistance and all federal programs, submit FAFSA to a federal processor (Title IV school code # 001999); also submit Financial Aid Transcript and Federal Income Tax forms. Approximately 90% of current students receive some form of financial assistance.

DEGREE REQUIREMENTS. *For M.D.:* satisfactory completion of 4-year program. All students must pass USMLE Step 1 prior to entering 3rd year; all students must take USMLE Step 2 prior to awarding of M.D.

School of Dentistry

Louisville, Kentucky 40242-0001
Telephone: (502)852-5081; fax: (502)852-1210
Internet site: http://www.dental.louisville.edu
E-mail: lkmccu)1@ulkyvm.louisville.edu

Established 1886. Located at health science center. Special programs: Summer programs for underrepresented minorities; prematriculation summer sessions; research program for D.M.D. students; externship between 3rd and 4th years; decelerated studies program available.

Annual tuition and fees: residents $6,860, nonresidents $17,580; equipment and supplies $2,900. Rooms and apartments available for both single and married students at the medical-dental dormitory. Contact Admissions Office for both on- and off-campus housing information. Annual housing, food, transportation, and personal expenses: approximately $13,300 (12 months).

Enrollment: 1st-year class 80; total full-time 285. First-year enrolled student information: 36 from out of state; 14 states represented; 25 women; average age 25; 5 underrepresented minorities; 4 other minorities.

Faculty: full-time 66; part-time 59.

Degrees conferred: D.M.D., D.M.D. -M.S. (Oral Biology).

RECRUITMENT PRACTICES AND POLICIES. School has diversity program and actively recruits women/minority applicants. Diversity contact: Admissions Office.

ADMISSION REQUIREMENTS FOR FIRST-YEAR APPLICANTS. Preference given to state residents; U.S. citizens and permanent residents only. *Undergraduate preparation.* Suggested predental courses: 3 courses in biology with labs, 2 courses in general chemistry with labs, 2 courses in organic chemistry with labs. 1 course in physics with lab. The junior-college transfer credit limit is 60 credits. Will consider applicants with only 3 years of undergraduate preparation; prefer applicants who will have a bachelor's degree prior to enrollment; all enrollees had bachelor's degree awarded prior to enrollment. Applicants should have at least a 2.75 GPA (A = 4) for serious consideration. *Regular application process.* Apply through AADSAS (file after June 1, before April 1), submit official transcripts for each school attended (should show at least 90 semester credits/135 quarter credits), service processing fee; at the same time as you send in AADSAS materials, submit official DAT scores directly to the Admissions Office. Submit to the Office of Student Affairs the following materials only after being contacted by an Admissions Officer: an application fee of $10 (nonresidents only); supplemental data information, official transcripts, predental committee evaluation and 2 recommendations from science professors, and current photograph. Interviews are by invitation only and generally for final selection. Preference given to applicants who apply by February 1. Combined degree applicants should contact the Office of Student Affairs for current information and specific requirements for admission. First-year students admitted in fall only. Rolling admission process. Notification starts in December and is finished when class is filled. Applicant's response to offer and $200 deposit due within 30 days if accepted prior to January 31; response and deposit due within 2 weeks if received after February 1. Phone: (502)852-5081, (800)334-8635, X5081.

ADMISSION REQUIREMENTS FOR ADVANCED-STANDING APPLICANTS. Accepts transfers from other accredited U.S. dental schools on a case-by-case basis. Admission limited to space available. Contact the Office of Student Affairs for current information and specific requirements for admission.

ADMISSION STANDARDS AND RECOGNITION. *For D.D.S.:* number of applicants 1,351; number enrolled 80; median DAT: ACAD 16.3, PAT 16.2; median GPA 3.34 (A = 4), median sciences GPA 3.18 (A = 4). Gorman rating 4.32 (scale: strong 4.01–4.49); this placed the school in the Top 30 of all U.S. dental schools.

FINANCIAL AID. Scholarships, minority scholarships, grants-in-aid, institutional loans, state loan programs, DEAL, HEAL, alternative loan programs, federal Perkins loans, Stafford subsidized and unsubsidized loans, and military service commitment scholarship programs are available. Assistantships/fellowships may be available for combined-degree candidates. Most financial aid is based on documented need. Institutional financial aid applications and information are available at the on-campus interview (by invitation). For merit scholarships, the selection criteria place heavy reliance on DAT and undergraduate GPA. Contact the university's Office of Financial Aid for current information; phone: (502)852-5211. For most financial assistance and all need-based programs, submit FAFSA to a federal processor (Title IV school code # 001999); also submit Financial Aid Tran-

script, Federal Income Tax forms, and Use of Federal Funds Certification. Approximately 90% of current students receive some form of financial assistance. Average award for residents $15,765, nonresidents $22,417.

DEGREE REQUIREMENTS. *For D.M.D.:* satisfactory completion of 4-year program. *For D.M.D.-M.S.:* generally a 4½–5½-year program.

LOYOLA UNIVERSITY CHICAGO
Chicago, Illinois 60611-2196
Internet site: http://www.luc.edu

Founded 1870. Private control. Roman Catholic affiliation—Jesuit. Semester system. Library: 1,349,000 volumes; 1,208,400 microforms; 11,454 periodicals/subscriptions; 245 PC work stations. Special programs: Postbaccalaureate premedical program for adults and underrepresented minorities, contact Pre Health Advisor, Post-Baccalaureate Program; phone (312)508-6054. The university's ranking in domestic higher education by NIH awards/grants was 100th, with 82 awards/grants received; total dollars received $14,075,125.

The university's graduate school includes: Institute of Human Resources and Industrial Relations, Institute of Pastoral Studies, Marcella Niehoff School of Nursing, School of Business, School of Education, School of Law, School of Social Work, Stritch School of Medicine.

Total university enrollment: 14,000.

Loyola University Medical Center
2160 South First Avenue
Maywood, Illinois 60153

Opened 1969. Located 12 miles W of Chicago. Private control. Medical center is a member of Council of Teaching Hospitals. School of Medicine is located at medical center. Special facilities: Foster G. McGaw Hospital. Nationally recognized programs in Endocrinology, Geriatrics, Otolaryngology.

Stritch School of Medicine
2160 South First Avenue
Maywood, Illinois 60153
Telephone: (708)216-3229
Internet site: http://www.luc.edu

Established 1870; a major consolidation occurred in 1920. Located at medical center. Library: 172,800 volumes/microforms; 2,500 current periodicals/subscriptions. Affiliated hospitals: Foster G. McGaw Hospital, Hines Veterans Administration Hospital. Special programs: Medical Humanities Program, summer programs for underrepresented minorities, Mentor Program.

Annual tuition: $27,710; fees $450. No on-campus housing available. Contact Admissions Office for off-campus housing information. Off-campus housing and personal expenses: approximately $14,021.

Enrollment: 1st-year class 130 (EDP 10); total full-time 519 (men 55%, women 45%). First-year statistics: 50% out of state; 50% women; average age 24; 15% minorities; 77% science majors.

Faculty: full-time 525, part-time/volunteers 400.

Degrees conferred: M.D., M.D.-Ph.D. (Anatomy, Biochemistry, Cell Biology, Genetics, Immunology, Molecular Biology, Neurosciences, Pathology, Pharmacology, Physiology).

RECRUITMENT PRACTICES AND POLICIES. School has diversity program and actively recruits women/minority applicants. Diversity contact: Associate Dean for Student Affairs; phone: (708)216-3220.

ADMISSION REQUIREMENTS FOR FIRST-YEAR APPLICANTS. Preference given U.S. citizens and permanent residents only. *Undergraduate preparation.* Suggested premed courses: 2 courses in biology with labs, 2 courses in inorganic chemistry with labs, 2 courses in organic chemistry with labs, 2 courses in physics with labs. Bachelor's degree from an accredited institution required; all applicants have bachelor's degrees awarded prior to enrollment. *Has EDP;* applicants must apply through AMCAS (official transcripts sent by mid-May) between June 1 and August 1. Early applications are encouraged. Submit secondary/supplemental application, a personal statement, and 2 recommendations to Admissions Office within 2 weeks of receipt of application. Interviews are by invitation only and generally for final selection. Notification normally begins October 1. *Regular application process.* Apply through AMCAS (file after June 1, before November 1); submit MCAT (will accept MCAT test results from 1995); official transcripts for each school attended (should show at least 90 semester credits/135 quarter credits, submit transcripts by mid-May to AMCAS), service processing fee. Submit an application fee of $50, a supplemental application, a personal comment/statement, preprofessional committee evaluation, and 2 recommendations from science faculty to Admissions Office within 2–3 weeks of receipt of supplemental materials. Interviews are by invitation only and generally for final selection. Dual-degree applicants must apply to, and be accepted by, both schools; contact the Admissions Office for current information and specific requirements for admission. First-year students admitted in fall only. Rolling admission process. Applicants are generally informed within a month from the date of the interview. The notification starts October 15 and is finished when class is filled. Applicant's response to offer due within 2 weeks of receipt of acceptance letter. School does maintain an alternate list. Phone: (708)216-3229.

ADMISSION REQUIREMENTS FOR TRANSFER APPLICANTS. Accepts transfers from other LCME-accredited U.S. medical schools. Admission limited to space available. Contact the Admissions Office for current information and specific requirements.

ADMISSION STANDARDS AND RECOGNITION. *For M.D.:* number of state-resident applicants 1,753, nonresidents 8,353; number of state residents interviewed 244, nonresidents 315; number of residents enrolled 65, nonresidents 65; median MCAT 9.5 (verbal reasoning 9.4; biological sciences 9.8; physical sciences 9.4); median GPA 3.5 (A = 4). Gorman rating 4.25 (scale: strong 4.01–4.49); school's ranking by NIH awards was 82nd, with 74 awards/grants received; total dollars awarded $12,056,100.

FINANCIAL AID. Scholarships, grants-in-aid, institutional loans, HEAL, alternative loan programs, federal Perkins loans, Stafford subsidized and unsubsidized loans, and service commitment scholarship programs are available. Assistantships/fellowships may be available for dual-degree candidates. Student aid is primarily in the form of loans. Financial aid applications and the *Guide for Student Financial Aid* are given out at the on-campus interview (by invitation). Contact the Financial Aid Office for current information; phone: (708)216-3227. For most financial assistance and all federal programs, submit FAFSA to a federal processor (Title IV school code # 001710); also submit Financial Aid Transcript and Federal Income Tax forms. Approximately 90% of current students receive some form of financial assistance. Average debt after graduation $98,900.

DEGREE REQUIREMENTS. *For M.D.:* satisfactory completion of 4-year program. All students must pass USMLE Step 1 prior to entering 3rd year; all students must take USMLE Step 2 prior to awarding of M.D. *For M.D.-Ph.D.:* generally a 7-year program.

MARQUETTE UNIVERSITY
Milwaukee, Wisconsin 53201-1881
Internet site: http://www.mu.edu

Founded 1881. Located in an urban area adjacent to downtown, 2 miles W of Lake Michigan. Private control, Roman Catholic affiliation—Jesuit. Semester system. Library: 700,000 volumes; 268,600 microforms; 9,400 periodicals/subscriptions; 69 PC work stations.

The university's graduate school includes: College of Arts and Sciences, College of Business Administration, College of Communication, College of Engineering, College of Nursing, School of Education, School of Dentistry, School of Law.

Total university enrollment at main campus: 10,450.

School of Dentistry

P.O. Box 1881, Room 144
Milwaukee, Wisconsin 63201-1881
Phone: (800)445-5285; (414)288-6505; fax: (414)288-3586
Internet site: http://www.dental.mu.edu
E-mail: admission@caries.dental.mu.edu

Established 1907. Located on university's campus. Affiliated hospitals: Children's Hospital of Wisconsin, Froedtert Memorial Luther Hospital, Sinai-Samaritan Medical Center, Zablocki U.S. Veteran's Hospital. Special programs: Pre-clinical Program (extends the 4-year program to 5), Summer Science Enrichment Program, Pre-enrollment Support Program (PESP). Postgraduate specialties: Dental Materials, Emergency Treatment, Endodontics, General Dentistry, Oral Medicine, Oral Surgery, Orthodontics, Pediatric Dentistry, Periodontics, Prosthodontics.

Annual tuition: residents $17,170, nonresidents $28,840; fees $900; equipment and supplies $6,025. On-campus rooms and apartments available for both single and married students. Contact the Office of Residence Life for both on- and off-campus housing information; phone: (414)288-7208. Dental students tend to live off-campus. Off-campus housing, food, transportation, and personal expenses: approximately $14,500.

Enrollment: 1st-year class 72; total full-time 288 (men 68%, women 32%). First-year enrolled student information: 51 from out of state; 19 states represented; 23 women; average age 25; 15 underrepresented minorities; 11 other minorities.

Faculty: full-time 79, part-time 210.

Degrees conferred: D.D.S., B.S.-D.D.S. (Marquette University, Mount Mary College), D.D.S.-M.S.

RECRUITMENT PRACTICES AND POLICIES. School has diversity program and actively recruits women/minority applicants. Diversity contact: Director of Multicultural Affairs, phone: (800)445-5385, (414)288-1533.

ADMISSION REQUIREMENT FOR B.S.-D.D.S. APPLICANTS. Contact the Office of Undergraduate Admissions at either Marquette University or Mount Mary College for current information and specific requirements for admission.

ADMISSION REQUIREMENTS FOR FIRST-YEAR APPLICANTS. Positions open to state residents are limited; U.S. citizens and permanent residents only. *Undergraduate preparation.* Suggested predental courses: 2 courses in biology with labs, 2 courses in inorganic chemistry with labs, 2 courses in organic chemistry with labs, 2 courses in physics with labs, 2 courses in English, 17 elective courses in nonsciences. There is no limitation on the number of junior-college credits taken. Will consider applicants with only 3 years of undergraduate preparation, prefer applicants who will have a bachelor's degree prior to enrollment; 75% of applicants have bachelor's degree awarded prior to enrollment. *Application process.* Apply through AADSAS (file after June 1, before April 1, applicants after April 1 should apply directly to the School of Dentistry), submit official transcripts for each school attended (should show at least 90 semester credits/135 quarter credits), service processing fee; at the same time as you send in AADSAS materials, submit an application fee of $25 and official DAT scores directly to the Admissions Office. TOEFL may be required of an applicant whose native language is other than English. Submit the following materials directly to the Admissions Office only after being contacted by an Admissions Officer: an official transcript, predental committee evaluation or 2 recommendations from science professors and recent photograph. Interviews are by invitation only and generally for final selection. Dual-degree applicants must apply to, and be accepted by both schools. Contact the Admissions Office for current information and specific requirements for admission. First-year students admitted in fall only. Rolling admission process. Notification starts on December 1 and is finished when class is filled. Applicant's response to offer and $750 deposit due within 30 days if accepted prior to January 15; response and deposit due within 2 weeks if received after January 16. School does maintain an alternate/waiting list. Phone: (414)288-3532.

ADMISSION REQUIREMENTS FOR ADVANCED-STANDING APPLICANTS. Accepts transfers from other accredited U.S. and Canadian dental schools, generally only at the sophomore level. Admission limited to space available. There is an advanced-standing program for graduates of foreign schools of dentistry. Contact the Admissions Office for current information and specific requirements for admission.

ADMISSION STANDARDS AND RECOGNITION. *For D.D.S.:* number of applicants 2,309; number enrolled

75; median DAT: ACAD 17.5, PAT 16.8; median GPA 3.32 (A = 4), median sciences GPA 3.23 (A = 4). Gorman rating 4.48 (scale: strong 4.01–4.49); this placed the school in the Top 20 of all U.S. dental schools.

FINANCIAL AID. Scholarships, merit scholarships, minority scholarships, grants, institutional loans, state loan programs, DEAL, HEAL, alternative loan programs, federal Perkins loans, Stafford subsidized and unsubsidized loans, and military service commitment scholarship programs are available. Assistantships/fellowships may be available for combined degree candidates. For merit scholarships, the selection criteria place heavy reliance on DAT and undergraduate GPA. The Marquette University financial aid applications and the *Guide to Financial-aid for Graduate and Professional Study* booklet are available by contacting the Financial Aid Office; phone; (414)288-1678. For most financial assistance and all need-based programs submit FAFSA to a federal processor (Title IV school code # 003863); also submit Financial Aid Transcript and Federal Income Tax forms, and Use of Federal Funds Certification. All current students receive some form of financial assistance. Average award for residents $22,400, nonresidents $39,481.

DEGREE REQUIREMENTS. *For B.S.-D.D.S.:* an 8–9-year program. *For D.D.S.:* satisfactory completion of 4-year program. *For D.D.S.-M.S.:* generally a 4½–5½-year program.

MARSHALL UNIVERSITY
Huntington, West Virginia 25755-2020
Internet site: http://www.marshal.edu

Founded 1837. Public control. Semester system. Special facilities: WMUL-FM, WPBY-TV, Robert C. Byrd Institute for Advanced Flexible Manufacturing Systems, Research and Economic Development Center. Library: 426,200 volumes; 198,814 microforms; 2,728 periodicals/subscriptions; 33 PC work stations.

The university's graduate school includes: College of Business, College of Education, College of Fine Arts, College of Liberal Arts, College of Science, School of Nursing, School of Medicine.

Total university enrollment at main campus: 13,164.

School of Medicine
1542 Spring Valley Drive
Huntington, West Virginia 25704
Phone: (304)696-7312, (800)544-7514
Internet site: http://musom.marshall.edu

Established in 1972 under the Veterans Administration Assistance and Health Training Act. Located adjacent to VA Hospital, 8 miles from university. Affiliated hospitals: Cabell Huntington Hospital, St. Mary's Hospital, VA Medical Center, River Park Hospital. Special programs: M.S. (Forensic Biomedical Science), Ph.D. (Biomedical Science).

Annual tuition: residents $9,202, nonresidents $21,282. On-campus housing available for both single and married students at university. Contact Director of Student Housing for both on- and off-campus housing information; phone: (304)696-2564. Medical students tend to live off-campus. Off-campus housing and personal expenses: approximately $13,400.

Enrollment: 1st-year class 48 (EDP 10); total full-time 205 (men 67%, women 33%). First-year statistics: 6% out of state; 8 schools represented; 35% women; average age 25; 19% minorities; 84% science majors.

Degree conferred: M.D.

RECRUITMENT PRACTICES AND POLICIES. School has diversity program and actively recruits women/minority applicants. Diversity contact: Associate Dean, Student Affairs and Academic Affairs; phone: (304)696-7229.

ADMISSION REQUIREMENTS FOR FIRST-YEAR APPLICANTS. Preference given to state residents; U.S. citizens and permanent residents only. *Undergraduate preparation.* Suggested premed courses: 2 courses in biology with labs, 2 courses in inorganic chemistry with labs, 2 courses in organic chemistry with labs, 2 courses in physics with labs, 2 courses in English, 2 courses in either behavioral or social sciences. Bachelor's degree from an accredited institution required; 94% of applicants have bachelor's degrees awarded prior to enrollment. *Has EDP* for state residents only; applicants must apply through AMCAS (official transcripts sent by mid-May) between June 1 and August 1. Early applications are encouraged. Submit supplemental application, a personal statement, and 3 letters of recommendation to Admissions Office within 2 weeks of receipt of application. Interviews are by invitation only and generally for final selection. Notification normally begins October 1. *Regular application process.* Apply through AMCAS (file after June 1, before December 1); submit MCAT (must be taken within the last 3 calendar years); official transcripts for each school attended (should show at least 90 semester credits/135 quarter credits, submit transcripts by mid-May to AMCAS), service processing fee. Submit an application fee of $30 ($50 nonresidents), a supplemental application, a personal statement, preprofessional committee evaluation and 2 recommendations from science faculty to Admissions Office within 2–3 weeks of the receipt of supplemental materials, but not later than December 31. Interviews are by invitation only and generally for final selection. Dual-degree applicants must apply to, and be accepted by, both schools; contact the Admissions Office for current information and specific requirements for admission. First-year students admitted in fall only. Rolling admission process. Notification starts on October 15 and is finished when class is filled. Applicant's response to offer and $100 deposit due within 2 weeks of receipt of acceptance letter. Phone: (304)696-7312; fax: (304)696-7272.

ADMISSION REQUIREMENTS FOR TRANSFER APPLICANTS. Accepts transfers from other accredited U.S. medical schools who are West Virginia residents. Admission limited to space available. Contact the Admissions Office for current information and specific requirements for admission.

ADMISSION STANDARDS AND RECOGNITION. *For M.D.:* number of state-resident applicants 339, nonresidents 817; number of state residents interviewed 275, nonresidents 15; number of residents enrolled 45, nonresidents 3; median MCAT 9.0 (verbal reasoning 9.6; biological sciences 8.8; physical sciences 8.7); median GPA 3.4 (A = 4). Gorman rating 3.13 (scale: acceptable plus 3.01–3.59); school's ranking by NIH awards/grants was 121st, with 7 awards/grants received; total dollars awarded $747,747.

FINANCIAL AID. Scholarships, grants-in-aid, state and institutional loans, HEAL, alternative loan programs, federal Perkins loans, Stafford subsidized and unsubsidized loans, and service commitment scholarship programs are available. Financial aid is primarily in the form of loans. Financial aid applications and information are given out at the on-campus interview (by invitation). Contact the Office of Financial Assistance for current information; phone: (304)696-3162. For most financial assistance and all federal programs, submit FAFSA to a federal processor (Title IV school code # G06869); also submit Financial Aid Transcript and Federal Income Tax forms. Approximately 90% of current students receive some form of financial assistance. Average debt after graduation $54,000.

DEGREE REQUIREMENTS. *For M.D.:* satisfactory completion of 4-year program. All students must pass USMLE Step 1 prior to entering 3rd year; all students must pass USMLE Step 2 prior to awarding of M.D.

UNIVERSITY OF MARYLAND AT BALTIMORE

Baltimore, Maryland 21201-1627
Internet site: http://www.umab.edu

Founded 1807. Public control. Semester system. Library: 322,500 volumes; 2,600 periodicals/subscriptions; 236 PC work stations. The university's ranking in domestic higher education by NIH awards/grants was 36th, with 321 awards/grants received; total dollars awarded $67,238,807.

The university's other graduate colleges/schools include: Graduate School of Basic Science, Baltimore College of Dentistry, Baltimore School of Medicine, School of Law, School of Pharmacy, School of Social Work.

Total university enrollment at main campus: 5,800.

University Health Center Baltimore City Campus

22 South Greene Street
Baltimore, Maryland 21201

Located in downtown Baltimore. Public control. University of Maryland Medical System is a member of Council of Teaching Hospitals. Special facilities: Aquatic Pathology Center, Cancer Center, Center for Vaccine Development, Clinical Stroke Research Center, Comprehensive Perinatal AIDS Research Center. Schools located at the Baltimore city campus are: Graduate School of Basic Science, School of Dentistry, School of Law, School of Nursing, School of Pharmacy, School of Social Work. Nationally recognized programs in AIDS, Gastroenterology, Neurology, Orthopedics, Pulmonary Disease, Urology.

School of Medicine

655 West Baltimore Street
Baltimore, Maryland 21201-1559
Phone: (410)706-7478.
Internet site: http://www.som1.ab.umd.edu
E-mail: infoxwell@schmed01.ab.umd.edu

Chartered in 1808 and is the 5th oldest medical school in the U.S. Located in downtown Baltimore. Library: 252,000 volumes/microforms; 3,100 current periodicals/subscriptions. Affiliated hospitals: University Hospital, Shock Trauma Center, Institute of Psychiatric and Human Behavior, Sudden Infant Death Syndrome Institute, University of Maryland Medical System. Special programs: summer programs for underrepresented minorities; prematriculation summer sessions.

Annual tuition: residents $12,749, nonresidents $23,849; fees $298. On-campus rooms available for single students only. Apartments are available a short distance from campus. Contact Housing Office for both on- and off-campus housing information; phone: (410)706-7767. Medical students tend to live off-campus. Off-campus housing and personal expenses: approximately $18,152.

Enrollment: 1st-year class 140 (EDP 10); total full-time 603 (men 51%, women 49%). First-year statistics: 12% out of state; 50% women; average age 25; 20% minorities; 71% science majors.

Degrees conferred: M.D., M.D.-Ph.D. (Anatomy, Biochemistry, Biomedical Engineering, Cell Biology, Epidemiology, Genetics, Immunology, Microbiology, Molecular Biology, Neurosciences, Pathology, Pharmacology, Physiology, Preventive Medicine).

RECRUITMENT PRACTICES AND POLICIES. School has diversity program and actively recruits women/minority applicants. Diversity contact: Assistant Dean of Student Affairs; phone: (410)706-7689.

ADMISSION REQUIREMENTS FOR FIRST-YEAR APPLICANTS. Preference given to state residents; U.S. citizens and permanent residents only. *Undergraduate preparation.* Suggested premed courses: 2 courses in biology with labs, 2 courses in inorganic chemistry with labs, 2 courses in organic chemistry with labs, 2 courses in physics with labs, 1 course in college math, 2 courses in English. Bachelor's degree from an accredited institution required; all applicants have bachelor's degree awarded prior to enrollment. *Has EDP* for state residents only; applicants must apply through AMCAS (official transcripts sent by mid-May) between June 1 and August 1. Early applications are encouraged. Submit secondary/supplemental application, a personal statement, and 2 recommendations to Admissions Office within 2 weeks of receipt of application. Interviews are by invitation only and generally for final selection. Notification normally begins October 1. *Application process.* Apply through AMCAS (file after June 1, before December 1); submit MCAT (will accept MCAT test results from 1995), official transcripts for each school attended (should show at least 90 semester credits/135 quarter credits, submit transcripts by mid-May to AMCAS), service processing fee. All residents and committee-selected nonresident applicants receive a Stage II application. Submit an application fee of $40, the Stage II application, a personal statement, preprofessional committee evaluation, and 2 recommendations from science faculty to Admissions Office within 2–3 weeks of the receipt of Stage II materials. Interviews are by invitation only and generally for final selection. Combined degree applicants must apply to, and be accepted by both schools; contact the Admissions Office for current information and specific requirements for admission. First-year students admitted in fall only. Rolling admission process. Notification starts on October 15 and is finished when class is filled. Applicant's response to offer due within 3 weeks of receipt of acceptance letter. School does maintain an alternate list. Phone: (410)706-7478.

ADMISSION REQUIREMENTS FOR TRANSFER APPLICANTS. Accepts transfers from other accredited U.S. medical schools into the 3rd and 4th years. Admission limited to space available. Contact the Admissions Office for current information and specific requirements for admission.

ADMISSION STANDARDS AND RECOGNITION. *For M.D.:* number of state-resident applicants 1,100, nonresidents 3,366; number of state residents interviewed 366, nonresidents 146; number of residents enrolled 126, nonresidents 18; median MCAT 9.7 (verbal reasoning 9.6; biological sciences 10.1; physical sciences 10.1); median GPA 3.56 (A = 4). Gorman rating 3.79 (scale: good 3.61-3.99); *U.S. News & World Report* ranked the school in the Top 25 of all U.S. medical schools in primary-care programs; medical ranking by NIH awards was 35th, with 269 awards/grants received; total dollars awarded $55,083,493.

FINANCIAL AID. Scholarships, dean's scholarships (primarily for nonresidents), grants, desegregation grants (residents), institutional loans, HEAL, alternative loan programs, NIH stipends, federal Perkins loans, Stafford subsidized and unsubsidized loans, and service commitment scholarship programs are available. Assistantships/fellowships may be available for combined degree candidates. Financial aid is based solely on demonstrated need. For scholarships, the selection criteria place heavy reliance on MCAT and undergraduate GPA. Contact the Financial Aid Office for current information; phone: (410)706-7347. For most financial assistance and all federal programs, submit FAFSA to a federal processor (Title IV school code # 002104); also submit Financial Aid Transcript and Federal Income Tax forms. Approximately 70% of current students receive some form of financial assistance. Average debt after graduation $60,523.

DEGREE REQUIREMENTS. *For M.D.:* satisfactory completion of 4-year program. All students must pass USMLE Step 1 prior to entering 3rd year. *For M.D.-Ph.D.:* generally a 6–7-year program.

Baltimore College of Dental Surgery, Dental School
666 West Baltimore Street, Room 4-A-22
Baltimore, Maryland 21201
Phone: (410)706-7422; fax: (410)706-0945
Internet site: http://www.ab.umd.edu

Established 1840; the first dental college in U.S. Located in downtown Baltimore. Special programs: externships, clerkships. Postgraduate specialties: Endodontics, General Dentistry, Oral and Maxillofacial Surgery, Orthodontics, Pediatric Dentistry, Periodontics, Prosthodontics.

Annual tuition: residents $9,631, nonresidents $20,715; fees $509; equipment and supplies $3,501. On-campus rooms available for single students only. Apartments are available a short distance from campus. Contact Housing Office for both on- and off-campus housing information; phone: (410)706-7767. Dental students tend to live off-campus. Off-campus housing, food, transportation, and personal expenses: approximately $12,500.

Enrollment: 1st-year class 98. First-year enrolled student information: 40 from out of state; 14 states and 1 foreign country represented; 41 women; average age 22; 13 underrepresented minorities; 24 other minorities.

Faculty: full-time/part-time/volunteers 250.

Degrees conferred: D.D.S., B.S.-D.D.S. (with Schools in the University of Maryland system only), D.D.S.-Ph.D. (Anatomy, Biochemistry, Microbiology, Oral Pathology, Physiology).

RECRUITMENT PRACTICES AND POLICIES. School has diversity program and actively recruits women/minority applicants. Diversity contact: Admissions Office.

ADMISSION REQUIREMENT FOR BACHELOR-D.D.S. APPLICANTS. For current information, specific requirements, and an application, contact the individual undergraduate colleges/schools within the University of Maryland system that have a joint-degree program with the Dental School.

ADMISSION REQUIREMENTS FOR FIRST-YEAR APPLICANTS. Preference given to state residents; U.S. citizens and permanent residents only. *Undergraduate preparation.* Suggested predental courses: 2 courses in biology with labs, 2 courses in inorganic chemistry with labs, 2 courses in organic chemistry with labs, 2 courses in physics with labs, 2 courses in English. The junior-college transfer credit limit is 60 credits, but must be validated by attendance at a college of arts and science. Will consider applicants with only 3 years of undergraduate preparation; prefer applicants who will have a bachelor's degree prior to enrollment; 93% of applicants have bachelor's degree awarded prior to enrollment. *Application process.* Apply through AADSAS (file after June 1, before February 15), submit official transcripts for each school attended (should show at least 90 semester cred-

its/135 quarter credits), service processing fee; at the same time as you send in AADSAS materials, submit an application fee of $50 and official DAT scores (taken no later than October of the year prior to the anticipated year of enrollment) directly to the Admissions Office. TOEFL may be required of an applicant whose native language is other than English. Submit the following materials only after being contacted by an Admissions Officer: a supplemental application, official transcripts, a predental committee evaluation, or 2 recommendations from science professors to the Admissions Office within 2 weeks. Interviews are by invitation only and generally for final selection. Dual-degree applicants must apply to, and be accepted by, both schools. First-year students admitted in fall only. Rolling admission process. Notification starts on December 1 and is finished when class is filled, but generally not later than August 1. Applicant's response to offer and $200 deposit due within 30 days if accepted prior to January 31; response and deposit due within 15 days if received after February 1. Phone: (410)706-7422.

ADMISSION REQUIREMENTS FOR ADVANCED-STANDING APPLICANTS. There is no formal advanced-standing program. In rare instances, consideration is given to students from accredited U.S. dental schools. Contact the Admissions Office for current information and specific requirements for admission.

ADMISSION STANDARDS AND RECOGNITION. *For D.D.S.:* number of applicants 1,915; number enrolled 98; median DAT: ACAD 18.0, PAT 17.0; median GPA 3.22 (A = 4), median sciences GPA 3.14 (A = 4). Gorman rating 4.17 (scale: strong 4.01–4.49); this placed the school in the Top 41 of all U.S. dental schools; the dental school's ranking by NIH awards/grants was 10th among dental schools, with 23 awards/grants received; total value of all awards/grants $4,072,594.

FINANCIAL AID. Scholarships, dean's scholarships, minority scholarships, grants-in-aid, tuition waivers, institutional loans, state loan programs, DEAL, HEAL, alternative loan programs, federal Perkins loans, Stafford subsidized and unsubsidized loans, and military service commitment scholarship programs are available. Assistantships/fellowships may be available for combined degree candidates. Institutional financial aid applications and information are generally available at the on-campus invitation interview. For scholarships, the selection criteria place heavy reliance on DAT and undergraduate GPA. Contact the Office of Student Financial Aid for current information; phone: (410)706-7347. For most financial assistance and all need-based programs, submit FAFSA to a federal processor (Title IV school code # 002104); also submit Financial Aid Transcript, Federal Income Tax forms, and Use of Federal Funds Certification. Approximately 63% of current students receive some form of financial assistance. Average award for residents $28,000, nonresidents $38,000.

DEGREE REQUIREMENTS. *For B.S.-D.D.S.:* generally a 7-year program. *For D.D.S.:* satisfactory completion of 4-year program; passage of Part II of the National Board Dental Examination. *For D.D.S.-Ph.D.:* generally a 6–7-year program.

UNIVERSITY OF MASSACHUSETTS
Amherst, Massachusetts 01003-0001

Founded 1863. The University of Massachusetts has campuses located in Boston, North Dartmouth, Lowell, and a medical center in Worcester. Public control. The university's ranking in domestic higher education by NIH awards was 42nd, with 273 awards/grants received; total dollars awarded $61,325,101.

Total university enrollment: 54,000.

University of Massachusetts Medical Center at Worcester
55 Lake Avenue North
Worcester, Massachusetts 01655-0115

Public control. The medical center is a member of Council of Teaching Hospitals. Schools located at medical center are: Graduate School of Biomedical Sciences, Graduate School of Nursing, Medical School. Nationally recognized programs in Endocrinology, Orthopedics, Urology.

Medical School
55 Lake Avenue North
Worcester, Massachusetts 01655-0115
Phone: (508)856-2323
Internet site: http://www.ummed.edu:8000
E-mail: admission@banyan.ummed.edu

Established 1970. Located at the medical center. Library: 114,000 volumes/microforms; 1,500 current periodicals/subscriptions. Affiliated hospitals: University Hospital, St. Vincent's Hospital, Worcester City Hospital, Worcester Memorial Hospital, Berkshire Memorial Center. Special programs: summer programs for underrepresented minorities.

Annual tuition: residents $10,187, fees $1,835. Limited on-campus rooms available for single students only. Contact Admissions Office for both on- and off-campus housing information; phone: (508)856-2323. Medical students tend to live off-campus. Off-campus housing and personal expenses: approximately $15,372.

Enrollment: 1st-year class 100 (EDP 10); total full-time 432 (men 50%, women 50%). First-year statistics: none from out of state; 50% women; average age 25; 6% minorities; 60% science majors.

Degrees conferred: M.D., M.D.-Ph.D. (Biomedical Sciences, Biochemistry and Molecular Biology, Cell Biology, Cellular and Molecular Physiology, Immunology and Virology, Molecular Genetics and Microbiology, Molecular Biology, Neurosciences, Pharmacology and Molecular Toxicology).

RECRUITMENT PRACTICES AND POLICIES. School has diversity program and actively recruits women/minority applicants. Diversity contact: Director of Education; phone: (508)856-3866.

ADMISSION REQUIREMENTS FOR FIRST-YEAR APPLICANTS. Accepts state residents only who are U.S. citizens and permanent residents. *Undergraduate preparation.* Suggested premed courses: 2 courses in biology with labs, 2 courses in inorganic chemistry with labs, 2 courses in organic chemistry with labs, 2 courses in physics with labs, 2 courses in English, 2 courses in calculus recommended; will not consider CLEP credit. Bachelor's degree from an accredited institution required; all applicants have bachelor's degree awarded prior to enrollment. *Has EDP* for state residents only; applicants must apply through AMCAS (official transcripts sent by mid-May) between June 1 and August 1. Early applications are encouraged. Submit secondary/supplemental application, a personal statement, and 2 recommendations to Admissions Office within 2 weeks of receipt of application. Interviews are by invitation only and generally for final selection. Notification normally begins October 15. *Regular application process.* Apply through AMCAS (file after June 1, before November 1); submit MCAT (will accept MCAT test results from the last 3 years), official transcripts for each school attended (should show at least 90 semester credits/135 quarter credits, submit transcripts by mid-May to AMCAS), service processing fee. Submit an application fee of $50, a supplemental application, a personal statement, preprofessional committee evaluation, and 2 recommendations from science faculty (must be received by December 1) to Admissions Office within 2–3 weeks of the receipt of supplemental materials, but not later than December 15.

Interviews are by invitation only and generally for final selection. M.D.-Ph.D. applicants must apply to, and be accepted by, both schools; contact the Admissions Office for current information and specific requirements for admission. First-year students admitted in fall only. Rolling admission process. Notification starts in October and is finished when class is filled. Applicant's response to offer and $100 deposit due within 2 weeks of receipt of acceptance letter. School does maintain an alternate list. Phone: (508)856-2323.

ADMISSION REQUIREMENTS FOR TRANSFER APPLICANTS. Accepts transfers from other accredited U.S. medical schools who are state residents. Admission limited to space available. Contact the Admissions Office after January 1 for current information and specific requirements for admission.

ADMISSION STANDARDS AND RECOGNITION. *For M.D.:* number of state-resident applicants 1,051, nonresidents 524; number of state residents interviewed 440, nonresidents none; number of residents enrolled 100, nonresidents none; median MCAT 10.0 (verbal reasoning 10.0; biological sciences 10.0; physical sciences 10.0); median GPA 3.50 (A = 4). Gorman rating 3.24 (scale: acceptable plus 3.01–3.59); *U.S. News & World Report* ranked the medical school in the Top 25 schools in primary-care programs; the school's ranking by NIH awards was 42nd, with 193 awards/grants received; total dollars awarded $49,468,352.

FINANCIAL AID. Scholarships, minority scholarships, grants, institutional loans, HEAL, alternative loan programs, learning contracts, federal Perkins loans, Stafford subsidized and unsubsidized loans, and service commitment scholarships to the commonwealth in primary care are available. Tuition waivers/stipends may be available for M.D.-Ph.D. candidates. Financial aid applications and information are given out at the on-campus interview (by invitation) or sent with the letter of acceptance. Contact the Financial Aid Office for current information; phone: (508)856-2265. For most financial assistance and all federal programs, submit FAFSA to a federal processor (Title IV school code # G09756); also submit Financial Aid Transcript and Federal Income Tax forms, and CSS Profile form. Approximately 75% of current students receive some form of financial assistance. Average debt after graduation $70,000.

DEGREE REQUIREMENTS. *For M.D.:* satisfactory completion of 4-year program. *For M.D.-Ph.D.:* generally a 6–7-year program.

MAYO CLINIC AND MAYO FOUNDATION

Rochester, Minnesota 55901
Internet site: http://www.mayo.edu

Founded 1863. There are three sites: Rochester, Minnesota, Jacksonville, Florida, Scottsdale, Arizona. Private control. One of the world's largest group practices. Special facilities: Mass Spectrometry Resource Laboratory, Analytical Nuclear Magnetic Resonance Resource Laboratory, Electron Microscopy Resource Laboratory, Molecular Biology Resource Laboratory, Biomedical Imaging Resource Laboratory, Cancer Center. The Mayo Clinic's ranking (grouped by all organizations, educational, medical, etc.) by NIH awards was 50th, with 223 awards/grants received; total dollars awarded $59,637,789.

The clinic and foundation's graduate schools include: Mayo Graduate School, Mayo Medical School, Mayo School of Health Related Sciences.

Mayo Medical Center

Rochester, Minnesota 55901

Private Control. The medical center is a member of Council of Teaching Hospitals. Nationally recognized programs in AIDS, Cancer, Cardiology, Endocrinology, Gastroenterology, Geriatrics, Gynecology, Neurology, Ophthalmology, Orthopedics, Otolaryngology, Pediatrics, Psychiatry, Pulmonary Disease, Rehabilitation, Rheumatology, Urology. *U.S. News & World Report*'s hospital/medical center national rankings for all hospitals placed the Mayo Clinic in the Top 20 of all U.S. hospitals.

Mayo Medical School

200 First Street, S.W.
Rochester, Minnesota 55905
Phone: (507)284-3671; fax: (507)284-2634
Internet site: http://www.mayo.edu

Library: 353,000 volumes/microforms; 4,300 current periodicals/subscriptions. Affiliated hospitals: Rochester Methodist Hospital, St. Mary's Hospital, Mayo Clinics.

Annual tuition: $19,800. No on-campus housing available. Contact Admissions Office for off-campus housing information. Off-campus housing and personal expenses: approximately $7,200 (single students).

Enrollment: 1st-year class 42 (EDP 2, M.D.-Ph.D. 6); total full-time 165 (men 50%, women 50%). First-year statistics: 80% out of state; 36 states represented; 50% women; average age 24; 18% minorities; 76% science majors.

Faculty: full-time 1,000.

Degrees conferred: M.D., M.D.-Ph.D. (Biochemistry, Biomedical Imaging, Biophysics, Immunology, Molecular Biology, Molecular Neurosciences, Pharmacology, Physiology, Tumor Biology).

RECRUITMENT PRACTICES AND POLICIES. School has diversity program and actively recruits women/minority applicants. Diversity contact: Associate Dean for Student Affairs; phone: (507)284-0339.

ADMISSION REQUIREMENTS FOR FIRST-YEAR APPLICANTS. Some preference given to state residents; U.S. citizens and permanent residents only. *Undergraduate preparation.* Suggested premed courses: 2 courses in biology with labs, 2 courses in inorganic chemistry with labs, 2 courses in organic chemistry with labs, 1 course in biochemistry, 2 courses in physics with labs. Bachelor's degree from an accredited institution required; all applicants have bachelor's degree awarded prior to enrollment. *Has EDP*; applicants must apply through AMCAS (official transcripts sent by mid-May) between June 1 and August 1. Early applications are encouraged. Submit secondary/supplemental application, a personal statement and 2 recommendations to Admissions Office within 2 weeks of receipt of application, but not later than September 1. Interviews are by invitation only and generally for final selection. Notification normally begins October 1. *Regular application process.* Apply through AMCAS (file after June 1, before December 1); submit MCAT (will accept MCAT test results from 1995), official transcripts for each school attended (should show at least 90 semester credits/135 quarter credits, submit transcripts by mid-May to AMCAS), service processing fee. A telephone interview is used in place of supplemental materials. Dual-degree applicants should contact the Admissions Office for current information and specific requirements for admission. First-year students admitted in fall only. Rolling admission process. Notification starts on October 15 and is finished when class is filled. Applicant's response to offer and $100 deposit due within 2 weeks of receipt of acceptance letter. School does maintain an alternate list. Application fee $60. Phone: (507)284-3671; fax: (507)284-2634.

ADMISSION REQUIREMENTS FOR TRANSFER APPLICANTS. Rarely considers transfer applicants. Contact the Admissions Office for current information and any change in transfer policy.

ADMISSION STANDARDS AND RECOGNITION. *For M.D.:* number of state-resident applicants 404, nonresidents 3,387; number of state residents interviewed 61, nonresidents 348; number of residents enrolled 8, nonresidents 34; median MCAT 11.0 (verbal reasoning 11.0; bi-

ological sciences 11.0; physical sciences 11.0); median GPA 3.7 (A = 4). Gorman rating 3.84 (scale: good 3.61–3.99); *U.S. News & World Report* ranked the medical school in the Top 25 of all U.S. medical schools.

FINANCIAL AID. Mayo scholarships (for residents of Minnesota, Florida, Arizona), merit scholarships, minority scholarships, grants, Mayo Student Loan Program, HEAL, alternative loan programs, federal Perkins loans, Stafford subsidized and unsubsidized loans, and service commitment scholarship programs are available. Stipends/tuition waivers may be available for dual-degree candidates. Financial aid applications and information are given out at the on-campus interview (by invitation). Mayo scholarships reduce tuition from $19,800 to $4,800 for residents of Minnesota, Florida, and Arizona and to $9,400 for other nonresidents. Contact the Financial Aid Office for current information; phone: (507)284-4839. For most financial assistance and all federal programs, submit FAFSA to a federal processor (Title IV school code # G11732); also submit Financial Aid Transcript and Federal Income Tax forms. Approximately 45% of students receive full-tuition scholarships. Average debt after graduation $53,000.

DEGREE REQUIREMENTS. *For M.D.:* satisfactory completion of 4-year program. All students must take both USMLE Step 1 and Step 2. *For M.D.-Ph.D.:* generally a 6–8-year program.

MEDICAL COLLEGE OF GEORGIA

Augusta, Georgia 30912-1003
Internet site: http://www.mcg.edu

Chartered 1828. School of Graduate Studies awarded its 1st degree in 1953. Public control. Quarter system. Library: 170,000 volumes; 6,000 microforms; 1,287 periodicals/subscriptions; 115 work stations. Special facilities: Alzheimer's Disease Center, Sickle Cell Center, Gene Data Bank, Institute of Molecular Medicine and Genetics. The medical college's ranking in domestic higher education by NIH awards was 101st, with 58 awards/grants received; total dollars awarded $13,188,308.

The college's other graduate colleges/schools include: School of Allied Health, School of Dentistry, School of Graduate Studies, School of Nursing.

Total enrollment at main campus: 2,061.

Medical College of Georgia Hospital and Clinics
1120 15th Street
Augusta, Georgia 30912

Member of Council of Teaching Hospitals. Special facilities: Shock Trauma Center, Children's Medical Center. Nationally recognized programs in Endocrinology, Neurology, Orthopedics, Urology.

School of Medicine
1120 15th Street, 170 Kelly Building
Augusta, Georgia 30912-4760
Phone: (706)721-3186; fax: (706)721-0959
Internet site: http://www,mcg.edu
E-mail: schmed.stadmin@mail.mcg.edu

Established 1828. Affiliated hospitals: Veterans Affairs Medical Center, Memorial Medical Center (Savannah), Dwight David Eisenhower Army Medical Center, (Ft. Gordon), Georgia Baptist Hospital (Atlanta). Special Programs: summer programs for underrepresented minorities.

Annual tuition: residents $6,174, nonresidents $21,819; fees $249. On-campus rooms and apartments available for both single and married students. Annual on-campus housing cost: $12,000 (room and board). Medical students tend to live on-campus. Contact Housing Office, Student Center, for both on- and off-campus housing information; phone: (706)721-3471.

Enrollment: 1st-year class 180 (EDP 50); total full-time 732 (men 68%, women 32%). First-year statistics: 2% out of state; 27% women; average age 24; 7–8% minorities.

Faculty: full-time 530, part-time/volunteers over 1,000.

Degrees conferred: M.D., M.D.-Ph.D. (Biochemistry, Molecular Biology, Cellular Biology and Anatomy, Endocrinology, Pharmacology and Toxicology, Physiology).

RECRUITMENT PRACTICES AND POLICIES. School has diversity program and actively recruits women/minority applicants. Diversity contact: Associate Dean, Special Academic Programs; phone: (706)721-2522.

ADMISSION REQUIREMENTS FOR FIRST-YEAR APPLICANTS. Preference given to state residents (up to 5% may be from out of state); U.S. citizens and permanent residents only. *Undergraduate preparation.* Suggested premed courses: 2 courses in biology with labs, 2 courses in inorganic chemistry with labs, 1 course in organic chemistry with lab, 1 course in advanced chemistry, 2 courses in physics with labs, 2 courses in English; 1 course in biochemistry highly recommended. Bachelor's degree from an accredited institution required; 99% of applicants have bachelor's degrees awarded prior to enrollment. *Has EDP for state residents only;* applicants must

apply through AMCAS (official transcripts sent by mid-May) between June 1 and August 1. Early applications are encouraged. Submit secondary/supplemental application, a personal statement, and 2 recommendations to Admissions Office within 2 weeks of receipt of application. On-campus interviews are by invitation only. Notification normally begins October 1. *Regular application process.* Apply through AMCAS (file after June 1, before December 1); submit MCAT (MCAT must be no more than 2 years old), official transcripts for each school attended (should show at least 90 semester credits/135 quarter credits, submit transcripts by mid-May to AMCAS), service processing fee. Submit the supplemental application, a personal statement, preprofessional committee evaluation, and 2 recommendations from science faculty to Admissions Office within 2–3 weeks of the receipt of supplemental materials. Interviews are by invitation only and generally for final selection. Dual-degree applicants must apply to, and be accepted by, both schools; contact the Admissions Office for current information and specific requirements for admission. First-year students admitted in fall only. Rolling admission process. Notification starts on October 15 and is finished when class is filled. Applicant's response to offer and $50 deposit due within 2 weeks of receipt of acceptance letter. School does maintain an alternate list. Admissions phone: (706)721-3186; E-mail: schmed.stadmin@mail.mcg.edu; M.D.-Ph.D. Director's phone: (706)721-6306; fax: (706)721-6829.

ADMISSION REQUIREMENTS FOR TRANSFER APPLICANTS. Accepts transfers from other accredited U.S. medical schools who are state residents. Admission limited to space available. Contact the Office of Associate Dean for Admissions after January 1 for current information and specific requirements for admission.

ADMISSION STANDARDS AND RECOGNITION. *For M.D.:* number of state-resident applicants 1,109, nonresidents 767; number of state residents interviewed 466, nonresidents 26; number of residents enrolled 177, nonresidents 3; median MCAT 9.3 (verbal reasoning 9.7; biological sciences 9.4; physical sciences 9.2); median GPA 3.49 (A = 4). Gorman rating 3.33 (scale: acceptable plus 3.01–3.59); School of Medicine's ranking by NIH awards was 81st, with 54 awards/grants received; total dollars awarded, $12,314,590.

FINANCIAL AID. Scholarships, merit scholarships, minority scholarships, grants, institutional loans, HEAL, alternative loan programs, NIH stipends, federal Perkins loans, Stafford subsidized and unsubsidized loans, and service commitment scholarship programs are available. Tuition waivers available for all M.D.-Ph.D. degree candidates. For merit scholarships, the selection criteria place heavy reliance on MCAT and undergraduate GPA. Contact the Office of Student Financial Aid for current information; phone: (706)721-4901. For most financial assistance and all federal programs, submit FAFSA to a federal processor (Title IV school code # 001579); also submit Financial Aid Transcript and Federal Income Tax forms. Approximately 85% of current students receive some form of financial assistance. Average debt after graduation $37,900.

DEGREE REQUIREMENTS. *For M.D.:* satisfactory completion of 4-year program. All students must pass USMLE Step 1 prior to entering 3rd year; all students must pass USMLE Step 2 prior to awarding of M.D. *For M.D.-Ph.D.:* generally a 7-year program

School of Dentistry
Augusta Georgia 30912-1020
Phone: (706)721-3587; fax: (702)721-6276
Internet site: http://www.mcg.edu

Established 1965. Located on medical college's campus. Semester system.

Annual tuition: residents $5,292; nonresidents $18,261; equipment and supplies $4,409. On-campus rooms and apartments available for both single and married students. Annual on-campus housing cost: $12,000. Dental students tend to live on-campus. Contact Housing Office for both on- and off-campus housing information; phone: (706)721-3471.

Enrollment: 1st-year class 56. First-year enrolled student information: 1 from out of state; 1 state represented; 19 women; average age 24; 7 underrepresented minorities; 3 other minorities.

Faculty: full-time 89.

Degrees conferred: D.M.D., D.M.D.-M.S. (Oral Biology), D.M.D.-Ph.D. (Oral Biology).

RECRUITMENT PRACTICES AND POLICIES. School has diversity program and actively recruits women/minority applicants. Diversity contact: Director, Minority Student Affairs; phone: (706)721-2821.

ADMISSION REQUIREMENTS FOR FIRST-YEAR APPLICANTS. Preference given to state residents; U.S. citizens and permanent residents only. *Undergraduate preparation.* Suggested predental courses: 2 courses in biology with labs, 2 courses in general chemistry with labs, 2 courses in organic chemistry with labs, 2 courses in physics with labs, 2 courses in English; 1 course in biochemistry strongly recommended. There is no limitation on the number of credits taken at a junior college. Will consider applicants with only 3 years of undergraduate

preparation; prefer applicants who will have a bachelor's degree prior to enrollment; 98% of applicants have bachelor's degrees awarded prior to enrollment. *Application process.* Apply directly to the Admissions Office of the School of Dentistry after July 1, before November 1. Submit application, official transcripts for each school attended (should show at least 90 semester credits/135 quarter credits), DAT scores (taken no later than October of the year prior to the year of intended enrollment; will consider scores up to 3 years old), and either a predental committee evaluation or 3 recommendations from professors in your major field of study. Interviews are by invitation only and generally for final selection. First-year students admitted in fall only. Rolling admission process. Notification starts on December 1 and is finished when class is filled, but never later than August 1. Applicant's response to offer and $50 deposit due within 30 days if accepted prior to February 28; response and deposit due within 2 weeks if received after March 1. School does maintain an alternate list. Phone: (706)721-3587; fax: (706)721-6276; E-mail: ossas@mail.msg.edu. For information on Joint-degree programs, contact Director, Graduate Programs; phone: (706)721-2526.

ADMISSION REQUIREMENTS FOR ADVANCED-STANDING APPLICANTS. Does not accept students with advanced standing.

ADMISSION STANDARDS AND RECOGNITION. *For D.M.D.:* number of applicants 213; number enrolled 56; median DAT: ACAD 17, PAT 17; median GPA 3.26 (A = 4), median sciences GPA 3.21 (A = 4). Gorman rating 4.14 (scale: strong 4.01–4.49); this placed the school in the Bottom 10 of all U.S. dental schools; the dental school's ranking by NIH awards was 28th among dental schools, with 4 awards/grants received; total value of all awards/grants $860,337.

FINANCIAL AID. Scholarships, merit scholarships, grants, institutional loans, state loan programs, DEAL, HEAL, alternative loan programs, federal Perkins loans, Stafford subsidized and unsubsidized loans, and armed forces service commitment scholarship programs are available. Assistantships/fellowships may be available for combined-degree candidates. Institutional financial aid applications and information are given out at the on-campus by invitation interview. Apply after January 1, before March 1. For merit scholarships, the selection criteria place heavy reliance on DAT and undergraduate GPA. Contact the medical college's Office of Student Financial Aid for current information; phone: (706)721-4901. For most financial assistance and all need-based programs, submit FAFSA to a federal processor (Title IV school code # 001579); also submit Financial Aid Transcript, Federal Income Tax forms, and Use of Federal Funds Certification. Approximately 86% of current students receive some form of financial assistance. Average award for residents $13,151.

DEGREE REQUIREMENTS. *For D.M.D.:* satisfactory completion of 4-year program (45 month) program. *For D.M.D.-M.S.:* generally a 4½–5½-year program. *For D.M.D.-Ph.D.:* generally a 6–7-year program.

MEDICAL COLLEGE OF OHIO AT TOLEDO

Toledo, Ohio 43699-0008
Internet site: http://www.mco.edu

Established 1969; graduated first class in 1972. Located south Toledo. State assisted. The state's only free-standing public medical college. Graduate-only institution. Semester system. Library: 125,000 volumes; 1,899 current periodicals/subscriptions; 63 PC work stations. Special facilities: transmissions electron microscopes, CAT scanner, MRI scanner. Special programs: Organ Transplant Center for Northwestern Ohio. The college's ranking in domestic higher education by NIH awards/grants was 125th, with 37 awards/grants received; total dollars awarded $7,021,987.

The college's graduate school includes: School of Allied Health, School of Nursing, School of Medicine.

Total university enrollment at main campus: 761.

Health Science Center

P.O. Box 10008
Toledo, Ohio 43699

State control. The Medical College of Ohio Hospital is a member of the Council of Teaching Hospitals. Special facilities: Medical College of Ohio Hospital. Nationally recognized programs in Endocrinology and Orthopedics.

School of Medicine

P.O. Box 10008
Toledo, Ohio 43699
Phone: (419)381-4229; fax: (419)381-4005
Internet site: http://www.mco.edu

Established 1969. Semester system with a traditional 4-year curriculum. Special programs: special admissions program with Bowling Green State University and University of Toledo; FLEX Program: a 5-year M.D. program for disadvantaged students. Affiliated hospitals: Medical College Hospital, Toledo Hospital, St. Vincent

Medical Center, Mercy Hospital, Toledo Mental Health Center, Coghlin Rehabilitation Hospital.

Annual tuition: residents $10,737, nonresidents $23,191; fees $770. No on-campus housing available. Contact the Admissions Office for off-campus housing information. Off-campus housing and personal expenses: approximately $8,600.

Enrollment: 1st-year class 140 (EDP 10); total full-time 570 (men 60%, women 40%). First-year statistics: 20% out of state; 40% women; average age 24; 14% minorities; 82% science majors.

Faculty: full-time 400, part-time/volunteers 1,100.

Degrees conferred: M.D., M.D.-M.S., M.D.-Ph.D. (Anatomy, Biochemistry, Microbiology, Molecular Biology, Neurosciences, Pathology, Pharmacology, Physiology).

RECRUITMENT PRACTICES AND POLICIES. School has diversity program and actively recruits women/minority applicants. Diversity contact: Associate Dean for Admissions and Minority Affairs; phone: (419)381-3438.

ADMISSION REQUIREMENTS FOR FIRST-YEAR APPLICANTS. Preference given to state residents; U.S. citizens and permanent residents only. *Undergraduate preparation.* Suggested premed courses: 2 courses in biology with labs, 2 courses in inorganic chemistry with labs, 2 courses in organic chemistry with labs, 2 courses in physics with labs, 2 courses in college math, 2 courses in English. Bachelor's degree from an accredited institution required; all applicants have bachelor's degree awarded prior to enrollment. *Has EDP* for state residents only; applicants must apply through AMCAS (official transcripts sent by mid-May) between June 1 and August 1. Early applications are encouraged. Submit supplemental application, a personal statement, and 2 recommendations to Admissions Office within 2 weeks of receipt of application. Interviews are by invitation only and generally for final selection. Notification normally begins October 1. *Regular application process.* Apply through AMCAS (file after June 1, before December 1); submit MCAT (will accept MCAT test results from 1995), official transcripts for each school attended (should show at least 90 semester credits/135 quarter credits, submit transcripts by mid-May to AMCAS), service processing fee. Submit an application fee of $30, a supplemental application, a personal statement, preprofessional committee evaluation, and 2 recommendations from science faculty to Admissions Office within 2–3 weeks of the receipt of supplemental materials. Preliminary review is completed by mid-December. Interviews are by invitation only and generally for final selection. Joint-degree applicants must apply to, and be accepted by, both schools; contact the Admissions Office for current information and specific requirements for admission. First-year students admitted in fall only. Rolling admission process. Notification starts October 15 and is finished when class is filled. Applicant's response to offer due within 2 weeks of receipt of acceptance letter. School does maintain an alternate list. Phone: (419)381-4229.

ADMISSION REQUIREMENTS FOR TRANSFER APPLICANTS. Accepts transfers from other accredited U.S. medical schools who are Ohio residents. Admission limited to space available. Contact the Admissions Office for current information and specific requirements for admission.

ADMISSION STANDARDS AND RECOGNITION. *For M.D.:* number of state-resident applicants 1,390, nonresidents 3,556; number of state residents interviewed 464, nonresidents 139; number of residents enrolled 118, nonresidents 22; median MCAT 9.1 (verbal reasoning 9.13; biological sciences 9.24; physical sciences 9.17); median GPA 3.48 (A = 4). Gorman rating 3.32 (scale: acceptable plus 3.01–3.59); the college's ranking by NIH awards/grants was 97th, with 34 awards/grants received; total dollars awarded $6,786,987.

FINANCIAL AID. Need-based scholarships, merit scholarships, minority scholarships, grants-in-aid, institutional loans, HEAL, alternative loan programs, NIH stipends, federal Perkins loans, Stafford subsidized and unsubsidized loans, and service commitment scholarship programs are available. Assistantships/fellowships may be available for dual-degree candidates. All accepted students receive financial-aid applications in early February. For merit scholarships, the selection criteria place heavy reliance on MCAT and undergraduate GPA. Contact the Financial Aid Office for current information; phone: (419)383-3436. For most financial assistance and all federal programs, submit FAFSA to a federal processor (Title IV school code # G07737); also submit Financial Aid Transcript and Federal Income Tax forms. Approximately 75% of current students receive some form of financial assistance. Average debt after graduation $70,000.

DEGREE REQUIREMENTS. *For M.D.:* satisfactory completion of 4-year program. All students must pass USMLE Step 1 and all students must take USMLE Step 2. *For M.D.-M.S.:* generally a 4½–5½-year program. *For M.D.-Ph.D.:* generally a 7-year program.

MEDICAL COLLEGE OF WISCONSIN
Milwaukee, Wisconsin 53226-0509
Internet site: http://www.mcw.edu

Founded 1913; was part of Marquette University. Became a free-standing independent medical school in 1967; name changed in 1970. Library: 244,000 volumes/microforms; 1,735 periodicals/subscriptions. Special facilities: Arthritis Institute, Biophysics Research Institute, Cancer Center, Cardiovascular Research Center, Center for Bioethics, Clinical Research Center, Digestive Disease Research Center, Foley Center for Aging, Health Policy Institute, Neurosciences Program, Spinal Cord Injury Center. The medical college's ranking in domestic higher education by NIH awards/grants was 66th, with 154 awards/grants received; total dollars awarded $36,542,795.

The Medical College of Wisconsin includes the Graduate School and the Medical School.

Total enrollment at main campus: 1,440.

Milwaukee Regional Medical Center
Milwaukee, Wisconsin 53226

Founded 1978. Located in the western suburban section of Milwaukee. Private control. The medical center includes Froedtert Memorial Lutheran Hospital, Children's Hospital of Wisconsin (both are members of the Council of Teaching Hospitals), Blood Center of Southeastern Wisconsin, Curative Rehabilitation Services, Milwaukee County Mental Health Division.

Medical School
8701 Watertown Plank Road
Milwaukee, Wisconsin 53226
Phone: (414)456-8246
Internet site: http://www.mcw.edu/medschool
E-mail: medschool@mcw.edu

Established 1913. Located at Milwaukee Regional Medical Center. The 1st and 2 years of study are primarily in basic medical sciences. Affiliated hospitals; Milwaukee County Medical Complex, Clement J. Zablocki Veterans Affairs Medical Center, Children's Hospital of Wisconsin, John L. Doyne Hospital, Froedtert Memorial Lutheran Hospital, Eye Institute. Special programs: Summer programs for underrepresented minorities (apprenticeship in medicine, apprenticeship in research).

Annual tuition: $15,044. No on-campus housing available. Safe and affordable housing is found in the immediate vicinity of the college. Contact Admissions Office for off-campus housing information. Off-campus housing and personal expenses: approximately $10,859.

Enrollment: 1st-year class 204 (EDP 40, M.S.T.P. 2); total full-time 807 (men 64%, women 36%). First-year statistics: 32% women; average age 25; 10% minorities; 65% science majors.

Faculty: full-time 811, part-time/volunteers 1,719.

Degrees conferred: M.D., M.D.-M.A. (Bioethics), M.D.-M.S. (Biophysics, Cellular Biology, Pathology, Pharmacology and Toxicology), M.D.-Ph.D. (Biochemistry, Biophysics, Biostatistics, Cellular Biology and Anatomy, Genetics, Microbiology, Pathology, Pharmacology and Toxicology, Physiology); has M.S.T.P.

RECRUITMENT PRACTICES AND POLICIES. School has diversity program and actively recruits women/minority applicants. Diversity contact: Associate Dean for Minority Affairs; phone: (414)456-8734.

ADMISSION REQUIREMENTS FOR FIRST-YEAR APPLICANTS. Preference given to state residents; U.S. citizens and permanent residents only. *Undergraduate preparation.* Suggested premed courses: 2 courses in biology with labs, 2 courses in general chemistry with labs, 2 courses in organic chemistry with labs, 2 courses in physics with labs, 1 course in college math, 2 courses in English. Bachelor's degree from an accredited institution required; 99% of applicants have bachelor's degree awarded prior to enrollment. *Has EDP*; applicants must apply through AMCAS (official transcripts sent by mid-May) between June 1 and August 1. Early applications are encouraged. Submit supplemental application, a personal statement, and 2 recommendations to Admissions Office within 2 weeks of receipt of application. Interviews are by invitation only and generally for final selection. Notification normally begins October 1. *Regular application process.* Apply through AMCAS (file after June 1, before November 1); submit MCAT (will accept MCAT test results from the last 3 years), official transcripts for each school attended (should show at least 90 semester credits/135 quarter credits, submit transcripts by mid-May to AMCAS), service processing fee. Submit an application fee of $60, a supplemental application, a personal statement, preprofessional committee evaluation, and 3 recommendations from science faculty to Admissions Office within 2–3 weeks of the receipt of supplemental materials. All foreign applicants must provide proof of financial support before they are eligible for consideration. Interviews are by invitation only and generally for final selection. M.S.T.P. and dual-degree applicants must apply to, and be accepted by, both schools; contact either the Director of M.S.T.P. (phone: (414)456-8641), the Graduate Office, Graduate School of Biomedical Sciences (phone: (414)456-4362), or the Admissions Office for current information and specific requirements for ad-

mission. First-year students admitted in fall only. Rolling admission process. Notification starts October 15 and is finished when class is filled. Applicant's response to offer and $100 deposit due within 2 weeks of receipt of acceptance letter. School does maintain an alternate list. Phone: (414)456-8246.

ADMISSION REQUIREMENTS FOR TRANSFER APPLICANTS. Accepts transfers from other LCME-accredited U.S. medical schools into the 2nd and 3rd years. Admission limited to space available. Contact the Admissions Office for current information and specific requirements for admission.

ADMISSION STANDARDS AND RECOGNITION. *For M.D.:* number of state-resident applicants 516, nonresidents 6,691; number of state residents interviewed 98, nonresidents 352; number of residents enrolled 98, nonresidents 106; median GPA 3.58 (A = 4). Gorman rating 3.23 (scale: acceptable plus 3.01–3.59); *U.S. News & World Report* ranked the school in the Top 25 of all U.S. medical schools in primary-care programs; the school's medical ranking by NIH awards was 52nd, with 149 awards/grants received; total dollars awarded $33,708,171.

FINANCIAL AID. Limited number of merit scholarships, grants-in-aid, tuition credits for Wisconsin residents, institutional loans, HEAL, alternative loan programs, NIH stipends, federal Perkins loans, Stafford subsidized and unsubsidized loans, and service commitment scholarship programs are available. M.S.T.P. candidates receive full tuition support and a stipend. Assistantships/fellowships may be available for dual-degree candidates. Financial aid applications should be initiated as soon as possible after the on-campus interview (by invitation). Most financial aid is based on demonstrated need and previous indebtedness. For scholarships, the selection criteria place heavy reliance on MCAT and undergraduate GPA. Contact the Student Financial Services Office for current information; phone: (414)456-8208. For most financial assistance and all federal programs, submit FAFSA to a federal processor (Title IV school code # 015611); also submit Financial Aid Transcript and Federal Income Tax forms; a credit report must be submitted prior to matriculation. Approximately 90% of current students receive some form of financial assistance. Average debt after graduation $81,000.

DEGREE REQUIREMENTS. *For M.D.:* satisfactory completion of 4-year program. All students must pass USMLE Step 1 prior to entering 3rd year; all students must take USMLE Step 2 and record a score. For M.D.-

M.A., M.S.: generally a 5–5½-year program. *For M.D.-Ph.D.:* generally a 7-year program.

UNIVERSITY OF MEDICINE AND DENTISTRY OF NEW JERSEY

Newark, New Jersey 07103-2400
Internet site: http://www.umdnj.edu

Founded 1970, became a free standing university in 1981. Public control. Graduate study-only institution. Quarter system. Special facilities: Center for Advanced Biotechnology and Medicine, Environmental and Occupational Health Science Center, New Jersey Cancer Institute, New Jersey Eye Institute. Library: 205,000 volumes; 22,219 microforms; 2,980 periodicals/subscriptions; 100 PC work stations. Special programs: B.A./B.S.-M.D. program. The university's ranking in domestic higher education by NIH awards was 54th, with 199 awards/grants received; total dollars awarded $48,050,716.

The university's other schools include: Graduate School of Biomedical Science, New Jersey Dental School, New Jersey Medical School, Robert Wood Johnson Medical School, School of Health Related Professions, School of Nursing, School of Osteopathic Medicine.

Total university enrollment at main campus: 4,476.

New Jersey Medical College

185 South Orange Avenue
Newark, New Jersey 07103-2714
Phone: (973)982-4631; fax: (973)982-7986
Internet site: http://www.umdnj.edu
E-mail: taylorbp@umdnj

Founded in 1954 as Seton Hall College of Medicine and Dentistry. Acquired by the state of New Jersey, 1965. Moved to Newark in 1977. Library: 77,000 volumes/microforms; 2,100 current periodicals/subscriptions. Affiliated hospitals: Beth Israel Hospital, University Hospital, East Orange Veterans Administration Hospital, Hackensack University Medical Center, Morristown Memorial Hospital, Children's Hospital of New Jersey, Kessler Institute, Berger Pines Hospital, St. Michael's Hospital of Patterson, Eye Institute of New Jersey, Jersey City Medical Center. Special programs: summer programs for underrepresented minorities; prematriculation summer sessions.

Annual tuition: residents $16,162, nonresidents $24,594; fees $1,200. No on-campus housing available. Contact Office of Student Affairs for off-campus housing information; phone: (973)982-4631. Off-campus housing and personal expenses: approximately $13,522.

Enrollment: 1st-year class 170 (EDP 3); total full-time 696 (men 65%, women 35%). First-year statistics: 8% out of state; 33.5% women; average age 25; 15% minorities; 66% science majors.

Faculty: full-time 640, part-time/volunteers 1,200.

Degrees conferred: M.D., B.S.-M.D. (in collaboration with Boston University, Drew University, Montclair State University, New Jersey Institute of Technology, Stevens Institute of Technology, Richard Stockton College of New Jersey), M.D.-Ph.D. (Anatomy, Biochemistry, Cell Biology, Microbiology and Molecular Genetics, Neurosciences, Oral Biology, Pathology, Pharmacology, Physiology).

RECRUITMENT PRACTICES AND POLICIES. School has diversity program and actively recruits women/minority applicants. Diversity contact: Assistant Dean for Minority Affairs, phone: (973)982-5431.

ADMISSION REQUIREMENT FOR BACHELOR-M.D. APPLICANTS. Request application information from one or more of the undergraduate institutions listed above. All undergraduate institutions have specific requirements for admissions; for current information and specific requirements, contact the individual Admissions Offices; phone: Drew University: (201)408-3802; NJIT; (201)596-3584; Stockton: (602)657-4514; College of New Jersey: (609)771-2021. Submit the application and all required admissions materials by the institution's application deadline.

ADMISSION REQUIREMENTS FOR FIRST-YEAR APPLICANTS. Preference given to state residents; U.S. citizens and permanent residents only. *Undergraduate preparation.* Suggested premed courses: 2 courses in biology with labs, 2 courses in inorganic chemistry with labs, 2 courses in organic chemistry with labs, 2 courses in physics with labs, 2 courses in English; 1 course in college math recommended. Bachelor's degree from an accredited institution required; 84% of applicants have bachelor's degree awarded prior to enrollment. *Has EDP* for state residents only; applicants must apply through AMCAS (official transcripts sent by mid-May) between June 1 and August 1. Early applications are encouraged. Submit secondary/supplemental application, a personal statement, and 2 recommendations to Admissions Office within 2 weeks of receipt of application. Interviews are by invitation only and generally for final selection. Notification normally begins October 1. *Regular application process.* Apply through AMCAS (file after June 1, before December 1); submit MCAT (will accept MCAT test results from the last 4 years), official transcripts for each school attended (should show at least 90 semester credits/135 quarter credits, submit transcripts by mid-May to AMCAS), service processing fee. Submit an application fee of $125, a supplemental application, a personal statement, preprofessional committee evaluation, and 2 recommendations from science faculty to Director of Admissions, within 2–3 weeks of the receipt of supplemental materials. Interviews are by invitation only and generally for final selection. Dual-degree applicants must apply to, and be accepted by, both schools; contact the Admissions Office for current information and specific requirements for admission. First-year students admitted in fall only. Rolling admission process. Notification starts on October 15 and is finished when class is filled. Applicant's response to offer and $100 deposit due within 2 weeks of receipt of acceptance letter. School does maintain an alternate list. Phone: (973)972-4631/5383; fax: (973)972-7986; E-mail: njms_admiss@umdnj.edu.

ADMISSION REQUIREMENTS FOR TRANSFER APPLICANTS. Accepts transfers from other accredited U.S. medical schools. Admission limited to space available. Contact the Admissions Office for current information and specific requirements for admission.

ADMISSION STANDARDS AND RECOGNITION. *For M.D.:* number of state-resident applicants 1,379, nonresidents 2,578; number of state residents interviewed 480, nonresidents 194; number of residents enrolled 157, nonresidents 3; median MCAT 9.8 (verbal reasoning 9.6; biological sciences 10.1; physical sciences 10.1); median GPA 3.44 (A = 4). Gorman rating 3.43 (scale: acceptable plus 3.01–3.59); the school's medical ranking by NIH awards/grants was 76th, with 60 awards/grants received; total dollars awarded $15,151,867.

FINANCIAL AID. Academic excellence scholarships, minority scholarships, grants-in-aid, institutional loans, HEAL, alternative loan programs, NIH stipends, federal Perkins loans, Stafford subsidized and unsubsidized loans, and service commitment scholarship programs are available. The UMDNJ financial aid applications and information are available at the on-campus interview (by invitation). All students are considered automatically for all financial aid they are eligible for. Assistantships/fellowships may be available for dual-degree candidates. For merit scholarships, the selection criteria place heavy reliance on MCAT and undergraduate GPA. Contact the Financial Aid Office for current information; phone: (973)972-4376. For most financial assistance and all federal programs, submit FAFSA to a federal processor (Title IV school code # 013645); also submit Financial Aid Transcript and Federal Income Tax forms. Approximately 70% of current students receive some form of financial assistance. Average debt after graduation $76,100.

DEGREE REQUIREMENTS. *For B.A./B.S.-M.D.:* generally a 7-year program (3 years undergraduate, 4 years of medical school). *For M.D.:* satisfactory completion of 4-year program. All students must pass USMLE Step 1 prior to entering 3rd year; all students must pass USMLE Step 2 prior to awarding of M.D. *For M.D.-Ph.D.:* generally a 7-year program.

Dental School
110 Bergen Street, Room B829
Newark, New Jersey 07103-2425
Phone: (973)972-4300

Established 1954; admitted first class in 1956. Special programs: Students for Dentistry Program (for underrepresented minorities); prematriculation summer sessions; summer research fellowships; externships. Postgraduate specialties: Endodontics, General Dentistry (AEGD), General Practice Residency, Oral and Maxillofacial Surgery, Oral Medicine, Orthodontics, Pediatric Dentistry, Periodontics, Prosthodontics.

Annual tuition: residents $14,492, nonresidents $22,679; fees $575; equipment and supplies $4,300. No on-campus housing available. Contact Housing Office for off-campus housing information; phone: (973)972-5362. Off-campus housing, food, transportation, and personal expenses: approximately $9,634.

Enrollment: 1st-year class 75. First-year enrolled student information: 10 from out of state; 7 states represented; 36 women; average age 24; 12 underrepresented minorities; 5 other minorities.

Degrees conferred: D.M.D., B.S.-D.M.D. (Fairleigh Dickinson University, Jersey City State College, Montclair State University, New Jersey Institute of Technology, Ramapo College, Stockton State College, Rowan University, Stevens Institute of Technology), D.M.D.-M.S. and D.M.D.-Ph.D. with the Graduate School of Biomedical Science (Anatomy, Biochemistry and Molecular Biology, Cell Biology, Injury Science, Laboratory Medicine and Pathology, Microbiology and Molecular Genetics, Neurosciences, Pharmacology and Toxicology, Physiology).

RECRUITMENT PRACTICES AND POLICIES. School has diversity program and actively recruits women/minority applicants. Diversity contact: Minority Affairs Office; phone: (973)972-3434.

ADMISSION REQUIREMENTS FOR B.S.-D.M.D. APPLICANTS. The admission requirements for each college are different and unique; contact the individual admissions offices for current policies and procedures.

ADMISSION REQUIREMENTS FOR FIRST-YEAR APPLICANTS. Preference given to state residents; U.S. citizens and permanent residents only. *Undergraduate preparation.* Suggested predental courses: 2 courses in biology with labs, 2 courses in inorganic chemistry with labs, 2 courses in organic chemistry with labs, 2 courses in physics with labs, 2 courses in English. There is no limitation on the number of junior college credits that may be taken. Will consider applicants with only 3 years of undergraduate preparation; prefer applicants who will have a bachelor's degree prior to enrollment; 72 out 75 applicants had bachelor's degree awarded prior to enrollment. *Application process.* Apply through AADSAS (file after June 1, before December 1), submit official transcripts for each school attended (should show at least 90 semester credits/135 quarter credits), service processing fee. Submit the following materials directly to the Office of Student Affairs only after being contacted by an Admissions Officer: an application fee, official transcripts, DAT scores, predental committee evaluation or 3 recommendations from science professors, photograph. Interviews are by invitation only and generally for final selection. Dual-degree applicants must apply to, and be accepted by, both schools. First-year students admitted in fall only. Rolling admission process. Notification starts in December and is finished when class is filled. Applicant's response to offer and $100 deposit due within 30 days if accepted prior to January 31; response and deposit due within 2 weeks if received after February 1.

ADMISSION REQUIREMENTS FOR ADVANCED-STANDING APPLICANTS. Accepts transfers from other accredited U.S. dental schools who surpass the minimum requirements for entrance of the current class. Admission limited to space available. There is no advanced-standing program for graduates of foreign schools of dentistry. Contact the Office of Student Affairs for current information and specific requirements for admission.

ADMISSION STANDARDS AND RECOGNITION. *For D.M.D.:* number of applicants 1,115; number enrolled 75; median DAT: ACAD 17.11, PAT 15.75; median GPA 3.12 (A = 4), median sciences GPA 3.05 (A = 4). Gorman rating 4.11 (scale: strong 4.01–4.49); this placed the school in the Bottom 10 of all U.S. dental schools; the dental school's ranking by NIH awards/grants was 17th among dental schools, with 7 awards/grants received; total value of all awards/grants $2,398,302.

FINANCIAL AID. Scholarships, MLK scholarships, grants, institutional loans, state loan programs, DEAL, HEAL, alternative loan programs; federal Perkins loans, Stafford subsidized and unsubsidized loans, and military service commitment scholarship programs are available. Assistantships/fellowships may be available for combined-degree candidates. Institutional financial aid applications and *Financial Aid Handbook* are available at the interview (by invitation). Most financial aid is based on demonstrated need. For scholarships, the selection criteria place heavy reliance on DAT and undergraduate GPA. Contact the Financial Aid Office for current information; phone: (973)972-4376. For most financial assistance and all need-based programs, submit FAFSA to a federal processor (Title IV school code # 013645); also submit Financial Aid Transcript, Federal Income Tax forms, and Use of Federal Funds Certification. Approximately 99% of current students receive some form of financial assistance. Average award resident $19,493 (79% loan), nonresidents $26,302 (79% loan).

DEGREE REQUIREMENTS. *For B.S.-D.M.D.:* a 6–7-year program. *For D.M.D.:* satisfactory completion of 4-year-program. *For D.M.D.-M.S.:* generally a 4½–5½-year program. *For D.M.D.-Ph.D.:* generally a 6–7-year program.

Robert Wood Johnson Medical College

675 Hoes Lane
Piscataway, New Jersey 08854-5635
Phone: (908)235-4576; fax: (908)235-5078
Internet site: http://www3.imdnj.edu/rwjms.html

Established 1961; formerly known as Rutgers Medical School; was a 2-year medical program. Located adjacent to Rutgers University. Has campuses in Piscataway and Camden. All basic science education is at Piscataway campus. Affiliated hospitals: Robert Wood Johnson University Hospital (New Brunswick), Cooper Hospital/Medical Center (Camden), Cancer Institute of New Jersey. Special facilities: Environmental and Occupational Health Science Institute (designated by NIH as a center of excellence). Special programs: Summer programs for underrepresented minorities; prematriculation summer sessions.

Annual tuition: residents $16,247, nonresidents $24,679; fees $1,150. No on-campus housing available. Contact Student Affairs Office for off-campus housing information. Off-campus housing and personal expenses: approximately $13,238.

Enrollment: 1st-year class 139 (EDP 6); total full-time 624 (men 59%, women 41%). First-year statistics: 13% out of state; 37% women; average age 25; 19% minorities; 65% science majors.

Degrees conferred: M.D., B.S.-M.D. (Rutgers University), M.D.-J.D., M.D.-M.P.H., M.D.-Ph.D. (Biochemistry, Biomedical Engineering, Cell Biology, Microbiology, Molecular Biology, Pharmacology, Physiology).

RECRUITMENT PRACTICES AND POLICIES. School has diversity program and actively recruits women/minority applicants. Diversity contact: Assistant Dean, Multicultural and Student Affairs, phone: (908)235-4060.

ADMISSION REQUIREMENT FOR BACHELOR-M.D. APPLICANTS. All applicants are students at Rutgers University and are selected at the end of their sophomore year. ACCESS-MEDUMDNJ: an articulation program for underrepresented minorities affiliated with Rutgers University, Seton Hall University, and College of New Jersey. For current information and specific requirements for admission, contact Director ACCESS-MED.

ADMISSION REQUIREMENTS FOR FIRST-YEAR APPLICANTS. Preference given to state residents; U.S. citizens and permanent residents only. *Undergraduate preparation.* Suggested premed courses: 2 courses in biology with labs, 2 courses in inorganic chemistry with labs, 2 courses in organic chemistry with labs, 2 courses in physics with labs, 1 course in college math, 2 courses in English. Bachelor's degree from an accredited institution required; all applicants have bachelor's degree awarded prior to enrollment. *Has EDP;* applicants must apply through AMCAS (official transcripts sent by mid-May) between June 1 and August 1. Early applications are encouraged. Submit secondary/supplemental application, a personal statement, and 2 recommendations to Admissions Office within 2 weeks of receipt of application. Interviews are by invitation only and generally for final selection. Notification normally begins October 1. *Regular application process.* Apply through AMCAS (file after June 1, before December 1); submit MCAT (will accept MCAT test results from the last 4 years), official transcripts for each school attended (should show at least 90 semester credits/135 quarter credits, submit transcripts by mid-May to AMCAS), service processing fee. Submit an application fee of $125, a supplemental application, a personal statement, preprofessional committee evaluation, and 2 recommendations from science faculty to Admissions Office within 2½–3 weeks of the receipt of supplemental materials. Interviews are by invitation only and generally for final selection. M.D.-Ph.D. degree applicants must apply to, and be accepted by, both schools; contact the Admissions Office for current information and specific requirements for admission. First-year stu-dents admitted in fall only. Rolling admission process. Notification starts in October and is finished when class is filled. Applicant's response to offer and $50 deposit due within 2 weeks of receipt of acceptance letter. School does maintain an alternate list. Phone: (908)235-4576; fax: (908)235-5635. *For M.D.-Ph.D.* contact the Graduate School of Biomedical Sciences: (908)235-5016.

ADMISSION REQUIREMENTS FOR TRANSFER APPLICANTS. Accepts transfers from other accredited U.S. medical schools. Admission limited to space available. Contact the Admissions Office for current information and specific requirements for admission.

ADMISSION STANDARDS AND RECOGNITION. *For B.A./B.S.-M.D.:* number of state-resident applicants 39, nonresidents 3; number of state residents interviewed 33, nonresidents 2; number of residents enrolled 12, nonresidents 0; median SAT verbal 596; math 735; high school median GPA 3.84 (A = 4). *For M.D.:* number of state-resident applicants 1,365, nonresidents 2,608; number of state residents interviewed 652, nonresidents 105; number of residents enrolled 121, nonresidents 18; median MCAT 9.6 (verbal reasoning 9.1; biological sciences 10.0; physical sciences 10.0); median GPA 3.54 (A = 4). Gorman rating 3.26 (scale: acceptable plus 3.01–3.59).

FINANCIAL AID. Scholarships, minority scholarships, grants-in-aid, institutional loans, HEAL, alternative loan programs, federal Perkins loans, Stafford subsidized and unsubsidized loans, and service commitment scholarship programs are available. Assistantships/fellowships may be available for dual-degree candidates. UMDNJ financial aid applications and information are given out at the on-campus interview (by invitation). Most financial aid is based on demonstrated need. For scholarships, the selection criteria place heavy reliance on MCAT and undergraduate GPA. Contact the university's Financial Aid Office for current information; phone: (973)972-7030. For most financial assistance and all federal programs, submit FAFSA to a federal processor (Title IV school code # 013645); also submit Financial Aid Transcript, Federal Income Tax forms, Statement of Educational Purpose and Default/Refund Statement. Approximately 80% of current students receive some form of financial assistance. Average debt after graduation $73,600.

DEGREE REQUIREMENTS. *For B.A./B.S.-M.D.:* a 7-year program. *For M.D.:* satisfactory completion of 4-year program. All students must pass USMLE Step 1 prior to entering 3rd year; all students must pass USMLE

Step 2 prior to awarding of M.D. *For M.D.-J.D.:* generally a 6½–8-year program. *For M.D.-M.P.H.:* generally a 5-year program; fieldwork experience. *For M.D.-Ph.D.:* generally a 7-year program.

School of Osteopathic Medicine
1 Medical Center Drive
Stratford, New Jersey 08084-1401
Phone: (609)566-6998
Internet site: http://www3.umdnj/edu
E-mail: wallacwss@umdnj.edu

Established 1976. Located in southern New Jersey. Special programs: Center for Health Promotion and Wellness. Affiliated hospitals: 3 Kennedy Memorial Hospital University Medical Center sites, Our Lady of Lourdes Hospital, Christ Hospital (Jersey City).

Annual tuition: residents $16,484, nonresidents $24,634. No on-campus housing available. Contact Admissions Office for assistance in finding off-campus housing. Off-campus housing and personal expenses: approximately $12,000.

Enrollment: 1st-year class 75; total full-time 266 (men 47%, women 53%). First-year statistics: 10% out of state; average age 24; 24% minorities.

Faculty: full-time 149, part-time 21

Degrees conferred: D.O., D.O.-Ph.D. with the Graduate School of Biomedical Sciences, Stratford Division (Cell and Molecular Biology).

RECRUITMENT PRACTICES AND POLICIES. School has diversity program and actively recruits women/minority applicants. Diversity contact: Admissions Office.

ADMISSION REQUIREMENTS FOR FIRST-YEAR APPLICANTS. Preference given to state residents; U.S. citizens and permanent residents only. *Undergraduate preparation.* Suggested premed courses: 2 courses in biology, 2 courses in inorganic chemistry, 2 courses in organic chemistry, 2 courses in physics, 1 course in college math, 2 courses in English, 2 courses in behavioral sciences. Bachelor's degree from an accredited institution required; all applicants have bachelor's degree awarded prior to enrollment. *Application process.* Apply through AACOMAS (file after June, before February 1), submit MCAT (will accept test results from last 3 years), submit official transcripts for each school attended (should show at least 90 semester credits/135 quarter credits), service processing fee. After a review of the AACOMAS application and supporting documents, a decision is made concerning which candidates should receive supplemental materials. The supplemental application, an application fee of $125, a personal statement, and 3 recommendations (1 from a D.O.) should be returned to Admissions Office as soon as possible. Joint-degree applicants must apply to, and be accepted by, both schools; contact the Admissions Office for current information and specific requirements for admission. Interviews are by invitation only and generally for final selection. In addition, international applicants must submit foreign transcripts to the World Education Service for translation and evaluation. TOEFL may be required of those applicants whose native language is other than English. First-year students admitted in fall only. Rolling admission process. Notification starts in January and is finished when class is filled. Applicant's response to offer due within 2 weeks of receipt of acceptance letter. Phone: (609)566-7050; fax: (609)566-6895.

ADMISSION REQUIREMENTS FOR TRANSFER APPLICANTS. Accepts transfers from other accredited U.S. osteopathic medical schools. Admission limited to space available. Contact the Admissions Office for current information and specific requirements for admission.

ADMISSION STANDARDS AND RECOGNITION. *For D.O.:* number of applicants 3,200; number enrolled 80; median MCAT 8.4; median GPA 3.46; the school's ranking by NIH awards/grants was 2nd among osteopathic schools, with 11 awards/grants received; total value of all awards/grants $2,651,988.

FINANCIAL AID. Scholarships, merit scholarships, MLK scholarships, grants, institutional loans, NOF, HEAL, alternative loan programs, NIH stipends, federal Perkins loans, Stafford subsidized and unsubsidized loans, service obligation scholarship programs, and military and national health service programs are available. Financial aid applications and information are generally available at the interview (by invitation); however, all accepted students are sent financial aid applications and information. All accepted applicants are considered for merit scholarships; the selection criteria place heavy reliance on MCAT and undergraduate GPA; all scholarships are renewable. Contact the Financial Aid Office for current information; phone: (609)566-6008. For most financial assistance and for all federal programs use FAFSA (Title IV school code # 031645); also submit Financial Aid Transcript and Federal Income Tax forms. Approximately 80% of current students receive some form of financial assistance. Average debt after graduation $73,000.

DEGREE REQUIREMENTS. *For D.O.:* satisfactory completion of 4-year program. All students must pass the National Board of Osteopathic Medical Examination Level I and II prior to the awarding of D.O. *For D.O.-Ph.D.:* generally a 7–8-year program.

MEHARRY MEDICAL COLLEGE
Nashville, Tennessee 37208-9989

Founded 1976. Private control. Semester system. Library: 58,000 volumes/microforms; 1,000 periodicals/subscriptions. Special programs: B.A./B.S.-M.D. program (annual undergraduate tuition $7,078).

The college's schools are: School of Allied Health Professions, School of Dentistry, School of Graduate Study and Research, School of Medicine.

Total enrollment: about 800.

School of Medicine
1005 D. B.Todd Boulevard
Nashville, Tennessee 37208
Phone: (615)327-6223; fax: (615)327-6228
Internet site: http://www.mmc.edu

Established 1876. Affiliated hospitals: George W. Hubbard Hospital, Meharry Comprehensive Health Center, Metro Nashville General Hospital, York Veterans Administration Medical Center, Blanchfield Army Community Hospital, Elam Community Health Center, Murfreesboro VA Hospital, United Neighbor Hood Health Services Medical Clinic, Matthew Walker Comprehensive Health Center.

Annual tuition: $17,800; fees $2,000. On-campus housing available for both single and married students. Contact Admissions Office for both on- and off-campus housing information. Off-campus housing and personal expenses: approximately $6,500.

Enrollment: 1st-year class 80; total full-time 385 (men 50%, women 50%). First-year statistics: 80% out of state; 51% women; average age 25; 82% minorities.

Degrees conferred: M.D., B.S.-M.D. (Fisk University), M.D.-M.S. (Medical Scholars Program), M.D.-Ph.D. (Biochemistry, Cell Biology, Microbiology, Molecular Biology, Neurosciences, Pharmacology, Physiology).

RECRUITMENT PRACTICES AND POLICIES. School has diversity program and actively recruits women/minority applicants. Diversity contact: Assistant Dean for Students/Academic Affairs; phone: (615)327-6713.

ADMISSION REQUIREMENT FOR BACHELOR-M.D. APPLICANTS. Preference given to state residents who are minority students. Students must apply by February 1 of freshmen year. Selection occurs after 1 semester at Fisk University. The applicants must have taken either SATs or ACTs.

ADMISSION REQUIREMENTS FOR FIRST-YEAR APPLICANTS. Preference given to state residents; U.S. citizens and permanent residents only. *Undergraduate preparation.* Suggested premed courses: 2 courses in biology with labs, 2 courses in general chemistry with labs, 2 courses in organic chemistry with labs, 2 courses in physics with labs, 2 courses in English. Bachelor's degree from an accredited institution required; 96% of applicants have bachelor's degree awarded prior to enrollment. *Has EDP* for state residents only; applicants must apply through AMCAS (official transcripts sent by mid-May) between June 1 and August 1. Early applications are encouraged. Submit secondary/supplemental application, a personal statement, 2 recommendations to Admissions Office within 2 weeks of receipt of application. Interviews are by invitation only and generally for final selection. Notification normally begins October 1. *Regular application process.* Apply through AMCAS (file after June 1, before December 15); submit MCAT (will accept MCAT test results from 1995), official transcripts for each school attended (should show at least 90 semester credits/135 quarter credits, submit transcripts by mid-May to AMCAS), service processing fee. Submit an application fee of $45, a supplemental application, a personal statement, preprofessional committee evaluation, and 2 recommendations from science faculty to Admissions Office within 2–3 weeks of the receipt of supplemental materials. Interviews are by invitation only and generally for final selection. Dual-degree applicants must apply to, and be accepted by, both schools; contact the Admissions Office for current information and specific requirements for admission. First-year students admitted in fall only. Rolling admission process. Notification starts on October 15 and is finished when class is filled. Applicant's response to offer and $300 deposit due within 3 weeks of receipt of acceptance letter. School does maintain an alternate list. Phone: (615)327-6951; E-mail: admissions@ccvax.mmc.edu.

ADMISSION REQUIREMENTS FOR TRANSFER APPLICANTS. Does not consider transfer applicants. Contact the Admissions Office for current information and any change in admissions policy.

ADMISSION STANDARDS AND RECOGNITION. *For M.D.:* number of state-resident applicants 299, nonresidents 5,154; number of state residents interviewed 32, nonresidents 303; number of residents enrolled 16, nonresidents 64; median MCAT 7.6 (verbal reasoning 7.7; biological sciences 7.8; physical sciences 7.2); median GPA 3.0 (A = 4). Gorman rating 3.37 (scale: acceptable plus 3.01–3.59); school's medical ranking by NIH awards was 85th, with 37 awards/grants received; total dollars awarded $10,350,194.

FINANCIAL AID. Limited scholarships, grants-in-aid, institutional loans, HEAL, alternative loan programs, federal Perkins loans, Stafford subsidized and unsubsidized loans, and service commitment scholarship programs are available. Assistantships/fellowships may be available for combined-degree candidates. Financial-aid applications and information are given out at the on-campus interview (by invitation). Contact the Financial Aid Office for current information; phone: (315)327-6826; E-mail: kendal16@ccvax.mmc.edu. For most financial assistance and all federal programs, submit FAFSA to a federal processor (Title IV school code # G03506); also submit Financial Aid Transcript and Federal Income Tax forms. Approximately 85% of current students receive some form of financial assistance.

DEGREE REQUIREMENTS. *For B.S.-M.D.:* a 7-year program. *For M.D.:* satisfactory completion of 4- or 5-year program. All students must pass USMLE Step 1 prior to entering 3rd year; all students must pass USMLE Step 2 prior to awarding of M.D. *For M.D.-M.S.:* generally a 4½–5½-year program. *For M.D.-Ph.D.:* generally a 7-year program.

School of Dentistry
1005 D. B. Todd Boulevard
Nashville, Tennessee 37208
Phone: (615)327-6207
Internet site: http://www.mmc.edu

Established 1876. Special facilities: Regional Research Center for Minority Oral Health. Affiliated hospitals: Metropolitan Nashville General Hospital, Alvin C. York Veterans Administration Medical Center. Postgraduate specialties: Oral and Maxillofacial Surgery.

Annual tuition: $17,820; fees $2,194; equipment and supplies $1,200. On-campus rooms and apartments available for both single and married students. Contact Admissions Office for both on- and off-campus housing information. Off-campus housing, food, transportation, and personal expenses: approximately $13,535.

Enrollment: 1st-year class 50; total full-time, 179. First-year enrolled student information: 49 from out of state; 17 states represented; 25 women; average age 25; 42 underrepresented minorities; 4 other minorities.

Degrees conferred: D.D.S., B.S.-D.D.S. (Fisk University).

RECRUITMENT PRACTICES AND POLICIES. School has diversity program and actively recruits women/minority applicants. Diversity contact: Assistant Dean for Students/Academic Affairs; phone: (615)327-6713.

ADMISSION REQUIREMENT FOR BACHELOR-D.D.S. APPLICANTS. Preference given to state residents who are minority applicants. Students must apply during freshmen year at Fisk University. Selection occurs after 1 semester at Fisk University.

ADMISSION REQUIREMENTS FOR FIRST-YEAR APPLICANTS. Preference given to state residents and residents of SREB states; U.S. citizens and permanent residents only. *Undergraduate preparation.* Suggested predental courses: 2 courses in biology/zoology with labs, 2 courses in general chemistry with labs, 2 courses in organic chemistry with labs, 2 courses in physics with labs, 2 courses in English. There is no limitation on the number of credits taken at an accredited junior college. Will consider applicants with only 3 years of undergraduate preparation; prefer applicants who will have a bachelor's degree prior to enrollment; all applicants have bachelor's degree awarded prior to enrollment. *Application process.* Apply through AADSAS (file after June 1, before December 1); submit official transcripts for each school attended (should show at least 90 semester credits/135 quarter credits), service processing fee. Submit the following materials only after being contacted by an Admissions Officer: an application fee of $45 (money order or cashier check), a supplemental application, official transcripts, official DAT scores (must have been taken within the last 3 years), predental committee evaluation or three letters of recommendations, and current photograph to Admissions Office and Records within 2 weeks of receipt of supplemental materials. Interviews are by invitation only and generally for final selection. First-year students admitted in fall only. Rolling admission process. Notification starts on December 1 and is finished when class is filled, but generally not later than July 15. Applicant's response to offer and $100 deposit due within 30 days if accepted prior to January 31; response and deposit due within 2 weeks if received after February 1. Phone: (615)327-6223.

ADMISSION REQUIREMENTS FOR ADVANCED-STANDING APPLICANTS. Accepts transfers from other accredited U.S. and Canadian dental schools. Admission limited to space available. Contact the Admissions Office for current information and specific requirements for admission.

ADMISSION STANDARDS AND RECOGNITION. *For D.D.S.:* number of applicants 1,313; number enrolled 50; median DAT: ACAD 15.5, PAT 15.5; median GPA 2.84 (A = 4), median sciences GPA 2.63 (A = 4). Gorman rating 4.3 (scale: strong 4.01-4.49); this placed the school in the Bottom 10 of all U.S. dental schools.

FINANCIAL AID. Limited scholarships, grants-in-aid, institutional loans, state loan programs, DEAL, HEAL, alternative loan programs, federal Perkins loans, Stafford subsidized and unsubsidized loans, and military service commitment scholarship programs are available. Institutional financial aid applications and information are given out at the on-campus interview (by invitation). Contact the medical college's Office of Financial Aid for current information; phone: (615)327-6826. For most financial assistance and all need-based programs, submit FAFSA to a federal processor (Title IV school code # G03506); also submit Financial Aid Transcript, Federal Income Tax forms, and Use of Federal Funds Certification. Approximately 83% of current students receive some form of financial assistance. Average award $37,708.

DEGREE REQUIREMENTS. *For B.S.-D.D.S.:* a 7-year program. *For D.D.S.:* satisfactory completion of 4-year program.

MERCER UNIVERSITY

Macon, Georgia 31207-0003
Internet site: http://www.mercer.edu

Founded 1833. Located in an urban area, 80 miles S of Atlanta. Coed. Private control—Baptist affiliation. Semester system. Library: 404,800 volumes; 241,000 microforms; 3,346 periodicals/subscriptions; 35 work stations.

The university's graduate colleges/schools: School of Education, School of Engineering, School of Medicine, Stetson School of Business and Economics, Walter F. George School of Law.

Total university enrollment at main campus: 5,000.

School of Medicine

Macon, Georgia 31207
Phone: (912)752-2524; fax: (912)752-2547
Internet site: http://www.mercer.edu
E-mail: kothanek.j@gain.mercer.edu

Established 1982. Located on university's campus. Affiliated hospitals: Medical Center of Central Georgia (Macon), Memorial Medical Center (Savannah), Floyd Medical Center (Rome), Putney Memorial Hospital (Albany), Medical Center (Columbus).

Annual tuition: $20,528. On-campus rooms and apartments available for both single and married students. Contact Admissions Office for both on- and off-campus housing information. Medical students tend to live off-campus. Off-campus housing and personal expenses: approximately $10,805.

Enrollment: 1st-year class 56 (EDP 12); total full-time 215 (men 62%, women 38%). First-year statistics: none from out of state; 35.7% women; average age 24; 1% minorities.

Degree conferred: M.D.

RECRUITMENT PRACTICES AND POLICIES. School has diversity program and actively recruits women/minority applicants. Diversity contact: Associate Dean for Admissions/Student Affairs; phone: (912)752-2542.

ADMISSION REQUIREMENTS FOR FIRST-YEAR APPLICANTS. Preference given to state residents; U.S. citizens and permanent residents only. *Undergraduate preparation.* Suggested premed courses: 2 courses in biology with labs, 2 courses in inorganic chemistry with labs, 2 courses in organic chemistry with labs, 2 courses in physics with labs; 1 course in biochemistry is highly recommended. Bachelor's degree from an accredited institution required; all applicants have bachelor's degree awarded prior to enrollment. *Has EDP* for state residents only; applicants must apply through AMCAS (official transcripts sent by mid-May) between June 1 and August 1. Early applications are encouraged. Submit secondary/supplemental application, a personal statement, and 2 recommendations to Admissions Office within 2 weeks of receipt of application. Interviews are by invitation only and generally for final selection. Notification normally begins October 15. *Regular application process.* Apply through AMCAS (file after June 1, before December 1); submit MCAT (will accept MCAT test results from the last 3 years), official transcripts for each school attended (should show at least 90 semester credits/135 quarter credits, submit transcripts by mid-May to AMCAS), service processing fee. Submit an application fee of $25, a supplemental application, a personal statement, preprofessional committee evaluation and 2 recommendations from science faculty, and a Certificate of Georgia Residency to Admissions Office within 2–3 weeks of the receipt of supplemental materials. First-year students admitted in fall only. Rolling admission process. Notification starts October 15 and is finished when class is filled. Applicant's response to offer and $100 deposit due within 10 days of receipt of acceptance letter. Phone: (912)752-2524; E-mail: kothanek.j@gain.mercer.edu.

ADMISSION REQUIREMENTS FOR TRANSFER APPLICANTS. Accepts transfers from other accredited U.S. medical schools who are Georgia residents into the 3rd year only. Admission limited to space available. Contact the Admissions Office for current information and specific requirements for admission.

ADMISSION STANDARDS AND RECOGNITION. *For M.D.:* number of state-resident applicants 753, nonresidents 596; number of state residents interviewed 174, nonresidents 0; number of residents enrolled 56, nonresidents 0; median MCAT 8.6 (verbal reasoning 8.9; biological sciences 8.6; physical sciences 8.0); median GPA 3.4 (A = 4). Gorman rating 3.05 (scale: acceptable plus 3.01–3.59); the school's medical ranking by NIH awards was 123rd, with 3 awards/grants received; total dollars awarded $372,755.

FINANCIAL AID. Scholarships, merit scholarships, institutional loans, HEAL, alternative loan programs, federal Perkins loans, Stafford subsidized and unsubsidized loans, and service commitment scholarship programs are available. Financial aid applications and information are available at the on-campus interview. For merit scholarships, the selection criteria place heavy reliance on MCAT and undergraduate GPA. Contact the Financial Aid Office for current information; phone: (912)752-2853. For most financial assistance and all federal programs, submit FAFSA to a federal processor (Title IV school code # E00560); also submit Financial Aid Transcript and Federal Income Tax forms. Approximately 88% of current students receive some form of financial assistance.

DEGREE REQUIREMENTS. *For M.D.:* satisfactory completion of 4-year program. All students must pass USMLE Step 1 prior to entering 3rd year; all students must pass USMLE Step 2 prior to awarding of M.D.

UNIVERSITY OF MIAMI
Coral Gables, Florida 33124
Internet site: http://www.miami.edu

Founded 1925. Located 12 miles SW of Miami. Private control. Semester system. Library: 2,030,000 volumes; 3,130,000 microforms; 19,550 periodicals/subscriptions. The university's ranking in domestic higher education by NIH awards/grants was 44th, with 206 awards/grants received; total dollars awarded $59,912,967. Special programs: B.S.-M.D. program (annual undergraduate tuition $17,700).

The university's graduate schools/colleges include: College of Arts and Science, College of Engineering, Graduate School of International Studies, Rosenstiel School of Marine and Atmospheric Science, School of Architecture, School of Business Administration, School of Communication, School of Education, School of Music, School of Nursing, School of Law, School of Medicine.

Total university enrollment at main campus: 13,541.

University of Miami–Jackson Memorial Medical Center
1611 N.W. 12 Avenue
Miami, Florida 33136

Private control. The medical center is a member of Council of Teaching Hospitals. Special facilities: Applebaum Magnetic Resonance Imaging Center, Bascombe Palmer Eye Institute/Anne Bates Leach Eye Hospital, Sylvester Comprehensive Cancer Center, Ryder Trauma Center, Diabetes Research Institute, Mailman Center for Child Development. Nationally recognized programs in AIDS, Gastroenterology, Neurology, Ophthalmology, Pediatrics.

School of Medicine
P.O. Box 016159
Miami, Florida 33101-6189
Phone: (305)243-6791; fax: (305)243-6548
Internet site: http://www.med.miami.edu
E-mail: miami-md@mednet.med.miami.edu

Established 1952. Located next to Jackson Memorial Hospital in the Civic Center area of Miami. Block curriculum system. Library: 180,000 volumes/microforms; 2,100 current periodicals/subscriptions. Affiliated hospitals: Jackson Memorial Hospital, Veterans Affairs Medical Center. Special programs: summer programs for underrepresented minorities.

Annual tuition: residents $24,190, nonresidents $30,070; fees $578. No on-campus housing available. Contact Admissions Office for off-campus housing information. Off-campus housing and personal expenses: approximately $12,840.

Enrollment: 1st-year class 140 (EDP 10); total full-time 578 (men 50%, women 50%). First-year statistics: 3% out of state; 47.9% women; average age 24; 10% minorities; 60% science majors.

Degrees conferred: M.D., B.S.-M.D., M.D.-Ph.D.

(Anatomy, Biochemistry, Biophysics, Cell Biology, Immunology, Microbiology, Molecular Biology, Neurosciences, Pharmacology, Physiology).

RECRUITMENT PRACTICES AND POLICIES. School has diversity program and actively recruits women/minority applicants. Diversity contact: Associate Dean for Minority Affairs; phone: (305)243-6865.

ADMISSION REQUIREMENT FOR BACHELOR-M.D. APPLICANTS (honors program in medicine). State residents only. Submit application, SAT I, SAT II (English, mathematics, science) or ACT, official high school transcripts with rank in class, and 3 letters of recommendations. Interviews are by invitation only at the College of Arts and Science, University of Miami, and generally for final selection. Apply to Admissions Office by January 1. Notification by April 1. Application fee $30. Phone: (305)284-4323; Financial Aid Office phone: (305)284-5212.

ADMISSION REQUIREMENTS FOR FIRST-YEAR APPLICANTS. Preference given to state residents; U.S. citizens and permanent residents only. *Undergraduate preparation.* Suggested premed courses: 2 courses in biology with labs, 2 courses in inorganic chemistry with labs, 2 courses in organic chemistry with labs, 2 courses in physics with labs, 2 courses in English; CLEP credit not accepted. Bachelor's degree from an accredited institution required; 77% of applicants have bachelor's degree awarded prior to enrollment. *Has EDP for state residents only;* applicants must apply through AMCAS (official transcripts sent by mid-May) between June 1 and August 1. Early applications are encouraged. Submit supplemental application, a personal statement and 2 recommendations to Admissions Office within 2 weeks of receipt of application. Interviews are by invitation only and generally for final selection. Notification normally begins October 1. *Regular application process.* Apply through AMCAS (file after June 1, before December 15); submit MCAT (will accept MCAT test results from last 3 years), official transcripts for each school attended (should show at least 90 semester credits/135 quarter credits, submit transcripts by mid-May to AMCAS), service processing fee. Submit an application fee of $50, a supplemental application, a personal statement, a preprofessional committee evaluation, and 2 recommendations from science faculty to Admissions Office within 2–3 weeks of the receipt of supplemental materials. Interviews are by invitation only and generally for final selection. Combined degree applicants must apply to, and be accepted by, both schools; contact the Admissions Office for current information and specific

requirements for admission. First-year students admitted in fall only. Rolling admission process. Notification starts October 1 and is finished when class is filled. Applicant's response to offer and $100 deposit due within 3 weeks of receipt of acceptance letter. School does maintain an alternate list. Phone: (305)243-6791; fax: (305)243-6548; E-mail: miamimd@mednet.med.miami.edu.

ADMISSION REQUIREMENTS FOR TRANSFER APPLICANTS. Accepts transfers from other accredited U.S. medical schools who are state residents. Admission limited to space available. Contact the Admissions Office after February 1 for current information and specific requirements for admission.

ADMISSION STANDARDS AND RECOGNITION. *For B.S.-M.D.:* number of applicants 150; number of state residents interviewed 80, nonresidents 32; number of enrolled 19; median SAT combined score, 1,388. *For M.D.:* number of state-resident applicants 1,401, nonresidents 1,469; number of state residents interviewed 304, nonresidents 12; number of residents enrolled 136, nonresidents 4; median MCAT 10.0 (verbal reasoning 10.0; biological sciences 10.0; physical sciences 10.0); median GPA 3.65 (A = 4). Gorman rating 3.78 (scale: good 3.61–3.99); the school's medical ranking by NIH awards was 38th, with 178 awards/grants received; total dollars awarded $51,265,401.

FINANCIAL AID. Scholarships, merit scholarships, minority scholarships, grants-in-aid, institutional loans, HEAL, alternative loan programs, federal Perkins loans, Stafford subsidized and unsubsidized loans, and service commitment scholarship programs are available. Assistantships/fellowships may be available for combined degree candidates. Financial aid applications and information are available at the on-campus interview (by invitation). For scholarships, the selection criteria place heavy reliance on MCAT and undergraduate GPA. Contact the Financial Aid Office for current information; phone: (305)243-6211. For most financial assistance and all federal programs, submit FAFSA to a federal processor (Title IV school code # E00533); also submit Financial Aid Transcript and Federal Income Tax forms. Approximately 80% of current students receive some form of financial assistance. Average debt after graduation $103,000.

DEGREE REQUIREMENTS. *For B.S.-M.D.:* a 6- or 7-year program. *For M.D.:* satisfactory completion of 4-year program. *For M.D.-Ph.D.:* generally a 7-year program.

MICHIGAN STATE UNIVERSITY

East Lansing, Michigan 48824-1020
Internet site: http://www.msu.edu

Founded 1855. Located 80 miles NW of Detroit. State control. Semester system. Library: 3.900,000 volumes; 4,800,000 microforms; 27,900 periodicals/subscriptions. Special facilities: Center for Environmental Toxicology, Clinical Center, Genetic Clinic, Hematology Oncology Clinic, Institute of Nutrition, Olin Health Center. Special programs: B.A./B.S.-M.D. (Medical Scholars Program); annual undergraduate tuition residents $4,336, nonresidents $11,366; postbaccalaureate premedical program for underrepresented minorities. The university's ranking in domestic higher education by NIH awards was 91st, with 93 awards/grants received; total dollars awarded $19,455,850.

The university's graduate schools/collegs include: College of Agriculture and Natural Resources, College of Arts and Letters, College of Communication Arts and Sciences, College of Education, College of Engineering, College of Human Ecology, College of Natural Science, College of Nursing, College of Social Science, Eli Broad Graduate School of Management, Institute of Environmental Toxicology, College of Human Medicine, College of Osteopathic Medicine, College of Veterinary Medicine.

Total university enrollment at main campus: 41,454.

Health-Care Complex

Located on campus. Schools located at the health-care complex are: College of Human Medicine, College of Osteopathic Medicine, College of Veterinary Medicine.

College of Human Medicine

A-239 Life Sciences
East Lansing, Michigan 48824-1317
Phone: (517)353-9620; fax: (517)432-0021
Internet site: http://www.chm.msu.edu
E-mail: MDAdmissions@msu.edu

First class entered in 1969. Located on main campus. Block/semester system. Special programs: Summer programs for underrepresented minorities (ABLE); Rural Physician Program. Affiliated hospitals: affiliated with 19 community hospitals in 6 Michigan communities.

Annual tuition: residents $15,430, nonresidents $32,824; fees $483. On-campus rooms and apartments available for both single and married students. Contact Director of Housing for both on- and off-campus housing information; phone: (517)355-7457. Off-campus housing and personal expenses: approximately $19,177.

Enrollment: 1st-year class 106 (EDP 4; Rural Physician Program 16); total full-time 483 (men 50%, women 50%). First-year statistics: 14% out of state (no more than 20% can be enrolled); 54% women; average age 26; 16% minorities; 71% science majors.

Faculty: full-time/part-time/volunteers 2,000.

Degrees conferred: M.D., B.A.-M.D. (Medical Scholars Program), M.D.-M.A., M.D.-M.S., M.D.-Ph.D. (Anatomy, Biochemistry, Cellular and Molecular Biology, Ecology and Evolutionary Biology, Epidemiology, Genetics, Health and Humanities, Microbiology, Neurosciences, Pathology, Pharmacology and Toxicology, Physiology), has M.S.T.P.

RECRUITMENT PRACTICES AND POLICIES. School has diversity program and actively recruits women/minority applicants; Diversity contact: Assistant Dean for Student Affairs, phone: (517)353-7140.

ADMISSION REQUIREMENT FOR BACHELOR-M.D. APPLICANTS. Suggested high school preparation: 3 years of basic science, 3 years of mathematics, 2 years of foreign languages, 4 years of English, 1 year of psychology/sociology. Preference given to state residents. Submit application, SAT I, or ACT, official high school transcripts with rank in class, and 3 letters of recommendation. Apply to Admissions Office by February 1. Interviews are by invitation only and generally for final selection. Contact the Officer of Admissions for current information; phone: (517)353-9620. Financial aid information is available through the university's Office of Financial Aid.

ADMISSION REQUIREMENTS FOR FIRST-YEAR APPLICANTS. Preference given to state residents; U.S. citizens and permanent residents only. *Undergraduate preparation.* Suggested premed courses: 2 courses in biology with labs, 2 courses in inorganic chemistry with labs, 2 courses in organic chemistry with labs, 2 courses in physics with labs, 1 course in college math, 2 courses in psychology/sociology, 2 courses in English, 6 other nonscience courses. Bachelor's degree from an accredited institution required; all applicants have bachelor's degree awarded prior to enrollment. *Has EDP* for state residents only; applicants must apply through AMCAS (official transcripts sent by mid-May) between June 1 and August 1. Early applications are encouraged. Submit secondary/supplemental application, a personal statement, and 2 recommendations to Admissions Office within 2 weeks of receipt of application. Interviews are by invitation only and generally for final selection. Notification normally begins October 1. *Regular application process.* Apply through AMCAS (file after June 1, before November 1); submit MCAT (will accept MCAT test results from 1995), official transcripts for each school attended (should show at least 90 semester credits/135 quarter credits, submit transcripts by mid-May to AMCAS), service processing fee. Submit an application fee of $55, a supplemental application, an autobiographical statement and 3 essays, preprofessional committee evaluation, and 2 recommendations from science faculty to Admissions Office within 2–3 weeks of the receipt of supplemental materials. Interviews are by invitation only and generally for final selection. M.D.-advanced-graduate-degree applicants must apply to, and be accepted by, both the medical school and the graduate school; contact the Admissions Office for current information and specific requirements for admission. First-year students admitted in fall only. Rolling admission process. Notification starts on October 15 and is finished when class is filled. Applicant's response to offer and $50 deposit due within 2 weeks of receipt of acceptance letter. School does maintain an alternate list. Phone: (517)353-9620; E-mail: mdadmissions@msu.edu.

ADMISSION REQUIREMENTS FOR TRANSFER APPLICANTS. Accepts transfers from other accredited U.S. medical schools into the 3rd year only. Admission limited to space available. Contact the Admissions Office for current information and specific requirements for admission.

ADMISSION STANDARDS AND RECOGNITION. *For B.A./B.S.-M.D. (Medical Scholars Program):* number of applicants 389; number interviewed 59; number enrolled 10; median SAT combined score 1,374, ACT 31; median GPA 4.1 (A = 4). *For M.D.:* number of state-resident applicants 1,359, nonresidents 2,267; number of state residents interviewed 297, nonresidents 132; number of residents enrolled 94, nonresidents 13; median MCAT 9.3 (verbal reasoning 9.7; biological sciences 9.4; physical sciences 8.6); median GPA 3.5 (A = 4). Gorman rating 3.77 (scale: good 3.61–3.99); *U.S. News & World Report* ranked the school in the Top 25 of all U.S. medical schools for primary-care programs; medical ranking by NIH awards/grants was 96th, with 33 awards/grants received; total dollars awarded, $7,015,429.

FINANCIAL AID. Scholarships, minority scholarships, grants-in-aid, institutional loans, HEAL, alternative loan programs, NIH stipends, federal Perkins loans, Stafford subsidized and unsubsidized loans, and service commitment scholarship programs are available. All financial aid is based on proven need. Assistantships/fellowships may be available for M.D.-advanced-graduate-degree candidates. Financial aid applications and information are available at the on-campus interview (by invitation). For scholarships, the selection criteria place heavy reliance on MCAT and undergraduate GPA. Contact the MSU Health Professions Financial Aid Office for current information; phone: (517)353-5188. Apply for financial aid as soon as possible after January 1. For most financial assistance and all federal programs, submit FAFSA to a federal processor (Title IV school code # 002290); also submit Financial Aid Transcript and Federal Income Tax forms. Approximately 75% of current students receive some form of financial assistance. Average debt after graduation $82,700.

DEGREE REQUIREMENTS. *For B.A./B.S.-M.D.:* an 8-year program. *For M.D.:* satisfactory completion of 4-year program. All students must pass USMLE Step 1 prior to entering 3rd year; all students must pass USMLE Step 2 prior to awarding of M.D. *For M.D.-M.S.:* generally a 4½–5½-year program. *For M.D.-Ph.D.:* generally a 7-year program.

College of Osteopathic Medicine
C110 East Fee Hall
East Lansing, Michigan 48824-1316
Phone: (517)353-7740, (517)355-3296
Internet site: http://www.com.msu.edu
E-mail: cpmadm@com.msu.edu

College opened in 1971. Located on main campus. Semester system.

Annual tuition: residents $15,430, nonresidents $32,824. On-campus rooms and apartments available for both single and married students. Contact Housing Office for both on- and off-campus housing information; phone: (517)353-7457. Off-campus housing and personal expenses: approximately $19,170.

Enrollment: 1st-year class 126; total full-time 512 (men 57%, women 43%). First-year statistics: 13% out of state; 48% women; average age 26; 14% underrepresented minorities; 11% other minorities; 67% science majors.

Degrees conferred: D.O., D.O.-M.S., D.O.-Ph.D. (Anatomy, Biochemistry, Microbiology, Pathology, Pharmacology and Toxicology, Physiology, Neuroscience [interdisciplinary]); has M.S.T.P.

RECRUITMENT PRACTICES AND POLICIES. School has diversity program and actively recruits women/minority applicants. Diversity contact: Assistant Dean.

ADMISSION REQUIREMENTS FOR FIRST-YEAR APPLICANTS. Preference given to state residents; U.S. citizens and permanent residents only. *Undergraduate preparation.* Suggested premed courses: 2 courses in biology, 2 courses in inorganic chemistry, 2 courses in organic chemistry, 2 courses in physics, 2 courses in English. Bachelor's degree from an accredited institution required; all applicants have bachelor's degree awarded prior to enrollment. *Has EDP* for state residents only; applicants must apply through AMCAS (official transcripts sent by mid-May) between June 1 and August 1. Early applications are encouraged. Submit secondary/supplemental application, a personal statement, and 2 recommendations to Admissions Office within 2 weeks of receipt of application. Interviews are by invitation only and generally for final selection. Notification normally begins October 1. *Application process.* Apply through AACOMAS (file after June 1, before December 1); submit MCAT (will accept test results from last 3 years), official transcripts for each school attended (should show at least 90 semester credits/135 quarter credits), service processing fee. After a review of the AACOMAS application and supporting documents, a decision is made concerning which candidates should receive supplemental materials. The supplemental application, an application fee of $60, a personal statement, and 3 recommendations (1 from a D.O.) should be returned to Admissions Office as soon as possible. International applicants are subject to Michigan State University's requirements for foreign students. Contact the Office of International Students and Scholars, 103 Center for International Programs, MSU, East Lansing, Michigan 48824 for current information and specific requirements for admission. Interviews are by invitation only and generally for final selection. Applicants to M.S.T.P. must be accepted by both the college and the graduate school. Request applications from both schools and mark M.S.T.P. clearly on both forms. First-year students admitted in fall only. Rolling admission process. Notification starts in October and is finished when class is filled. Applicant's response to offer and $100 deposit due within 2 weeks of receipt of acceptance letter. School does maintain an alternate list. Phone: (517)353-5188.

ADMISSION REQUIREMENTS FOR TRANSFER APPLICANTS.
Accepts transfers from other accredited U.S. osteopathic medical schools with a compelling reason and only into the 3rd year. Admission limited to space available. Contact Admissions Office for current information and specific requirements for admission.

ADMISSION STANDARDS AND RECOGNITION.
For D.O.: number of applicants 3,080; number interviewed 250–300; number enrolled 126; median MCAT 8.4; median GPA 3.0; the school's ranking by NIH awards/grants was 3rd among osteopathic schools, with 14 awards/grants received; total value of all awards/grants $2,284,099.

FINANCIAL AID. Scholarships, minority scholarships, grants, institutional loans, NOF, HEAL, alternative loan programs, NIH stipends, federal Perkins loans, Stafford subsidized and unsubsidized loans, service obligation scholarship programs, and military and National Health Service programs are available. All financial aid is based on documented need. Assistantships/fellowships may be available for M.S.T.P. applicants. Financial-aid applications and information are sent out periodically during the year. For scholarships, the selection criteria place heavy reliance on MCAT and undergraduate GPA. Contact the MSU Health Professions Financial Aid Office for current information; phone: (517)353-5188. For most financial assistance and all federal programs, submit FAFSA to a federal processor (Title IV school code # 002290); also submit Financial Aid Transcript and Federal Income Tax forms. Approximately 80% of current students receive some form of financial assistance. Average debt after graduation $82,000.

DEGREE REQUIREMENTS. *For D.O.:* satisfactory completion of Units I, II, and III. *For D.O.-M.S.:* generally a 5-year program. *For M.D.-Ph.D.:* generally a 7-year program.

UNIVERSITY OF MICHIGAN
Ann Arbor, Michigan 48109
Internet site: http://www.umich.edu

Founded 1817. Located 40 miles W of Detroit. Public control. Semester system. Library: 6,133,000 volumes; 3,472,100 microforms; 67,530 periodicals/subscriptions. Special programs: B.A./B.S.-M.D. program; annual undergraduate tuition: residents $6,915, nonresidents $22,173. The university's ranking in domestic higher education by NIH awards/grants was 5th, with 731 awards/grants received; total dollars awarded $194,357,783.

The university's other graduate colleges/schools: College of Architecture and Urban Planning, College of Pharmacy. Horace H. Rackham School of Graduate Studies includes: College of Engineering, College of Literature, Science and the Arts, School of Art and Design, School of Education, School of Information, School of Nursing, School of Public Policy; Medical School, School of Business Administration, School of Dentistry, School of Law, School of Music, School of Natural Resources and Environment, School of Public Health, School of Social Work.

Total university enrollment at main campus: 36,600.

University of Michigan Medical Center
1500 East Medical Center Drive
Ann Arbor, Michigan 48109-0603

University hospital opened in 1986. Public control. The medical center is a member of Council of Teaching Hospitals. Special facilities: Simpson Memorial Institute, Buhl Research Center for Human Genetics. Nationally recognized programs in AIDS, Cancer, Cardiology, Endocrinology, Gastroenterology, Geriatrics, Gynecology, Neurology, Orthopedics, Otolaryngology, Psychiatry, Pulmonary Disease, Rehabilitation, Rheumatology, Urology. *U.S. News & World Report*'s hospital/medical center national rankings for all hospitals placed the medical center in the Top 20 of all U.S. hospitals.

Medical School
M4130 Medical Science I Building
Ann Arbor, Michigan 48109-0611
Phone: (313)764-6317; fax: (313)936-3510
Internet site: http://www.med.umich.edu/medschool

Established 1850. Located at medical center. Library: 200,000 volumes/microforms; 3,000 current periodicals/subscriptions. Affiliated hospitals: University of Michigan Hospital, St. Joseph Mercy Hospital, Ann Arbor VA Hospital. Special facilities: Comprehensive Cancer Center, Geriatrics Center, Historical Center for the Health Sciences, Howard Hughes Medical Institute at University of Michigan, Kresge Hearing Research Institute, Mental Health Research Institute, Michigan Human Genome Center, Michigan Transplant Center, Multipurpose Arthritis and Musculoskeletal Disease Center, Center for Organogensis. Special programs: summer programs for underrepresented minorities; for information contact Director; phone: (313)763-1296; prematriculation summer sessions.

Annual tuition: residents $16,964, nonresidents $25,884; fees $175. Limited on-campus housing available. Contact Office of University Housing for both on- and off-campus housing information; phone: (313)763-3164. Medical students tend to live off-campus. Off-campus housing and personal expenses: approximately $14,000.

Enrollment: 1st-year class 170 (EDP 5, M.D.-Ph.D. approximately 8 each year); total full-time 653 (men 60%, women 40%). First-year statistics: 40% out of state; 41.8% women; average age 25; 15% minorities; 69% science majors.

Faculty: full-time 750.

Degrees conferred: M.D., B.A./B.S.-M.D. (Inteflex Program), M.D.-M.P.H., M.D.-M.S., M.D.-Ph.D. (Anatomy and Cell Biology, Biological Chemistry, Biology, Bioengineering, Biophysics, Biostatistics, Cellular and Molecular Biology, Chemistry, Epidemiology, Genetic Counseling (M.S.), Human Genetics, Medicinal Chemistry, Microbiology and Immunology, Molecular Biology, Neurosciences, Pathology, Pharmacology, Physiology); has M.S.T.P.

RECRUITMENT PRACTICES AND POLICIES. School has diversity program and actively recruits women/minority applicants. Diversity contact: Assistant Dean for Students and Minority Affairs; phone: (313)764-8185.

ADMISSION REQUIREMENT FOR BACHELOR-M.D. APPLICANTS. Open to both state residents and nonresidents. Submit application, application fee of $40, either SAT I or ACT, official high school transcripts with rank in class, 3 letters of recommendation to College of Literature, Science and Arts by January 10. Interviews are by invitation only and generally for final selection. Notification date is April 1. Applicant's response to offer and $200 deposit due within 1 month of receipt of acceptance letter. Advancement to the medical phase is based on overall undergraduate record and MCAT. For more complete information contact Inteflex Medical Program, Co-Director; phone: (313)764-9534.

ADMISSION REQUIREMENTS FOR FIRST-YEAR APPLICANTS. Preference given to state residents; U.S. citizens and permanent residents only. *Undergraduate preparation.* Suggested premed courses: 2 courses in biology with labs, 2 courses in inorganic chemistry with labs, 2 courses in organic chemistry with labs, 2 courses in physics with labs, 2 courses in English, 6 courses in nonscience/humanities. Bachelor's degree from an accredited institution required; all applicants have bachelor's degree awarded prior to enrollment. *Has EDP for state residents only;* applicants must apply through AMCAS (official transcripts sent by mid-May) between June 1 and August 1. Early applications are encouraged. Submit secondary/supplemental application, a personal statement, and 2 recommendations to Admissions Office within 2 weeks of receipt of application. Interviews are by invitation only and generally for final selection. Notification normally begins October 1. *Regular application process.* Apply through AMCAS (file after June 1, before December 1); submit MCAT (will accept MCAT test results from 1995), official transcripts for each school attended (should show at least 90 semester credits/135 quarter credits, submit transcripts by mid-May to AMCAS), service processing fee. All applicants are asked to submit an application fee of $55 and a supplemental application, but only 25% are asked to submit a preprofessional committee evaluation and 2 recommendations from science faculty. All requested materials should be returned to the Admissions Office within 2–3 weeks of the receipt of supplemental materials. Interviews are by invitation only and generally for final selection. M.S.T.P. and M.D.-Ph.D. applicants must apply to, and be accepted by, both the medical school and the graduate school; in addition there is a separate application; contact the Admissions Office for current information and specific admissions requirements or the M.S.T.P. Coordinator; phone: (734)764-6176; E-mail em.mstp2umich.edu. Students may also apply to M.S.T.P. during the fall of their first 2 years in medical school. First-year students admitted in fall only. Rolling admission process. Notification starts on December 1 and is finished when class is filled. Applicant's response to offer and $100 deposit due within 2 weeks of receipt of acceptance letter. School does maintain an alternate list. Phone: (313)764-6317.

ADMISSION REQUIREMENTS FOR TRANSFER APPLICANTS. Does not accept transfer applicants. All students must apply as 1st year applicants. Contact the Admissions Office for current information or modification of policy.

ADMISSION STANDARDS AND RECOGNITION. *For B.A./B.S.-M.D.:* number of state-resident applicants 243, nonresidents 489; number of state residents interviewed 125, nonresidents 51; number of residents enrolled 25, nonresidents 10; median resident SAT combined score 1,380, nonresidents 1,417; median GPA for both 4.1 (A = 4). *For M.D.:* number of state-resident applicants 1,101, nonresidents 4,464; number of state residents interviewed 290, nonresidents 323; number of residents enrolled 94, nonresidents 76; median MCAT 11.3 (verbal reasoning 11.3; biological sciences 11.0; physical sciences 11.0); median GPA 3.6 (A = 4). *Barron's Guide* placed the medical school among the top 25 most prestigious U.S. medical schools; Gorman rating 4.91 (scale: very strong 4.51–4.99); *U.S. News & World Report* ranked the medical school in the Top 25 of all U.S. medical schools; did not rank the medical school in the Top 25 in primary-care programs; medical school's ranking by NIH awards/grants was 9th, with 486 awards/grants received; total dollars awarded $129,672,760.

FINANCIAL AID. Scholarships, minority scholarships, grants-in-aid, institutional loans, HEAL, alternative loan programs, NIH stipends, federal Perkins loans, Stafford subsidized and unsubsidized loans, and service commitment scholarship programs are available. Students selected for M.S.T.P. receive full tuition, health insurance, and $15,000 stipend; assistantships/fellowships may be available for joint-degree candidates. Financial aid applications and information are given out at the on-campus interview (by invitation). For scholarships, the selection criteria place heavy reliance on MCAT and undergraduate GPA. Contact the Financial Aid Office for current information; phone: (313)763-4147; E-mail: medfinaid@umich.edu. For most financial assistance and all federal programs, submit FAFSA to a federal processor (Title IV school code # E00398); also submit Financial Aid Transcript and Federal Income Tax forms. Approximately 85% of current students receive some form of financial assistance. Average debt after graduation $73,500.

DEGREE REQUIREMENTS. *For B.A./B.S.-M.D.:* an 8-year program. *For M.D.:* satisfactory completion of 4-year program. All students must pass USMLE Step 1 prior to entering 3rd year; all students must pass USMLE Step 2 prior to awarding of M.D. *For M.D.-M.P.H.:* generally a 5-year program. *For M.D.-M.S.:* generally a 4½–5½-year program. *For M.D.-Ph.D.:* generally a 7–8-year program.

School of Dentistry
Ann Arbor, Michigan 48109-1078
Phone: (313)764-8006
Internet site: http://www.dent.umich.edu/dentsch

Established 1875. Located on main campus. Curriculum; the first 2 years are primarily basic science; many courses are taught in conjunction with the medical school faculty. Library: 56,000 volumes/microforms; 466 current periodicals/subscriptions. Affiliated hospitals: University Hospital, C. S. Mott Children's Hospital. Special programs: prematriculation summer sessions; externships; extramural clinical experiences. M.S. degrees and postgraduate specialties: Endodontics, General Dentistry, Dental Public Health (with the School of Public Health), Oral and Maxillofacial Pathology, Oral and Maxillofacial Surgery, Orthodontics, Pediatric Dentistry, Periodontics, Prosthodontics, Restorative Dentistry; Ph.D. (Oral Health Sciences).

Annual tuition: residents $13,838, nonresidents $25,050; fees $178; equipment and supplies $1,785. Limited on-campus housing available. Contact Office of University Housing for both on- and off-campus housing information; phone: (313)763-3164. Dental students tend to live off-campus. Off-campus housing, food, transportation, and personal expenses: approximately $14,000.

Enrollment: 1st-year class 101; total full-time 385. First-year enrolled student information: 40 from out of state; 13 states represented; 47 undergraduate institutions represented; 48 women; average age 23; 16 underrepresented minorities; 22 other minorities.

Faculty: full-time 135.

Degrees conferred: D.D.S., B.A.-D.D.S., D.D.S.-M.P.H., M.S. (Biomaterials, Dental Hygiene, Dental Public Health), D.D.S.-Ph.D. (Oral Health Sciences).

RECRUITMENT PRACTICES AND POLICIES. School has diversity program and actively recruits women/minority applicants. Diversity contact: Director of Minority Affairs; phone: (313)763-3342.

ADMISSION REQUIREMENT FOR BACHELOR-D.D.S. APPLICANTS. The bachelor's degree is earned only if a liberal arts college will award the degree independently. For more information, contact the Admissions Office.

ADMISSION REQUIREMENTS FOR FIRST-YEAR APPLICANTS. Preference given to state residents; U.S. citizens and permanent residents only. *Undergraduate preparation.* Suggested predental courses: 2 courses in biology with labs, 2 courses in inorganic chemistry with labs, 2 courses in organic chemistry with labs, 2 courses in physics with labs, 2 courses in English. The junior-college transfer-credit limit is 60 credits. Will consider applicants with only 3 years of undergraduate preparation; prefer applicants who will have a bachelor's degree prior to enrollment; 90% of applicants have bachelor's degrees awarded prior to enrollment. *Application process.* Apply through AADSAS (file after June 1, before February 1), submit official transcripts for each school attended (prefer at least 90 semester credits/135 quarter credits), service processing fee; at the same time as you send in AADSAS materials; submit official DAT scores (should be taken no later than October of the year prior to anticipated year of enrollment), official transcripts, predental committee evaluation or 2 recommendations from science professors and 1 recommendation from a nonscience professor, and a photograph directly to the Admissions Office. Submit the application fee of $50 only after being contacted by an Admissions Officer. To receive serious consideration, an applicant's GPA should be at least a 2.7 (A = 4) or better. Interviews are by invitation only and generally for final selection. Combined degree applicants must apply to, and be accepted by, both schools. First-year students admitted in fall only. Rolling admission process. Notification starts on December 1 and is finished when class is filled. Applicant's response to offer due within 30 days if accepted prior to January 31; response and deposit due within 15 days if received after February 1; preferred response time is immediately. School does maintain an alternate list. Phone: (313)763-3316.

ADMISSION REQUIREMENTS FOR ADVANCED-STANDING APPLICANTS. Accepts transfers from other accredited U.S. and Canadian dental schools; preference given to state residents. Admission limited to space available. There is an advanced-standing program for graduates of foreign schools of dentistry. Contact the Admissions Office for current information and specific requirements for admission.

ADMISSION STANDARDS AND RECOGNITION. *For D.D.S.:* number of applicants 1,448; number enrolled 101; median DAT: ACAD 18.51, PAT 17.12; median GPA 3.36 (A = 4), median sciences GPA 3.25 (A = 4). Gorman rating 4.91 (scale: very strong 4.51–4.99); this placed the school in the Top 5 of all U.S. dental schools; the dental school's ranking by NIH awards was 4th among dental schools, with 35 awards/grants received; total value of all awards/grants $6,015,227.

FINANCIAL AID. Scholarships, minority scholarships, research stipends, grants, institutional loans, state loan programs, DEAL, HEAL, alternative loan programs, federal Perkins loans, Stafford subsidized and unsubsidized loans, and military service commitment scholarship programs are available. Assistantships/fellowships may be available for combined-degree candidates. Institutional financial aid applications and information are generally available at the on-campus interview (by invitation), and applications are sent to all accepted applicants. For scholarships, the selection criteria place heavy reliance on DAT and undergraduate GPA. Contact the Office of Student Affairs and Financial Aid for current information; phone: (313)763-3313. All awards are made through the university's Office of Financial Aid. For most financial assistance and all need-based programs submit FAFSA to a federal processor (Title IV school code # 002325); also submit Financial Aid Transcript and Federal Income Tax forms, and Use of Federal Funds Certification. Approximately 82% of current students receive some form of financial assistance. Average award for residents $20,298, nonresidents $27,910.

DEGREE REQUIREMENTS. *For D.D.S.:* satisfactory completion of 4-year program. *For D.D.S.-M.P.H.:* generally a 5-year program. *For D.D.S.-M.S.:* generally a 4½–5½-year program; thesis/nonthesis option; research project. *For D.D.S.-Ph.D.:* generally a 6–7-year program; candidacy, dissertation, oral defense, final exam.

MIDWESTERN UNIVERSITY
Downers Grove, Illinois 60515-1235
Internet site: http://www.midwestern.edu
E-mail: mwuinfo@mmu.edu

Private control. Graduate study only. Semester system. Library: 84,000 volumes/microforms; 1,450 current periodicals/subscriptions; 41 PC work stations. The university's ranking by NIH awards/grants was 5th among schools of osteopathic medicine, with 2 awards/grants received; total dollars awarded $257,992.

The university's other graduate colleges include: Chicago College of Osteopathic Medicine, College of Allied Health Professions, College of Pharmacy; at the Arizona campus, the Arizona College of Osteopathic Medicine.

Total university enrollment: 1,204.

Chicago College of Osteopathic Medicine
555 31st Street
Downers Grove, Illinois 60515
Phone: (800)458-6253, (630)969-4400
Internet site: http://www.acom.edu
E-mail: admiss@midwestern.edu

Established 1900 as the College of Osteopathic Medicine and Surgery; merged and created Littlejohn College and Hospital; name changed to Chicago College in 1970. Located on main campus. Private control. Semester system. Affiliated hospitals: Chicago Osteopathic Hospital and Medical Center, Olympia Fields Osteopathic Hospital and Medical Center.

Annual tuition: residents $18,411, nonresidents $22,374. Limited on-campus housing available. Annual on-campus housing cost: single students $2,244 (room only), married students $4,863. Contact Housing Director for both on- and off-campus housing information, phone: (630)971-6400. Medical students tend to live off-campus. Off-campus housing and personal expenses: approximately $6,354.

Enrollment: 1st-year class 150; total full-time 638 (men 63%, women 37%). First-year statistics: 55% out of state; 40% women; average age 26; 67% science majors.

Degree conferred: D.O.

RECRUITMENT PRACTICES AND POLICIES. School has diversity program and actively recruits women/minority applicants. Diversity contact: Admissions Office.

ADMISSION REQUIREMENTS FOR FIRST-YEAR APPLICANTS. Preference given to state residents; U.S. citizens and permanent residents only. *Undergraduate*

preparation. Suggested premed courses: 2 courses in biology, 2 courses in inorganic chemistry, 2 courses in organic chemistry, 2 courses in physics, 2 courses in English. Bachelor's degree from an accredited institution required; all applicants have bachelor's degree awarded prior to enrollment. *Application process.* Apply through AACOMAS (file after June 1, before December 1); submit MCAT (will accept test results from last 3 years), official transcripts for each school attended (should show at least 90 semester credits/135 quarter credits), service processing fee. After a review of the AACOMAS application and supporting documents, a decision is made concerning which candidates should receive supplemental materials. Supplemental applications are sent to all students with a 2.75 (A = 4) science GPA. The supplemental application, an application fee of $50, a personal statement, and 3 recommendations (1 from a D.O.) should be returned to Admissions Office as soon as possible; not later than early January. Interviews are by invitation only and generally for final selection. First-year students admitted in fall only. Rolling admission process. Notification starts in October and is finished when class is filled. Applicant's response to offer and $250 deposit due within 2 weeks of receipt of acceptance letter. Phone: (630)969-4400; fax: (630)971-6086; E-mail: admiss@midwestern.edu.

ADMISSION REQUIREMENTS FOR TRANSFER APPLICANTS. Accepts transfers from other accredited U.S. osteopathic medical schools. Admission limited to space available. Contact the Admissions Office for current information and specific requirements for admission.

ADMISSION STANDARDS AND RECOGNITION. *For D.O.:* number of applicants 4,800; number enrolled 150; median MCAT 8.7; median GPA 3.5 (A = 4); the school's ranking by NIH awards/grants was 5th among osteopathic schools, with 2 awards/grants received; total value of all awards/grants $257,992.

FINANCIAL AID. Scholarships, institutional loans, NOF, HEAL, alternative loan programs, federal Perkins loans, Stafford subsidized and unsubsidized loans, service obligation scholarship programs, and military and National Health Service programs are available. Financial aid applications and information are available at the on-campus interview (by invitation). Contact the Financial Aid Office for current information. For most financial assistance and all financial programs, submit FAFSA to a federal processor (Title IV school code # 001657); also submit Financial Aid Transcript and Federal Income Tax forms. Approximately 87% of current students receive some form of financial assistance. Average debt after graduation $96,000.

DEGREE REQUIREMENTS. *For D.O.:* satisfactory completion of 4-year (a 45-month) program. All students must pass the National Board of Osteopathic Medical Examination Level I to advance to the 3rd year. All students must take the National Board of Osteopathic Medical Examination Level II prior to the awarding of D.O.

Arizona College of Osteopathic Medicine
19555 North 59th Avenue
Glendale, Arizona 85308
Phone: (800)458-6253 (Midwestern University's main office), (602)572-3215
Internet site: http://www.acom.edu or www.midwestern.edu

Established 1995. Located in the suburbs of Phoenix; newest school of osteopathic medicine. Semester system.
Annual tuition: $22,600. Limited on-campus housing available. Contact Manager of Residence Life for both on- and off-campus housing information; phone: (602)572-3848. Medical students tend to live off-campus. Off-campus housing and personal expenses: approximately $12,251.
Enrollment: 1st-year class 110 (men 68%; women 32%).
Degree conferred: D.O.

ADMISSION REQUIREMENTS FOR FIRST-YEAR APPLICANTS. *Undergraduate preparation.* Suggested premed courses: 2 courses in biology, 2 courses in inorganic chemistry, 2 courses in organic chemistry, 2 courses in physics, 2 courses in English. Bachelor's degree from an accredited institution required; all applicants have bachelor's degree awarded prior to enrollment. *Regular application process.* Apply through AACOMAS (file after June 1, before December 1); submit MCAT (will accept test results from last 3 years), official transcripts for each school attended (should show at least 90 semester credits/135 quarter credits), service processing fee. After a review of the AACOMAS application and supporting documents, a decision is made concerning which candidates should receive supplemental materials. The supplemental application, an application fee of $40, a personal statement, and 3 recommendations (1 from a D.O.) should be returned to Admissions Office as soon as possible. In addition, international applicants must submit foreign transcripts to the World Education Service for translation and evaluation. TOEFL may be required of those applicants whose native language is other than English. Interviews are by invitation only and generally for

final selection. First-year students admitted in fall only. Rolling admission process. Notification starts in October and is finished when class is filled. Applicant's response to offer and $100 deposit due within 2 weeks of receipt of acceptance letter. School does maintain an alternate list. Phone: (602)572-3215; E-mail: admiss@midwestern.edu.

ADMISSION REQUIREMENTS FOR TRANSFER APPLICANTS. Accepts transfers from other accredited U.S. osteopathic medical schools. Admission limited to space available. Contact the Admissions Office for current information and specific requirements for admission.

ADMISSION STANDARDS AND RECOGNITION. *For D.O.:* number of applicants 4,250; number enrolled 110; median MCAT 8.7; median GPA 3.3.

FINANCIAL AID. Scholarships, institutional loans, NOF, HEAL, alternative loan programs, federal Perkins loans, Stafford subsidized and unsubsidized loans, service obligation scholarship programs, and military and National Health Service programs are available. Financial aid applications and information are available from either the Arizona campus or from Downers Grove. Contact the Financial Aid Office for current information; phone Glendale: (602)572-3321, Downers Grove: (630)515-6035. For most financial assistance and all federal programs, submit FAFSA to a federal processor (Title IV school code # 001657); also submit Financial Aid Transcript and Federal Income Tax forms. Approximately 87% of current students receive some form of financial assistance.

DEGREE REQUIREMENTS. *For D.O.:* satisfactory completion of 4-year (45-month) program. All students must pass the National Board of Osteopathic Medical Examination Level I and all must take Level II prior to the awarding of D.O.

UNIVERSITY OF MINNESOTA, DULUTH
Duluth, Minnesota 55812-2596
Internet site: http://www.d.umn.eud/academic.html

Founded 1895. Public control. Quarter system. Library: 412,600 volumes; 375,200 microforms; 3,000 periodicals/subscriptions; 193 PC work stations. Special facilities: Alworth Institute of International Studies, Large Lakes Observatory, Marshall Performing Art Center, Natural Resource Research Institute, Tweed Museum

University of Minnesota, Duluth *155*

of Art. The University of Minnesota's ranking in domestic higher education by NIH awards/grants was 17th, with 521 awards/grants received; total dollars awarded $130,828,969.

The university's graduate school includes: College of Education and Human Service Professions, College of Liberal Arts, College of Science and Engineering, School of Business and Economics, School of Fine Arts, School of Medicine.

Total university enrollment at the campus: 7,348.

School of Medicine
10 University Drive
Duluth, Minnesota 55812
Phone: (218)726-8511; fax: (218)726-6235
Internet site: http://www.d.umn.edu/medweb
E-mail: jcarl10@ub.e.umn.edu

Established 1969. Quarter system. The medical program is a 2-year transfer program. Library: 66,000 volumes/microforms; 600 current periodicals/subscriptions. Affiliated hospitals: St. Mary's Medical Center, Miller-Dwan Medical Center, St. Luke's Hospital.

Annual tuition: residents $16,672; nonresidents $30,452; fees $593. On-campus housing available for both single and married students. Contact Housing Office for both on- and off-campus housing information; phone: (218)726-8178. Medical students tend to live off-campus. Off-campus housing and personal expenses: approximately $8,900.

Enrollment: 1st-year class 53; total full-time 116 (men 53%, women 47%). First-year statistics: 6% out of state; 50% women; average age 24; 17% minorities; 77% science majors.

Faculty: full-time 45, part-time/volunteers 280.

Degree conferred: none; a transfer program.

RECRUITMENT PRACTICES AND POLICIES. School has diversity program and actively recruits women/minority applicants. Diversity contact: Director; Center for American Indian and Minority Health; phone: (218)726-7235.

ADMISSION REQUIREMENTS FOR FIRST-YEAR APPLICANTS. Preference given to state residents and certain counties in Wisconsin; U.S. citizens and permanent residents only. *Undergraduate preparation.* Suggested premed courses: 2 courses in biology with labs, 2 courses in inorganic chemistry with labs, 2 courses in organic chemistry with labs, 2 courses in physics with labs, 1 course in calculus, 2 courses in English. Bachelor's degree from an accredited institution required; all appli-

cants have bachelor's degrees awarded prior to enrollment. *Has EDP;* applicants must apply through AMCAS (official transcripts sent by mid-May) between June 1 and August 1. Early applications are encouraged. Submit secondary/supplemental application, a personal statement, and 2 recommendations to Admissions Office within 2 weeks of receipt of application. Interviews are by invitation only and generally for final selection. Notification normally begins October 1. *Regular application process.* Apply through AMCAS (file after June 1, before November 15); submit MCAT (will accept MCAT test results from the last 3 years), official transcripts for each school attended (should show at least 90 semester credits/135 quarter credits, submit transcripts by mid-May to AMCAS), service processing fee. Submit an application fee of $50, a supplemental application, a personal statement, preprofessional committee evaluation, and 2 recommendations from science faculty to Admissions Office within 2–3 weeks of the receipt of supplemental materials. Interviews are by invitation only and generally for final selection. First-year students admitted in fall only. Rolling admission process. Notification starts in October and is finished when class is filled. Applicant's response to offer due within 2 weeks of receipt of acceptance letter. School does maintain an alternate/waiting list. Phone: (218)726-8511; E-mail: jcarl10@d.umn.edu.

ADMISSION REQUIREMENTS FOR TRANSFER APPLICANTS. Does not accept transfers; however, contact the Admissions Office for current information and any change in admission policy.

ADMISSION STANDARDS AND RECOGNITION. *For M.D.:* number of state-resident applicants 608, nonresidents 778; number of state residents interviewed 177, nonresidents 8; total accepted 80; number of residents enrolled 50, nonresidents 3; median MCAT 9.0 (verbal reasoning 9.1; biological sciences 9.4; physical sciences 8.9); median GPA 3.54 (A = 4). Gorman rating: N/A.

FINANCIAL AID. Scholarships, institutional loans, HEAL, alternative loan programs, federal Perkins loans, and Stafford subsidized and unsubsidized loans available. Financial-aid applications and information are available at the on-campus interview (by invitation). Contact the Financial Aid Office for current information; phone: (218)726-8786. For most financial assistance and all federal programs, submit FAFSA to a federal processor (Title IV school code # E00477); also submit Financial Aid Transcript and Federal Income Tax forms. Approximately 93% of current students receive some form of financial assistance.

DEGREE REQUIREMENTS. All students transfer to the University of Minnesota School of Medicine in Minneapolis.

UNIVERSITY OF MINNESOTA

Minneapolis, Minnesota 55455-0213
Internet site: http://www.umn.edu

Founded 1851. Coed. Public control. Quarter system. Library: 5,250,000 volumes; 5,000,000 microforms; 46,000 periodicals/subscriptions. The university's ranking in domestic higher education by NIH awards/grants was 17th, with 521 awards/grants received; total dollars awarded $130,828,969.

The university's graduate school includes: College of Agriculture, Food and Environmental Sciences, College of Architecture and Landscape Architecture, College of Biological Sciences, College of Education and Human Development, College of Human Ecology, College of Liberal Arts, College of Natural Resources, Hubert H. Humphrey Institute of Public Policy, Institute of Human Genetics, Institute of Technology, School of Nursing, Carlson School of Management, College of Pharmacy, College of Veterinary Medicine, Law School, Medical School, School of Dentistry, School of Public Health.

Total university enrollment at main campus: 37,000.

University of Minnesota Health Sciences Center

University of Minnesota Hospital and Clinics is a member of the Council of Teaching Hospitals. Schools located at health sciences center are the College of Pharmacy, Medical School, School of Dentistry, School of Nursing. Special facilities: Biomedical Engineering Center, Biomedical Engineering Institute, Biological Process Technology Institute, Cancer Center, Center for Bioethics, Center for Neuroscientific Databases, Children's Rehabilitation Center, Computational Biology Centers, Variety Club Heart Center, Virtual Genome Center. Nationally recognized programs in Cancer, Endocrinology, Geriatrics, Gynecology, Neurology, Orthopedics, Otolaryngology.

Medical School

P.O. Box 293
Minneapolis, Minnesota 55455-0310
Phone: (612)624-1122; fax: (612)624-4200
Internet site: http://www.med.umn.edu
E-mail: reilloo2@maroon.tc.umn.edu

Established 1888. Located on main campus. Quarter system. Library: 400,000 volumes/microforms.

Annual tuition: residents $16,702, nonresidents $30,482. On-campus accommodations available for both single and married students. On-campus housing cost per quarter: single students $1,593 (room and board). Contact Housing and Residential Life Office for on-campus housing information; phone: (612)624-2994. For off-campus information, contact Como Student Community Office; phone: (612)378-2434. Medical students tend to live off-campus. Off-campus housing and personal expenses: approximately $12,143.

Enrollment: 1st-year class 175 (EDP 20); total full-time 653 (men 59%, women 41%). First-year statistics: 10% out of state; 41.8% women; average age 25; 17% minorities; 70% science majors.

Faculty: full-time 900.

Degrees conferred: M.D., M.D.-Ph.D. (Biochemistry, Biomedical Engineering, Biophysics, Cell Biology, Genetics, Immunology, Microbiology, Molecular Biology, Neurosciences, Pharmacology, Physiology); has M.S.T.P.

RECRUITMENT PRACTICES AND POLICIES. School has diversity program and actively recruits women/minority applicants. Diversity contact: Assistant to the Dean for Student Affairs; phone: (612)624-9666.

ADMISSION REQUIREMENTS FOR FIRST-YEAR APPLICANTS. Preference given to state residents; U.S. citizens and permanent residents only. *Undergraduate preparation.* Suggested premed courses: 2 courses in biology with labs, 2 courses in inorganic chemistry with labs, 2 courses in organic chemistry with labs, 3 courses in physics with labs, 1 course in calculus, 2 courses in English, 1 course in biochemistry, 6 courses in behavioral sciences, social sciences, and humanities. Bachelor's degree from an accredited institution required; all applicants have bachelor's degree awarded prior to enrollment. *Has EDP;* applicants must apply through AMCAS (official transcripts sent by mid-May) between June 1 and August 1. Early applications are encouraged. Submit secondary/supplemental application, a personal statement, and 2 recommendations to Admissions Office within 2 weeks of receipt of application. Interviews are by invitation only and generally for final selection. Notification normally begins October 1. *Regular application process.* Apply through AMCAS (file after June 1, before November 15; submit MCAT (will accept MCAT test results from last 3 years), official transcripts for each school attended (should show at least 90 semester credits/135 quarter credits, submit transcripts by mid-May to AMCAS), service processing fee. Submit an application fee of $50, a supplemental application, a personal comment/statement, preprofessional committee evaluation, and 2 recommendations from science faculty to Admissions Office within 2–3 weeks of the receipt of supplemental materials, but not later than December 15. Interviews are by invitation only and generally for final selection. M.D.-Ph.D. degree applicants should contact the M.D.-Ph.D. Office for current information and specific requirements for admissions; phone; (612)625-3680. First-year students admitted in fall only. Rolling admission process. Notification starts on November 15 and is completed by May 15. Applicant's response to offer due within 2 weeks of receipt of acceptance letter. Phone: (612)624-1122; E-mail: reilloo2@maroon.tc. umn.edu.

ADMISSION REQUIREMENTS FOR TRANSFER APPLICANTS. Rarely accepts transfers except those from the School of Medicine, Duluth. Contact the Admissions Office for current information and any change in admissions policy.

ADMISSION STANDARDS AND RECOGNITION. *For M.D.:* number of state-resident applicants 857, nonresidents 1,473; number of state residents interviewed 659, nonresidents 105; total accepted 258; number of residents enrolled 162, nonresidents 13; median MCAT 10.0 (verbal reasoning 10.0; biological sciences 10.0; physical sciences 10.0); median GPA 3.59 (A = 4). *Barron's Guide* placed the medical school among the Top 25 most prestigious U.S. medical schools; Gorman rating 4.71 (scale: very strong 4.51–4.99); the medical school's ranking by NIH awards was 24th, with 314 awards/grants received; total dollars awarded $78,164,201.

FINANCIAL AID. Scholarships, merit scholarships, minority scholarships, grants-in-aid, institutional loans, HEAL, alternative loan programs, NIH stipends, federal Perkins loans, Stafford subsidized and unsubsidized loans, and service commitment scholarship programs are available. All M.D.-Ph.D. students are accepted into fully funded positions, which include stipends, tuition waivers, fees, and health insurance. Financial aid applications and information are generally available at the on-campus interview (by invitation). For merit scholarships, the selection criteria place heavy reliance on MCAT and undergraduate GPA. Contact the Financial Aid Office for current information; phone: (612)625-4998. For most financial assistance and all federal programs, submit FAFSA to a federal processor (Title IV school code # E00477); also submit Financial Aid Transcript, Federal Income Tax forms, and ACT-FFS Needs Analysis form. Approximately 90% of current students receive some form of financial assistance. Average debt after graduation $73,600.

DEGREE REQUIREMENTS. *For M.D.:* satisfactory completion of 4-year program. All students must pass USMLE Step 1 prior to entering 3rd year; all students must pass USMLE Step 2 prior to awarding of M.D. *For M.D.-Ph.D.:* generally a 7-year program.

School of Dentistry
15-106 Malcolm Moos Health Sciences Tower
515 Delaware Street, S.E.
Minneapolis, Minnesota 55455-0329
Phone: (612)625-7149; fax: (612)626-2654
Internet site: http://www.umn.edu
E-mail: kraski001@maroon.tc.umn.edu

Established 1888. Located at the university's health sciences center. Quarter system. Affiliated hospitals: University Hospital, Hennepin County Medical Center, VA Hospital. Special facilities: Dental Research Institute, Minnesota Dental Research Center for Biomaterials and Biomechanics, Minnesota Oral Health Clinical Research Center. Special programs: externships, summer research fellowships, foreign exchange in Denmark, Norway, Germany, and Peru. Postgraduate specialties: Basic medical sciences (Ph.D.), Endodontics (M.S.), Oral Biology (Ph.D.), Oral Health Services for Older Adults (M.S.), Oral Pathology, Oral and Maxillofacial Surgery (certificate), Orthodontics (M.S.), Pediatric Dentistry (M.S.), Periodontics (M.S.), Prosthodontics (M.S.), TMJ and Orofacial Pain (M.S.).

Annual tuition: residents $10,375, nonresidents $17,209; fees $475; equipment and supplies $1,693. On-campus rooms and apartments available for both single and married students. Contact Director of Housing for both on- and off-campus housing information; phone: (612)624-2994. Dental students tend to live off-campus. Off-campus housing, food, transportation, and personal expenses: approximately $8,189.

Enrollment: 1st-year class 86. First-year enrolled student information: 29 from out of state; 29 women; average age 24; 1 underrepresented minority; 7 other minorities.

Degrees conferred: D.D.S., B.A.-D.D.S., D.D.S.-M.S., D.D.S.-Ph.D.

RECRUITMENT PRACTICES AND POLICIES. School has diversity program and actively recruits women/minority applicants. Diversity contact: Officer of Minority Affairs; phone: (612)625-7149.

ADMISSION REQUIREMENT FOR EARLY ACCEPTANCE PROGRAM-D.D.S. APPLICANTS. For information and applications contact: undergraduate students should contact the School of Dentistry's Office of Enrollment Management. A bachelor's degree can be earned only if the liberal-arts college providing the preprofessional program will award the degree independently.

ADMISSION REQUIREMENTS FOR FIRST-YEAR APPLICANTS. Preference given to residents of Minnesota, Montana, South Dakota, North Dakota, Wisconsin, and the province of Manitoba. *Undergraduate preparation.* Suggested predental courses: 2 courses in biology with labs, 2 courses in general chemistry with labs, 2 courses in organic chemistry with labs, 2 courses in physics with labs, 1 course in college math, 2–3 courses in English, 1 course in psychology. The junior-college transfer credit limit is 64 semester/96 quarter credits. Will consider applicants with only 3 years of undergraduate preparation; prefer applicants who will have a bachelor's degree prior to enrollment; 86% of applicants have bachelor's degree awarded prior to enrollment. *Application process.* Apply through AADSAS (file after June 1, before January 1); submit official transcripts for each school attended (should show at least 87 semester credits/130 quarter credits), service processing fee. Submit the following materials only after being contacted by an Admissions Officer: an application fee of $50, a Minnesota application, official transcripts, DAT scores, predental committee evaluation or 3 University of Minnesota recommendations forms, personal statement, and Verification of Residency form to Office of Enrollment Management within 2 weeks of receipt of supplemental materials. A minimum of 2.5 GPA (A = 4) is required for consideration, but a substantially higher GPA is needed to be competitive. Interviews are by invitation only and generally for final selection. Dual-degree applicants should contact the Office of Enrollment Management for current information and specific requirements for admission. First-year students admitted in fall only. Rolling admission process. Notification starts on December 1 and is finished generally by April 1. Applicant's response to offer and $550 deposit due within 30 days if accepted prior to February 28; response and deposit due within 2 weeks if received after March 1. Phone: (612)625-7149.

ADMISSION REQUIREMENTS FOR ADVANCED-STANDING APPLICANTS. Transfer opportunities are extremely limited. Contact the Office of Enrollment Management for current information and specific requirements for admission.

ADMISSION STANDARDS AND RECOGNITION. *For D.D.S.:* number of applicants 948; number enrolled 86; median DAT: ACAD 18.22, PAT 17.71; median GPA 3.47 (A = 4), median sciences GPA 3.39 (A = 4). Gorman rating 4.76 (scale: very strong 4.51–4.99); this placed the school in the Top 15 of all U.S. dental schools; the school's ranking by NIH awards/grants was 12th among U.S. dental schools, with 16 awards/grants received; total value of all awards/grants $3,292,334.

FINANCIAL AID. Scholarships, merit scholarships, minority scholarships, grants-in-aid, institutional loans, state loan programs, DEAL, HEAL, alternative loan programs, federal Perkins loans, Stafford subsidized and unsubsidized loans, and military service commitment scholarship programs are available. Assistantships/fellowships may be available for combined degree candidates. Institutional financial aid applications and information are generally available at the on-campus by invitation interview. For merit scholarships, the selection criteria place heavy reliance on DAT and undergraduate GPA. Contact the Coordinator of Dental Financial Aid in the university's Office of Student Financial Aid for current information; phone: (612)324-1665/(800)400-UOFM. For most financial assistance and all need-based programs, submit FAFSA to a federal processor (Title IV school code # E00477); also submit Financial Aid Transcript, Federal Income Tax forms, and Use of Federal Funds Certification. Approximately 73% of current students receive some form of financial assistance. Average award resident $17,502, nonresident $22,031.

DEGREE REQUIREMENTS. *For B.A./B.S.-D.D.S.* (Early Acceptance Program): a 7–8-year program, depending on the undergraduate liberal arts college. *For D.D.S.:* satisfactory completion of 4-year program. *For D.D.S.-M.S.:* generally a 4½–5½-year program. *For D.D.S.-Ph.D.:* generally a 6–7-year program.

UNIVERSITY OF MISSISSIPPI
University, Mississippi 38677
Internet site: http://www.olemiss.edu

Founded 1848. Located 180 miles N of Jackson, 75 miles SE of Memphis, Tennessee. Public control. Semester system. Library: 940,700 volumes; 2,788,500 microforms; 9,467 periodicals/subscriptions; 156 PC work stations. The university's ranking in domestic higher education by NIH awards/grants was 111th, with 55 awards/grants received; total dollars awarded $10,034,693

The university's graduate school includes: College of Liberal Arts, School of Accounting, School of Business Administration, School of Education, School of Engineering, School of Law, School of Pharmacy.

Total university enrollment at main campus: 10,100.

University of Mississippi Medical Center
2500 North State Street
Jackson, Mississippi 39216

Public control. University hospitals and clinics is a member of Council of Teaching Hospitals. Schools/programs located at Medical Center are: graduate programs in medical sciences, School of Dentistry, School of Health Related Professions, School of Nursing.

School of Medicine
2500 North State Street
Jackson, Mississippi 39216-4505
Phone: (601)984-5010; fax: (601)984-5008
Internet site: http://www.umsmed.edu
E-mail: bmb@fiona.umsmed.edu

Established 1903 as a 2-year program; expanded to a 4-year program in 1955. Located at the medical center. Library: 161,000 volumes/microforms; 2,500 current periodicals/subscriptions. Affiliated hospitals: University Hospital and Clinics, Veterans Administration Medical Center, McBryde Rehabilitation Center for the Blind. Special programs: prematriculation summer sessions.

Annual tuition: residents $6,715, nonresidents $12,830; fees $115. On-campus dormitory rooms for women students only. Contact Housing Office for both on- and off-campus housing information; phone: (601)984-1491. Most medical students live off-campus. Off-campus housing and personal expenses: approximately $8,955.

Enrollment: 1st-year class 100 (EDP 10); total full-time 386 (men 70%, women 30%). First-year statistics: none from out of state; 29% women; average age 25; 15% minorities; 78% science majors.

Degrees conferred: M.D., M.D.-M.S., M.D.-Ph.D. (Anatomy, Biochemistry, Microbiology, Pathology, Pharmacology and Toxicology, Physiology, Preventive Medicine).

RECRUITMENT PRACTICES AND POLICIES. School has diversity program and actively recruits women/minority applicants. Diversity contact: Director of Minority Affairs; phone: (601)984-1340.

ADMISSION REQUIREMENTS FOR FIRST-YEAR APPLICANTS. Preference given to state residents; U.S. citizens and permanent residents only. *Undergraduate preparation.* Suggested premed courses: 2 courses in biology with labs, 2 courses in general or inorganic chemistry with labs, 2 courses in organic chemistry with labs, 2 courses in physics with labs, 2 course in college math, 2 courses in English, 2 courses in advanced sciences. Bachelor's degree from an accredited institution required; all applicants have bachelor's degrees awarded prior to enrollment. *Has EDP* for state residents only; applicants must apply through AMCAS (official transcripts sent by mid-May) between June 1 and August 1. Early applications are encouraged. Submit secondary/supplemental application, a personal statement, and 2 recommendations to Admissions Office within 2 weeks of receipt of

application. Interviews are by invitation only and generally for final selection. Notification normally begins October 1. *Regular application process.* Apply through AMCAS (file after June 1, before November 1); submit MCAT (will accept MCAT test results from the last 3 years), official transcripts for each school attended (should show at least 90 semester credits/135 quarter credits, submit transcripts by mid-May to AMCAS), service processing fee. Submit a supplemental application, a personal statement, preprofessional committee evaluation, and 2 recommendations from science faculty to Admissions Office within 2–3 weeks of the receipt of supplemental materials. Interviews are by invitation only and generally for final selection. Dual-degree applicants must apply to, and be accepted by, both schools; contact the Admissions Office for current information and specific requirements for admission. First-year students admitted in fall only. Rolling admission process. Notification starts on October 15 and is finished when class is filled. Applicant's response to offer and $50 deposit due within 15 days of receipt of acceptance letter. School does maintain an alternate list. Phone: (601)984-5010.

ADMISSION REQUIREMENTS FOR TRANSFER APPLICANTS. Accepts transfers from other accredited U.S. medical schools who are state residents into the 3rd year only. Admission limited to space available. Contact the Admissions Office for current information and specific requirements for admission.

ADMISSION STANDARDS AND RECOGNITION. *For M.D.:* number of state-resident applicants 313, nonresidents 270; number of state residents interviewed 193, nonresidents none; number of residents enrolled 100, nonresidents none; median MCAT 9.0 (verbal reasoning 9.0; biological sciences 9.0; physical sciences 9.0); median GPA 3.48 (A = 4). Gorman rating 3.39 (scale: acceptable plus 3.01–3.59); the school's medical ranking by NIH awards/grants was 93rd, with 43 awards/grants received; total dollars awarded $7,739,968.

FINANCIAL AID. Scholarships, merit scholarships, minority scholarships, grants-in-aid, institutional loans, state loan programs, HEAL, alternative loan programs, federal Perkins loans, Stafford subsidized and unsubsidized loans, and service commitment scholarship programs are available. Assistantships/fellowships may be available for dual-degree candidates. Part-time employment at Medical Center may be available. Financial aid applications and information are generally available at the on-campus interview (by invitation). For merit scholarships, the selection criteria place heavy reliance on MCAT and undergraduate GPA. Contact the Financial

Aid Office for current information; phone: (601)984-1717. For most financial assistance and all federal programs, submit FAFSA to a federal processor (Title IV school code # 004688); also submit Financial Aid Transcript and Federal Income Tax forms. Approximately 85% of current students receive some form of financial assistance. Average debt after graduation $46,500.

DEGREE REQUIREMENTS. *For M.D.:* satisfactory completion of 4-year program. All students must pass USMLE Step 1 prior to entering 3rd year; all students must pass USMLE Step 2 prior to awarding of M.D. *For M.D.-M.S.:* generally a 4½–5½-year program. *For M.D.-Ph.D.:* generally a 7-year program.

School of Dentistry
2500 North State Street
Jackson, Mississippi 39216-4505
Phone: (601)684-6009
Internet site: http://www.umc.edu/dentistry

Established 1973, admitted first class in 1975. Located at the medical center. All basic sciences faculty have joint appointments in both dental and medical schools. Affiliated hospital: University Hospital and Clinics. Special programs: externship, summer enrichment program for underrepresented minorities. Postgraduate specialties: Advanced Education in General Dentistry (AEGD), General Practice Residency.

Annual tuition: residents $4,400, nonresidents $10,400; fees $885; equipment and supplies $750. On-campus dormitory rooms for female students only. Contact Housing Office for both on- and off-campus housing information; phone: (601)984-1491. Most dental students live off-campus. Off-campus housing, food, transportation, and personal expenses: approximately $11,400.

Enrollment: 1st-year class 31. First-year enrolled student information: 0 from out of state; 9 women; average age 23; 2 underrepresented minorities.

Degree conferred: D.M.D.

RECRUITMENT PRACTICES AND POLICIES. School has diversity program and actively recruits women/minority applicants. Diversity contact: Office of Student Minority Affairs; phone: (601)984-1340.

ADMISSION REQUIREMENTS FOR FIRST-YEAR APPLICANTS. Nonresidents not considered, state residents must be U.S. citizens or permanent residents. *Undergraduate preparation.* Suggested predental courses: 2 courses in biology with labs, 2 courses in inorganic chemistry with labs, 2 courses in organic chemistry with labs, 2 courses in physics with labs, 2 courses in college math, 2 courses in English, 1 course in advanced biology or chemistry, 2 courses in social sciences. The junior-

college transfer credit limit is 65 credits. Will consider applicants with only 3 years of undergraduate preparation; prefer applicants who will have a bachelor's degree prior to enrollment; 28 out of 31 enrolled students had bachelor's degree awarded prior to enrollment. *Application process.* Request applications from the Division of Student Services and Records, University of Mississippi Medical Center. Apply directly to the School of Dentistry after July 1, before March 1. Submit official transcripts for each school attended (should show at least 90 semester credits/135 quarter credits), official DAT scores (will accept DAT test result from the last 3 years), an application, and predental committee evaluation or 3 recommendations from science professors to Office of Student Programs. Interviews are by invitation only and generally for final selection. First-year students admitted in fall only. Rolling admission process. Notification starts in December and is finished when class is filled, but generally not later than June 1. Applicant's response to offer due within 15 days of receipt of acceptance letter. Phone: (601)684-6009.

ADMISSION REQUIREMENTS FOR ADVANCED-STANDING APPLICANTS. Accepts transfers from other accredited U.S. and Canadian dental schools who are state residents. Admission limited to space available. There is no advanced-standing program for graduates of foreign schools of dentistry. Contact the Admissions Office for current information and specific requirements for admission.

ADMISSION STANDARDS AND RECOGNITION. *For D.D.S.:* number of applicants 121; number enrolled 31; median DAT: ACAD 16, PAT 16; median GPA 3.53 (A = 4), median sciences GPA 3.45 (A = 4). Gorman rating 4.05 (scale: strong 4.01–4.49); this placed the school in the Bottom 10 of all U.S. dental schools; the dental school's ranking by NIH awards was 40th among U.S. dental schools, with 1 award/grants received; total value of all awards/grants $62,500.

FINANCIAL AID. Need-based scholarships, merit scholarships, grants, institutional loans, state loan programs, DEAL, HEAL, alternative loan programs, federal Perkins loans, Stafford subsidized and unsubsidized loans, and military service commitment scholarship programs are available. Institutional financial aid applications and information are generally available at the on-campus interview (by invitation). Contact the Office of Student Financial Aid, Medical Center, for current information; phone: (601)984-1117. For most financial assistance and all need-based programs, submit FAFSA to a federal processor (Title IV school code # 004688); also submit Financial Aid

Transcript, Federal Income Tax forms, and Use of Federal Funds Certification. Approximately 89% of current students receive some form of financial assistance. Average award $15,000.

DEGREE REQUIREMENTS. *For D.M.D.:* satisfactory completion of 4-year program.

UNIVERSITY OF MISSOURI– COLUMBIA

Columbia, Missouri 65211
Internet site: http://www.missouri.edu

Founded 1839. Located 120 miles W of St. Louis. Public control. Semester system. Library: 2,500,000 volumes; 4,800,000 microforms. The university's ranking in domestic higher education by NIH awards/grants was 76th, with 135 awards/grants received; total dollars awarded $25,483,176.

The university's graduate schools includes: College of Agriculture, College of Arts and Science, College of Business and Public Administration, College of Education, College of Engineering, College of Human Environmental Science, School of Health Related Professions, School of Journalism, School of Law, School of Library and Information Science, School of Natural Resources, School of Nursing, College of Veterinary Medicine, School of Medicine.

Total university enrollment at main campus: 22,300.

Health Sciences Center

One Hospital Drive
Columbia, Missouri 65212
Internet site: http://www.hsc.missouri.edu

Located on the main campus. Public control. University of Missouri Hospital is a member of Council of Teaching Hospitals. Facilities at health sciences center: Mid-Missouri Mental Health Center, Harry S. Truman Veterans Administration Hospital, Howard A. Rusk Rehabilitation Center, Mason Institute of Ophthalmology, Cosmopolitan International Diabetes Center, Ellis-Fischel Cancer Center. Nationally recognized program in Orthopedics.

School of Medicine

One Hospital Drive
Columbia, Missouri 65212
Phone: (573)882-2923; fax: (573)884-4808
Internet site: http://www.miarms.missouri.edu
E-mail: shari_l_swindell@muccmail.missouri.edu

Established 1872 as a 2-year program; expanded to a 4-year program in 1956. Located on main campus. Semester block system. Library: 204,000 volumes/microforms; 2,000 current periodicals/subscriptions. Affiliated hospitals: University Hospital, University Clinics, Green Meadows Clinics and Crossroads West Clinic. Special programs: summer programs for underrepresented minorities.

Annual tuition: residents $14,254, nonresidents $28,458; fees $578. On-campus rooms and apartments available for both single and married students. Annual on-campus housing cost: single students $4,100 (room only), married students $3,700. Contact Residential Life Office for both on- and off-campus housing information; phone: (573)882-7275. Medical students tend to live off-campus. Off-campus housing and personal expenses: approximately $11,800.

Enrollment: 1st-year class 92 (EDP 10); total full-time 382 (men 57%, women 53%). First-year statistics: 3% out of state; 41% women; average age 25; 2% minorities; 77% science majors.

Faculty: full-time 329.

Degrees conferred: M.D., M.D.-M.S., M.D.-Ph.D. (Biochemistry, Biomedical Engineering, Genetics, Immunology, Microbiology, Pathology, Pharmacology, Physiology).

RECRUITMENT PRACTICES AND POLICIES. School has diversity program and actively recruits women/minority applicants. Diversity contact: Assistant Dean for Curriculum and Minority Affairs; phone: (573)882-9219.

ADMISSION REQUIREMENTS FOR FIRST-YEAR APPLICANTS. Strong preference given to state residents; U.S. citizens and permanent residents only. *Undergraduate preparation.* Suggested premed courses: 2 courses in biology with labs, 2 courses in inorganic chemistry with labs, 2 courses in organic chemistry with labs, 2 courses in physics with labs, 1 course in college math, 2 courses in English; 1 course in biochemistry is strongly encouraged. Bachelor's degree from an accredited institution required; all applicants have bachelor's degree awarded prior to enrollment. *Has EDP* for state residents only; applicants must apply through AMCAS (official transcripts sent by mid-May) between June 1 and August 1. Early applications are encouraged. Submit supplemental application, a personal statement, and 2 recommendations to Admissions Office within 2 weeks of receipt of application. Interviews are by invitation only and generally for final selection. Notification normally begins October 1 .*Regular application process.* Apply through AMCAS (file after June 1, before November 1); submit MCAT (will accept MCAT test results from the last 3 years), official transcripts for each school attended (should show at least 90 semester credits/135 quarter credits, submit transcripts by mid-May to AMCAS), service processing fee. Submit a supplemental application, a personal comment/statement, preprofessional committee evaluation, and 2 recommendations from science faculty to Admissions Office within 2–3 weeks of the receipt of supplemental materials. Interviews are by invitation only and generally for final selection. Combined degree applicants must apply to, and be accepted by, both schools; contact the Admissions Office for current information and specific requirements for admission. First-year students admitted in fall only. Rolling admission process. Notification starts on November 15 and is finished when class is filled. Applicant's response to offer and $100 deposit due within 2 weeks of receipt of acceptance letter. School does maintain an alternate list. Phone: (573)882-2923; E-mail: shari_l._swindell@muccmail.missouri.edu.

ADMISSION REQUIREMENTS FOR TRANSFER APPLICANTS. Accepts transfers from other accredited U.S. medical schools of state residents into the 3rd year only. Admission limited to space available. Contact the Admissions Office for current information and specific requirements for admission.

ADMISSION STANDARDS AND RECOGNITION. *For M.D.:* number of state-resident applicants 516, nonresidents 607; number of state residents interviewed 275, nonresidents 11; number of residents enrolled 91, nonresidents 1; median MCAT 9.8 (verbal reasoning 9.7; biological sciences 9.8; physical sciences 9.8); median GPA 3.7 (A = 4). Gorman rating 4.19 (scale: strong 4.01–4.49); medical school's ranking by NIH awards/grants was 88th, with 48 awards/grants received; total dollars awarded $8,858,525.

FINANCIAL AID. Scholarships, merit scholarships, minority scholarships, grants-in-aid, institutional loans, HEAL, alternative loan programs, federal Perkins loans, Stafford subsidized and unsubsidized loans, and service commitment scholarship programs are available. Assistantships/fellowships may be available for dual-degree candidates. Financial aid applications and information are sent to all accepted students. For merit scholarships, the selection criteria place heavy reliance on MCAT and undergraduate GPA. Contact the Financial Aid Office for current information; phone: (314)882-2923. For most financial assistance and all federal programs, submit FAFSA to a federal processor (Title IV school code # 002516); also submit Financial Aid Transcript and Federal Income Tax forms. Approximately 80% of current students receive some form of financial assistance. Average debt after graduation $62,500.

DEGREE REQUIREMENTS. *For M.D.:* satisfactory completion of 4-year program. All students must pass USMLE Step 1 prior to 4th year; all students must pass USMLE Step 2 prior to awarding of M.D. *For M.D.-M.S.:* generally a 4½–5½-year program. *For M.D.-Ph.D.:* generally a 6–8-year program.

UNIVERSITY OF MISSOURI–KANSAS CITY
Kansas City, Missouri 64110-2499
Internet site: http://www.umkc.edu

Founded 1929. Public control. Semester system. Library: 962,000 volumes; 1,813,413 microforms; 8,793 periodicals/subscriptions.

The university's other graduate colleges/schools: College of Arts and Science, Conservatory of Music, School of Biological Sciences, School of Business and Public Administration, School of Dentistry, School of Education, School of Graduate Studies, School of Law, School of Medicine, School of Nursing, School of Pharmacy.

Total university enrollment at main campus: 10,200.

School of Medicine
2411 Holmes
Kansas City, Missouri 64108-2292
Phone: (816)235-1870; fax: (816)235-5277
Internet site: http://research.med.umkc.edu

Established 1969. Located on main campus near both schools and affiliated community hospital. Primarily designed for high school graduates who are just beginning undergraduate study. Year-round program. Affiliated hospitals: Children's Mercy Hospital, St. Luke's Hospital, Truman Medical Center. Special programs: summer programs for underrepresented minorities; an alternative path for extended study and a combined baccalaureate-M.D.-Ph.D. program for a small number of highly qualified applicants is available.

Annual tuition beginning with year 3: residents $19,453, nonresidents $39,416; fees $676. All students are expected to live in university housing for year 1. Annual housing cost: $6,000.

Enrollment: 1st-year class 99; total full-time 371 (men 42%, women 58%). First-year statistics: 20% out of state; 66% women; average age 18; 11% minorities.

Degree conferred: B.S.-M.D.

RECRUITMENT PRACTICES AND POLICIES. School has diversity program and actively recruits women/minority applicants. Diversity contact: Director, Officer of Minority Affairs; phone: (816)235-1780.

ADMISSION REQUIREMENT FOR BACCALAURE-ATE-M.D. APPLICANTS. Preference given to state residents; no more than 10–15 nonresidents may be enrolled each year. All applicants must be graduates of accredited high schools. *Suggested high school preparation:* 3 years of science, 3 years of social studies, 1 year of fine arts, 2 years of foreign language, 4 years of mathematics, 4 years of English; 1 course in computer science is recommended. *Application process.* Request application materials from the University of Missouri Kansas City, Office of Admissions/Enrollment Services; phone: (816)235-1111; E-mail admit@umkc.edu. Submit application after August 1 before November 1, ACT, an official transcript with rank in class, a personal statement, and 3 letters of recommendation to the Council on Selection. All applicants must apply to, and be accepted by, both the School of Medicine and either the College of Arts and Sciences or the School of Biological Studies. Interviews are by invitation only and generally for final selection. First-year students admitted in fall only. Notification normally begins April 1. Applicant's response to offer and $100 deposit due May 1. Contact the Council on Selection for current information and specific requirements for admission. Phone: (816)235-1111.

ADMISSION REQUIREMENTS FOR TRANSFER APPLICANTS. Accepts transfers from other accredited U.S. institutions into year 3 who are residents of Missouri or adjacent counties of Kansas. Admission limited to space available. Contact the Admissions Office for current information and specific requirements for admission.

ADMISSION STANDARDS AND RECOGNITION. *For Baccalaureate-M.D.:* number of state-resident applicants 435, nonresidents 436; number of state residents interviewed 279, nonresidents 92; number of residents enrolled 87, nonresidents 12; median ACT 94 percentile. Medical school's ranking by NIH awards/grants was 110th, with 17 awards/grants received; total dollars awarded $2,857,181.

FINANCIAL AID. Scholarships, merit scholarships, minority scholarships, institutional loans, HEAL, alternative loan programs, federal Perkins loans, Stafford subsidized and unsubsidized loans, and service commitment scholarship programs are available. Financial aid applications and information are sent out with the application materials. Contact the university's Student Financial Aid Office for current information; phone: (816)235-1154. Apply no later than March 15. For most financial assistance and all federal programs, submit FAFSA to a federal processor (Title IV school code # 002518); also submit Financial Aid Transcript and Federal Income Tax forms.

DEGREE REQUIREMENTS. *For Baccalaureate-M.D.:* a 6-year (year-round) program. *For M.D.:* satisfactory completion of M.D. program. All students must pass USMLE Step 1 prior to entering 3rd year; all students must pass USMLE Step 2 prior to awarding of M.D.

School of Dentistry
650 East 25th Street, Room 416
Kansas City, Missouri 64108
Phone: (816)235-2080, (800)776-8652; fax: (816)235-2157
Internet site: http://www.umkc.edu/dentistry
E-mail: dds@smtpgate.umkc.edu

Established 1881 as the Kansas City Dental College. Merged with the Western Dental College in 1919. Joined the University of Kansas City, a private institution, in 1941; became part of the University of Missouri in 1963. Located a few miles north of the main campus in "Hospital Hill" area. Library: 25,000 volumes/microforms; 350 current periodicals/subscriptions. Affiliated hospitals: Kansas City Children's Mercy Hospital, Truman Medical Center. Postgraduate specialties: Diagnostic Sciences, General Dentistry, Oral and Maxillofacial Prosthetics, Oral and Maxillofacial Surgery, Orthodontics, Pediatric Dentistry, Periodontics, Prosthodontics.

Annual tuition: residents $12,538, nonresidents $25,220; fees $543; equipment and supplies $6,372. No on-campus housing available. Contact Off-campus Housing Association for both on- and off-campus housing information; phone: (816)235-1428. Off-campus housing, food, transportation, and personal expenses: approximately $10,520.

Enrollment: 1st-year class 79. First-year enrolled student information: 11 from out of state; 35 women; average age 24; 10 underrepresented minorities; 11 other minorities.

Degrees conferred: D.D.S., B.A.-D.D.S. (with University of Missouri, Kansas City), M.S. (Oral Biology), D.D.S.-Ph.D. (interdisciplinary degree in Oral Biology, Biomaterials).

RECRUITMENT PRACTICES AND POLICIES. School has diversity program and actively recruits women/minority applicants. Diversity contact: Minority Recruitment Program; phone: (816)235-2085, (800)776-8652.

ADMISSION REQUIREMENT FOR B.A.-D.D.S. APPLICANTS. For information and applications contact Director, Office of Student Programs; phone: (816)776-8652.

ADMISSION REQUIREMENTS FOR FIRST-YEAR APPLICANTS. Preference given to residents of Missouri, Kansas, Arkansas, New Mexico; U.S. citizens and permanent residents only. *Undergraduate preparation.* Suggested predental courses: 2 courses in biology with labs, 2 courses in general chemistry with labs, 2 courses in organic chemistry with labs, 2 courses in physics with labs, 2 courses in English. The junior-college transfer credit limit is 60 credits. Will consider applicants with only 2 years of undergraduate preparation; prefer applicants who will have a bachelor's degree prior to enrollment; 72 out of 79 enrolled students had bachelor's degree awarded prior to enrollment. *Application process.* Apply through AADSAS (file after June 1, before January 1; preference given to applications received by November 1); submit official transcripts for each school attended (should show at least 90 semester credits/135 quarter credits), service processing fee; at the same time as you send in AADSAS materials, submit official DAT scores directly to the Admissions Office. Submit the following materials only after being contacted by an Admissions Officer: an application fee of $25, a secondary/supplemental application, official transcripts, and predental committee evaluation or 3 letters of recommendation from science professors, application survey to Office of Student Program within 2 weeks of receipt of supplemental materials. Interviews are by invitation only and generally for final selection. First-year students admitted in fall only. Rolling admission process. Notification starts in December and is finished when class is filled. Applicant's response to offer and $200 deposit due within 30 days if accepted prior to January 31; response and deposit due within 15 days if received after February 1. School does maintain an alternate list. Phone: (816)235-2157; E-mail: dds@smtpgate.umkc.edu.

ADMISSION REQUIREMENTS FOR ADVANCED-STANDING APPLICANTS. Accepts transfers from other accredited U.S. and Canadian dental schools. Admission limited to space available. There is no advanced-standing program for graduates of foreign schools of dentistry. Contact the Admissions Office for current information and specific requirements for admission.

ADMISSION STANDARDS AND RECOGNITION. *For D.D.S.:* number of applicants 1,019; number enrolled 79; median DAT: ACAD 16.9, PAT 16.6; median GPA 3.30 (A = 4), median sciences GPA 3.23 (A = 4). Gorman rating 4.27 (scale: strong 4.01-4.49); this placed the school in the Top 35 of all U.S. dental schools; the dental school's ranking by NIH awards/grants was 22nd among U.S. dental schools, with 8 awards/grants received; total value of all awards/grants $1,617,429.

FINANCIAL AID. Scholarships, merit scholarships, minority scholarships, grants-in-aid, institutional loans, state loan programs, DEAL, HEAL, alternative loan programs; federal Perkins loans, Stafford subsidized and unsubsidized loans, and military service commitment scholarship programs are available. Request the School of Dentistry's *Financial Aid, Sources, Resources and Helpful Hints* from the Office of Student Programs. Institutional financial aid applications and information are generally available at the on-campus interview (by invitation). Contact the university's Financial Aid and Scholarship Office for current information; phone: (816)235-1154. For most financial assistance and all need-based programs, submit FAFSA to a federal processor (Title IV school code # 002518); also submit Financial Aid Transcript, Federal Income Tax forms, and Use of Federal Funds Certification. Approximately 84% of current students receive some form of financial assistance. Average award for residents $22,907, nonresidents $27,228.

DEGREE REQUIREMENTS. *For B.A.-D.D.S.:* a 6-year program. *For D.D.S.:* satisfactory completion of 4-year (8 semesters, 2 summer terms) program; passing grades on both Part I and II of National Board of Dental Examination.

MOREHOUSE SCHOOL OF MEDICINE
720 Westview Drive, S.W.
Atlanta, Georgia 30310-1495
Internet site: http://www.msm.edu

Founded 1978. One of 3 historically black medical institutions. Primary mission is to provide physicians for medically underserved rural and inner-city areas. Located in the heart of Atlanta. Private control. Semester system. Library: 59,200 volumes; 849 periodicals/subscriptions; 28 PC work stations. The school's medical-school ranking by NIH awards/grants was 81st, with 54 awards/grants received; total dollars awarded $12,314,590.

School of Medicine
720 Westview Drive, S.W.
Atlanta, Georgia
Phone: (404)752-1500
Internet site: http://www.msm.edu
E-mail: Karen@link.nium.edu

First M.D. class graduated in 1985. Special programs: prematriculation summer sessions. Affiliated hospitals: Grady Memorial Hospital, Southwest Community Hospital, Tuskegee Veterans Administration Medical Center (Alabama).

Annual tuition: $19,439; fees $1,986. No on-campus housing available. Contact Admissions Office for off-campus housing information. Off-campus housing and personal expenses: approximately $16,997.

Enrollment: 1st-year class 35 (EDP 1); total full-time 145 (men 41%, women 59%). First-year statistics: 45% out of state; 76.5% women; average age 25; 91% underrepresented minorities.

Faculty: full-time 171, part-time/volunteers 145.

Degrees conferred: M.D., M.D.-M.P.H. (with Clark Atlanta University), M.D.-Ph.D. (Biomedical Sciences).

RECRUITMENT PRACTICES AND POLICIES. School has diversity program and actively recruits women/minority applicants. Diversity contact: Associate Dean for Students Affairs and Curriculum; phone: (404)752-1651.

ADMISSION REQUIREMENTS FOR FIRST-YEAR APPLICANTS. Preference given to state residents; U.S. citizens and permanent residents only. *Undergraduate preparation.* Suggested premed courses: 2 courses in biology with labs, 2 courses in general/inorganic chemistry with labs, 2 courses in organic chemistry with labs, 2 courses in physics with labs, 2 courses in college math, 2 courses in English; courses in behavioral sciences strongly recommended. Bachelor's degree from an accredited institution required; all applicants have bachelor's degrees awarded prior to enrollment. *Has EDP for URM state residents only;* applicants must apply through AMCAS (official transcripts sent by mid-May) between June 1 and August 1. Early applications are encouraged. Submit secondary/supplemental application, a personal statement, and 2 recommendations to Admissions Office within 2 weeks of receipt of application. Interviews are by invitation only and generally for final selection. Noti-

fication normally begins October 15. *Application process.* Apply through AMCAS (file after June 1, before December 1); submit MCAT (will accept MCAT test results from 1995), official transcripts for each school attended (should show at least 90 semester credits/135 quarter credits, submit transcripts by mid-May to AMCAS), service processing fee. Submit an application fee of $45, a supplemental application, a personal statement, preprofessional committee evaluation, and 2 recommendations from science faculty to Admissions Office within 2–3 weeks of receipt of supplemental materials. Interviews are by invitation only and generally for final selection. Combined degree applicants must apply to, and be accepted by, both schools; contact the Admissions Office for current information and specific requirements for admission. First-year students admitted in fall only. Rolling admission process. Notification starts on December 20 and is finished when class is filled. Applicant's response to offer and $100 deposit due within 2 weeks of receipt of acceptance letter. Phone: (404)752-1650; fax: (404)752-1512; E-mail: karen@link.nium.edu.

ADMISSION REQUIREMENTS FOR TRANSFER APPLICANTS. Accepts transfers from other accredited U.S. medical schools into the 2nd year only. Admission limited to space available. Contact the Admissions Office for current information and specific requirements for admission.

ADMISSION STANDARDS AND RECOGNITION. *For M.D.:* number of state-resident applicants 433, nonresidents 2,495; number of state residents interviewed 100, nonresidents 119; number of residents enrolled 21, nonresidents 13; median MCAT 7.0 (verbal reasoning 6.9; biological sciences 7.2; physical sciences 6.8); median GPA N/A. Gorman rating 3.06 (scale: acceptable plus 3.01–3.59).

FINANCIAL AID. Scholarships, limited merit scholarships, minority scholarships, grants-in-aid, institutional loans, HEAL, alternative loan programs, federal Perkins loans, Stafford subsidized and unsubsidized loans, and service commitment scholarship programs are available. All financial aid is based on documented need. For merit awards, the selection criteria place heavy reliance on MCAT and undergraduate GPA. Contact the Office of Student Fiscal Affairs for current information; phone: (404)752-1656. For most financial assistance and all federal programs, submit FAFSA to a federal processor (Title IV school code # G24821); also submit Financial Aid Transcript and Federal Income Tax forms. Approximately

74% of current students receive some form of financial assistance.

DEGREE REQUIREMENTS. *For M.D.:* satisfactory completion of 4-year program. All students must pass USMLE Step 1 prior to entering 3rd year; all students must pass USMLE Step 2 prior to awarding of M.D.

MOUNT SINAI SCHOOL OF MEDICINE OF CITY UNIVERSITY OF NEW YORK
New York, New York 10029

Mount Sinai Medical Center
One Gustave L. Levy Place
New York, New York 10029

Established 1852. Public Control. Mount Sinai Hospital is a member of Council of Teaching Hospitals. Schools located at medical center are: Graduate School of Biological Sciences, Postgraduate School of Medicine. Special facilities: Division of Environment and Occupational Medicine, Clinical Genetics Center, Gerald A. Ruttenberg Cancer Center, Lucy Moses Cardiothoracic Center. Nationally recognized programs in AIDS, Cancer, Cardiology, Endocrinology, Gastroenterology, Geriatrics, Gynecology, Neurology, Otolaryngology, Rehabilitation, Rheumatology, Urology.

Mount Sinai School of Medicine
Annenberg Building, Room 5-04
One Gustave L. Levy Place, Box 1002
New York, New York 10029-6574
Phone: (212)241-6696
Internet site: http://www.mssm.edu

Established 1968. Officially affiliated with City University of New York. Library: 154,000 volumes/microforms; 2,500 current periodicals/subscriptions. Affiliated hospitals: Jewish Home and Hospital, North General Hospital, Queens General Hospital, St. Barnabas Health Care System, Newark Beth Israel Medical Center, Bronx Veterans Affairs Medical Center, Cabrini Medical Center, Elmhurst Medical Center, Englewood Hospital and Medical Center. Special programs: has an Early Acceptance Program with Amherst College, Brandeis University, Princeton University, Wesleyan University, Williams College, Cooper Union; a 7-year Biomedical Education Program with City College of City University of New York; prematriculation summer sessions.

Annual tuition: $23,125; fees $825. On-campus rooms and apartments available for both single and married students. Annual on-campus housing cost: $8,500. Contact Admissions Office for both on- and off-campus housing information. Medical students tend to live off-campus. Off-campus housing and personal expenses: approximately $12,000.

Enrollment: 1st-year class 110 (EDP 5); total full-time 483 (men 51%, women 49%). First-year statistics: 50% out of state; 50% women; average age 25; 43% science majors.

Faculty: full-time 1,000, part-time/volunteers 250.

Degrees conferred: M.D., M.D.-Ph.D. (Anatomy, Biochemistry, Biophysics, Cell Biology, Genetics, Immunology, Microbiology, Molecular Biology, Neurosciences, Pathology, Pharmacology, Physiology); has M.S.T.P.

RECRUITMENT PRACTICES AND POLICIES. School has diversity program and actively recruits women/minority applicants. Diversity contact: Assistant Dean, Student Affairs, phone: (212)241-8276.

ADMISSION REQUIREMENTS FOR FIRST-YEAR APPLICANTS. Preference given to state residents; U.S. citizens and permanent residents only. *Undergraduate preparation.* Suggested premed courses: 2 courses in biology with labs, 2 courses in inorganic chemistry with labs, 2 courses in organic chemistry with labs, 2 courses in physics with labs, 2 courses in college math, 2 courses in English. Bachelor's degree from an accredited institution required; all applicants have bachelor's degree awarded prior to enrollment. *Has EDP;* applicants must apply through AMCAS (official transcripts sent by mid-May) between June 1 and August 1. Early applications are encouraged. Submit secondary/supplemental application, a personal statement, and 2 recommendations to Admissions Office within 2 weeks of receipt of application. Interviews are by invitation only and generally for final selection. Notification normally begins October 1. *Regular application process.* Apply through AMCAS (file after June 1, before November 1); submit MCAT (will accept MCAT test results from the last 3 years), official transcripts for each school attended (should show at least 90 semester credits/135 quarter credits, submit transcripts by mid-May to AMCAS), service processing fee. Submit an application fee of $100, a supplemental application, a personal statement, preprofessional committee evaluation, and 2 recommendations from science faculty to Admissions Office within 2–3 weeks of receipt of supplemental materials. Two separate interviews by invitation only are required, and the second interview is generally for final selection. Dual-degree applicants apply by checking the appropriate box on the supplemental application; contact the Admissions Office for current information and specific requirements for admission. First-year students admitted in fall only. Rolling admission process. Notification starts November 15 and is finished when class is filled. Applicant's response to offer and $100 deposit due within 2 weeks of receipt of acceptance letter. School does maintain an alternate list. Phone: (212)241-6696; E-mail: admissions@smtlink.mssm.edu.

ADMISSION REQUIREMENTS FOR TRANSFER APPLICANTS. Accepts transfers from other accredited U.S. medical schools. Admission limited to space available. Contact the Admissions Office after January 1 for current information and specific requirements.

ADMISSION STANDARDS AND RECOGNITION. *For M.D.:* number of state-resident applicants 1,547, nonresidents 3,797; number of state residents interviewed 399, nonresidents 455; number of residents enrolled 58, nonresidents 52; median MCAT 10.2 (verbal reasoning 9.7; biological sciences 10.4; physical sciences 10.5); median GPA 3.52 (A = 4). Gorman rating 3.89 (scale: good 3.61–3.99); the school's medical-school ranking by NIH awards/grants was 29th, with 252 awards/grants received; total dollars awarded $66,381,916.

FINANCIAL AID. Scholarships, merit scholarships, minority scholarships, grants-in-aid, institutional loans, state incentive awards, HEAL, alternative loan programs, NIH stipends, federal Perkins loans, Stafford subsidized and unsubsidized loans, and service commitment scholarship programs are available. All M.S.T.P. students receive a full tuition waiver and a stipend. Financial aid applications and information are sent to all accepted students. Financial aid is based on demonstrated need. For scholarships, the selection criteria place heavy reliance on MCAT and undergraduate GPA. Contact the Financial Aid Office for current information; phone: (212)241-6696. For most financial assistance and all federal programs, submit FAFSA to a federal processor (Title IV school code # G07026); also submit Financial Aid Transcript and Federal Income Tax forms. Approximately 75% of current students receive some form of financial assistance. Average debt after graduation $86,935.

DEGREE REQUIREMENTS. *For M.D.:* satisfactory completion of 4-year program. All students must pass USMLE Step 1 prior to entering 3rd year; all students must pass USMLE Step 2 prior to awarding of M.D. *For M.D.-Ph.D.:* generally a 6–7-year program.

UNIVERSITY OF NEBRASKA AT OMAHA
Omaha, Nebraska 68101
Internet site: http://www.unomaha.edu

Founded 1908. Public control. Semester system. Library: 736,918 volumes; 7,753,914 microforms; 4,085 periodicals/subscriptions. Special facilities: Center for Afghanistan Studies, Aviation Institute Center for Faculty Development, Center for International Telecommunication Management, Center for Urban Education, Small Business Development Center.

The university's graduate studies and research includes the following: College of Arts and Sciences, College of Business Administration, College of Education, College of Fine Arts, College of Public Affairs and Community Service.

Total university enrollment at main campus: 15,000.

University of Nebraska Medical Center
600 South 42nd Street
Omaha, Nebraska 68198-0001

Public Control. Nebraska health system is a member of Council of Teaching Hospitals. Schools located at medical center are: College of Dentistry, College of Medicine, College of Nursing, College of Pharmacy, Graduate College, School of Allied Health. Special facilities: Geriatric Center, Eppley Cancer Research Institute, C. Louis Meyer Children's Rehabilitation Center. Nationally recognized programs in Cancer and Otolaryngology. The medical center's ranking in domestic higher education by NIH awards/grants was 97th, with 72 awards/grants received; total dollars awarded $15,712,930.

College of Medicine
Room 5017A Wittson Hall
600 South 42nd Street
Omaha, Nebraska 68198-6585
Phone: (404)559-6140; fax: (402)559-4148
Internet site: http://www.unmc.edu
E-mail: cfrank@unmc.edu

Established 1880. Located at the medical center. Library: 234,000 volumes/microforms; 2,200 current periodicals/subscriptions. Affiliated hospitals: University Medical Center, Veterans Affairs Hospital. Special programs: summer programs for high school juniors and seniors.

Annual tuition: residents $10,814, nonresidents $20,908; fees $1,521.50. No on-campus housing available. Contact Student Services Office for off-campus housing information; phone: (402)559-5221. Off-campus housing and personal expenses: approximately $14,501.

Enrollment: 1st-year class 120 (EDP 5); total full-time 488 (men 55%, women 45%). First-year statistics: 5% out of state; 46% women; average age 25; 75% science majors.

Faculty: full-time 395, part-time/volunteers 1,091.

Degrees conferred: M.D., M.D.-M.S., M.D.-Ph.D. (Anatomy and Cell Biology, Biochemistry, Genetics, Immunology, Medical Sciences, Molecular Biology, Pharmaceutical Sciences, Pharmacology, Physiology); has Scholars Program.

RECRUITMENT PRACTICES AND POLICIES. School has diversity program and actively recruits women/minority applicants. Diversity contact: Assistant Dean for Student and Multicultural Affairs, phone: (402)559-4437.

ADMISSION REQUIREMENTS FOR FIRST-YEAR APPLICANTS. Preference given to state residents; U.S. citizens and permanent residents only. *Undergraduate preparation.* Suggested premed courses: 2 courses in biology with labs, 2 courses in inorganic chemistry with labs, 2 courses in organic chemistry with labs, 2 courses in physics with labs, 1 course in college math, 1 course in English, 4 courses in humanities/social sciences. Advanced placement and CLEP are accepted in lieu of course work. Bachelor's degree from an accredited institution required; all applicants have bachelor's degree awarded prior to enrollment. *Has EDP*; applicants must apply through AMCAS (official transcripts sent by mid-May) between June 1 and August 1. Early applications are encouraged. Submit supplemental application, a personal statement, and 2 recommendations to Admissions Office within 2 weeks of receipt of application. Interviews are by invitation only and generally for final selection. Notification normally begins October 1. *Regular application process.* Apply through AMCAS (file after June 1, before November 1); submit MCAT (will accept MCAT test results from last 3 years), official transcripts for each school attended (should show at least 90 semester credits/135 quarter credits, submit transcripts by mid-May to AMCAS), service processing fee. All state residents and selected nonresidents are asked to submit a supplemental application and an application fee of $25, a personal statement, preprofessional committee evaluation, and 2 recommendations from science faculty to Admissions Office within 2–3 weeks of the receipt of supplemental materials. Interviews are by invitation only and generally for final selection. M.D.-Ph.D. degree applicants must submit 1 application but must be accepted to both schools; contact the Admissions Office for current

information and specific requirements for admission. First-year students admitted in fall only. Rolling admission process. Notification starts on January 1 and is finished when class is filled. Applicant's response to offer and $100 deposit due within 2 weeks of receipt of acceptance letter. School does maintain an alternate list. Phone: (404)559-6140; fax: (402)559-6148; E-mail: cfrank@unmc.edu.

ADMISSION REQUIREMENTS FOR TRANSFER APPLICANTS. Accepts transfers from other accredited U.S. medical schools. Admission limited to space available. Contact the Admissions Office after January 1 for current information and specific requirements.

ADMISSION STANDARDS AND RECOGNITION. *For M.D.:* number of state-resident applicants 393, nonresidents 843; number of state residents interviewed 380, nonresidents 45; number of residents enrolled 120, nonresidents 3; median MCAT 9.5 (verbal reasoning 9.3; biological sciences 9.7; physical sciences 9.2); median GPA 3.76 (A = 4). Gorman rating 3.66 (scale: good 3.61–3.99); the school's medical ranking by NIH awards/grants was 79th, with 65 awards/grants received; total dollars awarded $13,834,149.

FINANCIAL AID. Scholarships, some merit scholarships, grants-in-aid, institutional loans, HEAL, alternative loan programs, Primary Care Loan Program, federal Perkins loans, Stafford subsidized and unsubsidized loans and service commitment scholarship programs are available. Assistantships/fellowships may be available for combined-degree candidates. Financial aid applications and information are sent out with the letter of acceptance and are due back within 30 days of date of acceptance. For merit scholarships, the selection criteria place heavy reliance on MCAT and undergraduate GPA. Contact the Financial Aid Office for current information; phone: (404)559-4199. For most financial assistance and all federal programs, submit FAFSA to a federal processor (Title IV school code #006895); also submit Financial Aid Transcript and Federal Income Tax forms. Approximately 60% of current students receive some form of financial assistance. Average debt after graduation $78,000.

DEGREE REQUIREMENTS. *For M.D.:* satisfactory completion of 4-year program. All students must pass USMLE Step 1 prior to entering 3rd year; taking USMLE Step 2 is optional. *For M.D.-M.S.:* generally a 4½–5½-year program. *For M.D.-Ph.D.:* generally a 7-year program.

College of Dentistry

40th and Holdrege Street
Lincoln, Nebraska 68583-0740
Phone: (402)472-1363, (800)332-0235; fax: (402)472-5290
Internet site: http://www.unmc.edu
E-mail: gmcanfie@unmc.edu

Established 1899 as Lincoln Dental College, affiliated with University of Nebraska in 1917; became a part of the medical center in 1979. Located on Lincoln campus, 55 miles from medical center. Semester system. Basic-science courses are taught in first 2 years. Affiliated hospitals: University Hospital (Omaha), Veterans Administration Hospital (Lincoln). Postgraduate specialties: Endodontics, General Dentistry, General Practice Residency, Orthodontics, Pediatric Dentistry, Periodontics, Prosthodontics.

Annual tuition: residents $9,502, nonresidents $22,196; fees $486; equipment and supplies $3,228. On-campus rooms and apartments available for both single and married students. Contact Housing Office for both on- and off-campus housing information; phone: (402)472-3561. Dental students tend to live off-campus. Off-campus housing, food, transportation, and personal expenses: approximately $14,400.

Enrollment: 1st-year class 43; total full-time 160. First-year enrolled student information: 11 from out of state; 9 states, 1 foreign country represented; 19 women; average age 22; 4 underrepresented minorities; 1 other minority.

Faculty: full-time 138.

Degree conferred: D.D.S., M.S. (Oral Biology), Ph.D. (Oral Biology).

RECRUITMENT PRACTICES AND POLICIES. School has diversity program and actively recruits women/minority applicants. Diversity contact: Minority Student Affairs Office; phone: (402)559-4437.

ADMISSION REQUIREMENTS FOR FIRST-YEAR APPLICANTS. Preference given to residents of Nebraska, Wyoming, and North Dakota; U.S. citizens and permanent residents only. *Undergraduate preparation.* Suggested predental courses: 2 courses in biology with labs, 2 courses in inorganic chemistry with labs, 2 courses in organic chemistry with labs, 2–3 courses in physics with labs, 2 courses in English. There are no limitations on the number of junior-college credits taken. Will consider applicants with only 3 years of undergraduate preparation, prefer applicants who will have a bachelor's degree prior to enrollment; 25 out of 43 enrolled students have bachelor's degrees awarded prior to enrollment. *Application process.* Apply through AADSAS (file after July 1, before February 1); submit official transcripts for each school attended (should show at least 90 semester credits/135 quarter credits), service processing fee. TOEFL is required of an applicant whose native language is other than English. Submit the following materials only after being contacted by an Admissions Officer: an application fee of $25, a supplemental application, official transcripts, DAT scores (should be taken no later the October of the year preceding the anticipated year of enrollment) to Admissions Office within 2 weeks of receipt of supplemental materials. Recommendations are not required, but a predental committee evaluation would be appreciated. Interviews are by invitation only and generally for final selection. First-year students admitted in fall only. Rolling admission process. Notification starts on December 1 and is finished when class is filled. Applicant's response to offer and $200 deposit due within 30 days if accepted prior to January 31; response and deposit due within 15 days if received after February 1. Phone: (402)472-1363; E-mail: gmcanfie@unmc.edu.

ADMISSION REQUIREMENTS FOR ADVANCED-STANDING APPLICANTS. Accepts transfers from other accredited U.S. dental schools on an individual basis. Admission limited to space available. Contact the Admissions Office for current information and specific requirements for admission.

ADMISSION STANDARDS AND RECOGNITION. *For D.D.S.:* number of applicants 707; number enrolled 43; median DAT: ACAD 16.9, PAT 16.2; median GPA 3.67 (A = 4), median sciences GPA 3.56 (A = 4). Gorman rating 4.16 (scale: strong 4.01–4.49); this placed the school in the Bottom 10 of all U.S. dental schools.

FINANCIAL AID. Scholarships, merit scholarships, minority scholarships, grants-in-aid, institutional loans, state loan programs, DEAL, HEAL, alternative loan programs, federal Perkins loans, Stafford subsidized and unsubsidized loans, and military service commitment scholarship programs are available. Institutional financial aid applications and information are generally available at the on-campus interview (by invitation). For merit scholarships, the selection criteria place heavy reliance on DAT and undergraduate GPA. Contact the Financial Aid Office at medical center for current information; phone: (402)559-4199. For most financial assistance and all need-based programs, submit FAFSA to a federal processor (Title IV school code # 006895); also submit Financial Aid Transcript, Federal Income Tax forms, and Use of Federal

Funds Certification. Approximately 95% of current students receive some form of financial assistance. Average awards for residents $20,312, nonresidents $32,667.

DEGREE REQUIREMENTS. *For D.D.S.:* satisfactory completion of 4-year (45-month) program.

UNIVERSITY OF NEVADA, RENO
Reno, Nevada 89557-0035
Internet site: http://www.unr.edu

Founded 1864. Public control. Semester system. Library: 880,000 volumes; 2,720,000 microforms; 9,800 periodicals/subscriptions; 115 PC work stations. Special facility: Biological Science Center. The university's ranking in domestic higher education by NIH awards/grants was 126th, with 30 awards/grants received; total dollars awarded $6,845,756.

The university's graduate schools/colleges include: Center for Environmental Sciences and Engineering, College of Arts and Science, College of Business Administration, College of Education, College of Engineering, College of Human and Community Sciences, Donald W. Reynolds School of Journalism, M. C. Fleischmann College of Agriculture, Mackay School of Mines, College of Medicine.

Total university enrollment at main campus: approximately 12,000.

College of Medicine
Manville Building 357
Reno, Nevada 89557
Phone: (702)784-3063; fax: (702)784-6174
Internet site: http://www.unr.ed/med
E-mail: asa@scs.unr.edu

Established 1969. Located on Reno campus; the University Medical Center is located in Las Vegas. Semester system. Affiliated hospitals: University Medical Center, Veterans Administration Medical Center, Washoe Medical Center.

Annual tuition: residents $9,160; nonresidents $23,187; fees, $1,894. On-campus rooms and apartments available for both single and married students. Contact Housing Services Office for both on- and off-campus housing information; phone: (702)784-6107. Medical students tend to live off-campus. Off-campus housing and personal expenses: approximately $7,887.

Enrollment: 1st-year class 52 (EDP 2); total full-time 207 (men 60%, women 40%). First-year statistics: 20% out of state; 40% women; average age 24; 5% minorities; 86% science majors.

Degrees conferred: M.D., M.D.-Ph.D. (Biochemistry, Biomedical Engineering, Cell and Molecular Biology, Pharmacology, Physiology).

RECRUITMENT PRACTICES AND POLICIES. School has diversity program and actively recruits women/minority applicants. Diversity contact: Director of Recruitment; phone: (702)784-1317.

ADMISSION REQUIREMENTS FOR FIRST-YEAR APPLICANTS. High priority given to state residents, nonresidents with ties to Nevada, residents of western states without medical schools; U.S. citizens and permanent residents only. *Undergraduate preparation.* Suggested premed courses: 3 courses in biology with labs, 2 courses in inorganic chemistry with labs, 2 courses in organic chemistry with labs, 2 courses in physics with labs, 2 courses in behavioral sciences; demonstrated proficiency in English composition and expression. Bachelor's degree from an accredited institution required; all applicants have bachelor's degree awarded prior to enrollment. *Has EDP*; applicants must apply through AMCAS (official transcripts sent by mid-May) between June 1 and August 1. Early applications are encouraged. Submit supplemental application, a personal statement, and 2 recommendations to Office of Medical Admission and Student Affairs within 2 weeks of receipt of application. Interviews are by invitation only and generally for final selection. Notification normally begins October 1. *Regular application process.* Apply through AMCAS (file after June 1, before December 1); submit MCAT (will accept MCAT test results from the last 3 years), official transcripts for each school attended (should show at least 90 semester credits/135 quarter credits, submit transcripts by mid-May to AMCAS), service processing fee. Submit an application fee of $45, a supplemental application, a personal statement, preprofessional committee evaluation, and 2 recommendations from science faculty to Office of Medical Admission and Student Affairs within 2–3 weeks of the receipt of supplemental materials. Interviews are by invitation only and generally for final selection. M.D.-Ph.D. degree applicants must complete a supplemental M.D.-Ph.D. application and be accepted to both schools; contact the Admissions Office for current information and specific requirements for admission. First-year students admitted in fall only. Rolling admission process. Notification starts on January 15 and is finished when class is filled. Applicant's response to offer due within 2 weeks of receipt of acceptance letter. School does maintain an alternate list. Phone: (702)784-6063; E-mail: asa@scs.unr.edu.

ADMISSION REQUIREMENTS FOR TRANSFER APPLICANTS. Accepts transfers from other accredited U.S. and Canadian medical schools who are state residents or nonresidents with strong ties to state. Admission limited to space available. Contact the Admissions Office for current information and specific requirements for admission.

ADMISSION STANDARDS AND RECOGNITION. *For M.D.:* number of state-resident applicants 242, nonresidents 934; number of state residents interviewed 135, nonresidents 45; number of residents enrolled 47, nonresidents 5; median MCAT 9.4 (verbal reasoning 9.1; biological sciences 9.7; physical sciences 9.2); median GPA 3.6 (A = 4). Gorman rating 3.20 (scale: acceptable plus 3.01–3.59); college's medical ranking by NIH awards/grants was 98th, with 25 awards/grants received; total dollars awarded $5,919,756.

FINANCIAL AID. Scholarships, merit scholarships, grants-in-aid, institutional loans, HEAL, alternative loan programs, short-term loans, federal Perkins loans, Stafford subsidized and unsubsidized loans, and service commitment scholarship programs are available. Financial aid is based on documented need and merit. Assistantships/fellowships may be available for combined degree candidates. Financial aid applications and information are generally available at the on-campus interview (by invitation). For merit scholarships, the selection criteria place heavy reliance on MCAT and undergraduate GPA. Applicants from WICHE states must provide evidence that they have applied for WICHE support and have been denied in order to receive financial assistance from the College of Medicine. Contact the Financial Aid Office for current information; phone: (702)784-6063. For most financial assistance and all federal programs, submit FAFSA by February 15 (for priority consideration) to a federal processor (Title IV school code # 002568); also submit Financial Aid Transcript and Federal Income Tax forms. Approximately 80% of current students receive some form of financial assistance.

DEGREE REQUIREMENTS. *For M.D.:* satisfactory completion of 4-year program. All students must pass USMLE Step 1 prior to entering 3rd year; all students must pass USMLE Step 2 prior to awarding of M.D. *For M.D.-Ph.D.:* generally a 7-year program.

UNIVERSITY OF NEW ENGLAND
Biddeford, Maine 04005-9526

The university's charter dates back to 1831; however, the university was actually formed only in 1978; 20 minute drive from Portland. University has a suburban campus in Portland. Private control. Semester system. Library: 86,000 volumes/microforms; 1,280 current periodicals/subscriptions; 62 PC computer work stations. Special facilities: Alfond Center for Health Sciences, Center for Human Services.

The university's graduate programs include: College of Osteopathic Medicine, College of Professional and Continuing Studies.

Total university enrollment at main campus: 2,500.

College of Osteopathic Medicine
11 Hills Beach Road
Biddleford, Maine 04005-9599
Phone: (800)477-4UNE, (207)283-0171
Internet site: http://www.une.edu
E-mail: msinkewjz@mailbox.une.edu

College established 1970 as St. Francis College of Osteopathic Medicine; merged with university in 1978. Affiliated with 20 community hospitals and medical centers.

Annual tuition: $32,850. Limited on-campus housing available. Annual on-campus housing cost: single students $4,150 (room only), married students $5,250. Contact Graduate Housing Office for both on- and off-campus housing information. Medical students tend to live off-campus; phone: (207)283-0171, X2272. Off-campus housing and personal expenses: approximately $9,500.

Enrollment: 1st-year class 115; total full-time 369 (men 52%, women 48%). First-year statistics: 10% out of state; 50% women; average age 29; 8% minorities; 24% science majors.

Faculty: full-time 14; part-time 18.

Degree conferred: D.O.

ADMISSION REQUIREMENTS FOR FIRST-YEAR APPLICANTS. Preference given to students who will practice in New England; U.S. citizens and permanent residents only. *Undergraduate preparation.* Suggested premed courses: 2 courses in biology, 2 courses in inorganic chemistry, 2 courses in organic chemistry, 2 courses in physics, 1 course in college math, 2 courses in English. For serious consideration an applicant should have a 2.75 (A = 4) GPA or above. Bachelor's degree from an accredited institution required; all applicants have bachelor's degrees awarded prior to enrollment. *Application process.* Apply through AACOMAS (file after June 1, before January 1); submit MCAT (will accept test results from last 2 years, MCAT should be taken no later than September of the year prior to the year of anticipated enrollment), official transcripts for each school attended (should show at least 90 semester credits/135 quarter credits), service processing fee. After a review of the AACOMAS application and supporting documents, a decision is made concerning which candidates should receive supplemental materials. The supplemental application, an application fee of $55, a personal statement, and 3 recommendations (at least 2 from science faculty; 1 from a D.O. is highly recommended) should be returned to the Admissions Office as soon as possible. In addition, international applicants must submit foreign transcripts to the World Education Service for translation and evaluation. TOEFL may be required of those applicants whose native language is other than English. Interviews are by invitation only and generally for final selection. First-year students admitted in fall only. Rolling admission process. Notification starts in October and is finished when class is filled. Applicant's response to offer and $100 deposit due within 2 weeks of receipt of acceptance letter. Phone: (207)283-0171, X218; fax: (207)283-3249.

ADMISSION REQUIREMENTS FOR TRANSFER APPLICANTS. Accepts transfers from other accredited U.S. osteopathic medical schools. Admission limited to space available. Contact the Admissions Office for current information and specific requirements for admission.

ADMISSION STANDARDS AND RECOGNITION. *For D.O.:* number of applicants 3,500; number enrolled 115, median MCAT 8.3; median GPA 3.4 (A = 4); the school's ranking by NIH awards/grants was 6th among osteopathic schools, with 1 award/grant received; total value of all awards/grants $181,323.

FINANCIAL AID. Scholarships, minority scholarships, grants, institutional loans, Maine Osteopathic Loan Fund, NOF, HEAL, alternative loan programs, federal Perkins loans, Stafford subsidized and unsubsidized loans, service obligation scholarships programs, and military and National Health Service programs are available. Financial-aid applications and information are generally available at the on-campus interview (by invitation). For scholarships, the selection criteria place heavy reliance on MCAT and undergraduate GPA. Contact the Office of Graduate Financial Aid for current information; phone: (207)283-0171. For most financial assistance and all federal programs submit FAFSA to a federal processor (Title IV school code # 002050); also submit Financial Aid Transcript and Federal Income Tax forms. Approximately 80% of current students receive some form of financial assistance. Average debt after graduation $110,000.

DEGREE REQUIREMENTS. *For D.O.:* satisfactory completion of 4-year program.

UNIVERSITY OF NEW MEXICO
Albuquerque, New Mexico 87131-2039
Internet site: http://www.unm.edu

Founded 1889. Located 60 miles from Santa Fe, the state capital. Public control. Semester system. Library: 1,600,000 volumes; 5,000,000 microforms. Special facilities: Institute for Modern Optics, Museum of Southwestern Biology. The university's ranking in domestic higher education by NIH awards/grants was 75th, with 85 awards/grants received; total dollars awarded $25,595,768.

The university's graduate schools/colleges include: College of Arts and Science, College of Education, College of Engineering, College of Fine Arts, College of Nursing, College of Pharmacy, Robert O. Anderson Graduate School of Management, School of Architecture and Planning, School of Public Administration, School of Law, School of Medicine.

Total university enrollment at main campus: 23,600.

University of New Mexico Health Center
2211 Lomas Boulevard, N.E.
Albuquerque, New Mexico 87106

Public control. University hospital is a member of the Council of Teaching Hospitals. Schools located at health center are: College of Nursing, College of Pharmacy, School of Medicine. Special facilities: Cancer Research and Treatment Center, Carrie Tingley Hospital, Children's Hospital of New Mexico, Children's Psychiatric Hospital, Mental Health Center. Nationally recognized programs in Endocrinology, Urology.

School of Medicine
Basic Medical Sciences Building R 107
Albuquerque, New Mexico 87131-5166
Phone: (505)277-4766; fax: (505)277-2755
Internet site: http://hsc.unm.edu/som

Established 1961. Located on north campus. Affiliated hospitals: University Hospital, Mental Health Center, University of New Mexico Children's Psychiatric Hospital, Center for Noninvasive Diagnosis, International Cancer Center, Regional Federal Medical Center. Special programs: Summer programs for underrepresented minorities; prematriculation summer sessions.

Annual tuition: residents $5,966, nonresidents $16,961; fees $32. No on-campus housing available. Contact Admissions Office for off-campus housing information. Off-campus housing and personal expenses: approximately $16,000.

Enrollment: 1st-year class 73 (EDP 25); total full-time 302 (men 44%, women 56%). First-year statistics: 7% out of state; 56% women; average age 25; 40% ethnic minorities; 79% science majors.

Faculty: full-time/part-time 535, volunteers 900.

Degrees conferred: M.D., M.D.-M.S., M.D.-Ph.D. (Anatomy, Biochemistry, Biomedical Engineering, Biophysics, Cell Biology, Genetics, Immunology, Microbiology, Molecular Biology, Neurosciences, Pathology, Pharmacology, Physiology).

RECRUITMENT PRACTICES AND POLICIES. School has diversity program and actively recruits women/minority applicants. Diversity contact: Associate Dean, Officer of Cultural and Ethnic Programs; phone: (505)277-2728.

ADMISSION REQUIREMENTS FOR FIRST-YEAR APPLICANTS. Preference given to state residents; U.S. citizens and permanent residents only. *Undergraduate preparation.* Suggested premed courses: 2 courses in biology with labs, 2 courses in inorganic chemistry with labs, 2 courses in organic chemistry with labs, 2 courses in physics with labs, 2 courses in English; courses in biochemistry, calculus, and Spanish are strongly recommended. Bachelor's degree from an accredited institution required; 92% of applicants have bachelor's degrees awarded prior to enrollment. *Has EDP* for state residents (all nonregional applicants, including WICHE, and former state residents must apply as EDP applicants); applicants must apply through AMCAS (official transcripts sent by mid-May) between June 1 and August 1. Early applications are encouraged. Submit supplemental application, a personal statement, and 2 recommendations to Office of Admissions and Student Affairs within 2 weeks of receipt of application. Interviews are by invitation only and generally for final selection. Notification normally begins October 1. *Regular application process.* Apply through AMCAS (file after June 1, before December 1); submit MCAT (will accept MCAT test results from 1995), official transcripts for each school attended (should show at least 90 semester credits/135 quarter credits, submit transcripts by mid-May to AMCAS), service processing fee. All state residents are sent additional materials. Submit an application fee of $50, a supplemental application, a personal statement, preprofessional committee evaluation, and 2 recommendations from science faculty to Office of Admission and Student Affairs within 2–3 weeks of the receipt of supplemental materials. Interviews are by invitation only and generally for final selection. Dual-degree applicants must apply through

AMCAS and submit separate application to the Graduate Committee of the School of Medicine; contact the Office of Admission and Student Affairs for current information and specific requirements for admission. First-year students admitted in fall only. Rolling admission process. Notification starts March 15 and is finished when class is filled. Applicant's response to offer and $100 deposit due within 4 weeks of receipt of acceptance letter. School does maintain an alternate list. Phone: (505)277-4766; fax: (505)277-2755.

ADMISSION REQUIREMENTS FOR TRANSFER APPLICANTS. Occasionally accepts transfers from other accredited U.S. medical schools who are state residents with a compelling reason only. Admission limited to space available. Contact the Office of Admission and Student Affairs for current information and specific requirements for admission.

ADMISSION STANDARDS AND RECOGNITION. *For M.D.:* number of state-resident applicants 360, nonresidents 805; number of state residents interviewed 357, nonresidents 19; total accepted 90; number of residents enrolled 68, nonresidents 5; median MCAT 8.79 (verbal reasoning 8.85; biological sciences 9.04; physical sciences 8.47); median GPA 3.45 (A = 4). Gorman rating 3.29 (scale: acceptable plus 3.01–3.59); *U.S. News & World Report* ranked the school in the Top 25 of all U.S. medical schools in primary-care programs; medical school's ranking by NIH awards/grants was 72nd, with 61 awards/grants received; total dollars awarded $17,305,692.

FINANCIAL AID. Limited scholarship assistance, grants, institutional loans, HEAL, alternative loan programs, federal Perkins loans, Stafford subsidized and unsubsidized loans, and service commitment scholarship programs are available. Assistantships/fellowships may be available for combined-degree candidates. Financial aid applications and information are generally available at the on-campus interview (by invitation). Most financial aid is based on demonstrated need. Contact the Student Affairs Office for the current *Financial Aid Handbook*; phone: (505)277-8008. For most financial assistance and all federal programs, submit FAFSA to a federal processor (Title IV school code # G24593); also submit Financial Aid Transcript and Federal Income Tax forms. Approximately 80% of current students receive some form of financial assistance. Average debt after graduation $48,400.

DEGREE REQUIREMENTS. *For M.D.:* satisfactory completion of 4-year program. All students must pass

USMLE Step 1 prior to entering 3rd year; all students must take USMLE Step 2 prior to awarding of M.D. *For M.D.-M.S.:* generally 4½–5½-year program. *For M.D.-Ph.D.:* generally a 7-year program.

NEW YORK INSTITUTE OF TECHNOLOGY

Old Westbury, New York 11568-8000
Internet site: http://www.nyit.edu

Founded 1955. Located about 25 miles E of New York City. Private control. Library: 200,000 volumes; 580,000 microforms; 3,900 periodicals/subscriptions; 70 PC work stations. Special facilities: Center for Labor and Industrial Relations, Science and Technology Research Center, Video Center, Management Information Systems Center.

The university's graduate division includes: School of Allied Health and Life Science, School of Architecture, School of Arts, Sciences and Communication, School of Education, School of Engineering and Technology, School of Management.

Total university enrollment at main campus: 9,396.

College of Osteopathic Medicine

P.O. Box 8000
Old Westbury, New York 11568-8000
Phone: (516)626-6922
Internet site: http://www.nyit.edu/nycom/

Located adjacent to main campus. Special programs: Summer programs for underrepresented minorities. Affiliated with over 22 hospitals and clinics in New York and New Jersey.

Annual tuition: $21,400. No on-campus housing available. Contact Office of Student Affairs for off-campus housing information. Off-campus housing and personal expenses: approximately $13,810.

Enrollment: 1st-year class 205; total full-time 897 (men 58%, women 42%). First-year statistics: none from out of state; 43% women; average age 25.

Faculty: full-time 40, part-time 78.

Degrees conferred: D.O., D.O.-M.B.A., D.O.-M.S. (Clinical Nutrition).

RECRUITMENT PRACTICES AND POLICIES. School has diversity program and actively recruits women/minority applicants. Diversity contact: Office of Student Affairs.

ADMISSION REQUIREMENTS FOR FIRST-YEAR APPLICANTS. Preference given to state residents; U.S.

citizens and permanent residents only. *Undergraduate preparation.* Suggested premed courses: 2 courses in biology, 2 courses in inorganic chemistry, 2 courses in organic chemistry, 2 courses in physics, 2 courses in English. Bachelor's degree from an accredited institution required. For serious consideration an applicant should have a 2.75 GPA (A = 4) or better; all applicants have bachelor's degrees awarded prior to enrollment. *Application process.* Apply through AACOMAS (file after June 1, before December 1); submit MCAT (will accept test results from last 3 years), official transcripts for each school attended (should show at least 90 semester credits/135 quarter credits), service processing fee. After a review of the AACOMAS application and supporting documents, a decision is made concerning which candidates should receive supplemental materials. The supplemental application, an application fee of $60, a personal statement, and 3 recommendations (1 from a D.O.) should be returned to Admissions Office as soon as possible. In addition, international applicants must submit foreign transcripts to the World Education Service for translation and evaluation. TOEFL may be required of those applicants whose native language is other than English. Interviews are by invitation only and generally for final selection. Joint-degree applicants must apply to, and be accepted by, both schools; contact the Office of Student Affairs for current information and specific requirements for admission. First-year students admitted in fall only. Rolling admission process. Notification starts in January and is finished when class is filled. Applicant's response to offer and $500 deposit due within 2 weeks of receipt of acceptance letter. School does maintain an alternate list. Phone: (516)626-6947; fax: (516)626-6946.

ADMISSION REQUIREMENTS FOR TRANSFER APPLICANTS. Accepts transfers from other accredited U.S. osteopathic medical schools. Admission limited to space available. Contact the Office of Student Affairs for current information and specific requirements for admission.

ADMISSION STANDARDS AND RECOGNITION. *For D.O.:* number of applicants 4,700; number enrolled 205; median MCAT 7.3; median GPA 3.2.

FINANCIAL AID. Scholarships, merit scholarship, minority scholarships, grants-in-aid, New York State TAP, institutional loans, NOF, HEAL, alternative loan programs, federal Perkins loans, Stafford subsidized and unsubsidized loans, service obligation scholarship programs, and military and National Health Service programs are available. Financial aid applications and information are generally available at the on-campus interview (by invitation). Financial aid is primarily based on demonstrated need. Contact the Financial Aid Office for current information; phone: (516)686-7960. For most financial assistance and all federal programs submit FAFSA to a federal processor (Title IV school code # 002782); also submit Financial Aid Transcript and Federal Income Tax forms. Approximately 80% of current students receive some form of financial assistance.

DEGREE REQUIREMENTS. *For D.O.:* satisfactory completion of 4-year program. All students must pass the National Board of Osteopathic Medical Examination Part I and take part II prior to the awarding of D.O. *For D.O.-M.B.A., M.S.:* generally a 4½–5½-year program.

NEW YORK MEDICAL COLLEGE
Valhalla, New York 10595
Internet site: http://www.nymc.edu

Established 1896. Located about 25 miles N of New York City. Private control. Graduate study only. Semester system. Library: 148,000 volumes/microforms; 1,500 current periodicals/subscriptions; 20 PC work stations.

The medical college's graduate schools are: Graduate School of Basic Medical Sciences, Graduate School of Health Sciences, Medical College.

Total enrollment: 975.

Medical College
Sunshine Cottage
Valhalla, New York 10595
Phone: (914)993-4507; fax: (914)993-4976
Internet site: http://www.nymc.edu

Established 1860. Special programs: summer programs for underrepresented minorities; prematriculation summer sessions.

Annual tuition: $28,795; fees $1,580. No on-campus housing available. The college does have housing facilities within walking distance of the campus. Contact Director of Housing for off-campus housing information; phone: (914)993-4832. Off-campus housing and personal expenses: approximately $13,584.

Enrollment: 1st-year class 185 (EDP 10); total full-time 784 (men 64%, women 36%). First-year statistics: 70% out of state; 38% women; average age 25; 11% minorities; 68% science majors.

Faculty: full-time/part-time/volunteers 2,800.

Degrees conferred: M.D., M.D.-M.S., M.D.-Ph.D. (Basic Medical Sciences, Biochemistry, Cell Biology and Anatomy, Experimental Pathology, Genetics, Microbiol-

ogy and Immunology, Molecular Biology, Neurosciences, Pharmacology, Physiology).

RECRUITMENT PRACTICES AND POLICIES. School has diversity program and actively recruits women/minority applicants. Diversity contact: Associate Dean for Students Affairs, Director of Minority Affairs; phone: (914)993-4623.

ADMISSION REQUIREMENTS FOR FIRST-YEAR APPLICANTS. Preference given to state residents; U.S. citizens and permanent residents only. *Undergraduate preparation.* Suggested premed courses: 2 courses in biology with labs, 2 courses in inorganic chemistry with labs, 2 courses in organic chemistry with labs, 2 courses in physics with labs, 2 courses in English. Bachelor's degree from an accredited institution required; all applicants have bachelor's degree awarded prior to enrollment. *Has EDP*; applicants must apply through AMCAS (official transcripts sent by mid-May) between June 1 and August 1. Early applications are encouraged. Submit supplemental application, a personal statement, and 2 recommendations to Admissions Office within 2 weeks of receipt of application. Interviews are by invitation only and generally for final selection. Notification normally begins October 1. *Regular application process.* Apply through AMCAS (file after June 1, before December 1); submit MCAT (will accept MCAT test results from last 3 years), official transcripts for each school attended (should show at least 90 semester credits/135 quarter credits, submit transcripts by mid-May to AMCAS), service processing fee. Submit an application fee of $100, a supplemental application, a personal statement, preprofessional committee evaluation, and 2 recommendations from science faculty to Admissions Office within 2–3 weeks of the receipt of supplemental materials. Interviews are by invitation only and generally for final selection. First-year students admitted in fall only. Rolling admission process. Notification starts in October and is finished when class is filled. Applicant's response to offer and $100 deposit due within 2 weeks of receipt of acceptance letter. School does maintain an alternate list. M.D.-Ph.D. degree applicants apply during the first 2 years of medical school. Students are generally admitted to the combined degree program after the completion of all basic-science courses and when Step 1 of USMLE has been taken. For further information contact the Admissions Office; phone: (914)993-4507.

ADMISSION REQUIREMENTS FOR TRANSFER APPLICANTS. Accepts transfers from other accredited U.S. and Canadian medical schools. Admission limited to space available. Contact the Admissions Office after January 1 for current information and specific requirements for admission.

ADMISSION STANDARDS AND RECOGNITION. *For M.D.:* number of state-resident applicants 2,443, nonresidents 9,806; number of state residents interviewed 381, nonresidents 931; number of residents enrolled 59, nonresidents 143; median MCAT 10.0 (verbal reasoning 9.7; biological sciences 10.4; physical sciences 10.1); median GPA 3.20 (A = 4). Gorman rating 3.5 (scale: acceptable plus 3.01–3.59); the college's medical ranking by NIH awards/grants was 83rd, with 42 awards/grants received; total dollars awarded $11,792,708.

FINANCIAL AID. Scholarships, merit scholarships, minority scholarships, grants-in-aid, institutional loans, state incentive awards, HEAL, alternative loan programs, federal Perkins loans, Stafford subsidized and unsubsidized loans, and service commitment scholarship programs are available. Most financial aid is based on demonstrated need. Financial aid applications and information are generally available at the on-campus interview (by invitation). For scholarships, the selection criteria place heavy reliance on MCAT and undergraduate GPA. Contact the Office of Student Financial Planning for current information; phone: (914)993-4491. For most financial assistance and all federal programs, submit FAFSA to a federal processor (Title IV school code # G02784); also submit Financial Aid Transcript and Federal Income Tax forms. Approximately 85% of current students receive some form of financial assistance. Average debt after graduation $122,000.

DEGREE REQUIREMENTS. *For M.D.:* satisfactory completion of 4-year program. All students must take USMLE Step 1 prior to entering 3rd year; all students must take USMLE Step 2 prior to awarding of M.D. *For M.D.-M.S.:* generally a 4½–5½-year program. *For M.D.-Ph.D.:* generally a 7-year program.

NEW YORK UNIVERSITY
New York, New York 10012-1019
Internet site: http://www.nyu.edu

Founded 1831. Located in Greenwich Village at Washington Square. Private control. Semester system. Library: 3,650,000 volumes; 3,240,000 microforms; 28,700 periodicals/subscriptions; 50 PC work stations. Special program: B.A./B.S.-M.D. program (annual undergraduate tuition $20,756). The university's ranking in domestic higher education by NIH awards/grants was 30th, with 309 awards/grants received; total dollars awarded $80,128,411.

The university's other graduate colleges/schools: College of Dentistry, Gallatin School of Individualized Study, Graduate School of Arts and Science, Leonard M. Stern School of Business, Robert F. Wagner School of Public Service, School of Continuing Education, School of Education, School of Law, School of Medicine, Shirley M. Ehrenkranz School of Social Work, Tisch School of the Arts.

Total university enrollment at main campus: 33,900.

New York University Medical Center Complex
550 First Avenue
New York, New York 10016

Located in midtown Manhattan overlooking the East River. Private control. The medical center is a member of the Council of Teaching Hospitals. Facilities in close proximity to medical center are: Institute of Forensic Medicine, Institute for Crippled and Disabled, Millbank Laboratories, Hunter College–Bellevue School of Nursing, New York Infirmary. Special facilities: Bellevue Hospital Center, Veteran's Administration Hospital, Tisch Hospital, Skirball Institute of Biomolecular Medicine, Arnold and Marie Schwartz Health Care Center, Howard A. Rusk Institute of Rehabilitation Medicine. Nationally recognized programs in AIDS, Cardiology, Gastroenterology, Geriatrics, Gynecology, Neurology, Orthopedics, Otolaryngology, Psychiatry, Pulmonary Disease, Rehabilitation, Rheumatology. *U.S. News & World Report*'s hospital/medical center national rankings for all hospitals placed New York University Medical Center in the Top 20 of all U.S. hospitals.

School of Medicine
P.O. Box 1924
New York, New York 10016
Phone: (212)263-5290
Internet site: http://www.med.nyu.edu/MedSchool

Established 1841. Located at the medical center complex. Library: 170,000 volumes/microforms; 1,900 current periodicals/subscriptions. Affiliated hospitals: Bellevue Hospital, Brooklyn Hospital, Franklin Hospital, Goldwater Memorial Hospital, Gouverneur Diagnostic and Treatment Center, Hospital for Joint Disease Orthopedic Institute, Lenox Hill Hospital, New York Infirmary, New York Veteran's Hospital, North Shore University Hospital, Tisch Hospital. Special facilities: Skirball Institute of Biomedical Medicine, Arnold and Marie

Schwartz Health Care Center, Howard A. Rusk Institute of Rehabilitation Medicine.

Annual tuition: $26,015; fees $3,810. On-campus rooms and apartments available for both single and married students. Average on-campus living expense: $8,575. Housing information is sent to all accepted students.

Enrollment: 1st-year class 160; total full-time 666 (men 63%, women 37%). First-year statistics: 50% out of state; 35% women; average age 25; 36% minorities; 71% science majors.

Degrees conferred: M.D., B.A.-M.D. (New York University's College of Arts and Sciences), M.D.-Ph.D. (Biochemistry, Biophysics, Cell Biology, Genetics, Microbiology, Molecular Biology, Neurosciences, Pathology, Pharmacology, Physiology); has M.S.T.P.

RECRUITMENT PRACTICES AND POLICIES. School has diversity program and actively recruits women/minority applicants. Diversity contact: Associate Dean, Officer of Minority Student Services and Recruitment; phone: (212)263-8448.

ADMISSION REQUIREMENT FOR B.A.-M.D. APPLICANTS. Submit application; SAT I or ACT, 3 Achievements or 3 APs (AP English or English Achievement required), official high school transcripts with rank in class, 3 letters of recommendations, and an application fee of $45. Two interviews are required and are by invitation only (1 at the College of Arts and Science and 1 at the School of Medicine); generally for final selection. Apply to Admissions Office by January 15. Notification normally on April 1. Applicant's response to offer and $200 deposit due May 1. For current information and specific requirements, contact either the Office of Undergraduate Admission (phone: (212)998-4500) or the School of Medicine.

ADMISSION REQUIREMENTS FOR FIRST-YEAR APPLICANTS. Preference given to U.S. citizens and permanent residents only. *Undergraduate preparation.* Suggested premed courses: 2 courses in biology with labs, 2 courses in inorganic chemistry with labs, 2 courses in organic chemistry with labs, 2 courses in physics with labs, 2 courses in English; at least one course in genetics, embryology, developmental biology, and biochemistry are recommended. Bachelor's degree from an accredited institution required; all applicants have bachelor's degree awarded prior to enrollment. Does not have an EDP. *Application process.* Apply directly to School of Medicine's Office of Admission after August 15, before November 21. Submit MCAT (will accept MCAT test results from the last 3 years), official transcripts for each school attended (should show at least 90 semester credits/135 quarter credits, submit transcripts by mid-May to AMCAS), an application fee of $75; a personal statement, preprofessional committee evaluation, and 2 recommendations from science faculty directly to Admissions Office. Interviews are by invitation only and generally for final selection. Dual-degree applicants must request a supplemental M.D.-Ph.D. application; contact the Admissions Office for current information and specific requirements for admission. First-year students admitted in fall only. Rolling admission process. Notification starts December 20 and is finished when class is filled. Applicant's response to offer and $100 deposit due within 2 weeks of receipt of acceptance letter. School does maintain an alternate list. Phone: (212)263-5290; fax: (212)725-2140.

ADMISSION REQUIREMENTS FOR TRANSFER APPLICANTS. Rarely accepts transfer applicants and then only under exceptional circumstances. Contact the Admissions Office for current information and any change in transfer policy.

ADMISSION STANDARDS AND RECOGNITION. *For B.A.-M.D.:* number of applicants 325; number interviewed 11; number enrolled 3. *For M.D.:* number applicants 4,839; number interviewed 1,053; number of residents enrolled 78, nonresidents 84; median MCAT 11.0 (verbal reasoning 11.0; biological sciences 11.0; physical sciences 11.0); median GPA 3.5 (A = 4). *Barron's Guide* placed the School of Medicine among the Top 25 most prestigious U.S. medical school; Gorman rating 4.62 (scale: very strong 4.51–4.99); *U.S. News & World Report* ranked the school in the Top 25 of all U.S. medical schools; medical school's ranking by NIH awards/grants was 25th, with 254 awards/grants received; total dollars awarded $71,084,917.

FINANCIAL AID. Scholarships, merit scholarships, minority scholarships, grants-in-aid, New York State Tuition Assistance Program, institutional loans, state loans, HEAL, alternative loan programs, NIH stipends, federal Perkins loans, Stafford subsidized and unsubsidized loans, and service commitment scholarship programs are available. Assistantships/fellowships/stipends/tuition waivers may be available for dual-degree candidates. Financial aid applications and information are sent to all accepted students. For merit scholarships, the selection criteria place heavy reliance on MCAT and undergraduate GPA. Contact the Financial Aid Office for current information and the *Financial Aid Handbook*; phone: (212)263-5286. For most financial assistance and all federal programs, submit

FAFSA to a federal processor (Title IV school code # G24543); also submit Financial Aid Transcript and Federal Income Tax forms, and CSS Financial Aid Profile. Approximately 85% of current students receive some form of financial assistance. Average debt after graduation $73,000.

DEGREE REQUIREMENTS. *For B.A.-M.D.:* an 8-year program. *For M.D.:* satisfactory completion of 4-year program. Taking USMLE Steps 1 and 2 are optional. *For M.D.-Ph.D.:* generally a 6–7-year program.

College of Dentistry
345 East 24th Street, Room 1031W.
New York, New York 10010-4086
Phone: (212)988-9818; fax: (212)995-4240
Internet site: http://www.nyu.dent.edu
E-mail: dental.admissions@nyu.edu

Established 1896 as the New York College of Dentistry. The largest dental school in U.S. Located at the David B. Kriser Dental Center. Library: 36,000 volumes/microforms; 500 current periodicals/subscriptions. Special facilities: Center for Continuing Dental Education, Research Center for Minority Oral Health, David B. Kriser Oral Cancer Center, David B. Kriser Oro-Facial Pain Center, David B. Kriser Institute for the Rehabilitation of Disabled Dentists, Wachman Institute for Human Environmental Life Protection. Special programs: summer programs for underrepresented minorities. Postgraduate specialties: Endodontics, General Dentistry, Implant Dentistry, Oral and Maxillofacial Pathology, Oral and Maxillofacial Surgery, Orthodontics, Periodontics, Prosthodontics.

Annual tuition: $32,950; fees $775; equipment and supplies $3,900. On-campus rooms and apartments available for both single and married students. Contact Admissions Office for both on- and off-campus housing information. Dental students tend to live off-campus. Off-campus housing, food, transportation, and personal expenses: approximately $16,480.

Enrollment: 1st-year class 202; total full-time 785. First-year enrolled student information: 94 from out of state; 17 states represented; 79 women; average age 23; 5 underrepresented minority; 75 other minorities.

Degrees conferred: D.D.S., B.A.-D.D.S. (with Alfred University, Fairleigh Dickinson University, University of Hartford, NYU College of Arts and Sciences, Polytechnic University, Stevens Institute of Technology, Ramapo College, St. Francis College, Saint Peter's College, Wagner College, Caldwell College, Manhattan College, Manhattanville College, Mt. Saint Vincent, New Jersey Institute of Technology, Staten Island University, Stern College for Women, Yeshiva University, D.D.S.-M.B.A. (Stern School of Business); has M.S. Oral Biology.

RECRUITMENT PRACTICES AND POLICIES. School has diversity program and actively recruits women/minority applicants. Diversity contact: Office of Minority Affairs; phone: (212)998-9818.

ADMISSION REQUIREMENTS FOR FIRST-YEAR APPLICANTS. *Undergraduate preparation.* Suggested predental courses: 2 courses in biology with labs, 2 courses in inorganic chemistry with labs, 2 courses in organic chemistry with labs, 2 courses in physics with labs, 2 courses in English. The junior-college transfer-credit limit is 60 credits. Will consider applicants with only 3 years of undergraduate preparation; preference given to applicants who will have a bachelor's degree prior to enrollment; 193 out of 203 enrolled students have bachelor's degree awarded prior to enrollment. *Application process.* Apply through AADSAS (file after July 15, before April 1); submit official transcripts for each school attended (should show at least 90 semester credits/135 quarter credits), service processing fee. At the same time as you send in AADSAS materials, submit official DAT scores (test results should be from the last 3 years), a NYU College of Dentistry application and application fee of $35, official transcripts, predental committee evaluation or 3 recommendations from science professors, and signed passport photograph directly to the Office of Enrollment Services. Interviews are by invitation only and generally for final selection. Combined-degree applicants must apply to, and be accepted by, both schools. First-year students admitted in fall only. Rolling admission process. Notification starts on December 1 and is finished when class is filled. Applicant's response to offer and $500 deposit due within 15 days if accepted prior to January 1; response and deposit due within 2 weeks if received after January 1. A second deposit of $1,000 is due May 1. School does maintain an alternate list. Phone: (212)998-9818. For information on combined-degree programs contact the Associate Dean for Academic Affairs; phone: (212)998-9820.

ADMISSION REQUIREMENTS FOR ADVANCED-STANDING APPLICANTS. Accepts transfers from other accredited U.S. dental schools. Admission limited to space available. For graduates of foreign schools of dentistry, there is a 3-year dental program. Contact the Office of Enrollment Services for current information and specific requirements for admission.

ADMISSION STANDARDS AND RECOGNITION. *For D.D.S.:* number of applicants 2,395; number enrolled 202; median DAT: ACAD 18.10, PAT 16.46; median GPA

3.29 (A = 4), median sciences GPA 3.01 (A = 4). Gorman rating 4.64 (scale: very strong 4.51–4.99); this placed the school in the Top 15 of all U.S. dental schools; the dental school's ranking by NIH awards/grants was 23rd among dental schools, with 6 awards/grants received; total value of all awards/grants $1,565,429.

FINANCIAL AID. Limited number of full tuition dean's scholarships, minority student scholarships, grants-in-aid, institutional loans, state loan programs, DEAL, HEAL, alternative loan programs, federal Perkins loans, Stafford subsidized and unsubsidized loans, and military service commitment scholarship programs are available. Students accepted before January 1 will automatically be sent institutional financial-aid applications and information. Students accepted after January 1 should request financial-aid application and information directly from Financial Aid Office; phone: (212)998-9826. Most financial aid is based on demonstrated need. For merit scholarships, the selection criteria place heavy reliance on DAT and undergraduate GPA. For most financial assistance and all need-based programs, submit FAFSA to a federal processor (Title IV school code # 002785); also submit Financial Aid Transcript, Federal Income Tax forms, and Use of Federal Funds Certification. Approximately 93% of current students receive some form of financial assistance. Average award $27,565 (83% loan).

DEGREE REQUIREMENTS. *For B.A./B.S.-D.D.S.:* a 7-year program. *For D.D.S.:* satisfactory completion of 4-year program. *For D.D.S.-M.B.A.:* generally a 5½-year program. *For D.D.S.-M.S.:* generally a 4½–5½-year program.

UNIVERSITY OF NORTH CAROLINA AT CHAPEL HILL
Chapel Hill, North Carolina 27599
Internet site: http://www.unc.edu

Founded 1789. The first state university chartered in the U.S. Public control. Semester system. Library: 3,500,000 volumes; 2,730,000 microforms. The university's ranking in domestic higher education by NIH awards/grants was 14th with 545 awards/grants received; total dollars awarded $141,992,460.

The university's graduate schools/colleges include: College of Arts and Science, School of Education, School of Information and Library Science, School of Journalism and Mass Communications, School of Nursing, School of Public Health, School of Social Work, Kenan-Flagler Business School, School of Dentistry, School of Law, School of Medicine, School of Pharmacy.

Total university enrollment at main campus: 24,500.

University Medical Center
101 Manning Drive
Chapel Hill, North Carolina 27514

Public control. University of North Carolina Hospitals is a member of the Council of Teaching Hospitals. The other schools located at medical center are: School of Dentistry, School of Nursing, School of Pharmacy, School of Public Health. Special facilities: Biological Sciences Center, Cancer Research Center. Nationally recognized programs in AIDS, Cancer, Endocrinology, Gastroenterology, Geriatrics, Gynecology, Neurology, Ophthalmology, Otolaryngology, Rheumatology.

School of Medicine
CB# 7000, 130 MacNider Hall
Chapel Hill, North Carolina 27599-7000
Phone: (919)962-8331
Internet site: http://www.med.unc.edu
E-mail: esmann@med.unc.edu

Established 1879; expanded to 4-year school in 1952. Located on main campus. Library: 290,000 volumes/microforms; 4,590 current periodicals/subscriptions. Affiliated hospitals: University of North Carolina Hospitals. Special programs: Early Acceptance Commitment Plan for sophomores at University of North Carolina, Chapel Hill.

Annual tuition: residents $3,293, nonresidents $23,775; fees $769. On-campus rooms and apartments available for both single and married students. Annual on-campus housing cost: $3,385. Contact Director of Housing for both on- and off-campus housing information; phone: (919)966-5661. Medical students tend to live off-campus. Off-campus housing and personal expenses: approximately $10,541.

Enrollment: 1st-year class 160 (EDP 10); total full-time 674 (men 53%, women 47%). First-year statistics: 8% out of state; 50.6% women; average age 24; 24% minorities; 77% science majors.

Faculty: full-time 290, part-time 335.

Degrees conferred: M.D., M.D.-M.P.H. (Epidemiology, Maternal and Child Health, Health Policy and Administration), M.D.-Ph.D. (Anatomy, Biochemistry, Biomedical Engineering, Biophysics, Biostatistics, Epidemiology, Cell Biology, Genetics, Microbiology and Immunology, Molecular Biology, Parasitology, Pathology, Pharmacology, Physiology, Toxicology).

RECRUITMENT PRACTICES AND POLICIES. School has diversity program and actively recruits women/minority applicants. Diversity contact: Director of Medical Education; phone: (919)966-3641.

ADMISSION REQUIREMENTS FOR FIRST-YEAR APPLICANTS. Preference given to state residents. *Undergraduate preparation.* Suggested premed courses: 2 courses in biology with labs, 2 courses in inorganic chemistry with labs, 2 courses in organic chemistry with labs, 2 courses in physics with labs, 2 courses in English. Bachelor's degree from an accredited institution required; all applicants have bachelor's degrees awarded prior to enrollment. *Has EDP*; state residents and highly qualified nonresidents are encouraged to apply; applicants must apply through AMCAS (official transcripts sent by mid-May) between June 1 and August 1. Early applications are encouraged. Submit supplemental application, a personal statement, and 2 recommendations to Admissions Office within 2 weeks of receipt of application. Interviews are by invitation only and generally for final selection. Notification normally begins October 1. *Regular application process.* Apply through AMCAS (file after June 1, before November 15); submit MCAT (will accept MCAT test results from last 5 years), official transcripts for each school attended (should show at least 90 semester credits/135 quarter credits, submit transcripts by mid-May to AMCAS), service processing fee. Qualified applicants will receive both a supplemental and M.D.-Ph.D. application. Submit the supplemental application and an application fee of $60, a personal statement, preprofessional committee evaluation, and 2 recommendations from science faculty to Admissions Office within 2–3 weeks of the receipt of supplemental materials. Interviews are by invitation only and generally for final selection. First-year students admitted in fall only. Rolling admission process. Notification starts October 15 and is finished when class is filled. Applicant's response to offer and $100 deposit due within 3 weeks of receipt of acceptance letter. School does maintain an alternate list. Phone: (919)962-8331; E-mail: ismann@med.unc.edu. For current M.D.-Ph.D. information contact the Program Director; phone: (919)966-1435; fax: (919)966-1576; E-mail: epo@med. unc.edu.

ADMISSION REQUIREMENTS FOR TRANSFER APPLICANTS. Accepts transfers from other accredited U.S. medical schools into the 3rd year only and selected residents from Oral Surgery Program at UNC, Chapel Hill. Admission limited to space available. Contact the Admissions Office for current information and specific requirements.

ADMISSION STANDARDS AND RECOGNITION. *For M.D.:* number of state-resident applicants 1,063, nonresidents 1,972; number of state residents interviewed 794, nonresidents 111; number of residents enrolled 140, nonresidents 20; median MCAT 9.4 (verbal reasoning 9.8; biological sciences 9.3; physical sciences 9.1); median GPA 3.48 (A = 4). Gorman rating 4.47 (scale: strong 4.01–4.49); *U.S. News & World Report* ranked school in the Top 25 of all U.S. medical schools in primary-care programs; the medical school's ranking by NIH awards/grants was 14th, with 380 awards/grants received; total dollars awarded $102,268,058.

FINANCIAL AID. Merit scholarships, grants, institutional loans, HEAL, alternative loan programs, NIH stipends, federal Perkins loans, Stafford subsidized and unsubsidized loans, and service commitment scholarship programs are available. Assistantships/fellowships may be available for dual-degree candidates. For financial aid applications and information contact the Student Aid Section, phone: (919)962-6118; E-mail: caselin@med. unc.edu. For serious consideration for financial assistance, submit application by March 1. For merit scholarships, the selection criteria place heavy reliance on MCAT and undergraduate GPA. For most financial assistance and all federal programs, submit FAFSA to a federal processor (Title IV school code # 002974); also submit Financial Aid Transcript and Federal Income Tax forms. Approximately 85% of current students receive some form of financial assistance. Average debt after graduation $30,500.

DEGREE REQUIREMENTS. *For M.D.:* satisfactory completion of 4-year program. *For M.D.-Ph.D.:* generally a 6–7-year program.

School of Dentistry

CB #7450 Brauer Hall
Chapel Hill, North Carolina 27599-7450
Phone: (919)966-4565; fax: (919)966-7007
Internet site: http://www.unc.edu
E-mail: brunson.dentce@mhs.unc.edu

Accepted 1st class in 1950. Located on main campus. Special facilities: Dental Research Center. Special programs: Medical Educational Development Program, with School of Medicine; summer programs for underrepresented minorities. Postgraduate specialties: Endodontics, General Practice in Dentistry, Geriatric Dentistry, Oral and Maxillofacial Surgery, Oral Biology, Oral Epidemiology, Oral Radiology, Orthodontics, Pediatric Dentistry, Periodontics, Prosthodontics.

Annual tuition: residents $4,091, nonresidents $28,270; fees $2,354; equipment and supplies $1,500. On-campus rooms and apartments available for both single and married students. Contact Department of University Housing for both on- and off-campus housing information; phone: (919)962-5405. Dental students tend to live off-campus. Off-campus housing, food, transportation, and personal expenses: approximately $14,351.

Enrollment: 1st-year class 76. First-year enrolled student information: 12 from out of state; 6 states represented; 42 women; average age 24; 7 underrepresented minorities; 2 other minorities.

Faculty: full-time 84.

Degrees conferred: D.D.S., D.D.S.-M.P.H. (with School of Public Health), D.D.S.-M.S. (Oral Biology), D.D.S.-Ph.D. (Behavioral Sciences), has Institutional Dentist Scientists Program (NIH funded).

RECRUITMENT PRACTICES AND POLICIES. School has diversity program and actively recruits women/minority applicants. Diversity contact: Director, Counseling Services; phone: (919)966-4451.

ADMISSION REQUIREMENTS FOR FIRST-YEAR APPLICANTS. Priority given to state residents; U.S. citizens and permanent residents only. *Undergraduate preparation.* Suggested predental courses: 2 courses in biology with labs, 2 courses in inorganic chemistry with labs, 2 courses in organic chemistry with labs, 2 courses in physics with labs, 2 courses in English. The junior-college transfer credit limit is 64 credits. Will consider applicants with only 3 years of undergraduate preparation; prefer applicants who will have bachelor's degree awarded prior to enrollment; 71 out of 76 enrolled students have bachelor's degree awarded prior to enrollment. *Application process.* Apply through AADSAS (file after June 1, before November 1); submit official transcripts for each school attended (should show at least 96 semester credits/144 quarter credits), service processing fee; at the same time as you send in AADSAS materials request a supplemental application; submit an application fee of $60, official DAT scores (preference: April test results from applicant's junior year), predental committee evaluation or 2 academic-related recommendations to the Admissions and Students Affairs Office. TOEFL may be required of an applicant whose native language is other than English. Foreign-trained dentists wishing to enter as first-year students must submit acceptable scores on Part 1 of the National Board, Dental Exam. For Institutional Dental Scientist Program, contact the Admissions and Student Affairs Office for current information and specific requirements for admission. Interviews are by invitation only and generally for final selection. First-year students admitted in fall only. Rolling admission process. Notification starts December and is finished when class is filled, but no later than June 7. Applicant's response to offer and $200 deposit due within 30 days if accepted prior

to February 28; response and deposit due within 2 weeks if received after March 1. School does maintain an alternate list. Phone: (919)966-4565.

ADMISSION REQUIREMENTS FOR ADVANCED-STANDING APPLICANTS. Accepts transfers from other ADA-accredited U.S. dental schools, but only at midyear of 1st year. Preference is given to state residents. Admission limited to space available. There is no advanced-standing program for graduates of foreign schools of dentistry. Foreign-trained dentists can enter only as 1st-year students. Contact the Admissions and Student Affairs Office for current information and specific requirements for admission.

ADMISSION STANDARDS AND RECOGNITION. *For D.D.S.:* number of applicants 922; number enrolled 76; median DAT: ACAD 18.4, PAT 17.5; median GPA 3.29 (A = 4), median sciences GPA 3.27 (A = 4). Gorman rating 4.42 (scale: strong 4.01–4.49); this placed the school in the Top 25 of all U.S. dental schools; the dental school's ranking by NIH awards/grants was 5th among dental schools, with 25 awards/grants received; total value of all awards/grants $4,928,981.

FINANCIAL AID. Board of Governors Scholarships (for minority and disadvantaged students), Dental Scholars Program, merit scholarships, North Carolina School of Dentistry Minority Grants, institutional loans, North Carolina Loan Programs, DEAL, HEAL, alternative loan programs, federal Perkins loans, Stafford subsidized and unsubsidized loans, and military service commitment scholarship programs are available. All financial aid is based on documented need. Fellowships may be available for joint-degree candidates. Institutional financial aid applications and information are available after January 1. Apply for financial aid by March 1 (priority deadline). For scholarship assistance, the selection criteria place heavy reliance on DAT and undergraduate GPA. Contact the university's Office of Scholarships and Student Aid for current information; phone: (919)962-8936. For most financial assistance and all need-based programs, submit FAFSA to a federal processor (Title IV school code # 002974); also submit Financial Aid Transcript, Federal Income Tax forms, and Use of Federal Funds Certification. Approximately 85% of current students receive some form of financial assistance. Average awards for residents $13,292, nonresidents $26,838.

DEGREE REQUIREMENTS. *For D.D.S.:* satisfactory completion of 4-year program. *For D.D.S.-M.P.H.:* generally a 5–5½-year program. *For D.D.S.-M.S.:* generally a

4½–5½-year program. *For D.D.S.-Ph.D.,D.S.P.:* generally a 6–7-year program.

UNIVERSITY OF NORTH DAKOTA

Grand Forks, North Dakota 58202
Internet site: http://www.und.nodak.edu

Founded 1883. Located in the northeastern part of state, 320 miles NW of Minneapolis, 120 miles S of Winnipeg, Manitoba. Public control. Semester system. Library: 2,300,000 volumes; 800,000 microforms; 8,200 periodicals/subscriptions; 150 PC work stations.

The university's graduate schools/colleges include: Center for Aerospace, Center for Teaching and Learning, College of Arts and Science, College of Business and Public Administration, College of Fine Arts, College of Human Resources, School of Engineering and Mines, School of Nursing, School of Law, School of Medicine.

Total university enrollment at main campus: 11,500.

North Dakota Medical Center

Public control. Special facilities: USDA Human Nutrition Research Center, North Dakota Diabetes Ocular Research Center.

School of Medicine and Health Sciences

501 North Columbia Road, Box 9037
Grand Forks, North Dakota 58202-9037
Phone: (701)777-4221; fax: (701)777-4924
Internet site: http://www.med.und.nodak.edu
E-mail: jheit@mail.med.und.nodak.edu

Established 1905 as a basic-science school with a 2-year medical school. In 1981 approved as a 4-year medical school. Located on main campus but has campuses in Minot, Bismark, and Fargo. Library: 50,000 volumes/microforms; 1,000 current periodicals/subscriptions. Special facilities: Center for Rural Health. Affiliated hospitals: Rehabilitation Hospital, VA Hospital in Fargo, USAF Hospital in Grand Forks and Minot, PHS Hospitals and Clinics (part of the Indian Health Service). Special programs: Indians-into-Medicine (INMED); state of residency is not a factor in selection process.

Annual tuition: residents $9,986, nonresidents $24,943. On-campus rooms and apartments available for both single and married students. Annual on-campus housing cost: single students $2,750 (room only), married students $3,300. Contact Housing Office for both on- and off-campus housing information; phone: (701)777-4251. Medical students tend to live off-campus. Off-campus housing and personal expenses: approximately $11,114.

Enrollment: 1st-year class 57 (INMED, annually up to 7 qualified Native Americans); total full-time 235 (men 60%, women 40%). First-year statistics: 33% out of state; 43.9% women; average age 25; 17% minorities; 73% science majors.

Faculty: full-time 160, part-time/volunteers 91.

Degrees conferred: M.D., M.D.-Ph.D. (Anatomy, Biochemistry, Cell Biology, Immunology, Microbiology, Molecular Biology, Pharmacology, Physiology).

RECRUITMENT PRACTICES AND POLICIES. School has diversity program and actively recruits women/minority applicants. Diversity contact: College Coordinator; phone: (901)777-3037.

ADMISSION REQUIREMENTS FOR FIRST-YEAR APPLICANTS. Preference given to state residents, a limited number of Minnesota residents and WICHE applicants from states without medical schools; U.S. citizens and permanent residents only. *Undergraduate preparation.* Suggested premed courses: 2 courses in biology with labs, 2 courses in inorganic chemistry with labs, 2 courses in organic chemistry with labs, 2 courses in physics with labs, 1 course in college math, 2 courses in English, 1 psychology or social-science course. Bachelor's degree from an accredited institution required; 98% of applicants have bachelor's degree awarded prior to enrollment. Does not have EDP. *Application process.* Apply directly to the Office of Student Affairs and Admissions after July 1, before November 1. Submit the application and an application fee of $35, MCAT (will accept MCAT test results from last 3 years), official transcripts for each school attended (should show at least 90 semester credits/135 quarter credits), a personal statement, preprofessional committee evaluation, and 3 recommendations from science faculty to Office of Student Affairs and Admission. Interviews are by invitation only and generally for final selection. First-year students admitted in fall only. Rolling admission process. Notification starts December 15 and is finished when class is filled. Applicant's response to offer and $75 deposit due within 4 weeks of receipt of acceptance letter. Dual-degree applicants apply to M.D.-Ph.D. program after being accepted by the School of Medicine; contact the Office of Student Affairs and Admissions for current information and specific requirements for admission. Phone: (701)777-4221; fax: (701)777-4942.

ADMISSION REQUIREMENTS FOR TRANSFER APPLICANTS. Rarely accepts transfers from other accredited U.S. medical schools except under very unusual circumstances. Contact the Office of Student Affairs and

Admissions for current information and any modification in policy.

ADMISSION STANDARDS AND RECOGNITION. *For M.D.:* number of state-resident applicants 166, nonresidents 204; number of state residents interviewed 106, nonresidents 48; number of residents enrolled 43, nonresidents 14 (includes INMED, Minnesota, and WICHE students); median MCAT 9.0 (verbal reasoning 9.1; biological sciences 8.9; physical sciences 9.1); median GPA 3.61 (A = 4); Gorman rating 3.17 (scale: acceptable plus 3.01–3.59); medical school's ranking by NIH awards/grants was 115th, with 14 awards/grants received; total dollars awarded $1,618,064.

FINANCIAL AID. Scholarships, merit scholarships, minority scholarships, grants-in-aid, institutional loans, HEAL, alternative loan programs, federal Perkins loans, Stafford subsidized and unsubsidized loans and service commitment scholarship programs are available. Assistantships/fellowships may be available for dual-degree candidates. Immediately after acceptance financial aid applications and information are sent to students. All financial aid is based on demonstrated need. For scholarship assistance, the selection criteria place heavy reliance on MCAT and undergraduate GPA. Contact the Financial Aid Office for current information; phone: (701)777-2849; fax: (701)777-4942. For most financial assistance and all federal programs, submit FAFSA to a federal processor (Title IV school code # 003005); also submit Financial Aid Transcript and Federal Income Tax forms. Approximately 85% of current students receive some form of financial assistance. Average debt after graduation $69,400.

DEGREE REQUIREMENTS. *For M.D.:* satisfactory completion of 4-year program. *For M.D.-Ph.D.:* generally a 7-year program.

UNIVERSITY OF NORTH TEXAS
Denton, Texas 76203-6737
Internet site: http://www.unt.edu

Founded 1890. Located 38 miles NW of Dallas. Public control. Semester system. Special facilities: Institute for Studies in Addiction, Center for Network Neuroscience, University Center for Texas Studies. Library: 1,292,500 volumes; 2,902,000 microforms; 10,302 periodicals/subscriptions; 300 work stations.

The university's Robert B. Toulouse School of Graduate Studies includes: College of Arts and Sciences, College of Business Administration, College of Education, College of Music, School of Community Services, School of Library and Information Sciences, School of Merchandising and Hospitality Management, School of Visual Arts.

Total university enrollment at main campus: 24,900.

University of North Texas Science Center at Fort Worth
Fort Worth, Texas 76107-2699
Internet site: http://www.hsc.unt.edu

Public control. Library: 137,000 volumes; 2,142 periodicals/subscriptions. Special facilities: DNA Identity Lab. The Center's graduate schools are: Graduate School of Biomedical Sciences, Texas College of Osteopathic Medicine. The health science center's ranking in domestic higher education by NIH awards/grants was 157th, with 25 awards/grants received; total dollars awarded $3,518,350.

Texas College of Osteopathic Medicine
3500 Camp Bowie Boulevard
Fort Worth, Texas 76107-2699
Phone: (817)735-2000
Internet site: http://www.hsc.unt.edu

Founded 1970; became state supported in 1975. Located in the cultural district of Fort Worth. Semester system.

Annual tuition: residents $7,350, nonresidents $20,450. No on-campus housing available. Contact the Admissions Office for off-campus housing information. Off-campus housing and personal expenses: approximately $14,000.

Enrollment: 1st-year class 115; total full-time 429 (men 61%, women 39%). First-year statistics: 10% out of state; 40% women; average age 25; 21% minorities; 73% science majors.

Faculty: full-time 170, part-time/volunteers 300.

Degrees conferred: D.O., D.O.-M.S., D.O.-M.P.H., D.O.-Ph.D.

RECRUITMENT PRACTICES AND POLICIES. School has diversity program and actively recruits women/minority applicants. Diversity contact: Multicultural Affairs Office.

ADMISSION REQUIREMENTS FOR FIRST-YEAR APPLICANTS. Preference given to state residents; U.S. citizens and permanent residents only. *Undergraduate preparation.* Suggested premed courses: 2 courses in biology with labs, 2 courses in inorganic chemistry with labs, 2 courses in organic chemistry with labs, 2 courses in physics with labs, 2 courses in English. Bachelor's degree from an accredited institution required; all applicants have bachelor's degrees awarded prior to enrollment. *Has EDP* for state residents only; applicants must apply through AACOMAS (official transcripts sent by mid-May) between June 1 and August 1. Early applications are encouraged. Submit supplemental application, a personal statement, and 2 recommendations to Office of Medical Student Admission within 2 weeks of receipt of application. Interviews are by invitation only and generally for final selection. Notification normally begins October 15. *Regular application process.* Apply through AACOMAS (file after June 1, before December 1); submit MCAT (will accept test results from last 3 years), official transcripts for each school attended (should show at least 90 semester credits/135 quarter credits), service processing fee. After a review of the AACOMAS application and supporting documents, a decision is made concerning which candidates should receive supplemental materials. The supplemental application, an application fee of $50, a personal statement, and 3 recommendations (1 from a D.O.) should be returned to Admissions Office as soon as possible. In addition, international applicants must submit foreign transcripts to the World Education Service for translation and evaluation. Joint-degree applicants must apply to, and be accepted by, both schools; contact the Office of Medical Student Admissions for current information and specific requirements for admission. Interviews are by invitation only and generally for final selection. First-year students admitted in fall only. Rolling admission process. Notification starts January 15 and is finished when class is filled. Applicant's response to offer and $100 deposit due within 2 weeks of receipt of acceptance letter. School does maintain an alternate list. Phone: (817)735-2204, (800)535-TCOM; fax: (817)735-2225.

ADMISSION REQUIREMENTS FOR TRANSFER APPLICANTS. Accepts transfers from other accredited U.S. osteopathic medical schools. Admission limited to space available. Contact the Admissions Offices for current information and specific requirements.

ADMISSION STANDARDS AND RECOGNITION. *For D.O.:* number of applicants 2,200; number accepted 190; number enrolled 114; median MCAT 9.0; median GPA 3.45 (A = 4); the school's ranking by NIH awards/grants was 1st among osteopathic schools, with 25 awards/grants received; a total value of all awards/grants $3,518,350.

FINANCIAL AID. Scholarships, merit scholarship, minority scholarships, grants-in-aid, institutional loans, NOF, HEAL, alternative loan programs, HPSL, NIH stipends, DHPP, EFNSP, federal Perkins loans, Stafford subsidized and unsubsidized loans, service obligation scholarship programs, and military and National Health Service programs are available. Financial aid applications and information are generally available at the on-campus interview (by invitation). For scholarship assistance, the selection criteria place heavy reliance on MCAT and undergraduate GPA. Contact the Financial Aid Office for current information; phone: (800)346-TCOM. For most financial assistance and all federal programs, submit FAFSA to a federal processor (Title IV school code # 003954); also submit Financial Aid Transcript and Federal Income Tax forms. Approximately 80% of current students receive some form of financial assistance. Average debt after graduation $61,000.

DEGREE REQUIREMENTS. *For D.O.:* satisfactory completion of 4-year program. *For D.O.-M.S., M.P.H.:* generally a 4½–5½-year program. *For D.O.-Ph.D.:* generally a 7-year program.

NORTHEASTERN OHIO UNIVERSITY
Rootstown, Ohio 44272-0095
Internet site: http://www.neoucom.edu

Established in 1973 as a medical-school consortium; members of consortium are University of Akron, Kent State University, and Youngstown State University. Located approximately 35 miles SE of Cleveland. Public control. Semester system. Graduate-only institution. Library: 95,700 volumes; 4,518 microforms; 1,082 periodicals/subscriptions; 86 PC work stations. Special facilities: Electron Microscopy Laboratory, Institute for Humanities and Medicine, Institute for Biomedical Engineering (University of Akron). Special program: B.A./B.S.-M.D.

Total university enrollment: 417.

College of Medicine
Rootstown, Ohio 44272-0095
Phone: (330)325-2511; fax: (330)325-8372
Internet site: http://www.neoucom.edu
E-mail: admission@neoucom.edu

Established 1973. Public control.

Annual tuition: residents $11,214, nonresidents $21,924. On-campus housing available for 1st- and 2nd-year medical students at all 3 undergraduate institutions. Costs vary depending on where the student is enrolled. Contact Housing Office at each campus.

Enrollment: 1st-year class 15–20 (EDP 5); does not include B.S.-M.D. program; total full-time 417 (men 57%, women 43%). First-year statistics: 3% out of state; 43.8% women; 6% minorities.

Faculty: full-time/part-time/volunteers 1,500.

Degrees conferred: M.D., B.S.-M.D. (with University of Akron, Kent State University, Youngstown State University).

RECRUITMENT PRACTICES AND POLICIES. School has diversity program and actively recruits women/minority applicants. Diversity contact: Special Assistant to the President for Minority Affairs and Affirmative Action; phone: (330)325-2511.

ADMISSION REQUIREMENT FOR B.S.-M.D. APPLICANTS. Preference given to state residents; nonresidents are eligible to apply but are restricted to 10% of entering class. *High school preparation*: 4 years of mathematics, 4 years of science, 4 years of English, 2–3 years of foreign language, 3–4 years of social studies. Submit application and application fee, SAT I or ACT, official high school transcript, letters of recommendations. Apply to Associate Director of Admission at the College of Medicine after September 1, before December 31. Interviews are by invitation only and generally for final selection. Notification normally on April 1. Applicant's response to offer and $100 deposit due within 1–2 weeks from receipt of acceptance letter.

ADMISSION REQUIREMENTS FOR FIRST YEAR APPLICANTS (traditional M.D. program). Preference given to state residents; U.S. citizens and permanent residents only. *Undergraduate preparation.* Suggested premed courses: 2 courses in biology with labs, 2 courses in inorganic chemistry with labs, 2 courses in organic chemistry with labs, 2 courses in physics with labs, 1 course in college math, 2 courses in English. Bachelor's degree from an accredited institution required; all applicants have bachelor's degree awarded prior to enrollment. *Has EDP* for state residents and well-qualified nonresidents; applicants must apply through AMCAS (official transcripts sent by mid-May) between June 1 and August 1. Early applications are encouraged. Submit secondary/supplemental application, a personal statement, and 2 recommendations to Office of Admission and Institutional Research within 2 weeks of receipt of application. Interviews are by invitation only and generally for final selection. Notification normally begins October 1. *Regular application process.* Apply through AMCAS (file after June 1, before December 1); submit MCAT (will accept MCAT test results from the last 3 years), official transcripts for each school attended (should show at least 90 semester credits/135 quarter credits, submit transcripts by mid-May to AMCAS), service processing fee. Submit an application fee of $50, a supplemental applica-

tion, a personal statement, preprofessional committee evaluation, and 2 recommendations from science faculty to Office of Admission and Institutional Research within 2–3 weeks of the receipt of supplemental materials. Interviews are by invitation only and generally for final selection. First-year students admitted in fall only. Rolling admission process. Notification starts October 15 and is finished when class is filled. Applicant's response to offer due within 2 weeks of receipt of acceptance letter. School does maintain an alternate/waiting list. Phone: (330)325-2511.

ADMISSION REQUIREMENTS FOR TRANSFER APPLICANTS. Accepts transfers from other accredited U.S. medical schools only if space is available. Contact the Admissions Office after January 1 for current information and specific requirements.

ADMISSION STANDARDS AND RECOGNITION. *For B.S.-M.D.:* number of state-resident applicants 427, nonresidents 323; number of state residents interviewed 208, nonresidents 31; number of residents enrolled 92, nonresidents 13; median SAT 1,338, ACT 30; median GPA 3.84 (A = 4). *For M.D.:* number of state-resident applicants 781, nonresidents 411; number of state residents interviewed 138, nonresidents 4; number of residents enrolled 28, nonresidents 0; median MCAT 9.0 (verbal reasoning 9.4; biological sciences 9.1; physical sciences 8.8); median GPA 3.4 (A = 4). Gorman rating 3.15 (scale: acceptable plus 3.01–3.59); the college's medical ranking by NIH awards/grants was 117th, with 12 awards/grants received; total dollars awarded $1,348,347.

FINANCIAL AID. Need-based scholarships, merit scholarships, minority scholarships, grants-in-aid, institutional loans, HEAL, alternative loan programs, federal Perkins loans, Stafford subsidized and unsubsidized loans, and state service commitment tuition remission programs are available. Financial aid applications and information are generally available at the on-campus interview (by invitation). For need-based scholarships, the selection criteria place heavy reliance on MCAT and undergraduate GPA. Contact the Financial Aid Office for current information; phone: (330)325-2511. For most financial assistance and all federal programs, submit FAFSA to a federal processor (Title IV school code # G24544); also submit Financial Aid Transcript and Federal Income Tax forms. Approximately 75% of current students receive some form of financial assistance. Average debt after graduation $67,300.

DEGREE REQUIREMENTS. *For B.S.-M.D.:* a 6–7-year program. *For M.D.:* satisfactory completion of 4-year program.

NORTHWESTERN UNIVERSITY
Evanston, Illinois 60208
Internet site: http://www.nwu.edu

Founded 1851. Located 12 miles N of Chicago. Private control. Semester system. Library: 3,775,500 volumes; 2,887,000 microforms; 38,900 periodicals/subscriptions; 467 PC work stations. Special programs: B.A.-M.D. program (Honors Program in Medical Education [HPME]; annual undergraduate tuition $18,108). The university's ranking in domestic higher education by NIH awards/grants was 35th, with 297 awards/grants received; total dollars awarded $70,110,436.

The university's graduate schools/colleges include: College of Arts and Science, Division of Interdepartmental programs, Garret-Evangelical Theological Seminary, Integrated Graduate Programs in the Life Sciences, J. L. Kellogg Graduate School of Management, Robert R. McCormick School of Engineering and Applied Science, School of Education and Social Policy, School of Speech, Dental School, Medical School, Medill School of Journalism, School of Law, School of Music.

Total university enrollment at main campus: 17,900.

Northwestern Memorial Hospital
250 East Superior Street
Chicago, Illinois 60611

Private control. The hospital is a member of the Council of Teaching Hospitals. Special facilities: Asher Center for the Study and Treatment of Depressive Disorders, Buehler Center on Aging, McGaw Medical Center of Northwestern University, Cognitive Neurology and Alzheimer's Disease Center, Comprehensive AIDS Center, Feinberg Cardiovascular Research Institute, Feinberg Clinical Neuroscience Research Center, Immunobiology Center, Institute for Health Services Research and Policy Studies, Multipurpose Arthritis and Musculoskeletal Diseases Center, NU Prosthetic-Orthotic Center, Rober H. Lurie Cancer Center, Searle Family Center for Neurological Disorders. Nationally recognized programs in AIDS, Cancer, Cardiology, Gastroenterology, Geriatrics, Gynecology, Neurology, Orthopedics, Otolaryngology, Pulmonary Disease, Urology.

School of Medicine
303 East Chicago Avenue
Chicago, Illinois 60611
Phone: (312)503-8206
Internet site: http://www.nums.nwu.edu

Founded 1859. Located on university's lakefront campus. Tuition charged on the quarter system. Library: 228,000 volumes/microforms; 2,500 current periodicals/subscriptions. Affiliated hospitals: McGaw Medical Center Hospital, Northwestern Memorial Hospital, Children's Memorial (Evanston), Glenbrook Hospital, Rehabilitation Institute of Chicago, VA Lakeside Medical Center, Columbus-Cabrini Medical Center, St. Joseph's Hospital and Health Care Center. Special programs: Integrated Graduate Program in the Life Sciences (an interdisciplinary Ph.D. program).

Annual tuition: $29,057. On-campus rooms and apartments available for both single and married students. Contact Admissions Office for both on- and off-campus housing information. Medical students tend to live off-campus. Off-campus housing and personal expenses: approximately $15,282.

Enrollment: 1st-year class 170; total full-time 697 (men 62%, women 38%). First-year statistics: 65% out of state; 46.6% women; average age 22; 58% science majors.

Faculty: full-time/part-time/volunteers 2,200.

Degrees conferred: M.D., B.A.-M.D. (HPME), M.D.-M.M. (Kellogg Graduate School of Management), M.D.-M.P.H., M.D.-Ph.D. (Anatomy, Biochemistry, Biomedical Engineering, Biophysics, Cell Biology, Genetics, Immunology, Microbiology, Molecular Biology, Neurosciences, Pathology, Pharmacology, Physiology); has M.S.T.P.

RECRUITMENT PRACTICES AND POLICIES. School has diversity program and actively recruits women/minority applicants. Diversity contact: Assistant Dean of Minority Affairs; phone: (312)503-0461.

ADMISSION REQUIREMENT FOR B.S. (HPME)-M.D. APPLICANTS. *High school requirements:* 4 years of English, 4 years of mathematics, 1 year each of chemistry, physics, biology, 2 years of foreign language. Submit application and application fee of $50, SAT I or ACT, plus Achievements in Mathematics Level II, Chemistry, Writing, official high school transcript with rank in class, letters of recommendation. Apply to Undergraduate Office of Admission and Financial Aid by January 1; phone: (847)491-7271; E-mail: ug-admissions@nwu.edu. Notification April 1. Applicant's response to offer and $200 deposit due by May 1.

ADMISSION REQUIREMENTS FOR FIRST-YEAR APPLICANTS. Preference is given to U.S. citizens and permanent residents only. *Undergraduate preparation.* Suggested premed courses: 2 courses in biology with labs, 2 courses in inorganic chemistry with labs, 2 courses in organic chemistry with labs, 2 courses in physics with labs, 1 course in college math, 2 courses in English. Bachelor's degree from an accredited institution required; all applicants have bachelor's degree (including HPME awarded prior to enrollment). *Application process.* Apply through AMCAS (file after June 1, before October 15); submit MCAT (will accept MCAT test results from 1995); submit official transcripts for each school attended (should show at least 90 semester credits/135 quarter credits, submit transcripts by mid-May to AMCAS), service processing fee. Submit an application fee of $50, a supplemental application, a personal statement, preprofessional committee evaluation, and 2 recommendations from science faculty to Admissions Office within 2–3 weeks of the receipt of supplemental materials. Interviews are by invitation only and generally for final selection. M.D.-Ph.D. and dual-degree applicants must apply to and be accepted to both schools; contact the Admissions Office for current information and specific requirements for admissions or the J. L. Kellogg Graduate School; phone: (847)491-3308; for M.D.-Ph.D. program, phone: (312)503-5232; for M.D.-M.P.H., phone: (312)503-0696. First-year students admitted in fall only. Rolling admission process. Notification starts October 15 and is finished when class is filled. Applicant's response to offer due within 2 weeks of receipt of acceptance letter. School does maintain an alternate list. Phone: (312)503-8206.

ADMISSION REQUIREMENTS FOR TRANSFER APPLICANTS. Accepts transfers from other accredited U.S. medical schools. Admission limited to space available. Contact the Admissions Office for current information and specific requirements for admission.

ADMISSION STANDARDS AND RECOGNITION. *For B.A.-M.D.:* number of applicants 878; number interviewed 186; number enrolled 45; median SAT V 739, SAT M 767, English 749, Math II 778, Chem 718. *For M.D.:* number of state-resident applicants 1,347, nonresidents 7,293; number of state residents interviewed 161, nonresidents 331; number of residents enrolled 60, nonresidents 111; median MCAT 9.7 (verbal reasoning 9.7; biological sciences 9.8; physical sciences 9.6); median GPA 3.56 (A = 4). *Barron's Guide* placed the School of Medicine among the Top 25 most prestigious U.S. medical schools; Gorman rating 4.37 (scale: strong 4.01–4.49); *U.S. News & World Report* ranked the School of Medicine in the Top 25 of all U.S. medical schools; medical school's ranking by NIH awards/grants was 41st, with 193 awards/grants received; total dollars awarded $49,468,352.

FINANCIAL AID. Scholarships, merit scholarships, minority scholarships, grants-in-aid, institutional loans, HEAL, alternative loan programs, NIH stipends, federal Perkins loans, Stafford subsidized and unsubsidized loans, and service commitment scholarship programs are available. Assistantships/fellowships may be available for dual-degree candidates. Financial aid is based on demonstrated need. Financial aid applications and information are generally available at the on-campus interview (by invitation). For scholarship assistance, the selection criteria place heavy reliance on MCAT and undergraduate GPA. The school has a Debt Capping Grant Program for 3rd- and 4th-year students. Contact the Financial Aid Office for current information; phone: (312)503-8722. For most financial assistance and all federal programs, submit FAFSA to a federal processor (Title IV school code # E00295); also submit Financial Aid Transcript and Federal Income Tax forms. Approximately 60% of current students receive some form of financial assistance. Average debt after graduation $102,000.

DEGREE REQUIREMENTS. *For B.A.-M.D.:* a 7-year program. *For M.D.:* satisfactory completion of 4-year program. All students must take USMLE Step 1. *For M.D.-M.M.:* generally 5-year program. *For M.D.-M.P.H.:* generally a 4½–5½-year program. *For M.D.-Ph.D.:* generally a 7-year program.

NOVA SOUTHEASTERN UNIVERSITY
Fort Lauderdale, Florida 33314-7721
Internet site: http://www.nova.edu

Chartered 1964 as Nova University. Merged with Southeastern University of Health Sciences in 1994. Offers degree programs throughout the U.S. Located 3 miles W of Ft. Lauderdale. Private control. Semester system. Special facilities: Family Center for Child Development, Institute for Marine and Coastal Studies, Institute for Social Services to Families, Center for Youth Policy. Library: 313,000 volumes; 1,157,300 microforms; 8,073 periodicals/subscriptions; 90 PC work stations.

The university's graduate colleges/schools include: Abraham S. Fischler Center for the Advancement of Education, Center for Psychological Studies, Heal Professional Division–College of Allied Health, College of Dental Medicine, College of Optometry, College of Osteopathic Medicine, College of Pharmacy, Oceanography Center, School of Business and Entrepreneurship, School of Computer and Information Sciences, School of Social and Systemic Studies, Shepard Broad Law Center.

Total university enrollment at main campus: 15,739.

College of Osteopathic Medicine
3200 South University Drive
Ft. Lauderdale, Florida 33328
Phone: (954)262-1101
Internet site: http://www.nova.edu
E-mail: mweiner@hpd.nova.edu

Established 1979. Relocated from North Miami Beach to main campus in 1996. Semester system; first two years devoted to basic sciences. Special program: Rural Medicine Program.

Annual tuition: residents $18,500, nonresidents $21,750. No on-campus housing available. Contact Residential Life Office for off-campus housing information; phone: (954)262-7052. Off-campus housing and personal expenses: approximately $10,000.

Enrollment: 1st-year class 150; total full-time 551 (men 64%, women 36%). First-year statistics: 43% out of state; 42% women; average age 26; 87% science majors.

Faculty: full-time/part-time/volunteers 350.

Degrees conferred: D.O., D.O.-M.P.H. (for students already enrolled in the college).

ADMISSION REQUIREMENTS FOR FIRST-YEAR APPLICANTS. Preference given to state residents; U.S. citizens and permanent residents only. *Undergraduate preparation.* Suggested premed courses: 2 courses in biology, 2 courses in inorganic chemistry, 2 courses in organic chemistry, 2 courses in physics, 1 course in college math, 2 courses in English. Bachelor's degrees from an accredited institution required. 98% of applicants have bachelor's degrees awarded prior to enrollment. *Application process.* Apply through AACOMAS (file after June 1, before February 1); submit MCAT (will accept test results from last 3 years); official transcripts for each school attended (should show at least 90 semester credits/135 quarter credits), service processing fee. After a review of the AACOMAS application and supporting documents, a decision is made concerning which candidates should receive supplemental materials. The supplemental application, an application fee of $50, a personal statement, and 3 recommendations (1 from a D.O.) should be returned to Admissions Office as soon as possible. In addition, international applicants must submit foreign transcripts to the World Education Service for translation and evaluation. TOEFL may be required of those applicants whose native language is other than English. Interviews are by invitation only and generally for final selection. First-year students admitted in fall only. Rolling admission process. Notification starts in October and is finished when class is filled. Applicant's response to offer and $250 deposit due within 2 weeks of receipt of acceptance letter. School does maintain an alternate list. Phone: (954)262-1101, (800)356-0026; E-mail: mweiner@hpd.nova.edu.

ADMISSION REQUIREMENTS FOR TRANSFER APPLICANTS. Accepts transfers from other accredited U.S. osteopathic medical schools. Admission limited to space available. Contact the Admissions Offices for current information and specific requirements for admission.

ADMISSION STANDARDS AND RECOGNITION. *For D.O.:* number applicants 3,300; number enrolled 150; median MCAT 8.7; median GPA 3.4 (A = 4).

FINANCIAL AID. Scholarships, merit scholarships, full tuition minority scholarships, grants-in-aid, institutional loans, NOF, HEAL, alternative loan programs, federal Perkins loans, Stafford subsidized and unsubsidized loans, service obligation scholarships programs, and military and National Health Service programs are available. Financial aid applications and information are generally available at the on-campus interview (by invitation). For scholarships, the selection criteria place heavy reliance on MCAT and undergraduate GPA. Contact the Financial Aid Office for current information; phone: (954)262-3380. For most financial assistance and all federal programs, submit FAFSA to a federal processor (Title IV school code # 001509); also submit Financial Aid Transcript and Federal Income Tax forms. Approximately 75% of current students receive some form of financial assistance. Average debt after graduation $120,000.

DEGREE REQUIREMENTS. *For D.O.:* satisfactory completion of 4-year program. All students must take and pass the National Board of Osteopathic Medical Examination Parts I and II prior to the awarding of D.O.

College of Dental Medicine
3200 South University Drive
Ft. Lauderdale, Florida 33328
Phone: (954)262-7311; fax: (954)916-1782
Internet site: http://www.nova.edu/cwis/centers/hpd/dental

Established 1996. Located on main campus. Basic-science courses are taught by both the college and medical science's faculty. Postgraduate specialties: Endodontics, Orthodontics, Pediatric Dentistry, Periodontics.

Annual tuition: $25,500. No on-campus housing available. Contact Office of Residential Life for off-campus housing information; phone: (954)262-7052. Off-campus housing, food, transportation, and personal expenses: approximately $14,200.

Enrollment: 1st-year class N/A; total full-time N/A.
Faculty: full-time, part-time/volunteers: N/A.
Degree conferred: D.M.D.

RECRUITMENT PRACTICES AND POLICIES. School has diversity program and actively recruits women/minority applicants. Diversity contact: Admissions Office; phone: (954)262-1101.

ADMISSION REQUIREMENTS FOR FIRST-YEAR APPLICANTS. Preference given to state residents; U.S. citizens and permanent residents only. *Undergraduate preparation.* Suggested predental courses: 2 courses in biology with labs, 2 courses in general chemistry with labs, 2 courses in organic chemistry with labs, 2 courses in physics with labs, 2 courses in English. The junior-college transfer credit limit is 60 credits. For serious consideration applicants should have at least a 2.5 (A = 4) GPA. Will consider applicants with only 3 years of undergraduate preparation; prefer applicants who will have a bachelor's degree prior to enrollment; 98% of applicants have bachelor's degree awarded prior to enrollment. *Application process.* Apply through AADSAS (file after June 1, before April 1); submit official transcripts for each school attended (should show at least 90 semester credits/135 quarter credits), service processing fee; at the same time as you send in AADSAS materials, submit official DAT scores directly to the Admissions Office. TOEFL may be required of an applicant whose native language is other than English. Submit the following materials only after being contacted by an Admissions Officer: an application fee of $50, a secondary/supplemental application, official transcripts, and predental committee evaluation or 2 recommendations from science professors and 1 from a humanities professor to Admissions Office within 2 weeks of receipt of supplemental materials. Interviews are by invitation only and generally for final selection. First-year students admitted in fall only. Rolling admission process. Notification starts in December and is finished when class is filled, but generally not later than June 1. Applicant's response to offer and $500 deposit due within 30 days if accepted prior to January 1; response and deposit due within 2 weeks if received after January 1. School does maintain an alternate list. Phone: (954)262-1101, (800)356-0026; fax: (954)916-2282.

ADMISSION REQUIREMENTS FOR ADVANCED-STANDING APPLICANTS. Accepts transfers from other accredited U.S. dental schools. Admission limited to space available. Contact the Admissions Office for current information and specific requirements.

ADMISSION STANDARDS AND RECOGNITION. *For D.M.D.:* number of applicants 1,100. The college's first year was 1997; median DAT: ACAD N/A, PAT N/A; median GPA N/A (A = 4), median sciences GPA N/A (A = 4). Gorman rating N/A.

FINANCIAL AID. Limited number of scholarships, grants, institutional loans, state loan programs, DEAL, HEAL, alternative loan programs, federal Perkins loans, Stafford subsidized and unsubsidized loans, and military service commitment scholarship programs are available. Institutional financial aid applications and information are generally available at the on-campus interview (by invitation). For need-based scholarships, the selection criteria place heavy reliance on DAT and undergraduate GPA. Contact the Financial Aid Office for current information; phone: (954)262-1130. For most financial assistance and all need-based programs, submit FAFSA to a federal processor (Title IV school code # 001509); also submit Financial Aid Transcript, Federal Income Tax forms, and Use of Federal Funds Certification.

DEGREE REQUIREMENTS. *For D.M.D.:* satisfactory completion of 4-year program.

OHIO STATE UNIVERSITY
Columbus, Ohio 43210
Internet site: http://www.ohio-state.edu

Founded 1870. Located 2 miles N of downtown Columbus. Public control. Quarter system. Library: 4,860,000 volumes; 4,005,000 microforms; 33,360 periodicals/subscriptions; 370 PC work stations. Special programs: post-baccalaureate premedical program for adults and underrepresented minorities. The university's ranking in domestic higher education by NIH awards/grants was 50th, with 243 awards/grants received; total dollars awarded $51,620,890.

The university's graduate schools/colleges include: College of the Arts, College of Biological Sciences, College of Education, College of Engineering, College of Food Agriculture and Environmental Sciences, College of Human Ecology, College of Humanities, College of Mathematical and Physical Sciences, College of Nursing, College of Social and Behavioral Sciences, College of Social Work, Max M. Fisher College of Business, College of Dentistry, College of Law, College of Medicine, College of Optometry, College of Pharmacy, College of Veterinary Medicine.

Total university enrollment at main campus: 54,781.

Ohio State University Medical Center
410 West Tenth Avenue
Columbus, Ohio 43210

Located on main campus. Public control. Ohio State University hospitals are members of the Council of Teaching

Hospitals. Colleges located at medical center are: College of Dentistry, College of Medicine, College of Nursing, College of Optometry, College of Pharmacy. Special facilities: University Hospital, Arthur James Cancer Hospital and Research Institute, Davis Medical Research Center. Nationally recognized programs in Endocrinology, Gynecology, Otolaryngology, Pulmonary Disease, Rehabilitation.

College of Medicine

270-A Meiling Hall
370 West Ninth Avenue
Columbus, Ohio 43210-1238
Phone: (614)292-7137; fax: (614)292-1544
Internet site: http://www.med.ohio_state.edu
E-mail: admiss-med@osy.edu

Established 1914. Located on the south edge of the main campus. Quarter system. Library: 200,000 volumes/microforms; 2,200 current periodicals/subscriptions. Affiliated hospitals: University Hospital, Cleveland Clinic Foundation (*U.S. News & World Report*'s hospital/medical center national rankings for all hospitals placed Cleveland Clinic in the Top 20 of all U.S. hospitals), Columbus Children's Hospital, Arthur James Cancer Hospital and Research Institute, Mt. Carmel Hospital, Grant Hospital, Riverside Methodist Hospital, St. Ann's Hospital, St. Anthony Hospitals, Veterans Administration Clinic, Harding Hospital, Heart and Lung Institute. Special programs: Medical Humanities Program; Independent Study Program.

Annual tuition: residents $10,968, nonresidents $30,027; fees $246. On-campus rooms and apartments available for both single and married students. Contact Office of Housing Assignments for both on- and off-campus housing information; phone: (614)292-8226. Medical students tend to live off-campus. Off-campus housing and personal expenses: approximately $11,439.

Enrollment: 1st-year class 210 (EDP 10); total full-time 844 (men 63%, women 37%). First-year statistics: 20% out of state; 38% women; average age 25; 68% science majors.

Faculty: full-time/part-time/volunteers 1,700.

Degrees conferred: M.D., M.D.-Ph.D. (Anatomy, Biochemistry, Biomedical Engineering, Biophysics, Cell Biology, Genetics, Immunology, Microbiology, Molecular Biology, Neurosciences, Pathology, Pharmacology, Physiology); has M.S.T.P.

RECRUITMENT PRACTICES AND POLICIES. School has diversity program and actively recruits women/minority applicants. Diversity contact: Office of Minority Affairs; phone: (614)292-0964.

ADMISSION REQUIREMENTS FOR FIRST-YEAR APPLICANTS. Preference given to state residents; U.S. citizens and permanent residents only. *Undergraduate preparation.* Suggested premed courses: 2 courses in biology with labs, 2 courses in inorganic chemistry with labs, 2 courses in organic chemistry with labs, 2 courses in physics with labs, a course in biochemistry and molecular biology is strongly recommended. Bachelor's degree from an accredited institution required; all applicants have bachelor's degree awarded prior to enrollment. *Has EDP*; applicants must apply through AMCAS (official transcripts sent by mid-May) between June 1 and August 1. Early applications are encouraged. Submit secondary/supplemental application, a personal statement, and 2 recommendations to Admissions Office within 2 weeks of receipt of application. On-campus interviews are by invitation only and generally for final selection. Notification normally begins October 1. *Regular application process.* Apply through AMCAS (file after June 1, before November 1); submit MCAT (will accept MCAT test results from 1995), official transcripts for each school attended (should show at least 90 semester credits/135 quarter credits, submit transcripts by mid-May to AMCAS), service processing fee. Submit an application fee of $25, a supplemental application, a personal statement, preprofessional committee evaluation, and 2 recommendations from science faculty to Admissions Office within 30 days from the receipt of supplemental materials. On-campus interviews are by invitation only and generally for final selection. Dual-degree applicants must apply to, and be accepted by, both schools; contact the M.S.T.P. Office for current information and specific requirements for admission; phone: (614)282-7790. First-year students admitted in fall only. Rolling admission process. Notification starts in early October and is finished when class is filled. Applicant's response to offer and $25 deposit due within 2 weeks of receipt of acceptance letter. School does maintain an alternate list. Phone: (614)292-7137; E-mail: admiss-med@osu. edu.

ADMISSION REQUIREMENTS FOR TRANSFER APPLICANTS. Accepts transfers from other accredited U.S. medical schools into the 3rd year only. Admission limited to space available. Contact the Admissions Office for current information and specific requirements for admission.

ADMISSION STANDARDS AND RECOGNITION. *For M.D.:* number of state-resident applicants 1,469, nonresidents 3,138; number of state residents interviewed 455, nonresidents 226; number of residents enrolled 164, nonresidents 42; median MCAT 10.1 (verbal reasoning 10.0; biological sciences 10.3; physical sciences 10.3);

median GPA 3.5 (A = 4). Gorman rating 4.37 (scale: strong 4.01–4.49); the school's medical ranking by NIH awards/grants was 50th, with 147 awards/grants received; total dollars awarded $35,555,275.

FINANCIAL AID. Need-based scholarships, merit scholarships, minority scholarships, grants-in-aid, institutional loans, HEAL, alternative loan programs, NIH stipends, federal Perkins loans, Stafford subsidized and unsubsidized loans, and service commitment scholarship programs are available. M.S.T.P. fellowships, monthly stipends, and full-fee authorization available for dual-degree candidates. Financial aid applications and information are given out at the on-campus interview (by invitation). Most financial aid is based on demonstrated need. For scholarships, the selection criteria place heavy reliance on MCAT and undergraduate GPA; apply by March 1 for priority consideration. Contact the Financial Aid Office for current information; phone: (614)292-8771. For most financial assistance and all federal programs, submit FAFSA to a federal processor (Title IV school code # 003090); also submit Financial Aid Transcript and Federal Income Tax forms. Approximately 75% of current students receive some form of financial assistance. Average debt after graduation $60,000.

DEGREE REQUIREMENTS. *For M.D.:* satisfactory completion of 4-year program. All students must pass USMLE Step 1 prior to entering 3rd year; all students must pass USMLE Step 2 prior to awarding of M.D. *For M.D.-Ph.D.:* generally a 7-year program.

College of Dentistry
Box 195, Room 3173 Postle Hall
305 West 12th Avenue
Columbus, Ohio 43210
Phone: (614)292-3361; fax: (614)292-7619
Internet site: http://www.acs.ohio-state.edu/units/ dentistry
E-mail: dentadmit@osu.edu

Established 1890. In 1907, Ohio Medical University was merged with Starling Medical College; it became a part of Ohio State University in 1914. Located at the University Health Science Center since 1951. Quarter system. Basic sciences taught in first 6 quarters. Affiliated hospitals: Children's Hospital, University Hospital, Veterans Administration Hospital. Special programs: Externships. Postgraduate specialties: Dental Anesthesiology, Endodontics, General Dentistry (AEGD), General Practice Residency, Oral Pathology, Oral and Maxillofacial Surgery, Orthodontics, Pediatric Dentistry, Periodontics, Prosthodontics.

Annual tuition (3 quarters): residents $9,339, nonresidents $29,844; fees $588; equipment and supplies $2,400. On-campus rooms and apartments available for both single and married students. Contact Office of Housing Assignments for both on- and off-campus housing information; phone: (614)292-8266. Dental students tend to live off-campus. Off-campus housing, food, transportation, and personal expenses: approximately $836 per month.

Enrollment: 1st-year class 98. First-year enrolled student information: 11 from out of state; 5 states represented; 31 women; average age 24; 3 underrepresented minorities; 19 other minorities.

Degrees conferred: D.D.S., B.A./B.S.-D.D.S. (Ohio State University only), D.D.S.-M.P.H., D.D.S.-M.S., Ph.D. (Oral Biology).

RECRUITMENT PRACTICES AND POLICIES. School has diversity program and actively recruits women/minority applicants. Diversity contact: Admissions and Recruitment Officer; phone: (614)292-3361.

ADMISSION REQUIREMENTS FOR FIRST-YEAR APPLICANTS. Preference given to state residents (for serious consideration a nonresident should have at least a 3.1 [A = 4] GPA); U.S. citizens and permanent residents only. *Undergraduate preparation.* Suggested predental courses: 3 quarter courses in biology with labs, 3 quarter courses in inorganic chemistry with labs, 1 quarter course in organic chemistry with lab, 2 quarter courses in physics with labs, 2 quarter courses in English. There is no limitation on the number of junior-college credits taken, except required courses must be taken at a 4-year institution. Will consider applicants with only 3 years of undergraduate preparation; prefer applicants who will have a bachelor's degree prior to enrollment; 89 out of 98 enrolled students have bachelor's degrees awarded prior to enrollment. *Application process.* Apply through AADSAS (file after June 1, before January 1); submit official transcripts for each school attended (should show at least 90 semester credits/135 quarter credits), service processing fee; at the same time as you send in AADSAS materials, submit official DAT scores (taken not later than October of the year prior to anticipated year of enrollment) and transcripts directly to the Admissions Office. TOEFL may be required of an applicant whose native language is other than English. Submit the following materials only after being contacted by an Admissions Officer: an application fee of $30 ($40 for international students), a supplemental application, predental committee evaluation or 2 recommendations, at least 1 from a faculty member, and 20 hours of documented observation in a general-practice dental office to Admissions Office.

Canadian and other international applicants should contact the Offices of Admissions and Recruitment for additional requirements for admission. Interviews are by invitation only and generally for final selection. Dual-degree applicants must apply to, and be accepted by, both schools. First-year students admitted in fall only. Rolling admission process. Notification starts December 1 and is finished when class is filled. Applicant's response to offer and $475 deposit due within 30 days if accepted prior to January 1; response and deposit due within 15 days if received after February 1. School does maintain an alternate list. Phone: (614)292-3980; fax: (614)292-7619; E-mail: dentadmit@osu.edu.

ADMISSION REQUIREMENTS FOR ADVANCED-STANDING APPLICANTS. Accepts transfers from other accredited U.S. dental schools. Admission limited to space available. There is no advanced-standing program for graduates of foreign schools of dentistry. Contact the Admissions Office for current information and specific requirements for admission.

ADMISSION STANDARDS AND RECOGNITION. *For D.D.S.:* number of applicants 1,125; number enrolled 98; median DAT: ACAD 17.7, PAT 17.3; median GPA 3.27 (A = 4), median sciences GPA 3.10 (A = 4). Gorman rating 4.77 (scale: very strong 4.51–4.99); this placed the school in the Top 10 of all U.S. dental schools; the dental school's ranking by NIH awards/grants was 21st among dental schools, with 14 awards/grants received; total value of all awards/grants $1,630,682.

FINANCIAL AID. Ohio State scholarships, merit scholarships, minority scholarships, grants-in-aid, institutional loans, state loan programs, DEAL, HEAL, HPSL, alternative loan programs, federal Perkins loans, Stafford subsidized and unsubsidized loans, and military service commitment scholarship programs are available. All financial aid is based on documented need and is made in the form of loans and scholarships. Institutional financial aid applications and information are generally available at the on-campus interview (by invitation). For scholarship assistance, the selection criteria place heavy reliance on DAT and undergraduate GPA; priority application deadline is March 1. Contact the Financial Aid Office for current information; phone: (614)292-7764. For most financial assistance and all need-based programs, submit FAFSA to a federal processor (Title IV school code # 003090); also submit Financial Aid Transcript, Federal Income Tax forms, Use of Federal Funds Certification, and Selective Service Registration form for all males. Approximately 96% of current students receive some form

of financial assistance. Average award resident $17,214, nonresidents $35,553.

DEGREE REQUIREMENTS. *For B.A./B.S.-D.D.S.:* a 7–8-year program. *For D.D.S.:* satisfactory completion of 4-year program. *For D.D.S.-M.P.H.:* generally a 4½–5½-year program. *For D.D.S.-M.S.:* generally a 4½–5½-year program. *For D.D.S.-Ph.D.:* generally a 6–7-year program.

OHIO UNIVERSITY
Athens, Ohio 45701-2979
Internet site: http://www.ohiou.edu

Founded 1804. Oldest state-sponsored university W of Allegheny Mountains. Located 76 miles SE of Columbus. Public control. Quarter system. Library: 2,860,000 volumes; 2,800,000 microforms; 12,100 periodicals/subscriptions; 90 PC work stations. Special facilities: Avionics Engineering Center, Cartographic Center, Edison Biotechnology Center, Edwards Accelerator Laboratory, George Hill Center for Counseling and Research, Institute for Nuclear and Particle Physics, Kennedy Museum of American Art.

The university's graduate studies include: Center for International Studies, College of Arts and Sciences, College of Business, College of Communication, College of Education, College of Engineering, College of Fine Arts, College of Health and Human Services.

Total university enrollment at main campus: 27,300.

College of Osteopathic Medicine
102 Grosvenor Hall
Athens, Ohio 54701-2979
Phone: (614)593-4313
Internet site: http://www.tcom.ohiou.edu/oucom

Established 1975. Curriculum is divided into 4 phases. "Primary Care Continuum Curriculum" and alternative problem-solving track. Affiliated with 5 hospitals in Ohio that are Centers for Osteopathic Regional Education. Special programs: College is one of 25 medical schools selected for a Center of Excellence designation.

Annual tuition: residents $11,316, nonresidents $16,035. On-campus rooms and apartments available for both single and married students. Annual on-campus housing cost: single students $2,094 (room only), married students $5,556. Contact Housing Office for both on- and off-campus housing information; phone: (614)593-4088. Medical students tend to live off-campus. Off-campus housing and personal expenses: approximately $13,191.

Enrollment: 1st-year class 100; total full-time 410 (men 57%, women 43%). First-year statistics: 30% out of state (nonresidents must sign a service contract to practice medicine for 5 years in Ohio); 45% women; average age 25; 12% underrepresented minorities; 12% other minorities; 75% science majors.

Faculty: full-time 80, part-time/volunteers 400.

Degrees conferred: D.O., D.O.-Ph.D.

RECRUITMENT PRACTICES AND POLICIES. School has diversity program and actively recruits women/minority applicants. Diversity contact: Admissions Officer.

ADMISSION REQUIREMENTS FOR FIRST-YEAR APPLICANTS. Preference given to state residents; U.S. citizens and permanent residents only. *Undergraduate preparation.* Suggested premed courses: 2 courses in biology, 2 courses in inorganic chemistry, 2 courses in organic chemistry, 2 courses in physics, 2 courses in behavioral sciences, 2 courses in English; additional biological sciences are highly recommended. Bachelor's degree from an accredited institution required; all applicants have bachelor's degree awarded prior to enrollment. *Application process.* Apply through AACOMAS (file after June 1, before December 1); submit MCAT (will accept test results from last 3 years), official transcripts for each school attended (should show at least 90 semester credits/135 quarter credits), service processing fee. After a review of the AACOMAS application and supporting documents, a decision is made concerning which candidates should receive supplemental materials. The supplemental application, an application fee of $25, a personal statement, and 3 recommendations (1 from a D.O.) should be returned to Admissions Office as soon as possible. In addition, international applicants must submit foreign transcripts to the World Education Service for translation and evaluation. TOEFL may be required of those applicants whose native language is other than English. Interviews are by invitation only and generally for final selection. First-year students admitted in fall only. Rolling admission process. Notification starts in October and is finished when class is filled. Applicant's response to offer and $100 deposit due within 2 weeks of receipt of acceptance letter. School does maintain an alternate list. Phone: (800)345-1560, (614)593-4313; fax: (614)593-2256.

ADMISSION REQUIREMENTS FOR TRANSFER APPLICANTS. Accepts transfers from other accredited U.S. osteopathic medical schools. Admission limited to space available. Contact the Admissions Offices for current information and specific requirements for admission.

ADMISSION STANDARDS AND RECOGNITION. *For D.O.:* number of applicants 3,566, number enrolled 100; median MCAT 8.2; median GPA 3.4 (A = 4).

FINANCIAL AID. Scholarships, institutional loans, NOF, HEAL, alternative loan programs, federal Perkins loans, Stafford subsidized and unsubsidized loans, service obligation scholarship programs, and military and National Health Service programs are available. Financial aid applications and information are generally available at the on-campus interview (by invitation). For scholarships, the selection criteria place heavy reliance on MCAT and undergraduate GPA; apply by February 15 for priority consideration. Contact the Financial Aid Office for current information; phone: (614)593-2152. For most financial assistance and all federal programs, submit FAFSA to a federal processor (Title IV school code # E00306); also submit Financial Aid Transcript and Federal Income Tax forms. Approximately 80% of current students receive some form of financial assistance. Average debt after graduation $86,000.

DEGREE REQUIREMENTS. *For D.O.:* satisfactory completion of 4-phase program. All students must pass the National Board of Osteopathic Medical Examination Part I and take Part II.

OKLAHOMA STATE UNIVERSITY
Tulsa, Oklahoma 74107-1898

College of Osteopathic Medicine
1111 West 17th Street
Tulsa, Oklahoma 74107-1898
Phone: (918)582-1972, X8442, (800)677-1972
Internet site: http://osu.com.okstate.edu

Established 1972; became part of the university in 1988. Located on the west bank of Arkansas River. Semester system. Library: 88,100 volumes/microforms; 643 current periodicals/subscriptions; 15 PC computer work stations. Affiliated hospitals: Hillcrest Health Center (Oklahoma City), Tulsa Regional Medical Center, College Health Care Center.

Annual tuition: residents $9,300, nonresidents $15,500; fees $830. No on-campus housing. Contact Admissions Office for off-campus housing information. Off-campus housing and personal expenses: approximately $15,500.

Enrollment: 1st-year class 88; total full-time 349 (men 64%, women 36%). First-year statistics: 15% out of state;

32% women; average age 25; 23% minorities; 59% science majors.

Faculty: full-time 44, part-time/volunteers 150.
Degrees conferred: D.O., D.O.-Ph.D.

RECRUITMENT PRACTICES AND POLICIES. School has diversity program and actively recruits women/minority applicants. Diversity contact: Assistant Dean for Student Admissions and Advisement; phone: (800)377-1972.

ADMISSION REQUIREMENTS FOR FIRST-YEAR APPLICANTS. Preference given to state residents and to residents of states without a medical school; U.S. citizens and permanent residents only. *Undergraduate preparation.* Suggested premed courses: 2 courses in biology, 2 courses in general chemistry, 2 courses in organic chemistry, 2 courses in physics, 2 courses in English. In addition, an applicant should have taken at least 1 of the following: biochemistry, microbiology or molecular biology, embryology, histology, comparative anatomy or cellular biology. Bachelor's degree from an accredited institution required; all applicants have bachelor's degree awarded prior to enrollment. For serious consideration an applicant should have an overall 3.0 (A = 4) GPA, pre-professional 2.75 GPA, and an MCAT score of 7.0. *Application process.* Apply through AACOMAS (file after June 1, before December 1; November 1 is strongly encouraged); submit MCAT (will accept test results from last 3 years), official transcripts for each school attended (should show at least 90 semester credits/135 quarter credits), service processing fee. After a review of the AACOMAS application and supporting documents, a decision is made concerning which candidates should receive supplemental materials. The supplemental application, an application fee of $25, a personal statement, and 3 academic recommendations, 1 from a D.O., should be returned to Admissions Office as soon as possible, but not later than January 15. Dual-degree candidates should contact the Associate Dean for Basic Sciences and Graduate Studies for current information and specific requirements for admission. Interviews are by invitation only and generally for final selection. First-year students admitted in fall only. Rolling admission process. Notification starts in October and is finished when class is filled. Applicant's response to offer and $100 deposit due within 2 weeks of receipt of acceptance letter. School does maintain an alternate list. Phone: (918)561-8442.

ADMISSION REQUIREMENTS FOR TRANSFER APPLICANTS. Accepts transfers from other accredited U.S. osteopathic medical schools. Admission limited to space available. Contact the Admissions Office for current information and specific requirements for admission.

ADMISSION STANDARDS AND RECOGNITION. *For D.O.:* number of state-resident applicants 328, non-residents 1,779; number of state residents interviewed 190, nonresidents 30; number of residents enrolled 75, nonresidents 13; median MCAT 8.62; median GPA 3.44 (A = 4); science GPA 3.36; the school's ranking by NIH awards/grants was 7 among osteopathic schools, with 1 award/grant received; total value of all awards/grants $93,640.

FINANCIAL AID. Regents fee waivers, scholarships, Oklahoma Tuition Aid Grants, institutional loans, NOF, HEAL, alternative loan programs, federal Perkins loans, Stafford subsidized and unsubsidized loans, service obligation scholarship programs, and military and National Health Service programs are available. All financial aid is based on demonstrated need. Financial aid applications and information are generally available at the on-campus interview (by invitation). For scholarship assistance, the selection criteria place heavy reliance on MCAT and undergraduate GPA. Contact the Financial Aid Office for current information; phone: (918)561-8278. For most financial assistance and all federal programs, submit FAFSA to a federal processor (Title IV school code # G11282); also submit Financial Aid Transcript and Federal Income Tax forms. Approximately 85% of current students receive some form of financial assistance. Average debt after graduation $92,000.

DEGREE REQUIREMENTS. *For D.O.:* satisfactory completion of 4-year program. *For D.O.-Ph.D.:* generally a 6–7-year program

UNIVERSITY OF OKLAHOMA

Norman, Oklahoma 73019
Internet site: http://www.ou.edu

Founded 1890. Located 18 miles S of Oklahoma. Public control. Quarter system. Library: 2,430,,000 volumes; 3,394,000 microforms; 17,400 periodicals/subscriptions; 155 PC work stations. The university's ranking in domestic higher education by NIH awards/grants was 87th, with 90 awards/grants received; total dollars awarded $20,097,758.

The university's graduate colleges include: College of Architecture, College of Arts and Sciences, College of Business Administration, College of Education, College of Engineering, College of Fine Arts, College of Geosciences, College of Liberal Studies. Colleges located in

Oklahoma City: College of Allied Health, College of Nursing, College of Public Health, College of Dentistry, College of Law, College of Medicine, College of Pharmacy.

Total university enrollment: 19,400.

University of Oklahoma Health Center
Oklahoma City, Oklahoma 73190
Internet site: http://www.uokosc.edu

Public control. University Hospital is a member of the Council of Teaching Hospitals. Schools located at medical center are: College of Allied Health, College of Dentistry, College of Nursing, College of Pharmacy, College of Public Health, Graduate College. Special facilities: University Hospital, Veteran's Affairs Medical Center, Children's Hospital of Oklahoma, Presbyterian Hospital, Dean A. McGee Eye Institute, Oklahoma Medical Research Institute, O'Donoghue Rehabilitation Institute, Oklahoma Center for Neurosciences, Diagnostic Center for Alzheimer's Research, Molecular Pathogenesis of Eye Infection Research Center. Special affiliation: Member of the Oak Ridge Associated Universities (ORAU). Nationally recognized programs in Cancer, Endocrinology, Gynecology, Neurology, Orthopedics.

College of Medicine
P.O. Box 26901
Oklahoma City, Oklahoma 73190
Phone: (405)271-2331; fax: (405)271-3032
Internet site: http://www.uokhsc.edu
E-mail: doty-shaw@uokhsc.edu

Founded in 1900 as a 2-year school. Merged with Epworth Medical College in 1910. Located at health sciences center. Curriculum is 2 years of basic sciences, 2 years of clinical sciences. Affiliated hospitals: University Hospital, Veteran's Affairs Medical Center, Children's Hospital of Oklahoma, Presbyterian Hospital. Library: 210,000 volumes/microforms; 2,500 current periodicals/subscriptions. Special programs: prematriculation summer sessions.

Annual tuition: residents $9,107, nonresidents $21,961; fees $405. No on-campus housing available. Housing is available on the Norman campus. For information, contact Director of University Housing in Norman. Medical students tend to live off-campus. Off-campus housing and personal expenses: approximately $9,348.

Enrollment: 1st-year class 142; total full-time 584 (men 62%, women 38%). First-year statistics: up to 15% out of state each year; 39.4% women; average age 24; 17% minorities; 68% science majors.

Degrees conferred: M.D., M.D.-Ph.D. (Anatomy, Biochemistry, Biophysics, Cell Biology, Immunology, Microbiology, Molecular Biology, Neurosciences, Pathology, Pharmacology, Physiology).

RECRUITMENT PRACTICES AND POLICIES. School has diversity program and actively recruits women/minority applicants. Diversity contact: Office of Recruitment and Multicultural Services; phone: (405)271-3282.

ADMISSION REQUIREMENTS FOR FIRST-YEAR APPLICANTS. Preference given to state residents; U.S. citizens and permanent residents only. *Undergraduate preparation.* Suggested premed courses: 2 courses in biology with labs, 2 courses in inorganic chemistry with labs, 2 courses in organic chemistry with labs, 2 courses in physics with labs, 2 courses in English, 3 courses in humanities/social sciences. Bachelor's degree from an accredited institution required; 95% of applicants have bachelor's degree awarded prior to enrollment. Does not have EDP. *Application process.* Apply through AMCAS (file after June 1, before October 15); submit MCAT (will accept MCAT test results from last 3 years), official transcripts for each school attended (should show at least 90 semester credits/135 quarter credits, submit transcripts by mid-May to AMCAS), service processing fee. Submit a filing fee of $50, supplemental materials, preprofessional committee evaluation, and 3 recommendations from science faculty to Admissions Office no later than November 1. Interviews are by invitation only and generally for final selection. Dual-degree applicants must apply to, and be accepted by, both schools; contact the Admissions Office for current information and specific requirements for admission. First-year students admitted in fall only. Rolling admission process. Notification starts December 1 and is finished when class is filled. Applicant's response to offer and $100 deposit due within 2 weeks of receipt of acceptance letter. School does maintain an alternate list. Phone: (405)271-2331; E-mail: Doty- Shaw@uokhsc.edu.

ADMISSION REQUIREMENTS FOR TRANSFER APPLICANTS. Accepts transfers from other accredited U.S. medical schools; priority given to applicant's who have completed 2 years. Admission limited to space available. Contact the Admissions Office for current information and specific requirements for admission.

ADMISSION STANDARDS AND RECOGNITION. *For M.D.:* number of state-resident applicants 454, nonresidents 1,172; number of state residents interviewed 240, nonresidents 40; number of residents enrolled 135, nonresidents 7; median MCAT 9.44 (verbal reasoning 9.6; biological sciences 9.1; physical sciences 9.0); median GPA 3.59 (A = 4). Gorman rating 3.48 (scale: acceptable plus 3.01–3.59); the college's medical ranking by NIH awards/grants was 80th, with 66 awards/grants received; total dollars awarded $13,144,831.

FINANCIAL AID. Regents scholarships, fee waivers, minority scholarships, tuition-aid grants, institutional loans, HEAL, alternative loan programs, NIH stipends, federal Perkins loans, Stafford subsidized and unsubsidized loans, and Oklahoma Rural Education Loan Funds are available. Assistantships/fellowships may be available for dual-degree candidates. Financial aid applications and information are given out at the on-campus interview (by invitation). For scholarship assistance, the selection criteria place heavy reliance on MCAT and undergraduate GPA. Contact the Office of Financial Aid for current information; phone: (405)271-2118. For most financial assistance and all federal programs, submit FAFSA to a federal processor (Title IV school code # 005889); also submit Financial Aid Transcript and Federal Income Tax forms. Approximately 94% of current students receive some form of financial assistance. Average debt after graduation $54,270.

DEGREE REQUIREMENTS. *For M.D.:* satisfactory completion of 4-year program; the last 2 years are spent at either the Tulsa or Oklahoma City campus. All students must take USMLE Step 1 and Step 2 prior to graduation. *For M.D.-Ph.D.:* generally a 7-year program.

College of Dentistry
P.O. Box 26901
Oklahoma City, Oklahoma 73190
Phone: (405)271-3530; fax: (405)271-3423
Internet site: http://www.uokhsc.edu

Established 1972. Located at Health Sciences Center. Semester system. Special programs: Native American Center of Excellence. Postgraduate specialties: General Dentistry (AEGD), Oral and Maxillofacial Surgery, Orthodontics, Periodontics.

Annual tuition: residents $6,260, nonresidents $15,534; equipment and supplies $7,600 (includes a computer). No on-campus housing available. Contact Director of University Housing at Norman campus for on-campus housing information; phone: (405)325-2511. Dental students tend to live in community housing. Contact the Office of Student Affairs for local housing information. Off-campus housing, food, transportation, and personal expenses: approximately $11,000.

Enrollment: 1st-year class 54. First-year enrolled student information: 12 from out of state; 7 states represented; 16 women; average age 24.8; 8 underrepresented minorities; 8 other minorities.

Degree conferred: D.D.S.

RECRUITMENT PRACTICES AND POLICIES. School has diversity program and actively recruits women/minority applicants. Diversity contact: Native American Office; phone: (405)271-1976, or the Minority Affairs Office; phone: (405)271-2655.

ADMISSION REQUIREMENTS FOR FIRST-YEAR APPLICANTS. Preference given to state residents; U.S. citizens and permanent residents only. *Undergraduate preparation.* Suggested predental courses: 2 courses in biology with labs, 2 courses in inorganic chemistry with labs, 2 courses in organic chemistry with labs, 2 courses in physics with labs, 2 courses in English. There is no limitation on the number of junior-college credits taken; however, an applicant should have taken at lease 30 credits of upper-divisional course work at a 4-year institution. Will consider applicants with only 3 years of undergraduate preparation; prefer applicants who will have bachelor's degree prior to enrollment; 37 out of 54 enrolled students have bachelor's degree awarded prior to enrollment. *Application process.* Apply through AADSAS (file after June 1, before December 1); submit official transcripts for each school attended (should show at least 90 semester credits/135 quarter credits), service processing fee; at the same time as you send in AADSAS materials, submit an application fee of $50 (U.S. and naturalized citizens), $75 (permanent and international), a supplemental application, and official DAT scores (scores should be taken no later than October of the year prior to the anticipated year of enrollment) directly to the Admissions Office. TOEFL may be required of an applicant whose native language is other than English. Submit the following materials only after being contacted by an Admissions Officer: official transcripts and predental committee evaluation or 2 recommendations from science professors to Admissions Office within 2 weeks of being contacted. Interviews are by invitation only and generally for final selection. First-year students admitted in fall only. Rolling admission process. Notification starts December 1 and is finished when class is filled, generally no later than February 1. Applicant's response to offer and $500 deposit due within 30 days if accepted prior to December 15; response and deposit due within 2 weeks if received after January 15. School does maintain an alternate list. Phone: (405)271-3530; E-mail: susan-martin@uokhsc.edu.

ADMISSION REQUIREMENTS FOR ADVANCED-STANDING APPLICANTS. Accepts transfers from other accredited U.S. dental schools. Admission limited to space available. Contact the Admissions Office for current information and specific requirements for admission.

ADMISSION STANDARDS AND RECOGNITION. *For D.D.S.:* number of applicants 713; number enrolled 54; median DAT: ACAD 17.3, PAT 17.3; median GPA 3.33 (A = 4), median sciences GPA 3.22 (A = 4). Gorman rating 4.09 (scale: strong 4.01–4.49); this placed the school in the Bottom 10 of all U.S. dental schools.

FINANCIAL AID. Oklahoma tuition scholarships, minority scholarships, Oklahoma tuition-aid grants, institutional loans, state loan programs, DEAL, HEAL, alternative loan programs; federal Perkins loans, Stafford subsidized and unsubsidized loans, military service commitment scholarship programs are available. Institutional financial aid applications and information are generally available at the on-campus interview (by invitation). For scholarship assistance, the selection criteria place heavy reliance on DAT and undergraduate GPA; priority deadline is March 1; deadline for need-based programs is May 1. Contact the Office of Financial Aid for current information; phone: (405)271-2118. For most financial assistance and all need-based programs, submit FAFSA to a federal processor (Title IV school code # 005889); also submit Financial Aid Transcript, Federal Income Tax forms, and Use of Federal Funds Certification. Approximately 82% of current students receive some form of financial assistance. Average award for residents $18,634, nonresidents $30,089.

DEGREE REQUIREMENTS. *For D.D.S.:* satisfactory completion of 4-year (45-month) program.

OREGON HEALTH SCIENCES UNIVERSITY
Portland, Oregon 97201-3098
Phone: (503)494-8311
Internet site: http://www.ohsu.edu

Oregon's medical school was founded in 1887. In 1974 the University of Oregon's Schools of Dentistry, Medicine, and Nursing were unified at the University of Oregon Health Sciences Center in Portland; in 1981 it was renamed the Oregon Health Sciences University. It is now an independent nonprofit public corporation and an upper level/graduate institution. Located on top of Marquam Hill, a short distance from downtown. Library: 159,000 volumes/microforms; 2,615 periodicals/subscriptions; 32 PC work stations. Special facilities: Vollum Institute for Advanced Biomedical Research, Oregon Regional Primate Research Center, Center for

Research on Occupational and Environmental Toxicology, Biomedical Information Communication Center. University Hospital is a member of the Council of Teaching Hospitals and has nationally recognized programs in AIDS, Cancer, Cardiology, Endocrinology, Geriatrics, Gynecology, Neurology, Orthopedics, Otolaryngology, Rheumatology, Urology. The university's ranking in domestic higher education by NIH awards/grants was 48th, with 264 awards/grants received; total dollars awarded $53,647,400.

The university's other graduate schools include: School of Dentistry, School of Graduate Studies, School of Medicine, School of Nursing.

Total university enrollment at main campus: 1,757.

School of Medicine
3181 S.W. Sam Jackson Park Road
Portland, Oregon 97201-3098
Phone: (503)494-2998; fax: (503)494-3400
Internet site: http://www.ohsu.edu

Established 1887, name changed in 1974. A 4-year semitraditional program. Affiliated hospitals: Veteran's Administration Medical Center, Schriner's Hospital for Crippled Children, Good Samaritan Hospital and Medical Center, Doernbecher Memorial Hospital for Children, University Hospital.

Annual tuition: residents $16,037, nonresidents $31,968; fees $2,139. A residence hall is available on-campus; apartments available in surrounding area. Contact Housing Office for off-campus housing information; phone: (503)494-8665. Off-campus housing and personal expenses: approximately $12,414.

Enrollment: 1st-year class 96; total full-time 389 (men 54%, women 46%). First-year statistics: 40% out of state; 50% women; average age 25; 8% minorities; 58% science majors.

Degrees conferred: M.D., M.D.-M.P.H. (Epidemiology, Biostatistics), M.D.-Ph.D. (Behavioral Neuroscience, Biochemistry and Molecular Biology, Cell and Developmental Biology, Molecular and Medical Genetics, Molecular Microbiology and Immunology Neuroscience, Integrative Biomedical Sciences).

RECRUITMENT PRACTICES AND POLICIES. School has diversity program and actively recruits women/minority applicants. Diversity contact: Director, Multicultural Affairs; phone: (503)494-7574.

ADMISSION REQUIREMENTS FOR FIRST-YEAR APPLICANTS. Preference given to state residents, underrepresented minorities, and residents of WICHE states without a medical school; U.S. citizens and permanent residents only. *Undergraduate preparation.* Suggested premed courses: 2 courses in biology with labs, 2 courses in inorganic chemistry with labs, 2 courses in organic chemistry with labs, 2 courses in physics with labs, 2 courses in English, 2 courses in humanities, 2 courses in social sciences. Bachelor's degree from an accredited institution required; all applicants have bachelor's degrees awarded prior to enrollment. Does not have EDP. *Regular application process.* Apply through AMCAS (file after June 1, before October 15); submit MCAT (will accept MCAT test results from last 3 years), official transcripts for each school attended (should show at least 90 semester credits/135 quarter credits, submit transcripts by mid-May to AMCAS), service processing fee. After a preliminary evaluation supplemental materials may be requested. Submit an application fee of $60, secondary application, a personal statement, preprofessional committee evaluation, and 3 recommendations from science faculty to Office of Educational and Student Affairs within 2–3 weeks of the receipt of request for supplemental materials. Interviews are by invitation only and generally for final selection. M.D.-Ph.D. degree applicants will have a 2nd interview with the M.D.-Ph.D. selection committee. Contact the Office of Educational and Student Affairs for current information and specific requirements for admission. First-year students admitted in fall only. Rolling admission process. Notification starts November 1 and is finished when class is filled. Applicant's response to offer due within 2 weeks of receipt of acceptance letter. School does maintain an alternate list. Phone: (503)494-2998.

ADMISSION REQUIREMENTS FOR TRANSFER APPLICANTS. Accepts transfers from other accredited U.S. medical schools who are Oregon residents or their spouses. Admission limited to space available. Very few transfers have ever been accepted. Contact the Office of Educational and Student Affairs for current information and specific requirements for admission.

ADMISSION STANDARDS AND RECOGNITION. *For M.D.:* number of state-resident applicants 363, nonresidents 1,750; number of state residents interviewed 219, nonresidents 183; number of residents enrolled 54, nonresidents 42; median MCAT 10.0 (verbal reasoning 10.15; biological sciences 10.36; physical sciences 10.16); median GPA 3.56 (A = 4). Gorman rating 3.83 (scale: good 3.61–3.99); *U.S. News & World Report* ranked the school in the Top 25 of all U.S. medical schools in primary-care programs; medical school's ranking by NIH awards/grants was 45th, with 193 awards/grants received; total dollars awarded $40,218,250.

FINANCIAL AID. Scholarships, merit scholarships, minority scholarships, grants-in-aid, institutional loans, HEAL, alternative loan programs, federal Perkins loans, Stafford subsidized and unsubsidized loans, rural health service program, and service commitment scholarship programs are available. Most financial aid is based on documented need. Assistantships/fellowships may be available for dual-degree candidates. Financial aid information is generally available at the on-campus interview (by invitation). For scholarship assistance, the selection criteria place heavy reliance on MCAT and undergraduate GPA. Contact the Financial Aid Office for current information; phone: (503)494-8249. For most financial assistance and all federal programs, submit FAFSA to a federal processor (Title IV school code # 003223); also submit Financial Aid Transcript and Federal Income Tax forms. Approximately 92% of current students receive some form of financial assistance. Average debt after graduation $80,000.

DEGREE REQUIREMENTS. *For M.D.:* satisfactory completion of 4-year program. All students must take USMLE Step 1 and Step 2 prior to graduation. *For M.D.-M.P.H.:* generally a 5-year program. *For M.D.-Ph.D.:* generally a 6–8-year program.

School of Dentistry

611 S.W. Campus Drive
Portland, Oregon 97201-3097
Phone: (503)494-5274; fax: (503)494-4666
Internet site: http://www.ohsu.edu/sod
E-mail: cromleyn@ohsu.edu

Established 1898; became a part of the Oregon state system in 1945. Located on main campus. Quarter system. Special programs: 5th-year fellowship program; Disadvantaged Student Recruitment Program. Postgraduate specialties: Endodontics, Oral and Maxillofacial Surgery, Orthodontics, Periodontics.

Annual tuition: residents $9,114, nonresidents $18,885; fees $840; equipment and supplies $5,980. A residence hall is available on-campus; apartments available in surrounding area. Contact Director of Residence Hall Office for both on- and off-campus housing information; phone: (503)494-7747. Dental students tend to live off-campus. Off-campus housing, food, transportation, and personal expenses: approximately $9,214.

Enrollment: 1st-year class 70; total full-time 265. First-year enrolled student information: 20 from out of state; 10 states represented; 17 women; average age 25; 1 underrepresented minority; 7 other minorities.

Degrees conferred: D.M.D., D.M.D.-M.S. (Oral and Maxillofacial Surgery).

RECRUITMENT PRACTICES AND POLICIES. School has diversity program and actively recruits women/minority applicants. Diversity contact: Disadvantaged Student Recruitment Program; phone: (503)494-5274.

ADMISSION REQUIREMENTS FOR FIRST-YEAR APPLICANTS. Priority given to state residents and WICHE residents; U.S. citizens, and permanent residents only. *Undergraduate preparation.* Suggested predental courses: 1 year of biology with labs, 1 year of general chemistry with labs, 1 year of organic chemistry with labs, 1 year of physics with labs; biochemistry, microbiology, anatomy, and physiology are highly recommended. The junior-college transfer-credit limit is 60/90 credits, but an applicant must have completed at least 1 year at a 4-year institution prior to enrollment. Will consider applicants with only 3 years of undergraduate preparation; prefer applicants who will have bachelor's degree prior to enrollment; 68 out of 70 enrolled students have bachelor's degree awarded prior to enrollment. *Application process.* Apply through AADSAS (file after June 1, before December 1); submit official transcripts for each school attended (should show at least 90 semester credits/135 quarter credits), service processing fee; at the same time as you send in AADSAS materials, submit official DAT scores (taken no later than October of the year prior to the year of anticipated enrollment) directly to the Office of Admission and Student Affairs. TOEFL may be required of an applicant whose native language is other than English. Submit the following materials only after being contacted by an Admissions Officer: an application fee of $40, a supplemental application, official transcripts, predental committee evaluation, or 3 recommendations from science professors to the Office of Admission and Student Affairs immediately. Interviews are by invitation only and generally for final selection. Joint-degree applicants must apply to, and be accepted by, both schools; contact the Office of Admission and Student Affairs for current information and specific requirements for admission. First-year students admitted in fall only. Rolling admission process. Notification starts December 1 and is finished when class is filled. Applicant's response to offer and $500 deposit due within 15 days of the receipt of acceptance. School does maintain an alternate list. Phone: (503)494-5274; E-mail: cromleyn@ohsu.edu.

ADMISSION REQUIREMENTS FOR ADVANCED-STANDING APPLICANTS. Accepts transfers from other accredited U.S. dental schools. Admission limited to space available. There is no formal advanced-standing program for graduates of foreign schools of dentistry.

Contact the Office of Admission and Student Affairs for current information and specific requirements for admission.

ADMISSION STANDARDS AND RECOGNITION. *For D.M.D.:* number of applicants 996; number enrolled 70; median DAT: ACAD 19.2; median GPA 3.47 (A = 4), median sciences GPA 3.49 (A = 4). Gorman rating 4.33 (scale: strong 4.01–4.49); this placed the school in the Top 30 of all U.S. dental schools; the dental school's ranking by NIH awards/grants was 25th among dental schools, with 7 awards/grants received; total value of all awards/grants $1,179,519.

FINANCIAL AID. Scholarships, academic merit awards, minority scholarships, grants-in-aid, institutional loans, state loan programs, DEAL, HEAL, alternative loan programs, federal Perkins loans, Stafford subsidized and unsubsidized loans, and military service commitment scholarship programs are available. Assistantships/fellowships may be available for combined-degree candidates. Institutional financial aid applications and information are given out at the on-campus interview (by invitation). For academic merit awards (priority deadline March 1) the selection criteria place heavy reliance on DAT and undergraduate GPA. Contact the Office of Financial Aid for current information; phone: (503)494-7800. For most financial assistance and all need-based programs submit FAFSA to a federal processor (Title IV school code # 003223); also submit Financial Aid Transcript, Federal Income Tax forms, and Use of Federal Funds Certification. Approximately 95% of current students receive some form of financial assistance. Average award for residents $26,779, nonresidents $36,299.

DEGREE REQUIREMENTS. *For D.M.D.:* satisfactory completion of 4-year program. Students take Part I of the National Board Exam after their sophomore year and Part II in December of their senior year. *For D.M.D.-M.S.:* generally a 4½–5½-year program.

UNIVERSITY OF OSTEOPATHIC MEDICINE AND HEALTH SCIENCES
Des Moines, Iowa 50312-4104
Internet site: http://www.uomhs.edu

Private control. Graduate study only. Library: 28,000 volumes/microforms; 1,400 periodicals/subscriptions; 40 PC work stations. Special facilities: the university operates 5 clinics; an on-campus medical center opened in 1987.

The university's other graduate/professional colleges are: the College of Health Sciences, College of Podiatric Medicine and Surgery. Total university enrollment at main campus: 1,088.

College of Osteopathic Medicine and Surgery
3200 Grand Avenue
Des Moines, Iowa 50312
Phone: (515)271-1400; fax: (515)271-1545
Internet site: http://www.uomhs.edu
E-mail: doadmits@uomhs.edu

Established 1898 as the Dr. S. S. Still College of Osteopathic Medicine. Second-largest osteopathic school in U.S. Affiliated with Des Moines General Hospital and 12 other hospitals throughout the East and Midwest.

Annual tuition: $21,572. No on-campus housing available. Contact Off-campus Housing Office for information; phone: (515)271-1504. Off-campus housing and personal expenses: approximately $18,580.

Enrollment: 1st-year class 205; total full-time 804 (men 70%, women 30%). First-year statistics: 78% out of state; 38% women; average age 24; 67% science majors.

Faculty: full-time 59.

Degree conferred: D.O.

RECRUITMENT PRACTICES AND POLICIES. School has diversity program and actively recruits women/minority applicants. Diversity contact: Admissions Office.

ADMISSION REQUIREMENTS FOR FIRST-YEAR APPLICANTS. Preference given to state residents; U.S. citizens and permanent residents only. *Undergraduate preparation.* Suggested premed courses: 2 courses in biology, 2 courses in inorganic chemistry, 2 courses in organic chemistry, 2 courses in physics, 2 courses in English. Bachelor's degree from an accredited institution required; all applicants have bachelor's degrees awarded prior to enrollment. *Application process.* Apply through AACOMAS (file after June 1, before April 1); submit MCAT (will accept test results from last 2 years, 1 year is recommended), official transcripts for each school attended (should show at least 90 semester credits/135 quarter credits), service processing fee. After a review of the AACOMAS application and supporting documents, a decision is made concerning which candidates should receive supplemental materials. The supplementary application, an application fee of $50, a statement of purpose, and 3 recommendations (1 from a premed adviser and 2 from science faculty members) should be returned to Admissions Office as soon as possible. Interviews are by invitation only and generally for final selection. First-year students admitted in fall only. Rolling admission process. Notification starts in January and is finished when class is filled. Applicant's response to offer and $100 deposit due within 2 weeks of receipt of acceptance letter. School does maintain an alternate list. Phone: (515)271-1450, (800)240-2767, X1450; fax: (515)271-1578.

ADMISSION REQUIREMENTS FOR TRANSFER APPLICANTS. Accepts transfers from other accredited U.S. osteopathic medical schools. Admission limited to space available. Contact the Admissions Offices for current information and specific requirements.

ADMISSION STANDARDS AND RECOGNITION. *For D.O.:* number of applicants 4,420; number enrolled 205; median MCAT 8.2; median GPA 3.44 (A = 4).

FINANCIAL AID. Scholarships, merit scholarships, minority scholarships, grants-in-aid, institutional loans, NOF, HEAL, alternative loan programs, federal Perkins loans, Stafford subsidized and unsubsidized loans, service obligation scholarship programs, and military and National Health Service programs are available. Financial aid applications and information are given out at the on-campus interview (by invitation). For merit scholarships, the selection criteria place heavy reliance on MCAT and undergraduate GPA. Contact the Financial Aid Office for current information. For most financial assistance and all federal programs, submit FAFSA to a federal processor (Title IV school code # 015616); also submit Financial Aid Transcript and Federal Income Tax forms. Approximately 85% of current students receive some form of financial assistance. Average debt after graduation $120,000.

DEGREE REQUIREMENTS. *For D.O.:* satisfactory completion of 4-year program.

UNIVERSITY OF THE PACIFIC
Stockton, California 95211-0197
Internet site: http://www.uop.edu

Founded 1851. Private control. Semester system. Library: 437,000 volumes; 531,000 microforms; 2,652 periodicals/subscriptions; 48 work stations.

The university's graduate school includes: Conservatory of Music, School of Business and Public Administration, School of Education, McGeorge School of Law,

School of Dentistry (San Francisco), School of Pharmacy.

Total university enrollment at main campus: 5,850.

School of Dentistry

2155 Webster Street
San Francisco, California 94115
Phone: (415)929-6491; fax: (415)929-6654

Established 1896 as College of Physicians and Surgeons; amalgamated with University of the Pacific in 1962. Located in the Pacific Heights area of San Francisco. Quarter system. Special programs: International Dental Student Program. Postgraduate specialties: General Dentistry (AEGD), Orthodontics.

Annual tuition: $31,160; fees $1,150; equipment and supplies $9,600. Limited on-campus rooms and apartments available for both single and married students. Contact Office of Student Services for both on- and off-campus housing information; phone: (415)929-6491. Dental students tend to live off-campus. Off-campus housing, food, transportation, and personal expenses: approximately $12,040 (single students), $15,190 (married students).

Enrollment: 1st-year class 136; total full-time 525. First-year enrolled student information: 35 from out of state; 11 states represented; 48 women; average age 24; 7 underrepresented minorities; 49 other minorities.

Degrees conferred: D.D.S., B.A.-D.D.S. (5-, 6-, or 7-year programs available with University of the Pacific).

RECRUITMENT PRACTICES AND POLICIES. School has diversity program and actively recruits women/minority applicants. Diversity contact: Officer of Student Services; phone: (415)929-6491.

ADMISSION REQUIREMENT FOR BACHELOR-D.D.S. APPLICANTS. For information and applications contact: Admissions Office, University of the Pacific; phone: (209)946-2330.

ADMISSION REQUIREMENTS FOR FIRST-YEAR APPLICANTS. Preference given to state residents; U.S. citizens and permanent residents only. *Undergraduate preparation.* Suggested predental courses: 2 courses in biology with labs, 2 courses in inorganic chemistry with labs, 2 courses in organic chemistry with labs, 2 courses in physics with labs, 2 courses in English. Junior-college credits will be considered if transferred to a 4-year institution and counted as the equivalent of predental courses. Will consider applicants with only 3 years of undergraduate preparation; prefer applicants who will have bachelor's degree prior to enrollment; 134 out of 136 1st-year

students have bachelor's degree awarded prior to enrollment. *Application process.* Apply through AADSAS (file after June 1, before March 1); submit official transcripts for each school attended (should show at least 90 semester credits/135 quarter credits), service processing fee; at the same time as you send in AADSAS materials, submit official DAT scores (taken within the last 3 years), application fee of $75, and predental committee evaluation or 3 recommendations from science professors directly to the Admissions Office. TOEFL, TSE, and TWE are required of an applicant whose native language is other than English. Submit official transcripts to Admissions Office only after being contacted by an Admissions Officer. Interviews are by invitation only and generally for final selection. First-year students admitted in fall only. Rolling admission process. Notification starts December 1 and is finished when class is filled, but generally not later than July 1. Applicant's response to offer and $1,000 deposit due within 15 days of the receipt of the offer of acceptance. School does maintain an alternate list. Phone: (415)929-6491.

ADMISSION REQUIREMENTS FOR ADVANCED-STANDING APPLICANTS. Accepts transfers from other accredited U.S. dental schools, but only under unusual and compelling circumstances. Contact the Admissions Office for current information and specific requirements for admission.

ADMISSION REQUIREMENTS FOR INTERNATIONAL DENTAL STUDIES (IDS). For serious consideration an applicant must have a foreign dental degree comparable to a D.D.S., successful completion of Part I of the National Board Dental Examination, with a score of 75 or higher in each category, proof of proficiency in English language (at least 575 on TOEFL). Submit an application, application fee of $40, TOEFL (if English is not the applicant's native language), official translations and evaluations of all foreign credentials, the results of the National Board Dental Examination, and Certificate of Finance to Admissions Office. Apply by March 1. On-campus interviews and technical examinations are requested and generally used for final selection. Phone: (415)929-6688; E-mail: pking@uop.edu.

ADMISSION STANDARDS AND RECOGNITION. *For D.D.S.:* number of applicants 2,566; number enrolled 136; median DAT: ACAD 19.2, PAT 18.8; median GPA 3.21 (A = 4), median sciences GPA 3.12 (A = 4). Gorman rating 4.30 (scale: strong 4.01–4.49); this placed the school in the Top 30 of all U.S. dental schools; the school's ranking by NIH awards/grants was 39th among

U.S. dental schools, with 1 award/grant received; total value of all awards/grants was $93,000.

FINANCIAL AID. Scholarships, merit scholarships, minority scholarships, grants-in-aid, institutional loans, state loan programs, DEAL, HEAL, alternative loan programs; federal Perkins loans, Stafford subsidized and unsubsidized loans, and military service commitment scholarship programs are available. Assistantships/fellowships may be available for combined degree candidates. Institutional financial aid applications and information are sent to all applicants in early January. All financial aid is based on documented need. For scholarship assistance, the selection criteria place heavy reliance on DAT and undergraduate GPA. Contact the Financial Aid Office for current information; phone: (415)929-6452. For most financial assistance and all need-based programs, submit FAFSA to a federal processor (Title IV school code # 013292 or G04498); also submit Financial Aid Transcript, Federal Income Tax forms, and Use of Federal Funds Certification. Approximately 85% of current students receive some form of financial assistance. Average award $38,500.

DEGREE REQUIREMENTS. *For bachelor's-D.D.S.:* a 5-, 6- or 7-year program. *For D.D.S.:* satisfactory completion of a 4-academic-year or a 3-calendar-year program.

PENNSYLVANIA STATE UNIVERSITY
University Park, Pennsylvania 16802
Internet site: http://www.psu.edu

Founded 1855. Located 90 miles NW of Harrisburg. Public control. Semester system. Library: 2,680,000 volumes; 2,143,700 microforms; 24,628 periodicals/subscriptions. Special facilities: Bioprocessing Resource Center, Center for Biodiversity, Center for Bioremediation and Detoxification, Center of Health Policy Research, Center for Prevention Evaluation and Research, Gerontology Center, Particulate Materials Center, Whitaker Center for Medical Ultrasonic Transducer Engineering. University has branch campuses in Erie, Middletown, and Malvern. The university's ranking in domestic higher education by NIH awards/grants was 46th, with 280 awards/grants received; total dollars awarded $58,778,113.

The university's graduate school includes: College of Agricultural Sciences, College of Arts and Architecture, College of Communications, College of Earth and Mineral Sciences, College of Education, College of Engineering, College of Health and Human Development, College of Liberal Arts, Eberly College of Science, Mary Jean and Frank P. Smeal College of Business Administration.

Total university enrollment at main campus: 37,800.

Pennsylvania State University Milton S. Hershey Medical Center
500 University Drive
P.O. Box 850
Hershey, Pennsylvania 17033
Internet site: http://www.hmc.psu.edu

Founded 1966. Located about 8 miles from Harrisburg. Public control. The medical center is a member of the Council of Teaching Hospitals. Schools located at medical center are: Graduate School, College of Medicine. Special facilities: Penn State Center for Sports Medicine, University Hospital. Nationally recognized programs in Cancer, Gastroenterology, Urology.

College of Medicine
P.O. Box 850
Hershey, Pennsylvania 17033-0850
Phone: (717)531-8755; fax: (717)531-6225
Internet site: http://www.hmc.psu.edu
E-mail: hmcsaff@psu.edu

Established 1967. Located at the medical center. Library: 125,000 volumes/microforms; 1,800 current periodicals/subscriptions. Special programs: Overseas study program for selected 4th-year students.

Annual tuition: residents $17,500, nonresidents $24,694. On-campus rooms and apartments available for both single and married students. Annual on-campus housing cost: single students $2,817 (room only), married students $5,193. Contact Admissions Office for both on- and off-campus housing information. Some medical students live off-campus. Off-campus housing and personal expenses: approximately $10,985.

Enrollment: 1st-year class 105 (EDP 2); total full-time 445 (men 54%, women 46%). First-year statistics: 60% out of state; 41% women; average age 25; 19% minorities; 70% science majors.

Degrees conferred: M.D., M.D.-Ph.D. (Biochemistry and Molecular Biology, Bioengineering, Cell and Molecular Biology, Genetics, Integrative Bioscience, Microbiology and Immunology, Neurosciences, Pharmacology, Physiology).

RECRUITMENT PRACTICES AND POLICIES. School has diversity program and actively recruits women/minority applicants. Diversity contact: Associate Dean for Student Affairs; phone: (717)531-8651.

ADMISSION REQUIREMENTS FOR FIRST-YEAR APPLICANTS. Preference given to state residents; U.S. citizens and permanent residents only. *Undergraduate preparation.* Suggested premed courses: 2 courses in biology with labs, 2 courses in inorganic chemistry with labs, 2 courses in organic chemistry with labs, 2 courses in physics with labs, 2 courses in college math, 2 courses in humanities, 1 course in behavioral sciences. Bachelor's degree from an accredited institution required; all applicants have bachelor's degree awarded prior to enrollment. *Has EDP*; applicants must apply through AMCAS (official transcripts sent by mid-May) between June 1 and August 1. Early applications are encouraged. Submit secondary/supplemental application, a personal statement, and 2 recommendations to Admissions Office within 2 weeks of receipt of application. Notification normally begins October 1. *Regular application process.* Apply through AMCAS (file after June 1, before December 1); submit MCAT (will accept MCAT test results from 1995), official transcripts for each school attended (should show at least 90 semester credits/135 quarter credits, submit transcripts by mid-May to AMCAS), service processing fee. Submit an application fee of $40, a supplemental application, a personal statement, preprofessional committee evaluation, and 2 recommendations from science faculty to Admissions Office within 2–3 weeks of the receipt of supplemental materials, but not later than January 15. Interviews are by invitation only and generally for final selection. M.D.-Ph.D. degree applicants must apply to, and be accepted by, both schools; contact the Admissions Office for current information and specific requirements for admission. First-year students admitted in fall only. Rolling admission process. Notification starts October 15 and is finished when class is filled. Applicant's response to offer and $100 deposit due within 2 weeks of receipt of acceptance letter. School does maintain an alternate list. Phone: (717)531-8755; E-mail: hmcsaff@psu.edu.

ADMISSION REQUIREMENTS FOR TRANSFER APPLICANTS. Accepts transfers from other accredited U.S. medical schools. Admission limited to space available. Contact the Admissions Office for current information and specific requirements for admission.

ADMISSION STANDARDS AND RECOGNITION. *For M.D.:* number of state-resident applicants 1,391, nonresidents 6,052; number of state residents interviewed 224, nonresidents 390; number of residents enrolled 45, nonresidents 60; median MCAT 9.65 (verbal reasoning 9.4; biological sciences 9.9; physical sciences 9.8); median GPA 3.65 (A = 4). Gorman rating 3.67 (scale: good 3.61–3.99); *U.S. News & World Report* ranked the college in the Top 25 of all U.S. medical schools in primary-care education; medical school's ranking by NIH awards/grants was 62nd, with 128 awards/grants received; total dollars awarded $27,259,603.

FINANCIAL AID. Scholarships, merit scholarships, minority scholarships, grants-in-aid, institutional loans, HEAL, alternative loan programs, NIH stipends, federal Perkins loans, Stafford subsidized and unsubsidized loans, and service commitment scholarship programs are available. Assistantships/fellowships may be available for dual-degree candidates. Financial aid applications and information are generally available at the on-campus interview (by invitation). For scholarship assistance, the selection criteria place heavy reliance on MCAT and undergraduate GPA, suggested deadline February 15. Contact the Office of Student Affairs for current information; phone: (717)531-4103. For most financial assistance and all federal programs, submit FAFSA to a federal processor (Title IV school code # G06813); also submit Financial Aid Transcript and Federal Income Tax forms. Approximately 85% of current students receive some form of financial assistance; 60% receive funds from college sources. Average debt after graduation $85,000.

DEGREE REQUIREMENTS. *For M.D.:* satisfactory completion of 4-year program; research project. All students must pass USMLE Step 1 prior to entering 3rd year; all students must pass USMLE Step 2 prior to awarding of M.D. *For M.D.-Ph.D.:* generally a 7-year program.

UNIVERSITY OF PENNSYLVANIA
Philadelphia, Pennsylvania 19104
Internet site: http://www.upenn.edu

Founded 1740. Located 2 miles from the center of Philadelphia. Private control. Semester system. Library: 4,200,000 volumes; 1,500,000 microforms; 33,000 periodicals/subscriptions. Special programs: Postbaccalaureate premedical program for adults and underrepresented minorities located in the College of General Studies; phone (215)898-4847. The university's ranking in domestic higher education by NIH awards/grants was 3rd, with 798 awards/grants received; total dollars awarded $217,069,896.

The university's other graduate colleges/schools: Annenberg School of Communication, Graduate School of Education, Graduate School of Fine Arts, Law School, School of Arts and Science, School of Dental Medicine, School of Engineering and Applied Science, School of

Medicine, School of Nursing, School of Social Work, School of Veterinary Medicine, Wharton School.

Total university enrollment at main campus: 22,100.

Hospitals of the University of Pennsylvania
3400 Spruce Street
Philadelphia, Pennsylvania 19104

Private control. The hospitals are members of the Council of Teaching Hospitals. Special facilities: Institute on Aging, Center for Bioethics, Cancer Center for Clinical Epidemiology and Biostatistics, Center for Experimental Therapeutics, Deafness and Family Communication Center, Digestive and Liver Center, Institute for Environmental Medicine, Institute for Human Gene Therapy, Leonard Davis Institute of Health Economics, Institute for Medicine and Engineering, Institute for Neurological Sciences, Pennsylvania Muscle Institute, Center for Research on Reproduction and Women's Health. Nationally recognized programs in AIDS, Cancer, Cardiology, Endocrinology, Gastroenterology, Geriatrics, Gynecology, Neurology, Orthopedics, Otolaryngology, Psychiatry, Pulmonary Disease, Rheumatology, Urology. *Barron's Guide* placed the hospitals of the University of Pennsylvania among the Top 25 most prestigious U.S. Hospitals. *U.S. News & World Report*'s hospital/medical center national rankings for all hospitals placed hospitals of the University of Pennsylvania in the Top 20 of all U.S. hospitals.

School of Medicine
Edward J. Stemmler Hall, Ste 100
Philadelphia, Pennsylvania 19104-6056
Phone: (215)898-8001; fax: (215)573-6645
Internet site: http://www.med.upenn.edu

Established 1765; first medical school in the colonies. Located on the Irwin Campus in Philadelphia. A five-module curriculum. Library: 100,000 volumes/microforms; 2,000 current periodicals/subscriptions. Affiliated hospitals: Hospitals for the University of Pennsylvania, Children's Hospital of Philadelphia, Veteran's Administration of Philadelphia Hospital, Presbyterian Medical Center of Philadelphia, Pennsylvania Hospital, Phoenixville Hospital, Philadelphia General Hospital.

Annual tuition: $28,545. On-campus rooms and apartments available for both single and married students. Contact Department of Housing and Residence Life for on-campus housing information; phone: (215) 898-3676; for off-campus housing information contact the Office of Off-Campus Living; phone: (215) 898-8500. Medical students tend to live off-campus. Both on- and off-campus living and personal expenses: approximately $14,889.

Enrollment: 1st-year class 150 (M.S.T.P. 27); total full-time 684 (men 48%, women 52%). First-year statistics: 70% out of state; 43.7% women; average age 24; 19% minorities; 69% science majors.

Degrees conferred: M.D., M.D.-M.B.A., M.D.-Ph.D. (Biochemistry and Molecular Biology, Bioengineering, Cell and Molecular Biology, Epidemiology and Biostatistics, Genetics, Immunology, Neurosciences, Parasitology, Pharmacological Sciences); has M.S.T.P.

RECRUITMENT PRACTICES AND POLICIES. School has diversity program and actively recruits women/minority applicants; request "Information for Minority Applicants" materials. Diversity contact: Assistant Dean of Student Affairs and Director of Minority Affairs; phone: (215)898-4409.

ADMISSION REQUIREMENTS FOR FIRST-YEAR APPLICANTS. Some preference given to state residents; U.S. citizens and permanent residents only. *Undergraduate preparation.* Suggested premed courses: competence in biology, chemistry, physics, math, English. Bachelor's degree from an accredited institution required; all applicants have bachelor's degree awarded prior to enrollment. Does not have EDP. *Application process.* Apply through AMCAS (file after June 1, before November 1); submit MCAT (will accept MCAT test results from last 3 years), official transcripts for each school attended (should show at least 90 semester credits/135 quarter credits, submit transcripts by mid-May to AMCAS), service processing fee. Submit an application fee of $55, a supplemental application, a comment/statement, preprofessional committee evaluation, and 3 recommendations from science faculty to Admissions Office within 2–3 weeks of receipt of supplemental materials. Interviews are by invitation only and generally for final selection. All accepted students are considered for both the M.D.-Ph.D. and M.S.T.P.; contact the Admissions Office for current information and specific requirements for admission. First-year students admitted in fall only. Notification is in March. Applicant's response to offer and $100 deposit due within 2 weeks of receipt of acceptance letter. School does maintain an alternate list. Phone: (215)898-8001; fax: (215)898-0833.

ADMISSION REQUIREMENTS FOR TRANSFER APPLICANTS. Accepts transfers from other accredited U.S. medical schools, but only those with a compelling reason and only into the 3rd year. Admission limited to space available. Contact the Admissions Office for current information and specific requirements for admission.

ADMISSION STANDARDS AND RECOGNITION. *For M.D.:* number of state-resident applicants 1,041, nonresidents 7,511; number of state residents interviewed

161, nonresidents 788; number of residents enrolled 43, nonresidents 107; median MCAT 11.0 (verbal reasoning 11.0; biological sciences 11.0; physical sciences 11.0); median GPA 3.6 (A = 4). *Barron's Guide* placed the school among the Top 25 most prestigious U.S. medical schools; Gorman rating 4.91 (scale: very strong 4.51–4.99); *U.S. News & World Report* ranked the school in the Top 25 of all U.S. medical schools; the school's medical ranking by NIH awards/grants was 3rd, with 606 awards/grants received; total dollars awarded $175,206,976.

FINANCIAL AID. Scholarships, merit scholarships, minority scholarships, grants-in-aid, institutional low-interest loans, HEAL, alternative loan programs, NIH stipends (M.S.T.P.), federal Perkins loans, Stafford subsidized and unsubsidized loans, and service commitment scholarship programs are available. Assistantships/Franklin Medical School Fellowships may be available for combined degree candidates. Financial aid applications and information are generally available at the on-campus interview (by invitation). All accepted students are considered for the Gamble Scholars, selection is based on MCAT, undergraduate GPA, unique life experience, and leadership qualities. All financial aid documents should be received by April 15; notification is by May 15. Contact the Admissions and Financial Aid Office for current information; phone: (215)573-3423. For most financial assistance and all federal programs, submit FAFSA to a federal processor (Title IV school code # 009737); also submit Financial Aid Transcript and Federal Income Tax forms. Approximately 75% of current students receive some form of financial assistance. Average debt after graduation $81,000.

DEGREE REQUIREMENTS. *For M.D.:* satisfactory completion of 4-year program. All students must pass USMLE Step 1 prior to entering 3rd year; all students must pass USMLE Step 2 prior to awarding of M.D. *For M.D.-Ph.D., M.S.T.P.:* generally a 7-year program.

School of Dental Medicine
4001 Spruce Street
Philadelphia, Pennsylvania 19104-6003
Phone: (215)898-8943; fax: (215)898-5243
Internet site: http://www.upenn.edu

Established 1878 as the Thomas W. Evans Museum and Dental Institute. Name changed in 1964. Located on main campus. Library: 53,000 volumes/microforms; 435 current periodicals/subscriptions. Special facilities: Center for Oral Health Research. Special programs: foreign-exchange program at 17 different international locations; research fellowships; externships; Program for Advanced

Standing Students (PASS). Postgraduate specialties: Endodontics, General Dentistry, Dental Public Health, Oral and Maxillofacial Pathology, Oral and Maxillofacial Surgery, Orthodontics, Pediatric Dentistry, Periodontics, Prosthodontics.

Annual tuition: $31,700; fees $1,120; equipment and supplies $3,250. On-campus rooms and apartments available for both single and married students. Contact Graduate Housing Office for both on- and off-campus housing information; phone: (215)898-8271. Dental students tend to live off-campus. Off-campus housing, food, transportation, and personal expenses: approximately $12,980.

Enrollment: 1st-year class 92; total full-time 355. First-year enrolled student information: 72 from out of state; 15 states represented; 47 women; average age 24; 5 underrepresented minorities; 30 other minorities.

Faculty: full-time/part-time/volunteers 260.

Degrees conferred: D.M.D., B.S.-D.M.D. (with College of Arts and Sciences of the University of Pennsylvania, Lehigh University, Muhlenberg College, Rensselaer Polytechnic Institute, Villanova University), D.M.D.-M.B.A., M.S. (Oral Biology), D.D.S.-Ph.D. (no formal program but is available with special arrangements).

RECRUITMENT PRACTICES AND POLICIES. School has diversity program and actively recruits women/minority applicants. Diversity contact: Officer of Minority Affairs; phone: (215)898-5052.

ADMISSION REQUIREMENT FOR BACHELOR-D.D.S. APPLICANTS. For information and applications contact: School of Dental Medicine, Admissions Office; phone: (215)898-8943; or each individual undergraduate college listed above.

ADMISSION REQUIREMENTS FOR FIRST-YEAR APPLICANTS. Some preference given to state residents; U.S. citizens and permanent residents only. *Undergraduate preparation.* Suggested predental courses: 2 courses in biology with labs, 2 courses in inorganic chemistry with labs, 2 courses in organic chemistry with labs, 2 courses in physics with labs, 1 course in college math (calculus preferred), 1 course in English. The junior-college transfer credit limit is 60 credits, all earned before a student enters the 3rd year at a 4-year institution. Will consider applicants with only 3 years of undergraduate preparation; prefer applicants who will have a bachelor's degree prior to enrollment. For serious consideration an applicant should have at least 2.8 (A = 4) GPA; all applicants have bachelor's degrees awarded prior to enrollment. *Application process.* Apply through AADSAS (file after June 1, before February 1); submit official transcripts for each school attended (should show at least 90 semester credits/135 quarter credits), service processing fee; at the same time as you send in AADSAS materials, submit an application fee of $45 plus fee card, a supplemental application, official transcripts, official DAT scores, and predental committee evaluation or 2 recommendations from professors directly to the Admissions Office. TOEFL may be required of an applicant whose native language is other than English. Interviews are by invitation only and generally for final selection. First-year students admitted in fall only. Rolling admission process. Notification starts in December and is finished when class is filled. Applicant's response to offer and $1,000 deposit due within 30 days if accepted prior to January 1; response and deposit due within 2 weeks if received after January 1. School does maintain an alternate list. Phone: (215)898-5570.

ADMISSION REQUIREMENTS FOR ADVANCED-STANDING APPLICANTS. Accepts transfers from other accredited U.S. dental schools into the 3rd year only. Admission limited to space available. Submit application, application fee, current dental school official transcripts, and personal statement regarding reason for transfer. There is an advanced-standing program (PASS) for graduates of foreign schools of dentistry. Contact the Admissions Office or the Office of International Relations (phone: (215)898-0558) for current information and specific requirements for admission.

ADMISSION STANDARDS AND RECOGNITION. *For D.D.S.*: number of applicants 1,642; number enrolled 92; median DAT: ACAD 19.2, PAT 16.8; median GPA 3.37 (A = 4), median sciences GPA 3.26 (A = 4). Gorman rating 4.88 (scale: very strong 4.51–4.99); this placed the school in the Top 5 of all U.S. dental schools; the dental school's ranking by NIH awards/grants was 3rd among dental schools with 32 awards/grants received; total value of all awards/grants was $7,090,130.

FINANCIAL AID. Scholarships, institutional low-interest loans, state loan programs, DEAL, HEAL, alternative loan programs, federal Perkins loans, Stafford subsidized and unsubsidized loans, and military service commitment scholarship programs are available. Assistantships/fellowships may be available for combined-degree candidates. Institutional financial-aid applications and information are generally available at the on-campus interview (by invitation). All financial aid is based on documented need. For scholarship assistance, the selection criteria place heavy reliance on DAT and undergraduate GPA. Contact the Office of Financial Aid for current information; phone: (215)898-4550. For most financial assistance and all need-based programs, submit FAFSA

to a federal processor (Title IV school code # 009737); also submit Financial Aid Transcript, Federal Income Tax forms, and Use of Federal Funds Certification. Approximately 72% of current students receive some form of financial assistance. Average award $25,000.

DEGREE REQUIREMENTS. *For B.S.-D.M.D.*: generally a 7-year program. *For D.M.D.*: satisfactory completion of 4-year (45-month) program. *For D.M.D.-M.S.*: generally a 4½–5½-year program.

PHILADELPHIA COLLEGE OF OSTEOPATHIC MEDICINE

4170 City Avenue
Philadelphia, Pennsylvania 19131-1969
Phone: (215)879-6770
Internet site: http://www.pcom.edu
E-mail: admission@pcom.edu

Established 1899; largest osteopathic college in U.S. Private control. Semester system; first 2 year's focus is basic sciences. Library: 71,000 volumes/microforms; 785 current periodicals/subscriptions; 25 computer work stations; has MEDLINE, CANCERLINE, BIOEHTIC, HEALTH, PALINET, TOXLINE, DIALOG, OCLC. Special facilities: Anatomy Museum, Heart Lung Bypass Center; maintains 5 urban health-care centers in Philadelphia and 1 rural health-care center in Sullivan County, PA. Special programs: prematriculation summer sessions.

Annual tuition: $21,750; fees $175. No on-campus housing available. Contact Admissions Office for off-campus housing information. Off-campus housing and personal expenses: approximately $15,000.

Enrollment: 1st-year class 250; total full-time 973 (men 67%, women 33%). First-year statistics: 32% out of state; 40% women; average age 26; 13% minorities; 84% science majors.

Faculty: full-time 60, part-time/volunteers 700.

Degrees conferred: D.O., M.Sc. (Biomedical Science), Psy.D., D.O.-M.B.A. (St. Joseph's University), D.O.-M.P.H. (Temple University).

RECRUITMENT PRACTICES AND POLICIES. School has diversity program and actively recruits women/minority applicants. Diversity contact: Admissions Office.

ADMISSION REQUIREMENTS FOR FIRST-YEAR APPLICANTS. Some preference given to state residents; U.S. citizens and permanent residents only. *Undergraduate preparation.* Suggested premed courses: 2 courses in biology, 2 courses in inorganic chemistry, 2 courses in organic chemistry, 2 courses in physics, 2 courses in English. Bachelor's degree from an accredited institution required; all applicants have bachelor's degree awarded prior to enrollment. For serious consideration an applicant should have a 3.1 (A = 4) in both sciences and overall GPA. *Has EDP*; applicants must apply through AACOMAS (official transcripts sent by mid-May) between June 1 and July 15. Submit supplemental application, a personal statement, and 2 recommendations to Admissions Office within 2 weeks of receipt of application. Interviews are by invitation only and generally for final selection. Notification normally in October. *Regular application process.* Apply through AACOMAS (file after June 1, before February 1); submit MCAT (will accept test results from last 3 years), official transcripts for each school attended (should show at least 90 semester credits/135 quarter credits), service processing fee. After a review of the AACOMAS application and supporting documents, a decision is made concerning which candidates should receive supplemental materials. The supplemental application, an application fee of $50, a personal statement, and 3 recommendations (1 from a D.O.) should be returned to Admissions Office as soon as possible, but not later than March 1. For dual-degree programs students generally apply during their first year of medical school. Interviews are by invitation only and generally for final selection. First-year students admitted in fall only. Rolling admission process. Notification starts in October and is finished when class is filled. Applicant's response to offer and $500 deposit due within 2 weeks of receipt of acceptance letter. School does maintain an alternate list. Phone: (215)871-6719, (800)999-6998; fax: (215)871-6719; E-mail: admissions@pcom.edu.

ADMISSION REQUIREMENTS FOR TRANSFER APPLICANTS. Does not accept transfer applicants. Contact the Admissions Offices for current information and any change in policy.

ADMISSION STANDARDS AND RECOGNITION. *For D.O.:* number of applicants 5,846; number enrolled 205; median MCAT 8.2; median GPA 3.4; the school's ranking by NIH awards/grants was 8th among osteopathic schools, with 1 award/grant received; a total value of all awards/grants was $86,333.

FINANCIAL AID. Scholarships, merit scholarships, minority scholarships, grants-in-aid, institutional loans, NOF, HEAL, alternative loan programs, federal Perkins loans, Stafford subsidized and unsubsidized loans, service obligation scholarship programs, and armed forces and National Health Service programs are available. After acceptance offer is received, contact the Student Financial Aid Office for current information; phone: (215)871-6170; E-mail: em.fin_aid@pcom.edu. For most financial assistance and all federal programs, submit FAFSA to a federal processor (Title IV school code #015979); also submit Financial Aid Transcript and Federal Income Tax forms. Approximately 90% of current students receive some form of financial assistance. Average debt after graduation $119,000.

DEGREE REQUIREMENTS. *For D.O.:* satisfactory completion of 4-year program. All students must pass the National Board of Osteopathic Medical Examination Level I and take Part II. *For D.O.-M.B.A.- M.P.H.:* generally 5-year programs.

PIKEVILLE COLLEGE SCHOOL OF OSTEOPATHIC MEDICINE
241 Sycamore Street
Pikeville, Kentucky 41501
Phone: (606)432-9640
Internet site: http://www.pc.edu/som
E-mail: spayson@pc.edu

Received accreditation in 1997; 1st class will enter in 1999. Located in eastern Kentucky in the Appalachian region. Private control. Semester system.

Annual tuition: $22,000. No on-campus housing available at this time. Contact the Student Affairs Office for housing information. Off-campus housing and personal expenses: approximately $13,000–$16,000.

Enrollment: 1st-year class 60. First-year statistics: N/A.

Degree conferred: D.O.

RECRUITMENT PRACTICES AND POLICIES. School has diversity program and actively recruits women/minority applicants. Diversity contact: Student Affairs Office.

ADMISSION REQUIREMENTS FOR FIRST-YEAR APPLICANTS. Preference given to residents of the Appalachian region; U.S. citizens and permanent residents only. *Undergraduate preparation.* Suggested premed courses: 3 courses in biology, 2 courses in general chemistry, 2 courses in organic chemistry, 2 courses in physics, 2 courses in English. Bachelor's degree from an accredited institution required; all applicants will have bachelor's degrees awarded prior to enrollment. *Application process.* Apply through AACOMAS (file after June 1, before December 1); submit MCAT (will accept test results from last 5 years), official transcripts for each school attended (should show at least 90 semester credits/135 quarter credits), service processing fee. After a review of the AACOMAS application and supporting documents, a decision is made concerning which candidates should receive supplemental materials. The supplemental application, an application fee of $75, a personal statement, and 3 recommendations (1 from a D.O.) should be returned to Admissions Office as soon as possible. Interviews are by invitation only and generally for final selection. First-year students admitted in fall only. Rolling admission process. Notification starts in December and is finished when class is filled. Applicant's response to offer and $100 deposit due within 2 weeks of receipt of acceptance letter. Phone: (606)432-9639; E-mail: spayson@pc.edu.

ADMISSION REQUIREMENTS FOR TRANSFER APPLICANTS. Accepts transfers from other accredited U.S. osteopathic medical schools. Contact Admissions Offices for current information and specific requirements for admission.

ADMISSION STANDARDS AND RECOGNITION. *For D.O.:* number of applicants N/A; number enrolled N/A.

FINANCIAL AID. Scholarships, grants, institutional loans, NOF, HEAL, alternative loan programs, federal Perkins loans, Stafford subsidized and unsubsidized loans, service obligation scholarship programs, and military and National Health Service programs are available. Contact the Financial Aid Office for current information; phone: (606)437-3461. For most financial assistance and all federal programs, submit FAFSA to a federal processor (Title IV school code # 001980); also submit Financial Aid Transcript and Federal Income Tax forms.

DEGREE REQUIREMENTS. *For D.O.:* satisfactory completion of 4-year program. All students will have to take the National Board of Osteopathic Medical Examination Level I and II prior to the awarding of D.O.

UNIVERSITY OF PITTSBURGH

Pittsburgh, Pennsylvania 15261
Internet site: http://www.pitt.edu

Founded 1787. Located 3 miles from downtown Pittsburgh. Public control. Trimester system. Library: 3,296,000 volumes; 3,312,000 microforms; 23,290 periodicals/subscriptions. The university's ranking in domestic higher education by NIH awards/grants was 13th, with 558 awards/grants received; total dollars awarded $151,872,229.

The university's graduate colleges/schools: Center for Neuroscience, Faculty of Arts and Science, Graduate School of Public and International Affairs, Graduate School of Public Health, Joseph M. Katz Graduate School of Business, School of Dental Medicine, School of Education, School of Engineering, School of Health and Rehabilitation Science, School of Information Sciences, School of Law, School of Medicine, School of Nursing, School of Pharmacy, School of Social Work.

Total university enrollment at main campus: 26,100.

University of Pittsburgh Medical Center

200 Lothrop Street
Pittsburgh, Pennsylvania 15213

Public control. The medical center is a member of the Council of Teaching Hospitals. School of Medicine is located at medical center. Special facilities: hospitals located at medical center; Montefiore University Hospital, Presbyterian University Hospital, Western Psychiatric Institute and Clinic, Pillsbury Cancer Institute, Benedum Geriatric Center. Nationally recognized programs in Gastroenterology, Neurology, Orthopedics, Otolaryngology, Pulmonary Disease, Rheumatology.

School of Medicine

518 Scaife Hall
Pittsburgh, Pennsylvania 15261
Phone: (412)648-9891; fax: (412)648-8768
Internet site: http://www.omed.pitt.edu
E-mail: admissions@fsl.dean-med.pitt.edu

Established 1886 as Western Pennsylvania Medical College; began association with University of Pittsburgh in 1908. Located in Oakland district of Pittsburgh. Semester system. Library: 220,000 volumes/microforms; 5,000 current periodicals/subscriptions. Affiliated hospitals: Children's Hospital of Pittsburgh, Magee-Women's Hospital, Veterans Affairs Medical Center, Terrace Village Health Center. Special programs: Cancer Research, Gene Therapy, Tissue Engineering, Neuroscience.

Annual tuition: residents $20,190, nonresidents $27,102. No on-campus housing available. Contact Admissions Office for off-campus housing information. Off-campus housing and personal expenses: approximately $11,790.

Enrollment: 1st-year class 146 (EDP 4); total full-time 573 (men 53%, women 47%). First-year statistics: 40% out of state; 41.8% women; average age 25; 61% science majors.

Degrees conferred: M.D., M.D.-Ph.D. (Biochemistry and Molecular Genetics, Biomedical Engineering, Biophysics, Cell Biology and Physiology, Cellular and Molecular Pathology, Immunology, Molecular Virology and

Microbiology, Neurosciences, Pharmacology); has M.S.T.P.

RECRUITMENT PRACTICES AND POLICIES. School has diversity program and actively recruits women/minority applicants. Diversity contact: Director, Minority Program; phone: (412)648-8987.

ADMISSION REQUIREMENTS FOR FIRST-YEAR APPLICANTS. Preference given to state residents; U.S. citizens and permanent residents only. *Undergraduate preparation.* Suggested premed courses: 2 courses in biology with labs, 2 courses in inorganic chemistry with labs, 2 courses in organic chemistry with labs, 2 courses in physics with labs, 2 courses in English; a strong background in mathematics is strongly recommended. Bachelor's degree from an accredited institution required; all applicants have bachelor's degree awarded prior to enrollment. *Has EDP*; applicants must apply through AMCAS (official transcripts sent by mid-May) between June 1 and August 1. Early applications are encouraged. Submit secondary/supplemental application, a personal statement, and 2 recommendations to Admissions Office within 2 weeks of receipt of application. Interviews are by invitation only and generally for final selection. Notification normally begins October 1. *Regular application process.* Apply through AMCAS (file after June 1, before November 1); submit MCAT (will accept MCAT test results from the last 3 years), official transcripts for each school attended (should show at least 90 semester credits/135 quarter credits, submit transcripts by mid-May to AMCAS), service processing fee. An application for M.D.-Ph.D. program is included in each supplemental packet. Submit an application fee of $60, a supplemental application, a brief personal essay, preprofessional committee evaluation and 3 recommendations from science faculty, and M.D.-Ph.D. application to Admissions Office within 2–3 weeks of the receipt of supplemental materials, not later then December 12. Interviews are by invitation only and generally for final selection. M.D.-Ph.D. degree applicants should contact the Admissions Office or the M.D.-Ph.D. Program Office (phone: (415)648-9891) for current information and specific requirements for admission. First-year students admitted in fall only. Rolling admission process. Notification starts October 15 and is finished when class is filled. Applicant's response to offer and $100 deposit due within 2 weeks of receipt of acceptance letter. School does maintain an alternate list. Phone: (412)648-9891; E-mail: admissions@fsl.deanmed.pitt.edu.

ADMISSION REQUIREMENTS FOR TRANSFER APPLICANTS. Accepts transfers from other accredited U.S. medical schools into the 3rd year only. Admission limited to space available. Contact the Admissions Office for current information and specific requirements for admission.

ADMISSION STANDARDS AND RECOGNITION. *For M.D.:* number of state-resident applicants 1,210, nonresidents 4,694; number of state residents interviewed 287, nonresidents 469; number of residents enrolled 91, nonresidents 55; median MCAT 10.7 (verbal reasoning 10.5; biological sciences 10.9; physical sciences 10.6); median GPA 3.61 (A = 4). Gorman rating 4.30 (scale: strong 4.01–4.49); *U.S. News & World Report* ranked the school in the Top 25 of all U.S. medical schools; the school's medical ranking by NIH awards/grants was 13th, with 401 awards/grants received; total dollars awarded $108,218,209.

FINANCIAL AID. Scholarships, merit scholarships, minority scholarships, grants-in-aid, institutional loans, HEAL, alternative loan programs, NIH stipends, federal Perkins loans, Stafford subsidized and unsubsidized, and service commitment scholarship programs are available. Assistantships/fellowships may be available for M.D.-Ph.D. degree candidates. All financial aid is based on demonstrated need. Financial aid applications and information are generally available at the on-campus interview (by invitation). For scholarship assistance, the selection criteria place heavy reliance on MCAT and undergraduate GPA. Apply by February 15 (priority deadline). The first $8,500 of all packages is federal Stafford student loans. Contact the Office of Financial Aid for current information; phone: (415)648-8936. For most financial assistance and all federal programs, submit FAFSA to a federal processor (Title IV school code # E00516); also submit Financial Aid Transcript and Federal Income Tax forms; supplemental information must reach the Office of Financial Aid not later than April 1. Approximately 80% of current students receive some form of financial assistance. Average debt after graduation $90,300.

DEGREE REQUIREMENTS. *For M.D.:* satisfactory completion of 4-year program. All students must pass USMLE Step 1 prior to entering 3rd year; all students must pass USMLE Step 2 prior to awarding of M.D. *For M.D.-Ph.D.:* generally a 7-year program.

School of Dental Medicine
3501 Terrace Street, Room 216
Pittsburgh, Pennsylvania 15231-1945
Phone: (415)648-8424; fax: (412)648-9871
Internet site: http://www.pitt.edu/~pittdent
E-mail: dentadmn@vms.cis.pitt.edu

Established 1896. Special programs: Research Fellowships, Externships. Postgraduate specialties: Dental Anesthesiology, Endodontics, General Dentistry, Oral and Maxillofacial Surgery, Orthodontics, Periodontics, Maxillofacial Prosthodontics.

Annual tuition: residents $17,630, nonresidents $25,400; fees $610; equipment and supplies $3,990. On-campus housing available for both single and married students. Contact Office of Student Services for both on- and off-campus housing information; phone: (412)648-8422. Dental students tend to live off-campus. Off-campus housing, food, transportation, and personal expenses: approximately $12,000.

Enrollment: 1st-year class 81; total full-time 235. First-year enrolled student information: 23 from out of state; 12 states and 1 foreign country represented; 31 women; average age 24; 4 underrepresented minorities; 10 other minorities.

Degree conferred: D.M.D.

RECRUITMENT PRACTICES AND POLICIES. School has diversity program and actively recruits women/minority applicants. Diversity contact: Office of Minority Programs; phone: (412)648-7860.

ADMISSION REQUIREMENTS FOR FIRST-YEAR APPLICANTS. Preference given to state residents; U.S. citizens and permanent residents only. *Undergraduate preparation.* Suggested predental courses: 2 courses in biology with labs, 2 courses in inorganic chemistry with labs, 2 courses in organic chemistry with labs, 2 courses in physics with labs, 2 courses in English, 10 courses in nonsciences. Will consider applicants with only 3 years of undergraduate preparation; prefer applicants who have completed most of their required courses in a 4-year institution and will have bachelor's degree prior to enrollment. For serious consideration an applicant should have at least a 3.0 (A = 4) GPA; 75 out of 81 enrolled first-year students have their bachelor's degrees awarded prior to enrollment. *Application process.* Apply through AADSAS (file after August 1, before February 1); submit official transcripts for each school attended (should show at least 90 semester credits/135 quarter credits), service processing fee; at the same time as you send in AADSAS materials, submit an application fee of $35 ($50 for international applicants) and predental committee evaluation (preferred) or 3 recommendations from science professors to Office of Student Services. Interviews are by invitation only and generally for final selection. First-year students admitted in fall only. Rolling admission process. Notification starts December 1 and is finished when class is filled, but generally not later than August 1. Applicant's response to offer and $500 deposit due within 15 days of the receipt of acceptance offer. School does maintain an alternate list. Phone: (412)648-8437; E-mail: dentadmn @vms.cis.pitt.edu.

ADMISSION REQUIREMENTS FOR ADVANCED-STANDING APPLICANTS. Accepts transfers from other accredited U.S. dental schools. Admission limited to space available. There is no advanced-standing program for graduates of foreign schools of dentistry. Contact the Office of Student Services for current information and specific requirements.

ADMISSION STANDARDS AND RECOGNITION. *For D.M.D.:* number of applicants 1,576; number enrolled 81; median DAT: ACAD 17.0, PAT 16.0; median GPA 3.18 (A = 4), median sciences GPA 3.07 (A = 4). Gorman rating 4.55 (scale: very strong 4.51–4.99); this placed the school in the Top 15 of all U.S. dental schools; the dental school's ranking by NIH awards/grants was 24th among dental schools, with 7 awards/grants received; total value of all awards/grants $1,179,519.

FINANCIAL AID. Scholarships, institutional loans, state loan programs, DEAL, HEAL, alternative loan programs, federal Perkins loans, Stafford subsidized and unsubsidized loans, and military service commitment scholarship programs are available. Institutional financial-aid applications and information are generally available at the on-campus interview (by invitation). Contact the Office of Student Services for current information; phone: (412)624-7129. For most financial assistance and all need-based programs, submit FAFSA to a federal processor (Title IV school code # E00750); also submit Financial Aid Transcript, Federal Income Tax forms, and Use of Federal Funds Certification; all financial aid information must reach the Office of Student Services not later than April 1. Approximately 93% of current students receive some form of financial assistance. Average award for residents $30,000, nonresidents $37,000.

DEGREE REQUIREMENTS. *For D.M.D.:* satisfactory completion of 4-year program.

PONCE SCHOOL OF MEDICINE
P.O. Box 7004
Ponce, Puerto Rico 00732-7004
Phone: (787)840-2511, (787)844-3685

Formerly Catholic University of Puerto Rico, School of Medicine; reorganized 1980. Graduated 1st class in

1981. Private control. Semester system. Library: 23,700 volumes; 12,915 microforms; 302 periodicals/subscriptions; 8 work stations. Special facility: Research Center in Minority Institutions.

Annual tuition: $18,784; fees $1,844.80. No on-campus housing available. Contact Admissions Office for off-campus housing information. Off-campus housing and personal expenses: approximately $15,975.

Enrollment: 1st-year class 60 (EDP 3); total full-time 257 (men 58%, women 42%). First-year statistics: 25% from outside Puerto Rico; 44% women; average age 25; 100% minorities; 62% science majors.

Degree conferred: M.D.

Faculty: full-time 49, part-time 50.

ADMISSION REQUIREMENTS FOR FIRST-YEAR APPLICANTS. Preference given to residents of Puerto Rico; a limited number of applicants from mainland are accepted; U.S. citizens and permanent residents only. *Undergraduate preparation.* Suggested premed courses: 2 courses in biology with labs, 2 courses in inorganic chemistry with labs, 2 courses in organic chemistry with labs, 2 courses in physics with labs, 3 courses in college math, 2 courses in English, 2 courses in Spanish language. Bachelor's degree from an accredited institution required; 89% of applicants have bachelor's degrees awarded prior to enrollment. *Has EDP* for residents of Puerto Rico only; applicants must apply through AMCAS (official transcripts sent by mid-May) between June 1 and August 1. Early applications are encouraged. Submit supplemental application, a personal statement, and 2 recommendations to Admissions Office within 2 weeks of receipt of application. Interviews are by invitation only and generally for final selection. Notification normally begins October 1. *Regular application process.* Apply through AMCAS (file after June 1, before December 15); submit MCAT (will accept MCAT test results from the last 3 years), official transcripts for each school attended (should show at least 90 semester credits/135 quarter credits, submit transcripts by mid-May to AMCAS), service processing fee. Submit an application fee of $50, a supplemental application, a personal statement, preprofessional committee evaluation, and 3 recommendations from science faculty to Admissions Office within 2–3 weeks of the receipt of supplemental materials. Interviews are by invitation only and generally for final selection. First-year students admitted in fall only. Rolling admission process. Notification starts in October and is finished when class is filled. Applicant's response to offer and $1,000 deposit due within 20 working days of receipt of acceptance letter. School does maintain an alternate list. Phone: (787)840-2511, (787)844-3685.

ADMISSION REQUIREMENTS FOR TRANSFER APPLICANTS. Accepts transfers from other accredited U.S. medical schools. Admission limited to space available. Contact Admissions Office for current information and specific requirements for admission.

ADMISSION STANDARDS AND RECOGNITION. *For M.D.:* number of applications from residents of Puerto Rico 367, nonresidents 620; number of residents interviewed 162, nonresidents 35; number of residents enrolled 47, nonresidents 14; median MCAT N/A, median GPA 3.31. Gorman rating 3.04 (scale: acceptable plus 3.01–3.59); school's medical ranking by NIH awards/grants was 104th, with 6 awards/grants received; total dollars awarded $3,626,408.

FINANCIAL AID. Scholarships, grants-in-aid, institutional loans, HEAL, alternative loan programs, federal Perkins loans, Stafford subsidized and unsubsidized loans, and service commitment scholarship programs are available. Financial aid applications and information are mailed in February; awards are mailed in July. All financial aid is based on demonstrated need. Contact the Financial Aid Office for current information; phone: (787)840-2511. For most financial assistance and all federal programs, submit FAFSA to a federal processor (Title IV school code # 024824); also submit Financial Aid Transcript and Federal Income Tax forms. Approximately 85% of current students receive some form of financial assistance. Average debt after graduation $27,200.

DEGREE REQUIREMENTS. *For M.D.:* satisfactory completion of 4-year program. All students must pass USMLE Step 1 prior to entering 3rd year.

UNIVERSITY OF PUERTO RICO, RIO PIEDRAS

Rio Piedras, Puerto Rico 00931

Founded 1903. Located 8 miles S of San Juan. Public control. Semester system. Library: 4,100,000 volumes; 1,637,800 microforms; 4,966 periodicals/subscriptions. The university's ranking in domestic higher education by NIH awards/grants was 92nd, with 43 awards/grants received; total dollars awarded $19,315,835.

The university's other graduate colleges/schools: College of Education, College of Humanities, College of Social Sciences, Faculty of Natural Science, Graduate School of Business Administration, Graduate School of Librarianship, School of Architecture, School of Law, School of Public Communication.

Total university enrollment at main campus: 20,000.

Medical Sciences Campus
San Juan, Puerto Rico, 00936

Public control. Schools located at Medical Sciences Campus are: College of Allied Health Professions, Faculty of Biosocial Sciences, Graduate School of Public Health, School of Dentistry, School of Medicine, School of Nursing, School of Pharmacy. Total enrollment on campus: 2,700. Special facilities: Caribbean Primate Research Center, Puerto Rican Cancer Center, Plasmapheresis Unit, Center for Energy and Environment Research, Clinical Research Center.

School of Medicine
P.O. Box 365067
San Juan, Puerto Rico 00936-5067
Phone: (787)758-2525, X5213; fax: (787)282-7117
Internet site: http://www.upr.clu.edu
E-mail: R_aponte@rcnad.upr.clu.edu

Established 1949. Semester system. Library: 42,000 volumes/microforms; 1,600 current periodicals/subscriptions. Affiliated hospitals: Puerto Rico Medical Center, Hospital Consortium, University District Hospital.

Annual tuition: residents $5,500, nonresidents $10,500; fees, $686. No on-campus housing available. Contact Admissions Office for off-campus housing information. Off-campus housing and personal expenses: approximately $15,000.

Enrollment: 1st-year class 115; total full-time 439 (men 50%, women 50%). First-year statistics: 3% from outside Puerto Rico; 50% women; average age 24; 100% minorities.

Faculty: full-time 330; part-time/volunteers 150.

Degrees conferred: M.D., M.D.-M.P.H., M.D.-M.S., M.D.-Ph.D. (Anatomy, Biochemistry, Microbiology, Pharmacology, Physiology).

RECRUITMENT PRACTICES AND POLICIES. School has diversity program and actively recruits women/minority applicants. Diversity contact: Associate Director, Hispanic Center of Excellence; phone: (787)758-2525, X1810.

ADMISSION REQUIREMENTS FOR FIRST-YEAR APPLICANTS. Preference given to state residents; U.S. citizens and permanent residents only. *Undergraduate preparation.* Suggested premed courses: 2 courses in biology with labs, 2 courses in inorganic chemistry with labs, 2 courses in organic chemistry with labs, 2 courses in physics with labs, 3 courses in English, 3 courses in Spanish, 2 courses in behavioral and social sciences. Bachelor's degree from an accredited institution re-

quired; 70% of applicants have bachelor's degrees awarded prior to enrollment. Does not have EDP. *Application process.* Apply through AMCAS (file after June 1, before December 1); submit MCAT (will accept MCAT test results from last 3 years), official transcripts for each school attended (should show at least 90 semester credits/135 quarter credits, submit transcripts by mid-May to AMCAS), service processing fee. Submit an application fee of $15, a supplemental application, a personal statement, preprofessional committee evaluation, and 3 recommendations from science faculty to Admissions Office within 2–3 weeks of receipt of supplemental materials. Interviews are by invitation only and generally for final selection. Dual-degree applicants must apply to, and be accepted by, both schools/programs; contact the Admissions Office for current information and specific requirements for admission. First-year students admitted in fall only. Rolling admission process. Notification starts February 15 and is finished when class is filled. Applicant's response to offer and $100 deposit due within 15 days of receipt of acceptance letter. School does maintain an alternate list. Phone: (787)758-2525, X5213.

ADMISSION REQUIREMENTS FOR TRANSFER APPLICANTS. Accepts transfers from other accredited U.S. medical schools into the 3rd year only. Admission limited to space available. Contact the Admissions Office for current information and specific requirements.

ADMISSION STANDARDS AND RECOGNITION. *For M.D.:* number of applications from residents of Puerto Rico 360, nonresidents 595; number of residents interviewed 170, nonresidents 5; number of residents enrolled 112, nonresidents 3; median MCAT 7.3 (verbal reasoning 7.0; biological sciences 8.0; physical sciences 7.0); median GPA 3.59 (A = 4). Gorman rating 3.22 (scale: acceptable plus 3.01–3.59); the school's medical ranking by NIH awards/grants was 92nd, with 20 awards/grants received; total dollars awarded $8,191,366.

FINANCIAL AID. Scholarships, grants-in-aid, institutional loans, HEAL, alternative loan programs, NIH stipends, federal Perkins loans, Stafford subsidized and unsubsidized loans, and service commitment scholarship programs are available. Assistantships/fellowships may be available for dual-degree candidates. Most financial aid is based on demonstrated need. Financial aid applications and/or information are generally available at the on-campus interview (by invitation). For scholarships, the selection criteria place heavy reliance on MCAT and undergraduate GPA. Contact the Financial

Aid Office for current information; phone: (787)758-2525. For most financial assistance and all federal programs, submit FAFSA to a federal processor (Title IV school code # 003945); also submit Financial Aid Transcript and Federal Income Tax forms. Approximately 85% of current students receive some form of financial assistance.

DEGREE REQUIREMENTS. *For M.D.:* satisfactory completion of 4-year program. *For M.D.-M.S., M.P.H.:* generally a 4½–5½-year program. *For M.D.-Ph.D.:* generally a 7-year program.

School of Dentistry
P.O. Box 365067, Room 201
San Juan, Puerto Rico 00936-5067
Phone: (787)758-2525, X1113; fax: (787)282-7117
Internet site: http://www.upr.edu
E-mail: N_madera@rcmad.upr.clu.edu

Established 1956. Located at the Medical Sciences Campus. Postgraduate specialties: General Dentistry, Oral and Maxillofacial Surgery, Orthodontics, Pediatric Dentistry, Prosthodontics.

Annual tuition: $5,000; fees $105; equipment and supplies $6,265. No on-campus housing available. Contact Admissions Office for off-campus housing information. Off-campus housing, food, transportation, and personal expenses: approximately $15,000.

Enrollment: 1st-year class 45; total full-time 192. First-year enrolled student information: none from outside Puerto Rico; 25 women; average age 23; 45 are minorities.

Faculty: full-time 68, part-time/volunteers 21.

Degree conferred: D.M.D.

ADMISSION REQUIREMENTS FOR FIRST-YEAR APPLICANTS. Limited to residents of Puerto Rico only; U.S. citizens and permanent residents only. *Undergraduate preparation.* Suggested predental courses: 2 courses in biology with labs, 2 courses in general chemistry with labs, 2 courses in organic chemistry with labs, 2 courses in physics with labs, 4 courses in English, 4 courses in Spanish, 2 courses in social and behavioral sciences. The junior-college transfer credit limit is 60 credits. Will consider applicants with only 2 years of undergraduate preparation; prefer applicants who will have completed 3 years of predental courses prior to enrollment; 35 out of 45 enrolled 1st-year students have bachelor's degree awarded prior to enrollment. *Application process.* Apply through AADSAS (file after June 31, before December 15); submit official transcripts for each school attended (should show at least 90 semester cred-

its/135 quarter credits), service processing fee; at the same time as you send in AADSAS materials, submit official DAT scores, an application fee of $15, official transcripts, predental committee evaluation or 3 recommendations from science professors, and photograph directly to Admissions Office; phone: (787)758-2525, X1113; E-mail: N_madera@rcmad.upr.clu.edu. Interviews are by invitation only and generally for final selection. First-year students admitted in fall only. Rolling admission process. Notification starts in December and is finished when class is filled. Applicant's response to offer and $100 deposit due within 15 days of the receipt of the offer of admission.

ADMISSION REQUIREMENTS FOR ADVANCED-STANDING APPLICANTS. Accepts transfers from other accredited U.S. dental schools. Admission limited to space available. There is no advanced-standing program for graduates of foreign schools of dentistry. Contact the Admissions Office for current information and specific requirements for admission.

ADMISSION STANDARDS AND RECOGNITION. *For D.M.D.:* number of applications from residents of Puerto Rico 107, nonresidents 163; number of residents enrolled 45, nonresidents none; median DAT: ACAD 16.0, PAT 16.0; median GPA 3.29 (A = 4), median sciences GPA 3.12 (A = 4). Gorman rating 4.03 (scale: strong 4.01–4.49); this placed the school in the Bottom 10 of all U.S. dental schools; the dental school's ranking by NIH awards/grants was 41st among dental schools, with 1 award/grant received; total value of all awards/grants $50,223.

FINANCIAL AID. P.R. government scholarships, grants, institutional loans, state loan programs, DEAL, HEAL, alternative loan programs, federal Perkins loans, Stafford subsidized and unsubsidized loans, and military service commitment scholarship programs are available. Institutional financial aid applications and/or information are given out at the on-campus interview (by invitation). Contact the Office of Financial Aid for current information; phone: (787)758-2525. For most financial assistance and all need-based programs, submit FAFSA to a federal processor (Title IV school code # 003945); also submit Financial Aid Transcript, Federal Income Tax forms, and Use of Federal Funds Certification. 100% of current students receive some form of financial assistance.

DEGREE REQUIREMENTS. *For D.M.D.:* satisfactory completion of 4-year program.

UNIVERSITY OF ROCHESTER
Rochester, New York 14627-0416
Internet site: http://www.rochester.edu

Founded 1850. Located on the Genessee River. Private control. Semester system. Library: 2,882,000 volumes; 3,649,451 microforms; 11,460 periodicals/subscriptions; 141 PC work stations. Special facilities: Center for Advanced Technology, Center for Electronic Imaging Systems, Center for Environmental Health Sciences, Center for Visual Science, Community Centered Practice, Rochester Center for Biomedical Ultrasound. Special programs: B.A./B.S.-M.D. program (annual undergraduate tuition $19,630). The university's ranking in domestic higher education by NIH awards/grants was 31st, with 329 awards/grants received; total dollars awarded $80,519,231.

The university's graduate colleges/schools include: College of Arts and Sciences, Eastman School of Music (Downtown Rochester), Margaret Warner Graduate School of Education and Human Development, School of Medicine and Dentistry, School of Nursing, William E. Simon Graduate School of Business Administration.

Total university enrollment at main campus: 8,760.

University of Rochester Medical Center
601 Elmwood Avenue
Rochester, New York 14642
Internet site: http://www.urmc.rochester.edu

Private control. Strong Memorial Hospital is a member of the Council of Teaching Hospitals. Schools located at medical center are: School of Medicine and Dentistry, School of Nursing. Special facilities: AIDS Research and Treatment Facility, Bone Marrow Transplantation Center, Clinical Research Center, University of Rochester Cancer Center. Nationally recognized programs: Neurology, Urology.

School of Medicine and Dentistry
Medical Center Box 601
Rochester, New York 14642
Phone: (716)275-4539; fax: (716)273-1016
Internet site: http://www.urmc.rochester.edu
E-mail: admish@urmc.rochester.edu

Established 1920. Located at the medical center. The school's curriculum is interdisciplinary and integrated. Library: 200,000 volumes/microforms; 3,000 current periodicals/subscriptions. Affiliated hospital: Strong Memorial Hospital. Special programs: Summer programs for underrepresented minorities; International Medicine Program.

Annual tuition: $26,835; fees $1,780. No on-campus housing available. Apartment living is available near the medical center. Contact Admissions Office for off-campus housing information. Off-campus housing and personal expenses: approximately $13,300 (12 months), $11,300 (10 months).

Enrollment: 1st-year class 100; total full-time 397 (men 55%, women 45%). First-year statistics: 60% out of state; 25 states represented; 38.4% women; average age 24; 63% science majors.

Faculty: full- and part-time 535.

Degrees conferred: M.D., baccalaureate-M.D. (Rochester Early Medical Scholars, REMS), M.D.-M.B.A., M.D.-M.P.H., M.D.-M.S., M.D.-Ph.D. (Biochemistry, Biophysics, Genetics, Immunology, Microbiology, Molecular Biology, Neurobiology and Anatomy, Pathology, Molecular Pharmacology and Physiology); has M.S.T.P.

RECRUITMENT PRACTICES AND POLICIES. School has diversity program and actively recruits women/minority applicants. Diversity contact: Associate Dean for Minority Affairs; phone: (716)275-2842.

ADMISSION REQUIREMENT FOR BACCALAUREATE (REMS)-M.D. APPLICANTS. Recommended high school requirements: 4 years of English, 4 years of mathematics, 1 year each of chemistry, physics, biology, 2 years of foreign language, 4 years of social studies. Submit application, an application fee of $50, SAT I or ACT, plus Achievements in Mathematics Level II, Chemistry, Writing, official high school transcript with rank in class, 3 letters of recommendation to Office of Undergraduate Admission after October 15, before December 20; phone: (716)275-3221. For financial aid information, contact the Undergraduate Office of Financial Aid; phone; (716)275-3226. Interviews are by invitation only and generally for final selection. Notification April 1–15. Applicant's response to offer and $400 deposit returned by May 1.

ADMISSION REQUIREMENTS FOR FIRST-YEAR APPLICANTS. Preference given to U.S. citizens and permanent residents only. *Undergraduate preparation.* Suggested premed courses: 2 courses in biology with labs, 2 courses in inorganic chemistry with labs, 2 courses in organic chemistry with labs, 2 courses in physics with labs, 2 courses in English, 4–6 courses in humanities, social or behavioral sciences. Bachelor's degree from an accredited institution required; all applicants have bachelor's degree awarded prior to enrollment. Does not have EDP. *Application process.* Apply through AMCAS (file after June 1, before October 15); submit MCAT (will accept MCAT test results from the last 3 years), official transcripts for each school attended (should show at least 90 semester credits/135 quarter credits, submit transcripts by mid-May to AMCAS), service processing fee. Submit an application fee of $70, a supplemental application, a personal statement, preprofessional committee evaluation, and 3 recommendations from science faculty to Admissions Office within 2–3 weeks of the receipt of supplemental materials, but not later than December 1. Deadline for M.D.-Ph.D. program is November 15. Interviews are by invitation only and generally for final selection. Dual-degree applicants must apply to, and be accepted by, both schools; contact the Admissions Office for current information and specific requirements for admission. First-year students admitted in fall only. Rolling admission process. Notification starts November 1 and is finished when class is filled. Applicant's response to offer and $100 deposit due within 2 weeks of receipt of acceptance letter. School does maintain an alternate list. Phone: (716)275-4542.

ADMISSION REQUIREMENTS FOR TRANSFER APPLICANTS. Accepts transfers from other accredited U.S. and Canadian medical schools with a compelling reason. Admission limited to space available. Contact the Admissions Office after February 1 for current information and specific requirements for admission.

ADMISSION STANDARDS AND RECOGNITION. *For baccalaureate-M.D.:* number of state-resident applicants 308, nonresidents 484; number of state residents interviewed 14, nonresidents 25; number of residents enrolled 4, nonresidents 6; median SATV 720, SATM 760. *For M.D.:* number of state-resident applicants 1,112, nonresidents 2,977; number of state residents interviewed 187, nonresidents 431; number of residents enrolled 38, nonresidents 61; median MCAT 10.0 (verbal reasoning 9.3; biological sciences 10.3; physical sciences 10.4); median GPA 3.6 (A = 4). Gorman rating 4.68 (scale: very strong 4.51–4.99); *U.S. News & World Report* ranked the school in the Top 25 of all U.S. medical schools in primary-care preparation; medical school's ranking by NIH awards was 26th, with 269 awards/grants received; total dollars awarded $70,474,469.

FINANCIAL AID. Scholarships, merit scholarships, minority scholarships, grants-in-aid, institutional loans, HEAL, alternative loan programs, NIH stipends, federal Perkins loans, Stafford subsidized and unsubsidized loans, and service commitment scholarship programs are available. Assistantships/fellowships may be available for dual-degree candidates. Financial-aid applications and information are generally available at the on-campus interview (by invitation); applications should be returned not later than April 15 for serious consideration. All financial aid is based on demonstrated need. All financial aid packages begin with the Stafford loan programs as the base award. For scholarships, the selection criteria place heavy reliance on MCAT and undergraduate GPA. Contact the Financial Aid Office for current information; phone: (716)275-4523; E-mail: finaid@urms.rochester.edu. For most financial assistance and all federal programs, submit FAFSA to a federal processor (Title IV school code # G24601); also submit Financial Aid Transcript, Federal Income Tax forms, and NEED ACCESS financial statement. Approximately 80% of current students receive some form of financial assistance. Average debt after graduation $81,200.

DEGREE REQUIREMENTS. For baccalaureate-M.D. (REMS): an 8-year program. *For M.D.:* satisfactory completion of 4-year program. *For M.D.-M.B.A.:* generally a 5–5½-year program. *For M.D.-M.S., M.P.H.:* generally a 4½–5½-year program. *For M.D.-Ph.D., M.S.T.P.:* generally a 7-year program.

RUSH UNIVERSITY
Chicago, Illinois 60612-3832
Internet site: http://www.rushu.rush.edu

Private control. Library: 596,600 volumes/microforms; 2,147 periodicals/subscriptions. Special facilities: Computer Research Institute, Comparative Research Center, Electron Microscope.

The university's colleges/schools are: College of Health Sciences, College Nursing, Graduate College, Rush Medical College.

Total university enrollment at main campus: 1,477.

Rush–Presbyterian–St. Luke's Medical Center
1653 West Congress Parkway
Chicago, Illinois 60612
Phone: (312)942-5000
Internet site: http://www.rpslmc.edu

Private control. Rush–Presbyterian–St. Luke's Medical Center is a member of the Council of Teaching Hospitals. The university is located at the medical center. Special facility: Johnston R. Bowman Health Center for the Elderly. Nationally recognized programs in AIDS, Cancer, Cardiology, Gastroenterology, Geriatrics, Gynecology, Orthopedics, Otolaryngology, Pulmonary Disease.

Rush Medical College

524 Academic Facility
600 South Paulina Street
Chicago, Illinois 60612
Phone: (312)942-6913; fax: (312)942-2333
Internet site: http://www.rushu.rush.edu
E-mail: medical@rush.edu

Established 1837; closed in 1942. Reopened in 1971 and merged with Presbyterian–St. Luke's Medical Center. Located on the university's campus. Semester system; traditional 4-year curriculum. Library: 97,000 volumes/microforms; 2,050 current periodicals/subscriptions. Affiliated hospitals: Holy Family Medical Center, Illinois Masonic Medical Center, Lake Forest Hospital, Oak Park Hospital, Riverside Medical Center, Rush-Copley Medical Center, Rush North Shore Medical Center, Westlake Community Hospital, Johnston R. Bowman Health Center for the Elderly. Special programs: primary-care preceptorships.

Annual tuition: $25,825; fees $1,600. On-campus rooms and apartments available for both single and married students. Annual on-campus housing cost: single students $3,600 (room only), married students $7,200. Contact Admissions Office for both on- and off-campus housing information. Medical students tend to live off-campus. Off-campus housing and personal expenses: approximately $13,400.

Enrollment: 1st-year class 120 (EDP 10); total full-time 489 (men 53%, women 47%). First-year statistics: 14% out of state; 49% women; average age 25; 10% minorities; 70% science majors.

Degrees conferred: M.D., M.D.-M.S., M.D.-Ph.D. (Anatomy, Biochemistry, Biophysics, Immunology, Medical Physics, Microbiology, Molecular Biology, Neurosciences, Pharmacology, Physiology).

RECRUITMENT PRACTICES AND POLICIES. School has diversity program and actively recruits women/minority applicants. Diversity contact: Assistant Dean, Minority Affairs; phone: (312)942-5481.

ADMISSION REQUIREMENTS FOR FIRST-YEAR APPLICANTS. Preference given to state residents; U.S. citizens and permanent residents only. *Undergraduate preparation.* Suggested premed courses: 2 courses in biology with labs, 2 courses in inorganic chemistry with labs, 2 courses in organic chemistry with labs, 2 courses in physics with labs, 2 courses in English. Bachelor's degree from an accredited institution required; all applicants have bachelor's degree awarded prior to enrollment. *Has EDP* for state residents only; applicants must apply through AMCAS (official transcripts sent by mid-May)

between June 1 and August 1. Early applications are encouraged. Submit secondary/supplemental application, a personal statement, and 2 recommendations to Admissions Office within 2 weeks of receipt of application. Interviews are by invitation only and generally for final selection. Notification normally begins October 1. *Regular application process.* Apply through AMCAS (file after June 1, before November 1); submit MCAT (will accept MCAT test results from the last 3 years), official transcripts for each school attended (should show at least 90 semester credits/135 quarter credits, submit transcripts by mid-May to AMCAS), service processing fee. Submit an application fee of $45, a supplemental application, a personal statement, preprofessional committee evaluation, and 3 recommendations from science faculty to Admissions Office within 2–3 weeks of the receipt of supplemental materials. Interviews are by invitation only and generally for final selection. Concurrent-degree applicants must apply to, and be accepted by, both schools; contact the Admissions Office for current information and specific requirements for admission. First-year students admitted in fall only. Rolling admission process. Notification starts October 15 and is finished when class is filled. Applicant's response to offer and $100 deposit due within 2 weeks of receipt of acceptance letter. School does maintain an alternate list. Phone: (312)942-6913.

ADMISSION REQUIREMENTS FOR TRANSFER APPLICANTS. Accepts transfers from other accredited U.S. medical schools. Admission limited to space available. Contact the Admissions Office for current information and specific requirements.

ADMISSION STANDARDS AND RECOGNITION. *For M.D.:* number of state-resident applicants 1,840, nonresidents 3,633; number of state residents interviewed 400, nonresidents 56; number of residents enrolled 104, nonresidents 16; median MCAT 9.0 (verbal reasoning 9.0; biological sciences 9.0; physical sciences 9.0); median GPA 3.51 (A = 4). Gorman rating 3.36 (scale: acceptable plus 3.01–3.59); college's medical ranking by NIH awards was 122nd, with 5 awards/grants received; total dollars awarded $570,227.

FINANCIAL AID. Limited scholarships, minority scholarships, grants-in-aid, institutional loans, HEAL, alternative loan programs, federal Perkins loans, Stafford subsidized and unsubsidized loans, and service commitment scholarship programs are available. Assistantships/fellowships may be available for concurrent-degree candidates. Financial aid applications and information are sent out with the acceptance letter. Apply for financial aid not later than May 1. Financial aid is based on demonstrated need. Financial aid packages consist primarily of loans. Contact the Rush University's Office of Student Financial Aid for current information; phone: (312)942-6256. For most financial assistance and all federal programs, submit FAFSA to a federal processor (Title IV school code # 009800); also submit Financial Aid Transcript and Federal Income Tax forms. Approximately 80% of current students receive some form of financial assistance. Average debt after graduation $106,000.

DEGREE REQUIREMENTS. *For M.D.:* satisfactory completion of 4-year program. All students must pass USMLE Step 1 prior to entering 3rd year; all students must take USMLE Step 2 prior to awarding of M.D. *For M.D.-M.S.:* generally a 4½–5½-year program. *For M.D.-Ph.D.:* generally a 7-year program.

ST. LOUIS UNIVERSITY

St. Louis, Missouri 63103-2097
Internet site: http://www.slu.edu

Founded 1818; received charter in 1832 and became first University W of Mississippi. Located in midtown St. Louis. Private control; Roman Catholic–Jesuit. Semester system. Library: 1,460,000 volumes; 1,100,000 microforms; 12,800 periodicals/subscriptions. The university's ranking in domestic higher education by NIH awards/grants was 93rd, with 90 awards/grants received; total dollars awarded $18,099,520.

The university's graduate schools/colleges include: College of Arts and Sciences, School of Allied Health Professions, School of Nursing, School of Public Health, School of Social Services, School of Business Administration, School of Law, School of Medicine.

Total university enrollment at main campus: 11,200.

St. Louis University Health Sciences Center

3635 Vista at Grand Boulevard
St. Louis, Missouri 63110

Private control. St. Louis University Hospital is a member of the Council of Teaching Hospitals. Schools located at health sciences center are: School of Allied Health Professions, School of Medicine, School of Nursing. Special facilities: Firmin Desloge Hospital, Bordley Pavilion, David P. Wohl Memorial Mental Health Institute, Cardinal Glennon Hospital for Children, SLU-Anheuser Busch Eye Institute, Institute of Molecular Virology. Nationally recognized programs in Endocrinology, Gastroenterology, Geriatrics, Orthopedics.

School of Medicine

1402 South Grand Boulevard
St. Louis, Missouri 63104
Phone: (314)577-8205; fax: (314)577-8214
Internet site: http://www.slu.edu/colleges/med
E-mail: mcpeters@slu.edu

Established 1836. Semester system; classical curriculum structure. Library: 113,000 volumes/microforms; 1,765 current periodicals/subscriptions. Affiliated hospitals: Deaconess Medical Center, DePaul Medical Center, St. John's Mercy Medical Center, St. Mary's Health Center, St. Louis Veterans Administration Hospital. Special programs: summer programs for underrepresented minorities.

Annual tuition: $28,248; fees $1,080. Housing available for both single and married students at the university's graduate residence facilities. Contact Office of Housing for both on- and off-campus housing information; phone: (314)977-2797. Medical students tend to live off-campus. Off-campus housing and personal expenses: approximately $13,075.

Enrollment: 1st-year class 152 (EDP 6); total full-time 599 (men 65%, women 35%). First-year statistics: 70% out of state; 26 states represented; 38.8% women; average age 24; 2% minorities; 71% science majors.

Faculty: full-time 570, part-time/volunteers 900.

Degrees conferred: M.D., M.D. with Distinction in Research, M.D. in Community Service, M.D.-M.P.H., M.D.-Ph.D. (Anatomy and Neuroanatomy-Neuroscience, Biochemistry, Cell and Molecular Biology, Molecular Microbiology and Immunology, Neurobiology, Pathology, Pharmacological, Physiological Sciences).

RECRUITMENT PRACTICES AND POLICIES. School has diversity program and actively recruits women/minority applicants. Diversity contact: Assistant Dean for Multicultural Affairs; phone: (314)268-5398.

ADMISSION REQUIREMENTS FOR FIRST-YEAR APPLICANTS. Some preference given to applicants from St. Louis University; U.S. citizens and permanent residents only. *Undergraduate preparation.* Suggested premed courses: 2 courses in biology with labs, 2 courses in inorganic chemistry with labs, 2 courses in organic chemistry with labs, 2 courses in physics with labs, 2 courses in English, 4 courses in humanities and behavioral science; biochemistry is strongly recommended. Bachelor's degree from an accredited institution required; all applicants have bachelor's degree awarded prior to enrollment. *Has EDP;* applicants must apply through AMCAS (official transcripts sent by mid-May) between June 1 and August 1. Early applications are encouraged. Submit secondary/supplemental application, a personal statement, and 2 recommendations to Admissions Office within 2 weeks of receipt of application. Interviews are by invitation only and generally for final selection. Notification normally begins October 1. *Regular application process.* Apply through AMCAS (file after June 1, before December 15); submit MCAT (will accept MCAT test results from the last 3 years), official transcripts for each school attended (should show at least 90 semester credits/135 quarter credits, submit transcripts by mid-May to AMCAS), service processing fee. Submit an application fee of $100, a supplemental application, a personal statement, a preprofessional committee evaluation, and 3 recommendations from science faculty to Admissions Office within 2–3 weeks of the receipt of supplemental materials. Interviews are by invitation only and generally for final selection. M.D.-Ph.D. degree applicants must submit a separate M.D.-Ph.D. application by December 15; contact the Admissions Office for current information and specific requirements for admission. First-year students admitted in fall only. Rolling admission process. Notification starts in October and is finished when class is filled. Applicant's response to offer and $100 deposit due within 2 weeks of receipt of acceptance letter. School does maintain a summer alternate list. Phone: (314)577-8205.

ADMISSION REQUIREMENTS FOR TRANSFER APPLICANTS. Accepts transfers from other accredited U.S. medical schools. Admission limited to space available. Contact the Dean of Admissions for current information and specific requirements for admission.

ADMISSION STANDARDS AND RECOGNITION. *For M.D.:* number of state-resident applicants 349, nonresidents 5,013; number of state residents interviewed 163, nonresidents 1,042; number of residents enrolled 48, nonresidents 102; median MCAT 10.6 (verbal reasoning 10.3; biological sciences 10.8; physical sciences 10.8); median GPA 3.69 (A = 4). Gorman rating 4.24 (scale: strong 4.01–4.49); the school's medical ranking by NIH awards was 74th, with 81 awards/grants received; total dollars awarded $16,594,144.

FINANCIAL AID. Scholarships, minority scholarships, grants-in-aid, institutional loans, HEAL, alternative loan programs, primary-care loans, federal Perkins loans, Stafford subsidized and unsubsidized loans, and service commitment scholarship programs are available. All financial aid is based on demonstrated need. Tuition remission and stipends are available for M.D.-Ph.D. degree candidates. Financial aid applications and information are sent to all accepted students. Contact the Office of Student Financial Aid for current information; phone:

(314)577-8617. For most financial assistance and all federal programs, submit FAFSA to a federal processor (Title IV school code # 002506); also submit Financial Aid Transcript, Federal Income Tax forms, and credit report. Approximately 80% of current students receive some form of financial assistance.

DEGREE REQUIREMENTS. *For M.D.:* satisfactory completion of 4-year program. All students must pass USMLE Step 1 prior to entering 3rd year; all students must pass USMLE Step 2 prior to awarding of M.D. *For M.D.-Ph.D.:* generally a 7-year program.

UNIVERSITY OF SOUTH ALABAMA

Mobile, Alabama 36688-0002
Internet site: http://www.usouthal.edu

Founded 1964. Public control. Quarter system. Library: 463,700 volumes; 861,000 microforms; 3,765 periodicals/subscriptions. Special facilities: Big Creek Lake Biological Station, Cancer Research Center, Coastal Research and Development Center, Primate Center. Special programs: B.A./B.S.-M.D. program (annual undergraduate tuition for residents $2,382, nonresidents $3,807). The university's ranking in domestic higher education by NIH awards/grants was 113th, with 45 awards/grants received; total dollars awarded $8,921,982.

The university's graduate schools/colleges include: College of Allied Health Professions, College of Arts and Sciences, College of Business and Management Studies, College of Education, College of Engineering, College of Nursing, Division of Computer and Information Sciences, College of Medicine.

Total university enrollment at main campus: 11,800.

University of South Alabama Medical Center

2451 Fillingim Street
Mobile, Alabama 36617

Founded 1831. Public control. The medical center is a member of the Council of Teaching Hospitals. Special facilities: Level I Trauma Center, U.S.A. Cancer Center.

College of Medicine

2015 MSB
Mobile, Alabama 36688-0002
Phone: (334)460-7176; fax: (334)460-6278
Internet site: http://www.usouthal.edu

Established 1967; 1st class admitted in 1973. Located in the Springhill section of Mobile. The first 2 years cover the basic sciences; then students follow a track system. Library: 69,000 volumes/microforms; 2,500 current periodicals/subscriptions. Affiliated hospitals: U.S.A. Medical Center, U.S.A. Knollwood Hospital, U.S.A. Doctors Hospital.

Annual tuition: residents $7,650 (residents of Mississippi Gulf Coast and Florida Panhandle qualify for in-state tuition), nonresidents $14,650; fees $667. On-campus furnished residence halls available for single students. University-owned housing adjacent to campus available for both single and married students. Contact Housing Office for both on- and off-campus housing information; phone: (334)460-6195. Off-campus housing and personal expenses: approximately $10,845.

Enrollment: 1st-year class 64 (EDP 10); total full-time 263 (men 62%, women 38%). First-year statistics: 10% out of state; 37.5% women; average age 24; 13% minorities.

Faculty: full-time 217, part-time 22.

Degrees conferred: M.D., B.S.-M.D., M.D.-Ph.D. (Anatomy, Biochemistry, Cell Biology, Genetics, Immunology, Microbiology, Molecular Biology, Neurosciences, Pharmacology, Physiology).

RECRUITMENT PRACTICES AND POLICIES. School has diversity program and actively recruits women/minority applicants. Diversity contact: Assistant Dean, Office of Special Programs and Student Affairs; phone: (334)460-7613.

ADMISSION REQUIREMENT FOR BACHELOR-M.D. APPLICANTS. Preference given to state residents; nonresidents may apply. Submit application, SAT I or ACT, official high school transcripts, letters of recommendation to U.S.A. Office of Admissions by March 1. Interviews are by invitation only and generally for final selection. Notification normally begins April 15. Applicant's response to offer due by July 1. Application fee $25. Phone: (334)460-6146.

ADMISSION REQUIREMENTS FOR FIRST-YEAR APPLICANTS. Preference given to state residents; U.S. citizens and permanent residents only. *Undergraduate preparation.* Suggested premed courses: 2 courses in biology with labs, 2 courses in inorganic chemistry with labs, 2 courses in organic chemistry with labs, 2 courses in physics with labs, 2 courses in college math (calculus strongly recommended), 2 courses in English, 2 courses in humanities. Bachelor's degree from an accredited institution required; all applicants have bachelor's degree awarded prior to enrollment. *Has EDP* for state residents only; applicants must apply through AMCAS (official transcripts sent by mid-May) between June 1 and August 1. Early applications are encouraged. Submit the final application, a personal statement, and 2 recommendations to Admissions Office within 2 weeks of receipt of application. Interviews are by invitation only and generally for

final selection. Notification normally begins October 1. *Application process.* Apply through AMCAS (file after June 1, before November 15); submit MCAT (will accept MCAT test results from the last 3 years), official transcripts for each school attended (should show at least 90 semester credits/135 quarter credits, submit transcripts by mid-May to AMCAS), service processing fee. After a preliminary review of AMCAS report, a final application is sent to selected applicants. Return final application, an application fee of $25, photograph, preprofessional committee evaluation, and 3 recommendations from science faculty to Admissions Office within 2–3 weeks of receiving the materials. Interviews are by invitation only and generally for final selection. Dual-degree applicants must apply to, and be accepted by, both schools; contact the Admissions Office for current information and specific requirements for admission. First-year students admitted in fall only. Rolling admission process. Notification starts October 15 and is finished when class is filled. Applicant's response to offer and $100 deposit due within 2 weeks of receipt of acceptance letter. School does maintain an alternate list. Phone: (344)460-7076.

ADMISSION REQUIREMENTS FOR TRANSFER APPLICANTS. Accepts transfers from other accredited U.S. medical schools. Admission limited to space available. Contact the Admissions Office for current information and specific requirements for admission.

ADMISSION STANDARDS AND RECOGNITION. *For B.S.-M.D.:* number of state-resident applicants 90, nonresidents 45; number of state residents interviewed 25, nonresidents 10; number of residents enrolled 10, nonresidents 5. *For M.D.:* number of state-resident applicants 520, nonresidents 788; number of state residents interviewed 232, nonresidents 6; number of residents enrolled 59, nonresidents 5; median MCAT 9.7 (verbal reasoning 9.8; biological sciences 9.9; physical sciences 9.6); median GPA 3.6 (A = 4). Gorman rating 3.10 (scale: acceptable plus 3.01–3.59); the college's medical ranking by NIH awards was 90th, with 40 awards/grants received; total dollars awarded $8,424,654.

FINANCIAL AID. Scholarships, limited number of state scholarships, minority scholarships, grants-in-aid, institutional loans, HEAL, alternative loan programs, state loan programs, federal Perkins loans, Stafford subsidized and unsubsidized loans, and service commitment scholarship programs are available. Assistantships/fellowships may be available for dual-degree candidates. All financial aid is based on demonstrated need. Financial aid applications and information are generally available at the on-campus interview (by invitation); return financial aid application not later than April 1. For scholarships, the selection criteria place heavy reliance on MCAT and undergraduate GPA. Contact the Office of Financial Aid for current information; phone: (334)460-7918. For most financial assistance and all federal programs, submit FAFSA to a federal processor (Title IV school code # 001057); also submit Financial Aid Transcript and Federal Income Tax forms. Approximately 85% of current students receive some form of financial assistance. Average debt after graduation $52,000.

DEGREE REQUIREMENTS. *For B.S.-M.D.*: an 8-year program; undergraduates in program must maintain 3.5 (A = 4) overall GPA and a 3.4 GPA in sciences and must score above the national norm on the MCATs to continue on to the College of Medicine. A formal assessment is conducted after the undergraduate has completed 96 quarter hours. *For M.D.:* satisfactory completion of 4-year program. All students must pass USMLE Step 1 prior to entering 3rd year; all students must pass USMLE Step 2 prior to awarding of M.D. *For M.D.-Ph.D.:* generally a 7-year program.

MEDICAL UNIVERSITY
OF SOUTH CAROLINA
Charleston, South Carolina 29425-0002
Internet site: http://www.musc.edu

Founded 1824. Located in downtown Charleston. State-assisted medical college. Semester system. Library: 212,000 volumes; 2,480 periodicals/subscriptions; 50 PC work stations. Special facilities: McCauley Dental Museum. Special programs: Postbaccalaureate premedical program for minorities (PREP); all minority resident applicants are automatically considered for this program. The university's ranking in domestic higher education by NIH awards/grants was 72nd, with 119 awards/grants received; total dollars awarded $26,854,823.

The university's colleges are: College of Graduate Studies, College of Health Professions, College of Medicine, College of Nursing, College of Pharmacy.

Total university enrollment at main campus: 2,285.

Medical University of South Carolina
Medical Center
171 Ashley Avenue
Charleston, South Carolina 29425

Public control. The medical center is a member of the Council of Teaching Hospitals. All the university's colleges are located at medical center. Facilities include: Children's Hospital, Digestive Disease Center, Hollings Cancer Center, MUSC Transplant Center, Psychiatric Institute, Storm Eye Institute, University Hospital.

College of Medicine
171 Ashley Avenue
Charleston, South Carolina 29425-7012
Phone: (803)792-3281; fax: (803)792-3764
Internet site: http://www.musc.edu
E-mail: taylorwl@musc.edu

Established 1824 and is the South's oldest medical school. Semester system. Affiliated hospitals: Charleston Memorial Hospital, Medical University Hospital, Veterans Administration Hospital. Special programs: summer programs for underrepresented minorities; Early Assurance Program (for state residents only).

Annual tuition: residents $7,332, nonresidents $21,264. No on-campus housing available. Contact Office of Enrollment Services for off-campus housing information. Off-campus housing and personal expenses: approximately $12,500.

Enrollment: 1st-year class 135 (EDP 15); total full-time 584 (men 60%, women 40%). First-year statistics: 10% out of state; 40.6% women; average age 24; 23% minorities; 60% science majors.

Faculty: full-time 731, part-time/volunteers 599.

Degrees conferred: M.D., M.D.-Ph.D. (Anatomy, Biochemistry, Cell Biology, Genetics, Immunology, Microbiology, Molecular Biology, Pathology, Pharmacology, Physiology).

RECRUITMENT PRACTICES AND POLICIES. School has diversity program and actively recruits women/minority applicants. Diversity contact: Director, University Diversity and Executive Assistant; phone: (803)792-2146.

ADMISSION REQUIREMENTS FOR FIRST-YEAR APPLICANTS. Preference given to state residents; U.S. citizens and permanent residents only. *Undergraduate preparation.* Suggested premed courses: 2 courses in biology with labs, 2 courses in inorganic chemistry with labs, 2 courses in organic chemistry with labs, 2 courses in physics with labs, 1 course in college math, 2 courses in English. Bachelor's degree from an accredited institution required; all applicants have bachelor's degree awarded prior to enrollment. *Has EDP* for state residents only; applicants must apply through AMCAS (official transcripts sent by mid-May) between June 1 and August 1. Early applications are encouraged. Submit secondary/supplemental application, a personal statement, and 2 recommendations to Office of Enrollment Services within 2 weeks of receipt of application. Interviews are by invitation only and generally for final selection. Notification normally begins October 1. *Regular application process.* Apply through AMCAS (file after June 1, before December 1); submit MCAT (will accept MCAT test results from the last 3 years), official transcripts for each school attended (should show at least 90 semester credits/135 quarter credits, submit transcripts by mid-May to AMCAS), service processing fee. Submit an application fee of $45, a supplemental application, a personal statement, preprofessional committee evaluation, and 3 recommendations from science faculty to Office of Enrollment Services within 2–3 weeks of the receipt of supplemental materials. Interviews are by invitation only and generally for final selection. Dual-degree applicants must apply to, and be accepted by, both schools; contact the Office of Enrollment Services for current information and specific requirements for admission. First-year students admitted in fall only. Rolling admission process. Notification starts in October and is finished when class is filled. Applicant's response to offer and $100 deposit due within 2 weeks of receipt of acceptance letter. School does maintain an alternate list. Phone: (803)792-3281.

ADMISSION REQUIREMENTS FOR TRANSFER APPLICANTS. Accepts transfers from other accredited U.S. medical schools. Admission limited to space available. Contact the Office of Enrollment Services for current information and specific requirements.

ADMISSION STANDARDS AND RECOGNITION. *For M.D.:* number of state-resident applicants 585, nonresidents 2,596; number of state residents interviewed 364, nonresidents 101; number of residents enrolled 123, nonresidents 12; median MCAT 9.0 (verbal reasoning 9.0; biological sciences 9.0; physical sciences 9.0); median GPA 3.46 (A = 4). Gorman rating 3.40 (scale: acceptable plus 3.01–3.59); the college's medical ranking by NIH awards was 64th, with 115 awards/grants received; total dollars awarded $26,285,086.

FINANCIAL AID. State scholarships, James B. Edwards Scholars Program, grants-in-aid, institutional loans, HEAL, alternative loan programs, federal Perkins loans, Stafford subsidized and unsubsidized loans, and service commitment scholarship programs are available. Assistantships/fellowships may be available for dual-degree candidates. Financial aid applications and information are available after February 1. For James B. Edwards Scholars Program, the selection criteria place heavy reliance on MCAT and undergraduate GPA. Contact the Office of Student Services for current information; phone: (803)792-2636; fax: (803)792-2535. For most financial assistance and all federal programs, submit FAFSA to a federal processor (Title IV school code

003438); also submit Financial Aid Transcript and Federal Income Tax forms. Approximately 85% of current students receive some form of financial assistance. Average debt after graduation $66,800.

DEGREE REQUIREMENTS. *For M.D.:* satisfactory completion of 4-year program. All students must pass USMLE Step 1 prior to beginning 3rd year. *For M.D.-Ph.D.:* generally a 7-year program.

College of Dental Medicine
171 Ashley Avenue
Charleston, South Carolina 29425-2970
Phone: (803)792-3281; fax: (803)792-3764
Internet site: http://www.musc.edu
E-mail: javedt@musc.edu

Established 1967. Located at medical center. Curriculum: basic science courses are covered in the first 2 years. Special facilities: McCauley Museum of Dental History. Special programs: Summer programs for underrepresented minorities. Postgraduate specialties: General Dentistry (AEGD), General Practice Residency, Oral and Maxillofacial Surgery, Pediatric Dentistry, Periodontics.

Annual tuition: residents $6,403, nonresidents $18,607; fees $450; equipment and supplies $4,000. No on-campus housing available. Contact Office of Student Housing for off-campus housing information. Off-campus housing and personal expenses: approximately $12,500.

Enrollment: 1st-year class 55; total full-time 183. First-year enrolled student information: 8 from out of state; 16 women; average age 24; 4 underrepresented minorities; 5 other minorities.

Faculty: full-time 59, part-time 20.

Degrees conferred: D.M.D.; has D.M.S.T.

RECRUITMENT PRACTICES AND POLICIES. School has diversity program and actively recruits women/minority applicants. Diversity contact: Office of Minority Affairs; phone: (803)792-2146.

ADMISSION REQUIREMENTS FOR FIRST-YEAR APPLICANTS. Preference given to state residents; U.S. citizens and permanent residents only. *Undergraduate preparation.* Suggested predental courses: 2 courses in biology with lab, 2 courses in inorganic chemistry with labs, 2 courses in organic chemistry with labs, 1 course in physics with lab, 2 courses in college math, 2 courses in English, 2 additional sciences (electives), 13 additional courses; biochemistry, microbiology, comparative anatomy, genetics, histology, recommended. The junior-college transfer-credit limit is 60 credits, and all credits must be earned before the applicant enters the 3rd year of undergraduate study. Will consider applicants with only 3 years of undergraduate preparation; prefer applicants who will have a bachelor's degree prior to enrollment; 53 out of 55 enrolled first-year students have bachelor's degrees awarded prior to enrollment. *Application process.* Apply through AADSAS (file after June 1, before December 1); submit official transcripts for each school attended (should show at least 90 semester credits/135 quarter credits), service processing fee; at the same time as you send in AADSAS materials, submit official DAT scores directly to the Office of Enrollment Services. Submit the following materials only after being contacted by an Admissions Officer: an application fee of $45, a supplemental application, official transcripts, and 3 references (forms are provided) to Office of Enrollment Services within 2 weeks of receipt of the requested materials. Interviews are by invitation only and generally for final selection. D.M.S.T. applicants must apply to, and be accepted by, both the College of Dentistry and College of Graduate Studies; contact the Office of Enrollment Services for current information and specific requirements for admission. First-year students admitted in fall only. Rolling admission process. Notification starts December 1 and is finished when class is filled, but generally not later than June 1. Applicant's response to offer and matriculation fee due within 30 days of the receipt of the acceptance offer. School does maintain an alternate list. Phone: (803)792-2344.

ADMISSION REQUIREMENTS FOR ADVANCED-STANDING APPLICANTS. Accepts transfers from other accredited U.S. dental schools. Admission limited to space available. There is no advanced-standing program for graduates of foreign schools of dentistry. Contact the Office of Enrollment Services for current information and specific requirements for admission.

ADMISSION STANDARDS AND RECOGNITION. *For D.M.D.:* number of applicants 726; number enrolled 55; median DAT: ACAD 17.0, PAT 17.0; median GPA 3.18 (A = 4). Gorman rating 4.21 (scale: strong 4.01–4.49); this placed the school in the Top 40 of all U.S. dental schools.

FINANCIAL AID. State scholarships, minority scholarships, institutional loans, state loan programs, DEAL, HEAL, alternative loan programs, federal Perkins loans, Stafford subsidized and unsubsidized loans, and military service commitment scholarship programs are available. Assistantships/fellowships may be available for D.M.S.T. candidates. Institutional financial aid applications and information are available by contacting the Office of Student Services; phone: (803)792-2536. For most financial assistance and all need-based programs, submit FAFSA to a federal processor (Title IV school code # 003438); also submit Financial Aid Transcript, Federal Income Tax forms, and Use of Federal Funds Certification. Approximately 90% of current students receive some form of financial assistance. Average award for residents $18,879, nonresidents $26,286.

DEGREE REQUIREMENTS. *For D.M.D.:* satisfactory completion of 4-year program. *For D.M.S.T.:* generally an additional 1–3 years beyond D.M.D.

UNIVERSITY OF SOUTH CAROLINA
Columbia, South Carolina 29208
Internet site: http://www.sc.edu

Founded 1801. Located in downtown Columbia. Public control. Semester system. Library: 2,714,000 volumes; 4,186,700 microforms; 17,940 periodicals/subscriptions; 289 work stations. The university's ranking in domestic higher education by NIH awards/grants was 124th, with 42 awards/grants received; total dollars awarded $7,094,212.

The university's graduate schools/colleges include: College of Applied Professional Sciences, College of Business Administration, College of Criminal Justice, College of Education, College of Engineering, College of Interdisciplinary Studies, College of Journalism, College of Liberal Arts, College of Library and Information Sciences, College of Nursing, College of Science and Mathematics, College of Social Work, School of Music, School of Public Health, College of Pharmacy, School of Law, School of Medicine.

Total university enrollment at main campus: 26,300.

School of Medicine
Columbia, South Carolina 29208
Phone: (803)733-3325; fax: (803)733-3328
Internet site: http://www.med.sc.edu
E-mail: witch@dcsmsrver.med.sc.edu

Established 1974; accepted 1st class in 1977. Located adjacent to Dorn Veterans Hospital. Semester system for first 2 years of medical study. Library: 86,000 volumes/microforms; 1,200 current periodicals/subscriptions. Affiliated hospitals and clinics: Alzheimer's Day Care Center, Center for Developmental Disabilities, Child Abuse Recovery Center, Children's Immunology Center, Clinical Genetics Center, Geriatric Assessment Clinic, Martin Primary Health Care Center (Winnsboro), Palmetto Children's Clinic, Palmetto Senior Care, University Specialty Clinics/University Primary Care, Bone Marrow Transplantation Program, Trauma Center of Richland Memorial Hospital, William S. Hall Psychiatric

Institute, Dorn Veterans Hospital, Moncrief Army Hospital, Greenville Memorial Hospital.

Annual tuition: residents $7,753, nonresidents $20,507. On-campus apartments available for married students only. Contact Housing Service, USC, 1215 Blossom Street, Columbia, S.C. for both on- and off-campus housing information; phone: (803)777-4571. Off-campus housing and personal expenses: approximately $14,445.

Enrollment: 1st-year class 72 (EDP 12); total full-time 285 (men 61%, women 39%). First-year statistics: 7% out of state; 34.7% women; average age 25; 4% minorities; 79% science majors.

Faculty: full-time 162, part-time/volunteers 15.

Degrees conferred: M.D., M.D.-M.P.H., M.D.-Ph.D. (Anatomy, Cell Biology, Immunology, Microbiology, Neurosciences, Pathology, Pharmacology, Physiology).

RECRUITMENT PRACTICES AND POLICIES. School has diversity program and actively recruits women/minority applicants. Diversity contact: Associate Dean for Minority Affairs; phone: (803)733-1531.

ADMISSION REQUIREMENTS FOR FIRST-YEAR APPLICANTS. Preference given to state residents; U.S. citizens and permanent residents only. *Undergraduate preparation.* Suggested premed courses: 2 courses in biology with labs, 2 courses in inorganic chemistry with labs, 2 courses in organic chemistry with labs, 2 courses in physics with labs, 2 courses in college math (calculus recommended), 2 courses in English. Bachelor's degree from an accredited institution required; 98% of applicants have bachelor's degree awarded prior to enrollment. *Has EDP*; applicants must apply through AMCAS (official transcripts sent by mid-May) between June 1 and August 1. Early applications are encouraged. Submit secondary/supplemental application, a personal statement, and 2 recommendations to Manager of Enrollment Services within 2 weeks of receipt of application. Interviews are by invitation only and generally for final selection. Notification normally begins October 1. *Regular application process.* Apply through AMCAS (file after June 1, before December 1); submit MCAT (will accept MCAT test results from the last 3 years), official transcripts for each school attended (should show at least 90 semester credits/135 quarter credits, submit transcripts by mid-May to AMCAS), service processing fee. Submit an application fee of $20, a supplemental application, a personal statement, preprofessional committee evaluation, and 3 recommendations from science faculty to Manager of Enrollment Services within 2–3 weeks of the receipt of supplemental materials, but not later than January 15. Interviews are by invitation only and generally for final selection. Combined degree applicants must apply

to, and be accepted by, both schools; contact the Assistant Dean for Graduate Studies for current information and specific requirements for admission; phone: (803)733-3100. First-year students admitted in fall only. Rolling admission process. Decisions are sent out on October 15, November 15, and December 15. Applicant's response to offer and $100 deposit due within 2 weeks of receipt of acceptance letter. School does maintain an alternate list. Phone: (803)733-3325.

ADMISSION REQUIREMENTS FOR TRANSFER APPLICANTS. Accepts transfers from other accredited U.S. medical schools. Admission limited to space available. Contact the Manager of Enrollment Services after January 1 for current information and specific requirements for admission.

ADMISSION STANDARDS AND RECOGNITION. *For M.D.:* number of state-resident applicants 478, nonresidents 1,029; number of state residents interviewed 261, nonresidents 107; number of residents enrolled 66, nonresidents 6; median MCAT 9.2; median GPA 3.39 (A = 4). Gorman rating 3.10 (scale: acceptable plus 3.01–3.59); the school's medical ranking by NIH awards was 114th, with 13 awards/grants received; total dollars awarded $1,773,557.

FINANCIAL AID. Scholarships, grants-in-aid, institutional loans, state loan programs, HEAL, alternative loan programs, primary-care loans, federal Perkins loans, Stafford subsidized and unsubsidized loans, and service commitment scholarship programs are available. Assistantships/fellowships may be available for dual-degree candidates. Financial aid applications and information are generally available at the on-campus interview (by invitation). For scholarships, the selection criteria place heavy reliance on MCAT and undergraduate GPA. Contact the Office of Student Services for current information; phone: (803)733-3135. For most financial assistance and all federal programs, submit FAFSA to a federal processor (Title IV school code # 003448); also submit Financial Aid Transcript and Federal Income Tax forms. Approximately 84% of current students receive some form of financial assistance. Average debt after graduation $57,000.

DEGREE REQUIREMENTS. *For M.D.:* satisfactory completion of 4-year program. All students must pass USMLE Step 1 prior to entering 3rd year; all students must pass USMLE Step 2 prior to awarding of M.D. *For M.D.-M.P.H.:* generally a 5–5½-year program. *For M.D.-Ph.D.:* generally a 6–7-year program.

UNIVERSITY OF SOUTH DAKOTA

Vermillion, South Dakota 57069-2390
Internet site: http://www.usd.edu

Founded 1882. Located 60 miles S of Sioux Falls, South Dakota, 40 miles from Sioux City, Iowa. Public control. Semester system. Library: 667,100 volumes; 645,000 microforms; 8,147 periodicals/subscriptions; 138 computer work stations.

The university's graduate schools/colleges include: College of Arts and Science, College of fine Arts, School of Business, School of Education, School of Law, School of Medicine.

Total university enrollment at main campus: 7,750.

School of Medicine

414 East Clark Street
Vermillion, South Dakota 57069-2390
Phone: (605)677-5233; fax: (605)377-5109
Internet site: http://www.usd.edu/med/som

Established 1907 as a 2-year school of basic medical sciences. Expended to a 4-year degree granting institution in 1974. Clinical training is in Yankton, Sioux Falls, and Rapid City. Located on main campus. Semester system. Library: 79,000 volumes/microforms; 1,000 current periodicals/subscriptions. Special programs: Programs to identify and assist Native Americans; Primary Care Preceptorship Program; specialty in family medicine for state of South Dakota.

Annual tuition: residents $11,075, nonresidents $24,650. On-campus rooms and apartments available for both single and married students. Annual on-campus housing cost: $1,850 for married students, $3,600 (including board) for single students. Contact Resident Services for both on- and off-campus housing information; phone: (605)677-5663. Medical students tend to live off-campus. Off-campus housing and personal expenses: approximately $11,500.

Enrollment: 1st-year class 50; total full-time 203 (men 53%, women 47%). First-year statistics: 2% out of state; 52% women; average age 25; 6% minorities; 88% science majors.

Degrees conferred: M.D., M.D.-Ph.D. (Anatomy, Biochemistry, Microbiology, Molecular Biology, Pharmacology, Physiology).

RECRUITMENT PRACTICES AND POLICIES. School has diversity program and actively recruits women/minority applicants. Diversity contact: Director of Admissions; phone: (605)677-5156.

ADMISSION REQUIREMENTS FOR FIRST-YEAR APPLICANTS. Priority given to state residents and nonresidents with ties to South Dakota; U.S. citizens and permanent residents only. *Undergraduate preparation.* Suggested premed courses: 2 courses in biology with labs, 2 courses in general chemistry with labs, 2 courses in organic chemistry with labs, 2 courses in physics with labs, 2 courses in college math (calculus preferred), 2 courses in English. Bachelor's degree from an accredited institution required; 98% of applicants have bachelor's degrees awarded prior to enrollment. Does not have EDP. *Application process.* Apply through AMCAS (file after June 1, before November 15); submit MCAT (will accept MCAT test results from the last 3 years), official transcripts for each school attended (should show at least 90 semester credits/135 quarter credits, submit transcripts by mid-May to AMCAS), service processing fee. Submit an application fee of $15, a supplemental application, a personal statement, preprofessional committee evaluation, and 3 recommendations from science faculty to Admissions Office within 2–3 weeks of the receipt of supplemental materials. Interviews are by invitation only and generally for final selection. Dual-degree applicants must apply to, and be accepted by, both schools; contact the Admissions Office for current information and specific requirements for admission. First-year students admitted in fall only. Rolling admission process. Notification starts December 22 and is finished when class is filled. Applicant's response to offer and $100 deposit due within 2 weeks of receipt of acceptance letter. School does maintain an alternate list. Phone: (605)677-5233.

ADMISSION REQUIREMENTS FOR TRANSFER APPLICANTS. Accepts transfers from other accredited U.S. medical schools, but only under exceptional circumstances. Contact the Admissions Office for current information and specific requirements.

ADMISSION STANDARDS AND RECOGNITION. *For M.D.:* number of state-resident applicants 152, nonresidents 840; number of state residents interviewed 152, nonresidents 23; number of residents enrolled 49, nonresidents 1; median MCAT 8.2 (verbal reasoning 8.3; biological sciences 8.8; physical sciences 8.8); median GPA 3.57 (A = 4). Gorman rating 3.16 (scale: acceptable plus 3.01–3.59); the school's medical ranking by NIH awards was 118th, with 12 awards/grants received; total dollars awarded $1,257,291.

FINANCIAL AID. Limited scholarships, grants-in-aid, institutional loans, HEAL, alternative loan programs, federal Perkins loans, Stafford subsidized and unsubsidized loans, and state service commitment scholarship programs are available. Assistantships/fellowships may be available for dual-degree candidates. Most financial aid is based on documented need. Financial aid applications and information are generally available at the on-campus interview (by invitation). For scholarships, the selection criteria place heavy reliance on MCAT and undergraduate GPA. Contact the Financial Aid Office for current information; phone: (605)377-5112. For most financial assistance and all federal programs, submit FAFSA to a federal processor (Title IV school code # 003474); also submit Financial Aid Transcript and Federal Income Tax forms. Approximately 88% of current students receive some form of financial assistance. Average debt after graduation $86,900.

DEGREE REQUIREMENTS. *For M.D.:* satisfactory completion of 4-year program. All students must pass USMLE Step 1 prior to entering 3rd year; all students must pass USMLE Step 2 prior to awarding of M.D. *For M.D.-Ph.D.:* generally a 7-year program.

UNIVERSITY OF SOUTH FLORIDA
Tampa, Florida 33620-9951
Internet site: http://www.usf.edu

Founded 1656. Public control. Semester system. Special facilities: Florida Institute of Oceanography, Gerontology Center, Institute for At-Risk Infants, Children, Youth and Their Families, Institute for Biomolecular Science, Institute on Aging. Library: 1,500,000 volumes; 4,000,000 microforms; 10,000 periodicals/subscriptions. Special program: Premedical Honors Program; contact the Director of Honors Program for current information; phone: (813)974-3087. The university's ranking in domestic higher education by NIH awards/grants was 112th, with 68 awards/grants received; total dollars awarded $9,592,278.

The university's graduate colleges include: College of Architecture, College of Arts and Sciences, College of Business Administration, College of Education, College of Engineering, College of Fine Arts, College of Nursing, College of Public Health, College of Medicine.

Total university enrollment at main campus: 30,900.

College of Medicine
Box 3
12901 Bruce D. Downs Boulevard
Tampa, Florida 33612-4799
Phone: (813)974-2229; fax: (803)974-4990
Internet site: http://www.med.usf.edu

Established 1971. Located at the health sciences center in the NE section of Tampa. Semester system; first 2 years are concentrated in the basic sciences. Affiliated hospitals and primary teaching facilities: USF Medical Clinics, Tampa General Hospital (a member of the Council of Teaching Hospitals), James S. Haley Veterans Hospital, Tampa Unit, Shriners Hospital for Crippled Children, H. Lee Moffitt Cancer Center. Special programs: Honors Program with undergraduates at university.

Annual tuition: residents $9,825, nonresidents $25,500. On-campus rooms and apartments available for both single and married students. Contact Admissions Office for both on- and off-campus housing information; phone: (813)974-2764. Medical students tend to live off-campus. Off-campus housing and personal expenses: approximately $11,500.

Enrollment: 1st-year class 96 (EDP 29); total full-time 386 (men 67%, women 33%). First-year statistics: none from out of state; 33% women; average age 23; 25% minorities.

Faculty: full-time 445.

Degrees conferred: M.D., M.D.-M.P.H., M.D.-Ph.D. (available under certain conditions).

RECRUITMENT PRACTICES AND POLICIES. School has diversity program and actively recruits women/minority applicants. Diversity contact: Associate Dean; phone: (813)974-3393.

ADMISSION REQUIREMENTS FOR FIRST-YEAR APPLICANTS. Accepts only state residents; they must be U.S. citizens and permanent residents. *Undergraduate preparation.* Suggested premed courses: 2 courses in biology with labs, 2 courses in inorganic chemistry with labs, 2 courses in organic chemistry with labs, 2 courses in physics with labs, 2 courses in college math, 2 courses in English. Bachelor's degree from an accredited institution required; all applicants have bachelor's degrees awarded prior to enrollment. *Has EDP* for state residents only; applicants must apply through AMCAS (official transcripts sent by mid-May) between June 1 and August 1. Early applications are encouraged. Submit secondary/supplemental application, a personal statement, and 2 recommendations to Admissions Office within 2 weeks of receipt of application. Interviews are by invitation only and generally for final selection. Notification normally begins October 1. *Regular application process.* Apply through AMCAS (file after June 1, before December 1); submit MCAT (will accept MCAT test results from the last 3 years), official transcripts for each school attended (should show at least 90 semester credits/135 quarter credits, submit transcripts by mid-May to AMCAS), service processing fee. After a preliminary review a selected group of applicants will be sent a formal USF application. Submit an application fee of $20, the USF application, preprofessional committee evaluation, and 3 recommendations from science faculty to Admissions Office within 2–3 weeks of the receipt of supplemental materials. Interviews are by invitation only and generally for final selection. Dual-degree applicants must apply to, and be accepted by, both schools; contact the Admissions Office for current information and specific requirements for admission. First-year students admitted in fall only. Rolling admission process. Notification starts October 15 and is finished when class is filled. Applicant's response to offer due within 2 weeks of receipt of acceptance letter. Phone: (813)974-2229.

ADMISSION REQUIREMENTS FOR TRANSFER APPLICANTS. Accepts transfers who are state residents from other accredited U.S. medical schools, but only with unusual circumstances or a special hardship. Contact the Admissions Office after Janaury 15 for current information and specific requirements for admission.

ADMISSION STANDARDS AND RECOGNITION. *For M.D.:* number of state-resident applicants 1,444, nonresidents 491; number of state residents interviewed 377, nonresidents 0; number of residents enrolled 96, nonresidents 0; median MCAT 9.9 (verbal reasoning 9.7; biological sciences 10.2; physical sciences 10.2); median GPA 3.7 (A = 4). Gorman rating 3.41 (scale: acceptable plus 3.01–3.59); the school's medical ranking by NIH awards was 94th, with 50 awards/grants received; total dollars awarded $7,343,991.

FINANCIAL AID. Limited funds available for institutional scholarships and loans, HEAL, alternative loan programs, federal Perkins loans, Stafford subsidized and unsubsidized loans, and service commitment scholarship programs are available. Assistantships/fellowships may be available for dual-degree candidates. Financial aid is based on documented need. Financial aid applications and information are generally available at the on-campus interview (by invitation). Contact the Financial Aid Office for current information; phone: (813)974-2068. For most financial assistance and all federal programs, submit FAFSA to a federal processor (Title IV school code # E00568); also submit Financial Aid Transcript and Federal Income Tax forms. Approximately 80% of current students receive some form of financial assistance. Average debt after graduation $65,000.

DEGREE REQUIREMENTS. *For Premedical Honors Program:* a 7- or 8-year track available. *For M.D.:* satisfactory completion of 4-year program. *For M.D.-M.P.H.:*

generally a 4½–5½-year program. *For M.D.-Ph.D.:* generally a 7-year program.

UNIVERSITY OF SOUTHERN CALIFORNIA
University Park
Los Angeles, California 90089-0913
Internet site: http://www.usc.edu

Founded 1880. Located 3½ miles from downtown Los Angeles. Private control. Semester system. Library: 3,100,000 volumes; 3,900,000 microforms; 38,000 periodicals/subscriptions; 334 computer work stations. Special programs: B.A.-M.D. program (began in 1993; annual undergraduate tuition $19,140). The university's ranking in domestic higher education by NIH awards/grants was 22nd, with 268 awards/grants received; total dollars awarded $96,108,230.

The university's graduate schools/colleges include: Annenberg School of Communication, College of Letters, Arts and Sciences, Graduate School of Business Administration, Institute of Safety and Systems Management, Leonard Davis School of Gerontology, School of Architecture, School of Cinema-Television, School of Dentistry, School of Engineering, School of Fine Arts, School of Independent Health Professions, School of Music, School of Pharmacy, School of Public Administration, School of Social Work, School of Theatre, School of Urban and Regional Planning, Law School, School of Medicine.

Total university enrollment at main campus: 28,000.

Los Angeles County and USC Medical Center
1200 North State Street
Los Angeles, California 90033

Public control. Located in NE Los Angeles, about 7 miles from University Park Campus. One of the largest teaching centers in the U.S. The medical center is a member of the Council of Teaching Hospitals. Nationally recognized programs in AIDS, Pulmonary Disease, Rheumatology.

School of Medicine
1975 Zonal Avenue (KAM-100C)
Los Angeles, California 90033
Phone: (213)342-2552
Internet site: http://www.hsc.usc.edu
E-mail: medadmit@hsc.usc.edu

Established 1885. Located on the health science campus across the street from the medical center. Semester system. Library: 315,000 volumes/microforms; 3,500 current periodicals/subscriptions. Special facilities: Center for Molecular Medicine, USC Norris Cancer Hospital, Doheny Eye Institute, USC Hospital, USC Institute for Genetic Medicine. Special programs: Research Scholars Program.

Annual tuition: $30,197; fees $1,172. No on-campus housing available. Contact Admissions Office for off-campus housing information. Off-campus housing and personal expenses: approximately $12,950.

Enrollment: 1st-year class 150; total full-time 631 (men 56%, women 44%). First-year statistics: 20% out of state; 15 states represented; 156 colleges/universities represented; 46% women; average age 24; 21% minorities; 68% science majors.

Faculty: full-time 1,000, part-time/volunteers 3,700.

Degrees conferred: M.D., B.A.-M.D., M.D.-Ph.D. (Anatomy and Cell Biology, Biochemistry, Genetics, Microbiology, Pharmacology and Nutrition, Physiology and Biophysics, Preventive Medicine).

RECRUITMENT PRACTICES AND POLICIES. School has diversity program and actively recruits women/minority applicants. Diversity contact: Assistant Dean for Minority Affairs; phone: (213)342-1050.

ADMISSION REQUIREMENT FOR B.A.-M.D. APPLICANTS. Program is open to both residents and non-residents. *High school requirements:* 4 years of English, 4 years of mathematics, 1 year each of chemistry, physics, biology, 2 years of foreign language, 4 years of social sciences. Submit application, SAT I or ACT, plus Achievements in Mathematics Level II, Chemistry, Writing, official high school transcript with rank in class, letters of recommendation to Undergraduate Office, College Academic Services of the College of Letters, Arts and Sciences by December 15. For current information contact the College Academic Services Office; Phone: (213)740-5930; Web site: http://www.usc.edu/dept/las/cas/md.html. Notification April 1. Applicant's response to offer and $200 deposit must be returned by May 1.

ADMISSION REQUIREMENTS FOR FIRST-YEAR APPLICANTS. Preference given to state residents; U.S. citizens and permanent residents only. *Undergraduate preparation.* Suggested premed courses: 2 courses in biology with labs, 2 courses in inorganic chemistry with labs, 2 courses in organic chemistry with labs, 2 courses in physics with labs, 1 course in molecular biology, 2 courses in English, 6 courses in humanities and social sciences; courses in math, statistics, and computers as a tool are recommended. Bachelor's degree from an accredited institution required; all applicants have bachelor's degrees awarded prior to enrollment. *Has EDP*; applicants

must apply through AMCAS (official transcripts sent by mid-May) between June 1 and August 1. Early applications are encouraged. Submit secondary/supplemental application, a personal statement, and 2 recommendations to Admissions Office within 2 weeks of receipt of application. Interviews are by invitation only and generally for final selection. Notification normally begins October 1. *Regular application process.* Apply through AMCAS (file after June 1, before November 1); submit MCAT (will accept MCAT test results from the last 2 years), official transcripts for each school attended (should show at least 90 semester credits/135 quarter credits, submit transcripts by mid-May to AMCAS), service processing fee. Submit an application fee of $70, a supplemental application, a personal statement, preprofessional committee evaluation, and 3 recommendations from science faculty to Admissions Office within 2–3 weeks of the receipt of supplemental materials. International applicants must have completed at least 1 year of study in an accredited U.S. college or university prior to submitting an application. Interviews are by invitation only and generally for final selection. Joint-degree applicants must apply to, and be accepted by, both schools; contact the Admissions Office for current information and specific requirements for admission. First-year students admitted in fall only. Rolling admission process. Notification starts January 1 and is finished when class is filled. Applicant's response to offer and $100 deposit due within 2 weeks of receipt of acceptance letter. School does maintain an alternate list. Phone: (213)342-2552; E-mail: medadmit@hsc.usc.edu. Applicants for the Research Scholars Program apply after their 1st or 2nd year in medical school and must identify a faculty mentor/preceptor and present a description of the proposed research program.

ADMISSION REQUIREMENTS FOR TRANSFER APPLICANTS. Accepts transfers from other accredited U.S. medical schools who have completed their 2nd year of medical school. Admission limited to space available. Contact the Admissions Office after January 15 for current information and specific requirements.

ADMISSION STANDARDS AND RECOGNITION. *For B.A.-M.D.:* number of applicants 520; number interviewed 130; number enrolled 35; median SAT combined score 1,476; median GPA 4.18 (A = 4). *For M.D.:* number of state-resident applicants 4,185, nonresidents 2,324; number of interviewed 800; number of residents enrolled 125, nonresidents 25; median MCAT 10.3 (verbal reasoning 10.0; biological sciences 10.7; physical sciences 10.5); median GPA 3.5 (A = 4). Gorman rating 4.20 (scale: strong 4.01–4.49); the school's medical ranking by NIH awards was 33rd, with 148 awards/grants received; total dollars awarded $56,627,847.

FINANCIAL AID. Scholarships, merit scholarships, minority scholarships, grants-in-aid, institutional loans, HEAL, alternative loan programs, federal Perkins loans, Stafford subsidized and unsubsidized loans, and service commitment scholarship programs are available. All financial assistance is based on documented need. Assistantships/fellowships/stipends may be available for combined degree candidates and the Research Scholars Program. Financial aid applications and information are generally available at the on-campus interview (by invitation). For scholarships, the selection criteria place heavy reliance on MCAT and undergraduate GPA. Contact the Financial Aid Office for current information; phone: (213)342-1016. For most financial assistance and all federal programs, submit FAFSA to a federal processor (Title IV school code # 001328); also submit Financial Aid Transcript and Federal Income Tax forms. Approximately 75% of current students receive some form of financial assistance. Average debt after graduation $108,000.

DEGREE REQUIREMENTS. *For B.A.-M.D.:* an 8-year program; acceptable GPA and MCAT scores required for advancement to the School of Medicine. *For M.D.:* satisfactory completion of 4-year program. All students must pass USMLE Step 1 prior to entering 3rd year; all students must pass USMLE Step 2 prior to awarding of M.D. *For M.D.-Ph.D.:* generally a 7-year program.

School of Dentistry
925 West 34th Street, Room 216
Los Angeles, California 90089-0641
Phone: (213)740-2841; fax: (213)740-8109
Internet site: http://www.usc.edu/hsc/dental
E-mail: scdental@hsc.usc.edu

Established 1897. Trimester system. Special programs: International Student D.D.S. Program.

Annual tuition: $34,998; fees $500, equipment and supplies $8,726. No on-campus housing available. Contact Admissions Office for off-campus housing information. Off-campus housing, food, transportation, and personal expenses: approximately $14,312.

Enrollment: 1st-year class 142; total full-time 617. First-year enrolled student information: 21 from out of state; 10 states represented; 41 women; average age 24; 7 underrepresented minorities; 67 other minorities.

Degrees conferred: D.D.S., D.D.S.-M.B.A., D.D.S.-M.S. (Gerontology), M.S. (Craniofacial Biology, through the graduate school), Ph.D. (Craniofacial Biology, through the graduate school).

RECRUITMENT PRACTICES AND POLICIES. School has diversity program and actively recruits women/minority applicants. Diversity contact: Admissions Office and Student Affairs; phone: (213)740-2841.

ADMISSION REQUIREMENTS FOR FIRST-YEAR APPLICANTS. Preference given to state residents; U.S. citizens and permanent residents only. *Undergraduate preparation.* Suggested predental courses: 2 courses in biology with labs, 2 courses in inorganic chemistry with labs, 2 courses in organic chemistry with labs, 2 courses in physics with labs, 2 courses in English. There is no limitation on the number of junior-college credits taken. Will consider applicants with only 2 years of undergraduate preparation; prefer applicants who will have bachelor's degree prior to enrollment. *Application process.* Apply through AADSAS (file after June 1, before March 1); submit official transcripts for each school attended (should show at least 90 semester credits/135 quarter credits), service processing fee; at the same time as you send in AADSAS materials, submit an application fee of $50, and request official DAT scores sent directly to the Admissions Office and Student Affairs. TOEFL may be required of an applicant whose native language is other than English. Submit the following materials only after being contacted by an Admissions Officer: official transcripts, predental committee evaluation or 2 recommendations from science professors, and a photograph to Admissions Office and Student Affairs. Interviews are by invitation only and generally for final selection. D.D.S.-M.B.A. applicants are considered after 1 year of study at the School of Dentistry. First-year students admitted in fall only. Rolling admission process. Notification starts December 1 and is finished when class is filled. Applicant's response to offer and $300 school fee due within 30 days if accepted prior to January 1; response and deposit due within 2 weeks if received after February 1. School does maintain an alternate list. Phone: (213)740-2841; E-mail: scadmit@hsc.usc.edu.

ADMISSION REQUIREMENTS FOR ADVANCED-STANDING APPLICANTS. Accepts transfers from other accredited U.S. and Canadian dental schools. Admission limited to space available. Contact the Admissions Office for current information and specific requirements for admission.

ADMISSION REQUIREMENTS FOR INTERNATIONAL APPLICANTS. Request application materials from International Student Program. Submit completed application, score from National Dental Board Part 1, proof of English proficiency or TOEFL scores, 2 letters of recommendation from former teachers, an accurate account of clinical experience, documentary proof of a licence to practice dentistry from a ministry of health, official dental-school documents (transcripts), and a certificate of a dental degree to the Office of International Student Programs. In addition, submit a notarized Statement of Financial Support to cover the costs of tuition and expenses for 2 years. Application deadline is October 1. (Program begins in April.) Contact the International Student Program for current information and requirements for admission. Phone: (213)740-2841.

ADMISSION STANDARDS AND RECOGNITION. *For D.D.S.:* number of applicants 2,062; number enrolled 142; median DAT: ACAD 18.0, PAT 17.0; median GPA 3.35 (A = 4), median sciences GPA 3.35 (A = 4). Gorman rating 4.51 (scale: very strong 4.51–4.99); this placed the school in the Top 20 of all U.S. dental schools; the dental school's ranking by NIH awards/grants was 8th among dental schools, with 19 awards/grants received; total value of all awards/grants $4,554,531.

FINANCIAL AID. Scholarships, merit scholarships, minority scholarships, grants-in-aid, institutional loans, state loan programs, DEAL, HEAL, alternative loan programs, federal Perkins loans, Stafford subsidized and unsubsidized loans, and military service commitment scholarship programs are available. Institutional financial aid applications and information are generally available at the on-campus interview (by invitation). For scholarships, the selection criteria place heavy reliance on DAT and undergraduate GPA. Contact the Financial Aid Office for current information; phone: (213)740-2841. For most financial assistance and all need-based programs submit FAFSA to a federal processor (Title IV school code # 001328); also submit Financial Aid Transcript, Federal Income Tax forms, and Use of Federal Funds Certification. Approximately 75% of current students receive some form of financial assistance.

DEGREE REQUIREMENTS. *For D.D.S.:* satisfactory completion of 4-year (11 consecutive 14-week trimesters) program. *For D.D.S.* (International Student Program): generally a 2-year program: passage of both Part I and II of ADA National Board Exams; oral comprehensive exam.

SOUTHERN ILLINOIS UNIVERSITY
Carbondale, Illinois 62901-6806
Internet site: http://www.siu.edu

Founded 1869. Located 100 miles SE of St. Louis, Missouri. Public control. Semester system. Library:

2,000,000 volumes; 2,000,000 microforms; 15,000 periodicals/subscriptions. Special program: postbaccalaureate premedical program for underrepresented minorities (MEDPREP).

The university's graduate schools/colleges include: College of Agriculture, College of Business and Administration, College of Education, College of Engineering, College of Liberal Arts, College of Communication and Media Arts, College of Science, School of Social Work, School of Law, School of Medicine.

Total university enrollment at main campus: 11,000.

Memorial Medical Center
800 North Rutledge
Springfield, Illinois 62781

Public control. Medical center is a member of the Council of Teaching Hospitals.

School of Medicine
801 North Rutledge
Springfield, Illinois 62794-1226
Phone: (217)782-2860; fax: (217)785-5538
Internet site: http://www.siumed.edu

Established 1969. The 1st year is spent in Carbondale. Library in Springfield: 113,000 volumes/microforms; 1,600 current periodicals/subscriptions. Affiliated hospitals: Memorial Hospital (Carbondale), Memorial Medical Center (Springfield), St. John's Hospital and Pavilion (Springfield).

Annual tuition: residents $13,691, nonresidents $38,285; fees $1,449. No on-campus housing available in either Carbondale or Springfield. Contact Admissions Office for both on- and off-campus housing information. Off-campus housing and personal expenses: approximately $7,520.

Enrollment: 1st-year class 72 (EDP 15); total full-time 290 (men 53%, women 47%). First-year statistics: 0 from out of state; 42% women; average age 24; 0 minority representation; 81% science majors.

Degrees conferred: M.D., M.D.-J.D.

RECRUITMENT PRACTICES AND POLICIES. School has diversity program and actively recruits women/minority applicants. Diversity contact: Assistant Dean, Minority Affairs; phone: (618)453-1650.

ADMISSION REQUIREMENTS FOR FIRST-YEAR APPLICANTS. Preference given to state residents from central and southern Illinois; U.S. citizens and permanent residents only. *Undergraduate preparation.* Suggested premed courses: 2 courses in biology with labs, 2 courses in inorganic chemistry with labs, 2 courses in organic chemistry with labs, 2 courses in physics with labs, 2 courses in college math, including statistics, 2 courses in English. Bachelor's degree from an accredited institution required; 98% of applicants have bachelor's degree awarded prior to enrollment. *Has EDP* for both state residents and nonresidents (nonresidents must apply through EDP); applicants must apply through AMCAS (official transcripts sent by mid-May) between June 1 and August 1. Early applications are encouraged. Submit supplemental application, a personal statement, and 2 recommendations to Office of Student Affairs within 2 weeks of receipt of application. Interviews are by invitation only and generally for final selection. Notification normally begins October 1. *Regular application process.* Apply through AMCAS (file after June 1, before November 15); submit MCAT (will accept MCAT test results from the last 3 years), official transcripts for each school attended (should show at least 90 semester credits/135 quarter credits, submit transcripts by mid-May to AMCAS), service processing fee. Submit an application fee of $50, a supplemental application, a personal statement, preprofessional committee evaluation, and 3 recommendations from science faculty to Admissions Office within 2–3 weeks of the receipt of supplemental materials. Interviews are by invitation only and generally for final selection. M.D.-J.D. degree applicants must apply to, and be accepted by, both schools; contact the Admissions Office for current information and specific requirements for admission. First-year students admitted in fall only. Rolling admission process. Notification starts October 15 and is finished when class is filled. Applicant's response to offer and $100 deposit due within 2 weeks of receipt of acceptance letter. School does maintain an alternate list. Phone: (217)782-6013.

ADMISSION REQUIREMENTS FOR TRANSFER APPLICANTS. Accepts transfers from other accredited U.S. medical schools into the 2nd year of study only. Preference given to central and southern Illinois residents. Admission limited to space available. Contact the Office of Student Affairs for current information and specific requirements for admission.

ADMISSION STANDARDS AND RECOGNITION. *For M.D.:* number of state-resident applicants 1,413, nonresidents 552; number of state residents interviewed 172, nonresidents 7; number of residents enrolled 72, nonresidents none; median MCAT 9.3 (verbal reasoning 10.0; biological sciences 10.0; physical sciences 9.0); median GPA 3.45 (A = 4). Gorman rating 3.28 (scale: acceptable plus 3.01–3.59); *U.S. News & World Report* ranked the school in the Top 25 of all U.S. medical schools in

primary-care preparation; medical ranking by NIH awards was 106th, with 25 awards/grants received; total dollars awarded $3,064,838.

FINANCIAL AID. Scholarships, merit scholarships, minority scholarships, grants-in-aid, institutional loans, HEAL, alternative loan programs, federal Perkins loans, Stafford subsidized and unsubsidized loans, and Illinois Health Improvement Associate Loans are available. Financial aid applications and information are generally available at the on-campus interview (by invitation). Scholarships and grants limited to students with demonstrated exceptional need. Contact the Financial Aid Office for current information; phone: (217)785-2224. For most financial assistance and all federal programs, submit FAFSA to a federal processor (Title IV school code # E00569); also submit Financial Aid Transcript and Federal Income Tax forms. Approximately 85% of current students receive some form of financial assistance. Average debt after graduation $54,900.

DEGREE REQUIREMENTS. *For M.D.:* satisfactory completion of 4-year program. All students must pass USMLE Step 1 prior to graduation. *For M.D.-J.D.:* generally a 6-year program.

School of Dental Medicine
2800 College Avenue, Building 273, Room 2300
Alton, Illinois 62002-4978
Phone: (618)474-7170; fax: (618)474-7150
Internet site: http://www.siue.edu/dmsch
E-mail: sdmapps@siue.edu

Established 1969. Located near both St. Louis and Edwardsville. Special program: prematriculation summer sessions.

Annual tuition: residents $7,410, nonresidents $22,230; fees $665; equipment and supplies $5,350. No on-campus housing available. Contact Admissions Office for off-campus housing information. Off-campus housing, food, transportation, and personal expenses: approximately $10,228.

Enrollment: 1st-year class 50; total full-time 200. First-year enrolled student information: 2 from out of state; 12 women; average age 23; 4 underrepresented minorities; 2 other minorities.

Faculty: full-time 42, part-time 49.

Degrees conferred: D.M.D., B.S.-D.D.S. (Edwardsville).

RECRUITMENT PRACTICES AND POLICIES. School has diversity program and actively recruits women/minority applicants. Diversity contact: Office of Minority Affairs; phone: (618)474-7190.

ADMISSION REQUIREMENTS FOR FIRST-YEAR APPLICANTS. Preference given to state residents; U.S. citizens and permanent residents only. *Undergraduate preparation.* Suggested predental courses: 2 courses in biology with labs, 2 courses in inorganic chemistry with labs, 2 courses in organic chemistry with labs, 2 courses in physics with labs, 2 courses in English. The junior-college transfer credit limit is 60 credits. Will consider applicants with only two years of undergraduate preparation; prefer applicants who will have a bachelor's degree prior to enrollment; 44% of applicants have bachelor's degree awarded prior to enrollment. *Application process.* Apply through AADSAS (file after June 1, before March 1); official transcripts for each school attended (should show at least 90 semester credits/135 quarter credits), service processing fee; at the same time as you send in AADSAS materials, submit an application fee of $20, an official transcript, and DAT scores to Office of Admissions and Records. Interviews are by invitation only and generally for final selection. First-year students admitted in fall only. Rolling admission process. Notification starts December 1 and is finished when class is filled, but not later than August 1. Applicant's response to offer and $80 deposit due within 30 days if accepted prior to February 28; response and deposit due within 2 weeks if received after March 1. School does maintain an alternate list. Phone: (618)474-7170.

ADMISSION REQUIREMENTS FOR ADVANCED-STANDING APPLICANTS. Accepts transfers from other accredited U.S. dental schools. Admission limited to space available. There is no advanced-standing program for graduates of foreign schools of dentistry. Contact the Office of Admissions and Records for current information and specific requirements for admission.

ADMISSION STANDARDS AND RECOGNITION. *For D.D.S.:* number of applicants 758; number enrolled 50; median DAT: ACAD 17.3, PAT 17.8; median GPA 3.14 (A = 4), median sciences GPA 3.04 (A = 4). Gorman rating 4.06 (scale: strong 4.01–4.49); this placed the school in the Bottom 10 of all U.S. dental schools.

FINANCIAL AID. Scholarships, merit scholarships, minority scholarships, tuition waivers, SIU-SDM loans, state loan programs, DEAL, HEAL, alternative loan programs, federal Perkins loans, Stafford subsidized and unsubsidized loans, and military service commitment scholarship programs are available. Most financial aid is based on demonstrated need. Institutional financial aid applications and information are generally available at the on-campus interview (by invitation). Contact the Financial Aid Office for current information; phone: (618)474-4175. For most financial assistance and all need-based programs submit FAFSA to a federal processor (Title IV school code # E00606); also submit Financial Aid Transcript, Federal Income Tax forms, and Use of Federal Funds Certification. Approximately 84% of current students receive some form of financial assistance. Average award resident $20,904.

DEGREE REQUIREMENTS. *For B.S.-D.M.D.:* a 7-year program. *For D.M.D.:* satisfactory completion of 4-year program.

STANFORD UNIVERSITY
Stanford, California 94305-9991
Internet site: http://www.stanford.edu

Founded 1891. Located near Palo Alto, 30 miles S of San Francisco. Private control. Semester system. Library: 6,500,000 volumes; 4,500,000 microforms; 43,800 periodicals/subscriptions; 600 computer work stations. The university's ranking in domestic higher education by NIH awards/grants was 9th, with 556 awards/grants received; total dollars awarded $167,465,890.

The university's graduate schools: Graduate School of Business, Law School, School of Earth Sciences, School of Education, School of Engineering, School of Humanities and Sciences, School of Medicine.

Total university enrollment at main campus: 14,000.

Stanford University Medical Center
300 Pasteur Drive
Stanford, California 94305

Center opened in 1959. Located on main campus. Private control. Stanford University Hospital and University of California at San Francisco merged in 1997 and became the UCSF/Stanford Health Care System. Stanford University Hospital is a member of the Council of Teaching Hospitals. The Medical Center consists of the School of Medicine, Stanford Clinics and Hospital, and Lucile Salter Packard Children's Hospital. Nationally recognized programs in AIDS, Cancer, Cardiology, Endocrinology, Gastroenterology, Geriatrics, Gynecology, Neurology, Orthopedics, Otolaryngology, Pediatrics, Psychiatry, Pulmonary Disease, Rheumatology, Urology. *U.S. News & World Report*'s hospital/medical center national rankings for all hospitals placed Stanford Hospital in the Top 20 of all U.S. hospitals.

School of Medicine
851 Welch Road, Room 154
Palo Alto, California 94304-1677
Phone: (650)723-6861; fax: (650)725-4599
Internet site: http://www.med.stanford.edu

Established 1858 as a medical department of the College of the Pacific; Stanford School of Medicine was established in 1958. Located 35 miles S of San Francisco. Quarter system. Library: 350,000 volumes/microforms; 3,000 current periodicals/subscriptions. Special programs: Early Matriculation Programs for underrepresented minorities and financially disadvantaged students; prematriculation summer sessions.

Annual tuition: $26,992; fees $607. On-campus apartments are available for both single and married students. Annual on-campus housing cost: single students $3,150 (room only), married students $3,300–$6,600. Contact Housing Assignment Service for on-campus housing information. Contact the Office of Community Housing Services for off-campus housing information. Off-campus housing and personal expenses: approximately $14,000.

Enrollment: 1st-year class 86 (EDP 2); total full-time 465 (men 57%, women 43%). First-year statistics: 50% out of state; 42% women; average age 24; 11% minorities; 40% science majors.

Faculty: full-time 600, part-time/volunteers 1,200.

Degrees conferred: M.D., M.D.-M.S., M.D.-Ph.D. (Biochemistry, Biomedical Engineering, Biophysics, Cancer Biology, Developmental Biology, Epidemiology, Genetics, Immunology, Medical Information Sciences, Microbiology, Molecular and Cell Biology, Neurosciences, Molecular Pharmacology, Structural Biology); has M.S.T.P.

RECRUITMENT PRACTICES AND POLICIES. School has diversity program and actively recruits women/minority applicants. Diversity contact: Associate Dean for Student Affairs; phone: (650)725-8589.

ADMISSION REQUIREMENTS FOR FIRST-YEAR APPLICANTS. Preference given to U.S. and permanent residents. *Undergraduate preparation.* Suggested premed courses: 2 courses in biology with labs, 2 courses in inorganic chemistry with labs, 2 courses in organic chemistry with labs, 2 courses in physics with labs; courses in calculus, physical chemistry, behavioral sciences, and biochemistry strongly encouraged; knowledge of a foreign language also desirable. Bachelor's degree from an accredited institution required; all applicants have bachelor's degrees awarded prior to enrollment. *Has EDP;* applicants must apply through AMCAS (official transcripts sent by mid-May) between June 1 and August 1.

Early applications are encouraged. Submit supplemental application, a personal statement, and 2 recommendations to Admissions Office within 2 weeks of receipt of application. Interviews are by invitation only and generally for final selection. Notification normally begins October 1. *Regular application process.* Apply through AMCAS (file after June 1, before November 1); submit MCAT (will accept MCAT test results from the last 3 years), official transcripts for each school attended (should show at least 90 semester credits/135 quarter credits, submit transcripts by mid-May to AMCAS), service processing fee. Submit an application fee of $55, a supplemental application, a personal statement, preprofessional committee evaluation, and 3 recommendations from science faculty to Admissions Office within 2–3 weeks of the receipt of supplemental materials. International applicants must have studied for at least 1 year at either an accredited U.S., Canadian, or UK institution. Interviews are by invitation only and generally for final selection. The request for an M.S.T.P. application form is on the supplementary application. Contact the M.S.T.P. Office for current information; phone: (650)723-6176. Joint-degree applicants must apply to, and be accepted by, both schools; contact the Admissions Office for current information and specific requirements for admission. First-year students admitted in fall only. Rolling admission process. Notification starts October 15 and is finished when class is filled. Applicant's response to offer due within 2 weeks of receipt of acceptance letter. School does maintain an alternate list. Phone: (650)723-6861.

ADMISSION REQUIREMENTS FOR TRANSFER APPLICANTS. Stanford School of Medicine does not accept transfer students.

ADMISSION STANDARDS AND RECOGNITION. *For M.D.:* number of state-resident applicants 2,723, nonresidents 4,001; number of state residents interviewed 237, nonresidents 237; number of residents enrolled 46, nonresidents 40; median MCAT 10.6 (verbal reasoning 10.0; biological sciences 11.0; physical sciences 11.0); median GPA 3.6 (A = 4). *Barron's Guide* placed school among the Top 25 most prestigious U.S. medical schools; Gorman rating 4.85 (scale: very strong 4.51–4.99); *U.S. News & World Report* ranked the school in the Top 25 of all U.S. medical schools; the school's medical ranking by NIH awards was 7th, with 448 awards/grants received; total dollars awarded $144,937,282.

FINANCIAL AID. Stanford Medical Students Scholars Program, grants, institutional loans, HEAL, alternative loan programs, U.S. Public Health Service Training Grants, federal Perkins loans, and Stafford subsidized and unsubsidized loans available. Assistantships and research opportunities may be available for joint-degree candidates. All financial aid is based on demonstrated need. International students are not eligible for financial aid. Financial-aid applications and information are generally available at the on-campus interview (by invitation). Contact the Financial Aid Office for current information; phone: (650)723-6959. For most financial assistance and all federal programs, submit FAFSA to a federal processor (Title IV school code # G24552); also submit Financial Aid Transcript and Federal Income Tax forms. Approximately 80% of current students receive some form of financial assistance. Average debt after graduation $48,890.

DEGREE REQUIREMENTS. *For M.D.:* satisfactory completion of 4–6 year program (the completion of 230 units in approved courses and a clerkship). All students must pass USMLE Step 1 prior to entering 3rd year; all students must pass USMLE Step 2 prior to awarding of M.D. *For D.D.-M.S.:* generally a 4½–5½-year program. *For M.D.-Ph.D., M.S.T.P.:* generally a 7-year program.

STATE UNIVERSITY OF NEW YORK AT STONY BROOK
Stony Brook, New York 11794-4433
Internet site: http://www.sunysb.edu

Founded 1957. Located 60 miles E of New York City, on Long Island's North Shore. Public control. Semester system. Library: 1,777,000 volumes; 2,484,000 microforms; 11,100 periodicals/subscriptions. The university's ranking in domestic higher education by NIH awards/grants was 55th, with 199 awards/grants received; total dollars awarded $45,492,015.

The university's graduate schools/colleges include: College of Arts and Sciences, College of Engineering and Applied Sciences, Institute for Terrestrial and Planetary Atmospheres, Marine Sciences Research Center, School of Dental Medicine, School of Health Technology and Management, School of Medicine, School of Nursing, School of Professional Development and Continuing Studies, School of Social Welfare.

Total university enrollment at main campus: 17,310.

SUNY Health Science Center
HSC Level 4
Stony Brook, New York 11794
Internet site: http://www.hsc.sunysb.edu

Public Control. University hospital is a member of the Council of Teaching Hospitals. Schools located at health science center are: School of Allied Health Professions, School of Dental Medicine, School of Nursing, School of Social Welfare.

School of Medicine
Level 4, Room 147
Health Science Center
Stony Brook, New York 11794-8434
Phone: (516)444-2113; fax: (516)444-2202
Internet site: http://www.hsc.sunysb.edu/som
E-mail: admissions@dean.som.sunysb.edu

Established 1971. Located at health science center. Semester system. Library: 238,000 volumes/microforms; 4,400 current periodicals/subscriptions. Affiliated hospitals: University Hospital, Nassau County Medical Center, Northport VA Hospital, Winthrop University Hospital. Special programs: M.S.T.P. combines research training at the School of Medicine with research at Cold Spring Harbor Laboratory and Brookhaven National Laboratory.

Annual tuition: residents $11,085, nonresidents $22,185; fees $170. On-campus rooms and apartments available for both single and married students. Annual on-campus housing cost: double room $3,460 (room only), meal plan $1,800; apartments per month range from $544–$1,099. Contact Student Affairs Office for both on- and off-campus housing information; phone: (516)632-6750. Medical students tend to live off-campus. Off-campus living expenses: approximately $15,900.

Enrollment: 1st-year class 100 (EDP 5, M.S.T.P. 5–6 each year); total full-time 421 (men 56%, women 43%). First-year statistics: 2% out of state; 44% women; average age 25; 9% underrepresented minorities; 27% other minorities; 90% science majors.

Faculty: full-time, 500 part-time 40.

Degrees conferred: M.D., M.D.-Ph.D. (Anatomy, Biochemistry, Biomedical Engineering, Biophysics, Cell Structure, Cellular Immunology, Computer Graphics and Molecular Modeling, Developmental Biology and Genetics, Epidemiology, Endocrinology, Genetic Toxicology, Membrane Biology and Biophysics, Molecular Biology and Molecular Genetics, Molecular Virology, Neuropharmacology, Pharmacology, Physiology, Tumorigenesis, Structure and Physical Biochemistry, Vertebrate Morphology, Virology); has M.S.T.P.

RECRUITMENT PRACTICES AND POLICIES. School has diversity program and actively recruits women/minority applicants. Diversity contact: Associate Dean for Student and Minority Affairs; phone: (516)444-2341.

ADMISSION REQUIREMENTS FOR FIRST-YEAR APPLICANTS. Priority given to state residents; U.S.

citizens and permanent residents only; nonresidents are encouraged to apply for M.D.-Ph.D. program. *Undergraduate preparation.* Suggested premed courses: 2 courses in biology with labs, 2 courses in inorganic chemistry with labs, 2 courses in organic chemistry with labs, 2 courses in physics with labs, 2 courses in English. Bachelor's degree from an accredited institution required; 98% of applicants have bachelor's degree awarded prior to enrollment. *Has EDP* for state residents only; applicants must apply through AMCAS (official transcripts sent by mid-May) between June 1 and August 1. Early applications are encouraged. Submit supplemental application, a personal statement, and 2 recommendations to Admissions Office within 2 weeks of receipt of application. Interviews are by invitation only and generally for final selection. Notification normally begins October 1. *Regular application process.* Apply through AMCAS (file after June 1, before November 15); submit MCAT (will accept MCAT test results from last 4 years), official transcripts for each school attended (should show at least 90 semester credits/135 quarter credits, submit transcripts by mid-May to AMCAS), service processing fee. Submit an application fee of $65, a supplemental application, a personal statement, preprofessional committee evaluation, and 2 recommendations from science faculty to Admissions Office within 2–3 weeks of the receipt of supplemental materials. Interviews are by invitation only and generally for final selection. M.S.T.P. is coordinated through the School of Medicine. A separate interview is required. Candidates should have had research experience. A formal application to the graduate school has to be made not later than the middle of the 2nd year of medical school. Applicants must apply to, and be accepted by, both schools. Contact the Admissions Office for current information and specific requirements for admission. First-year students admitted in fall only. Rolling admission process. Notification starts October 15 and is finished when class is filled. Applicant's response to offer and $100 deposit due within 15 days of receipt of acceptance letter. School does maintain an alternate list. Phone: (516)444-2113.

ADMISSION REQUIREMENTS FOR TRANSFER APPLICANTS. Accepts transfers from other accredited U.S. medical schools into the 3rd year only. Preference is given to state residents. Admission limited to space available. Contact the Admissions Office for current information and specific requirements for admission.

ADMISSION STANDARDS AND RECOGNITION. *For M.D.:* number of state-resident applicants 2,852, nonresidents 919; number interviewed 789; number of residents enrolled 98, nonresidents 2; median MCAT 10.3 (verbal reasoning 10.0; biological sciences 11.0; physical sciences 11.0); median GPA 3.53 (A = 4). Gorman rating 4.15 (scale: strong 4.01–4.49); the school's medical ranking by NIH awards/grants was 59th, with 115 awards/grants received; total dollars awarded $29,568,346.

FINANCIAL AID. Scholarships, merit scholarships, minority scholarships, grants-in-aid, institutional loans, HEAL, alternative loan programs, NIH stipends, federal Perkins loans, Stafford subsidized and unsubsidized loans, and service commitment scholarship programs are available. M.S.T.P. students receive funding from NIH in the form of a stipend plus tuition waivers. Assistantships/fellowships may be available for combined degree candidates. Financial aid applications and information are given out at the on-campus interview (by invitation). For scholarship assistance, the selection criteria place heavy reliance on MCAT and undergraduate GPA. Contact the Office of Student Affairs for current information, but applicants are encouraged to apply by March 1 for serious consideration; phone: (516)444-2341. For most financial assistance and all federal programs, submit FAFSA to a federal processor (Title IV school code # 002838); also submit Financial Aid Transcript and Federal Income Tax forms. Approximately 85% of current students receive some form of financial assistance. Average debt after graduation $61,000.

DEGREE REQUIREMENTS. *For M.D.:* satisfactory completion of 4-year program. It is recommended that all students take USMLE Step 1 and Step 2, but it is not required. *For M.D.-Ph.D., M.S.T.P.:* generally a 6–7-year program.

School of Dental Medicine

Rockland Hall, Room J 115
Stony Brook, New York 11794-8709
Phone: (516)632-8980; fax: (516)632-9705
Internet site: http://www.sunysb.edu

Established 1973. Located on main campus. Affiliated hospitals: University Hospital, Long Island Jewish Hospital, Montefiore Hospital, Northport Veteran's Affairs Hospital. Postgraduate specialties: General Dentistry (AEGD), Orthodontics, Periodontics, Program in Dental Care for Developmentally Disabled.

Annual tuition: residents $10,840, nonresidents $21,600; equipment and supplies $4,633. On-campus rooms and apartments available for both single and married students. Annual on-campus housing cost: double room $3,460 (room only), meal plan $1,800; apartments per month range from $544–$1,099. Contact Student Affairs Office for both on- and off-campus housing information; phone: (516)632-6750. Dental students tend to live off-campus. Off-campus housing, food, transportation, and personal expenses: approximately $15,900.

Enrollment: 1st-year class 24; total full-time 90. First-year enrolled student information: none from out of state; 16 women; average age 24; 1 underrepresented minority; 9 other minorities.

Degrees conferred: D.D.S., M.S. and Ph.D. are offered through the graduate school.

RECRUITMENT PRACTICES AND POLICIES. School has diversity program and actively recruits women/minority applicants. Diversity contact: Office of Academic Affairs, Admissions and Financial Aid; phone: (516)632-8980.

ADMISSION REQUIREMENTS FOR FIRST-YEAR APPLICANTS. Preference given to state residents; U.S. citizens and permanent residents only. *Undergraduate preparation.* Suggested predental courses: 2 courses in biology with labs, 2 courses in inorganic (general) chemistry with labs, 2 courses in organic chemistry with labs, 2 courses in physics with labs, 2 courses in college math; 1 course in biochemistry and 1 in a social science or English strongly suggested. No more than 2 science prerequisites can be taken at a junior college. Will consider applicants with only 3 years of undergraduate preparation but strongly prefer applicants who will have bachelor's degree prior to enrollment; all applicants have bachelor's degree awarded prior to enrollment. *Application process.* Apply through AADSAS (file after July 1, before January 15); submit official transcripts for each school attended (should show at least 90 semester credits/135 quarter credits), service processing fee; at the same time as you send in AADSAS materials; submit an application fee of $75, official transcripts, DAT scores (DAT should be taken no later than October of the year preceding the anticipated year of enrollment), predental committee evaluation, or 2 recommendations from science professors to the Admissions Office. Interviews are by invitation only and generally for final selection. First-year students admitted in fall only. Rolling admission process. Notification starts in December and is finished when class is filled not later than August 28. Applicant's response to offer and $200 deposit due within 30 days if accepted prior to January 31; response and deposit due within 2 weeks if received after February 1. School does maintain an alternate list. Phone: (516)632-8480.

ADMISSION REQUIREMENTS FOR ADVANCED-STANDING APPLICANTS. Accepts transfers from other accredited U.S. dental schools; however, an applicant should expect to complete at least 3 years of study at the dental school. Admission limited to space available. Contact the Admissions Office for current information and specific requirements for admission.

ADMISSION STANDARDS AND RECOGNITION. *For D.D.S.:* number of applicants 795; number enrolled 39; median DAT: ACAD 18.53, PAT 16.63; median GPA 3.36 (A = 4), median sciences GPA 3.3 (A = 4). Gorman rating 4.36 (scale: strong 4.01–4.49); this placed the school in the Top 25 of all U.S. dental schools; the dental school's ranking by NIH awards/grants was 26th among dental schools, with 5 awards/grants received; total value of all awards/grants $1,014,115.

FINANCIAL AID. Scholarships, merit scholarships, minority scholarships, grants-in-aid, institutional loans, Tuition Assistance Program (TAP), state loan programs, DEAL, HEAL, alternative loan programs, federal Perkins loans, Stafford subsidized and unsubsidized loans, and military service commitment scholarship programs are available. Institutional financial-aid applications and information are given out at the on-campus interview (by invitation). For scholarship assistance, the selection criteria place heavy reliance on DAT and undergraduate GPA. Contact the Financial Aid Office for current information; phone: (516)632-8980. For most financial assistance and all need-based programs submit FAFSA to a federal processor (Title IV school code # 002838); also submit Financial Aid Transcript, Federal Income Tax forms, and Use of Federal Funds Certification. 100% of current students receive some form of financial assistance.

DEGREE REQUIREMENTS. *For D.D.S.:* satisfactory completion of 4-year (43-month) program.

STATE UNIVERSITY OF NEW YORK HEALTH SCIENCE CENTER AT BROOKLYN

Brooklyn, New York 11203-2098
Internet site: http://www.hscbrooklyn.edu

Founded 1860; merged with the State University of New York in 1950. Formerly known as Downstate Medical Center; named changed in 1986. Public control. Semester system. Library: 330,000 volumes/microforms.

Special facilities: centerwide core facilities for DNA synthesis and purification, videoimaging, protein sequencing, and cell sorting; electron microscopy. Special programs: B.A.-M.D. program (annual undergraduate tuition residents $3,200, nonresidents $6,800); the center's ranking in domestic higher education by NIH awards/grants was 98th, with 45 awards/grants received; total dollars awarded $15,020,373.

The center's other graduate colleges/schools are: College of Medicine, College of Nursing, School of Graduate Studies.

Total university enrollment at main campus: 1,639.

University Hospital of Brooklyn
SUNY Health Science Center
445 Lenox Road
Box 23
Brooklyn, New York 11794

Public control. University Hospital is a member of Council of Teaching Hospitals.

College of Medicine
450 Clarkson Avenue, Box 60M
Brooklyn, New York 11203-2098
Phone: (718)270-2446
Internet site: http://www.hscbrooklyn.edu
E-mail: imontano@netmail.hscbrooklyn.edu

Established 1860 as Long Island College Hospital. Located in Flatbush section of Brooklyn. Affiliated hospitals: University Hospital, Kings County Hospital. Special programs: Summer programs for underrepresented minorities, prematriculation summer sessions.

Annual tuition: residents $11,060, nonresidents $22,160; fees $220. On-campus rooms and apartments available for both single and married students. Annual on-campus living expenses: $10,450. Contact Housing Office for both on- and off-campus housing information; phone: (718)270-1466.

Enrollment: 1st-year class 180 (EDP 20); total full-time 771 (men 60%, women 40%). First-year statistics: none from out of state; 41.6% women; average age 25; 14% minorities.

Faculty: full-time/ part-time/volunteers 2,500.

Degrees conferred: M.D., B.A.-M.D. (Brooklyn College), M.D.-Ph.D. (Anatomy and Cell Biology, Biochemistry, Biophysics, Microbiology and Immunology, Neurosciences, Pharmacology, Physiology).

RECRUITMENT PRACTICES AND POLICIES. School has diversity program and actively recruits women/minority applicants. Diversity contact: Associate Dean for Minority Affairs; phone: (718)270-3765.

ADMISSION REQUIREMENT FOR B.A.-M.D. APPLICANTS. Preference given to state residents; will consider nonresidents. *Recommended high school preparation*: 4 years of English, 3 years of science, 3 years of mathematics, 3 years of social studies. Submit application, SAT I, 3 Achievements or ACT, official high school transcript with rank in class, and 3 letters of recommendation. Apply to Director of Admissions, Brooklyn College, after November 1, before December 30. Interviews are by invitation only and generally for final selection. Notification date is on April 1. Applicant's response to offer due May 1. Phone: (718)951-5044.

ADMISSION REQUIREMENTS FOR FIRST-YEAR APPLICANTS. Preference given to state residents; U.S. citizens and permanent residents only. *Undergraduate preparation*. Suggested premed courses: 2 courses in biology with labs, 2 courses in inorganic chemistry with labs, 2 courses in organic chemistry with labs, 2 courses in physics with labs, 2 courses in English; biochemistry, mathematics, and an advanced science course recommended. Bachelor's degree from an accredited institution required; 98% of applicants have bachelor's degree awarded prior to enrollment. *Has EDP* for state residents only; applicants must apply through AMCAS (official transcripts sent by mid-May) between June 1 and August 1. Early applications are encouraged. Submit supplemental application, a personal statement, and 2 recommendations to Director of Admissions within 2 weeks of receipt of application. Interviews are by invitation only and generally for final selection. Notification normally begins October 1. *Regular application process*. Apply through AMCAS (file after June 1, before December 15); submit MCAT (will accept MCAT test results from 1995), official transcripts for each school attended (should show at least 90 semester credits/135 quarter credits, submit transcripts by mid-May to AMCAS), service processing fee. Submit an application fee of $65, a supplemental application, a personal statement, preprofessional committee evaluation, and 2 recommendations from science faculty to Director of Admissions within 2–3 weeks of the receipt of supplemental materials. Interviews are by invitation only and generally for final selection. M.D.-Ph.D. degree applicants must apply to, and be accepted by, both schools; contact the Admissions Office for current information and specific requirements for admission; M.D.-Ph.D. phone: (718)270-2740. First-year students admitted in fall only. Rolling admission process. Notification starts October 15 and is finished when class is filled. Applicant's response to offer and $100 deposit due within 2 weeks of receipt of acceptance letter. School does maintain an alternate list. Phone: (718)270-2446; E-mail: imontano@netmail.hscbrooklyn.edu.

ADMISSION REQUIREMENTS FOR TRANSFER APPLICANTS. Accepts transfers from other accredited U.S. medical schools; preference given to state residents. Admission limited to space available. Contact the Director of Admissions after January 1 for current information and specific requirements.

ADMISSION STANDARDS AND RECOGNITION. *For B.A./B.S.-M.D.:* number of state-resident applicants 300, nonresidents 61; number of state residents interviewed 59, nonresidents 1; number of residents enrolled 22, nonresidents 0; median SAT combined 1,430; median GPA 94 (scale 0–100). *For M.D.:* number of state-resident applicants 2,278, nonresidents 2,290; number of state residents interviewed 741, nonresidents 26; number of residents enrolled 184, nonresidents 1; median MCAT 9.6 (verbal reasoning 9.0; biological sciences 10.0; physical sciences 10.0); median GPA 3.53 (A = 4). Gorman rating 3.71 (scale: good 3.61–3.99); college's medical ranking by NIH awards/grants was 77th, with 45 awards/grants received; total dollars awarded $15,020,373.

FINANCIAL AID. Scholarships, merit scholarships, minority scholarships, grants-in-aid, institutional loans, state loans, Tuition Assistance Program (TAP), HEAL, alternative loan programs, federal Perkins loans, Stafford subsidized and unsubsidized loans, and service commitment scholarship programs are available. Assistantships/fellowships may be available for dual-degree candidates. Financial aid applications and information are given out at the on-campus interview (by invitation). Most financial aid is based on demonstrated need. For scholarships, the selection criteria place heavy reliance on MCAT and undergraduate GPA. Contact the Financial Aid Office for current information; phone: (718)270-2488. For most financial assistance and all federal programs, submit FAFSA to a federal processor (Title IV school code # 002839); also submit Financial Aid Transcript and Federal Income Tax forms. Approximately 80% of current students receive some form of financial assistance. Average debt after graduation $59,900.

DEGREE REQUIREMENTS. *For B.A.-M.D.:* generally an 8-year program; 7-year option available. *For M.D.:* satisfactory completion of 4-year program. All students must pass USMLE Step 1 prior to entering 3rd year; all students must pass USMLE Step 2 prior to awarding of M.D. *For M.D.-Ph.D.:* generally a 7-year program.

STATE UNIVERSITY OF NEW YORK HEALTH SCIENCE CENTER AT SYRACUSE

750 East Adams Street
Syracuse, New York 13210-2334
Internet site: http://www.hscsyr.edu

Founded 1834; merged with the State University of New York in 1950. Name changed from Upstate Medical Center in 1986. Public control. Semester system. Library: 175,000 volumes; 1,400 periodicals/subscriptions; 26 PC work stations. Special programs: B.A./B.S.-M.D. program (annual undergraduate tuition $3,200, at Binghamton University). A clinical campus is located in Binghamton, New York. The University Hospital is a member of the Council of Teaching Hospitals. The university's ranking in domestic higher education by NIH awards was 114th, with 40 awards/grants received; total dollars awarded $9,012,797.

The health sciences center's graduate colleges are: the College of Graduate Studies, College of Health Related Professions, College of Medicine, College of Nursing.

Total enrollment: 1,235.

College of Medicine
155 Elizabeth Blackwell Street
Syracuse, New York 13210
Phone: (315)464-4570; fax: (315)464-8867
Internet site: http://www.hscsyr.edu

Established 1834 as Geneva Medical College. Joined Syracuse University in 1872; transferred to SUNY in 1950. Fourteenth-oldest medical college in U.S. Affiliated hospitals: St. Joseph's Hospital and Health Center, Community General Hospital and Van Duyn Home and Hospital, U.S. Veteran's Administration Medical Center, Crouse-Irving Hospital, Richard H. Hutchings Psychiatric Center; in Binghamton, United Health Services, Our Lady of Lourdes Hospital, Robert Packer Hospital. Special programs: Rural Medical Program; prematriculation summer sessions.

Annual tuition: residents $11,093, nonresidents $22,193. On-campus rooms and apartments available for both single and married students. Annual on-campus housing cost: single students $3,030 (room only); board is $240 per month. Contact Director of Residential Life for both on- and off-campus housing information; phone: (315)464-5106. Medical students tend to live off-campus.

Off-campus housing and personal expenses: approximately $9,000.

Enrollment: 1st-year class 150 (EDP 5); total full-time 606 (men 53%, women 47%). First-year statistics: 7% out of state; 50–60 colleges represented; 45.6% women; average age 24.

Faculty: full-time/part-time/volunteers 1,667.

Degrees conferred: M.D., B.S.-M.D. (Binghamton University), M.D.-Ph.D. (Anatomy, Biochemistry, Cell and Molecular Biology, Microbiology and Immunology, Molecular Biology, Neurosciences, Pharmacology, Physiology).

RECRUITMENT PRACTICES AND POLICIES. School has diversity program and actively recruits women/minority applicants. Diversity contact: Director, Officer of Minority Affairs; phone: (315)464-5433.

ADMISSION REQUIREMENT FOR B.S.-M.D. APPLICANTS. UMEDS is for state residents only who are from underrepresented minorities. Address all inquiries to: Early Acceptance/UMEDS, College of Medicine, SUNY Health Sciences Center, P.O. Box 1000, Binghamton, NY 13902; phone; (607)770-8515.

ADMISSION REQUIREMENTS FOR FIRST-YEAR APPLICANTS. Preference given to state residents; U.S. citizens and permanent residents only. *Undergraduate preparation.* Suggested premed courses: 2 courses in biology with labs, 2 courses in inorganic chemistry with labs, 2 courses in organic chemistry with labs, 2 courses in physics with labs, 2 courses in English. Bachelor's degree from an accredited institution required; all applicants have bachelor's degrees awarded prior to enrollment. *Has EDP* for state residents only; applicants must apply through AMCAS (official transcripts sent by mid-May) between June 1 and August 1. Early applications are encouraged. Submit supplemental application, a personal statement, and 2 recommendations to Admissions Office within 2 weeks of receipt of application. Interviews are by invitation only and generally for final selection. Notification normally begins October 1. *Regular application process.* Apply through AMCAS (file after June 1, before November 1); submit MCAT (will accept MCAT test results from 1995), official transcripts for each school attended (should show at least 90 semester credits/135 quarter credits, submit transcripts by mid-May to AMCAS), service processing fee. Submit an application fee of $60, a supplemental application, a personal statement, preprofessional committee evaluation, and 2 recommendations from science faculty to Admissions Office within 2–3 weeks of the receipt of supplemental materials. Interviews are by invitation only and generally for final selection. Dual-degree applicants must apply to, and be accepted by, both schools; contact the Admissions Office for current information and specific requirements for admission. First-year students admitted in fall only. Rolling admission process. Notification starts October 15 and is finished when class is filled. Applicant's response to offer due within 2 weeks of receipt of acceptance letter. School does maintain an alternate/waiting list. Phone: (315)464-4570.

ADMISSION REQUIREMENTS FOR TRANSFER APPLICANTS. Accepts transfers from other accredited U.S. medical schools and selected foreign medical schools. Admission limited to space available. Contact the Admissions Office after January 1 for current information and specific requirements for admission.

ADMISSION STANDARDS AND RECOGNITION. *For B.S.-M.D.:* number of applicants 12; number interviewed 11; number enrolled 3. *For M.D.:* number of state-resident applicants 2,824, nonresidents 979; number of state residents interviewed 598, nonresidents 82; number of residents enrolled 137, nonresidents 10; median MCAT 9.0 (verbal reasoning 9.0; biological sciences 9.0; physical sciences 9.0); median GPA 3.54 (A = 4). Gorman rating 3.69 (scale: good 3.61–3.99); the college's medical ranking by NIH awards/grants was 87th, with 40 awards/grants received; total dollars awarded $9,012,797.

FINANCIAL AID. Tuition Assistance Program (TAP), grants-in-aid, institutional loans, state loans, HEAL, alternative loan programs, federal Perkins loans, Stafford subsidized and unsubsidized loans, and service commitment scholarship programs are available. Assistantships/fellowships may be available for M.D.-Ph.D. degree candidates. Financial aid applications and information are sent out to all accepted students. Contact the Financial Aid Committee for current information; phone: (315)464-4329. For most financial assistance and all federal programs, submit FAFSA to a federal processor (Title IV school code # 002840); also submit Financial Aid Transcript and Federal Income Tax forms. Approximately 78% of current students receive some form of financial assistance. Average debt after graduation $55,000.

DEGREE REQUIREMENTS. *For B.S.-M.D.:* generally an 8-year program. *For M.D.:* 4-year program. All students must pass USMLE Step 1 and take Step 2. *For M.D.-Ph.D.:* generally a 7-year program.

TEMPLE UNIVERSITY
Philadelphia, Pennsylvania 19122
Internet site: http://www.temple.edu

Founded 1894. Located 2 miles N of downtown. State-related control. Semester system. Library: 2,265,000 volumes; 2,462,700 microforms; 15,437 periodicals/subscriptions; 400 computer work stations. The university's ranking in domestic higher education by NIH awards/grants was 85th, with 97 awards/grants received; total dollars awarded $21,680,215.

The university's graduate schools/colleges include: College of Arts and Science, College of Education, College of Engineering, College of Health, Physical Education, Recreation and Dance, Ester Boyer College of Music, School of Business and Management, School of Communications and Theater, School of Social Administration, Tyler School of Art, School of Law; health center includes: College of Allied Health Professions, School of Dentistry, School of Medicine, School of Pharmacy.

Total university enrollment at main campus: 30,700.

Temple University Health Center
3401 North Broad Street
Philadelphia, Pennsylvania 19140
Phone: (215)707-2000

Public control. University Hospital is a member of the Council of Teaching Hospitals. Schools located at medical center: College of Allied Health Professions, School of Dentistry, School of Medicine, School of Pharmacy. Special facilities: Functional Gastrointestinal Diseases Center, Heart Transplantation Program, Multiple Sclerosis Center, Center for Sports Medicine. Nationally recognized programs in Cardiology, Endocrinology, Neurology, Otolaryngology, Pulmonary Disease, Rheumatology.

School of Medicine
Student Faculty Center, Suite 305
Broad and Ontario Street
Philadelphia, Pennsylvania 19140
Phone: (215)707-3656; fax: (215)707-3923
Internet site: http://www.temple.edu/medschool
E-mail: gmorton@nimbus.ocis.temple.edu

Established 1901. Located at health science campus in downtown Philadelphia. First 2 years are primarily basic medical sciences. Affiliated hospitals: Abington Memorial Hospital, Albert Einstein Medical Center, Conemaugh Valley Memorial Hospital, Fox Chase Cancer Center, Frankford Hospital, Jeanes Hospital, JFK Memorial Hospital, Lancaster General Hospital, Mercy Hospital, Montgomery Hospital, Moss Rehabilitation Hospital, Northeastern Hospital, Philadelphia Geriatric Center, Reading Hospital, Sacred Heart Hospital, Shriners Hospital for Crippled Children, Temple University Hospital, Veterans Administration Medical Center. Special facilities: Fels Research Institute, Thrombosis Research Center. Special programs: Recruitment, Admission and Retention Programs (ARP) for minorities; prematriculation summer sessions.

Annual tuition: residents $22,684, nonresidents $27,788. No university-related housing available. Contact Admissions Office for off-campus housing information. Off-campus housing and personal expenses: approximately $14,600.

Enrollment: 1st-year class 187 (EDP 4, M.D.-Ph.D. approximately 3 students each year); total full-time 729 (men 61%, women 39%). First-year statistics: 35% out of state; 43% women; average age 25; 20% minorities; 64% science majors.

Faculty: full-time 495, part-time/volunteers 1,500.

Degrees conferred: M.D., M.D.-Ph.D. (Anatomy and Cell Biology, Biochemistry, Microbiology and Immunology, Molecular Biology, Pathology, Pharmacology, Physiology).

RECRUITMENT PRACTICES AND POLICIES. School has diversity program and actively recruits women/minority applicants. Diversity contact: Assistant Dean; phone: (215)707-3653.

ADMISSION REQUIREMENTS FOR FIRST-YEAR APPLICANTS. Preference given to state residents; U.S. citizens and permanent residents only. *Undergraduate preparation.* Suggested premed courses: 2 courses in biology with labs, 2 courses in inorganic chemistry with labs, 2 courses in organic chemistry with labs, 2 courses in physics with labs, 2 courses in humanities. Bachelor's degree from an accredited institution required; all applicants have bachelor's degree awarded prior to enrollment. *Has EDP*; applicants must apply through AMCAS (official transcripts sent by mid-May) between June 1 and August 1. Early applications are encouraged. Submit supplemental application, a personal statement, and 2 recommendations to Admissions Office within 2 weeks of receipt of application. Interviews are by invitation only and generally for final selection. Notification normally begins October 1. *Regular application process.* Apply through AMCAS (file after June 1, before December 1); submit MCAT (will accept MCAT test results from the last 3 years), official transcripts for each school attended (should show at least 90 semester credits/135 quarter credits, submit transcripts by mid-May to AMCAS), service processing fee. Submit an application fee of $55, a supplemental application, a personal statement, prepro-fessional committee evaluation, and 3 recommendations from science faculty to Admissions Office within 2–3 weeks of the receipt of supplemental materials, but not later than January 15. Interviews are by invitation only and generally for final selection. M.D.-Ph.D. degree applicants must apply to, and be accepted by, both schools; contact the Director, M.D.-Ph.D. Program, for current information and specific requirements for admission; phone: (215)707-4375; fax: (215)707-3005; E-mail: mdphd@blue.temple.edu. First-year students admitted in fall only. Rolling admission process. Notification starts October 15 and is finished August 15. Applicant's response to offer and $100 deposit due within 2 weeks of receipt of acceptance letter. School does maintain an alternate list. Phone: (215)707-3656; fax: (215)707-3932.

ADMISSION REQUIREMENTS FOR TRANSFER APPLICANTS. Accepts transfers from other accredited U.S. medical schools into both the 2nd and 3rd years. Admission limited to space available. Contact the Admissions Office for current information and specific requirements for admission.

ADMISSION STANDARDS AND RECOGNITION. *For M.D.:* number of state-resident applicants 1,412, nonresidents 7,080; number of state residents interviewed 479, nonresidents 626; number of residents enrolled 121, nonresidents 66; median MCAT 10.0 (verbal reasoning 10.0; biological sciences 10.3; physical sciences 9.7); median GPA 3.4 (A = 4). Gorman rating 4.17 (scale: strong 4.01–4.49); the school's medical ranking by NIH awards was 70th, with 85 awards/grants received; total dollars awarded $18,335,513.

FINANCIAL AID. Scholarships, minority scholarships, grants-in-aid, institutional loans, HEAL, alternative loan programs, federal Perkins loans, Stafford subsidized and unsubsidized loans, and service commitment scholarship programs are available. Assistantships/stipends and tuition waivers may be available for dual-degree candidates. Almost all financial aid is based on demonstrated need. Financial aid applications and information are generally available at the on-campus interview (by invitation). The initial source of financial assistance is the Stafford loans. Contact the Financial Aid Office for current information; phone: (215)707-2667; fax: (215)707-2917. For most financial assistance and all federal programs, submit FAFSA to a federal processor (Title IV school code # E00352); also submit Financial Aid Transcript and Federal Income Tax forms. Approximately 80% of current students receive some form of financial assistance. Average debt after graduation $105,000.

DEGREE REQUIREMENTS. *For M.D.:* satisfactory completion of 4-year program. All students must pass USMLE Step 1 prior to entering 3rd year; all students must pass USMLE Step 2 prior to awarding of M.D. *For M.D.-Ph.D.:* generally a 7-year program.

School of Dentistry
3223 North Broad Street
Philadelphia, Pennsylvania 17140
Phone: (215)707-2801
Internet site: http://www.temple.edu/dentistry

Established 1863. Second-oldest dental school in U.S. Affiliated with Temple University in 1907. Located on health science campus. Semester system. Postgraduate specialties: Endodontics, General Dentistry (AEGD), Oral Surgery, Orthodontics, Periodontics, Prosthodontics.

Annual tuition: residents $19,224, nonresidents $26,916; fees $280, equipment and supplies $5,380. Limited on-campus housing available. Contact Housing Office for both on- and off-campus housing information; phone: (215)707-7663. Off-campus housing, food, transportation, and personal expenses: approximately $10,308.

Enrollment: 1st-year class 119; total full-time 500. First-year enrolled student information: 43 from out of state; 19 states represented; 34 women; average age 25; 14 underrepresented minorities; 41 other minorities.

Faculty: full-time 54, part-time 81.

Degrees conferred: D.M.D., B.A.-D.M.D. (with Juniata College, Wilkes-Barre University), D.M.D.-M.B.A.

RECRUITMENT PRACTICES AND POLICIES. School has diversity program and actively recruits women/minority applicants. Diversity contact: Director of Admissions; phone: (800)441-4363.

ADMISSION REQUIREMENT FOR B.S.-D.M.D. APPLICANTS. For information and applications contact the undergraduate colleges listed above.

ADMISSION REQUIREMENTS FOR FIRST-YEAR APPLICANTS. Preference given to state residents; U.S. citizens and permanent residents only. *Undergraduate preparation.* Suggested predental courses: 2 courses in biology with labs, 2 courses in inorganic chemistry with labs, 2 courses in organic chemistry with labs, 2 courses in physics with labs, 2 courses in English; histology, biochemistry, mammalian anatomy, physiology, and microbiology are strongly suggested. For serious consideration an applicant should have at least a 3.0 (A = 4) science GPA. The junior-college credit is considered for non-science credit only. Will consider applicants with only 3 years of undergraduate preparation; prefer applicants who will have bachelor's degree prior to enrollment; 117 out of 119 1st-year students have bachelor's degree awarded prior to enrollment. *Application process.* Apply through AADSAS (file after August 30, before March 15); submit official transcripts for each school attended (should show at least 90 semester credits/135 quarter credits), service processing fee; at the same time as you send in AADSAS materials, submit official DAT scores (scores should be submitted from April test of applicant's junior year) directly to the Admissions Office and Student Affairs. TOEFL may be required of an applicant whose native language is other than English. Submit the following materials only after being contacted by an Admissions Officer: an application fee of $30, official transcripts, a predental committee evaluation, or 2 recommendations from science professors to Admissions Office and Student Affairs. Interviews are by invitation only and generally for final selection. D.M.D.-M.B.A. degree applicants must apply to, and be accepted by, both schools; contact the Admissions Office for current information and specific requirements for admission. First-year students admitted in fall only. Rolling admission process. Notification starts December 1 and is finished when class is filled, but generally not later than August 1. Applicant's response to offer and $750 deposit due within 30 days if accepted prior to January 31; response and deposit due within 15 days if received after February 1. School does maintain an alternate list. Phone: (800)441-4363.

ADMISSION REQUIREMENTS FOR ADVANCED-STANDING APPLICANTS. Accepts transfers from other accredited U.S. dental schools under exceptional circumstances, but only into the 1st year. Admission limited to space available. There is no advanced-standing program for graduates of foreign schools of dentistry. Contact the Admissions Office and Student Affairs for current information and specific requirements for admission.

ADMISSION STANDARDS AND RECOGNITION. *For D.M.D.:* number of applicants 2,383; number enrolled 119; median DAT: ACAD 18.2, PAT 17.3; median GPA 3.18 (A = 4), median sciences GPA 3.21 (A = 4). Gorman rating 4.41 (scale: strong 4.01–4.49); this placed the school in the Top 25 of all U.S. dental schools; the dental school's ranking by NIH awards/grants was 35th among all U.S. dental schools, with 2 awards/grants received; total value of all awards/grants $298,121.

FINANCIAL AID. Tuition scholarships, minority scholarships, institutional loans, state loan programs, DEAL, HEAL, alternative loan programs, federal Perkins loans, Stafford subsidized and unsubsidized loans, and military service commitment scholarship programs are available. Institutional financial aid applications and information are generally available at the on-campus interview (by invitation). For scholarships, the selection criteria place heavy reliance on DAT and undergraduate GPA. Contact the Office of Financial Aid for current information; phone: (215)707-2667, 707-8978. For most financial assistance and all need-based programs, submit FAFSA to a federal processor (Title IV school code # E00353); also submit Financial Aid Transcript, Federal Income Tax forms, and Use of Federal Funds Certification. Approximately 93% of current students receive some form of financial assistance. Average award for residents $5,000, nonresidents $7,400.

DEGREE REQUIREMENTS. *For B.S.-D.M.D.:* a 7-year program. *For D.M.D.:* satisfactory completion of 4-year program. *For D.M.D.-M.B.A.* generally a 5½–6½-year program.

UNIVERSITY OF TENNESSEE, MEMPHIS
Memphis, Tennessee 38163-0002
Internet site: http://www.utmrm.edu

Founded 1911. Public control. Semester system. Library: 263,000 volumes; 300,000 microforms; 2,000 periodicals/subscriptions; 25 PC work stations. Special facilities: Stout Neuroscience Mass Spectrometry Laboratory, Memorial Research Center, Clinical Research Center, Molecular Resource Center, Center for Neurosciences, Materials Science Toxicology Laboratory. The university's ranking in domestic higher education by NIH awards/grants was 84th, with 107 awards/grants received; total dollars awarded $21,705,753.

The university's graduate colleges include: College of Allied Health Sciences, College of Dentistry, College of Graduate Health Sciences, College of Medicine, College of Nursing, College of Pharmacy.

University of Tennessee Memphis Health Science Center
877 Jefferson Avenue
Memphis, Tennessee 38103

Public control. Regional medical center at Memphis is a member of the Council of Teaching Hospitals. Special facilities: Crump Memorial Women's Hospital and Newborn Center, Gailor Clinic, Elvis Presley Memorial Trauma Center.

School of Medicine
790 Madison Avenue
Memphis, Tennessee 38163-2166
Phone: (901)448-5559; fax: (901)448-7255
Internet site: http://www.utmem.edu

Established 1851. Located at health science center. In Knoxville, Chattanooga, and Memphis, 45-month program with clinical experience. Library: 172,000 volumes/microforms; 1,200 current periodicals/ subscriptions. Affiliated hospitals: Baptist Memorial Hospital and Clinic, Veterans Administration Medical Center, LeBoheur Children's Medical Center, St. Jude Children's Research Hospital, Memphis Mental Health Institute, UT Family Practice Center at St. Francis Hospital, Campbell Clinic, Semmes-Murphey Clinic, Methodist Hospital, St. Joseph Hospital. Special programs: summer programs for high school and undergraduate college students.

Annual tuition: residents $9,469, nonresidents $18,133. Two on-campus dormitories available for single students. Contact Housing Office for both on- and off-campus housing information; phone: (901)448-5609. Medical students tend to live off-campus. Off-campus housing and personal expenses: approximately $10,665.

Enrollment: 1st-year class 165 (up to 15 students each year are selected for Clinic Scholars Program); total full-time 683 (men 62%, women 38%). First-year statistics: 10% out of state; 43% women; average age 24; 13% minorities; 86% science majors.

Degrees conferred: M.D., M.D.-Ph.D. (Anatomy, Biochemistry, Cell Biology, Immunology, Microbiology, Molecular Biology, Neurosciences, Pathology, Pharmacology, Physiology).

RECRUITMENT PRACTICES AND POLICIES. School has diversity program and actively recruits women/minority applicants. Diversity contact: Assistant Dean, Admissions and Students; phone: (901)448-7228.

ADMISSION REQUIREMENTS FOR FIRST-YEAR APPLICANTS. Preference given to state residents; U.S. citizens and permanent residents only. Applications are accepted from the state's 8 neighboring states only (Mississippi, Arkansas, Missouri, Kentucky, Virginia, North Carolina, Georgia, and Alabama). *Undergraduate preparation.* Suggested premed courses: 2 courses in biology with labs, 2 courses in inorganic chemistry with labs, 2 courses in organic chemistry with labs, 2 courses in physics with labs, 2 courses in English, 14 courses of electives. Bachelor's degree from an accredited institution required; 98% of applicants have bachelor's degree awarded prior to enrollment. Does not have EDP. *Application process.* Apply through AMCAS (file after June 1,

before November 15); submit MCAT (will accept MCAT test results from the last 4 years), official transcripts for each school attended (should show at least 90 semester credits/135 quarter credits, submit transcripts by mid-May to AMCAS), service processing fee. Submit an application fee of $50, a supplemental application, a personal statement, preprofessional committee evaluation, and 3 recommendations from science faculty to Admissions Office within 2–3 weeks of the receipt of supplemental materials. Interviews are by invitation only and generally for final selection. Combined degree applicants must apply to, and be accepted by, both schools; contact the Admissions Office for current information and specific requirements for admission. For information on Medical Students Research Fellowships Program contact the Officer of the Associate Dean for Research, Room A, 331 Coleman Building. First-year students admitted in fall only. Rolling admission process. Notification starts October 15 and is finished April 1. Applicant's response to offer and $100 deposit due within 2 weeks of receipt of acceptance letter. Phone: (901)448-5559.

ADMISSION REQUIREMENTS FOR TRANSFER APPLICANTS. Accepts transfers from other accredited U.S. medical schools into the 3rd year only who were state residents at the time of admission to their current medical school. Admission limited to space available. Contact the Admissions Office for current information and specific requirements.

ADMISSION STANDARDS AND RECOGNITION. *For M.D.:* number of state-resident applicants 679, nonresidents 1,280; number of state residents interviewed 317, nonresidents 69; number of residents enrolled 153, nonresidents 12; median MCAT 9.3 (verbal reasoning 9.0; biological sciences 10.0; physical sciences 9.0); median GPA 3.50 (A = 4). Gorman rating 3.62 (scale: good 3.61–3.99); the school's medical ranking by NIH awards was 69th, with 96 awards/grants received; total dollars awarded $20,303,244.

FINANCIAL AID. Merit scholarships, minority scholarships, grants-in-aid, institutional loans, HEAL, alternative loan programs, NIH stipends, federal Perkins loans, Stafford subsidized and unsubsidized loans, and conditional grants for Clinical Scholars Program are available. All financial aid is based on demonstrated need. Assistantships/fellowships may be available for dual-degree candidates. Financial aid applications and *Student Handbook* are mailed to all accepted students. For scholarships, the selection criteria place heavy reliance on MCAT and undergraduate GPA. Contact the Office of Financial Aid for current information; phone: (901)448-

5568. For most financial assistance and all federal programs, submit FAFSA to a federal processor (Title IV school code # E006725); also submit Financial Aid Transcript and Federal Income Tax forms. Approximately 80% of current students receive some form of financial assistance. Average debt after graduation $63,000.

DEGREE REQUIREMENTS. *For M.D.:* satisfactory completion of 45-month program. All students must pass USMLE Step 1 prior to entering 3rd year; all students must pass USMLE Step 2 prior to awarding of M.D. *For M.D.-Ph.D.:* generally a 7-year program.

College of Dentistry
875 Union Avenue
Memphis, Tennessee 38163
Phone: (800)788-0400, (901)488-6201; fax (901)448-7104
Internet site: http://chanc.utmem.dent.edu
E-mail: P.dowdle@utmem.dent.edu

Established 1878. Located at the health science center. Special programs: summer programs for underrepresented minorities; research fellowships; externships. Postgraduate specialties: General Dentistry (AEGD), Oral and Maxillofacial Surgery, Pediatric Dentistry, Periodontics.

Annual tuition: residents $5,744; nonresidents $13,454; fees $1,076; equipment and supplies, $6,693. Two on-campus dormitories available for single students. Contact Housing Office for both on- and off-campus housing information; phone: (901)448-5609. Dental students tend to live off-campus. Off-campus housing and personal expenses: approximately $10,665.

Enrollment: 1st-year class 80; total full-time 310. First-year enrolled student information: 24 from out of state; 7 states represented; 18 women; average age 24; 9 underrepresented minorities; 2 other minorities.

Degree conferred: D.D.S. Dental students may pursue an M.S. or Ph.D. in the College of Graduate Studies, although no formal program has been established.

RECRUITMENT PRACTICES AND POLICIES. School has diversity program and actively recruits women/minority applicants. Diversity contact: Minority Affairs Office; phone: (901)448-5640.

ADMISSION REQUIREMENTS FOR FIRST-YEAR APPLICANTS. Preference given to state residents and residents of Arkansas; U.S. citizens and permanent residents only. *Undergraduate preparation.* Suggested predental courses: 2 courses in biology with labs, 2 courses in inorganic chemistry with labs, 2 courses in organic chemistry with labs, 2 courses in physics with labs, 2

courses in English, 13 courses of electives. The junior-college transfer credit limit is 60 credits. For serious consideration an applicant should have at least a 2.5 (A = 4) GPA. Will consider applicants with only 3 years of undergraduate preparation; prefer applicants who will have a bachelor's degree prior to enrollment; 75 out of 80 enrolled 1st-year students have bachelor's degree awarded prior to enrollment. *Application process.* Apply directly to the Admissions Offices (file after June 1, before December 1). Submit an official transcript for each school attended (should show at least 90 semester credits/135 quarter credits), official DAT scores, and predental committee evaluation or 2 recommendations from science professors to Admissions Office. Interviews are by invitation only and generally for final selection. First-year students admitted in fall only. Rolling admission process. Notification starts December 1 and is finished when class is filled, but generally not later than August 15. Applicant's response to offer and $200 deposit due within 30 days if accepted prior to February 28; response and deposit due within 15 days if received after March 1. School does maintain an alternate list. Phone: (901)448-6201.

ADMISSION REQUIREMENTS FOR ADVANCED-STANDING APPLICANTS. Accepts transfers from other accredited U.S. dental schools. Admission limited to space available. There is an advanced-standing program for graduates of foreign schools of dentistry. Contact the Admissions Office for current information and specific requirements for admission.

ADMISSION STANDARDS AND RECOGNITION. *For D.D.S.:* number of applicants 250; number enrolled 80; median DAT: ACAD 16.9, PAT 16.2; median GPA 3.22 (A = 4), median sciences GPA 3.13 (A = 4). Gorman rating 4.24 (scale: strong 4.01–4.49); this placed the school in the Top 40 of all U.S. dental schools; the dental school's ranking by NIH awards/grants was 34th, among U.S. dental schools, with 4 awards/grants received; total value of all awards/grants was $317,374.

FINANCIAL AID. Scholarships, merit scholarships, minority scholarships, grants-in-aid, institutional loans, state loan programs, DEAL, HEAL, alternative loan programs, federal Perkins loans, Stafford subsidized and unsubsidized loans, and military service commitment scholarship programs are available. Institutional financial aid applications and information are sent to all accepted students. All financial aid is based on demonstrated need. For scholarship consideration the selection criteria place heavy reliance on DAT and undergraduate GPA. Contact the Office of Student Financial Aid for current information; phone: (901)448-5609. For most financial assistance and all need-based programs, submit FAFSA to a federal processor (Title IV school code # 006725); also submit Financial Aid Transcript, Federal Income Tax forms, and Use of Federal Funds Certification. Approximately 88% of current students receive some form of financial assistance. Average award for residents $18,325, nonresidents $26,347.

DEGREE REQUIREMENTS. *For D.D.S.:* satisfactory completion of 4-year program.

TEXAS A&M UNIVERSITY
College Station, Texas 77843-1244
Internet site: http://thunder.tamu.edu

Founded 1876. Located 100 miles N of Houston. Semester system. Library: 2,169,000 volumes; 4,323,500 microforms; 17,322 periodicals/subscriptions; 400 computer work stations. Special facilities: Institute for Bioscience and Technology, Center for Biotechnology, Nuclear Science Center, Space Research Center, Cyclotron Institute. The university's ranking in domestic higher education by NIH awards/grants was 132nd, with 39 awards/grants received; total dollars awarded $6,244,821.

The university's Office of Graduate Studies includes: College of Agriculture and Life Sciences, College of Architecture, College of Education, College of Engineering, College of Geosciences and Maritime Studies, College of Liberal Arts, College of Science, Intercollegiate Faculty of Nutrition, Intercollegiate Faculty of Toxicology, Lowry Mays College Graduate School of Business, College of Medicine, College of Veterinary Medicine.

Total university enrollment at main campus: 41,800.

Texas A&M Health Science Center
College Station, Texas 77843-1114

College of Medicine
159 Joe H. Reynolds Medical Building
College Station, Texas 77843-1114
Phone: (409)845-7744; fax: (409)847-8663
Internet site: http://hsc.tamu.edu; http://thunder.tamu.edu
E-mail: fgmaldonado@tamu.edu

Established 1971. The college's administrative offices are on the main campus, and the basic sciences are all taught at College Station. The clinical campus is in Temple, Texas, consisting of Olin E. Teague Veterans Center, Scott and White Clinic and Hospital, Central Texas Medical Center, Darnell Army Hospital (Ft. Hood). Semester

system. Library: 71,000 volumes/microforms; 1,900 current periodicals/subscriptions. Special programs: Summer programs for underrepresented minorities (Bridge to Science Program).

Annual tuition: residents $7,592, nonresidents $20,692; fees $1,400. Limited on-campus housing available. Contact university's Director of Campus Housing for both on- and off-campus housing information; phone: (409)845-1741. Medical students tend to live off-campus. Off-campus housing and personal expenses: approximately $13,300.

Enrollment: 1st-year class 64; total full-time 226 (men 60%, women 40%). First-year statistics: 2% out of state; 39% women; average age 25; 15% minorities; 92% science majors.

Faculty: full-time/part-time/volunteers 818.

Degrees conferred: M.D., M.D.-Ph.D. (Anatomy, Biochemistry, Biomedical Engineering, Biophysics, Cell Biology, Genetics, Immunology, Microbiology, Molecular Biology, Neurosciences, Pathology, Pharmacology, Physiology).

RECRUITMENT PRACTICES AND POLICIES. School has diversity program and actively recruits women/minority applicants. Diversity contact: Coordinator Special Programs; phone: (409)862-4065.

ADMISSION REQUIREMENTS FOR FIRST-YEAR APPLICANTS. Preference given to state residents; by state mandate nonresident enrollment may not exceed 10%; U.S. citizens and permanent residents only. *Undergraduate preparation.* Suggested premed courses: 2 courses in biology with labs, 1 course in an advanced biological science, 2 courses in inorganic chemistry with labs, 2 courses in organic chemistry with labs, 2 courses in physics with labs, 1 course in calculus, 2 courses in English. Bachelor's degree from an accredited institution required; all applicants have bachelor's degrees awarded prior to enrollment. Does not have EDP. *Application process.* Request applications from the Director of Admission. Apply after May 1, before November 1. Submit MCAT (will accept MCAT test results from the last 4 years), official transcripts for each school attended (should show at least 90 semester credits/135 quarter credits), an application fee of $45, a personal statement, preprofessional committee evaluation, and at least 2 recommendations from science required in support of application. Interviews are by invitation only and generally for final selection. M.D.-Ph.D. degree applicants must apply to, and be accepted by, both schools; contact the Admissions Office for current information and specific requirements for admission. First-year students admitted in fall only. Rolling admission process. Notification dates are November 15, December 15, January 15, and February 15. Applicant's response to offer due within 2 weeks of receipt of acceptance letter. Phone: (409)845-7743; fax: (409)862-4946; E-mail: fgmaldonado@tamu.edu.

ADMISSION REQUIREMENTS FOR TRANSFER APPLICANTS. Rarely accepts transfer applicants. Contact the Admissions Office for current information, specific requirements, or modification of admission policy.

ADMISSION STANDARDS AND RECOGNITION. *For M.D.:* number of state-resident applicants 1,433, nonresidents 143; number of state residents interviewed 394, nonresidents 7; number of residents enrolled 63, nonresidents 1; median MCAT 9.3; median GPA 3.64 (A = 4). Gorman rating 3.09 (scale: acceptable plus 3.01–3.59); the college's medical ranking by NIH awards was 113th, with 18 awards/grants received; total dollars awarded $2,443,034.

FINANCIAL AID. Grants, institutional loans, HEAL, alternative loan programs, federal Perkins loans, Stafford subsidized and unsubsidized loans, and service commitment scholarship programs are available. Most financial aid is based on demonstrated need. Most aid is in the form of long-term loans. Assistantships/fellowships may be available for M.D.-Ph.D. degree candidates. Financial-aid applications and information are generally available at the on-campus interview (by invitation). Contact the Office of Student Affairs for current information; phone: (409)845-7743; E-mail: J.falk@tamu.edu. For most financial assistance and all federal programs, submit FAFSA to a federal processor (Title IV school code # 003632); also submit Financial Aid Transcript and Federal Income Tax forms. Approximately 90% of current students receive some form of financial assistance. Average debt after graduation $63,300.

DEGREE REQUIREMENTS. *For M.D.:* satisfactory completion of 4-year program. All students must pass USMLE Step 1 prior to entering 3rd year; all students must pass USMLE Step 2 prior to awarding of M.D. *For M.D.-Ph.D.:* generally a 7-year program.

Baylor College of Dentistry
P.O. Box 660677
3302 Gaston Avenue
Dallas, Texas 75266-0677
Phone: (214)828-8200
Internet site: http://www.tambcd.edu

Established 1905 as the State Dental College; joined Baylor University in 1918; left Baylor in 1971 and in 1996 joined the Texas A&M system. Located about 1 mile from downtown Dallas in the Baylor medical center complex. Public control. Library: 36,000 volumes/microforms; 600 current periodicals/subscriptions. Postgraduate specialties: Endodontics, General Dentistry, Oral and Maxillofacial Pathology, Oral and Maxillofacial Surgery, Orthodontics, Pediatric Dentistry, Periodontics, Prosthodontics.

Annual tuition: residents $5,400, nonresidents $16,200; equipment and supplies $6,500. No on-campus housing available. Contact Housing Office for off-campus housing information; phone: (214)828-8210. Off-campus housing, food, transportation, and personal expenses: approximately $11,700.

Enrollment: 1st-year class 85; total full-time 35 (210 men, 142 women). First-year enrolled student information: 4 from out of state; 42 women; average age 24; 18 underrepresented minorities; 17 other minorities.

Faculty: full-time 82, part-time 111.

Degrees conferred: D.D.S., B.A.-D.D.S., D.D.S.-M.P.H.

RECRUITMENT PRACTICES AND POLICIES. School has diversity program and actively recruits women/minority applicants. Diversity contact: Office of Multicultural Services; phone: (214)828-8236.

ADMISSION REQUIREMENTS FOR BACHELOR-D.D.S. APPLICANTS. For information and applications contact the Admissions Office for current list of affiliated undergraduate institutions.

ADMISSION REQUIREMENTS FOR FIRST-YEAR APPLICANTS. Preference given to state residents and surrounding states without dental schools; U.S. citizens and permanent residents only. *Undergraduate preparation.* Suggested predental courses: 2 courses in biology with labs, 2 courses in inorganic chemistry with labs, 2 courses in organic chemistry with labs, 2 courses in physics with labs, 2 courses in English. The junior-college transfer credit limit is 60 credits. Will consider applicants with only 2 years of undergraduate preparation; prefer applicants who will have bachelor's degree prior to enrollment; 97% of applicants have bachelor's degree awarded prior to enrollment. *Application process.* State residents request application from college; nonresidents apply through AADSAS (suggested deadline November 1). Submit official transcripts for each school attended (should show at least 90 semester credits/135 quarter credits), service processing fee; at the same time as you send in AADSAS materials, submit official DAT scores directly to the Admissions Office. TOEFL may be required of an applicant whose native language is other than English. Submit the following materials only after being contacted by an Admissions Officer: an application fee of $35, a supplemental application, official transcripts, predental committee evaluation or 2 recommendations from professors in your major field of study, and photograph to Admissions Office within 2 weeks of receipt of supplemental materials, but not later than March 1. Interviews are by invitation only and generally for final selection. Dual-degree applicants must apply to, and be accepted by, both schools; contact the Admissions Office for current information and specific requirements for admission. First-year students admitted in fall only. Rolling admission process. Notification starts December 1 and is finished when class is filled. Applicant's response to offer and $200 deposit due within 30 days if accepted prior to January 31; response and deposit due within 2 weeks if received after February 1. School does maintain an alternate list. Phone: (214)828-8230.

ADMISSION REQUIREMENTS FOR ADVANCED-STANDING APPLICANTS. Accepts transfers from other accredited U.S. dental schools. Admission limited to space available. There is an advanced-standing program for graduates of foreign schools of dentistry; students are generally accepted into the 2nd year of study only. Contact the Admissions Office for current information and specific requirements for admission.

ADMISSION STANDARDS AND RECOGNITION. *For D.D.S.:* number of applicants 1,470; number enrolled 90; median DAT: ACAD 17.7, PAT 16.2; median GPA 3.27 (A = 4); median sciences GPA 3.20 (A = 4). Gorman rating 4.35 (scale: strong 4.01–4.49); this placed the school in the Top 25 of all U.S. dental schools; the school's ranking by NIH awards/grants was 30th among U.S. dental schools, with 7 awards/grants received; total value of all awards/grants was $819,166.

FINANCIAL AID. Scholarships, merit scholarships, minority scholarships, grants-in-aid, institutional loans, state loan programs, DEAL, HEAL, alternative loan programs, federal Perkins loans, Stafford subsidized and unsubsidized loans, and military service commitment scholarship programs are available. Institutional financial aid applications and information are generally available at the on-campus interview (by invitation). Most financial aid is based on demonstrated need. For scholarship assistance, the selection criteria place heavy reliance on DAT and undergraduate GPA. Contact the Financial Aid Office for current information; phone: (214)828-8236. For most financial assistance and all need-based programs, submit FAFSA to a federal processor (Title IV school code # 004948); also submit Financial Aid Transcrip, Federal Income Tax forms, and Use of Federal Funds Certification. Approximately 90% of current students receive some form of financial assistance. The awards range from $2,700 to $27,400. Average debt after graduation $57,200.

DEGREE REQUIREMENTS. *For baccalaureate-D.D.S.:* generally a 6–7-year program depending on the undergraduate institution. *For D.D.S.:* satisfactory completion of 4-year program. *For D.D.S.-M.P.H.:* generally a 5–6-year program.

TEXAS TECH UNIVERSITY
Lubbock, Texas 79409
Internet site: http://www.ttu.edu

Founded 1923. Coed. Public control. Semester system. Library: 507,000 volumes; 287,000 microforms; 17,556 periodicals/subscriptions; 170 computer work stations.

The university's graduate schools/colleges include: College of Agricultural Sciences and Natural Resources, College of Architecture, College of Arts and Sciences, College of Business Administration, College of Education, College of Engineering, College of Human Sciences, School of Law, School of Medicine.

Total university enrollment at main campus: 24,200.

Health Sciences Center
Founded 1979. Located adjacent to main campus. Schools located at health sciences center are: Graduate School of Biomedical Sciences, School of Allied Health, School of Medicine, School of Nursing, School of Pharmacy.

School of Medicine
Lubbock, Texas 79430-0001
Phone: (806)743-2297; fax: (806)743-3021
Internet site: http://www.ttu.edu

Established 1969. Located at health sciences center. Library: 225,000 volumes/microforms; 1,600 current periodicals/subscriptions. All medical students spend first 2 years in basic sciences at Lubbock campus; the 3rd and 4th years are spent in either Lubbock, Amarillo, or El Paso. Affiliated hospitals: Northwest Texas Hospital, Veterans Administration Hospital; regional health centers in Amarillo, El Paso, and Odessa.

Annual tuition: residents $6,550, nonresidents $19,650; fees $1,247. On-campus housing available during first 2 years; none during years 3 and 4. Contact Admissions Office for both on- and off-campus housing information. Medical students tend to live off-campus. Off-campus housing and personal expenses: approximately $9,461.

Enrollment: 1st-year class 120 (EDP 5); total full-time 467 (men 75%, women 25%). First-year statistics: 2% from out of state (up to 10% each year can be from out of state); 25% women; average age 24; 12% underrepresented minorities; 10 other minorities; 80% science majors.

Faculty: full-time 314, part-time/volunteers 775.

Degrees conferred: M.D., M.D.-M.B.A., M.D.-Ph.D. (Anatomy, Cell Biology and Biochemistry, Genetics, Microbiology and Immunology, Molecular Biology, Pharmacology, Physiology).

RECRUITMENT PRACTICES AND POLICIES. School has diversity program and actively recruits women/minority applicants. Diversity contact: Assistant Dean for Minority Affairs; phone: (806)743-2890.

ADMISSION REQUIREMENTS FOR FIRST-YEAR APPLICANTS. Applicants from Texas, southwestern Oklahoma, eastern New Mexico given preference; U.S. citizens and permanent residents only. *Undergraduate preparation.* Suggested premed courses: 2 courses in biology with labs, 2 courses in inorganic chemistry with labs, 2 courses in organic chemistry with labs, 2 courses in physics with labs, 2 courses in English. Bachelor's degree from an accredited institution required; 99% of applicants have bachelor's degree awarded prior to enrollment. *Has EDP;* applicants must apply directly to Admissions Office between June 15 and August 1. Early applications are encouraged. Submit application and application fee of $40, MCAT, official transcripts, a personal statement, and 2 recommendations to Admissions Office. Interviews are by invitation only and generally for final selection. Notification normally begins October 1. *Regular application process.* Apply directly to the Admissions Office after June 15, before November 1. Submit MCAT (will accept MCAT test results from the last 3 years), official transcripts for each school attended (should show at least 90 semester credits/135 quarter credits, submit transcripts by mid-May to AMCAS), an application and application fee of $40, a personal statement, preprofessional committee evaluation, and 3 recommendations from science faculty to Admissions

Office. Interviews are by invitation only and generally for final selection. Dual-degree applicants must apply to, and be accepted by, both schools; contact the Admissions Office for current information and specific requirements for admission. First-year students admitted in fall only. Rolling admission process. Notification starts October 15 and is finished when class is filled. Applicant's response to offer is due within 2 weeks of receipt of acceptance letter, but not latter than April 1. School does maintain an alternate list. Phone: (806)743-2297.

ADMISSION REQUIREMENTS FOR TRANSFER APPLICANTS. Accepts transfers from other accredited U.S. medical schools into the 3rd year only and only from the school's service area. Admission limited to space available. Contact the Admissions Office for current information and specific requirements for admission.

ADMISSION STANDARDS AND RECOGNITION. *For M.D.:* number of state-resident applicants 1,677, nonresidents 20; number of state residents interviewed 355, nonresidents 2; number of residents enrolled 117, nonresidents 3; median MCAT 9.3 (verbal reasoning 9.4; biological sciences 9.4; physical sciences 9.1); median GPA 3.59 (A = 4). Gorman rating 3.27 (scale: acceptable plus 3.01–3.59); school's medical ranking by NIH awards was 107th, with 25 awards/grants received; total dollars awarded $3,064,838.

FINANCIAL AID. Scholarships, merit scholarships, minority scholarships, grants-in-aid, institutional loans, HEAL, alternative loan programs, federal Perkins loans, Stafford subsidized and unsubsidized loans, and service commitment scholarship programs are available. Assistantships/fellowships may be available for dual-degree candidates. All financial aid is based on demonstrated need. Financial aid applications and information are generally available at the on-campus interview (by invitation). Applications are not processed until after an applicant has been accepted. For scholarship assistance, the selection criteria place heavy reliance on MCAT and undergraduate GPA. Contact the Director of Student Financial Aid for current information; phone: (806)743-3025. For most financial assistance and all federal programs, submit FAFSA to a federal processor (Title IV school code # 016024); also submit Financial Aid Transcript and Federal Income Tax forms. Approximately 65% of current students receive some form of financial assistance. Average debt after graduation $72,000.

DEGREE REQUIREMENTS. *For M.D.:* satisfactory completion of 4-year program. All students must pass

USMLE Step 1 prior to entering third year. *For M.D.-M.B.A.:* generally a 4–4½-year program. *For M.D.-Ph.D.:* generally a 7-year program.

UNIVERSITY OF TEXAS MEDICAL BRANCH AT GALVESTON

Galveston, Texas 77555
Internet site: http://www.utmb.edu

Founded 1891. Public control. Semester system. Library: 240,000 volumes; 4,000 microforms; 3,000 periodicals/subscriptions; 75 PC work stations. Special facilities: Biomedical Engineering Center, Collaborating Center for Tropical Medicine, Hispanic Center for Excellence, Marine Biomedical Institute, Molecular Science Institute, Institute for Medical Humanities, Sealy Center for Structural Biology, Shriner's Burn Institute. Special programs: Postbaccalaureate premedical program for minorities. The university's ranking in domestic higher education by NIH awards/grants was 61st, with 196 awards/grants received; total dollars awarded $42,687,568.

The university's graduate schools are: Graduate School of Biomedical Sciences, School of Allied Health Sciences, School of Medicine.

Total university enrollment at main campus: 2,200.

University of Texas Medical Branch Hospitals at Galveston

301 University Boulevard
Galveston, Texas 77555

State-owned medical center. The hospitals are members of the Council of Teaching Hospitals. Nationally recognized program in Endocrinology.

School of Medicine

G-210, Ashbel Smith Building
Galveston, Texas 77555-1317
Phone: (409)772-3517; fax: (409)772-5753
Internet site: http://www.utmb.edu
E-mail: pwylie@mspo4.med.utmb.edu

Established 1881. Affiliated hospitals/clinics: John Sealy Hospital, Shriner's Hospital for Crippled Children, Galveston Burn Unit, Birth Defects Center. Special programs: prematriculation summer sessions.

Annual tuition: residents $6,550, nonresidents $19,650; fees $461. Limited on-campus housing available for single students, none for married students. Contact Admissions Office for both on- and off-campus housing information; phone: (409)772-1898. Medical students tend to live off-campus. Off-campus housing and personal expenses: approximately $12,000.

Enrollment: 1st-year class 200; total full-time 820 (men 59%, women 41%). First-year statistics: 10% out of state; 36% women; average age 24; 50% minorities.

Faculty: full-time 920, part-time/volunteers 643.

Degrees conferred: M.D., M.D.-M.A. (Medical Humanities), M.D.-M.M.S. (Medical Sciences), M.D.-M.S. (Allied Health, Cellular Physiology and Molecular Biophysics, Microbiology, Pharmacology and Toxicology, Preventive Medicine and Community Health), M.D.-Ph.D. (Cell Biology, Cellular Physiology and Molecular Biophysics, Experimental Pathology, Human Biological Chemistry and Genetics, Medical Humanities, Microbiology, Neurosciences, Pharmacology and Toxicology, Preventive Medicine and Community Health).

RECRUITMENT PRACTICES AND POLICIES. School has diversity program and actively recruits women/minority applicants. Diversity contact: Associate Dean for Student Affairs and Admissions; phone: (409)772-1442.

ADMISSION REQUIREMENTS FOR FIRST-YEAR APPLICANTS. Ninety percent of class must be from state; U.S. citizens and permanent residents only. *Undergraduate preparation.* Suggested premed courses: 4 courses in biology with labs, 2 courses in inorganic chemistry with labs, 2 courses in organic chemistry with labs, 2 courses in physics with labs, 1 course in calculus, 2 courses in English. Bachelor's degree from an accredited institution required; 98% of applicants have bachelor's degrees awarded prior to enrollment. Does not have EDP. *Application process.* Obtain all application forms and procedural information from the University of Texas System Medical and Dental Application Center at Austin (78701). Submit application after April 15, before October 15. Submit MCAT (will accept MCAT test results from the last 3 years and results from April test date), official transcripts for each school attended (should show at least 90 semester credits/135 quarter credits), an application fee of $45 (for 1 school, $5 for each additional school), nonresidents $80 (for one school, $10 for each additional school), a personal statement, preprofessional committee evaluation, and 3 recommendations from science faculty. Interviews are by invitation only and generally for final selection. Combined degree applicants must apply to, and be accepted by, both schools; contact the Admissions Office for current information and specific requirements for admission. First-year students admitted in fall only. Rolling admission process. Notification starts January 15 and is finished when class is filled. Applicant's response to offer due within 2 weeks of receipt of acceptance letter. School does maintain an alternate list. Phone: (409)772-3517; E-mail: pwylie@mspo4.med.utmb.edu.

ADMISSION REQUIREMENTS FOR TRANSFER APPLICANTS. Accepts transfers from other accredited U.S. medical schools under exceptional circumstances and only into the 3rd year; preference given to state residents. Admission limited to space available. Contact the Admissions Office for current information and specific requirements for admission.

ADMISSION STANDARDS AND RECOGNITION. *For M.D.:* number of state-resident applicants 2,667, nonresidents 662; number of state residents interviewed 1,135, nonresidents 97; number of residents enrolled 188, nonresidents 12; median MCAT 9.0 (verbal reasoning 9.0; biological sciences 9.0; physical sciences 9.0); median GPA 3.50 (A = 4). Gorman rating 3.74 (scale: good 3.61–3.99); the school's medical ranking by NIH awards was 44th, with 193 awards/grants received; total dollars awarded $42,347,153.

FINANCIAL AID. Scholarships, disadvantaged scholarships, grants-in-aid, institutional loans, HEAL, alternative loan programs, federal Perkins loans, Stafford subsidized and unsubsidized loans, and service commitment scholarship programs are available. Graduate assistantships/fellowships may be available for combined degree candidates. Financial aid is based on demonstrated need. Financial aid applications and information are sent to all accepted students. For scholarships, the selection criteria place heavy reliance on MCAT and undergraduate GPA. Contact the Office of Student Financial Planning and Management for current information; phone: (409)772-4955. For most financial assistance and all federal programs, submit FAFSA to a federal processor (Title IV school code # 013976); also submit Financial Aid Transcript and Federal Income Tax forms. Approximately 76% of current students receive some form of financial assistance. Average debt after graduation $62,000.

DEGREE REQUIREMENTS. *For M.D.:* satisfactory completion of 4-year program. All students must pass USMLE Step 1 prior to entering 3rd year; all students must pass USMLE Step 2 prior to awarding of M.D. *For M.D.-M.A.,-M.M.S.-M.S.:* generally from 4½–5½-year programs. *For M.D.-Ph.D.:* generally a 6–7-year program.

THE UNIVERSITY OF TEXAS HEALTH SCIENCE CENTER AT HOUSTON

Houston, Texas 77225-0036
Internet site: http:// www.uthouston.edu

Founded 1972. Located 2 miles SW of downtown. Public control. Semester system. Library: 268,400 volumes/microforms; 2,745 periodicals/subscriptions; 90 PC work stations. Special facilities: AIDS Education and Training Center for Texas and Oklahoma, Center on Aging, Center for Health Policy Studies, Center for Health Promotion Research, Center for Infectious Diseases, Center for the Prevention of Injury and Violence, Epidemiology Research Center, Health Policy Institute, Houston Center for Bone Research Human Genetics Center, Human Nutrition Center, Neuroscience Research Center, Positron Diagnostic and Research Center, Southwest Center for Occupational and Environmental Health, Southwest Center for Prevention Research, Speech and Hearing Institute, UT Mental Sciences Institute. The university's ranking in domestic higher education by NIH awards/grants was 49th, with 188 awards/grants received; total dollars awarded $63,102,838.

The university's graduate colleges/schools include: Graduate School of Biomedical Sciences, Dental School, Houston Medical School, School of Nursing, School of Public Health.

Total university enrollment at main campus: 3,100.

Texas Medical Center

Established 1972. Public control. Member of the Council of Teaching Hospitals. Special facilities at medical center complex: University Children's Hospital, Texas Kidney Institute, Jesse H. and Mary Gibbs Jones Medical Surgical Center, Harris County Psychiatric Center, University of Texas, M. D. Anderson Cancer Center (nationally recognized for Cancer, Endocrinology, Gastroenterology, Gynecology, Otolaryngology, Urology; also a member of the Council of Teaching Hospitals), Lyndon Baines Johnson County Hospital, St. Joseph Hospital, San Jose Clinic, Southwest Memorial Hospital.

Houston Medical School

P.O. Box 20708
Houston, Texas 77225
Phone: (713)500-5116; fax: (713)500-0604
Internet site: http://www.med.uth.tmc.edu

Established 1969. Semester system. Special programs: summer programs for underrepresented minorities, prematriculation summer sessions. Affiliated hospitals: Herman Hospital, University of Texas, M. D. Anderson Cancer Center, Lyndon Baines Johnson County Hospital,

St. Joseph Hospital, San Jose Clinic, Southwest Memorial Hospital.

Annual tuition: residents $7,798, nonresidents $20,898; fees $1,003. On-campus rooms and apartments available for both single and married students. Two student residences are located within the medical center. Annual on-campus housing cost: single students $5,400 (room only), married students $7,200. Contact Housing Office for both on- and off-campus housing information; phone: (713)792-8112. Off-campus housing and personal expenses: approximately $11,565.

Enrollment: 1st-year class 200; total full-time 831 (men 53%, women 47%). First-year statistics: 4% out of state; 47% women; average age 23; 21% minorities; 67% science majors.

Faculty: full-time 640, part-time/volunteers 1,430.

Degrees conferred: M.D., M.D.-M.P.H., M.D.-M.S., M.D.-Ph.D. (Anatomy, Biochemistry, Cell Biology, Genetics, Immunology, Microbiology, Neurosciences, Pathology, Pharmacology, Physiology).

RECRUITMENT PRACTICES AND POLICIES. School has diversity program and actively recruits women/minority applicants. Diversity contact: Associate Dean for Educational Programs; phone: (713)567-4427.

ADMISSION REQUIREMENTS FOR FIRST-YEAR APPLICANTS. Ninety percent of class must be from state; U.S. citizens and permanent residents only. *Undergraduate preparation.* Suggested premed courses: 4 courses in biology with labs, 2 courses in inorganic chemistry with labs, 2 courses in organic chemistry with labs, 2 courses in physics with labs, 1 course in calculus, 2 courses in English. Bachelor's degree from an accredited institution required. 99% of applicants have bachelor's degrees awarded prior to enrollment. Does not have EDP. *Application process.* Obtain all application forms and procedural information from the University of Texas System Medical and Dental Application Center at Austin (78701). File application after June 15, before October 15. Submit MCAT (will accept MCAT test results from the last 3 years); official transcripts for each school attended (should show at least 90 semester credits/135 quarter credits), an application fee of $45 (for one school, $5 for each additional school), nonresidents $80 (for one school, $10 for each additional school), a personal statement, preprofessional committee evaluation, and 3 recommendations from science faculty. Interviews are by invitation only and generally for final selection. Combined degree applicants must apply to, and be accepted by, both schools; contact the Admissions Office for current information and specific requirements for admission.

First-year students admitted in fall only. Rolling admission process. Notification starts January 15 and is finished when class is filled. Applicant's response to offer due within 2 weeks of receipt of acceptance letter. School does maintain an alternate list. Phone: (713)500-5116.

ADMISSION REQUIREMENTS FOR TRANSFER APPLICANTS. Houston Medical School does not accept transfer applicants. Contact the Admissions Office for current information and any modification in policy.

ADMISSION STANDARDS AND RECOGNITION. *For M.D.:* number of state-resident applicants 2,680, nonresidents 791; number of state residents interviewed 1,011, nonresidents 17; number of residents enrolled 197, nonresidents 3; median MCAT 9.0 (verbal reasoning 9.0; biological sciences 9.3; physical sciences 8.8); median GPA 3.54 (A = 4). Gorman rating 3.46 (scale: acceptable plus 3.01–3.59); school's medical ranking by NIH awards was 51st, with 147 awards/grants received; total dollars awarded $34,093,028.

FINANCIAL AID. Scholarships, merit scholarships, minority scholarships, grants-in-aid, institutional loans, HEAL, alternative loan programs, NIH stipends, federal Perkins loans, Stafford subsidized and unsubsidized loans, and service commitment scholarship programs are available. Assistantships/fellowships may be available for combined degree candidates. Financial aid applications and information are generally available at the on-campus interview (by invitation). For scholarships, the selection criteria place heavy reliance on MCAT and undergraduate GPA. Contact the Office of Student Financial Aid at the Health Science Center for current information; phone: (713)500-3860. For most financial assistance and all federal programs, submit FAFSA to a federal processor (Title IV school code # 013956); also submit Financial Aid Transcript and Federal Income Tax forms. Approximately 60% of current students receive some form of financial assistance. Average debt after graduation $68,000.

DEGREE REQUIREMENTS. *For M.D.:* satisfactory completion of 4-year program. *For M.D.-M.P.H.:* generally a 5-year program. *For M.D.-Ph.D.:* generally a 6–7-year program.

Dental Branch
36516 John Freeman Avenue
Houston, Texas 77225
Phone: (713)500-4021
Internet site: http://www.db.uth.tmc.edu

Established 1905 as the Texas Dental College; joined University of Texas in 1943. Located at Texas Medical Center. Affiliated hospitals and clinics: Hermann Hospital, Harris County Hospital District, Methodist Hospital, Veterans Administration Medical Center, Institute for Rehabilitation and Research, Rusk Elementary School–based clinic, Bering Dental Clinics of Houston; clinics in Laredo, Brownsville, Huntsville, and Richmond. Postgraduate specialties: Endodontics, General Dentistry (AEGD), Dental Public Health (M.P.H.), Oral Pathology, Oral and Maxillofacial Surgery, Orthodontics, Pediatric Dentistry, Periodontics, Prosthodontics.

Annual tuition: residents $5,400, nonresidents $16,200; equipment, supplies, and other expenses $4,096. On-campus rooms and apartments available for both single and married students. Two student residences are located within the medical center. Annual on-campus housing cost: single students $5,400 (room only), married students $7,200. Contact Housing Office for both on- and off-campus housing information; phone: (713)792-8112. Off-campus housing and personal expenses: approximately $12,000.

Enrollment: 1st-year class 65; total full-time 260. First-year enrolled student information: 3 from out of state; 24 women; average age 23; 2 underrepresented minorities; 22 other minorities.

Degrees conferred: D.D.S., D.D.S.-M.P.H., M.S.

RECRUITMENT PRACTICES AND POLICIES. School has diversity program and actively recruits women/minority applicants. Diversity contact: Admissions Office; phone: (713)500-4021.

ADMISSION REQUIREMENTS FOR FIRST-YEAR APPLICANTS. Preference given to state residents; U.S. citizens and permanent residents only. *Undergraduate preparation.* Suggested predental courses: 2 courses in biology with labs, 2 courses in inorganic chemistry with labs, 2 courses in organic chemistry with labs, 2 courses in physics with labs, 1 course in biochemistry, 2 courses in English. There is no limitation on the number of junior-college credits that can be taken. Will consider applicants with only 3 years of undergraduate preparation; prefer applicants who will have a bachelor's degree prior to enrollment; For serious consideration an applicant should have at least a 3.0 GPA (A = 4); 57 out of 65 enrolled 1st-year students have bachelor's degrees awarded prior to enrollment. *Application process.* Request all application forms and procedural information from University of Texas System Medical and Dental Application Center at Austin (78701). Apply through either the University of Texas System Medical and Dental Application Center at Austin

(78701) or AADSAS (file after April 1, before November 1); submit official transcripts for each school attended (should show at least 90 semester credits/135 quarter credits), service processing fee; at the same time as you send materials to UTSMDAC/AADSAS, submit the following materials directly to the Office of Student Affairs at the dental branch: a photo, Health Professions Advisory Evaluation, official transcripts, and DAT scores (should be taken at least 8 months prior to the anticipated date of enrollment). Interviews are by invitation only and generally for final selection. Dual-degree applicants must apply to, and be accepted by, both schools; contact the Admissions Office for current information and specific requirements for admission. First-year students admitted in fall only. Rolling admission process. Notification starts December 1 and is finished when class is filled, but not later than July 15. Applicant's response to offer and $30 deposit due within 45 days if accepted prior to December 31; response and deposit due within 15 days if received after January 1. School does maintain an alternate list. Phone: (713)500-4151; fax: (713)500-4425.

ADMISSION REQUIREMENTS FOR ADVANCED-STANDING APPLICANTS. Accepts transfers from other accredited U.S. and Canadian dental schools. Admission limited to space available. There is an advanced standing program for graduates of foreign schools of dentistry. Contact the Office of Student Affairs for current information and specific requirements for admission.

ADMISSION STANDARDS AND RECOGNITION. *For D.D.S.:* number of applicants 852; number enrolled 207; median DAT: ACAD 17.8, PAT 16.3; median GPA 3.32 (A = 4), median sciences GPA 3.25 (A = 4). Gorman rating 4.34 (scale: strong 4.01–4.49); this placed the school in the Top 30 of all U.S. dental schools; the school's ranking by NIH awards/grants was 16th among dental schools, with 11 awards/grants received; total value of all awards/grants $2,746,676.

FINANCIAL AID. Scholarships, grants, institutional loans, state loan programs, DEAL, HEAL, alternative loan programs, federal Perkins loans, Stafford subsidized and unsubsidized loans, and military service commitment scholarship programs are available. Most financial aid is based on demonstrated need. Institutional financial aid applications and information are sent out with the letter of acceptance. Financial aid applications will not be accepted by the Financial Aid Office unless a tuition deposit has been received. Contact the Financial Aid Office for current information; phone: (713)500-3860. For most financial assistance and all need-based programs submit

FAFSA to a federal processor (Title IV school code # 013956); also submit Financial Aid Transcript, Federal Income Tax forms, and Use of Federal Funds Certification. Approximately 80% of current students receive some form of financial assistance. Average award $20,853.

DEGREE REQUIREMENTS. *For D.D.S.:* satisfactory completion of 4-year program. *For D.D.S.-M.P.H.:* generally a 5-year program.

THE UNIVERSITY OF TEXAS HEALTH SCIENCE CENTER AT SAN ANTONIO
7703 Floyd Curl Drive
San Antonio, Texas 78284
Phone: (210)597-7000
Internet site: http://www.uthscsa.edu

Founded 1972. Located 8 miles N of downtown San Antonio. Public control. Semester system. Library: 206,000 volumes/microforms; 2,500 periodicals/subscriptions. Special facilities: Center for Research in Reproductive Biology, Scanning Electron Microscope, University-Industry Cooperative Research Center, Institute of Biotechnology. The health science center's ranking in domestic higher education by NIH awards/grants was 59th, with 203 awards/grants received; total dollars awarded $43,103,751.

The health science center's graduate colleges/schools include: Dental School, Graduate School of Biomedical Sciences, Medical School, School of Allied Health Professions, School of Nursing.

Total university enrollment at main campus: 2,300.

Medical School at San Antonio
7703 Floyd Curl Drive
San Antonio, Texas 78274-7701
Phone: (210)567-2665; fax: (210)567-2685
Internet site: http://www.uthscsa.edu
E-mail: eliker@uthscas.edu

Established 1959. Affiliated hospitals: University Hospital, Brady-Green Community Health Center, Audie Murphy Veteran Hospital, Wilford Hall USAF Hospital, Brooke Army Hospital, Aerospace Medical Division of USAF, Baptist Memorial Hospital, Santa Rosa Medical Center. Curriculum is designed to have the first 2 years of study devoted primarily to basic sciences.

Annual tuition: residents $7,071, nonresidents $20,171; fees $375. No on-campus housing available. Off-campus housing is available within walking distance of school. Contact Office of Student Services for off-campus housing information. Off-campus housing and personal expenses: approximately $15,400.

Enrollment: 1st-year class 200; total full-time 830 (men 60%, women 40%). First-year statistics: 7.5% out of state; 44.5% women; average age 24; 18% minorities; 55% science majors.

Faculty: full-time 900.

Degrees conferred: M.D., M.D.-Ph.D. (Biochemistry, Cell Biology, Genetics, Immunology, Microbiology, Molecular Biology, Neurosciences, Pharmacology, Physiology).

RECRUITMENT PRACTICES AND POLICIES. School has diversity program and actively recruits women/minority applicants. Diversity contact: Medical Dean's Office; phone: (210)567-4427.

ADMISSION REQUIREMENTS FOR FIRST-YEAR APPLICANTS. Ninety percent of class must be from state; U.S. citizens and permanent residents only. *Undergraduate preparation.* Suggested premed courses: 4 courses in biology with labs, 2 courses in inorganic chemistry with labs, 2 courses in organic chemistry with labs, 2 courses in physics with labs, 1 course in calculus, 2 courses in English. Bachelor's degree from an accredited institution required. 98% of applicants have bachelor's degrees awarded prior to enrollment. Does not have EDP. *Application process.* Obtain all application forms and procedural information from the University of Texas System Medical and Dental Application Center at Austin (78701). File application after April 15, before October 15. Submit MCAT (will accept MCAT test results from the last 3 years); official transcripts for each school attended (should show at least 90 semester credits/135 quarter credits), an application fee of $45 (for one school, $5 for each additional school), nonresidents $80 (for one school, $10 for each additional school), a personal statement, preprofessional committee evaluation, and 3 recommendations from science faculty. Interviews are by invitation only and generally for final selection. For M.D.-Ph.D. degree applicants there are no additional materials required; contact the Associate Dean, Graduate School of Biomedical Science, for current information on the 2nd interview required for the program; phone: (210)567-3711. First-year students admitted in fall only. Rolling admission process. Notification starts January 15 and is finished when class is filled. Applicant's response to offer due within 14 days of receipt of acceptance letter. School does maintain an alternate list. Phone: (210)567-2665.

ADMISSION REQUIREMENTS FOR TRANSFER APPLICANTS. Transfer applicants are not considered.

Contact the Admissions Office for current information and any modifications in policy.

ADMISSION STANDARDS AND RECOGNITION. *For M.D.:* number of state-resident applicants 2,638, nonresidents 728; number of state residents interviewed 1,031, nonresidents 200; total number accepted 269; number of residents enrolled 185, nonresidents 15; median MCAT 10.0 (verbal reasoning 10.0; biological sciences 10.0; physical sciences 10.0); median GPA 3.51 (A = 4). Gorman rating 3.73 (scale: good 3.61–3.99); the school's medical ranking by NIH awards was 48th, with 170 awards/grants received; total dollars awarded $37,034,808.

FINANCIAL AID. Limited scholarships, institutional loans, HEAL, alternative loan programs, federal Perkins loans, Stafford subsidized and unsubsidized loans, and service commitment scholarship programs are available. Assistantships/fellowships may be available for M.D.-Ph.D. degree candidates. Financial aid applications and information are sent out with the letter of acceptance. For scholarships, the selection criteria place heavy reliance on MCAT and undergraduate GPA. Contact the Office of Student Services for current information; phone: (210)567-2635. For most financial assistance and all federal programs, submit FAFSA to a federal processor (Title IV school code # 010115); also submit Financial Aid Transcript and Federal Income Tax forms. Approximately 90% of current students receive some form of financial assistance. Average debt after graduation $76,000.

DEGREE REQUIREMENTS. *For M.D.:* satisfactory completion of 4-year program. *For M.D.-Ph.D.:* generally a 6–7-year program.

Dental School
7703 Floyd Curl Drive
San Antonio, Texas 78284-7702
Phone: (210)567-3181
Internet site: http://www.uthscsa.eud
E-mail: serna@uthscsa.edu

Established 1970. Located at South Texas Medical Center. Special programs: Research fellowships, externships. Postgraduate specialties: Endodontics (M.S.), General Dentistry, Dental Diagnostic Sciences (M.S.), Dental Public Health, Oral and Maxillofacial Surgery, Pediatric Dentistry, Periodontics (M.S.), Prosthodontics (M.S.).

Annual tuition: residents $5,400, nonresidents $16,200; fees $230, equipment and supplies $1,400. No on-campus housing available. Off-campus housing is available within walking distance of school. Contact Office of Student Services for off-campus housing information. Off-campus housing, food, transportation, and personal expenses: approximately $15,400.

Enrollment: 1st-year class 90; total full-time 351. First-year enrolled student information: 4 from out of state; 3 states represented; 30 women; average age 24; 14 underrepresented minorities; 13 other minorities.

Faculty: full-time 137, part-time/volunteers 97.

Degrees conferred: D.D.S., B.S.-D.D.S. (with Abilene Christian University, Incarnate Word College, Prairie View A&M University, Sam Houston State University, Southwest Texas State University, St. Mary's University, Texas A&I University, West Texas A&M University, University of Texas Pan American, University of Texas at San Antonio, Texas Wesleyan University), D.D.S.-M.S., D.D.S.-Ph.D. (with Graduate School of Biomedical Sciences).

RECRUITMENT PRACTICES AND POLICIES. School has diversity program and actively recruits women/minority applicants. Diversity contact: Minority Affairs and Special Programs Officer; phone: (210)567-2671.

ADMISSION REQUIREMENT FOR BACHELOR-D.D.S. APPLICANTS. For information on the Early Acceptance Program, contact program directors at each of the undergraduate institutions listed above. Admission to the programs generally takes place during the students freshmen year.

ADMISSION REQUIREMENTS FOR FIRST-YEAR APPLICANTS. Preference given to state residents; U.S. citizens and permanent residents only. *Undergraduate preparation.* Suggested predental courses: 2 courses in biology with labs, 2 courses in inorganic chemistry with labs, 2 courses in organic chemistry with labs, 2 courses in physics with labs. There is no limitation on the number of junior-college credits taken. Will consider applicants with only 3 years of undergraduate preparation; prefer applicants who will have bachelor's degree prior to enrollment; 98% of applicants have bachelor's degree awarded prior to enrollment. *Application process.* Request all application forms and procedural information from University of Texas System Medical and Dental Application Center, 702 Colorado, Suite 620, Austin (78701); phone: (512)499-4785. Apply through either the University of Texas System Medical and Dental Application Center at Austin (78701) or AADSAS (file after April 1, before November 1); submit official transcripts for each school attended (should show at least 90 semester credits/135 quarter credits), service processing fee; at the same time as you send materials to UTSMDAC/AADSAS, submit the following materials directly to the Office of the Registrar at the dental branch: a photo, Health Professions Advisory Evaluation, official transcripts, and DAT scores (should be taken at least 8 months prior to the anticipated date of enrollment). Interviews are by invitation only and generally for final selection. Dual-degree applicants must apply to, and be accepted by, both schools; contact the Admissions Office for current information and specific requirements for admission. First-year students admitted in fall only. Rolling admission process. Notification starts December 1 and is finished when class is filled, but not later than early August. Applicant's Statement of Intent to Enroll due within 30 days if accepted prior to January 15; response and deposit due within 14 days if received after January 15. School does maintain an alternate list. Phone: (210)567-2674; fax: (210)567-6271; E-mail: carr@uthscsa.edu.

ADMISSION REQUIREMENTS FOR ADVANCED STANDING APPLICANTS. There is no specific program of advanced standing for U.S. citizens and permanent residents; each applicant is considered on a case-by-case basis. There is an advanced standing program for graduates of foreign schools of dentistry. Contact the Office of the Registrar for current information and specific requirements for admission.

ADMISSION STANDARDS AND RECOGNITION. *For D.D.S.:* number of applicants 549, number enrolled 90; median DAT: ACAD 18.0, PAT 17.6; median GPA 3.41 (A = 4), median sciences GPA 3.36 (A = 4). Gorman rating 4.28 (scale: strong 4.01–4.49); this placed the school in the Top 35 of all U.S. dental schools.

FINANCIAL AID. Limited scholarships, institutional loans, state loan programs, DEAL, HEAL, alternative loan programs, federal Perkins loans, Stafford subsidized and unsubsidized loans, and military service commitment scholarship programs are available. Assistantships/fellowships may be available for combined-degree candidates. Institutional financial aid applications and information are available after January 1. Submit applications as soon as possible. Most financial aid is based on demonstrated need. For scholarship assistance, the selection criteria place heavy reliance on DAT and undergraduate GPA. Contact the Financial Aid Office for current information; phone: (210)567-2635. For most financial assistance and all need-based programs submit FAFSA to a federal processor (Title IV school code # 010115); also submit Financial Aid Transcript, Federal Income Tax forms, and Use of Federal Funds Certification. Approximately 90% of current students receive some form of financial assistance. Average award for residents $20,237, nonresidents $21,324.

DEGREE REQUIREMENTS. *For B.S.-D.D.S.:* generally a 7-year program. *For D.D.S.:* satisfactory completion of 4-year program. *For D.D.S.-M.S.:* generally a 4½–6-year program. *For D.D.S.-Ph.D.:* generally a 7-year program.

THE UNIVERSITY OF TEXAS SOUTHWESTERN MEDICAL CENTER AT DALLAS

Dallas, Texas 75235-9002
Internet site: http://www.swmed.edu

Founded 1943. Located 3 miles N of downtown. Public control. Semester system. Library: 225,000 volumes; 10,000 microforms; 2,000 periodicals/subscriptions. Special facilities: Howard Hughes Medical Institute, Zale Lipshy Hospital, Cain Center for Biomedical Research, James Collins Center for Biomedical Research, Cecil H. and Ida Green Center for Reproductive Biology Sciences, Robert T. Hayes Center for Mineral Metabolism Research, Erik Jonsson Center for Research on Molecular Genetics and Human Disease, Kimberly Clark Center for Breast Cancer Research, Eugene McDermott Center for Human Growth and Development, Eugene McDermott Center for Pain Management, Mobility Foundation Center for Rehabilitation Research, W. A. "Tex" and Deborah Moncrief Jr. Center for Cancer Genetics, Harry Moss Heart Center, Harold C. Simmons Arthritis Research Center, Harold C. Simmons Comprehensive Cancer Center, Kent Waldrep Foundation Center for Basic Neuroscience Research, Cancer Immunobiology Center, Center for Basic Research in Transplantation Immunology, Nuclear Medicine Center. The university's ranking in domestic higher education by NIH awards/grants was 28th, with 311 awards/grants received; total dollars awarded $86,496,266.

The university's graduate schools at Dallas include: Southwestern Graduate School of Biomedical Sciences, School of Allied Health Sciences, Southwestern Medical School.

Total university enrollment at main campus: 1,529.

University of Texas Southwestern Medical Center
Dallas, Texas 95235

Public Control. Member of the Council of Teaching Hospitals. Special facilities at medical center complex: Parkland Memorial Hospital, Children's Medical Center (member of the Council of Teaching Hospitals), St. Paul Hospital (member of the Council of Teaching Hospitals), Zale Lipshy Hospital (member of the Council of Teaching Hospitals), City of Dallas Health Department, Institute of Forensic Sciences. Hospitals within the complex have nationally recognized programs in AIDS, Endocrinology, Gynecology, Pediatrics, Pulmonary Disease, Rheumatology, Urology. *Barron's Guide* placed the medical center among the Top 25 most prestigious U.S. hospitals/medical centers.

Southwestern Medical School

5323 Harry Hines Boulevard
Dallas, Texas 75235-9096
Phone: (214)648-2670; fax: (214)648-3289
Internet site: http://www.swmed.edu
E-mail: admissions@mednet.swmed.edu

Established 1943. Library: 175,000 volumes/microforms; 2,400 current periodicals/subscriptions. Affiliated hospitals: Baylor University Medical Center, John Peter Smith Hospital (Fort Worth), Charlton Methodist Hospital, Presbyterian Hospital of Dallas, Timberlawn Psychiatric Hospital, University of Texas Health Science Center at Tyler, Veterans Administration Medical Center.

Annual tuition: residents $7,216, nonresidents $20,346; fees $696. No on-campus housing available. Contact Admissions Office for off-campus housing information. Off-campus housing and personal expenses: approximately $15,885.

Enrollment: 1st-year class 201; total full-time 830 (men 65%, women 35%). First-year statistics: 10% out of state; 40% women; average age 24; 11% minorities; 74% science majors.

Degrees conferred: M.D., M.D.-M.A. (Biomedical Communications), M.D.-M.S. (Biomedical Engineering, with University of Texas at Arlington, Radiological Sciences, Rehabilitation Counseling Psychology), M.D.-Ph.D. (Biochemistry and Molecular Biology, Biomedical Engineering, Cell Regulation, Clinical Psychology, Genetics and Development, Immunology, Integrative Biology, Molecular Biophysics, Molecular Microbiology, Neurosciences, Radiological Sciences); has M.S.T.P.

RECRUITMENT PRACTICES AND POLICIES. School has diversity program and actively recruits women/minority applicants. Diversity contact: Assistant Dean for Minority Student Affairs; phone: (214)648-2168.

ADMISSION REQUIREMENTS FOR FIRST-YEAR APPLICANTS. Ninety percent of class must be from state; U.S. citizens and permanent residents only. *Undergraduate preparation.* Suggested premed courses: 4 courses in biology with labs, 2 courses in inorganic chemistry with labs, 2 courses in organic chemistry with labs, 2 courses in physics with labs, 1 course in calculus, 2 courses in English. Bachelor's degree from an accredited institution required; 98% of applicants have bachelor's

degrees awarded prior to enrollment. Does not have EDP. *Application process.* Obtain all application forms and procedural information from the University of Texas System Medical and Dental Application Center at Austin (78701). File application after April 15, before October 15. Submit MCAT (will accept MCAT test results from the last 3 years and will accept results from April test date), official transcripts for each school attended (should show at least 90 semester credits/135 quarter credits), an application fee of $45 (for one school, $5 for each additional school), nonresidents $80 (for one school, $10 for each additional school), a personal statement, preprofessional committee evaluation, and 3 recommendations from science faculty to UTSMDAC, Austin (78701). Interviews are by invitation only and generally for final selection. Combined degree applicants must apply to, and be accepted by, both schools; contact the Admissions Office for current information and specific requirements for admission. Students apply for M.S.T.P. during their first 2 years of medical school. First-year students admitted in fall only. Rolling admission process. Notification starts January 15 and is finished when class is filled. Applicant's response to offer due within 2 weeks of receipt of acceptance letter. School does maintain an alternate list. Phone: (214)648-5617.

ADMISSION REQUIREMENTS FOR TRANSFER APPLICANTS. Rarely accepts transfer applicants and only if space is available. Contact the Admissions Office for current information and specific requirements for admission.

ADMISSION STANDARDS AND RECOGNITION. *For M.D.:* number of state-resident applicants 2,565, nonresidents 853; number of state residents interviewed 690, nonresidents 116; number of residents enrolled 181, nonresidents 20; median MCAT 10.4 (verbal reasoning 10.0; biological sciences 11.0; physical sciences 10.0); median GPA 3.60 (A = 4). *Barron's Guide* placed medical school among the Top 25 most prestigious U.S. medical schools; Gorman rating 3.76 (scale: good 3.61-3.99); *U.S. News & World Report* ranked the school in the Top 25 of all U.S. medical schools; the school's medical ranking by NIH awards was 21st, with 311 awards/grants received; total dollars awarded $86,496,266.

FINANCIAL AID. A limited number of scholarships from memorial funds and foundations, institutional loans, HEAL, alternative loan programs, NIH stipends, federal Perkins loans, Stafford subsidized and unsubsidized loans, and service commitment scholarship programs are available. Assistantships/fellowships may be available for combined degree candidates. Most financial aid is awarded based on demonstrated need. For scholarship consideration, the selection criteria place heavy reliance on MCAT and undergraduate GPA. Financial aid applications and information are available by contacting the Office of the Registrar; phone: (214)648-3606. For most financial assistance and all federal programs, submit FAFSA to a federal processor (Title IV school code # 010019); also submit Financial Aid Transcript and Federal Income Tax forms. Approximately 80% of current students receive some form of financial assistance. Average debt after graduation $62,500.

DEGREE REQUIREMENTS. *For M.D.:* satisfactory completion of 4-year program. All students must pass USMLE Step 1 prior to entering 4th year. *For M.D.-M.A.,-M.S.:* generally 4½–5½-year program. *For M.D.-Ph.D.:* generally a 6–7-year program.

THOMAS JEFFERSON UNIVERSITY
Philadelphia, Pennsylvania
Internet site: http://www.tju.edu

Founded 1924. Located in historic Philadelphia. Private control. Semester system. Library: 170,000 volumes; 10,634 microforms; 2,210 periodicals/subscriptions; 70 work stations. Special facilities: Jefferson Institute of Molecular Medicine, Kimmel Cancer Institute. Special programs: B.S.-M.D. program; postbaccalaureate program/Pre-Health Program with University of Pennsylvania, College of General Studies, Bryn Mawr College, and University of Delaware. The university's ranking in domestic higher education by NIH awards/grants was 51st, with 206 awards/grants received; total dollars awarded $50,406,358.

The university's graduate colleges include: College of Allied Health Sciences, College of Graduate Studies, Jefferson Medical College.

Total university enrollment at main campus: 1,280.

Thomas Jefferson University Hospital
11th and Walnut Street
Philadelphia, Pennsylvania 19107

Private control. The hospital is a member of the Council of Teaching Hospitals. Nationally recognized programs in Gynecology, Orthopedics, Rehabilitation.

Jefferson Medical College
1025 Walnut Street
Philadelphia, Pennsylvania 19107-5083
Phone: (215)955-6983; fax: (215)923-6939
Internet site: http://www.tju.edu

Established 1824, one of the oldest medical colleges in the nation and currently the largest. Semester system; first 2 years are spent in studying the basic sciences. Affiliated hospitals: Thomas Jefferson University Hospital, Stein Research Center, Wills Eye Hospital, Veterans Administration Hospital. Special facility: Bodine Center for Radiation Therapy. Special programs: prematriculation summer sessions; a decelerated program available during first 2 years.

Annual tuition: $25,990. On-campus apartments available for both single and married students. Contact Housing Office for both on- and off-campus housing information; phone: (215)955-8913. Medical students tend to live off-campus. Off-campus housing and personal expenses: approximately $14,300.

Enrollment: 1st-year class 223 (EDP 20); total full-time 902 (men 68%, women 32%). First-year statistics: 56% out of state; however, most students come from Delaware, Pennsylvania, New Jersey, and New York; 29 states and 82 different undergraduate institutions represented; 35% women; average age 24; 8% minorities; 78% science majors.

Faculty: full-time 689, part-time/volunteers 3,000.

Degrees conferred: M.D., B.S.-M.D. (with Penn State University), M.D.-M.B.A. (with Widener University), M.D.-M.H.A. (Widener University), M.D.-Ph.D. (Biochemistry, Cell Biology, Genetics, Immunology, Microbiology and Molecular Virology, Molecular Biology, Pathology, Molecular Pharmacology and Structural Biology, Physiology).

RECRUITMENT PRACTICES AND POLICIES. School has diversity program and actively recruits women/minority applicants. Diversity contact: Assistant Dean for Student Affairs and Special Programs; phone: (215)503-6763.

ADMISSION REQUIREMENT FOR B.S.-M.D. APPLICANTS. Both state residents and nonresidents encouraged to apply. *High school requirements:* 4 units of English, 1 1/2 units of algebra, 1 unit of geometry, 3 units of sciences, 5 units of social studies, humanities, and/or arts. Submit application and application fee of $40, SAT I, official high school transcript with rank in class, 3 letters of recommendation. Apply to Admissions Office at Penn State University, Box 3000, Penn State University, after September 1, before November 30. Phone: (814)865-5471. Interviews are by invitation only and generally for final selection. Notification March 1. Applicant's response to offer and $225 deposit returned by May 1. Classes begin in June.

ADMISSION REQUIREMENTS FOR FIRST-YEAR APPLICANTS. Preference given to U.S. citizens, permanent residents, and children of alumni and faculty. *Un-*

dergraduate preparation. Suggested premed courses: 2 courses in biology with labs, 2 courses in inorganic chemistry with labs, 2 courses in organic chemistry with labs, 2 courses in physics with labs. Bachelor's degree from an accredited institution required; 91% of applicants have bachelor's degree awarded prior to enrollment (21 students are from Penn State University/Jefferson accelerated program). *Has EDP;* applicants must apply through AMCAS (official transcripts sent by mid-May) between June 1 and August 1. Early applications are encouraged. Submit secondary/supplemental application, a personal statement, and 2 recommendations to Admissions Office within 2 weeks of receipt of application. Interviews are by invitation only and generally for final selection. Notification normally begins October 1. *Regular application process.* Apply through AMCAS (file after June 1, before November 15); submit MCAT (will accept MCAT test results from the last 3 years), official transcripts for each school attended (should show at least 90 semester credits/135 quarter credits, submit transcripts by mid-May to AMCAS), service processing fee. Submit an application fee of $65, a supplemental application, a personal statement, preprofessional committee evaluation, and 3 recommendations from science faculty to Admissions Office within 2–3 weeks of the receipt of supplemental materials, but no later than January 15. Interviews are by invitation only and generally for final selection. M.D.-Ph.D. degree applicants must apply to, and be accepted by, both schools; contact the Director of Admission and Recruitment of the College of Graduate Studies for current information and specific requirements for admission; phone: (215)955-0155. First-year students admitted in fall only. Rolling admission process. Notification starts October 15 and is finished when class is filled. Applicant's response to offer and $100 deposit due within 2 weeks of receipt of acceptance letter. School does maintain an alternate list. Phone: (215)955-6983.

ADMISSION REQUIREMENTS FOR TRANSFER APPLICANTS. Accepts transfers from other accredited U.S. medical schools into the 3rd year but only with a compelling reason. Admission limited to space available. Contact the Admissions Office after December 1 for current information and specific requirements for admission.

ADMISSION STANDARDS AND RECOGNITION. *For B.S.-M.D.:* number of applicants 541; number interviewed 117; number enrolled 24; median combined SAT 1510. *For M.D.:* number of state-resident applicants 1,440, nonresidents 9,739; number of state residents interviewed 233, nonresidents 516; number of residents enrolled 98, nonresidents 124; median MCAT 9.9 (verbal reasoning 9.8; biological sciences 9.8; physical sciences

10.0); median GPA 3.5 (A = 4). Gorman rating 3.49 (scale: acceptable plus 3.01–3.59); the college's medical ranking by NIH awards was 40th, with 205 awards/grants received; total dollars awarded $50,011,137.

FINANCIAL AID. Scholarships, merit scholarships, minority scholarships, grants-in-aid, institutional loans, HEAL, alternative loan programs, federal Perkins loans, Stafford subsidized and unsubsidized loans, primary-care service commitment scholarship programs are available. Fellowships, tuition waivers, and stipends may be available for M.D.-Ph.D. degree candidates. All financial aid is based on demonstrated need. Financial aid applications and the *Financial Aid Handbook* are available after December 18. Financial aid applications must be completed and returned no later than April 1. For scholarships, the selection criteria place heavy reliance on MCAT and undergraduate GPA. Contact the Office of Student Financial Aid for current information; phone: (215)955-5855. For most financial assistance and all federal programs, submit FAFSA to a federal processor (Title IV school code # 010021); also submit Financial Aid Transcript and Federal Income Tax forms. Approximately 76% of current students receive some form of financial assistance. Average debt after graduation $92,000.

DEGREE REQUIREMENTS. *For B.S.-M.D.:* a 6-calendar-year program; a 3.5 GPA (A = 4) at Penn State University and MCATS are required. *For M.D.:* satisfactory completion of 4-year program. All students must pass USMLE Step 1 prior to entering 3rd year; all students must pass USMLE Step 2 prior to awarding of M.D. *For M.D.-M.B.A.:* generally a 5½–6-year program. *For M.D.-Ph.D.:* generally a 7-year program.

TOURO UNIVERSITY

College of Osteopathic Medicine
1210 Scott Street
San Francisco, California
Phone: (888)880-SFDO (California), (888)887-SFDO (outside California)
Internet site: http://www.sfcom.edu

Established 1997. Located in center of San Francisco. Private control. Semester system.

Annual tuition: $22,270; fees $2,900. No on-campus housing available. Contact Director of Admissions and Relations for off-campus housing information. Off-campus housing and personal expenses: approximately $15,000.

Enrollment: 1st-year class approximately 125; total full-time N/A.

Degree conferred: D.O.

RECRUITMENT PRACTICES AND POLICIES. School has diversity program and actively recruits women/minority applicants. Diversity contact: Director of Admissions and Relations.

ADMISSION REQUIREMENTS FOR FIRST-YEAR APPLICANTS. Preference given to U.S. citizens and permanent residents only. *Undergraduate preparation.* Suggested premed courses: 2 courses in biology, 2 courses in inorganic chemistry, 2 courses in organic chemistry, 2 courses in physics, 2 courses in English; 1 course in biochemistry is strongly recommended. Bachelor's degree from an accredited institution required; all applicants have bachelor's degree awarded prior to enrollment. For serious consideration an applicant should have at least a 3.0 GPA (A = 4). *Application process.* Apply through AACOMAS (file after June 1, before February 1); submit MCAT (will accept test results from last 3 years), official transcripts for each school attended (should show at least 90 semester credits/135 quarter credits), service processing fee. After a review of the AACOMAS application and supporting documents, a decision is made concerning which candidates should receive supplemental materials. Submit the supplemental application, an application fee of $50, a personal statement, and 1 recommendation from the premed committee, 2 from science faculty members, and 1 from a D.O. to Admissions Office as soon as possible. In addition, international applicants must submit foreign transcripts to the World Education Service for translation and evaluation. TOEFL may be required of those applicants whose native language is other than English. Interviews are by invitation only and generally for final selection. First-year students admitted in fall only. Rolling admission process. Notification starts in October and is finished when class is filled. Applicant's response to offer and $1,000 deposit due within 2 weeks of receipt of acceptance letter.

ADMISSION REQUIREMENTS FOR TRANSFER APPLICANTS. Will accept transfers from other accredited U.S. osteopathic medical schools. Admission limited to space available. Contact the Director of Admissions and Relations for current information and specific requirements for admission.

ADMISSION STANDARDS AND RECOGNITION. *For D.O.:* number of state-resident applicants N/A, nonresidents N/A.

FINANCIAL AID. Scholarships, grants, institutional loans, NOF, HEAL, alternative loan programs, federal Perkins loans, Stafford subsidized and unsubsidized loans, service obligation scholarship programs, and military and National Health Service programs are available. Financial aid applications and information will probably be available at the on-campus interview (by invitation). Contact the Financial Aid Office for current information. For most financial assistance and all federal programs, submit FAFSA to a federal processor (Title IV school code # N/A); also submit Financial Aid Transcript and Federal Income Tax forms.

DEGREE REQUIREMENTS. *For D.O.:* satisfactory completion of 4-year program.

TUFTS UNIVERSITY
Medford, Massachusetts 02155
Internet site: http://www.tufts.edu

Founded 1852. Located 5 miles NW of Boston. Private control. Semester system. Special facilities: Center for Applied Child Development, Electro-Optics Technology Center, Center for Environmental Management, Lincoln Filene Center for Sciences and Math Teaching, Science and Technology Center. Library: 739,700 volumes; 1,098,500 microforms; 3,465 periodicals/subscriptions. The university's ranking in domestic higher education by NIH awards/grants was 64th, with 149 awards/grants received; total dollars awarded $37,060,232.

The university's graduate colleges/schools include: Fletcher School of Law and Diplomacy, Graduate School of Arts and Sciences, College of Engineering, Sackler School of Graduate Biomedical Sciences, School of Dental Medicine, School of Medicine, School of Nutrition Science and Policy, School of Veterinary Medicine.

Total university enrollment at main campus: 8,500.

Health Science Center
750 Washington Street
Boston, Massachusetts 02111

Located in downtown Boston. Private control. New England Medical Center is a member of the Council of Teaching Hospitals. Schools located at health science center are: Sackler School of Graduate Biomedical Sciences, School of Dental Medicine, School of Medicine, School of Nutrition Science and Policy, School of Veterinary Medicine. Special facilities: Sackler Center for Health Communication, New England Medical Center. The medical center has nationally recognized programs in AIDS, Cardiology, Endocrinology, Gastroenterology, Geriatrics, Rheumatology, Urology.

School of Medicine
136 Harrison Avenue
Boston, Massachusetts 02111
Phone: (617)636-6571
Internet site: http://www.tufts.edu/med

Established 1893. Located at health science center. Library: 109,000 volumes/microforms; 1,500 current periodicals/subscriptions. Affiliated/associated hospitals: New England Medical Center, Baystate Medical Center, Boston Veteran's Administration Medical Center, Eastern Maine Medical Center, Faulkner Hospital, Fahey Hitchcock Medical Center, Newton-Wellesley Hospital, Lemuel Shattuck Hospital, Saint Elizabeth's Medical Center of Boston. Special programs: prematriculation summer sessions.

Annual tuition: $31,805; fees $345. On-campus rooms available for single students only. Annual on-campus housing cost: single students $5,930 (room only). Contact Office of Educational Affairs for both on- and off-campus housing information; phone: (617)636-6621. Medical students tend to live off-campus. Off-campus housing and personal expenses: approximately $14,134.

Enrollment: 1st-year class 165 (EDP 3); total full-time 676 (men 59%, women 41%). First-year statistics: 70% out of state; 43% women; average age 24; 8% minorities; 78% science majors.

Degrees conferred: M.D., M.D.-M.B.A. (with Northeastern University and Brandeis University), M.D.-M.P.H., M.D.-M.S., M.D.-Ph.D. (Biochemistry, Cell Biology, Genetics, Immunology, Microbiology, Molecular Biology, Neurosciences, Pharmacology, Physiology); has M.S.T.P.

RECRUITMENT PRACTICES AND POLICIES. School has diversity program and actively recruits women/minority applicants. Diversity contact: Assistant Director of Student Services; phone: (617)636-6576.

ADMISSION REQUIREMENTS FOR FIRST-YEAR APPLICANTS. Some preference given to state residents; U.S. citizens and permanent residents only. *Undergraduate preparation.* Suggested premed courses: 2 courses in biology with labs, 2 courses in inorganic chemistry with labs, 2 courses in organic chemistry with labs, 2 courses in physics with labs, 2 courses in English; calculus, statistics, and computer science are recommended. Bachelor's degree from an accredited institution required; all applicants have bachelor's degrees awarded prior to enrollment. *Has EDP;* applicants must apply through AMCAS (official transcripts sent by mid-May) between June 1 and August 1. Early applications are encouraged. Submit secondary/supplemental application, a personal statement, and 2 recommendations to Admissions Office

within 2 weeks of receipt of application. Interviews are by invitation only and generally for final selection. Notification normally begins October 1. *Regular application process.* Apply through AMCAS (file after June 1, before November 1); submit MCAT (will accept MCAT test results from the last 3 years), official transcripts for each school attended (should show at least 90 semester credits/135 quarter credits, submit transcripts by mid-May to AMCAS), service processing fee. Submit an application fee of $95, a secondary application, a personal statement, preprofessional committee evaluation, and 3 recommendations from science faculty to Admissions Office within 2–3 weeks of the receipt of supplemental materials. Interviews are by invitation only and generally for final selection. Combined-degree applicants must submit a separate application to the program of their choice; contact the Office of Special Programs (phone: (617)636-6571) for current information and specific requirements for admission. First-year students admitted in fall only. Rolling admission process. Notification starts December 1 and is finished when class is filled. Applicant's response to offer and $100 deposit due within 2 weeks of receipt of acceptance letter. School does maintain an alternate list. Phone: (617)636-6571.

ADMISSION REQUIREMENTS FOR TRANSFER APPLICANTS. Accepts transfers from LCME-accredited U.S. medical schools into both the 2nd and 3rd years. Admission limited to space available; in some years there are no openings. Contact the Admissions Office for current information and specific requirements for admission.

ADMISSION STANDARDS AND RECOGNITION. *For M.D.:* number of state-resident applicants 916, nonresidents 10,584; number of state residents interviewed 163, nonresidents 666; number of residents enrolled 48, nonresidents 120; median MCAT 9.5 (verbal reasoning 9.6; biological sciences 9.8; physical sciences 9.6); median GPA 3.54 (A = 4). Gorman rating 4.46 (scale: strong 4.01–4.49); the school's medical ranking by NIH awards was 55th, with 122 awards/grants received; total dollars awarded $31,191,111.

FINANCIAL AID. Scholarships, merit scholarships, minority scholarships, grants-in-aid, institutional loans, HEAL, alternative loan programs, NIH stipends, federal Perkins loans, Stafford subsidized and unsubsidized loans, service commitment scholarship programs are available. Research assistantships/fellowships (they provide both tuition waivers and a stipend) are available for combined degree candidates. Financial aid applications should be filed as soon as possible after January 1. For scholarship assistance, the selection criteria place heavy reliance on MCAT and undergraduate GPA. Contact the Financial Aid Office for current information; phone: (617)636-6574. For most financial assistance and all federal programs, submit FAFSA to a federal processor (Title IV school code # E00520); also submit Financial Aid Transcript and Federal Income Tax forms. Approximately 75% of current students receive some form of financial assistance; 33% of students receive aid directly from School of Medicine. Average debt after graduation $117,000.

DEGREE REQUIREMENTS. *For M.D.:* satisfactory completion of 4-year program. All students must pass USMLE Step 1 prior to entering 3rd year; all students must pass USMLE Step 2 prior to awarding of M.D. *For M.D.-M.B.A.:* generally a 5-year program. *For M.D.-M.P.H.:* generally a 4½–5-year program. *For M.D.-Ph.D.:* generally a 7-year program.

School of Dental Medicine
One Kneeland Street
Boston, Massachusetts 02111
Phone: (617)636-6639
Internet site: http://www.tufts.edu/dental
E-mail: jenlewis@infonet.tufts.edu

Established 1868 as Boston Dental College, joined Tufts College in 1899. Located at health science center. Special programs: International Student Program, summer research fellowships. Postgraduate specialties: Endodontics, General Practice Residency (GPR), Oral and Maxillofacial Surgery, Orthodontics, Pediatric Dentistry, Periodontics, Prosthodontics.

Annual tuition: $28,800; equipment, supplies, and other expenses: $6,500. On-campus rooms available for single students only. Annual on-campus housing cost: single students $5,930 (room only). Contact Admissions Office for both on- and off-campus housing information; phone: (617)636-6639. Dental students tend to live off-campus. Off-campus housing, food, transportation, and personal expenses: approximately $13,000.

Enrollment: 1st-year class 148; total full-time 724. First-year enrolled student information: 114 from out of state; 26 states and 4 foreign countries represented; 59 women; average age 24; 4 underrepresented minorities; 65 other minorities.

Faculty: full-time 29, part-time 365.

Degrees conferred: D.M.D., B.S.-D.M.D. (Adelphi University), D.M.D.-M.S. (Dental Sciences).

RECRUITMENT PRACTICES AND POLICIES. School has diversity program and actively recruits women/minority applicants. Diversity contact: Minority Affairs Office; phone: (617)636-6639.

ADMISSION REQUIREMENT FOR B.S.-D.M.D. APPLICANTS. For information and applications contact the Undergraduate Office of Admission, Adelphi University, Garden City, New York 11530; phone: (516)877-3033.

ADMISSION REQUIREMENTS FOR FIRST-YEAR APPLICANTS. There is a contractual arrangement with the state of New Mexico. Preference given to applicants with a 3.2 GPA (A = 4). *Undergraduate preparation.* Suggested predental courses: 2 courses in biology with labs, 2 courses in inorganic chemistry with labs, 2 courses in organic chemistry with labs, 2 courses in physics with labs, 2 courses in English. The junior-college transfer credit limit is 60 credits, and all must be earned before entering a 4-year institution. Will consider applicants with only 2 years of undergraduate preparation; prefer applicants who will have bachelor's degree prior to enrollment; all applicants have bachelor's degree awarded prior to enrollment. *Application process.* Apply through AADSAS (file after June 1, before March 1); submit official transcripts for each school attended (should show at least 90 semester credits/135 quarter credits), service processing fee; at the same time as you send in AADSAS materials, submit official DAT scores directly to the Office of Admission and Student Affairs. TOEFL may be required of an applicant whose native language is other than English. Submit the following materials immediately after being contacted by the Office of Admission: an application fee of $55, official transcripts, and predental committee evaluation or 2 recommendations from senior science professors to the Office of Admission and Student Affairs. Interviews are by invitation only and generally for final selection. Combined degree applicants must apply to, and be accepted by, both schools; contact the Office of Admissions and Student Affairs for current information and specific requirements for admission. First-year students admitted in fall only. Rolling admission process. Notification starts in December and is finished when class is filled. Applicant's response to offer and $1,500 deposit due within 30 days if accepted prior to January 31; response and deposit due within 2 weeks if received after February 1. School does maintain an alternate list. Phone: (617)636-6639; E-mail: jenlewis@infonet.tufts.edu.

ADMISSION REQUIREMENTS FOR ADVANCED-STANDING APPLICANTS. Accepts transfers from other accredited U.S. dental schools. Admission limited to space available. There is an advanced-standing program for graduates of foreign schools of dentistry (International Student Program); generally international graduates are admitted into the 2nd year only. Contact the Office of Admission and Student Affairs for current information and specific requirements for admission.

ADMISSION STANDARDS AND RECOGNITION. *For D.M.D.:* number of applicants 2,647; number enrolled 148; median DAT: ACAD 17.8, PAT 16.8; median GPA 3.2 (A = 4), median sciences GPA 3.12 (A = 4). Gorman rating 4.85 (scale: very strong 4.51–4.99); this placed the school in the Top 10 of all U.S. dental schools; the dental school's ranking by NIH awards/grants was 37th among dental schools, with 2 awards/grants received; total value of all awards/grants $154,186.

FINANCIAL AID. Scholarships, merit scholarships, minority scholarships, grants-in-aid, Tufts loan program, state loan programs, DEAL, HEAL, alternative loan programs, federal Perkins loans, Stafford subsidized and unsubsidized loans, and military service commitment scholarship programs are available. Assistantships/fellowships may be available for combined degree candidates. Institutional financial aid applications and information are sent to all accepted students who submit a tuition deposit. For scholarships, the selection criteria place heavy reliance on DAT and undergraduate GPA. Contact the Financial Aid Office for current information; phone: (617)636-6639. For most financial assistance and all need-based programs, submit FAFSA to a federal processor (Title IV school code # E00519); also submit Financial Aid Transcript, Federal Income Tax forms, and Use of Federal Funds Certification. Approximately 80% of current students receive some form of financial assistance. Average award $41,300.

DEGREE REQUIREMENTS. *For B.S.-D.M.D.:* a 7-year program. *For D.M.D.:* satisfactory completion of 4-year program. *For D.M.D.* (International Student Program): a 2-year-and-3-month program. *For D.D.S.-M.S.:* generally a 4½–5½-year program.

TULANE UNIVERSITY

New Orleans, Louisiana 70118-5669
Internet site: http://www.tulane.edu

Founded 1834. Private control. Semester system. Special facilities: Center for Archaeology, Delta Regional Primate Research Center, Endocrine Poly-Peptide and Cancer Institute, Haywood Genetics Center, Institute for Health Services, Lindy N. Boggs Center for Energy and Biotechnology, Tulane Cancer Center, Tulane Research and Teaching Center, Tulane/Xavier Center for Bioenvironmental Research, U.S.-Japan Cooperative Biomedical Research Laboratories. Library: 2,200,000 volumes; 2,405,300 microforms; 14,846 periodicals/subscriptions. The university's ranking in domestic higher education by NIH awards/grants was 73rd, with 94 awards/grants received; total dollars awarded $26,652,092.

The university's graduate colleges/schools: Graduate School, A. B. Freeman Business School, Law School, School of Architecture, School of Engineering, School of Medicine, School of Public Health and Tropical Medicine, School of Social Work.

Total university enrollment at main campus: 11,100.

Tulane University Medical Center

1415 Tulane Avenue
New Orleans, Louisiana 70112

Private control. The university's hospital and clinics are members of the Council of Teaching Hospitals. Schools located at medical center are: School of Medicine, School of Public Health and Tropical Medicine. Special facilities: Tulane University and Columbia HCA Healthcare Corporation.

School of Medicine

1430 Tulane Avenue, SL67
New Orleans, Louisiana 70112-2699
Phone: (504)588-5187; fax: (504)599-6735
Internet site: http://www.mcl.tulan.edu
E-mail: medsch@tmcpop.tmc.tulane.edu

Established 1834. Located in downtown New Orleans. Semester system. First 2 years are dedicated primarily to basic sciences. Affiliated hospitals: Charity Hospital of New Orleans, Tulane Medical Center Hospital and Clinics, Medical Center of Louisiana in New Orleans, Veterans Affairs Hospital. Special programs: summer programs for underrepresented minorities (MedREP); prematriculation summer sessions (PRIME).

Annual tuition: $29,000; fees $1,341. On-campus rooms and apartments available for both single and married students. Annual on-campus housing cost: single students $4,500 (room only), married students $4,815. Contact Director of Housing for both on- and off-campus housing information; phone: (504)865-5724. Medical students tend to live off-campus. Off-campus housing and personal expenses: approximately $12,000.

Enrollment: 1st-year class 148 (EDP 10); total full-time 599 (men 55%, women 45%). First-year statistics:

85% out of state; 37 states represented; 82 colleges represented; 47% women; average age 24; 7% minorities; 65% science majors.

Degrees conferred: M.D., M.D.-M.P.H., M.D.-Ph.D. (Anatomy, Biochemistry, Biomedical Engineering, Cell Biology, Genetics, Immunology, Microbiology, Molecular Biology, Neurosciences, Pathology, Pharmacology, Physiology).

RECRUITMENT PRACTICES AND POLICIES. School has diversity program and actively recruits women/minority applicants. Diversity contact: Associate Dean for Student Services; phone: (504)588-5327.

ADMISSION REQUIREMENTS FOR FIRST-YEAR APPLICANTS. Some preference given to state residents; U.S. citizens and permanent residents only. *Undergraduate preparation.* Suggested premed courses: 2 courses in biology with labs, 2 courses in inorganic chemistry with labs, 2 courses in organic chemistry with labs, 2 courses in physics with labs, 2 courses in English. Bachelor's degree from an accredited institution required; 99% of applicants have bachelor's degrees awarded prior to enrollment. *Has EDP*; applicants must apply through AMCAS (official transcripts sent by mid-May) between June 1 and August 1. Early applications are encouraged. Submit supplemental application, a personal statement, and 2 recommendations to Admissions Office within 2 weeks of receipt of application. Interviews are by invitation only and generally for final selection. Notification normally begins October 1. *Regular application process.* Apply through AMCAS (file after June 1, before December 15); submit MCAT (will accept MCAT test results from the last 3 years), official transcripts for each school attended (should show at least 90 semester credits/135 quarter credits; submit transcripts by mid-May to AMCAS), service processing fee. Submit an application fee of $95, a supplemental application, a personal statement, preprofessional committee evaluation, and 3 recommendations from science faculty to Admissions Office within 2–3 weeks of the receipt of supplemental materials, but not later than January 31. Interviews are by invitation only and generally for final selection. Dual-degree applicants must apply to, and be accepted by, both schools; contact the Admissions Office for current information and specific requirements for admission. First-year students admitted in fall only. Rolling admission process. Notification starts October 15 and is finished when class is filled. Applicant's response to offer and $500 deposit due within 3 weeks of receipt of acceptance letter. School does maintain an alternate list. Phone: (504)588-5187.

ADMISSION REQUIREMENTS FOR TRANSFER APPLICANTS. Accepts transfers from other accredited U.S. medical schools into both the 2nd and 3rd year class. Admission limited to space available. Contact the Admissions Office for current information and specific requirements for admission.

ADMISSION STANDARDS AND RECOGNITION. *For M.D.:* number of state-resident applicants 628, nonresidents 10,154; number of state residents interviewed 136, nonresidents 647; number of residents enrolled 25, nonresidents 125; median MCAT 10.0 (verbal reasoning 10.0; biological sciences 10.0; physical sciences 10.0); median GPA 3.46 (A = 4). Gorman rating 4.70 (scale: very strong 4.51–4.99); the school's medical ranking by NIH awards was 73rd, with 79 awards/grants received; total dollars awarded $16,665,862.

FINANCIAL AID. Limited number of scholarships, minority scholarships, grants-in-aid, institutional loans, HEAL, alternative loan programs, externships, federal Perkins loans, Stafford subsidized and unsubsidized loans, and service commitment scholarship programs are available. Assistantships/fellowships may be available for dual-degree candidates. Most financial aid is based on demonstrated need. Financial aid applications and information are generally available at the on-campus interview (by invitation). For scholarships, the selection criteria place heavy reliance on MCAT and undergraduate GPA. Contact the Financial Aid Office for current information; phone: (504)585-6135. For most financial assistance and all federal programs, submit FAFSA to a federal processor (Title IV school code # 002029); also submit Financial Aid Transcript and Federal Income Tax forms. Approximately 85% of current students receive some form of financial assistance.

DEGREE REQUIREMENTS. *For M.D.:* satisfactory completion of 4-year program. Taking USMLE Step 1 and Step 2 is optional. *For M.D.-Ph.D.:* generally a 7-year program.

UNIFORMED SERVICES UNIVERSITY OF THE HEALTH SCIENCES
Bethesda, Maryland 20814-4799
Internet site: http://www.usuhs.mil

Founded 1972. Located on the grounds of the National Naval Medical Center. Federal control. Semester system. Special affiliations: Armed Forces Institute of Pathology, National Library of Medicine, NIH, U.S. Armed Forces Radiobiology Research Institute, Walter Reed Army Institute of Research.

The university's schools include: Graduate School of Nursing, School of Medicine.

Total university enrollment at main campus: 757

F. Edward Hebert School of Medicine

Room A-10411
4301 Jones Bridge Road
Bethesda, Maryland 20814-4799
Phone: (800)772-1743, (301)295-3101; fax (301)295-3454
Internet site: http://www.usuhs.mil
E-mail: stavish@usuhsb.usuhs.mil

Admitted 1st class 1976. The academic year is 48 weeks in duration. Library: 117,700 volumes/microforms; 1,345 current periodicals/subscriptions; 40 PC work stations. Special programs: 20% of clinical experience may be taken in other areas of the world.

Annual tuition: There is no tuition charge. No on-campus housing available. Annual living expenses are expected to be covered by the student's annual salary.

Enrollment: 1st-year class 165; total full-time 673 (men 72.5%, women 27.5%). First-year statistics: 24% from northern states, 30% from southern states, 36% from western states, 10% from central states; 28% women; average age 24; 20% minorities; 75% science majors.

Faculty: full-time 1,100, part-time 1,500.

Degrees conferred: M.D., M.P.H., M.S., M.T.M.H., D.P.H., Ph.D.

RECRUITMENT PRACTICES AND POLICIES. School has diversity program and actively recruits women/minority applicants. Diversity contact: Office of Minority Affairs; phone: (301)295-9560.

ADMISSION REQUIREMENTS FOR FIRST-YEAR APPLICANTS. Preference given to U.S. citizens, both military and civilian, between the ages of 18 and 30. *Undergraduate preparation.* Suggested premed courses: 2 courses in biology with labs, 2 courses in inorganic chemistry with labs, 2 courses in organic chemistry with labs, 2 courses in physics with labs, 1 course in calculus, 2 courses in English. Bachelor's degree from an accredited institution required; all applicants have bachelor's degree awarded prior to enrollment. *Application process.* Apply through AMCAS (file after June 1, before November 1); submit MCAT (will accept MCAT test results from the last 3 years), official transcripts for each school attended (should show at least 90 semester credits/135 quarter credits, submit transcripts by mid-May to AMCAS), service processing fee. No supplementary application fee required. Submit a supplemental application, a photograph, a personal statement, preprofessional committee evalua-

tion, and 3 recommendations from science faculty to Admissions Office within 2–3 weeks of the receipt of supplemental materials. Interviews are by invitation only and generally for final selection. First-year students admitted in fall only. Rolling admission process. Notification starts November 1 and is finished when class is filled. Applicant's response to offer due within 2 weeks of receipt of acceptance letter. Prior to enrollment a student can expect to have a background check performed and will have to pass a medical examination.

ADMISSION REQUIREMENTS FOR TRANSFER APPLICANTS. School does not accept transfer applicants.

ADMISSION STANDARDS AND RECOGNITION. *For M.D.:* number of applicants 3,380; number interviewed 526; number enrolled 165; median MCAT 10.2 (verbal reasoning 9.9; biological sciences 10.2; physical sciences 10.4); median GPA 3.51 (A = 4). Gorman rating 3.18 (scale: acceptable plus 3.01–3.59); the school's medical ranking by NIH awards was 125th, with 2 awards/grants received; total dollars awarded $247,763.

FINANCIAL AID. Upon matriculation the student becomes an active reserve officer in one of the military service branches. They receive a full salary, free health benefits for the student and his/her family, a housing allowance, commissary privileges, and 30 days paid leave.

DEGREE REQUIREMENTS. *For M.D.:* satisfactory completion of 4-year program. All students must pass USMLE Step 1 prior to entering 3rd year; all students must pass USMLE Step 2 prior to awarding of M.D. Upon graduation there is a military commitment of not less than 7 years on active duty and 6 years of inactive ready reserve.

Union University

Schenectady, New York 12308-2311
Internet site: http://www.union.edu

Founded 1795. Located across the Hudson River from Albany. Private control. Semester system. Library: 500,000 volumes; 618,600 microforms; 1,970 periodicals/subscriptions. The university's ranking in domestic higher education by NIH awards/grants was 135th, with 37 awards/grants received; total dollars awarded $5,866,530.

The university's graduate colleges/schools: Union College, Albany Law School, Albany Medical College, Albany College of Pharmacy.

Total university enrollment at main campus: 2,300.

Albany Medical Center
New Scotland Road
Albany, New York 12208

Private control. The medical center is a member of the Council of Teaching Hospitals. The schools located at medical center are Albany Medical College and the Graduate Program in Biological and Medical Sciences. Special facility: Joint Center for Cancer and Blood Disorders; has a nationally recognized program in Urology.

Albany Medical College
47 New Scotland Avenue
Albany, New York 12208-3479
Phone: (518)262-5521; fax: (518)262-5887
Internet site: http://www.amc.edu

Established 1839; one of the oldest medical schools in the country. Semester system. Library: 124,000 volumes/microforms; 2,563 current periodicals/subscriptions. Affiliated hospitals: Albany Medical Center Hospital, Albany Veterans Administration Medical Center, Capital District Psychiatric Center. Special programs: Summer programs for underrepresented minorities (STEP); Minority High School Research Apprenticeship Program.

Annual tuition: residents $25,278, nonresidents $26,613. On-campus rooms and apartments available for single students only. Annual on-campus housing cost: single students $2,475 (room only). Contact Student Affairs Office for both on- and off-campus housing information; phone: (518)262-5634. Medical students tend to live off-campus. Off-campus housing and personal expenses: approximately $12,500.

Enrollment: 1st-year class 130; total full-time 542 (men 48.5%, women 51.5%). First-year statistics: 60% out of state; 60% women; average age 24; 6% underrepresented minorities; 30% other minorities.

Faculty: full-time 54, part-time 35.

Degrees conferred: M.D., B.A.-M.D. (Siena College), B.S.-M.D. (Rensselaer Polytechnic Institute), M.D.-Ph.D. (Biochemistry, Cell Biology, Immunology, Microbiology, Molecular Biology, Neurosciences, Pathology, Pharmacology, Physiology).

RECRUITMENT PRACTICES AND POLICIES. School has diversity program and actively recruits women/minority applicants. Diversity contact: Director of Minority Affairs; phone: (518)262-5824.

ADMISSION REQUIREMENT FOR BACHELOR-M.D. APPLICANTS. No preference given to state residents. Submit application after September 1, before December 1, with a $45 application fee (R.P.I. and Siena College); $75 medical college. SAT I and SAT II in math-

ematics, writing, and physics, chemistry or biology or ACT, official high school transcripts with rank in class, 3 letters of recommendation required in support of application. Interviews are by invitation only and generally for final selection. Notification is between February and March 15. Applicant's response to offer and $200 (Siena), $250 (R.P.I.) deposit, due by May 1. All undergraduates must take MCAT before continuing on to medical college. Current undergraduate tuition: R.P.I. $19,075, Siena College $11,840. For current information and additional requirements, contact the Admissions Office; phone: R.P.I. (818)276-6813, Siena College (518)783-2423, Albany Medical College (518)262-5435.

ADMISSION REQUIREMENTS FOR FIRST-YEAR APPLICANTS. Preference given to U.S. citizens and permanent residents. *Undergraduate preparation.* Suggested premed courses: 2 courses in biology with labs, 2 courses in inorganic chemistry with labs, 2 courses in organic chemistry with labs, 2 courses in physics with labs; proficiency in English required. Enrollment at an accredited undergraduate institution required; 65% of applicants have bachelor's degrees awarded prior to enrollment. Does not have EDP. *Application process.* Apply through AMCAS (file after June 1, before November 1); submit MCAT (will accept MCAT test results from the last 3 years), official transcripts for each school attended (should show at least 90 semester credits/135 quarter credits, submit transcripts by mid-May to AMCAS), service processing fee. Submit a supplemental application, a personal statement, and preprofessional committee evaluation or three recommendations from science faculty to Admissions Office within 2–3 weeks of the receipt of supplemental materials. There is no application fee. Interviews are by invitation only and generally for final selection. Dual-degree applicants must apply to, and be accepted to both the college and the graduate program; contact the Admissions Office for current information and specific requirements for admission. First-year students admitted in fall only. Rolling admission process. Notification starts October 15 and is finished when class is filled. Applicant's response to offer and $100 deposit due within 2 weeks of receipt of acceptance letter. School does maintain an alternate list. Phone: (518)262-5521.

ADMISSION REQUIREMENTS FOR TRANSFER APPLICANTS. Accepts students from other accredited U.S. medical schools with a compelling need to transfer, but only into the 2nd or 3rd year. Admission limited to space available. Contact the Admissions Office for current information and specific requirements for admission.

ADMISSION STANDARDS AND RECOGNITION. *For B.A./B.S.-M.D.:* R.P.I. Program—number of state-resident applicants 72, nonresidents 371; number of state residents interviewed 35, nonresidents 59; number of residents enrolled 7, nonresidents 9; median SAT V 710, SAT M 740; Siena College Program—number of state-resident applicants 189, nonresidents 170; number of state residents interviewed 22, nonresidents 14; number of residents enrolled 9, nonresidents 3; median SAT V 680, SAT M 690. *For M.D.*: number of state-resident applicants 2,301, nonresidents 7,385; number of state residents interviewed 222, nonresidents 471; number of residents enrolled 28, nonresidents 56; median MCAT 9.9 (verbal reasoning 9.8; biological sciences 10.2; physical sciences 9.8); median GPA 3.4 (A = 4); science GPA 3.3. Gorman rating 3.82 (scale: good 3.61–3.99); the college's medical ranking by NIH awards was 99th, with 37 awards/grants received; total dollars awarded $5,866,530.

FINANCIAL AID. Scholarships, merit scholarships, minority scholarships, grants-in-aid, institutional loans, HEAL, alternative loan programs, federal W/S program, federal Perkins loans, Stafford subsidized and unsubsidized loans, and service commitment scholarship programs are available. Financial aid applications and information are generally available at the on-campus interview (by invitation). Most financial aid is based on documented need. For scholarships, the selection criteria place heavy reliance on MCAT and undergraduate GPA. A financial aid announcement is sent to all applicants by January 15 with reference. All application materials should be received no later than April 1. Contact the Financial Aid Office for current information; phone: (518)262-5434. For most financial assistance and all federal programs, submit FAFSA to a federal processor (Title IV school code # G02887); also submit Financial Aid Transcript and Federal Income Tax forms. Approximately 80% of current students receive some form of financial assistance. Average debt after graduation $96,665.

DEGREE REQUIREMENTS. *For B.A.-M.D.* (Siena College): an 8-year program. *For B.S.-M.D. (R.P.I.):* a 6-calendar-year program. *For M.D.:* satisfactory completion of 4-year program. All students must take USMLE Step 1 and Step 2 and record a score. *For M.D.-Ph.D.:* generally a 7-year program.

UNIVERSITY OF UTAH

Salt Lake City, Utah 84112-9401
Internet site: http://www.utah.edu

Founded 1850. Public control. Semester system. Special facilities: Center for Biopolymers at Interfaces, Howard Hughes Medical Institute, Matheson Center for Health Care Studies, Radiobiology Laboratory, Rocky Mountain Center for Occupation and Environmental Health. Library: 3,089,400 volumes; 3,126,000 microforms; 21,807 periodicals/subscriptions; 186 work stations. The university's ranking in domestic higher education by NIH awards/grants was 34th, with 282 awards/grants received; total dollars awarded $70,920,034. The university's graduate school includes: College of Engineering, College of Fine Arts, College of Health, College of Humanities, College of Mines and Earth Sciences, College of Law, College of Nursing, College of Science, College of Social and Behavioral Science, Graduate School of Architecture, Graduate School of Business, Graduate School of Education, Graduate School of Social Work, College of Pharmacy, School of Medicine.

Total university enrollment at main campus: 27,100.

Utah Health Sciences Center

50 North Medical Drive
Salt Lake City, Utah 84132
Internet site: http://www.utah.edu/health

Public control. University of Utah Hospital is a member of the Council of Teaching Hospitals. Schools located at health sciences center are: College of Health, College of Nursing, College of Pharmacy, School of Medicine. Special facilities: Eccles Institute for Human Genetics, Howard Hughes Medical Institute, Intermountain Burn Center, Moran Eye Institute, Rocky Mountain Center for Occupational and Environmental Health, Utah Cancer Center, Utah Genome Center. Nationally recognized programs in Cardiology, Gynecology, Orthopedics, Pulmonary Disease.

School of Medicine

50 North Medical Drive
Salt Lake City, Utah 84132
Phone: (801)581-7498; fax: (801)585-3300
Internet site: http://medstat.med.utah.edu
E-mail: dean.admission@hsc.utah.edu

Established 1905 as a 2-year school; expanded to 4-year program in 1943. Located at health sciences center. A new curriculum instituted in 1997; emphasis in first 2 years is still basic medical sciences. Library: 100,000 volumes/microforms; 1,750 current periodicals/subscriptions. Special program: prematriculation summer sessions.

Annual tuition: residents $7,189, nonresidents $15,319; fees $440. On-campus rooms and apartments available for both single and married students. Annual on-campus housing cost: single students $2,125 (room only), married students $5,688. Contact Director of Residential

Living for both on- and off-campus housing information; phone: (801)581-8667. Medical students tend to live off-campus. Off-campus housing and personal expenses: approximately $12,173.

Enrollment: 1st-year class 100 (EDP 10); total full-time 395 (men 70%, women 30%). First-year statistics: 25% out of state; 28% women; average age 25; 2% minorities; 74% science majors.

Faculty: full-time/part-time/volunteers: approximately 800.

Degrees conferred: M.D., M.D.-M.S.P.H., M.D.-M.P.H., M.D.-Ph.D. (Biochemistry, Bioengineering, Cell and Molecular Biology, Human Genetics, Immunology, Neurobiology and Neuroanatomy, Oncological Sciences, Pharmacology and Toxicology, Physiology).

RECRUITMENT PRACTICES AND POLICIES. School has diversity program and actively recruits women/minority applicants. Diversity contact: Director, Health Sciences Minority Affairs; phone: (801)585-2430.

ADMISSION REQUIREMENTS FOR FIRST-YEAR APPLICANTS. Preference given to Utah and Idaho state residents; U.S. citizens and permanent residents only. *Undergraduate preparation.* Suggested premed courses: 2 courses in biology with labs, 2 courses in inorganic chemistry with labs, 2 courses in organic chemistry with labs, 2 courses in physics with labs, 2 courses in English. Bachelor's degree from an accredited institution required; all applicants have bachelor's degree awarded prior to enrollment. *Has EDP;* all nonresidents are required to apply under EDP. Applicants must apply through AMCAS (official transcripts sent by mid-May) between June 1 and August 1. Early applications are encouraged. Submit secondary/supplemental application, a personal statement, and 2 recommendations to Medical School Admissions Office within 2 weeks of receipt of application. Interviews are by invitation only and generally for final selection. Notification normally begins October 1. *Regular application process.* Apply through AMCAS (file after June 1, before October 15); submit MCAT (will accept MCAT test results from the last 3 years), official transcripts for each school attended (should show at least 90 semester credits/135 quarter credits, submit transcripts by mid-May to AMCAS), service processing fee. Submit an application fee of $50, a supplemental application, a personal statement, preprofessional committee evaluation, and 3 recommendations from science faculty to Admissions Office within 2–3 weeks of the receipt of supplemental materials. Interviews are by invitation only and generally for final selection. M.D.-Ph.D. degree applicants must apply to the School of Medicine first, then

submit a letter requesting admission to M.D.-Ph.D. program. The letter should include a description of the applicant's research experience and future goal. Contact Program Administrator for additional information and specific requirements for admission; phone: (801)585-6408; E-mail; janet.bassett@medschool.med.utah.edu. Combined degree applicants must apply to, and be accepted by, both schools. Contact the Medical School Admissions Office for current information and specific requirements for admission. First-year students admitted in fall only. Rolling admission process. Notification starts October 15 and is finished when class is filled. Applicant's response to offer and $100 deposit due within 2 weeks of receipt of acceptance letter. School does maintain an alternate list. Phone: (801)581-7498; E-mail: dean.admission@hsc.utah.edu.

ADMISSION REQUIREMENTS FOR TRANSFER APPLICANTS. Rarely accepts transfers applicants. Contact the Medical School Admissions Office for current information and any modification in policy.

ADMISSION STANDARDS AND RECOGNITION. *For M.D.:* number of state-resident applicants 393, nonresidents 954; number of state residents interviewed 284, nonresidents 168; number of residents enrolled 75, nonresidents 25; median MCAT 10.2 (verbal reasoning 10.0; biological sciences 10.6; physical sciences 10.5); median GPA 3.6 (A = 4). Gorman rating 3.81 (scale: good 3.61–3.99); the school's medical ranking by NIH awards was 39th, with 192 awards/grants received; total dollars awarded $50,131,137.

FINANCIAL AID. A very limited number of scholarships, grants-in-aid, institutional loans, HEAL, alternative loan programs, NIH stipends, federal Perkins loans, Stafford subsidized and unsubsidized loans, and service commitment scholarship programs are available. Assistantships/fellowships may be available for dual-degree candidates. Financial aid applications and information are generally available at the on-campus interview (by invitation). Contact the Financial Aid Office for current information; phone: (801)581-6474. For most financial assistance and all federal programs, submit FAFSA to a federal processor (Title IV school code # 003675); also submit Financial Aid Transcript and Federal Income Tax forms. Approximately 75% of current students receive some form of financial assistance. Average debt after graduation $57,280.

DEGREE REQUIREMENTS. *For M.D.:* satisfactory completion of 4-year program. All students must take

USMLE Step 1 and Step 2 and record scores. *For M.D.-M.S.P.H, M.P.H.:* generally 4½–5½-year programs. *For M.D.-Ph.D.:* generally a 7–8-year program.

VANDERBILT UNIVERSITY
Nashville, Tennessee 37240-1001
Internet site: http://www.vanderbilt.edu

Founded 1873. Located 1½ miles W of downtown Nashville, the state capital. Private control. Semester system. Library: 2,000,000 volumes; 1,800,000 microforms; 16,000 periodicals/subscriptions. The university's ranking in domestic higher education by NIH awards/grants was 21st, with 379 awards/grants received; total dollars awarded $96,642,969.

The university's graduate colleges/schools: Divinity School, Graduate School, Owen Graduate School of Management, Peabody College, School of Engineering, School of Law, School of Medicine, School of Nursing.

Total university enrollment at main campus: 10,000.

Vanderbilt University Medical Center
1161 21st Avenue, South
Nashville, Tennessee 37232

Private control. Vanderbilt University Hospital is a member of the Council of Teaching Hospitals. Schools located at medical center are: School of Medicine, School of Nursing. Special facilities: Newman Clinical Research Center, Cooperative Care Center, Kim Dayani Human Performance Center, Stallworth Rehabilitation Center, Vanderbilt Child and Adolescent Psychiatric Hospital, Vanderbilt Clinic. *Barron's Guide* placed Vanderbilt University Hospital among the Top 25 most prestigious U.S. medical schools. Nationally recognized programs in Cancer, Endocrinology, Neurology, Otolaryngology, Pulmonary Disease.

School of Medicine
209 Light Hall
21st Avenue at Garland Avenue
Nashville, Tennessee 37232-0685
Phone: (615)322-2145; fax: (615)343-8397
Internet site: http://www.mc.vanderbilt.edu/medschool
E-mail: medsch.admis@mcmail.vanderbilt.edu

Established 1873. Semester system. Library: 164,000 volumes/microforms; 2,200 current periodicals/subscriptions. Affiliated hospitals: Vanderbilt University Hospital, Nashville VA Hospital, Metro General Hospital, St. Thomas Hospital. Affiliated medical schools are located

in Stockholm and Paris. Special program: premedical summer institute for underrepresented minorities.

Annual tuition: $24,280; fees $1,200. On-campus apartments available for both single and married students. Contact Office of Residential Affairs for both on- and off-campus housing information; phone: (615)322-2591. Medical students tend to live off-campus. Off-campus housing and personal expenses: approximately $10,610.

Enrollment: 1st-year class 104 (EDP 5); total full-time 413 (men 65%, women 35%). First-year statistics: 85% out of state; 36% women; average age 23; 5% minorities; 80% science majors.

Faculty: full-time 980, part-time/volunteers 868.

Degrees conferred: M.D., M.D.-M.P.H., M.D.-Ph.D. (Biochemistry, Biomedical Engineering, Cell Biology, Microbiology and Immunology, Molecular Biology, Pathology, Pharmacology, Molecular Physiology and Biophysics); has M.S.T.P.

RECRUITMENT PRACTICES AND POLICIES. School has diversity program and actively recruits women/minority applicants. Diversity contact: Associate Dean for Students Affairs; phone: (615)322-6109.

ADMISSION REQUIREMENTS FOR FIRST-YEAR APPLICANTS. Preference given to U.S. citizens and permanent residents only. *Undergraduate preparation.* Suggested premed courses: 2 courses in biology with labs, 2 courses in inorganic chemistry with labs, 2 courses in organic chemistry with labs, 2 courses in physics with labs, 2 courses in English. Bachelor's degree from an accredited institution required; all applicants have bachelor's degrees awarded prior to enrollment. *Has EDP;* applicants must apply through AMCAS (official transcripts sent by mid-May) between June 1 and August 1. Early applications are encouraged. Submit secondary application, a personal statement, and 2 recommendations to Admissions Office within 2 weeks of receipt of application. Interviews are by invitation only and generally for final selection. Notification normally begins October 1. *Regular application process.* Apply through AMCAS (file after June 1, before October 15); submit MCAT (will accept MCAT test results from the last 3 years), official transcripts for each school attended (should show at least 90 semester credits/135 quarter credits, submit transcripts by mid-May to AMCAS), service processing fee. Submit an application fee of $50, a secondary application, a personal statement, preprofessional committee evaluation, and 3 recommendations from science faculty to Medical School Admission Office within 2–3 weeks of the receipt of supplemental materials, but not later than January 15. Interviews are by invitation only and generally for final selection. M.D.-Ph.D. degree applicants must complete the M.S.T.P. section on the secondary application; contact the Medical School Admissions Office or Interdisciplinary Programs Office (phone: (800)810-8993; fax: (615)343-0749) for current information and specific requirements for admission. First-year students admitted in fall only. Rolling admission process. Notification starts October 15 and is finished when class is filled. Applicant's response to offer due within 2 weeks of receipt of acceptance letter. School does maintain an alternate list. Phone: (615)322-2145.

ADMISSION REQUIREMENTS FOR TRANSFER APPLICANTS. Accepts transfers from other accredited U.S. medical schools after the 2nd year only. Admission limited to space available and is extremely limited. Contact the Medical School Admissions Office for current information and specific requirements for admission.

ADMISSION STANDARDS AND RECOGNITION. *For M.D.:* number of state-resident applicants 315, nonresidents 3,121; number of state residents interviewed 32, nonresidents 604; number of residents enrolled 32, nonresidents 94; median MCAT 11.2 (verbal reasoning 10.5; biological sciences 11.4; physical sciences 11.5); median GPA 3.75 (A = 4). *Barron's Guide* placed the school among the Top 25 most prestigious U.S. medical schools; Gorman rating 4.65 (scale: very strong 4.51–4.99); *U.S. News & World Report* ranked the school in the Top 25 of all U.S. medical schools; the school's medical ranking by NIH awards was 23rd, with 309 awards/grants received; total dollars awarded $80,730,742.

FINANCIAL AID. Limited scholarship assistance, G. Canby Robinson Scholars Program (international students are eligible to participate in this program), grants-in-aid, institutional loans, HEAL, alternative loan programs, NIH stipends, federal Perkins loans, Stafford subsidized and unsubsidized loans, and service commitment scholarship programs are available. Scholarships and NIH grants may be available for M.D.-Ph.D. degree candidates; in addition there may be funds available at the department level. Most financial aid is based on demonstrated need. Financial aid applications and information are sent to all interviewed applicants in January. For scholarship assistance, the selection criteria tend to place heavy reliance on MCAT and undergraduate GPA. Contact the Financial Aid Office for current information; phone: (615)343-6310; fax: (615)343-8397. For most financial assistance and all federal programs, submit FAFSA to a federal processor (Title IV school code #E00459); also submit Financial Aid Transcript and Federal Income Tax forms. Approximately 81% of current students receive some form of financial assistance. Average debt after graduation $77,000.

DEGREE REQUIREMENTS. *For M.D.:* satisfactory completion of 4-year program. *For M.D.-M.P.H.:* generally 5–6-year program. *For M.D.-Ph.D.:* generally a 6–7-year program.

UNIVERSITY OF VERMONT
Burlington, Vermont 05405-0160
Internet site: http://www.uvm.edu

Founded 1791. Located 95 miles S of Montreal, Canada, and located on the eastern shore of Lake Champlain. Public control. Semester system. Library: 1,110,000 volumes; 851,000 microforms; 8,000 periodicals/subscriptions; 38 PC work stations. Special facilities: Bruker 250-MHz Nuclear Magnetic Resonance Facility, Vermont Regional Cancer Center. Special programs: Postbaccalaureate premedical program for adults and underrepresented minorities; contact the UVM Student Service Advisor; phone: (802)656-2085, (800)639-3210. The university's ranking in domestic higher education by NIH awards/grants was 78th, with 98 awards/grants received; total dollars awarded $24,292,519.

The university's graduate colleges includes: College of Agriculture and Life Sciences, College of Arts and Sciences, College of Education and Social Service. College of Engineering and Mathematics, School of Allied Health Sciences, School of Business Administration, School of Natural Resources, School of Nursing, College of Medicine.

Total university enrollment at main campus: 9,350.

College of Medicine
C-225 Given Building
Burlington, Vermont 05405
Phone: (802)656-2154; fax: (802)656-8577
Internet site: http://www.med.uvm.edu

Established 1822. Curriculum is based on a 3-phase system. Library: 100,000 volumes/microforms; 1,400 current periodicals/subscriptions. Affiliated hospitals: Fletcher Allen Health Care Medical Center (a member of the Council of Teaching Hospitals), Medical Center Hospital of Vermont, Maine Medical Center (Portland), Champlain Valley Physicians Hospital (Plattsburgh, New York).

Annual tuition: residents $17,327, nonresidents $29,827; fees $661. Limited on-campus housing available. Annual on-campus housing cost: single students $5,200 (room only). Contact Housing Services Office for both on- and off-campus housing information; phone: (802)721-8395. Medical students tend to live off-campus. Off-campus housing and personal expenses: approximately $14,648.

Enrollment: 1st-year class 93 (EDP 15); total full-time 376 (men 48%, women 52%). First-year statistics: 60% out of state; 59% women; average age 26; 13% minorities; 57% science majors.

Faculty: full-time 284, part-time/volunteers 600.

Degrees conferred: M.D., M.D.-Ph.D. (Anatomy and Neurobiology, Biochemistry, Biophysics, Cell and Molecular Biology, Genetics, Molecular Microbiology and Molecular Genetics, Molecular Biology, Neurosciences, Pathology, Pharmacology, Molecular Physiology and Biophysics).

RECRUITMENT PRACTICES AND POLICIES. School has diversity program and actively recruits women/minority applicants. Diversity contact: Associate Dean for Student Affairs and Admissions; phone: (802)656-2150.

ADMISSION REQUIREMENTS FOR FIRST-YEAR APPLICANTS. Preference given to residents of Vermont and Maine; U.S. citizens and permanent residents only. *Undergraduate preparation.* Suggested premed courses: 2 courses in biology with labs, 2 courses in inorganic chemistry with labs, 2 courses in organic chemistry with labs, 2 courses in physics with labs, 2 courses in English. Bachelor's degree from an accredited institution required; all applicants have bachelor's degree awarded prior to enrollment. *Has EDP*; applicants must apply through AMCAS (official transcripts sent by mid-May) between June 1 and August 1. Early applications are encouraged. Submit supplemental application, a personal statement, and 2 recommendations to Admissions Office within 2 weeks of receipt of application. Interviews are by invitation only and generally for final selection. Notification normally begins October 1. *Regular application process.* Apply through AMCAS (file after June 1, before November 1); submit MCAT (will accept MCAT test results from the last 4 years), official transcripts for each school attended (should show at least 90 semester credits/135 quarter credits, submit transcripts by mid-May to AMCAS), service processing fee. Submit an application fee of $75, a supplemental application, a personal statement, preprofessional committee evaluation, and 3 recommendations from science faculty to Admissions Office within 2–3 weeks of the receipt of supplemental materials, but not later than January 15. Interviews are by invitation only and generally for final selection. M.D.-Ph.D. degree applicants must apply to, and be accepted by, both

schools; the graduate work generally begins in the summer prior to the 1st year; contact the Admissions Office for current information and specific requirements for admission. First-year students admitted in fall only. Rolling admission process. Notification starts in December and is finished when class is filled. Applicant's response to offer and $100 deposit due within 2 weeks of receipt of acceptance letter. School does maintain an alternate list. Phone: (802)656-2154.

ADMISSION REQUIREMENTS FOR TRANSFER APPLICANTS. Accepts transfers from other accredited U.S. medical schools into the 3rd year only. Admission limited to space available. Contact the Admissions Office after January 1 for current information and specific requirements for admission.

ADMISSION STANDARDS AND RECOGNITION. *For M.D.:* number of state-resident applicants 103, non-residents 8,259; number of state residents interviewed 95, nonresidents 563; number of residents enrolled 39, nonresidents 54; median MCAT 9.0 (verbal reasoning 9.2; biological sciences 9.0; physical sciences 9.0); median GPA 3.40 (A = 4). Gorman rating 3.64 (scale: good 3.61–3.99); the school's medical ranking by NIH awards was 66th, with 91 awards/grants received; total dollars awarded $23,159,607.

FINANCIAL AID. Scholarships, merit scholarships, minority scholarships, grants-in-aid, UVM 21st Century Loan Program, HEAL, alternative loan programs, federal Perkins loans, Stafford subsidized and unsubsidized loans and service commitment scholarship programs are available. Assistantships/fellowships may be available for M.D.-Ph.D. degree candidates. Financial aid applications and information are generally available at the on-campus by invitation interview. For scholarship assistance, the selection criteria place heavy reliance on MCAT and undergraduate GPA. Contact the Financial Aid Office for current information; phone: (802)656-8293. For most financial assistance and all federal programs, submit FAFSA prior to March 1 to a federal processor (Title IV school code # 003696); also submit Financial Aid Transcript and Federal Income Tax forms. Approximately 80% of current students receive some form of financial assistance. Average debt after graduation $90,000.

DEGREE REQUIREMENTS. *For M.D.:* satisfactory completion of 45-month program. Taking USMLE Step 1 and Step 2 are optional. *For M.D.-Ph.D.:* generally a 6–7-year program.

VIRGINIA COMMONWEALTH UNIVERSITY

Richmond, Virginia 23284-3051
Internet site: http://www.vcu.edu

Founded 1838. University formed by merger of Richmond Professional Institute and Medical College of Virginia in 1968. Public control. Semester system. Special facilities: Anderson Art Gallery, Burn Trauma Clinic, Institute of Biotechnology, Business Management Center, Center for Drug and Alcohol Studies, Massey Cancer Center, Sickle Cell Anemia Center, Institute of Statistics, Transplant Center, Virginia Center on Aging. Library: 1,200,000 volumes; 2,500,000 microforms; 10,200 periodicals/subscriptions; 78 PC work stations. The university's ranking in domestic higher education by NIH awards/grants was 63rd, with 160 awards/grants received; total dollars awarded $39,296,634.

The university's School of Graduate Studies includes: Center for Environmental Studies, Center for Public Policy, College of Humanities and Sciences, School of Allied Health Professions, School of Business, School of Education, School of Engineering, School of Medicine Graduate Programs, School of Nursing, School of Pharmacy Graduate Programs, School of Social Work, School of the Arts; the Medical College of Virginia includes: School of Dentistry, School of Medicine, School of Pharmacy.

Total university enrollment at main campus: 21,300.

Medical College of Virginia Hospitals

P.O. Box 980510
Richmond, Virginia 23298

Located in downtown Richmond. Public control. Medical College of Virginia Hospitals are members of the Council of Teaching Hospitals. Schools located at medical college campus: School of Allied Health Professions, School of Dentistry, School of Medicine, School of Nursing, School of Pharmacy. Special facilities: Massey Cancer Center, Virginia Center on Aging.

Medical College of Virginia

P.O. Box 980565
Richmond, Virginia 23298-0565
Phone: (804)808-9629; fax: (804)828-1246
Internet site: http://www.vcu.edu

Established 1838 as a medical department at Hampden-Sidney College; in 1954 it became Medical College of Virginia, a totally independent institution. Located near the financial and governmental areas of downtown. The basic medical sciences are included in the first 2 years. Affiliated hospitals: Medical College of Virginia Hospitals (includes West, Main and North Hospitals),

A. D. Williams Memorial Clinic, VA Hospital. Library: 247,000 volumes/microforms; 3,400 current periodicals/subscriptions. Special facility: Medical College of Virginia Clinical Research Center. Special programs: Summer programs for underrepresented minorities, prematriculation summer sessions; guaranteed admissions program with VCU undergraduate schools.

Annual tuition: residents $10,883, nonresidents $25,883; fees $1,049. On-campus rooms and apartments available for both single and married students. Annual on-campus living, transportation, and personal expenses: $16,525. Contact Admissions Office for both on- and off-campus housing information. Medical students may live off-campus. Off-campus housing and personal expenses: approximately $16,000.

Enrollment: 1st-year class 172 (EDP 30); total full-time 683 (men 60%, women 40%). First-year statistics: 30% out of state; 41% women; average age 23; 8.7% minorities; 59% science majors.

Faculty: full-time 765, part-time/volunteers 750.

Degrees conferred: M.D., M.D.-Ph.D. (Anatomy, Biochemistry, Molecular Biophysics, Cell Biology, Human Genetics, Microbiology and Immunology, Neurosciences, Pathology, Pharmacology, Physiology).

RECRUITMENT PRACTICES AND POLICIES. School has diversity program and actively recruits women/minority applicants. Diversity contact: Assistant Director of Admissions or Office of Health Careers Opportunity Program (HCOP); phone (804)828-9629.

ADMISSION REQUIREMENTS FOR FIRST-YEAR APPLICANTS. Preference given to state residents; U.S. citizens and permanent residents only. *Undergraduate preparation.* Suggested premed courses: 2 courses in biology with labs, 2 courses in inorganic chemistry with labs, 2 courses in organic chemistry with labs, 2 courses in physics with labs, 2 courses in college math, 2 courses in English. Bachelor's degree from an accredited institution required; all applicants have bachelor's degrees awarded prior to enrollment. *Has EDP*; MCV encourages applicants with science interests to apply under EDP; applicants must apply through AMCAS (official transcripts sent by mid-May) between June 1 and August 1. Early applications are encouraged. Submit supplemental application, a personal statement, and 2 recommendations to Admissions Office within 2 weeks of receipt of application. Interviews are by invitation only and generally for final selection. Notification normally begins October 1. *Regular application process.* Apply through AMCAS (file after June 1, before December 1); submit MCAT (will accept MCAT test results from the last 3 years), official transcripts for each school attended (should show at least 90 semester credits/135 quarter credits, submit transcripts by mid-May to AMCAS), service processing fee. Submit an application fee of $75, a supplemental application, a personal statement, preprofessional committee evaluation, and 3 recommendations from science faculty to Admissions Office within 2–3 weeks of the receipt of supplemental materials, but not later than December 1. Interviews are by invitation only and generally for final selection. M.D.-Ph.D. degree applicants must submit the M.D.-Ph.D. application. A second interview, by invitation, is required. Contact the Admissions Office or the M.D.-Ph.D. Program Director (phone: (804)828-7600) for current information and specific requirements for admission. First-year students admitted in fall only. Rolling admission process. Notification starts October 15 and is finished when class is filled. Applicant's response to offer and $100 deposit due within 2 weeks of receipt of acceptance letter. School does maintain an alternate list. Phone: (804)828-9629.

ADMISSION REQUIREMENTS FOR TRANSFER APPLICANTS. Accepts transfers from other LCME-accredited U.S. and Canadian medical schools into the 3rd year only. Admission limited to space available. State residents given preference. Contact the Admissions Office for current information and specific requirements for admission.

ADMISSION STANDARDS AND RECOGNITION. *For M.D.:* number of state-resident applicants 1,151, non-residents 4,151; number of state residents interviewed 423, nonresidents 499; number of residents enrolled 119, nonresidents 53; median MCAT 9.9 (verbal reasoning 9.9; biological sciences 10.0; physical sciences 9.8); median GPA 3.42 (A = 4). Gorman rating 3.08 (scale: acceptable plus 3.01–3.59); the college's medical ranking by NIH awards was 49th, with 152 awards/grants received; total dollars awarded $37,012,689.

FINANCIAL AID. Scholarships, merit scholarships, minority scholarships, grants-in-aid, institutional loans, HEAL, alternative loan programs, NIH stipends, federal Perkins loans, Stafford subsidized and unsubsidized loans, service commitment scholarships, and Virginia medical scholarships are available. For M.D.-Ph.D. financial assistance is available to cover tuition and fees and receive a stipend. Financial aid applications and information are generally available by mid-January and must be returned not later than March 15. For scholarships, the selection criteria place heavy reliance on MCAT and undergraduate GPA. Contact the Financial Aid Office for current information; phone: (804)828-4006. For most financial assistance and all federal programs, submit

FAFSA to a federal processor (Title IV school code # 003735); also submit Financial Aid Transcript and Federal Income Tax forms. Approximately 90% of current students receive some form of financial assistance. Approximately 55% of new students receive some sort of scholarship assistance. Average debt after graduation $74,600.

DEGREE REQUIREMENTS. *For M.D.:* satisfactory completion of 4-year program. All students must take the USMLE Step 1 and Step 2 and record a score. *For M.D.-Ph.D.:* generally a 7-year program.

School of Dentistry
520 North 12th Street, Room 309
Richmond, Virginia 23298-0566
Phone: (804)828-9196; fax: (804)828-2588
Internet site: http://views.vcu.edu/dentistry

Established 1893. Postgraduate specialties: Dental Anesthesia, Endodontics, General Dentistry, General Practice Residency, Oral and Maxillofacial Surgery, Orthodontics, Pediatric Dentistry, Periodontics, Prosthodontics.

Annual tuition: residents $8,698, nonresidents $20,636; fees $975; equipment and supplies $3,630. On-campus rooms and apartments available for both single and married students. Annual on-campus living expenses: $16,525. Contact Admissions Office for both on- and off-campus housing information. Dental students may live off-campus. Off-campus housing, food, transportation, and personal expenses: approximately $13,000.

Enrollment: 1st-year class 80; total full-time 312. First-year enrolled student information: 21 from out of state; 26 women; average age 25; 5% underrepresented minorities; 12 other minorities.

Degrees conferred: D.D.S., B.S.-D.D.S. (students may earn a B.S. degree only if it is awarded by their predental institution), D.D.S.-M.S., D.D.S.-Ph.D.

RECRUITMENT PRACTICES AND POLICIES. School has diversity program and actively recruits women/minority applicants. Diversity contact: Director, Health Careers Opportunity Program (HCOP); phone: (804)828-4200.

ADMISSION REQUIREMENTS FOR FIRST-YEAR APPLICANTS. Preference given to state residents; U.S. citizens and permanent residents only. *Undergraduate preparation.* Suggested predental courses: 2 courses in biology with labs, 2 courses in inorganic chemistry with labs, 2 courses in organic chemistry with labs, 2 courses in physics with labs, 2 courses in English; courses in microbiology, biochemistry, animal physiology, genetics, immunology, behavioral sciences, and embryology are strongly recommended. The junior-college transfer credit limit is 60 credits. Will consider applicants with only 3 years of undergraduate preparation; prefer applicants who will have bachelor's degree prior to enrollment; all applicants have bachelor's degree awarded prior to enrollment. *Application process.* Apply through AADSAS (file after May 1, before January 1); submit official transcripts for each school attended (should show at least 90 semester credits/135 quarter credits), service processing fee; at the same time as you send in AADSAS materials, submit official DAT scores (DAT should be taken no later than October of the year prior to the year of anticipated enrollment), application fee of $50, and official transcripts directly to the Admissions Office and Student Affairs. TOEFL may be required of an applicant whose native language is other than English. Submit the following materials to the Admissions Office and Student Affairs only after being contacted by an Admissions Officer: a VCU application, predental committee evaluation or 2 recommendations from science professors, and a photograph. Interviews are by invitation only and generally for final selection. Dual-degree applicants must apply to, and be accepted by, both the School of Dentistry and the School of Basic Sciences; contact the Office of Admissions and Student Affairs for current information and specific requirements for admission. First-year students admitted in fall only. Rolling admission process. Notification starts December 1 and is finished when class is filled, but generally not later than August 1. Applicant's response to offer and $200 deposit due within 30 days if accepted prior to January 31; response and deposit due within 2 weeks if received after February 1. School does maintain an alternate list. Phone: (804)828-9196.

ADMISSION REQUIREMENTS FOR ADVANCED-STANDING APPLICANTS. Accepts transfers from other accredited U.S. and Canadian dental schools into both the 2nd and 3rd years of study. Admission limited to space available. There is an advanced-standing program for graduates of foreign schools of dentistry. Contact the Office of Admissions and Student Affairs for current information and specific requirements for admission.

ADMISSION STANDARDS AND RECOGNITION. *For D.D.S.:* number of applicants 1,370; number enrolled 80; median DAT: ACAD 18.0, PAT 17.6; median GPA 3.32 (A = 4), median sciences GPA 3.31 (A = 4). Gorman rating 4.15 (scale: strong 4.01–4.49); this placed the school in the Top 45 of all U.S. dental schools; the dental school's ranking by NIH awards/grants was 29th among dental schools, with 1 award/grant received; total value of awards/grants $860,337.

FINANCIAL AID. Scholarships, minority scholarships, grants-in-aid, institutional loans, state loan programs, DEAL, HEAL, alternative loan programs, federal Perkins loans, Stafford subsidized and unsubsidized loans, Rural Virginia Dental Scholarships, and military service commitment scholarship programs are available. Assistantships/fellowships may be available for combined degree candidates. Institutional financial aid applications and information are generally available at the on-campus interview (by invitation). For scholarship assistance the selection criteria place heavy reliance on DAT and undergraduate GPA. Contact the Financial Aid Office for current information; phone: (804)828-9196. For most financial assistance and all need-based programs, submit FAFSA to a federal processor (Title IV school code # 003735); also submit Financial Aid Transcript, Federal Income Tax forms, and Use of Federal Funds Certification. Approximately 90% of current students receive some form of financial assistance. Average award for residents $20,402, nonresidents $24,722.

DEGREE REQUIREMENTS. *For D.D.S.:* satisfactory completion of 4-year program. *For D.D.S.-M.S.:* generally a 4½–5½-year program. *For D.D.S.-Ph.D.:* generally a 7-year program.

UNIVERSITY OF VIRGINIA

Charlottesville, Virginia 22903-3196
Internet site: http://www.virginia.edu

Founded 1819. Located 66 miles W of Richmond, 120 miles SW of Washington, D.C. Public control. Semester system. Library: 4,165,800 volumes; 4,386,000 microforms; 39,084 periodicals/subscriptions; 325 computer work stations. The university's ranking in domestic higher education by NIH awards/grants was 38th, with 326 awards/grants received; total dollars awarded $67,238,907.

The university's graduate colleges/schools: Colgate Darden Graduate School of Business Administration, Curry School of Education, Graduate School of Arts and Sciences, McIntire School of Commerce, School of Architecture, School of Engineering and Applied Science, School of Law, School of Medicine, School of Nursing.

Total university enrollment at main campus: 17,700.

University of Virginia Medical Center

Jefferson Park Avenue
Charlottesville, Virginia 22908

Public control. The medical center is a member of the Council of Teaching Hospitals. Special facilities: Kluge Children's Rehabilitation Center, Surgery Oncology

Clinic. Nationally recognized programs in Cancer, Endocrinology, Neurology, Orthopedics, Otolaryngology, Rheumatology, Urology.

School of Medicine
Health Sciences Center, Box 235
Charlottesville, Virginia 22908
Phone: (804)924-5571; fax: (804)982-2586
Internet site: http://www.med.virginia.edu

Established 1825, it is one of the oldest medical schools in the South. Located on University of Virginia's campus. Library: 153,000 volumes/microforms; 3,000 current periodicals/subscriptions. The University of Virginia medical center is the primary teaching facility. Special programs: Summer programs for underrepresented minorities; prematriculation summer sessions; Summer Research Program.

Annual tuition: residents $10,174, nonresidents $22,850; fees $936. On-campus rooms and apartments available for single students; limited on-campus housing available for married students. Annual on-campus housing cost: single students $3,420 (room only). Contact Office Housing for both on- and off-campus housing information; phone: (804)924-6873. Off-campus housing and personal expenses: approximately $11,500.

Enrollment: 1st-year class 139 (M.D.-Ph.D. 4); total full-time 556 (men 56%, women 44%). First-year statistics: 35% out of state; 47.5% women; average age 24; 15% minorities; 62% science majors.

Faculty: full-time 702, part-time 39.

Degrees conferred: M.D., M.D.-Ph.D. (Biochemistry, Biology, Biomedical Engineering, Biophysics, Cell Biology, Chemistry, Microbiology, Molecular Physiology and Biological Physics, Neurosciences, Pharmacology); has M.S.T.P.

RECRUITMENT PRACTICES AND POLICIES. School has diversity program and actively recruits women/minority applicants. Diversity contact: Associate Dean; phone: (804)924-1867.

ADMISSION REQUIREMENTS FOR FIRST-YEAR APPLICANTS. Preference given to state residents; U.S. citizens and permanent residents only. *Undergraduate preparation.* Suggested premed courses: 2 courses in biology with labs, 2 courses in inorganic chemistry with labs, 2 courses in organic chemistry with labs, 2 courses in physics with labs. Bachelor's degree from an accredited institution required; all applicants have bachelor's degrees awarded prior to enrollment. Does not have EDP. *Application process.* Apply through AMCAS (file after June 1, before November 1); submit MCAT (will accept MCAT test results from the last 2 years), official transcripts for each school attended (should show at least 90 semester credits/135 quarter credits, submit transcripts by mid-May to AMCAS), service processing fee. Submit an application fee of $50, a supplemental application, a personal statement, preprofessional committee evaluation, and 3 recommendations from science faculty to Director of Admissions within 2–3 weeks of the receipt of supplemental materials. Interviews are by invitation only and generally for final selection. For M.S.T.P., M.D.-Ph.D. degree applicants there is a separate application included in the supplemental application materials; contact the Director of Admissions or Graduate Program Office (phone: (804)924-1294) for current information and specific requirements for admission. First-year students admitted in fall only. Rolling admission process. Notification starts in October and is finished when class is filled. Applicant's response to offer and $100 deposit due within 3 weeks of receipt of acceptance letter. School does maintain an alternate list. Phone: (804)924-5571.

ADMISSION REQUIREMENTS FOR TRANSFER APPLICANTS. Accepts transfers from other LCME-accredited U.S. medical schools into the 3rd year only. Preference given to state residents. Admission limited to space available. Contact the Director of Admissions for current information and specific requirements for admission.

ADMISSION STANDARDS AND RECOGNITION. *For M.D.:* number of state-resident applicants 1,042, nonresidents 3,837; number of state residents interviewed 213, nonresidents 263; number of residents enrolled 91, nonresidents 48; median MCAT 10.5 (verbal reasoning 10.32; biological sciences 10.65; physical sciences 10.77); median GPA 3.57 (A = 4). Gorman rating 4.48 (scale: strong 4.01–4.49); *U.S. News & World Report* ranked the school in the Top 25 of all U.S. medical schools; the school's medical ranking by NIH awards was 36th, with 246 awards/grants received; total dollars awarded $51,688,775.

FINANCIAL AID. Scholarships, minority scholarships, grants-in-aid, institutional loans, HEAL, alternative loan programs, NIH stipends, federal Perkins loans, Stafford subsidized and unsubsidized loans, service commitment scholarships, and Virginia medical scholarship programs are available. Assistantships/fellowships/stipends/tuition waivers may be available for M.D.-Ph.D., M.S.T.P. dual-degree candidates. Most financial aid is based on documented need. Financial aid applications and information are generally available at the on-campus interview (by invitation). For scholarship assistance, the selection criteria place heavy reliance on MCAT and undergraduate GPA.

Contact the Financial Aid Office for current information; phone: (804)924-0033. For most financial assistance and all federal programs, submit FAFSA by March 1 to a federal processor (Title IV school code # 003745); also submit Financial Aid Transcript and Federal Income Tax forms. The priority deadline for the receipt of all financial aid information is April 1. Approximately 80% of current students receive some form of financial assistance. Average debt after graduation $49,500.

DEGREE REQUIREMENTS. *For M.D.:* satisfactory completion of 4-year program. All students must take USMLE Step 1 and recieve a passing score on the USMLE Step 2 prior to awarding of M.D. *For M.D.-Ph.D., M.S.T. P.:* generally a 6–7-year program.

WAKE FOREST UNIVERSITY

Winston-Salem, North Carolina 27109
Internet site: http://www.wfu.edu

Founded 1834. Located 3 miles N of Winston-Salem. Private control. Baptist affiliation. Semester system. Library: 1,299,800 volumes; 1,602,300 microforms; 17,585 periodicals/subscriptions; 100 computer work stations. Special programs: postbaccalaureate premedical program for students who have not achieved admission to medical school. The university's ranking in domestic higher education by NIH awards/grants was 49th, with 193 awards/grants received; total dollars awarded $52,389,555.

The university's graduate colleges/schools: Graduate School, Babcock Graduate School of Management, Bowman Gray School of Medicine, School of Law.

Total university enrollment at main campus: 5,750.

Wake Forest University Medical Center

Winston-Salem, North Carolina 27157

Private control. School of Medicine is located at medical center. Special facilities: J. Paul Sticht Center on Aging and Rehabilitation, Comprehensive Rehabilitation Plaza, Level I Trauma Center.

Bowman Gray School of Medicine

Medical Center Boulevard
Winston-Salem, North Carolina 27157-1090
Phone: (336)716-4264; fax: (336)716-5807
Internet site: http://www.bgsm.edu
E-mail: medadmit@bgsm.edu

Established 1902, renamed in 1941. Located at medical center. The primary teaching hospital is North Carolina Baptist Hospital; the hospital is a member of the Council of Teaching Hospitals and has nationally recognized programs in Cancer, Cardiovascular, Geriatrics, Gynecology, Neurology, Orthopedics, Otolaryngology, Rheumatology, Urology. Other affiliated hospitals are: Forsyth Memorial Hospital, Kate Bitting Reynolds Health Center, Northwest Area Health Education Center, Brenner Children's Hospital, Reynolds Health Center, Moses Cone Hospital (Greensboro), Catawba Memorial Hospital (Hickory). Library: 130,000 volumes/microforms; 3,800 current periodicals/subscriptions. Special programs: prematriculation summer sessions.

Annual tuition: $24,000. No on-campus housing available to students. Contact Office of Student Affairs for off-campus housing information. Off-campus housing and personal expenses: approximately $14,225.

Enrollment: 1st-year class 110 (EDP 4); total full-time 449 (men 66%, women 34%). First-year statistics: 40% out of state; 17 states represented; 48 colleges represented; 33.6% women; average age 23; 14% minorities; 68% science majors.

Faculty: full-time 700, part-time/volunteers 542.

Degrees conferred: M.D., M.D.-M.B.A. (with Babcock Graduate School of Management), M.D.-M.S. (Epidemiology), M.D.-Ph.D. (Biochemistry, Biology, Cancer Biology, Chemistry, Medical Engineering, Microbiology and Immunology, Molecular Genetics, Neurobiology, Neurosciences, Molecular and Cellular Pathobiology, Pharmacology, Physiology).

RECRUITMENT PRACTICES AND POLICIES. School has diversity program and actively recruits women/minority applicants. Diversity contact: Director of Minority Affairs; phone: (336)716-4201.

ADMISSION REQUIREMENTS FOR FIRST-YEAR APPLICANTS. Preference given to state residents; U.S. citizens and permanent residents only. *Undergraduate preparation.* Suggested premed courses: 2 courses in biology with labs, 2 courses in either general or inorganic chemistry with labs, 2 courses in organic chemistry with labs, 2 courses in physics with labs, 2 courses in English. Bachelor's degree from an accredited institution required; all applicants have bachelor's degrees awarded prior to enrollment. *Has EDP;* applicants must apply through AMCAS (official transcripts sent by mid-May) between June 1 and August 1. Early applications are encouraged. Submit secondary/supplemental application, a personal statement, and 2 recommendations to Admissions Office within 2 weeks of receipt of application. Interviews are by invitation only and generally for final selection. Notification normally begins October 1. *Regular application process.* Apply through AMCAS (file after June 1, before

November 1); submit MCAT (will accept MCAT test results from the last 3 years), official transcripts for each school attended (should show at least 90 semester credits/135 quarter credits, submit transcripts by mid-May to AMCAS), service processing fee. Submit an application fee of $55, a supplemental application, a personal statement, preprofessional committee evaluation, and 3 recommendations from science faculty to Office of Medical School Admission within 2–3 weeks of the receipt of supplemental materials. Interviews, by invitation only, are held from October through March, generally for final selection. Joint-degree applicants must apply to, and be accepted by, both schools; GRE for the graduate school, GMAT for Babcock Graduate School of Management. M.D.-Ph.D. begins in the summer prior to the 1st year of medical school. Contact the Office of Medical School Admissions or the M.D.-Ph.D. Program Director (phone: (336)716-4332; E-mail: dbass@bgsm.edu) for current information and specific requirements for admission. First-year students admitted in fall only. Rolling admission process. Notification starts October 15 and is finished when class is filled. Applicant's response to offer and $100 deposit due within 2 weeks of receipt of acceptance letter. School does maintain an alternate list. Admissions Office phone: (336)716-4264.

ADMISSION REQUIREMENTS FOR TRANSFER APPLICANTS. Accepts transfers from other LCME-accredited U.S. medical schools. Admission limited to space available. Contact the Office of Medical School Admissions for current information and specific requirements for admission.

ADMISSION STANDARDS AND RECOGNITION. *For M.D.:* number of state-resident applicants 868, nonresidents 7,016; number of state residents interviewed 302, nonresidents 247; number of residents enrolled 59, nonresidents 49; median MCAT 9.9 (verbal reasoning 10.0; biological sciences 9.9; physical sciences 9.8); median GPA 3.4 (A = 4). Gorman rating 4.32 (scale: strong 4.01–4.49); *U.S. News & World Report* ranked the school in the Top 25 of all U.S. medical schools in primary-care programs; the school's medical ranking by NIH awards was 37th, with 189 awards/grants received; total dollars awarded $51,461,570.

FINANCIAL AID. Scholarships, academic merit awards, minority scholarships, North Carolina Tuition Remission Grants, institutional loans, HEAL, alternative loan programs, NIH stipends, federal Perkins loans, Stafford subsidized and unsubsidized loans, and service commitment scholarship programs are available. Assistantships/

fellowships may be available for joint-degree candidates. All financial aid is based on demonstrated need. Financial aid applications and information, as well as personal financial counseling, are generally available at the on-campus interview (by invitation). For scholarships, the selection criteria are based on need and academic standing. Contact the Financial Aid Office for current information; phone: (336)716-2889. For most financial assistance and all federal programs, submit FAFSA to a federal processor (Title IV school code # E00524); also submit Financial Aid Transcript and Federal Income Tax forms. Approximately 85% of current students receive some form of financial assistance. Average debt after graduation $73,000.

DEGREE REQUIREMENTS. *For M.D.:* satisfactory completion of 4-year program. All students must pass USMLE Step 1 prior to entering 3rd year; all students must pass USMLE Step 2 prior to awarding of M.D. *For M.D.-M.B.A.:* generally a 5–5½-year program. *For M.D.-Ph.D.:* generally a 7-year program.

WASHINGTON UNIVERSITY

St. Louis, Missouri 63130-4899
Internet site: http://www.wustl.edu

Founded 1853. Private control. Semester system. Library: 3,000,000 volumes; 2,700,000 microforms; 19,000 periodicals/subscriptions. Special facilities: Center for Mental Health Research, McDonnell Center for Cellular and Molecular Neurobiolgy. The university's ranking in domestic higher education by NIH awards/grants was 7th, with 637 awards/grants received; total dollars awarded $181,801,320.

The university's graduate colleges/schools: Graduate School of Arts and Science (includes the Division of Biology and Biomedical Sciences), George Warren Brown School of Social Work, John M. Olin School of Business, School of Architecture, School of Art, School of Engineering and Applied Science (includes Sever Institute of Technology), School of Law, School of Medicine.

Total university enrollment at main campus: 11,600.

Washington University Medical Center

216 South Kingshighway
St. Louis, Missouri 63110

Located on the eastern edge of Forrest Park. Private control. Both St. Louis Children's Hospital and Barnes-Jewish Hospital are members of the Council of Teaching Hospitals. Special facilities: Howard Hughes Institute, Central Institute for the Deaf. Barnes-Jewish Hospital has nationally recognized programs in AIDS, Cancer, Cardiology, Endocrinology, Gastroenterology, Geriatrics, Gynecology, Neurology, Ophthalmology, Orthopedics, Otolaryngology, Pediatrics, Psychiatry, Pulmonary Disease, Rehabilitation, Rheumatology, Urology. *Barron's Guide* placed Barnes-Jewish Hospital among the Top 25 most prestigious U.S. hospitals/medical centers; *U.S. News & World Report*'s hospital/medical center national rankings placed Barnes-Jewish Hospital in the top 20 of all U.S. hospitals.

School of Medicine
660 South Euclid Avenue, #8107
St. Louis, Missouri 63110
Phone: (314)362-6858; fax: (314)362-4658
Internet site: http://medschool.wustl.edu
E-mail: wumscoa@molly.wustl.edu

The Medical Department of Washington University was established in 1899 when both St. Louis Medical College (1942) and Missouri Medical College (1840) joined Washington University. The primary teaching hospitals are Barnes-Jewish Hospital and St. Louis Children's Hospital. Other affiliated hospitals are: St Louis Regional Medical Center, John Cochran Veterans Administration Medical Center, Malcolm Bliss Mental Health Center, Ellis Fischel Cancer Center, Shriner's Hospital for Crippled Children, Barnard Hospital, and since 1993 the BJC Health System (the largest academically linked health system in U.S.). Library: 367,000 volumes/microforms; 3,200 current periodicals/subscriptions. Special programs: summer programs for underrepresented minorities; prematriculation summer sessions.

Annual tuition: $28,800. On-campus housing available for single students only. Contact Admissions Offices for both on- and off-campus housing information. Medical students tend to live off-campus. Annual on and off-campus living and personal expenses: approximately $11,300.

Enrollment: 1st-year class 120; total full-time 481 (men 52%, women 28%). First-year statistics: 90% out of state; 34 states represented; 54 colleges represented; 49% women; average age 24; 11% minorities; 67% science majors.

Faculty: full-time 1,191, part-time/volunteers 1,230.

Degrees conferred: M.D., M.D.-M.A., M.D.-M.S., M.D.-Ph.D. (Biochemistry, Bioorganic Chemistry, Developmental Biology, Immunology, Microbial Pathogenesis, Molecular Biophysics, Molecular Cell Biology, Molecular Genetics, Molecular Microbiology, Neurosciences); has M.S.T.P.

RECRUITMENT PRACTICES AND POLICIES. School has diversity program and actively recruits women/minority applicants. Diversity contact: Associate Dean, Diversity Program; phone: (314)362-6854; E-mail: wumscoa@msnotes.wustl.edu.

ADMISSION REQUIREMENTS FOR FIRST-YEAR APPLICANTS. Some preference given to state residents; U.S. citizens and permanent residents only. *Undergraduate preparation.* Suggested premed courses: 2 courses in biology with labs, 2 courses in inorganic chemistry with labs, 2 courses in organic chemistry with labs, 2 courses in physics with labs, 1 course in college math, 2 courses in English. Bachelor's degree from an accredited institution required; 98% of applicants have bachelor's degrees awarded prior to enrollment. Does not have EDP. *Application process.* Apply through AMCAS (file after June 1, before December 1); submit MCAT (will accept MCAT test results from the last 2 years), official transcripts for each school attended (should show at least 90 semester credits/135 quarter credits, submit transcripts by mid-May to AMCAS), service processing fee. All applicants should submit an application fee of $50, a personal statement, preprofessional committee evaluation, and 3 recommendations from science faculty to Admissions Office by November 15. Interviews are by invitation only and generally for final selection. A separate application is required for M.S.T.P. (M.D.-Ph.D.) degree applicants; request application from M.S.T.P. Program Administrator; phone: (800)852-4625; E-mail: sullvab@medicine.wustl.edu. First-year students admitted in fall only. Rolling admission process. Notification starts October 15 and is finished when class is filled. Applicant's response to offer and $100 deposit due within 2 weeks of receipt of acceptance letter. School does maintain an alternate list. Phone: (314)362-6858; E-mail: wumscoa@msnotes.wustl.edu.

ADMISSION REQUIREMENTS FOR TRANSFER APPLICANTS. Accepts transfers from other LCME-accredited U.S. medical schools into the 3rd year only and considers only those with a compelling reason. Admission limited to space available. Contact the Admissions Office for current information and specific requirements for admission.

ADMISSION STANDARDS AND RECOGNITION. *For M.D.:* number of state-resident applicants 252, nonresidents 6,247; number of state residents interviewed 51, nonresidents 1,078; number of residents enrolled 11, nonresidents 111; median MCAT 11.6 (verbal reasoning 11.1; biological sciences 11.9; physical sciences 12.1); median GPA 3.75 (A = 4). *Barron's Guide* placed school among the Top 25 most prestigious U.S. medical schools; Gorman rating 4.76 (scale: very strong 4.51–4.99); *U.S.*

News & World Report ranked the school in the Top 25 of all U.S. medical schools; the school's medical ranking by NIH awards was 5th, with 582 awards/grants received; total dollars awarded $170,283,701.

FINANCIAL AID. Scholarships, merit scholarships, minority scholarships, Olins Fellowship for Women (application deadline February 1), institutional loans, HEAL, alternative loan programs, NIH stipends, federal Perkins loans, Stafford subsidized and unsubsidized loans, and service commitment scholarship programs are available. Stipends and tuition remission are available for M.S.T.P. (M.D.-Ph.D.) degree candidates. Financial aid applications and information are generally available at the on-campus interview (by invitation). Immediately upon the receipt of the letter of acceptance, the Financial Aid Application should be submitted. For scholarships, the selection criteria place heavy reliance on MCAT, undergraduate GPA, and personal achievement. Contact the Financial Aid Office for current information; phone: (314)362-6845; E-mail: money@msnotes.wustl.edu. For most financial assistance and all federal programs, submit FAFSA to a federal processor (Title IV school code # G24620); also submit Financial Aid Transcript and Federal Income Tax forms. Approximately 90% of current students receive some form of financial assistance. Average debt after graduation $55,360.

DEGREE REQUIREMENTS. *For M.D.:* satisfactory completion of 4-year program. Taking the USMLE Step 1 and Step 2 is only recommended. *For M.D.-M.A.:* generally a 4½–5-year program. *For M.D.-Ph.D.:* generally a 6–7-year program.

UNIVERSITY OF WASHINGTON
Seattle, Washington 98195
Internet site: http://www.washington.edu

Founded 1861. Located 3 miles from downtown Seattle. Public control. Quarter system. Library: 5,400,700 volumes; 6,255,700 microforms; 56,700 periodicals/subscriptions; 531 computer work stations. Special facilities: Applied Physics Laboratory, Botanical and Drug Plant Garden, Institute on Aging, Institute for Nuclear Theory, Interdisciplinary Graduate Program in Biomolecular Structure and Design, Laboratory of Radiation Biology, Regional Primate Research Center, Research Center in Oral Biology. The university's ranking in domestic higher education by NIH awards/grants was 2nd, with 809 awards/grants received; total dollars awarded $226,073,536.

The university's graduate schools include: College of Architecture and Urban Planning, College of Arts and Sciences, College of Education, College of Engineering, College of Forest Resources, College of Ocean and Fishery Sciences, Graduate School of Library and Information Sciences, Graduate School of Public Affairs, School of Business Administration, School of Nursing, School of Public Health and Community Medicine, School of Social Work, School of Dentistry, School of Law, School of Medicine.

Total university enrollment at main campus: 35,600.

University of Washington Medical Center/University of Washington Academic Medical Center
1959 NE Pacific Street, RC-35
Seattle, Washington 98195

Public control. Medical center is a member of the Council of Teaching Hospitals. Schools located at medical center are School of Dentistry, School of Medicine, School of Nursing, School of Pharmacy, School of Public Health and Community Medicine, School of Social Work. Special facilities: Virginia Merrill Bloedel Hearing Research Center, Keck Center for the Advanced Studies of Neural Signalling, Markey Molecular Medicine Center, Center for Research on AIDS and Sexually Transmitted Diseases. Nationally recognized programs in AIDS, Cancer, Cardiology, Endocrinology, Gastroenterology, Geriatrics, Gynecology, Neurology, Ophthalmology, Orthopedics, Otolaryngology, Pediatrics, Psychiatry, Pulmonary Disease, Rehabilitation, Rheumatology, Urology. *U.S. News & World Report*'s hospital/medical center national rankings for all hospitals placed the medical center in the Top 20 of all U.S. hospitals.

School of Medicine
Health Science Center A-300, Box 356340
Seattle, Washington 98195-6340
Phone: (206)543-7212; fax: (206)543-3639
Internet site: http://www.washington.edu/medical/som
E-mail: ashuwsom@u.washington.edu

Established 1945. Located at the Warren G. Magnuson Health Science Center. Primary teaching facilities are: the University of Washington Medical Center and the Harborview Medical Center. Other affiliated hospitals are spread throughout the Northwest. Quarter system. Special programs: Summer programs for minorities (MMEP); prematriculation summer sessions; WWAMI Program. (For residents of Alaska, with 10 students; Montana, with 20 students; Idaho, with 16 students, receive part of their basic medical-science instruction at their home-state university. Wyoming, with 10 students, was added in 1997.)

Annual tuition: residents $8,490, nonresidents $21,402. On-campus rooms and apartments available for both single and married students. Annual on-campus housing cost: single students $3,377 (room only), married students $4,634. Contact Student Services Office for both on- and off-campus housing information; phone (206)543-4059. Medical students tend to live off-campus. Off-campus housing and personal expenses: approximately $12,560.

Enrollment: 1st-year class 166 (M.D.-Ph.D. approximately 8–12 each year); total full-time 698 (men 53%, women 47%). First-year statistics: 10% out of state (Alaska, Montana, Idaho, Wyoming are considered residents because of WWAMI Program); 50% women; average age 24; 10% minorities; 47% science majors.

Faculty: full-time 1,336, part-time/volunteers 3,741.

Degrees conferred: M.D., M.D.-Ph.D. (Biochemistry, Bioengineering, Biomathematics/Biostatistics, Biological Structure, Cancer Research, Epidemiology, Environmental Health, Genetics, Immunology, Microbiology, Molecular Biotechnology, Molecular and Cellular Biology, Neurobiology, Pathology, Pharmacology, Physiology and Biophysics, Zoology); has M.S.T.P.

RECRUITMENT PRACTICES AND POLICIES. School has diversity program and actively recruits women/minority applicants. Diversity contact: Director, Minority Affairs Program; phone: (206)685-2489. The MMED home page is at http://weber.u.washington.edu/~dolson/mmep.html.

ADMISSION REQUIREMENTS FOR FIRST-YEAR APPLICANTS. Preference given to WWAMI Program participants and considered as state residents; U.S. citizens and permanent residents only. *Undergraduate preparation.* Suggested premed courses: 2 courses in biology with labs, 3 courses in chemistry with labs, 1 course in physics with labs, 2 other science courses; proficiency in English. Bachelor's degree from an accredited institution required; all applicants have bachelor's degree awarded prior to enrollment. Does not have EDP. *Application process.* Apply through AMCAS (file after June 1, before November 1); submit MCAT (will accept MCAT test results from the last 3 years), official transcripts for each school attended (should show at least 90 semester credits/135 quarter credits, submit transcripts by mid-May to AMCAS), service processing fee. Submit an application fee of $35, a supplemental application, 300-word autobiographical statement, 3 recommendations from science faculty, and a signed form authorizing a criminal background check to Admissions Office within 2–3 weeks of the receipt of supplemental materials, but not later than

January 15. Interviews are by invitation only and generally for final selection. M.S.T.P. degree applicants must submit an M.S.T.P. application; a supplemental application is then sent to applicants considered eligible; the M.S.T.P. interview is with a single M.S.T.P. selection committee for acceptance into both schools. Contact the Admissions Office or the M.S.T.P. Coordinator (phone: (206)685-0762; E-mail: mkl@u.washington.edu) for current information and specific requirements for admission. First-year students admitted in fall only. Rolling admission process. Notification starts November 1 and is finished when class is filled. Applicant's response to offer and $100 deposit due within 2 weeks of receipt of acceptance letter. School does maintain an alternate list. Phone: (206)543-7212. On-line catalog available at http://www.washington.edu/students/crscat/index.html.

ADMISSION REQUIREMENTS FOR TRANSFER APPLICANTS. Does not consider transfer applicants. Contact the Admissions Office for current information and any modification to policy.

ADMISSION STANDARDS AND RECOGNITION. *For M.D.:* number of state-resident applicants 1,023, nonresidents 2,580; number of state residents interviewed 719, nonresidents 96; number of residents enrolled: Washington 107, Alaska 10, Montana 20, Idaho 16, nonresidents 13; median MCAT 10.1 (verbal reasoning 10.0; biological sciences 10.4; physical sciences 10.0); median GPA 3.54 (A = 4). Gorman rating 4.39 (scale: strong 4.01–4.49); *U.S. News & World Report* ranked the school in both the Top 25 of all U.S. medical schools and in the Top 25 medical schools in primary-care programs; the school's medical ranking by NIH awards was 5th, with 582 awards/grants received; total dollars awarded $170,283,701.

FINANCIAL AID. Scholarships, merit scholarships, minority scholarships, grants-in-aid, institutional loans, HEAL, alternative loan programs, NIH stipends, federal Perkins loans, Stafford subsidized and unsubsidized loans, service commitment scholarship programs are available. Assistantships/fellowships/stipends/tuition waivers may be available for M.S.T.P. degree candidates. Financial aid applications and information are available in January. All financial aid is based on demonstrated need. Contact the Financial Aid Office for current information; phone: (206)685-2520. For most financial assistance and all federal programs, submit FAFSA not later than February 28 to a federal processor (Title IV school code # 003798); also submit Financial Aid Transcript and Federal Income Tax forms. Approximately 82% of current students receive some form of financial assistance. Average debt after graduation $60,100.

DEGREE REQUIREMENTS. *For M.D.:* satisfactory completion of 4-year program. All students must pass USMLE Step 1 prior to entering 3rd year; all students must pass USMLE Step 2 prior to awarding of M.D. *For M.D.-Ph.D., M.S.T.P.:* generally a 6–7-year program.

School of Dentistry
Box 356365
Seattle, Washington 98795-6365
Phone: (206)543-5840; fax: (206)616-2612
Internet site: http://www.dental.washington.edu
E-mail: evrgreen@u.washinton.edu

Established 1945. Located at the health science center. Quarter system. Special facilities: Regional Clinical Dental Research Center. Special programs: summer programs for underrepresented minorities; research fellowships; externships. Postgraduate specialties: Endodontics (M.S.D.), Dental Public Health, Oral Medicine (M.S.D.), Oral and Maxillofacial Surgery, Orthodontics (M.S.D.), Pediatric Dentistry, Periodontics (M.S.D.), Prosthodontics (M.S.D.), Restorative Dentistry.

Annual tuition: residents $8,058, nonresidents $20,709; fees $2,480, equipment and supplies $1,245. On-campus rooms and apartments available for both single and married students. Contact university's Housing Assignment Office for both on- and off-campus housing information; phone: (206)543-4059. Dental students tend to live off-campus. Off-campus housing, food, transportation, and personal expenses: approximately $11,000.

Enrollment: 1st-year class 55; total full-time 263. First-year enrolled student information: 9 from out of state; 18 women; average age 25; 7 underrepresented minorities; 15 other minorities.

Faculty: full-time 73, part-time 46.

Degrees conferred: D.D.S., M.S.D., D.D.S.-M.S. (Oral Biology), D.D.S.-Ph.D. (Anatomy, Oral Biology, Oral Pathology, Pharmacology, Physiology).

RECRUITMENT PRACTICES AND POLICIES. School has diversity program and actively recruits women/minority applicants. Diversity contact: Health Sciences Minority Student Program; phone: (206)685-1834.

ADMISSION REQUIREMENTS FOR FIRST-YEAR APPLICANTS. Preference given to state and WICHE residents; U.S. citizens and permanent residents only. *Undergraduate preparation.* Suggested predental courses: 2 courses in biology with labs, 2 courses in organic chem-

istry with labs, 2 courses in physics with labs, 1 course in biochemistry, 1 course in microbiology. There is no limitation on the number of junior-college credits taken. Will consider applicants with only 3 years of undergraduate preparation; prefer applicants who will have bachelor's degrees prior to enrollment. For serious consideration an application should have at least a 3.0 (A = 4) GPA in predental courses; 51 out of 55 enrolled students have bachelor's degree awarded prior to enrollment. *Application process.* Apply through AADSAS (file after June 1, before December 1); submit official transcripts for each school attended (should show at least 90 semester credits/135 quarter credits), service processing fee; at the same time as you send in AADSAS materials, submit official DAT scores (DAT should be taken no later than October 1 year prior to the anticipated year of enrollment) directly to the Office of Student Affairs. TOEFL may be required of an applicant whose native language is other than English. Submit the following materials only after being contacted by an Admissions Officer: an application fee of $35, a secondary/supplemental application, official transcripts, DAT scores, predental committee evaluation, 2 recommendations from science faculty members, and a signed form authorizing a criminal background check to the Office of Student Affairs within 2 weeks of receipt of supplemental materials. Interviews are by invitation only and generally for final selection. Joint-degree applicants must apply to, and be accepted by, both schools; contact the Office of Student Affairs for current information and specific requirements for admission. First-year students admitted in fall only. Rolling admission process. Notification starts December 1 and is finished when class is filled. Applicant's response to offer and $100 deposit due within 30 days if accepted prior to January 31; response and deposit due within 2 weeks if received after February 1. School does maintain an alternate list. Phone: (206)543-5840; E-mail: evrgreen@u.washington.edu.

ADMISSION REQUIREMENTS FOR ADVANCED-STANDING APPLICANTS. Rarely accepts transfers except under exceptional circumstances. There is an advanced-standing program for graduates of foreign schools of dentistry. Contact the Office of Student Affairs for current information and specific requirements for admission.

ADMISSION STANDARDS AND RECOGNITION. *For D.D.S.:* number of applicants 1,018; number enrolled 55; median DAT: ACAD 20.0, PAT 20.0; median GPA 3.41 (A = 4), median sciences GPA 3.43 (A = 4). Gorman rating 4.79 (scale: very strong 4.51–4.99); this placed the school in the Top 10 of all U.S. dental schools; the school's ranking by NIH awards/grants was 1st among dental schools, with 38 awards/grants received; total value of all awards/grants $17,948,059.

FINANCIAL AID. Scholarships, merit scholarships, minority scholarships, grants-in-aid, institutional loans, state loan programs, DEAL, HEAL, alternative loan programs; federal Perkins loans, Stafford subsidized and unsubsidized loans, and military service commitment scholarship programs are available. Assistantships/fellowships/tuition waivers may be available for combined-degree candidates. Institutional financial aid applications and information are available in January. Apply by February 28. For scholarships, the selection criteria place heavy reliance on DAT and undergraduate GPA. Contact the university's Office of Financial Aid for current information; phone: (206)543-5840. For most financial assistance and all need-based programs submit FAFSA to a federal processor (Title IV school code #003798); also submit Financial Aid Transcript, Federal Income Tax forms, and Use of Federal Funds Certification. Approximately 80% of current students receive some form of financial assistance.

DEGREE REQUIREMENTS. *For D.D.S.:* satisfactory completion of 4-year program. *For D.D.S.-M.S.:* generally a 4½–5½-year program. *For D.D.S.-Ph.D.:* generally a 7-year program.

WAYNE STATE UNIVERSITY
Detroit, Michigan 48202
Internet site: http://www.wayne.edu

Founded 1868. Public control. Semester system. Library: 2,960,000 volumes; 3,400,000 microforms; 24,600 periodicals/subscriptions. Special facilities: Addiction Research Center, Bioengineering Center, Center for Molecular Medicine and Genetics, Cryogenics Laboratory, Institute of Gerontology, Institute of Chemical Toxicology. Special programs: Postbaccalaureate premedical program for underrepresented minorities; contact the Recruitment Office; phone: (313)577-1598. The university's ranking in domestic higher education by NIH awards/grants was 53rd, with 207 awards/grants received; total dollars awarded $48,553,011.

The university's graduate schools include: College of Education, College of Engineering, College of Fine, Performing and Communication Arts, College of Liberal Arts, College of Nursing, College of Science, College of Urban, Labor and Metropolitan Affairs, Law School, School of Business Administration, School of Social Work, College of Pharmacy and Allied Health Professions, School of Medicine.

Total university enrollment at main campus: 31,185.

Detroit Receiving Hospital and University Health Center/Detroit Medical Center
4201 St. Antoine Boulevard
Detroit, Michigan 48201

Located in the north central area of Detroit. Public control. Both centers are members of the Council of Teaching Hospitals. Special facilities: Children's Hospital, Rehabilitation Institute, Veterans Administration Hospital, Kresge Eye Institute, Wayne State University Comprehensive Sickle Cell Center, Karmanas Cancer Center, Gershenson Radiation Oncology Center, Gamma Knife.

School of Medicine
540 East Canfield
Detroit, Michigan 48201
Internet site: http://www.med.wayne.edu

Established 1868. Fourth-largest medical school in U.S. Located at the medical center. Curriculum is made up of 4 periods. Library: 163,000 volumes/microforms; 1,200 current periodicals/subscriptions. Affiliated hospitals: Detroit Receiving Hospital, University Hospital, Harper Hospital, Grace Hospital, Hutzel Hospital. Special programs: Summer programs for underrepresented minorities; prematriculation summer sessions.

Annual tuition: residents $10,499, nonresidents $20,572; fees $350. No on-campus housing available. Contact School of Medicine Student Organizations Office for housing information packet. Off-campus housing and personal expenses: approximately $13,900.

Enrollment: 1st-year class 256 (EDP 35); total full-time 1,049 (men 61%, women 39%). First-year statistics: 5% out of state; 40% women; average age 25; 15% minorities.

Faculty: full-time 800.

Degrees conferred: M.D., M.D.-M.S. (Anatomy and Cell Biology, Biochemistry and Molecular Biology, Community Health Services, Immunology and Microbiology, Molecular Biology and Genetics, Physical Medicine & Rehabilitation, Physiology, Psychiatry, Radiological Physics), M.D.-Ph.D. (Anatomy and Cell Biology, Biochemistry and Molecular Biology, Immunology and Microbiology, Medical Physics, Molecular Biology and Genetics, Pathology, Pharmacology, Physiology).

RECRUITMENT PRACTICES AND POLICIES. School has diversity program and actively recruits women/minority applicants. Diversity contact: Assistant Dean for Student Affairs; phone: (313)577-1463.

ADMISSION REQUIREMENTS FOR FIRST-YEAR APPLICANTS. Preference given to state residents and residents of medically underrepresented areas of Michigan; U.S. citizens and permanent residents only. *Undergraduate preparation.* Suggested premed courses: 2 courses in biology with labs, 2 courses in inorganic chemistry with labs, 2 courses in organic chemistry with labs, 2 courses in physics with labs, 2 courses in English. Bachelor's degree from an accredited institution required; all applicants have bachelor's degrees awarded prior to enrollment. *Has EDP* for state residents only; applicants must apply through AMCAS (official transcripts sent by mid-May) between June 1 and August 1. Early applications are encouraged. Submit secondary/supplemental application, a personal statement, and 2 recommendations to Admissions Office within 2 weeks of receipt of application. Interviews are by invitation only and generally for final selection. Notification normally begins October 1. About 15% of class is allocated to EDP. *Application process.* Apply through AMCAS (file after June 1, before December 1); submit MCAT (will accept MCAT test results from the last 3 years), official transcripts for each school attended (should show at least 90 semester credits/135 quarter credits, submit transcripts by mid-May to AMCAS), service processing fee. Submit an application fee of $30, a supplemental application, a personal statement, preprofessional committee evaluation, and 3 recommendations from science faculty to Admissions Office within 2–3 weeks of the receipt of supplemental materials. Interviews are by invitation only and generally for final selection. Combined degree applicants must apply to, and be accepted by, both schools; there is no special combined degree process. Contact the Admissions Office or the Office of Research and Academic Programs (phone: (313)577-1455; fax: (313)577-1348) for current M.S., Ph.D. information, and specific requirements for admission. First-year students admitted in fall only. Rolling admission process. Notification starts October 15 and is finished when class is filled. Applicant's response to offer and $50 deposit due within 3 weeks of receipt of acceptance letter. School does maintain an alternate list. Phone: (313)577-1466.

ADMISSION REQUIREMENTS FOR TRANSFER APPLICANTS. Accepts transfers from other accredited U.S. and Canadian medical schools into both the 2nd and 3rd year. Admission limited to space available. Contact the Admissions Office for current information and specific requirements for admission.

ADMISSION STANDARDS AND RECOGNITION. *For M.D.:* number of state-resident applicants 1,513, nonresidents 2,518; number of state residents interviewed 664, nonresidents 95; number of residents enrolled 245, nonresidents 11; median MCAT 8.9 (verbal reasoning 8.8; biological sciences 8.8; physical sciences 9.1); median GPA 3.5 (A = 4). Gorman rating 4.18 (scale: strong 4.01–4.49); the school's medical ranking by NIH awards was 47th, with 154 awards/grants received; total dollars awarded $37,374,449.

FINANCIAL AID. Scholarships, merit scholarships, minority scholarships, grants-in-aid for Michigan residents, institutional loans, HEAL, alternative loan programs, federal Perkins loans, Stafford subsidized and unsubsidized loans, and service commitment scholarship programs are available. Assistantships/fellowships/tuition scholarships may be available for dual-degree candidates. Financial-aid applications and information are generally available at the on-campus interview (by invitation). Financial aid is awarded based on academic performance, financial need, and availability of funding. Contact the Office of Scholarships and Financial Aid for current information; phone: (313)577-1039. For most financial assistance and all federal programs, submit FAFSA to a federal processor (Title IV school code # E00570); also submit Financial Aid Transcript and Federal Income Tax forms. Approximately 85% of current students receive some form of financial assistance.

DEGREE REQUIREMENTS. *For M.D.:* satisfactory completion of 4-year program. All students must pass USMLE Step 1 prior to entering 3rd year; all students must take USMLE Step 2 and record a score. *For M.D.-M.S.:* generally a 4½–5½-year program. *For M.D.-Ph.D.:* generally a 7-year program.

WEST VIRGINIA COLLEGE OF OSTEOPATHIC MEDICINE

400 North Lee Street
Lewisburg, West Virginia 24901-1128
Internet site: http://www.wvsom.edu

Founded 1974 as Greenbrier College of Osteopathic Medicine; became part of West Virginia State System of Higher Education in 1976. Located in rural Appalachia. Public control. Three-phase system. Library: 18,660 volumes; 680 periodicals/subscriptions; 11 PC work stations.

Annual tuition: residents $10,750, nonresidents $27,400. No on-campus housing available. Contact Admissions Office for off-campus housing information. Off-campus housing and personal expenses: approximately $15,000.

Enrollment: 1st-year class 65; total full-time 261 (men 58%, women 42%). First-year statistics: 31% out of state; 42% women; average age 28; 8% minorities.

Faculty: full-time 39, part-time 4.

Degree conferred: D.O.

RECRUITMENT PRACTICES AND POLICIES. School has diversity program and actively recruits women/minority applicants. Diversity contact: Director of Admissions and Registrar.

ADMISSION REQUIREMENTS FOR FIRST-YEAR APPLICANTS. Preference given to state residents, then to SREB contract states, and then residents of southern Appalachian states; U.S. citizens and permanent residents only. *Undergraduate preparation.* Suggested premed courses: 2 courses in biology, 2 courses in inorganic chemistry, 2 courses in organic chemistry, 2 courses in physics, 2 courses in English, 14 elective courses. Bachelor's degree from an accredited institution required; all applicants have bachelor's degree awarded prior to enrollment. For serious consideration an applicant should have at least 2.5 (A = 4) GPA. *Application process.* Apply through AACOMAS (file after June 1, before December 1); submit MCAT (will accept test results from last 3 years), official transcripts for each school attended (should show at least 90 semester credits/135 quarter credits), service processing fee. After a review of the AACOMAS application and supporting documents, a decision is made concerning which candidates should receive supplemental materials. The supplemental application, an application fee of $35, $75 for nonresidents, a personal statement, and 3 recommendations (1 from a D.O.) should be returned to Admissions Office as soon as possible, not later than February 28. Interviews are by invitation only and generally for final selection. First-year students admitted in fall only. Rolling admission process. Notification starts in November and is finished when class is filled. Applicant's response to offer and $500 (state resident), $2,000 (nonresident) deposit due within 2 weeks of receipt of acceptance letter. School does maintain an alternate/waiting list. CPR Certification is required prior to enrollment. Phone: (304)645-6270, X373; fax: (304)645-4859.

ADMISSION REQUIREMENTS FOR TRANSFER APPLICANTS. Accepts transfers from other accredited U.S. osteopathic medical schools. Admission limited to space available. Contact the Admissions Offices for current information and specific requirements for admission.

ADMISSION STANDARDS AND RECOGNITION. *For D.O.:* number of applicants 2,420; number enrolled 65; median MCAT 7.3; median GPA 3.40 (A = 4).

FINANCIAL AID. Tuition-fee waivers, scholarships, grants, institutional loans, NOF, HEAL, alternative loan programs, West Virginia Board of Trustees Medical Student Loan Program, federal Perkins loans, Stafford subsidized and unsubsidized loans, service obligation scholarship programs, and armed forces and National Health Service programs are available. Financial aid applications and information are given out at the on-campus interview (by invitation). Contact the Financial Aid Office for current information; phone: (304)645-6270. For most financial assistance and all federal programs, submit FAFSA to a federal processor (Title IV school code # 011245); also submit Financial Aid Transcript and Federal Income Tax forms. Approximately 85% of current students receive some form of financial assistance. Average debt after graduation $86,342.

DEGREE REQUIREMENTS. *For D.O.:* satisfactory completion of 4-year program.

WEST VIRGINIA UNIVERSITY
Morgantown, West Virginia 26506-6009
Internet site: http://www.wvu.edu

Founded 1867. Located 70 miles S of Pittsburgh. Public control. Semester system. Library: 1,344,200 volumes; 2,512,100 microforms; 10,800 periodicals/subscriptions; 120 computer work stations. The university's ranking in domestic higher education by NIH awards/grants was 136th, with 38 awards/grants received; total dollars awarded $5,806,160.

The university's other graduate colleges/schools: College of Agriculture and Forestry, College of Business and Economics, College of Creative Arts, College of Engineering and Mineral Resources, College of Human Resources and Education, College of Law, Eberly College of Arts and Science, Perley Isaac Reed School of Journalism, School of Dentistry, School of Medicine, School of Nursing, School of Pharmacy, School of Physical Education, School of Social Work.

Total university enrollment at main campus: 21,500.

Health Sciences Center
Morgantown, West Virginia 26506

Founded 1968. Public control. The university hospital is a member of the Council of Teaching Hospitals. The health sciences center has divisions in Charleston and Wheeling. Schools located at health sciences center are: School of Dentistry, School of Medicine, School of Nursing, School of Pharmacy. Special facilities: Mary Babb Randolph Cancer Center.

School of Medicine

P.O. Box 9815
Morgantown, West Virginia 26506-9111
Phone: (304)293-3521; fax: (304)293-7968
Internet site: http://www.hsc.wvu.edu/som
E-mail: dhall@wvuhscl.hsc.wvu.edu

Established 1902 as a 2-year medical program; 4-year program in 1960. Located at health sciences center. Basic medical sciences are presented in first two years; one-third of the medical students will complete the degree in Charleston Division. Affiliated hospitals: Ruby Memorial Hospital, Chestnut Ridge Psychiatric Hospital, Health South Mountainview Regional Rehabilitation. Library: 265,000 volumes/microforms; 2,200 current periodicals/subscriptions. Special programs: summer programs for underrepresented minorities (Health Careers Opportunity Program).

Annual tuition: residents $9,202, nonresidents $21,282. Limited on-campus rooms and apartments available for both single and married students. Annual on-campus housing cost: single students $3,175 (room only), married students $3,475. Contact Housing and Residential Life Office for both on- and off-campus housing information; phone: (304)293-5840. Off-campus housing and personal expenses: approximately $13,430.

Enrollment: 1st-year class 88 (EDP 8); total full-time 349 (men 54%, women 46%). First-year statistics: 5% out of state; 50% women; average age 24; 84% science majors.

Faculty: full-time 472.

Degrees conferred: M.D., M.D.-Ph.D. (Anatomy, Biochemistry, Microbiology and Immunology, Neurosciences [Multidisciplinary], Pharmacology and Toxicology, Physiology).

RECRUITMENT PRACTICES AND POLICIES. School has diversity program and actively recruits women/minority applicants. Diversity contact: Associate Dean for Student Affairs; phone: (304)293-2408.

ADMISSION REQUIREMENTS FOR FIRST-YEAR APPLICANTS. Preference given to state residents; U.S. citizens and permanent residents only. *Undergraduate preparation.* Suggested premed courses: 2 courses in biology with labs, 2 courses in inorganic chemistry with labs, 2 courses in organic chemistry with labs, 2 courses in physics with labs, 2 courses in English, 2 courses in behavioral or social sciences; courses in calculus, biochemistry, and cell/molecular biology are strongly encouraged. Bachelor's degree from an accredited institution required; 97% of applicants have bachelor's degree awarded prior to enrollment. *Has EDP for state residents only; appli-*cants must apply through AMCAS (official transcripts sent by mid-May) between June 1 and August 1. Early applications are encouraged. Submit supplemental application, a personal statement, and 2 recommendations to Admissions Office within 2 weeks of receipt of application. Interviews are by invitation only and generally for final selection. Notification normally begins October 1. *Regular application process.* Apply through AMCAS (file after June 1, before November 15); submit MCAT (will accept MCAT test results from the last 2 years), official transcripts for each school attended (should show at least 90 semester credits/135 quarter credits, submit transcripts by mid-May to AMCAS), service processing fee. Submit an application fee of $45, a supplemental application, a personal statement, preprofessional committee evaluation, and 3 recommendations from science faculty to Admissions Office within 2–3 weeks of the receipt of supplemental materials. Interviews are by invitation only and generally for final selection. Combined degree applicants must apply to, and be accepted by, both schools. All admission requirements apply for both the School of Medicine and the graduate program. Contact the Admissions Office for current information and specific requirements for admission. First-year students admitted in fall only. Rolling admission process. Notification starts October 15 and is finished when class is filled. Applicant's response to offer and $100 deposit due within 2 weeks of receipt of acceptance letter. School does maintain an alternate list. Phone: (304)293-3521.

ADMISSION REQUIREMENTS FOR TRANSFER APPLICANTS. Accepts transfers from other accredited U.S. medical schools who can offer a compelling reason for transfer and are in good standing. Preference given to state residents. Admission limited to space available. Contact the Admissions Office for current information and specific requirements for admission.

ADMISSION STANDARDS AND RECOGNITION. *For M.D.:* number of state-resident applicants 327, nonresidents 1,121; number of state residents interviewed 250, nonresidents 36; number of residents enrolled 84, nonresidents 4; median MCAT 9.0 (verbal reasoning 9.1; biological sciences 9.3; physical sciences 8.7); median GPA 3.61 (A = 4). Gorman rating 3.47 (scale: acceptable plus 3.01–3.59); the school's medical ranking by NIH awards was 102nd, with 31 awards/grants received; total dollars awarded $4,421,770.

FINANCIAL AID. Scholarships, merit scholarships, minority scholarships, grants-in-aid, institutional loans, HEAL, alternative loan programs, federal Perkins loans,

Stafford subsidized and unsubsidized loans, and service commitment scholarship programs are available. Assistantships/fellowships may be available for combined degree candidates. Financial aid applications and information are generally available at the on-campus interview (by invitation). For scholarships, the selection criteria place heavy reliance on MCAT and undergraduate GPA. Contact the Financial Aid Office for current information; phone: (303)293-3706. For most financial assistance and all federal programs, submit FAFSA to a federal processor (Title IV school code # 003827); also submit Financial Aid Transcript and Federal Income Tax forms. Approximately 80% of current students receive some form of financial assistance. Average debt after graduation $78,000.

DEGREE REQUIREMENTS. *For M.D.:* satisfactory completion of 4-year program. All students must pass USMLE Step 1 prior to entering 3rd year; all students must pass USMLE Step 2 prior to awarding of M.D. *For M.D.-Ph.D.:* generally a 7-year program.

School of Dentistry
P.O. Box 9815
1170 Health Science North
Morgantown, West Virginia 26506-9815
Phone: (304)293-3521
Internet site: http://www.hsc.uvw.edu/sod

Established 1951. Located at health sciences center. Semester system plus summer sessions. Postgraduate specialties: Dental Hygiene, Endodontics, General Dentistry (AEGD), Oral and Maxillofacial Surgery, Orthodontics, Prosthodontics.

Annual tuition: residents $6,599, nonresidents $15,146; equipment and supplies $9,135. Limited on-campus rooms and apartments available for both single and married students. Annual on-campus housing cost: single students $3,175 (room only), married students $3,475. Contact Housing and Residential Life Office for both on- and off-campus housing information; phone: (304)293-5840. Off-campus housing, food, transportation, and personal expenses: approximately $13,430.

Enrollment: 1st-year class 41; total full-time 169. First-year enrolled student information: 21 from out of state; 11 states represented; 9 women; average age 23; 2 underrepresented minorities; 2 other minorities.

Faculty: full-time 55, part-time 2.

Degrees conferred: D.D.S., M.S., D.D.S.-M.D. (available on an individualized basis), D.D.S.-Ph.D.

RECRUITMENT PRACTICES AND POLICIES. School has diversity program and actively recruits women/minority applicants. Diversity contact: Office of Admissions and Records.

ADMISSION REQUIREMENTS FOR FIRST-YEAR APPLICANTS. Preference given to state residents; U.S. citizens and permanent residents only. *Undergraduate preparation.* Suggested predental courses: 2 courses in biology with labs, 2 courses in inorganic chemistry with labs, 2 courses in organic chemistry with labs, 2 courses in physics with labs, 2 courses in English. The junior-college transfer credit limit is 72 credits. Will consider applicants with only 3 years of undergraduate preparation; prefer applicants who will have a bachelor's degree prior to enrollment; 26 out of 41 1st-year students will have bachelor's degree awarded prior to enrollment. *Application process.* Apply through AADSAS (file after June 1, before February 15); submit official transcripts for each school attended (should show at least 90 semester credits/135 quarter credits), service processing fee; at the same time as you send in AADSAS materials, submit official DAT scores directly to the Office of Admissions and Records. Submit the following materials immediately after being contacted by an Admissions Officer: an application fee of $45, official transcripts, and predental committee evaluation or 3 recommendations—one each from a biology, chemistry, and physics professor, to Office of Admission and Records. Interviews are by invitation only and generally for final selection. Combined degree applicants must apply to, and be accepted by, both schools; contact the Office of Admission and Records for current information and specific requirements for admission. First-year students admitted in fall only. Rolling admission process. Notification starts December 1 and is finished when class is filled. Applicant's response to offer and $100 deposit due within 30 days if accepted prior to January 31; response and deposit due within 2 weeks if received after February 1. School does maintain an alternate list. Phone: (304)293-3521.

ADMISSION REQUIREMENTS FOR ADVANCED-STANDING APPLICANTS. Rarely considers transfer applicants available. There is no advanced-standing program for graduates of foreign schools of dentistry. Contact the Office of Admissions and Records for current information and any modification in policies.

ADMISSION STANDARDS AND RECOGNITION. *For D.D.S.:* number of applicants 1,187; number enrolled 41; median DAT: ACAD 17.0, PAT 16.0; median GPA 3.45 (A = 4), median sciences GPA 3.21 (A = 4). Gorman rating 4.18 (scale: strong 4.01–4.49); this placed the school in the Top 40 of all U.S. dental schools.

FINANCIAL AID. West Virginia University Dental Scholarships, Board of Regents Scholarships, minority fellowship, grants-in-aid, institutional loans, state loan programs, DEAL, HEAL, alternative loan programs, federal Perkins loans, Stafford subsidized and unsubsidized loans, and military service commitment scholarship programs are available. Assistantships/fellowships may be available for combined degree candidates. Institutional financial aid applications and information are given out at the on-campus interview (by invitation). For scholarships, the selection criteria place heavy reliance on DAT and undergraduate GPA. Contact the Senior Financial Aid Counselor in the university's Student Financial Aid Office for current information; phone: (304)293-3706. For most financial assistance and all need-based programs, submit FAFSA to a federal processor (Title IV school code # 003827); also submit Financial Aid Transcript, Federal Income Tax forms, and Use of Federal Funds Certification. Approximately 78% of current students receive some form of financial assistance. Average award for residents $18,370, nonresidents $27,625.

DEGREE REQUIREMENTS. *For D.D.S.:* satisfactory completion of 4-year program. *For D.D.S.-Ph.D.:* generally a 6–7-year program.

WESTERN UNIVERSITY OF HEALTH SCIENCES
Pomona, California 91766-1889
Internet site: http://www.westernu.edu

Founded 1977 as the College of Osteopathic Medicine of the Pacific; named changed in 1996. Located 35 miles E of Los Angeles. Private control. Semester system. Library: 18,000 volumes; 350 periodicals/subscriptions; 30 PC work stations. Special facilities: partner with San Bernardino County's Arrowhead Medical Center in an Academic Center for Excellence in the Health Sciences at San Bernardino County's Arrowhead Medical Center.

The university's other graduate colleges/schools includes: College of Pharmacy, School of Allied Health Professions.

Total university enrollment at main campus: 982.

Western University Medical Center
College of Osteopathic Medicine
College Plaza
309 East Second Street
Pomona, California, 91766-1889
Phone: (909)469-5200
Internet site: http://www.westernu.edu

Established 1977. Curriculum based on a 3-phase system. Special program: summer anatomy program for underrepresented minorities.

Annual tuition: $22,430; fees $665. No on-campus housing available. Contact Admissions Office for off-campus housing information. Off-campus housing and personal expenses: approximately $14,936.

Enrollment: 1st-year class 170; total full-time 687 (men 58%, women 42%). First-year statistics: 28% out of state; 40% women; average age 29; 31% other minorities.

Faculty: full-time 42, part-time/volunteers 1,000.

Degree conferred: D.O.

RECRUITMENT PRACTICES AND POLICIES. School has diversity program and actively recruits women/minority applicants. Diversity contact: Director of Admissions.

ADMISSION REQUIREMENTS FOR FIRST-YEAR APPLICANTS. Preference given to state residents; U.S. citizens and permanent residents only. *Undergraduate preparation.* Suggested premed courses: 2 courses in biology, 2 courses in inorganic chemistry, 2 courses in organic chemistry, 2 courses in physics, 2 courses in behavioral sciences, 2 courses in English. Bachelor's degree from an accredited institution required; all applicants have bachelor's degrees awarded prior to enrollment. *Has EDP*; applicants must apply through AACOMAS before June 15. Early applications are encouraged. Submit supplemental application, a personal statement, and 3 recommendations to Admissions Office within 2 weeks of receipt of application, but not later than August 1. For serious consideration an applicant should have at least a 3.30 (A = 4) in both sciences and overall GPA and a minimum average MCAT of 9.0. Interviews are by invitation only and generally for final selection. Notification normally begins in October. *Regular application process.* Apply through AACOMAS (file after June 1, before December 1); submit MCAT (will accept test results from last 3 years), official transcripts for each school attended (should show at least 90 semester credits/135 quarter credits), service processing fee. After a review of the AACOMAS application and supporting documents, a decision is made concerning which candidates should receive supplemental materials. The supplemental application, an application fee of $60, a personal statement, and 3 recommendations (1 from a D.O.) should be returned to Admissions Office as soon as possible, but not later than February 15. Interviews are by invitation only and generally for final selection. First-year students admitted in fall only. Rolling admission process. Notification starts in October and is finished when class is filled. Applicant's response to offer and $100 deposit due within 2 weeks of receipt of acceptance letter. School does maintain an alternate list. Phone: (909)623-5335; fax: (909)469-5570.

ADMISSION REQUIREMENTS FOR TRANSFER APPLICANTS. Accepts transfers from other accredited U.S. osteopathic medical schools. Admission limited to space available. Contact the Admissions Offices for current information and specific requirements for admission.

ADMISSION STANDARDS AND RECOGNITION. *For D.O.:* number applicants 4,000; number of enrolled 170; median MCAT 8.33; median GPA 3.3 (A = 4); science GPA 3.2.

FINANCIAL AID. Scholarships, grants, California State Graduate Fellowships, institutional loans, NOF, HEAL, alternative loan programs, federal Perkins loans, Stafford subsidized and unsubsidized loans, service obligation scholarship programs, armed forces and National Health Service programs are available. Financial aid applications and *Financial Aid Handbook* are generally available at the on-campus interview (by invitation). All financial aid is based on demonstrated need. Contact the Financial Aid Office for current information; phone: (909)469-5350. For most financial assistance and all federal programs, submit FAFSA to a federal processor (Title IV school code # 024827); also submit Financial Aid Transcript and Federal Income Tax forms. Approximately 75% of current students receive some form of financial assistance. Average debt after graduation $110,000.

DEGREE REQUIREMENTS. *For D.O.:* satisfactory completion of 4-year program. All students must take the National Board of Osteopathic Medical Examination Part I.

UNIVERSITY OF WISCONSIN

Madison, Wisconsin 53706-1380
Internet site: http://www.wisc.edu

Founded 1848. Located 120 miles N of Chicago. Public control. Semester system. Special facilities: Institute on Aging, Biotechnology Center, McArdle Cancer Research Laboratory, Institute for Enzyme Research, Synchrotron Radiation Center, Waisman Center on Mental Retardation and Human Development, Wisconsin Regional Primate Center, Wisconsin Cancer Center. Library: 5,530,000 volumes; 4,100,000 microforms; 46,100 periodicals/subscriptions. The university's ranking in domestic higher education by NIH awards/grants was 18th,

with 540 awards/grants received; total dollars awarded $124,389,718.

The university's graduate schools include: College of Agriculture and Life Sciences, College of Engineering, College of Letters and Science, Institute for Environmental Studies, Institute for Molecular Biology, School of Business, School of Education, School of Family Resources and Consumer Sciences, School of Pharmacy, Law School, Medical School, School of Nursing, School of Veterinary Medicine.

University of Wisconsin Hospitals and Clinics
600 Highland Avenue
Madison, Wisconsin 53792

Located on the campus. Public control. The hospital is a member of the Council of Teaching Hospitals. Schools located at the center are: Medical School, School of Allied Health, School of Nursing, School of Pharmacy. Special facilities: Wisconsin Clinical Cancer Center, Psychiatric Research Institute. Nationally recognized programs in AIDS, Cancer, Endocrinology, Gastroenterology, Geriatrics, Gynecology, Neurology, Ophthalmology, Otolaryngology, Pulmonary Disease, Rheumatology.

Medical School
Medical Sciences Center, Room 1140
1300 University Avenue
Madison, Wisconsin 53706
Phone: (608)263-4925; fax: (608)262-2327
Internet site: http://www.biostat.wisc.edu
E-mail: janice.waisman@mail.admin.wisc.edu

Initiated a 2-year program in 1907, expanded to 4 years in 1924. Located at the health science center. Library: 162,000 volumes/microforms; 2,000 current periodicals/subscriptions. Affiliated hospital: University of Wisconsin Hospital and Clinics. Special facilities: Biotechnology Center, Cardiovascular Research Center, Center for Neuroscience, Center for Tobacco Research and Intervention, Clinical Nutrition Center, Environmental Toxicology Center, General Clinical Research Center, Institute on Aging, Prevention Center, Primate Research Center, UW Comprehensive Cancer Center, Waisman Center on Mental Retardation and Human Development. Special programs: Medical Scholars Program (for up to 50 high school seniors; conditional admission to the medical school); prematriculation summer sessions.

Annual tuition: residents $14,780, nonresidents $21,630. On-campus rooms and apartments available for both single and married students. Contact Assignments Office for both on- and off-campus housing information; phone: (608)262-2522. Medical students tend to live off-campus. Off-campus housing and personal expenses: approximately $10,000.

Enrollment: 1st-year class 143 (EDP 20); total full-time 607 (men 53%, women 47%). First-year statistics: 20% out of state; 48% attended the University of Wisconsin; 42% women; average age 23; 15% minorities; 70% science majors.

Degrees conferred: M.D., B.S.-M.D., M.D.-M.S., M.D.-Ph.D. (Anatomy, Biochemistry, Biophysics, Cell Biology, Genetics, Immunology, Microbiology, Molecular Biology, Neurosciences, Pathology, Pharmacology, Physiology); has M.S.T.P.

RECRUITMENT PRACTICES AND POLICIES. School has diversity program and actively recruits women/minority applicants. Diversity contact: Assistant Dean for Minority Affairs; phone: (608)263-3713.

ADMISSION REQUIREMENT FOR BACHELOR-M.D. APPLICANTS. Only state residents are eligible. For serious consideration an applicant must have taken 4 years of English, 4 years of mathematics, 3 years of science, 3 years of social studies, 2 years of foreign language. In addition, the applicant should have at least a 3.8 (A = 4) high school GPA, rank in the top 5% of his/her class, and have either a combined SAT score of 1,300 or an ACT score of 30. Submit application, SAT I, SAT III, or ACT, official high school transcripts, letters of recommendations. Apply to Medical Schools Admissions Office by January 1. Interviews are not required. Notification is mailed on April 1; the applicant's deadline is May 1.

ADMISSION REQUIREMENTS FOR FIRST-YEAR APPLICANTS. Preference given to state residents; U.S. citizens, and permanent residents who have taken all their undergraduate work at an accredited U.S. or Canadian institution. *Undergraduate preparation.* Suggested premed courses: 2 courses in biology with labs, 2 courses in inorganic chemistry with labs, 2 courses in organic chemistry with labs, 2 courses in physics with labs, 2 courses in college math. Bachelor's degree from an accredited institution required; 97% of applicants have bachelor's degree awarded prior to enrollment. *Has EDP* for state residents only; applicants must apply through AMCAS (official transcripts sent by mid-May) between June 1 and August 1. Early applications are encouraged. Submit secondary/supplemental application, a personal statement, and 2 recommendations to Admissions Office within 2 weeks of receipt of application. Interviews are by invitation only and generally for final selection. Notification normally begins October 1. *Regular application process.* Apply through AMCAS (file after June 1, before Novem-

ber 1); submit MCAT (will accept MCAT test results from the last 3 years), official transcripts for each school attended (should show at least 90 semester credits/135 quarter credits, submit transcripts by mid-May to AMCAS), service processing fee. Submit an application fee of $45, a supplemental application, a personal statement, preprofessional committee evaluation, and 3 recommendations from science faculty to the Admission Committee within 2–3 weeks of the receipt of supplemental materials, but not later than December 1. Interviews are by invitation only and generally for final selection. In addition, M.D.-Ph.D. integrated-degree applicants must submit a supplemental application and there is a separate interview (by invitation only). GRE is required for most fellowship consideration. Contact the Admissions Office or Student Services Coordinator (phone: (608)262-1348; E-mail: msmith @facstaff.wisc.edu) for current information and any additional requirements for admission. First-year students admitted in fall only. Rolling admission process. Notification starts November 15 and is finished when class is filled. Applicant's response to offer due within 2 weeks of receipt of acceptance letter. School does maintain an alternate list. Phone: (608)263-4925; fax: (608)263-2327.

ADMISSION REQUIREMENTS FOR TRANSFER APPLICANTS. Transfer applicants from other accredited U.S. medical schools are rarely considered and then only into the 3rd year. Contact the Admissions Office for current information and specific requirements for admission.

ADMISSION STANDARDS AND RECOGNITION. *For B.A./B.S.-M.D.:* number of state-resident applicants 300; number of residents enrolled 45; median ACT 32; median GPA 3.96 (A = 4). *For M.D.:* number of state-resident applicants 631, nonresidents 2,062; number of state residents interviewed 164, nonresidents 51; number of residents enrolled 119, nonresidents 24; median MCAT 9.8 (verbal reasoning 9.6; biological sciences 10.1; physical sciences 9.6); median GPA 3.51 (A = 4). Gorman rating 4.42 (scale: strong 4.01–4.49); *U.S. News & World Report* ranked the school in the Top 25 of all U.S. medical schools in primary-care programs; medical ranking by NIH awards was 28th, with 274 awards/grants received; total dollars awarded $67,038,214.

FINANCIAL AID. Grants, institutional loans, HEAL, alternative loan programs, NIH stipends, federal Perkins loans, Stafford subsidized and unsubsidized loans, and service commitment scholarship programs are available. Assistantships/fellowships/stipends may be available for M.D.-Ph.D. degree candidates. Financial aid applications and information are generally available at the on-campus interview (by invitation). All financial aid is based on proven need and generally is in the form of long-term loan. Contact the Financial Aid Office for current information; phone: (608)262-3060. For most financial assistance and all federal programs, submit FAFSA to a federal processor (Title IV school code # 003895); also submit Financial Aid Transcript and Federal Income Tax forms. Approximately 85% of current students receive some form of financial assistance. Average debt after graduation $57,701.

DEGREE REQUIREMENTS. *For B.A./B.S.-M.D.:* generally a 7–9-year program. *For M.D.:* satisfactory completion of 4-year program. All students must pass USMLE Step 1 prior to entering 3rd year; all students must pass USMLE Step 2 prior to awarding of M.D. *For M.D.-M.S.:* generally a 4½–5½-year program. *For M.D.-Ph.D., M.S.T.P.:* generally a 7-year program.

WRIGHT STATE UNIVERSITY
Dayton, Ohio 45435
Internet site: http://www.wright.edu

Founded in 1964; became an independent unit in 1967. Public control. Quarter system. Library: 676,300 volumes; 1,231,000 microforms; 5,312 periodicals/subscriptions; 152 PC work stations. Special facilities: Region II Cancer Resource Center, Biomedical Imaging Laboratory, Cox Research Center, Center for Artificial Intelligence Application. The university's ranking in domestic higher education by NIH awards/grants was 137th, with 24 awards/grants received; total dollars awarded $5,557,398.

The university's graduate studies includes: College of Business and Administration, College of Education and Human Services, College of Engineering and Computer Science, College of Liberal Arts, College of Science and Mathematics, Interdisciplinary Programs, School of Medicine, School of Professional Psychology.

Total university enrollment at main campus: 15,700.

School of Medicine
P.O. Box 1751
Dayton, Ohio 45401-0927
Phone: (937)775-2934; fax: (937)775-3322
Internet site: http://www.med.wright.edu
E-mail: som_saa@desire.wright.edu

Established 1973. Located on main campus in Fairborn. Curriculum emphasis is on primary care. Affiliated hospitals: Children's Hospital Medical Center, Franciscan Medical Center, Good Samaritan Hospital and Health Center, Greene Memorial Hospital, Kettering Medical Center (a member of the Council of Teaching Hospitals), Miami Valley Hospital (a member of the Council of Teaching Hospitals), USAF Medical Center at Wright-Patterson Air Base, Veterans Affairs Medical Center (a member of the Council of Teaching Hospitals). Special programs: prematriculation summer sessions.

Annual tuition: residents $10,641, nonresidents $14,058; fees $1,847. On-campus rooms and apartments available for both single and married students. Annual on-campus housing cost: single students $4,800 (room only), married students $5,472. Contact Office of Residence Services for both on- and off-campus housing information; phone: (937)775-4172. Medical students tend to live off-campus. Off-campus housing and personal expenses: approximately $15,000.

Enrollment: 1st-year class 90 (EDP 5); total full-time 372 (men 47%, women 53%). First-year statistics: 10% out of state; 55.6% women; average age 23; 11% minorities; 68% science majors.

Faculty: full-time 240, part-time/volunteers 1,200.

Degrees conferred: M.D., M.D.-Ph.D. (Anatomy, Biochemistry, Immunology, Microbiology, Pathology, Pharmacology, Physiology).

RECRUITMENT PRACTICES AND POLICIES. School has diversity program and actively recruits women/minority applicants. Diversity contact: Assistant Dean; phone: (937)873-2934.

ADMISSION REQUIREMENTS FOR FIRST-YEAR APPLICANTS. Preference given to state residents; U.S. citizens and permanent residents only. *Undergraduate preparation.* Suggested premed courses: 2 courses in biology with labs, 2 courses in inorganic chemistry with labs, 2 courses in organic chemistry with labs, 2 courses in physics with labs, 2 courses in college math, 2 courses in English. Bachelor's degree from an accredited institution required; 98% of applicants have bachelor's degree awarded prior to enrollment. *Has EDP for state residents only;* applicants must apply through AMCAS (official transcripts sent by mid-May) between June 1 and August 1. Early applications are encouraged. Submit supplemental application, a personal statement, and 2 recommendations to Admissions Office within 2 weeks of receipt of application. Interviews are by invitation only and generally for final selection. Notification normally begins October 1. *Regular application process.* Apply through AMCAS (file after June 1, before November 1); submit MCAT (will accept MCAT test results from the last 3 years), official transcripts for each school attended (should show at least 90 semester credits/135 quarter credits, submit transcripts by mid-May to AMCAS), service processing fee. Submit an application fee of $30, a supplemental application, a personal statement, prepro- fessional committee evaluation, and 3 recommendations from science faculty to Admissions Office within 2–3 weeks of the receipt of supplemental materials, but not later than January 15. Interviews are by invitation only and generally for final selection. Dual-degree applicants must apply to, and be accepted by, both schools; contact the Admissions Office for current information and spe- cific requirements for admission. First-year students admitted in fall only. Rolling admission process. Notifi- cation starts October 15 and is finished when class is filled. Applicant's response to offer due within 2 weeks of receipt of acceptance letter. School does maintain an al- ternate list. Phone: (937)775-2934.

ADMISSION REQUIREMENTS FOR TRANSFER AP- PLICANTS. Accepts transfers from other accredited U.S. medical schools into the 3rd year only. Admission limited to space available. Contact the Admissions Office for current information and specific requirements for ad- mission.

ADMISSION STANDARDS AND RECOGNITION. *For M.D.:* number of state-resident applicants 1,375, non- residents 2,207; number of state residents interviewed 388, nonresidents 44; number of residents enrolled 81, nonresidents 9; median MCAT 8.50; median GPA 3.49. Gorman rating 3.07 (scale: acceptable plus 3.01–3.59); the school's medical ranking by NIH awards was 100th, with 22 awards/grants received; total dollars awarded $5,092,019.

FINANCIAL AID. Scholarships, grants, institutional loans, HEAL, alternative loan programs, federal Perkins loans, Stafford subsidized and unsubsidized loans, and service commitment scholarship programs are available. Financial aid applications and information are generally available at the on-campus interview (by invitation). For scholarships, the selection criteria place heavy reliance on MCAT and undergraduate GPA. Contact the Office of Financial Aid Services for current information; phone: (937)775-2934. For most financial assistance and all fed- eral programs, submit FAFSA by April 1 to a federal processor (Title IV school code # 003078); also submit Financial Aid Transcript and Federal Income Tax forms. Approximately 90% of current students receive some form of financial assistance.

DEGREE REQUIREMENTS. *For M.D.:* satisfactory completion of 4-year program. *For M.D.-Ph.D.:* gener- ally a 7-year program.

YALE UNIVERSITY
New Haven, Connecticut 06520
Internet site: http://www.yale.edu

Founded 1701. Located 80 miles NE of New York City. Private control. Semester system. Special facilities: Bass Center for Molecular and Structural Biology, Boyer Cen- ter for Molecular Medicine, Kline Chemistry Research Laboratory, Josiah Willard Gibbs Research Laboratories for Biology, Physics, Molecular Biology, Biophysics, Kline Biology Tower for Research and Graduate Training in the Biological Sciences. Library: 10,600,000 volumes; 5,000,000 microforms; 55,000 periodicals/subscriptions. The university's ranking in domestic higher education by NIH awards/grants was 6th, with 686 awards/grants re- ceived; total dollars awarded $187,219,234.

The university's graduate schools: Divinity School, Graduate School of Arts and Science, Law School, School of Architecture, School of Art, School of Drama, School of Forestry and Environmental Studies, School of Management, School of Medicine, School of Music, School of Nursing.

Total university enrollment at main campus: 11,000.

Yale–New Haven Medical Center
20 York Street
New Haven, Connecticut 06504

Private control. Yale–New Haven Hospital is a member of the Council of Teaching Hospitals. Schools located at medical center are: School of Medicine, School of Nurs- ing. *Barron's Guide* placed Yale–New Haven Hospital among the Top 25 most prestigious U.S. hospital/medical centers. Nationally recognized programs in AIDS, Cancer, Cardiology, Endocrinology, Gastroenterology, Geriatrics, Gynecology, Otolaryngology, Psychiatry, Pul- monary Disease, Rheumatology, Urology.

School of Medicine
367 Cedar Street
New Haven, Connecticut 06510
Phone: (203)785-2643; fax: (203)785-3234
Internet site: http://info.med.yale.edu/medadmit
E-mail: medicalschool.admission@quickmail.yale.edu

Established 1810. Located at the medical center. Se- mester system. The first 2 years of study are spent in the basic medical sciences. Affiliated hospitals: Yale–New Haven Hospital, West Haven Veteran's Administration Hospital, Bridgeport Hospital, Danbury Hospital, Green- wich Hospital, Griffin Hospital, Derby Hospital of Saint Raphael, New Haven, Lawrence and Memorial Hospitals, New London Norwalk Hospital, Saint Mary's Hospital, Waterbury Saint Vincent's Medical Center, Bridgeport

Waterbury Hospital. Library: 360,000 volumes/microforms; 2,500 current periodicals/subscriptions. Special programs: summer programs for underrepresented minorities.

Annual tuition: $26,975; fees $150. On-campus rooms and apartments available for both single and married students. Contact Housing Department for both on- and off-campus housing information; phone: (203)432-9756. Off-campus housing and personal expenses: approximately $13,000.

Enrollment: 1st-year class 101 (EDP 5); total full-time 481 (men 50%, women 50%). First-year statistics: 90% out of state; 50% women; average age 24; 17% underrepresented minorities; 27% other minorities; 80% science majors.

Degrees conferred: M.D., M.P.H., Dr.P.H., M.D.-J.D., M.D.-M.P.H., M.D.-Ph.D. (Biology, Cell Biology, Cellular and Molecular Physiology, Chemistry, Computer Science, Engineering and Applied Science, Epidemiology and Public Health, Experimental Pathology, Genetics, Immunobiology, Molecular Biophysics and Biochemistry, Molecular Cell Biology, Neurobiology, Neurosciences, Pharmacology); has M.S.T.P.

RECRUITMENT PRACTICES AND POLICIES. School has diversity program and actively recruits women/minority applicants. Diversity contact: Office of Multicultural Affairs; phone: (203)785-7545.

ADMISSION REQUIREMENTS FOR FIRST-YEAR APPLICANTS. Preference given to U.S. citizens and permanent residents. *Undergraduate preparation.* Suggested premed courses: 2 courses in biology with labs, 2 courses in inorganic chemistry with labs, 2 courses in organic chemistry with labs, 2 courses in physics with labs; bachelor's degree from an accredited institution required; 98% of applicants have bachelor's degrees awarded prior to enrollment. *Has EDP;* applicants apply directly to the Yale School of Medicine between June 1 and August 1. Early applications are encouraged. Submit the application, MCAT, official transcripts, a personal statement, and 3 recommendations to Admissions Office. Interviews are by invitation only and generally for final selection. Notification normally begins October 1. *Regular application process.* Apply directly to the Yale School of Medicine after May 1, before October 15; apply by October 1 for M.D.-Ph.D; all supplemental materials must be received by October 15. Submit MCAT (will accept MCAT test results from the last 3 years), official transcripts for each school attended (should show at least 90 semester credits/135 quarter credits), an application fee of $55, and 3 recommendations to the Admissions Office. All addi-

tional materials must arrive no later than November 15. Card E should be sent directly to M.D.-Ph.D. program. Interviews are by invitation only and generally for final selection. Combined degree applicants should obtain application and admission information directly from the School of Medicine's specific department or the School of Law (M.D.-J.D.) at Yale University. Contact the Admissions Office for current information and specific requirements for admission. First-year students admitted in fall only. Notification starts March 15 and is finished by March 31. Applicant's response to offer and $100 deposit due within 3 weeks of receipt of acceptance letter. Phone: (203)785-2643.

ADMISSION REQUIREMENTS FOR TRANSFER APPLICANTS. Yale does not accept transfer applicants. On rare occasions, if a compelling case can be made, the school will consider applicants on a case-by-case basis. Contact the Admissions Offices for current information and specific requirements for admission.

ADMISSION STANDARDS AND RECOGNITION. *For M.D.:* number of state-resident applicants 156, nonresidents 3,472; number of state residents interviewed 38, nonresidents 812; number of residents enrolled 9, nonresidents 92; median MCAT 11.2 (verbal reasoning 10.7; biological sciences 11.5; physical sciences 11.2); median GPA 3.72 (A = 4). *Barron's Guide* placed the school among the Top 25 most prestigious U.S. medical schools; Gorman rating 4.89 (scale: very strong 4.51–4.99); *U.S. News & World Report* ranked the school in the Top 25 of all U.S. medical schools; the school's medical ranking by NIH awards was 4th, with 606 awards/grants received; total dollars awarded $170,773,935.

FINANCIAL AID. Scholarships, merit scholarships, minority scholarships, grants-in-aid, institutional loans, HEAL, alternative loan programs, NIH stipends, federal Perkins loans, Stafford subsidized and unsubsidized loans, and service commitment scholarship programs are available. Assistantships/fellowships/stipends may be available for M.D.-Ph.D. combined degree candidates. All financial aid is based on documented need. Financial-aid applications and information are generally available at the on-campus interview (by invitation) or are sent out to all applicants in January. Contact the Financial Aid Office for current information; phone: (203)785-2645. For most financial assistance and all federal programs, submit FAFSA to a federal processor (Title IV school code # E00450); also submit Financial Aid Transcript and Federal Income Tax forms. Approximately 90% of current students receive some form of financial assistance. Average debt after graduation $76,644.

DEGREE REQUIREMENTS. *For M.D.:* satisfactory completion of 4-year program; thesis. All students must pass USMLE Step 1 prior to entering 3rd year; all students must pass USMLE Step 2 prior to awarding of M.D. *For M.D.-M.P.H.:* generally 5–5½-year program. *For M.D.-Ph.D.,-J.D.:* generally 6–7-year program.

YESHIVA UNIVERSITY
New York, New York, 10033-3201
Internet site: http://www.yu.edu

Founded 1886. Private control. Semester system. Special facilities: Center for Research in Cancer, Rose Fitzgerald Kennedy Center for Research in Mental Retardation and Human Development, Jack and Pearl Resnik Gerontology Center, Center for Psychological Intervention. Library: 1,013,700 volumes; 1,120,000 microforms; 10,100 periodicals/subscriptions; 200 computer work stations. The university's ranking in domestic higher education by NIH awards/grants was 29th with 264 awards/grants received; total dollars awarded $83,187,824.

The university's graduate colleges/schools: Albert Einstein College of Medicine, Azrieli Graduate School of Jewish Education and Administration, Benjamin N. Cardoza School of Law, Bernard Revel Graduate School, Ferkauf Graduate School of Psychology, Wurzweiler School of Social Work.

Total university enrollment at main campus: 5,400.

Jacobi Medical Center
Pelham Parkway South and Eastchester Road
Bronx, New York 10461

Formerly Bronx Municipal Hospital. Public control. The medical center is a member of the Council of Teaching Hospitals.

Albert Einstein College of Medicine
Jack and Pearl Resnick Campus
1300 Morris Park Avenue
Bronx, New York 10461
Phone: (718)430-2106, fax: (718)430-8825
Internet site: http://www.aecom.yu.edu
E-mail: admission@aecom.yu.edu

Established 1955. Located in the northeast Bronx, adjacent to Jacobi Medical Center. The college has 2 postgraduate divisions, the Sue Golding Graduate Division of Medical Science and the Belfer Institute for Advanced Biomedical Studies. Affiliated hospitals: Jacobi Medical Center, North Central Bronx Hospital, Beth Israel Medical Center, Montefiore Medical Center (the medical center is a member of the Council of Teaching Hospitals),

Bronx Lebanon Hospital Center, Long Island Jewish Medical Center, Catholic Medical Center. Library: 200,000 volumes/microforms; 2,400 current periodicals/subscriptions. Special facilities: Allman Research Center, Irwin S. and Sylvia Chanin Institute for Cancer Research, Arthur B. and Diane Belfer Educational Center for Health Sciences, Louis E. and Dora Rousso Center. Special programs: Biomedical Sciences Pathways, International Health Fellowships, and programs in Israel, Germany, France, Sweden, and Japan; prematriculation summer sessions.

Annual tuition: $28,200; fees $1,600. The college operates 2 apartment complexes for both single and married students. Contact Housing Office for both on- and off-campus housing information; phone: (718)430-3552. Annual housing, food, and personal expenses: approximately $9,800.

Enrollment: 1st-year class 178; total full-time 720 (men 55%, women 45%). First-year statistics: 50% out of state; 23 states represented; 64 undergraduate institutions represented; 45.6% women; average age 23; 8% minorities; 71% science majors.

Faculty: full-time approximately 1,000.

Degrees conferred: M.D., M.D.-Ph.D. (Anatomy and Structural Biology, Biochemistry, Cell Biology, Developmental and Molecular Biology, Microbiology and Immunology, Molecular Genetics, Molecular Pharmacology, Neurosciences, Pathology, Physiology and Biophysics); has M.S.T.P.

RECRUITMENT PRACTICES AND POLICIES. School has diversity program and actively recruits women/minority applicants. Diversity contact: Office of Minority Student Affairs; phone: (718)901-8712.

ADMISSION REQUIREMENTS FOR FIRST-YEAR APPLICANTS. Preference given to state residents; U.S. citizens and permanent residents only. *Undergraduate preparation.* Suggested premed courses: 2 courses in biology with labs, 2 courses in general chemistry with labs, 2 courses in organic chemistry with labs, 2 courses in physics with labs, 1 course in college math, 2 courses in English. Bachelor's degree from an accredited institution required; all applicants have bachelor's degree awarded prior to enrollment. *Has EDP;* applicants must apply through AMCAS (official transcripts sent by mid-May) between June 1 and August 1. Early applications are encouraged. Submit supplemental application, a personal statement, and 2 recommendations to Admissions Office within 2 weeks of receipt of application. Interviews are by invitation only and generally for final selection. Notification normally begins October 1. *Regular application process.* Apply through AMCAS (file after June 1, before

December 1); submit MCAT (will accept MCAT test results from the last 3 years), official transcripts for each school attended (should show at least 90 semester credits/135 quarter credits, submit transcripts by mid-May to AMCAS), service processing fee. Submit an application fee of $75, a supplemental application, a personal statement, preprofessional committee evaluation, and 3 recommendations from science faculty to Admissions Office within 2–3 weeks of the receipt of supplemental materials; supporting documentation must be received by December 31. Interviews are by invitation only and generally for final selection. M.S.T.P. applicants must complete a M.S.T.P. application in addition to the regular application; contact the Admissions Office for current information and specific requirements for admission. First-year students admitted in fall only. Rolling admission process. Notification starts January 15 and is finished when class is filled. Applicant's response to offer and $100 deposit due within 2 weeks of receipt of acceptance letter. School does maintain an alternate list. Phone: (718)430-2106; fax: (718)430-8825; E-mail: admissions @alcom.yu.edu.

ADMISSION REQUIREMENTS FOR TRANSFER APPLICANTS. Does not accept transfer applicants. Contact the Admissions Office for current information and any modification of policy.

ADMISSION STANDARDS AND RECOGNITION. *For M.D.:* number of state-resident applicants 2,359, non-residents 7,178; number of state residents interviewed 578, nonresidents 1,131; number of residents enrolled 85, nonresidents 93; median MCAT 10.6 (verbal reasoning 10.0; biological sciences 10.9; physical sciences 10.9); median GPA 3.62 (A = 4). *Barron's Guide* placed the college among the Top 25 most prestigious U.S. medical schools; Gorman rating 4.28 (scale: strong 4.01–4.49); *U.S. News & World Report* ranked the college in the Top 25 of all U.S. medical schools; the college's medical ranking by NIH awards was 22nd, with 260 awards/grants received; total dollars awarded $82,708,444.

FINANCIAL AID. Scholarships, merit scholarships, minority scholarships, grants-in-aid, institutional loans, HEAL, alternative loan programs, NIH stipends, federal Perkins loans, Stafford subsidized and unsubsidized loans, and service commitment scholarship programs are available. M.S.T.P. carries a full tuition scholarship and a stipend. All financial aid is based on documented need. Financial aid applications and information are generally available at the on-campus interview (by invitation). For scholarships, the selection criteria place heavy reliance on MCAT and undergraduate GPA. Contact the Student Finance Office for current information; phone: (718)430-2336. For most financial assistance and all federal programs, submit FAFSA to a federal processor (Title IV school code # G09895); also submit Financial Aid Transcript and Federal Income Tax forms. Approximately 75% of current students receive some form of financial assistance; 50% of students receive institutional loans and scholarships. Average debt after graduation $75,000.

DEGREE REQUIREMENTS. *For M.D.:* satisfactory completion of 4-year program. All students must pass USMLE Step 1 prior to entering 3rd year; all students must pass USMLE Step 2 prior to awarding of M.D. *For M.D.-Ph.D., M.S.T.P.:* generally a 7-year program.

Indexes

DENTAL SCHOOLS

A

Alabama at Birmingham, University of, School of Dentistry, Birmingham, AL

B

Baylor College of Dentistry, Dallas, TX; see Texas A&M University System
Boston University, School of Dental Medicine, Boston, MA
Buffalo, University at, School of Dentistry, Buffalo, NY

C

California at Los Angeles, University of, School of Dentistry, CA
California at San Francisco, University of, School of Dentistry, CA
Case Western Reserve University, School of Dentistry, Cleveland, OH
Columbia University, School of Dental and Oral Surgery, New York, NY
Creighton University, School of Dentistry, Omaha, NE

H

Harvard University, Harvard School of Dental Medicine, Boston, MA
Howard University, College of Dentistry, Washington, DC

I

Indiana University, School of Dentistry, Indianapolis, IN
Iowa, University of, School of Dentistry, Iowa City, IA

L

Loma Linda University, School of Dentistry, Loma Linda, CA
Louisiana State University, School of Dentistry, New Orleans, LA

M

Marquette University, School of Dentistry, Milwaukee, WI
Maryland at Baltimore, University of, Baltimore Dental College of Dental Surgery, Dental School, Baltimore, MD
Medical College of Georgia, School of Dentistry, Augusta, GA
Medical University of South Carolina, College of Dental Medicine, Charleston, SC
Medicine and Dentistry of New Jersey, University of, New Jersey Dental School, Newark, NJ
Meharry Medical College, School of Dentistry, Nashville, TN
Michigan, University of, School of Dentistry, Ann Arbor, MI
Minnesota, University of, School of Dentistry, Minneapolis, MN
Mississippi, University of, School of Dentistry, Jackson, MS
Missouri at Kansas City, University of, School of Dentistry, Kansas City, MO

N

Nebraska, University of, College of Dentistry, Lincoln, NE
New York University, College of Dentistry, David B. Kriser Dental Center, New York, NY
North Carolina, University of, School of Dentistry, Chapel Hill, NC

Northwestern University, Dental School, Chicago, IL
Nova Southeastern University, College of Dental Medicine, Ft. Lauderdale, FL

O

Ohio State University, College of Dentistry, Columbus, OH
Oklahoma, University of, College of Dentistry, Oklahoma City, OK
Oregon Health Sciences University, School of Dentistry, Portland, OR

P

Pacific, University of the, School of Dentistry, San Francisco, CA
Pennsylvania, University of, School of Dental Medicine, Philadelphia, PA
Pittsburgh, University of, School of Dental Medicine, Pittsburgh, PA

S

Southern California, University of, School of Dentistry, Los Angeles, CA
SUNY at Stony Brook, School of Dental Medicine, Stony Brook, NY

T

Tennessee at Memphis, University of, College of Dentistry, Memphis, TN
Texas A&M University System, Baylor College of Dentistry, Dallas, TX
Texas Health Science Center, University of, Houston Dental Branch, Houston, TX
Texas Health Science Center at San Antonio, University of, Dental School, San Antonio, TX

V

Virginia Commonwealth University, Medical College of Virginia, School of Dentistry, Richmond, VA

W

Washington, University of, School of Dentistry, Seattle, WA
West Virginia University, School of Dentistry, Morgantown, WV

MEDICAL SCHOOLS

A

Alabama at Birmingham, University of, School of Medicine, Birmingham, AL
Albany Medical College; see Union University, NY
Albert Einstein College of Medicine; see Yeshiva University, NY
Allegheny University, Medical College of Pennsylvania/Hahnemann School of Medicine, Philadelphia, PA
Arizona, University of, College of Medicine, Tucson, AZ
Arkansas, University of, College of Medicine, Little Rock, AR

B

Baylor College of Medicine, Houston, TX
Boston University, School of Medicine, Boston, MA
Bowman Gray School of Medicine; see Wake Forest University, NC
Brown University, School of Medicine, Providence, RI
Buffalo, University at, School of Medicine and Biomedical Sciences, Buffalo, NY

C

California at Davis, University of, School of Medicine, Davis, CA
California at Irvine, University of, College of Medicine, Irvine, CA
California at Los Angeles, University of, School of Medicine, Los Angeles, CA
California at San Diego, University of, School of Medicine, San Diego, CA
California at San Francisco, University of, School of Medicine, San Francisco, CA

Case Western Reserve University, School of Medicine, Cleveland, OH
Central del Caribe, Universidad, School of Medicine, Bayamón, PR
Chicago Medical School; see Finch University of Health Sciences, IL
Chicago, University of, Pritzker School of Medicine, Chicago, IL
Cincinnati, University of, College of Medicine, Cincinnati, OH
Colorado Health Sciences Center, University of, School of Medicine, Denver, CO
Columbia University, College of Physicians and Surgeons, New York, NY
Connecticut, University of, School of Medicine, Farmington, CT
Cornell University, Medical College, New York, NY
Creighton University, School of Medicine, Omaha, NE

D

Dartmouth College, Dartmouth Medical School, Hanover, NH
Duke University, School of Medicine, Durham, NC

E

East Carolina University, School of Medicine, Greenville, NC
East Tennessee State University, James H. Quillen College of Medicine, Johnson City, TN
Eastern Virginia Medical School of the Medical College of Hampton Roads, Norfolk, VA
Emory University, School of Medicine, Atlanta, GA

F

Finch University of Health Sciences, Chicago Medical School, North Chicago, IL
Florida, University of, College of Medicine, Gainesville, FL

G

George Washington University, School of Medicine, Washington, DC
Georgetown University, School of Medicine, Washington, DC

H

Harvard University, Harvard Medical School, Boston, MA
Hawaii, University of, John A. Burns School of Medicine, Honolulu, HI

Howard University, College of Medicine, Washington, DC

I

Illinois at Chicago, University of, College of Medicine, Chicago, IL
Indiana University, School of Medicine, Indianapolis, IN
Iowa, University of, College of Medicine, Iowa City, IA

J

Jefferson Medical College; see Thomas Jefferson University, PA
Johns Hopkins University, School of Medicine, Baltimore, MD

K

Kansas, University of, School of Medicine, Kansas City, KS
Kentucky, University of, College of Medicine, Lexington, KY

L

Loma Linda University, School of Medicine, Loma Linda, CA
Louisiana State University, School of Medicine, New Orleans, LA
Louisiana State University, School of Medicine, Shreveport, LA
Louisville, University of, School of Medicine, Louisville, KY
Loyola University Chicago, Stritch School of Medicine, Maywood, IL

M

Marshall University, School of Medicine, Huntington, WV
Maryland at Baltimore, University of, School of Medicine, Baltimore, MD
Massachusetts, University of, Medical School, Worcester, MA
Mayo Medical School, Rochester, MN
Medical College of Georgia, School of Medicine, Augusta, GA
Medical College of Ohio, Toledo, OH
Medical College of Pennsylvania/Hahnemann School of Medicine; see Allegheny University of the Health Sciences, PA
Medical College of Virginia; see Virginia Commonwealth University, VA
Medical College of Wisconsin, Milwaukee, WI
Medical University of South Carolina, College of Medicine, Charleston, SC

OSTEOPATHIC SCHOOLS

Health Sciences, University of, College of Osteopathic Medicine, Kansas City, MO

Kirksville College of Osteopathic Medicine, Kirksville, MO

Lake Erie College of Osteopathic Medicine, Erie, PA

Medicine and Dentistry of New Jersey, University of, School of Osteopathic Medicine, Stratford, NJ

Michigan State University, College of Osteopathic Medicine, Lansing, MI

Midwestern University, Arizona College of Osteopathic Medicine, Glendale, AZ

Midwestern University, Chicago College of Osteopathic Medicine, Downers Grove, IL

New England, University of, College of Osteopathic Medicine, Biddeford, ME

New York Institute of Technology, New York College of Osteopathic Medicine, Old Westbury, NY

North Texas Health Sciences Center, University of, Texas College of Osteopathic Medicine, Ft. Worth, TX

Nova Southeastern University, College of Osteopathic Medicine, Ft. Lauderdale, FL

Ohio University College of Osteopathic Medicine, Athens, OH

Oklahoma State University, College of Osteopathic Medicine, Tulsa, OK

Osteopathic Medicine and Health Sciences, University of, Des Moines, IA

Philadelphia College of Osteopathic Medicine, Philadelphia, PA

Touro College, College of Osteopathic Medicine, San Francisco, CA

Western University of Health Sciences, Pomona, CA

West Virginia School of Osteopathic Medicine, Lewisburg, WV

MEDICAL AND DENTAL SCHOOLS BY STATE

Alabama

University of Alabama at Birmingham, School of Dentistry

University of Alabama at Birmingham, School of Medicine

University of South Alabama, College of Medicine

Arizona

Arizona College of Osteopathic Medicine; see Midwestern University, IL

University of Arizona, College of Medicine

Arkansas

University of Arkansas for Medical Sciences, College of Medicine

California

University of California at Davis, School, of Medicine

University of California at Irvine, College of, Medicine

University of California at Los Angeles, School of Dentistry

University of California at Los Angeles, School of Medicine

University of California at San Diego, School of Medicine

University of California at San Francisco, School of Dentistry

University of California at San Francisco, School of Medicine

Loma Linda University, School of Dentistry

Loma Linda University, School of Medicine

Touro College, College of Osteopathic Medicine

University of the Pacific, School of Dentistry

University of Southern California, School of Dentistry

University of Southern California, School of Medicine

Stanford University, School of Medicine

Western University, College of Osteopathic Medicine of the Pacific

Colorado

University of Colorado, School of Dentistry

University of Colorado, School of Medicine

Connecticut

University of Connecticut, School of Dental Medicine

University of Connecticut, School of Medicine

Yale University, School of Medicine

District of Columbia

George Washington University, School of Medicine and Health Sciences

Georgetown University, School of Medicine

Howard University, College of Dentistry

Howard University, College of Medicine

Florida

University of Florida, College of Dentistry

University of Florida, College of Medicine, J. Hillis Miller Health Center

University of Miami, School of Medicine

Nova Southeastern University Health Professions Division, College of Osteopathic Medicine

University of South Florida, College of Medicine

Georgia

Emory University, School of Medicine

Medical College of Georgia, School of Dentistry

Medical College of Georgia, School of Medicine

Mercer University, School of Medicine

Morehouse School of Medicine

Hawaii

University of Hawaii, John A. Burns School of Medicine

Illinois

University of Chicago, Pritzker School of Medicine

Finch University of Health Sciences/Chicago Medical School

University of Illinois at Chicago, Health Sciences Center, College of Dentistry

University of Illinois at Chicago, Health Sciences Center, College of Medicine

Loyola University of Chicago, Stritch School of Medicine

Midwestern University, Arizona College of Osteopathic Medicine

Midwestern University, Chicago College of Osteopathic Medicine

Northwestern University Dental School

Northwestern University Medical School

West Virginia

Marshall University, School of Medicine
West Virginia School of Osteopathic Medicine
West Virginia University, School of Dentistry
West Virginia University, School of Medicine, Health Sciences Center

Wisconsin

Marquette University, School of Dentistry
Medical College of Wisconsin
University of Wisconsin Medical School

MEDICAL AND DENTAL SCHOOLS—PRIVATE

A

Albany Medical College; see Union University, NY
Albert Einstein College of Medicine; see Yeshiva University, NY
Allegheny University, Medical College of Pennsylvania/Hahnemann School of Medicine, Philadelphia, PA
Arizona College of Osteopathic Medicine, AZ; see Midwestern University

B

Baylor College of Medicine, Houston, TX
Boston University, Henry B. Goldman School of Dental Medicine, Boston, MA
Boston University, School of Medicine, Boston, MA
Bowman Gray School of Medicine; see Wake Forest University, NC
Brown University, School of Medicine, Providence, RI

C

Case Western Reserve University, School of Dentistry, Cleveland, OH
Case Western Reserve University, School of Medicine, Cleveland, OH
Central del Caribe, Universidad, School of Medicine, Bayamón, PR
Chicago College of Osteopathic Medicine, IL; see Midwestern University
Chicago Medical School; see Finch University of Health Sciences, IL
Chicago, University of, Pritzker School of Medicine, Chicago, IL

College of Osteopathic Medicine of the Pacific, CA; see Western University of Health Sciences
Columbia University, College of Physicians and Surgeons, New York, NY
Columbia University, School of Dental and Oral Surgery, New York, NY
Cornell University, Medical College, New York, NY
Creighton University, School of Dentistry, Omaha, NE
Creighton University, School of Medicine, Omaha, NE

D

Dartmouth College, Dartmouth Medical School, Hanover, NH
Detroit Mercy, University of, School of Dentistry, Detroit, MI
Duke University, School of Medicine, Durham, NC

E

Eastern Virginia Medical School of the Medical College of Hampton Roads, Norfolk, VA
Emory University, School of Medicine, Atlanta, GA

F

Finch University of Health Sciences, Chicago Medical School, North Chicago, IL

G

George Washington University, School of Medicine and Health Sciences, Washington, DC
Georgetown University, School of Medicine, Washington, DC

H

Harvard University, Harvard Medical School, Boston, MA
Harvard University, Harvard School of Dental Medicine, Boston, MA
Health Sciences, University of, College of Osteopathic Medicine, Kansas City, MO
Howard University, College of Dentistry, Washington, DC
Howard University, College of Medicine, Washington, DC

J

Jefferson Medical College; see Thomas Jefferson University, PA

Johns Hopkins University, School of Medicine, Baltimore, MD

K

Kirksville College of Osteopathic Medicine, Kirksville, MO

L

Lake Erie College of Osteopathic Medicine, Erie, PA
Loma Linda University, School of Dentistry, Loma Linda, CA
Loma Linda University, School of Medicine, Loma Linda, CA
Loyola University of Chicago, Stritch School of Medicine, Maywood, IL

M

Marquette University, School of Dentistry, Milwaukee, WI
Mayo Clinic and Mayo Foundation, Mayo Medical School, Rochester, MN
Medical College of Pennsylvania/Hahnemann School of Medicine; see Allegheny University of the Health Sciences, PA
Meharry Medical College, School of Dentistry, Nashville, TN
Meharry Medical College, School of Medicine, Nashville, TN
Mercer University, School of Medicine, Macon, GA
Miami, University of, School of Medicine, Miami, FL
Midwestern University, Arizona College of Osteopathic Medicine, Glendale, AZ
Midwestern University, Chicago College of Osteopathic Medicine, Downers Grove, IL
Morehouse School of Medicine, Atlanta, GA

N

New England, University of College of Osteopathic Medicine, Biddeford, ME
New York Institute of Technology, New York College of Osteopathic Medicine, Old Westbury, NY
New York Medical College, Valhalla, NY
New York University, College of Dentistry, David B. Kriser Dental Center, New York, NY
New York University, School of Medicine, New York, NY
Northwestern University, Dental School, Chicago, IL
Northwestern University, Medical School, Chicago, IL

MEDICAL AND DENTAL SCHOOLS—PUBLIC

MEDICAL SCHOOLS OFFERING COMBINED B.A./B.S.–M.D. PROGRAMS

[1]Medical schools offering programs combined within their own parent institution.
[2]Program is limited to state residents.

JOINT/DUAL-DEGREE PROGRAMS

D.D.S.-M.B.A.

Case Western Reserve University
Columbia University
New York University
University of Southern California

D.D.S.-M.P.H.

University of California at Los Angeles
Columbia University
University of Michigan
University of North Carolina
Ohio State University
Texas A&M University System, Baylor
    College of Dentistry
University of Texas, Houston

D.D.S.-M.S.

University at Buffalo
University of California at Los
    Angeles
University of California at San
    Francisco
Case Western Reserve University
University of Chicago
Columbia University
Loma Linda University
Marquette University
University of Minnesota
University of North Carolina
Ohio State University
University of Southern California
University of Texas at San Antonio
Virginia Commonwealth University
University of Washington

D.D.S.-M.S.D.

Indiana University
University of Washington
West Virginia University

D.D.S.-Ph.D.

University at Buffalo
University of California at Los
    Angeles
University of California at San
    Francisco
Case Western Reserve University
University of Illinois at Chicago
University of Maryland
University of Michigan
University of Minnesota
University of Missouri—Kansas City
University of Utah
West Virginia University

D.M.D.-M.B.A.

University of Pennsylvania
Temple University

D.M.D.-M.D.

University of Connecticut
Harvard University
University of Kentucky

D.M.D.-M.P.P.

Harvard University

D.M.D.-M.P.H.

University of Connecticut
Harvard University

D.M.D.-M.S.

Medical College of Georgia
University of Louisville
University of Medicine and Dentistry of
    New Jersey
Oregon Health Sciences University
Tufts University

D.M.D.-Ph.D.

Medical College of Georgia
University of Medicine and Dentistry of
    New Jersey
University of Pennsylvania

D.O.-M.B.A.

New York Institute of Technology
Philadelphia College of Osteopathic
    Medicine

D.O.-M.P.H.

University of North Texas
Nova Southeastern University
Philadelphia College of Osteopathic
    Medicine

D.O.-M.S.

Michigan State University
New York Institute of Technology
University of North Texas

D.O.-Ph.D.

Michigan State University
University of Medicine and Dentistry of
    New Jersey
University of North Texas
University of Ohio
Oklahoma State University

D.S.T.P.

University of Iowa
University of San Francisco

M.D.-M.A.

Boston University
University of California at Davis
University of Chicago
Duke University
Medical College of Wisconsin
Michigan State University
University of Texas, Southwestern
    Medical College
Washington University

M.D.-M.B.A.

Boston University
University at Buffalo
University of California at Davis
University of California at Irvine
University of Chicago
University of Colorado Health Sciences
    Center
Dartmouth Medical School
Duke University
Georgetown University
University of Pennsylvania
University of Rochester
Texas Tech University
Thomas Jefferson University
Tufts University
Wake Forest University

M.D.-J.D.

University of Chicago
Duke University
University of Medicine and Dentistry of
    New Jersey, Robert Wood Johnson
    Medical College
Southern Illinois University
Yale University

M.D.-M.H.A.

Thomas Jefferson University

M.D.-M.M.

Northwestern University

M.D.-M.M.S.

University of Texas at Galveston

M.D.-M.P.A.

Boston University

M.D.-M.P.H.

Allegheny University
University of Arizona
Baylor College of Medicine
Boston University
University at Buffalo
University of California at Davis
University of California at Los Angeles
University of California at San Diego
University of California at San Francisco
Columbia University
University of Connecticut
Duke University
Emory University
George Washington University
Harvard University
Johns Hopkins University
Louisiana State University
University of Medicine and Dentistry of
    New Jersey, Robert Wood Johnson
    Medical School
University of Michigan
Morehouse School of Medicine
University of North Carolina
Northwestern University
Oregon Health Sciences University
University of Puerto Rico
University of Rochester
St. Louis University
University of South Carolina
University of South Florida
University of Texas, Houston
Tufts University
Tulane University
University of Utah
Vanderbilt University
Yale University

M.D.-M.P.P.

Harvard University

M.D.-M.S.

Allegheny University
University of Arkansas
Boston University
Brown University
University at Buffalo
University of California at Davis
University of California at San Francisco
University of Cincinnati
Finch University of Health Sciences
University of Illinois at Chicago
University of Iowa
University of Kentucky
Loma Linda University
Medical College of Ohio
Medical College of Wisconsin
Meharry Medical College
Michigan State University
University of Michigan

University of Mississippi
University of Missouri at Columbia
University of Nebraska
University of New Mexico
New York Medical College
University of Puerto Rico
University of Rochester
Rush University
Stanford University
University of Texas at Galveston
University of Texas, Houston
University of Texas, Southwestern
Tufts University
Wake Forest University
Washington University
Wayne State University
University of Wisconsin

M.D.-M.S.E

Johns Hopkins University

M.D.-Ph.D.

University of Alabama at Birmingham[1]
University of Arizona
University of Arkansas
Baylor College of Medicine[1]
Boston University
Brown University
University at Buffalo
University of California at Davis
University of California at Irvine
University of California at Los Angeles[1]
University of California at San Diego[1]
University of California at San
    Francisco[1]
Case Western Reserve University[1]
University of Chicago[1]
University of Cincinnati
University of Colorado Health Sciences
    Center
Columbia University[1]
University of Connecticut
Cornell University[1]
Creighton University
Dartmouth Medical School
Duke University[1]
East Carolina University
East Tennessee State University
Emory University[1]
Finch University of Health Sciences
University of Florida
George Washington University
Georgetown University
Harvard University[3]
University of Hawaii
Howard University
University of Illinois at Chicago
Indiana University
University of Iowa[1]
Johns Hopkins University[1]

University of Kansas
University of Kentucky
Loma Linda University
Louisiana State University at New
    Orleans
Louisiana State University at Shreveport
Loyola University Chicago
Marshall University
University of Maryland at Baltimore
University of Massachusetts
Mayo Medical School
Medical College of Georgia
Medical College of Ohio
Medical College of Wisconsin
Medical University of South Carolina
University of Medicine and Dentistry of
    New Jersey, New Jersey Medical
    School
University of Medicine and Dentistry of
    New Jersey, Robert Wood Johnson
    Medical School
Meharry Medical College
University of Miami
University of Michigan
Michigan State University
University of Minnesota
University of Mississippi
University of Missouri—Columbia
Morehouse School of Medicine
Mount Sinai School of Medicine
University of Nebraska
University of Nevada
New York Medical College
New York University
University of North Carolina
University of North Dakota
Northwestern University
Ohio State University
University of Oklahoma
Oregon Health Sciences University
University of Pennsylvania
Pennsylvania State University
University of Pittsburgh[4]
University of Rochester[1]
Rush University
University of South Alabama
University of South Carolina
University of South Dakota
University of Southern California
Stanford University[1]
St. Louis University
SUNY at Stony Brook Health Sciences
    Center[1]
SUNY Health Sciences Center at
    Syracuse
Temple University
University of Tennessee at Memphis
Texas A&M University
University of Texas at Galveston
University of Texas, Houston
University of Texas at San Antonio
University of Texas, Southwestern[1]
Texas Tech University

Thomas Jefferson University
Tufts University[1]
Tulane University
Union University
University of Utah
Vanderbilt University[1]

University of Vermont
University of Virginia
Virginia Commonwealth University
Wake Forest University
Washington University[1]
University of Washington[1]

Wayne State University
West Virginia University
University of Wisconsin
Wright State University
Yale University[1]
Yeshiva University[1]

[1]Indicates U.S. Medical Scientist Training Programs supported by NIH in 1997.
[2]In cooperation with Rockefeller University-Sloan Kettering Institute.
[3]In cooperation with MIT.
[4]In cooperation with Carnegie Mellon University.

Members of the National Institutes of Health

Listed below are the 24 separate institutes, centers, and divisions which make up the NIH.

National Cancer Institute (NCI)

National Eye Institute (NEI)

National Heart, Lung, and Blood Institute (NHLBI)

National Human Genome Research Institute (NHGRI)

National Institute on Aging (NIA)

National Institute on Alcohol Abuse and Alcoholism (NIAAA)

National Institute of Allergy and Infectious Diseases (NIAID)

National Institute of Arthritis and Musculoskeletal and Skin Diseases (NIAMS)

National Institute of Child Health and Human Development (NICHD)

National Institute on Deafness and Other Communication Disorders (NIDCD)

National Institute of Dental Research (NIDR)

National Institute of Diabetes and Digestive and Kidney Diseases (NIDDK)

National Institute on Drug Abuse (NIDA)

National Institute of Environmental Health Sciences (NIEHS)

National Institute of General Medical Sciences (NIGMS)

National Institute of Mental Health (NIMH)

National Institute of Neurological Disorders and Stroke (NINDS)

National Institute of Nursing Research (NINR)

National Library of Medicine (NLM)

National Center for Research Resources (NCRR)

John E. Fogarty International Center (FIC)

Warren Grant Magnuson Clinical Center (CC)

Division of Computer Research and Technology (DCRT)

Center for Scientific Review (CSR)

Directory of the Federation of State Medical Boards (FSMB), including Puerto Rico and the District of Columbia

STATE AGENCY CONTACT INFORMATION

Alabama

Alabama State Board of Medical
  Examiners
P.O. Box 946
Montgomery, AL 36101-0946
(334)242-4116

Alaska

Alaska State Medical Board
3601 C Street, Suite 722 Anchorage, AK
  99503-5986
(907)269-8160

Arizona

Arizona Board of Osteopathic Examiners
  in Medicine and Surgery
141 East Palm Lane, Suite 205
Phoenix, AZ 85004
(602)255-1747

Arizona State Board of Medical
  Examiners
1651 East Morten Avenue, Suite 210
Phoenix, AZ 85020
(602)255-3751

Arkansas

Arkansas State Medical Board
2100 Riverfront Drive, Suite 200
Little Rock, AR 72202-1793
(501)296-1802

California

Medical Board of California
1426 Howe Avenue, Suite 54
Sacramento, CA 95825-3236
Licensure inquiries: (916)263-2499

Osteopathic Medical Board of California
2720 Gateway Oaks Drive, Suite 350
Sacramento, CA 95833
(910)263-3100

Colorado

Colorado Board of Medical Examiners
1560 Broadway, Suite 1300
Denver, CO 80202-5140
(303)894-7690

Connecticut

Connecticut Department of Public Health
Physician Licensure Department
P.O. Box 340308
Hartford, CT 06134-0308
(860)509-7586

Delaware

Delaware Board of Medical Practice
Cannon Building, Suite 203
861 Silver Lake Boulevard
Dover, DE 19903
(302)739-4522

District of Columbia

District of Columbia
Board of Medicine

614 H Street, N.W., Room 108
Washington, DC 20001
(202)727-5365

Florida

Florida Board of Medicine
Northwood Centre, # 60
1940 North Monroe Street
Tallahassee, FL 32399-0770
(904)488-0595

Florida Board of Osteopathic Medicine
Northwood Centre, # 60
1940 North Monroe Street
Tallahassee, FL 32399-0757
(904)922-6725

Georgia

Georgia Composite State Board of
  Medical Examiners
166 Pryor Street, S.W.
Atlanta, GA 30303-3465
(404)656-3913

Hawaii

Hawaii Board of Medical Examiners
Department of Commerce and Consumer
  Affairs
P.O. Box 3469
Honolulu, HI 96801
(808)586-2708

Idaho

Idaho State Board of Medicine
P.O. Box 83720

Statehouse Mail
Boise, ID 83720-0058
(208)334-2822

Illinois

Illinois Department of Professional
    Regulation
James R. Thompson Center
100 West Randolph Street, Suite 9-300
Chicago, IL 60601
(312)814-4500

Indiana

Indiana Health Professions Bureau
402 West Washington Street, Room 041
Indianapolis. IN 46204
(317)232-2960

Iowa

Iowa State Board of Medical Examiners
State Capitol Complex
Executive Hills West
1209 East Court Avenue
Des Moines, IA 50319-0180
(515)281-5171

Kansas

Kansas State Board of Healing Arts
235 S.W. Topeka Boulevard
Topeka, KS 66603-3068
(913)296-7413

Kentucky

Kentucky Board of Medical Licensure
Hurstbourne Office Park
310 Whittington Parkway, Suite 1B
Louisville, KY 40222
(502)429-8046

Louisiana

Louisiana State Board of Medical
    Examiners
P.O. Box 30250
New Orleans, LA 70190-0250
(504)524-6763

Maine

Maine Board of Licensure in Medicine
137 State House Station
Two Bangor Street
Augusta, ME 04333-0137
(207)287-3605

Maine Board of Osteopathic Licensure
142 State House Station
Two Bangor Street

Augusta, ME 04333-0142
(207)287-2480

Maryland

Maryland Board of Physician Quality
    Assurance
P.O. Box 2571
Baltimore, MD 21215-0095
General number: (410)764-4777 or   '
    (800)492-6836

Massachusetts

Massachusetts Board of Registration in
    Medicine
10 West Street, 3rd Floor
Boston, MA 02111
(617)727-3086

Michigan

Michigan Board of Medicine
P.O. Box 30670
Lansing, MI 48909-7518
(517)373-6873

Michigan Board of Osteopathic Medicine
    and Surgery
P.O. Box J0670
Lansing, MI 48909-7518
(517)373-6873

Minnesota

Minnesota Board of Medical Practice
University Park Plaza
2829 University Avenue, S.E., Suite 400
Minneapolis, MN 55414-3246
(612)617-2130

Mississippi

Mississippi State Board of Medical
    Licensure
3000 Old Canton Road, Suite 111
Jackson, MS 39216
(601)354-6645

Missouri

Missouri State Board of Registration for
    the Healing Arts
P.O. Box 4
Jefferson City, MO 65102
(314)751-0098

Montana

Montana Board of Medical Examiners
P.O. Box 200513
Helena, MT 59620-0513
(406)444-4284

Nebraska

Nebraska Department of Health
P.O. Box 94986
Lincoln, NE 68509-4986
(402)471-2115

Nevada

Nevada State Board of Medical
    Examiners
P.O. Box 7238
Reno, NV 89510
(702)688-2559

Nevada State Board of Osteopathic
    Medicine
2950 East Flamingo Road, Suite E-3
Las Vegas, NV 89121-5208
(702)732-2147

New Hampshire

New Hampshire Board of Medicine
2 Industrial Park Drive, Suite 8
Concord, NH 03301-8520
(603)271-1203

New Jersey

New Jersey State Board of Medical
    Examiners
140 East Front Street, 2nd Floor
Trenton, NJ 08608
(609)826-7100

New Mexico

New Mexico Board of Osteopathic
    Medical Examiners
P.O. Box 25101
Santa Fe, NM 87504
(505)827-7171

New Mexico State Board of Medical
    Examiners
Lamy Building, 2nd Floor
491 Old Santa Fe Trail
Santa Fe, NM 87501
(505)827-5022

New York

New York State Board for Medicine
Room 3023
Cultural Education Center
Empire State Plaza
Albany, NY 12230
(518)474-3841

North Carolina

North Carolina Medical Board
P.O. Box 20007

Raleigh, NC 27619-0007
(919)828-1212

North Dakota

North Dakota State Board of Medical
 Examiners
City Center Plaza
418 East Broadway, Suite 12
Bismarck, ND 5850l
(701)328-6500

Ohio

State Medical Board of Ohio
77 South High Street, 17th Floor
Columbus, OH 43266-0315
(614)466-3934

Oklahoma

Oklahoma State Board of Medical
 Licensure and Supervision
P.O. Box 18256
Oklahoma City, OK 73154-0256
(405)848-6841

Oklahoma Board of Osteopathic
 Examiners
4848 North Lincoln Boulevard, Suite 100
Oklahoma City, OK 73105-3321
(405)528-8625

Oregon

Oregon Board of Medical Examiners
620 Crown Plaza
500 S.W. First Avenue
Portland, OR 97201-5826
Licensure inquiries: (503)229-5770 (calls
 accepted from 8:00 A.M. to 11:30 A.M.)

Pennsylvania

Pennsylvania State Board of Medicine
P.O. Box 2649
Harrisburg, PA l7105-2649
(717)787-2381

Pennsylvania State Board of Osteopathic
 Medicine
P.O. Box 2649
Harrisburg, PA 17105-2649
(717)783-4858

Puerto Rico

Board of Medical Examiners of Puerto
 Rico
Call Box 13969
San Juan, PR 00908
(787)782-8989

Rhode Island

Rhode Island Board of Medical
 Licensure and Discipline
Department of Health Cannon Building,
 Room 205
Three Capitol Hill
Providence, RI 02918-5097
(401)277-3855

South Carolina

South Carolina Department of LLR
Board of Medical Examiners
P.O. Box 11289
Columbia, SC 29221-1289
(803)896-4500

South Dakota

South Dakota State Board of Medical
 and Osteopathic Examiners
1323 South Minnesota Avenue
Sioux Falls, SD 57105
(605)336-1965

Tennessee

Tennessee Board of Medical Examiners
426 5th Avenue, North
Cordell Hall Building, 1st Floor
Nashville, TN 37247-1010
(615)532-4384

Tennessee Board of Osteopathic
 Examiners
426 5th Avenue, North
Cordell Hall Building, 1st Floor
Nashville, TN 37247- 1010
(615)532-5081

Texas

Texas State Board of Medical Examiners
P.O. Box 2018
Austin, TX 78768-2018
(800)248-4062

Utah

Utah Department of Commerce Division
 of Occupational and Professional
 Licensing
P.O. Box 146741
Salt Lake City, UT 84114-6741
(801)530-6628

Vermont

Vermont Board of Medical Practice
109 State Street
Montpelier, VT 05609-1106
(803)828-2673

Virginia

Virginia Board of Medicine
6606 West Broad Street, 4th Floor
Richmond, VA 23230-1717
(804)662-7005

Washington

Washington Medical Quality Assurance
 Commission
P.O. Box 47866
Olympia, WA 98504-7866
(360)753-2844

Washington Board of Osteopathic
 Medicine and Surgery Department of
 Health
P.O. Box 47866
1300 S.E. Quince Street
Olympia, WA 98504-7866
(360)586-5962

West Virginia

West Virginia Board of Medicine
101 Dee Drive
Charleston, WV 2531 1
(304)558-2921

West Virginia Board of Osteopathy
334 Penco Road
Weirton, WV 26062
(304)723-4638

Wisconsin

Wisconsin Medical Examining Board
Department of Regulation and Licensing
P.O. Box 85
Madison, W1 53708-8935
(608)266-2811

Wyoming

Wyoming Board of Medicine
211 West 19th Street,
Colony Building, 2nd Floor
Cheyenne, WY 82002
(307)778-7053

Directory of State Dental Agencies, including Puerto Rico and the District of Columbia

STATE DENTAL AGENCY CONTACT INFORMATION

Alabama

Ms. Dianne E. Pool, Administrative
  Secretary
State Board of Dental Examiners of
  Alabama
2327 Pansy Street, Suite B
Huntsville, AL 35801
(205)533-4638; fax: (205)533-4690

Alaska

Ms. Katherine Hazelton, Licensing
  Examiner
Alaska State Board of Dental Examiners
Department of Commerce and Economic
  Development
P.O. Box 110806
Juneau, AK 99811-0806
(907)465-2542; fax: (907)465-2974

Arizona

Ms. Julie Chapko, Deputy Director
Arizona State Board of Dental
  Examiners
5060 N. 19th Avenue, #406
Phoenix, AZ 85015
(602)255-3696; fax: (602)255-3589

Arkansas

Ms. Judith Safly, Executive Director
Arkansas State Board of Dental
  Examiners
101 E. Capitol, Suite 111
Little Rock, AR 72201
(501)682-2085; fax: (501)682-3543

California

Ms. Lori Hubble
State of California Board of Dental
  Examiners
1432 Howe Avenue, # 85
Sacramento, CA 95825
(916)263-2306; fax: (916)263-2140

Colorado

Licensure Clerk
Colorado State Board of Dental
  Examiners
1560 Broadway, Suite 1310
Denver, CO 80202
(303)894-7758; fax: (303)894-7764

Connecticut

Ms. Norma Shea
Connecticut State Dental Commis-
  sion
Department of Public Health
Division of Medical Quality
  Assurance
410 Capitol Avenue
P.O. Box 340308
Hartford, CT 06134-0308
(860)509-7562; fax: (860)509-7553

Delaware

Ms. Sheila H. Wolfe, Administrative
  Assistant
Delaware State Board of Dental
  Examiners
P.O. Box 1401
Cannon Building, Suite 203
Dover, DE 19903
(302)739-4522, Ext. 218;
  fax: (302)739-2711

District of Columbia

Ms. Barbara A. Boyer
Examination Specialist
District of Columbia Board of
  Dentistry
Department of Consumer and Regulatory
  Affairs
614 "H" Street, N.W., Room 923
Washington, D.C. 20001
(202)727-7463; fax: (202)727-7662

Florida

Mr. Audie B. Wilson
Florida Board of Dentistry
1940 N. Monroe Street
Tallahassee, FL 32399-0765
(904)488-6015; fax: (904)922-3040

Georgia

Ms. Elaine Stewart, Administrative
  Secretary
Georgia Board of Dentistry
166 Pryor Street, S.W.
Atlanta, GA 30303
(404)656-3925; fax: (404)656-3960

Hawaii

Ms. Jodi Leandro, Licensing
  Examiner
State Board of Dental Examiners
Department of Commerce and Consumer
  Affairs
P.O. Box 3469
Honolulu, HI 96801
(808)586-2711; fax: (808)586-2689

Idaho

Ms. Susan Miller
Idaho State Board of Dentistry
P.O. Box 83720
Boise, ID 83720-0021
(208)334-2369; fax: (208)334-3247

Illinois

Licensure Maintenance Unit
Illinois State Board of Dentistry
Department of Professional Regulation
    and Education
320 W. Washington, 3rd Floor
Springfield, IL 62786
(217)782-0458; fax: (217)782-7645

Indiana

Ms. Maryann Seyfried, Director
Licensing Division
Indiana State Board of Dental Examiners
Health Professions Bureau
402 W. Washington, Room 041
Indianapolis, IN 46204
(317)233-4413; fax: (317)233-4236

Iowa

Ms. Linda Picketing, Administrative
    Secretary
Iowa Board of Dental Examiners
Executive Hills West
1209 E. Court
Des Moines, IA 50319
(515)281-5157; fax: (515)281-7969

Kansas

Ms. Marianne Spano, Staff Secretary
Kansas Dental Board
3601 S.W. 29th Street, Suite 134
Topeka, KS 66614-2062
(913)273-0780

Kentucky

Dr. Linda O'Laughlin, Executive
    Secretary
Kentucky Board of Dentistry
10101 Linn Station Road, # 540
Louisville, KY 40223
(502)423-0573; fax: (502)423-1239

Louisiana

Ms. Linda M. Foto, Administrative
    Assistant
Louisiana State Board of Dentistry
1515 Poydras Street, Suite 1850
New Orleans, LA 70112
(504)568-8574; fax: (504)568-8598

Maine

Ms. Irene Boucher, Executive Secretary
Maine Board of Dental Examiners
43 State House Station
Augusta, ME 04333
(207)287-3333; fax: same as phone

Maryland

Ms. Deborah Welch, License Coordinator
Maryland State Board of Dental
    Examiners
Metro-Executive Center
4201 Patterson Avenue
Baltimore, MD 21215-2299
(410)764-4730; fax: (410)358-0128

Massachusetts

Ms. Genevieve J. Schaefer, Clerk
Massachusetts Board of Registration in
    Dentistry
100 Cambridge Street, Room 1514
Boston, MA 02202
(617)727-9928; fax: (617)727-2197

Michigan

Ms. Carol Johnson, Licensing
    Administrator
Michigan Board of Dentistry
Department of Commerce
P.O. Box 30018
Lansing, MI 48909
(517)373-9102; fax: (517)373-2179

Minnesota

Ms. Karen Ramsey
Minnesota Board of Dentistry
2829 University Avenue, S.E., Suite 450
Minneapolis, MN 55414
(612)617-2250; fax: (612)617-2260

Mississippi

Administrative Assistant
Mississippi State Board of Dental
    Examiners
600 E. Amite Street, Suite 100
Jackson, MS 39201-2801
(601)944-9622; fax: (601)944-9624

Missouri

Ms. Kimberly Bax
Missouri Dental Board
3605 Missouri Boulevard
Jefferson City, MO 65109
(537)751-0043; fax: (573)751-8216

Montana

Ms. Sharon McCullough, Administrator
Montana Board and Dentistry
Arcade Building, Lower Level
111 N. Jackson
P.O. Box 200513
Helena, MT 59620-0407
(406)444-3745; fax: (406)444-1667

Nebraska

Ms. Becky WiseIl, Board Coordinator
Nebraska Board of Examiners in
    Dentistry
Professional and Occupational Licensure
    Division
301 Centennial Mall South
P.O. Box 94986
Lincoln, NE 68509-5007
(402)471-4915; fax: (402)471-3577

Nevada

Ms. Linda Riggs
Nevada Board of Dental Examiners
2225 E. Renaissance Drive
Las Vegas, NV 89119
(702)486-7044; fax: (702)486-7046

New Hampshire

Ms. Patticia A. Thompson,
    Administrative Assistant
New Hampshire Board of Dental
    Examiners
2 Industrial Park Drive
Concord, NH 03301-8520
(603)271-4561; fax: (603)271-6702

New Jersey

Ms. Kim Mayer
New Jersey State Board of Dentistry
124 Halsey Street
P.O. Box 45005
Newark, NJ 07101
(973)504-6405; fax: (973)648-3481

New Mexico

Ms. Renee Trujillo
New Mexico Board of Dental Health
    Care
P.O. Box 25101
Sante Fe, NM 87504-5101
(505)827-7165; fax: (505)827-7095

New York

Ms. Jeanne Riberdy
New York State Board of Dentistry
Room 3035, Cultural Education Center

Albany, NY 12230
(518)474-3838; fax: (518)473-6995

North Carolina

Ms. Gwen Rogers, Administrative
  Secretary
North Carolina State Board of Dental
  Examiners
3716 National Drive, Suite 221
P.O. Box 32270
Raleigh, NC 27622-2270
(919)781-4901; fax: (919)571-8457

North Dakota

Dr. Wayne Mattern, Executive Director
North Dakota Board of Dentistry
P.O. Box 7246
Bismarck, ND 58507-7246
(701)223-1474; fax: (701)224-0038

Ohio

Ms. Suzarme E. Curry, Administrative
  Secretary
Ohio State Dental Board
77 S. High Street, 18th Floor
Columbus, OH 43266-0306
(614)466-2580; fax: (614)752-8995

Oklahoma

Ms. Linda C. Campbell, Executive
  Director
Board of Governors of Registered
  Dentists
6501 N. Broadway, # 220
Oklahoma City, OK 73116
(405)848-1364; fax: (405)848-3279

Oregon

Ms. Teresa Haynes
Oregon Board of Dentistry
1515 S.W. Fifth Avenue, Suite 602
Portland, OR 97201
(503)229-5520; fax: (503)229-5120

Pennsylvania

Ms. June L. Hamer, Administrative
  Assistant
Pennsylvania State Board of Dentistry
P.O. Box 2649
Harrisburg, PA 17105
(717)787-7162; fax (717)787-7769

Puerto Rico

Ms. Cecilia Montalvo, Secretary of the
  Board
Puerto Rico Board of Dental Examiners

Department of Health
Call Box 10200
San Juan, PR 00908
(787)725-8161; fax: (787)725-7903

Rhode Island

Ms. Gail Giuliano
Rhode Island State Board of Examiners
  in Dentistry
Department of Health
Three Capitol Hill, # 404
Providence, RI 02908-5097
(401)277-2151; fax: (401)277-1250

South Carolina

Ms. Annie N. Heyward
South Carolina State Board of
  Dentistry
P.O. Box 11329/Dept. LLR
Columbia, SC 29211-1329
(803)734-4215; fax: (803)734-4216

South Dakota

Ms. Leigh Ann Cooper, Staff
  Assistant
South Dakota State Board of Dentistry
P.O. Box 1037
106 W. Capitol
Pierre, SD 57501
(605)224-1282; fax: (605)224-7426

Tennessee

Mr. William H. Oden, Administrator
Tennessee Board of Dentistry
426 5th Avenue, North
Cordell Hull Building, 1st Floor
Nashville, TN 37247-1010
(615)532-5073; fax: (615)532-5164

Texas

Ms. Sherri Sanders
Texas State Board of Dental
  Examiners
333 Guadalupe, Tower 3, Suite 800
Austin, TX 78701
(512)463-6400; fax: (512)463-7452

Utah

Licensing Specialist
Utah Board of Dentists and Dental
  Hygienists
Division of Occupational and
  Professional Licensing
P.O. Box 45805
Salt Lake City, UT 84145-0805
(801)530-6633 or 6623;
  fax: (801)530-6511

Vermont

Ms. Diane W. Lafaille, Staff
  Assistant / Executive Secretary
Vermont Board of Dental
  Examiners
Secretary of State Office
109 State Street
Montpelier, VT 05609-1106
(802)828-2390; fax: (802)828-2496

Virginia

Ms. Para Horner, Administrative
  Assistant
Virginia Board of Dentistry
6606 W. Broad Street, 4th Floor
Richmond, VA 23230-1717
(804)662-9906; fax: (804)662-9943

Washington

Ms. Lisa R. Anderson, Program
  Manager
Washington State Dental Health Care
  Quality Assurance Commission
1112 S.E. Quince Street
P.O. Box 47867
Olympia, WA 98504-7867
(360)586-6898; fax: (360)664-9077

West Virginia

James G. Anderson, III, Esq., Executive
  Secretary
West Virginia Board of Dental
  Examiners
P.O. Drawer 1459
Beckley, WV 25802-1459
(304)252-8266; fax: (304)252-2779

Wisconsin

Ms. Barbara Powers, Program
  Assistant
Wisconsin Dentistry Examining
  Board
P.O. Box 8935
1400 E. Washington Avenue
Madison, WI 53708
(608)266-5441; fax: (608)267-0644

Wyoming

Ms. Barbara Wickel, Executive
  Secretary
Wyoming Board of Dental
  Examiners
P.O. Box 272
Kemmerer, WY 83101
(307)877-9649; fax: (307)877-9649 *51
  (press *51 after beep to fax)